NEW ENGLAND HIKING

The Complete Guide to More Than 350 of the Best Hikes in New England

by Michael Lanza

ISBN 1-57354-021-8

Foghorn Press
Rights Department
P.O. Box 77845
San Francisco, CA 94107
foghorn@well.com

To order individual books, visit the Foghorn Press web site at www.foghorn.com, or call 1-800-FOGHORN (364-4676) or (707) 773-4260. Foghorn Press titles are distributed to the book trade by Publishers Group West, based in Emeryville, California. To contact your local sales representative, call 1-800-788-3123.

Library of Congress ISSN Data:
May 1997

New England Hiking
The Complete Guide to More Than 350 of the Best Hikes in New England
First Edition
ISSN: 1093-2720

Leave No Trace, Inc., is a program dedicated to maintaining the integrity of outdoor recreation areas through education and public awareness. Foghorn Press is a proud supporter of this program and its ethics.

The Foghorn Press Commitment

Foghorn Press is committed to the preservation of the environment. We promote Leave No Trace principles in our guidebooks. Additionally, our books are printed with soy-based inks on 100 percent recycled paper, which has a 50 percent post-consumer waste content.

Printed in the United States of America

NEW ENGLAND HIKING

The Complete Guide to More Than 350 of the Best Hikes in New England

by Michael Lanza

To Monty, a good friend and fellow mountain traveler who is deeply missed.

Contents

Maps

Introduction

Dear fellow hiker,

I have a single black-and-white photograph from what was probably my first hike up a New England mountain. It shows two friends and I standing on a rocky summit. In the distance, clouds blot out much of the sky. The wind lifts our hair and fills our shirts; it appears to be a cool day in early autumn.

I no longer recall what peak we hiked, only that it was in southern New Hampshire and that the hike had been the idea of one of my friends; I was tagging along on an outing that seemed like something I might enjoy. In fact, my recollection of the entire day amounts to little more than a lingering sense of the emotions it generated for me—kind of an artifact of memory, like an arrowhead dug up somewhere.

I was perhaps 18 or 20 years old, and standing on top of that little mountain struck me as quite possibly the most intense and wonderful thing I'd ever done.

Of course, at that age, most people have had little experience with things intense and wonderful. But I found that as my fascination with high places grew, so did the inspiration that began on that first summit.

I have since done much hiking all over New England, and taken my thirst for that feeling to bigger mountains out West—hiking, backpacking, and climbing in the Sierra Nevada, the Cascades and Olympics, the Tetons and Wind River Range, the Rockies from Colorado to Alberta, and the mountains of Alaska. My work has allowed me to spend the better part of recent summers wandering the West.

When Foghorn Press asked me to author this book, I realized I would spend a summer at home for a change, hiking those New England trails I had not yet visited but which belong in a guide this comprehensive. While I expected to sorely miss the West, instead I found myself enjoying a reunion of sorts with my hiking roots. I finally got to many places throughout New England that had been on my tick list for some time. And, to my surprise, the hikes I relished most were those I had known the least about, those scattered trails which for various reasons attract relatively few hikers.

This book is the product of many days on the trail, and a reflection of many personal memories. As you use it to explore New England's backcountry, I urge you to walk lightly, to do your part to help preserve these fragile places, and to venture beyond the popular, well-beaten paths to lesser-known destinations. I hope this book helps you find the same kind of experiences I have enjoyed in these mountains and forests—to discover your own arrowhead.

—Michael Lanza

How to Use This Book

New England Hiking is divided into six chapters: Maine, New Hampshire, Vermont, Massachusetts, Rhode Island, and Connecticut. A map at the beginning of each chapter shows where all the trailheads for hikes in that state are located.

For Maine trails:
see pages 1–84
For New Hampshire trails:
see pages 85–172
For Vermont trails:
see pages 173–236
For Massachusetts trails:
see pages 237–298
For Rhode Island trails:
see pages 299–318
For Connecticut trails:
see pages 319–356

There are two ways to search for the perfect hike:

1. If you know the name of the specific trail you would like to hike, or the name of the surrounding geographical area or nearby feature (town, national or state park or forest, mountain, lake, river, etc.), look it up in the index beginning on page 365 and turn to the corresponding page. Page numbers for trails featured in this book are listed in bold type.

2. If you want to find out about hiking possibilities in a particular part of a state, turn to the map at the beginning of that chapter. You can identify an area where you would like to hike and find out which hikes are available, then turn to the corresponding numbers for those hikes.

See the bottom of every page for a reference to corresponding maps.

What the Ratings Mean

Every hike in this book has been rated on a scale of 1 to 10 for its overall appeal, and on a scale of 1 to 5 for difficulty.

The overall rating is based largely on scenic qualities, although it also takes into account how crowded a trail is and whether or not you'll hear the noise of nearby civilization.

The difficulty rating is primarily based on the steepness of a trail and how rugged it is, as well as how sustained the more difficult sections of the hike are. A relatively flat, open, clearly marked trail is rated 1, while a hike involving substantial elevation gain—usually 2,000 to 4,000 vertical feet or more—and significant amounts of steep terrain with difficult footing or scrambling earns a 5.

Overall Rating

1 2 3 4 5 6 7 8 9 10

Poor .... Fair .... Great

Difficulty

1 2 3 4 5

A stroll .... Moderate .... A real butt-kicker!

Trail Names, Distances, and Times

Each trail in this book has a number, name, and listings on mileage and estimated time needed to complete the hike. The trail's number allows you to find it easily on the corresponding chapter map. The name is either the actual name of the trail (as listed on signposts and maps) or a name I gave to a series of trails or a loop trail. In these cases, the trail name is taken from the major destination or focal point of the hike. Most of the mileage listings are precise, though a few are very good estimates. All mileages and approximate times refer to round-trip travel, unless specifically noted as one way. In the case of one-way hikes, a car shuttle is advised. The estimated time is based on how long I feel an average adult in moderate physical condition would take to complete the hike. Actual times can vary widely, especially on longer hikes.

User Groups

I have designated a list of user groups permitted on each trail, including hikers, bikes, dogs, horses, hunters, cross-country skiers, snowshoers, and wheelchair users. While this book is intended primarily as a hiking guide, it includes some trails that are mediocre hikes yet excellent mountain biking or cross-country skiing routes. The snowshoe reference is intended as a guide for beginners; experienced snowshoers know that many of New England's bigger mountains can be climbed on snowshoes in winter, but this book deliberately avoids recommending snowshoeing any trail for which advanced winter mountaineering skills are needed. As always, the individual must make the final judgment regarding safety issues in winter.

Wheelchair accessibility is indicated usually when it was so stated by the land or facility manager, but concerned persons should call to find out if their specific needs will be met. The hunting reference is included to remind hikers that they need to be aware of the hunting season when hiking, and that they may be sharing a trail with hunters, in which case they should take the necessary precautions (wearing a bright color, preferably fluorescent orange) to avoid an accident in the woods. Hunting is a popular sport throughout New England; the season varies from state to state but generally extends from fall into early winter. Call the state departments of Fish and Game or park and forest offices to find out actual dates.

Maps

This section lists relevant maps for the hike in question. When several maps are mentioned, you might want to ask the seller about a map's detail, weatherproofness, range, and scale when deciding which one to obtain. Consider also which maps will cover other hikes that interest you. Prices are usually indicative of quality and detail. I've also listed the appropriate USGS (United States Geologic Survey) map or maps covering that area. Be advised that many USGS maps do not show trails or forest roads, and that trail locations may not be accurate if the map has not been updated recently. All of New England is covered by the standard 7.5-minute series maps (scale 1:24,000), except Massachusetts, which is covered by 15-minute series (1:25,000). Three indexes cover New England, showing the 7.5-minute and 15-minute maps: Maine; New Hampshire/Vermont; and Massachusetts/Connecticut/Rhode Island.

To order 7.5-minute or 15-minute series maps from the USGS, or the New England index maps, write to USGS Map Sales, Federal Center, Box 25286, Denver, CO 80225.

A private company called The Map Shack also sells the 7.5-minute or 15-minute series maps for $6 each plus a $5 shipping fee. To order, contact The Map Shack, 959 Main Street, Winchester, MA 01890; (617) 721-4943 or (800) 617-MAPS/6277. Outdoor gear retailers sometimes carry USGS maps, but the selection tends to be limited.

About the Trail Notes

The trail notes for each hike provide a detailed description intended to give the reader some idea of what kind of terrain to expect, what you might see, and how to follow the hike from beginning to end. I've sometimes added a special note about the hike, or a suggestion on how to combine it with a nearby hike or expand upon your outing in some other way. Also, there are a couple of terms used throughout the book that reflect the history of land usage in New England. While some New Englanders may be familiar with them, others may not. Forest roads are generally dirt or gravel roads maintained by the land manager and are typically not open to motor vehicles except those of the manager. Woods roads, or "old woods roads," are abandoned thoroughfares—many were formerly public routes between colonial communities—now heavily overgrown but recognizable as a wide path. Their condition can vary greatly.

Leave No Trace

Trails throughout New England receive heavy use, and many land managers constantly wrestle with issues of impact and access. Understand that your behavior can affect future access to trails, both on public and private land. Respect rules. Help preserve your favorite places by supporting the organizations responsible for maintaining them (usually listed for each hike in the following chapters). One of the best ways to avoid contributing to the degradation of popular trails is to use this book to its fullest potential: It contains more than 350 hikes, so check out some of those lesser-known spots you have never seen, or maybe never even heard of.

Never assume water sources to be safe. Either carry water from a source you know is reliable, or filter, treat, or boil any water on the trail.

When staying overnight in a backcountry area, practice low-impact, or Leave-No-Trace, camping. Again, while other information sources (including some public land management agencies) provide more in-depth advice on this subject, a few good rules to remember include:

- Choose a campsite at least 200 feet from trails and water sources, unless you're using a designated site. Make sure your site bears no evidence of your stay when you leave.
- Avoid building campfires; cook with a backpacking stove.
- Carry out everything you carry in.
- Do not leave any food behind, even buried, as animals will dig it up. Learn how to hang food appropriately to keep it from bears. Black bears have spread their range over most of New England in recent years, and problems have arisen in isolated backcountry areas where human use is heavy.
- Bury human waste beneath six inches of soil at least 200 feet from any water source. Burn and bury, or carry out, used toilet paper.
- Even biodegradable soap is harmful to the environment, so simply wash your cooking gear with water away from any streams or ponds.

A Last Word about Safety

There are many sources for those who want to expand their outdoor skills, including hiking clubs, guidebooks, and commercial programs. This book lacks the space to fully cover issues of safety, but I do want to give a brief warning about hiking in the mountains of New England. Few parts of the country contain mountains that are at once so potentially dangerous and so accessible to millions of people. Hikers who are unfamiliar with New England's mountains must bear in mind that, although they are relatively low compared with many western ranges, some of the worst weather recorded anywhere in the world occurs regularly up here.

Conditions vary widely across the region. Connecticut's hills can often be hiked year-round by the inexperienced, while New Hampshire's Presidential Range typically claims one or two lives every winter. The winter of 1995–96 saw a record six people die in that range, some of them experienced hikers and climbers who in all likelihood were simply overwhelmed by extreme cold and wind. It is significant to note that many mountaineers train for major peaks in Alaska and elsewhere by climbing in the Whites during winter. Snow and freezing rain can occur every month in northern New England's peaks. The higher mountains see hurricane-force winds year-round—winds that have literally lifted adults off the ground. On any hike, know what conditions to expect and prepare for the worst.

Maine

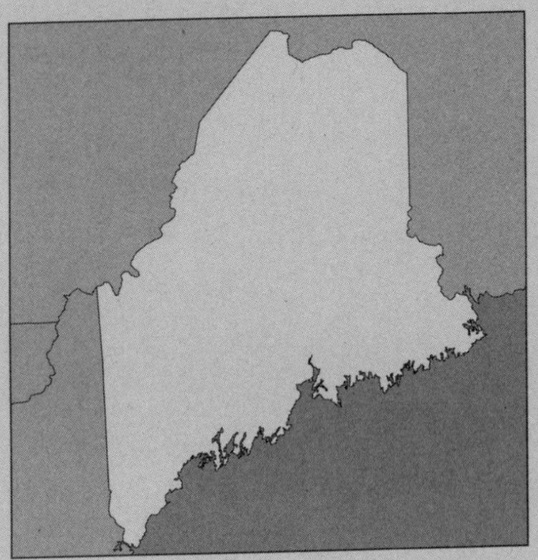

Overall Rating

1 2 3 4 5 6 7 8 9 10

Poor .... Fair .... Great

Difficulty

1 2 3 4 5

A stroll .... Moderate ...... A real butt-kicker!

Northern Maine

Adjoining Maps: South: Southern Maine .... *page* 3

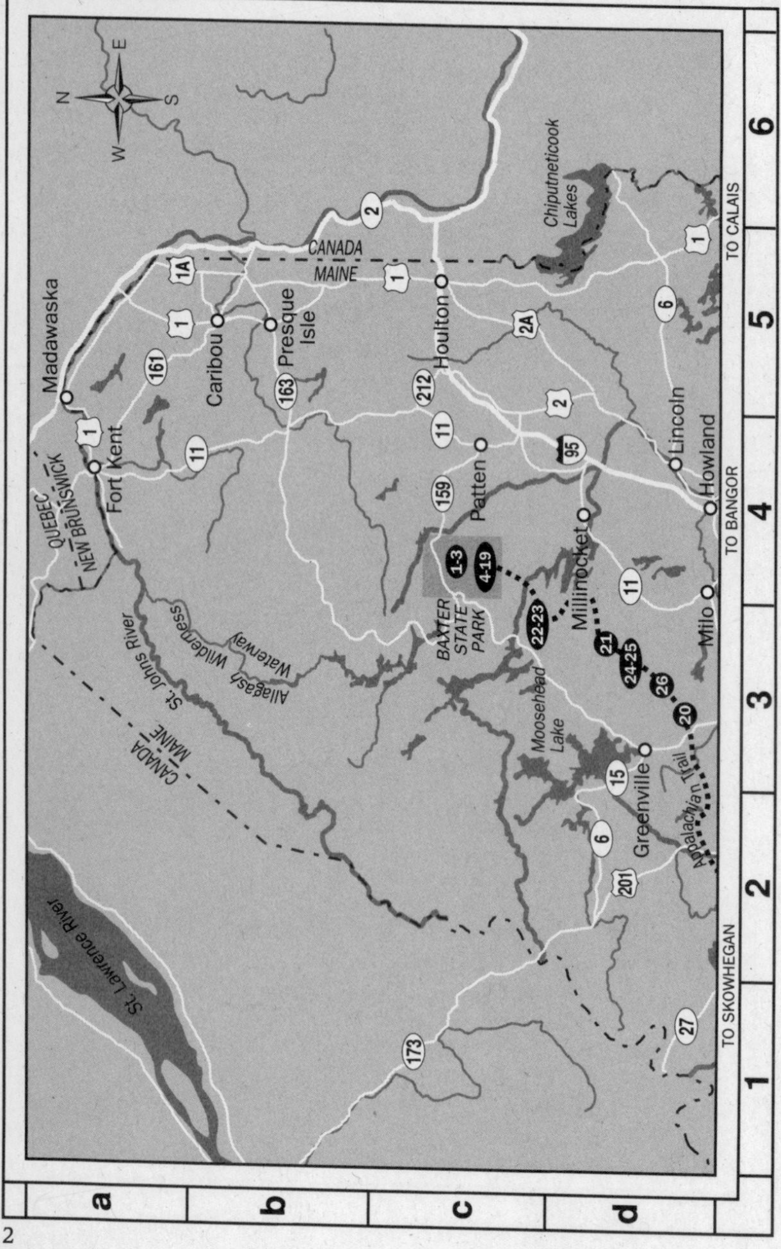

Southern Maine

Adjoining Maps: North: Northern Maine .... *page* 2
West: New Hampshire .... *pages* 86-87

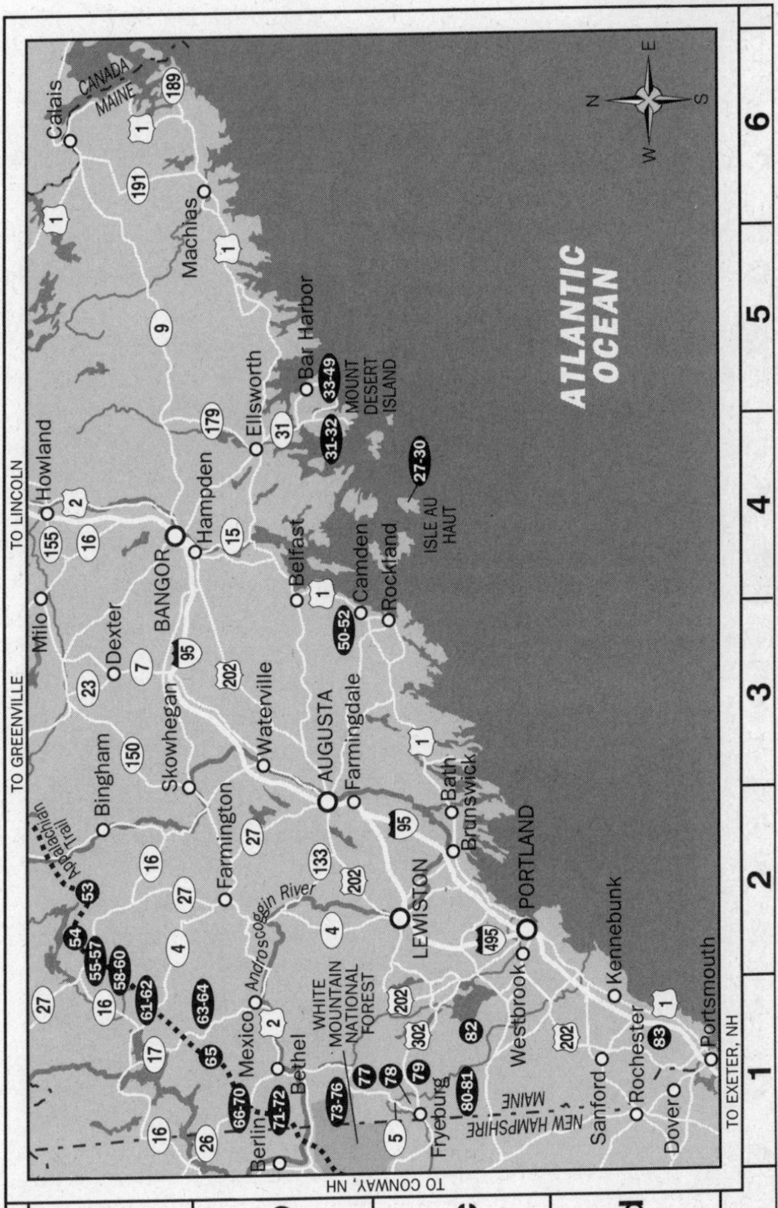

Maine features:

Northern Maine Map—page 2

MAINE

Sprawling over more than 33,000 square miles—roughly the area of the other five New England states combined—Maine offers a variety and remoteness of hiking experiences matched in New England perhaps only by New Hampshire. Maine's most prominent mountains comprise the northernmost reaches of the Appalachian chain, stretching from White Mountain National Forest in western Maine to Baxter State Park in the far north. The Appalachian Trail forms the backbone of the trails network through this region of vast wilderness lakes and rugged peaks, extending 281 miles through Maine alone.

Most of the hikes fall within three regions: the western lakes and mountains; the lower hills and mountains in the southwest; and the "Down East" coastal area around Acadia National Park and Camden Hills State Park. The trails come under the management of agencies as diverse as the state-run Bureau of Parks and Lands, the U.S. Forest Service, and the National Park Service.

Some hikes are on private land left open to public use in keeping with a long-standing tradition in Maine—a state where more than 90 percent of the total land area is privately held. Consequently, the descriptions of

Southern Maine Map—page 3

these hikes do not list any contact agency for additional information; in other words, you explore these places with the understanding that you are solely responsible for yourself. Bear in mind that while most of these private-land trails have been open to public use for many years, access can be cut off. Obey any no trespassing signs, and assume that hunting is allowed in season unless posted otherwise.

Along the Appalachian Trail (AT) in Maine, dogs are discouraged and horses, bikes, hunting, and possession of firearms are prohibited. Cross-country skiing and snowshoeing are welcome, though winter conditions can be extremely harsh and long stretches of the trail are not conducive to skiing. The Maine Appalachian Trail Club maintains the AT and some side trails through most of the state.

Acadia National Park

Occupying only about 40,000 acres, most of that on Mount Desert Island just off Maine's "Down East" coast, Acadia National Park is one of the country's smallest, yet most popular, national parks. Glaciers carved a unique landscape here of mountains rising as high as 1,500 feet virtually out of the ocean—most of them thrusting bare summits into the sky—and innumerable islands, bays, and coves that collaborate to create a hiking environment unlike any other in New England.

Acadia boasts more than 120 miles of hiking trails and 45 miles of carriage roads ideal for mountain biking, snowshoeing, or cross-country skiing. Many of the hikes described in this chapter are relatively short, but lead nonetheless to spectacular views of mountains, ocean, and islands. Although the well-blazed trails can be steep and rugged, most of these hikes are suitable for children.

July and August are crowded months on Mount Desert Island. Late spring and early fall are good times to visit, though the weather is cool. Snowfall can be rare in winter in this maritime environment.

Isle au Haut, the outermost island in Penobscot Bay, harbors a remote outpost of Acadia National Park. Lying southwest of Mount Desert Island, Isle au Haut (pronounced "Eyel a Ho" locally) is reached by a mailboat/ferry from Stonington, Maine. The national park maintains a primitive presence on the southern half of the island, with 18 miles of hiking trails, a couple of dirt roads, and a campground with five lean-to shelters less than a quarter of a mile from the boat landing at Duck Harbor.

Hiking the rocky coastal trails and low hills is the primary activity on Isle au Haut. Park rangers discourage bikes because of the limited roads, and bikes are prohibited from hiking trails. No wheelchair facilities are available. Dogs must be on a leash in the park and are prohibited from the campground. The island rarely gets enough snow for winter activities. The shore at Duck Harbor, near the campground, is a great place to catch the sunset.

Hiking trails are well marked with blue blazes and signs at intersections. But some trails are a bit overgrown in spots, which can create confusion—particularly where false trails diverge

Northern Maine Map—page 2

from marked trails. Watch closely for blazes.

Isle au Haut can be visited on a day trip or for overnight stays. From mid-June through early September (except Sundays), the ferry makes morning and late-afternoon trips between Stonington and the landing at Duck Harbor, the starting point for the four hikes described in this chapter. The ferry operates year-round to the Town Landing on Isle au Haut. Getting off the ferry at the Town Landing leaves you with a five-mile hike to the campground at Duck Harbor.

At least a couple of days are needed to get in much hiking. Camping reservations cost $25 per site regardless of the number of nights (limited to five nights from June 15 to September 15, and three the rest of the year), with a maximum of six people per lean-to. You can pitch a tent inside the lean-to only (which is advised in early summer, when the mosquitoes are vicious).

Request an Isle au Haut camping reservation form from Acadia National Park, P.O. Box 177, Bar Harbor, ME 04609; (207) 288-3338. Reservation forms are accepted only if postmarked on or after April 1.

For information on ferry schedules, contact the Isle au Haut Ferry Company, Stonington, ME 04681; (207) 367-5193. To reach the ferry dock, drive on Route 15 to Main Street in Stonington and turn left at Bartlett's Market; the ferry landing is past the firehouse, at the end of the pier. The round-trip ferry ride costs $20 per adult and $10 per child.

Baxter State Park

The state's flagship parkland, Baxter State Park, lies deep in the woods of northern Maine west of Millinocket. With more than 201,000 acres, it remains as close to true wilderness as managed lands can be. Baxter provides a sort of hiking experience that's increasingly rare in most of New England: remote and untamed.

Maine's highest peak, 5,267-foot Mount Katahdin, dominates the rugged topography of the park's south end and attracts the bulk of hiker traffic; its trails and summit can be crowded places in summer and early fall. But Baxter Park boasts 45 other mountains, many of them with trails to summits as nice as anything east of the Rockies—and much less trampled than Katahdin. On a Saturday one sunny Labor Day weekend, when hundreds of hikers flocked to Katahdin, a companion and I hiked a loop over the Brothers and Mount Coe and counted just 10 other people. The next day I spent a half-hour alone on the open ridge of Doubletop in the morning, and had the sweeping view from Old Jay Eye Rock on Mount O-J-I to myself that afternoon. That Labor Day, I trod up and down Traveler Mountain for several hours without encountering another soul.

Baxter Park is open from May 15 through October 15, and from December 1 through the end of March, subject to weather. Its trails are open to hiking only. Bikes are permitted only on maintained park roads. Dogs are not allowed in the park. Winter access is tightly regulated by park authorities; for more information, contact the park at 64 Balsam Drive, Millinocket, ME 04462-2190; (207) 723-5140. Hunting is prohibited.

An entrance fee of $8 per vehicle is charged at the gatehouse, but vehicles bearing a Maine registration enter at no charge. The park's entrance closes daily at 8:30 P.M. There are no public water sources in Baxter Park; treat your water, or bring an adequate supply with you. No permits are required for hiking, but advance reservations for camping within Baxter State Park are strongly recommended—the nearest private campgrounds are an hour outside the park.

1 South Branch Falls

1.0 mi/1.0 hr 

Location: In northern Baxter State Park; Northern Maine map page 2, grid c4.

User groups: Hikers only. No wheelchair facilities. This trail may be difficult to snowshoe because of severe winter weather, and is not suitable for skis. Bikes, dogs, and hunting are prohibited.

Access, fees: An entrance fee of $8 per vehicle is charged at the gatehouse, except to vehicles bearing a Maine registration, which enter for free. The park's entrance closes at 8:30 P.M.

Directions: Take Interstate 95 in Maine to exit 56 for Medway/Millinocket. Drive on Route 157 west through East Millinocket to Millinocket. Follow signs for Baxter State Park; the park's Togue Pond gatehouse is 18 miles from Millinocket. Just beyond the gatehouse, take the dirt perimeter road's left fork and drive 34.8 miles. Turn right at a sign for South Branch Pond Campground. Drive 1.3 miles to a turnout on the right. Or, from the junction of Routes 11 and 159 in Patten, drive west on Route 159 to Shin Pond and follow the access road to Baxter State Park's Matagamon Gatehouse, which is 24 miles from Patten. From the gatehouse, drive about 7.3 miles and turn left at the sign for South Branch Pond Campground.

Maps: For a map of trails in the park, get the excellent "Baxter State Park and Katahdin" map for $4.95 from the DeLorme Mapping Company, (800) 253-5081; or the "Baxter Park-Katahdin" map for $2.95 from the Appalachian Mountain Club, (800) 262-4455. For topographic maps of the area, request Wassataquoik Lake and The Traveler from the USGS.

Contact: Baxter State Park, 64 Balsam Drive, Millinocket, ME 04462-2190; (207) 723-5140.

Trail notes: This stretch of South Branch Ponds Brook might more aptly be called South Branch Gorge, since the biggest vertical drop the stream makes is about four feet. But the stream cuts a narrow channel through rock in a scenic gorge about a quarter-mile long. From the parking area, follow the trail for half a mile, descending gently at first, then somewhat steeply for the last tenth of a mile to the stream. Take one of the short side paths that leads to views of the gorge before heading back the way you came.

2 North Traveler Mountain

5.0 mi/3.5 hrs 

Location: In northern Baxter State Park; Northern Maine map page 2, grid c4.

User groups: Hikers only. No wheelchair facilities. This trail may be difficult to snowshoe because of severe winter weather, and is not suitable for skis. Bikes, dogs, and hunting are prohibited.

Access, fees: An entrance fee of $8 per vehicle is charged at the gatehouse, except to vehicles bearing a Maine registration, which enter for free. The park's entrance closes at 8:30 P.M.

Directions: Take Interstate 95 in Maine to exit 56 for Medway/Millinocket. Drive on Route 157 west through East Millinocket to Millinocket. Follow signs for Baxter State Park; the park's Togue Pond gatehouse is 18 miles from Millinocket. Just beyond the gatehouse, take the dirt perimeter road's left fork and drive 34.8 miles. Turn right at a sign for South Branch Pond Campground. Drive 2.1 miles to a parking area on the left, before the campground. Or, from the junction of Routes 11 and 159 in Patten, drive west on Route 159 to Shin Pond and follow the access road to Baxter State Park's Matagamon Gatehouse, which is 24 miles from Patten. From the gatehouse, drive about 7.3 miles and turn left at the sign for South Branch Pond Campground.

Maps: For a map of trails in the park, get the excellent "Baxter State Park and Katahdin" map for $4.95 from the DeLorme Mapping Company, (800) 253-5081; or the "Baxter Park-Katahdin" map for $2.95 from the Appalachian Mountain Club, (800) 262-4455. For topographic maps of the area, request Wassataquoik Lake and The Traveler from the USGS.

Contact: Baxter State Park, 64 Balsam Drive, Millinocket, ME 04462-2190; (207) 723-5140.

Trail notes: Traveler Mountain feels less like New England than possibly any other mountain in the region. With much of its sprawling upper ridges denuded by fires years ago and kept bare by a harsh climate, I half expect to see mountain goats grazing and hear the chirps of marmots up here. What you will hear, however, is next to nothing, enjoying absolute solitude for several hours on Traveler. The North Traveler Trail climbs a ridge to the north peak, with almost continuous sweeping views.

From the parking area, walk the road into the campground, toward the northernmost of the South Branch Ponds. (Traveler Mountain defines the skyline to the left, or east, above the pond.) Bear left through the campground, passing several sites, and turn right (south) onto the Pogy Notch Trail, which parallels the pond. In a tenth of a mile, turn left onto the blue-blazed North Traveler Trail, immediately ascending the fairly steep, rocky ridge. Just three-tenths of a mile from the pond, you emerge onto open ledges with your first views of the two South Branch Ponds, across to the South Branch Mountains, and south toward Katahdin. The views only improve as you continue up the ridge, where loose stones can make footing difficult and false summits can make the hike seem longer than its five miles. The trail passes through a nice little birch grove, with fresh blueberries for the picking along the way (I ate my share on an early September hike). Follow the blazes and cairns to the open summit, where there are views in every direction, including of the wilderness to the north. Due south is the 3,541-foot summit of The Traveler, connected to North Traveler by a trailless, three-mile ridge. Descend the way you came up.

❸ Peak of the Ridges

7.2 mi/6.0 hrs

Location: In northern Baxter State Park; Northern Maine map page 2, grid c4.

User groups: Hikers only. No wheelchair facilities. This trail may be difficult to snowshoe because of severe winter weather, and is not suitable for skis. Bikes, dogs, and hunting are prohibited.

Access, fees: An entrance fee of $8 per vehicle is charged at the gatehouse, except to vehicles bearing a Maine registration, which enter for free. The park's entrance closes at 8:30 P.M.

Directions: Take Interstate 95 in Maine to exit 56 for Medway/Millinocket. Drive on Route 157 west through East Millinocket to Millinocket. Follow signs for Baxter State Park; the park's Togue Pond gatehouse is 18 miles from Millinocket. Just beyond the gatehouse, take the dirt perimeter road's left fork and drive 34.8 miles. Turn right at a sign for South Branch Pond Campground. Drive 2.1 miles to a parking area on the left, before the campground. Or, from the junction of Routes 11 and 159 in Patten, drive west on Route 159 to Shin Pond and follow the access road to Baxter State Park's Matagamon Gatehouse, which is 24 miles from Patten. From the gatehouse, drive about 7.3 miles and turn left at the sign for South Branch Pond Campground.

Maps: For a map of trails in the park, get the excellent "Baxter State Park and Katahdin" map for $4.95 from the DeLorme Mapping Company, (800) 253-5081; or the "Baxter Park-Katahdin" map for $2.95 from the Appalachian Mountain Club, (800) 262-4455. For topographic maps of the area, request Wassataquoik Lake and The Traveler from the USGS.

Contact: Baxter State Park, 64 Balsam Drive, Millinocket, ME 04462-2190; (207) 723-5140.

Trail notes: Like the North Traveler hike (hike number 2), this 7.2-mile round-trip trek to the Peak of the Ridges on Traveler Mountain follows a long, open ridge, but is longer and more arduous, making it even more remote and challenging.

From the parking area, walk the road into the campground, toward the northernmost of the South Branch Ponds. Bear left through the campground, passing several sites, and turn right (south) onto the Pogy Notch Trail, which parallels the pond. In a mile, the trail passes a junction with the Howe Brook Trail, then crosses an often-dry streambed; follow the blue blazes to the left, eventually turning away from the streambed. Within another four-tenths of a mile, the trail turns left and ascends steeply a tenth of a mile to another junction. Turn left onto the Center Ridge Trail, which climbs relentlessly and at times steeply. But you don't have to go far to enjoy your first views of the two South Branch Ponds, across to the South Branch Mountains, and south toward Katahdin. After crossing an extensive talus field— where following the trail can be difficult, so watch carefully for blazes and cairns—the trail terminates at the Peak of the Ridges, a high point about a mile west of the 3,541-foot summit of The Traveler, and connected to it by a trailless ridge. Follow the same route back to your car.

4 Russell Pond/ Davis Pond Loop

19.0 mi/3.0 days  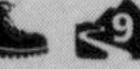

Location: In central Baxter State Park; Northern Maine map page 2, grid c4.

User groups: Hikers only. No wheelchair facilities. This trail may be difficult to snowshoe because of severe winter weather, and is not suitable for skis. Bikes, dogs, and hunting are prohibited.

Access, fees: An entrance fee of $8 per vehicle is charged at the gatehouse, except to vehicles bearing a Maine registration, which enter for free. The park's entrance closes at 8:30 P.M. A fee of $6 per person per night is charged for lean-to shelters and tent sites (minimum $12 per night per shelter) and $7 per person per night for a bunkhouse. Advance reservations for backcountry campsites are recommended. On this hike, Russell Pond has a bunkhouse (capacity 13), four tent sites, and four lean-tos (capacity four to eight); Davis Pond has one lean-to (capacity six).

Directions: Take Interstate 95 in Maine to exit 56 for Medway/Millinocket. Drive on

Route 157 west through East Millinocket to Millinocket. Follow signs for Baxter State Park; the park's Togue Pond gatehouse is 18 miles from Millinocket. Just beyond the gatehouse, take the dirt perimeter road's right fork and drive 8.1 miles to Roaring Brook Campground. The Russell Pond Trail begins beside the ranger station (where there is a hiker register).

Maps: For a map of trails in the park, get the excellent "Baxter State Park and Katahdin" map, for $4.95 from the DeLorme Mapping Company, (800) 253-5081; or the "Baxter Park–Katahdin" map for $2.95 from the Appalachian Mountain Club, (800) 262-4455. For topographic maps of the area, request Mount Katahdin and Katahdin Lake from the USGS.

Contact: Baxter State Park, 64 Balsam Drive, Millinocket, ME 04462-2190; (207) 723-5140.

Trail notes: Ever since I backpacked this loop with two friends several years ago, I've longed to get back and repeat it. Visitors to this magnificent park who hike only Katahdin—especially on a busy weekend like Labor Day—may not get a sense of remoteness. But Baxter is far enough removed from the rest of the world that if you wander away from the big mountain, you're in some real wilderness. My friends and I saw only a handful of other backpackers at Russell Pond and hikers on the popular Chimney Pond Trail, and one day we saw more moose (two) than people (none). I give this loop a difficulty rating of 4 only because of the steep climbs to Davis Pond in the Northwest Basin, and above Davis Pond to the Northwest Plateau. Much of this loop is easy hiking that fit backpackers can accomplish in fairly short days. (In fact, here's a confession that speaks volumes about the terrain: I forgot my boots at home on this trip and had to backpack three days in beat-up old sneakers—but had no problem other than being the butt of incessant jokes from my friends.) The loop is spread over three days to take advantage of two excellent backcountry camping areas at Russell and Davis Ponds. At the latter, you will have the lean-to and pristine hanging valley to yourselves.

From Roaring Brook Campground, follow the Russell Pond Trail north a relatively flat seven miles to Russell Pond Campground, where there is a ranger and canoes can be rented for a small fee. Listen for early morning or evening splashes in the pond—it's probably a moose grazing. On day two, head southwest on the Northwest Basin Trail, which climbs gradually alongside rock-strewn Wassataquoik Stream, passing small pools that invite a very chilly swim. It's a bit more than five miles to the Davis Pond lean-to.

The final day takes you up the Northwest Basin Trail onto the rocky, alpine area of the Northwest Plateau. Turn left onto the Hamlin Ridge Trail, passing over Hamlin Peak (4,751 feet), one of Maine's dozen 4,000-footers. The trail descends the open, rocky Hamlin Ridge, with constant views down into the cliff-ringed North Basin to your left (north) and toward Katahdin on the right (south). About two miles from Hamlin Peak, you will reach the North Basin Trail. To the right, it's less than a mile downhill to Chimney Pond (via the Chimney Pond Trail for the final three-tenths of a mile); this hike, however, turns left, following the North Basin Trail a short distance to the North Basin Cutoff, where you turn right. (For a view into the North Basin, continue straight ahead on the North Basin Trail for three-tenths of a mile to Blueberry Knoll; once you've enjoyed the vista, double back to the Cutoff.) Follow the Cutoff for a bit more than a half mile to the Chimney Pond Trail; turn left, and it's another 2.3 miles to Roaring Brook Campground.

Southern Maine Map—page 3

❺ South Turner Mountain

4.0 mi/3.0 hrs 

Location: In southern Baxter State Park; Northern Maine map page 2, grid c4.

User groups: Hikers only. No wheelchair facilities. This trail may be difficult to snowshoe because of severe winter weather, and is not suitable for skis. Bikes, dogs, and hunting are prohibited.

Access, fees: An entrance fee of $8 per vehicle is charged at the gatehouse, except to vehicles bearing a Maine registration, which enter for free. The park's entrance closes at 8:30 P.M.

Directions: Take Interstate 95 in Maine to exit 56 for Medway/Millinocket. Drive on Route 157 west through East Millinocket to Millinocket. Follow signs for Baxter State Park; the park's Togue Pond gatehouse is 18 miles from Millinocket. Just beyond the gatehouse, take the dirt perimeter road's right fork and drive 8.1 miles to Roaring Brook Campground. The Russell Pond Trail begins beside the ranger station (where there is a hiker register).

Maps: For a map of trails in the park, get the excellent "Baxter State Park and Katahdin" map for $4.95 from the DeLorme Mapping Company, (800) 253-5081; or the "Baxter Park–Katahdin" map for $2.95 from the Appalachian Mountain Club, (800) 262-4455. For topographic maps of the area, request Mount Katahdin and Katahdin Lake from the USGS.

Contact: Baxter State Park, 64 Balsam Drive, Millinocket, ME 04462-2190; (207) 723-5140.

Trail notes: Though just 3,122 feet in elevation, South Turner's craggy summit gives a rare view of the entire Katahdin massif from the east side. It's so overshadowed by the big mountain that many hikers don't even know about it—enhancing your chances for a summit in solitude. Sandy Stream Pond is a good place for moose viewing in the early morning or at dusk. You might combine this four-mile hike with the Sandy Stream Pond/Whidden Ponds Loop (hike number 6).

From the ranger station, follow the Russell Pond Trail a quarter mile, then turn right onto the South Turner Mountain Trail/Sandy Stream Pond Trail. You'll soon reach the southeast shore of Sandy Stream Pond, which the trail follows. As you come around the far end of the pond, the South Turner Mountain Trail turns right (the Whidden Pond Trail leads left) and soon begins the steep ascent of South Turner; much of the trail cuts through dense forest. The final stretch breaks out of the trees to wide views. Descend the same way you came.

❻ Sandy Stream Pond/ Whidden Ponds Loop

1.5 mi/1.0 hr 

Location: In southern Baxter State Park; Northern Maine map page 2, grid c4.

User groups: Hikers only. No wheelchair facilities. This trail may be difficult to snowshoe because of severe winter weather, and is not suitable for skis. Bikes, dogs, and hunting are prohibited.

Access, fees: An entrance fee of $8 per vehicle is charged at the gatehouse, except to vehicles bearing a Maine registration, which enter for free. The park's entrance closes at 8:30 P.M.

Directions: Take Interstate 95 in Maine to exit 56 for Medway/Millinocket. Drive on Route 157 west through East Millinocket to Millinocket. Follow signs for Baxter State Park; the park's Togue Pond gatehouse is 18 miles from Millinocket. Just beyond the gatehouse, take the dirt perimeter road's right fork and drive 8.1 miles to Roaring

Brook Campground. The Russell Pond Trail begins beside the ranger station (where there is a hiker register).

Maps: For a map of trails in the park, get the excellent "Baxter State Park and Katahdin" map for $4.95 from the DeLorme Mapping Company, (800) 253-5081; or the "Baxter Park–Katahdin" map for $2.95 from the Appalachian Mountain Club, (800) 262-4455. For topographic maps of the area, request Mount Katahdin and Katahdin Lake from the USGS.

Contact: Baxter State Park, 64 Balsam Drive, Millinocket, ME 04462-2190; (207) 723-5140.

Trail notes: This relatively flat, easy loop hits two nice ponds where moose are often seen, especially early in the morning or around dusk. I sat with friends on rocks on the shore of Sandy Stream Pond one morning and watched a huge bull moose casually grazing on underwater plants. And the view across the first Whidden Pond toward the North Basin of Hamlin and Howe Peaks is terrific. Start this hike early enough, and you could catch the sunrise hitting the North Basin and moose at Sandy Stream Pond. You might also want to combine it with a jaunt up South Turner Mountain (hike number 5).

From the ranger station, follow the Russell Pond Trail a quarter mile, then turn right onto the South Turner Mountain Trail/Sandy Stream Pond Trail. You'll soon reach the southeast shore of Sandy Stream Pond, which the trail follows. As you come around the far end of the pond, the South Turner Mountain Trail leads right; this hike turns left onto the Whidden Pond Trail, following it for a mile to the first of the Whidden Ponds (also the largest and the only one directly accessed by a trail). You might turn right onto the Russell Pond Trail and walk along the pond's shore for a bit. Eventually, turn back (south) on the Russell Pond Trail for the easy hike of a bit more than a mile back to Roaring Brook Campground.

7 Hamlin Peak

9.5 mi/6.0 hrs 

Location: In southern Baxter State Park; Northern Maine map page 2, grid c4.

User groups: Hikers only. No wheelchair facilities. This trail may be difficult to snowshoe because of severe winter weather, and is not suitable for skis. Bikes, dogs, and hunting are prohibited

Access, fees: An entrance fee of $8 per vehicle is charged at the gatehouse, except to vehicles bearing a Maine registration, which enter for free. The park's entrance closes at 8:30 P.M.

Directions: Take Interstate 95 in Maine to exit 56 for Medway/Millinocket. Drive on Route 157 west through East Millinocket to Millinocket. Follow signs for Baxter State Park; the park's Togue Pond gatehouse is 18 miles from Millinocket. Just beyond the gatehouse, take the dirt perimeter road's right fork and drive 8.1 miles to Roaring Brook Campground. The Chimney Pond Trail begins beside the ranger station (where there is a hiker register).

Maps: For a map of trails in the park, get the excellent "Baxter State Park and Katahdin" map for $4.95 from the DeLorme Mapping Company, (800) 253-5081; or the "Baxter Park–Katahdin" map for $2.95 from the Appalachian Mountain Club, (800) 262-4455. For topographic maps of the area, request Mount Katahdin and Katahdin Lake from the USGS.

Contact: Baxter State Park, 64 Balsam Drive, Millinocket, ME 04462-2190; (207) 723-5140.

Trail notes: Hamlin Peak, at 4,751 feet, is Maine's second-highest peak and one of a dozen 4,000-footers in the state, though it's also considered part of the Katahdin massif. Swarms of hikers climb Katahdin on a busy summer weekend, but far fewer venture up onto Hamlin—and they are missing much. The constant views along the Hamlin Ridge, both into the North Basin and back toward the South Basin and Katahdin, are among the most magnificent in Maine.

From Roaring Brook Campground, follow the Chimney Pond Trail an easy 2.3 miles to just beyond the Basin Ponds. (Don't bypass the short side path leading right to the southernmost of the Basin Ponds, where there's a great view across the water of your destination, Hamlin Ridge, and the North Basin.) Turn right onto the North Basin Cutoff, which soon meets up with the North Basin Trail. To the right a short distance is Blueberry Knoll and views into the North Basin and South Basin (experienced hikers will see that it's possible to bushwhack down to the pair of tiny ponds on the floor of North Basin and explore that rugged glacial cirque). This hike turns left (southwest) onto the North Basin Trail, and soon takes a right and begins ascending the Hamlin Ridge Trail. Two miles farther you reach Hamlin Peak, a mound of rocks slightly higher than the surrounding vast tableland, or plateau. Descend the way you came.

Special note: Another enjoyable way of hiking Hamlin, for visitors making this peak part of an extended stay in Baxter State Park, is from Chimney Pond Campground, which is 3.3 miles from Roaring Brook Campground via the Chimney Pond Trail. Backpack in to Chimney Pond (be sure to make your camping reservations months in advance), and hike Hamlin Peak via the Chimney Pond, North Basin, and Hamlin Ridge Trails (four miles, 2.5 hours). Chimney Pond is a good staging point for hikes of Katahdin, or even to begin the North of Katahdin backpacking loop (hike number 4) in the reverse direction.

8 Mount Katahdin: Knife Edge Loop

9.3 mi/9.0 hrs 

Location: In southern Baxter State Park; Northern Maine map page 2, grid c4.

User groups: Hikers only. No wheelchair facilities. This trail may be difficult to snowshoe because of severe winter weather, and is not suitable for skis. Bikes, dogs, and hunting are prohibited.

Access, fees: An entrance fee of $8 per vehicle is charged at the gatehouse, except to vehicles bearing a Maine registration, which enter for free. The park's entrance closes at 8:30 P.M.

Directions: Take Interstate 95 in Maine to exit 56 for Medway/Millinocket. Drive on Route 157 west through East Millinocket to Millinocket. Follow signs for Baxter State Park; the park's Togue Pond gatehouse is 18 miles from Millinocket. Just beyond the gatehouse, take the dirt perimeter road's right fork and drive 8.1 miles to Roaring Brook Campground. The Chimney Pond Trail begins beside the ranger station (where there is a hiker register).

Maps: For a map of trails in the park, get the excellent "Baxter State Park and Katahdin" map for $4.95 from the DeLorme Mapping Company, (800) 253-5081; or the "Baxter Park–Katahdin" map for $2.95 from the Appalachian Mountain Club, (800) 262-4455. For topographic maps of the area, request Mount Katahdin and Katahdin Lake from the USGS.

Contact: Baxter State Park, 64 Balsam Drive, Millinocket, ME 04462-2190; (207) 723-5140.

Trail notes: This long, rugged loop hike offers a mountain experience like no other in New England, and is the best way to take in as much of Maine's greatest mountain as possible in a day. The hike encompasses

Chimney Pond (set deep in the vast glacial cirque known as the South Basin), a challenging scramble up the Cathedral Trail, Katahdin's four peaks, the infamous Knife Edge, and the exposed Keep Ridge. Don't underestimate its length, difficulty, or dangers: two of my several visits to the 5,267-foot Katahdin have come on the heels of the deaths of hikers on the Knife Edge (one fell, two were struck by lightning). Once you're on the Knife Edge, there's no alternate descent route—you have to continue on it.

Follow the mostly easy Chimney Pond Trail 3.3 miles to the pond camping area (many visitors make this hike and go no farther, because the views from Chimney Pond are so beautiful). Behind the Chimney Pond ranger station, pick up the Cathedral Trail, which climbs steeply up a rockslide and the right flank of Katahdin's sweeping headwall, passing the three prominent stone buttresses known as the Cathedrals. You can scramble off-trail onto each of the Cathedrals for great views of the South Basin.

At 1.4 miles from Chimney Pond, bear left where the trail forks, soon reaching the Saddle Trail and more level ground. Turn left (southeast) and walk two-tenths of a mile to the main summit, Baxter Peak, where a large sign marks the northern terminus of the Appalachian Trail. Continue straight over the summit (southeast) on the Knife Edge Trail, following an increasingly narrow, rocky ridge that runs 1.1 miles to Katahdin's Pamola Peak. The trail hooks left at South Peak, and the stretch from there to Pamola becomes precipitous. At times, the footpath is barely two feet wide, with abrupt drops to either side. At Chimney Peak, you'll scramble down the vertical wall of a cleft in the ridge, a spot known to intimidate more than a few hikers. Then you'll scramble up the other side (not as difficult) onto Pamola Peak. From there, turn right (east) on the Helon Taylor Trail, which descends a long ridge, much of it open, for 3.1 miles to the Chimney Pond Trail. Turn right and walk a tenth of a mile to Roaring Brook Campground.

9 Katahdin Traverse

10.9 mi. one way/
10.0 hrs or 1–2 days

Location: In southern Baxter State Park; Northern Maine map page 2, grid c4.

User groups: Hikers only. No wheelchair facilities. This trail may be difficult to snowshoe because of severe winter weather, and is not suitable for skis. Bikes, dogs, and hunting are prohibited.

Access, fees: An entrance fee of $8 per vehicle is charged at the gatehouse, except to vehicles bearing a Maine registration, which enter for free. The park's entrance closes at 8:30 P.M.

Directions: Take Interstate 95 in Maine to exit 56 for Medway/Millinocket. Drive on Route 157 west through East Millinocket to Millinocket. Follow signs for Baxter State Park; the park's Togue Pond gatehouse is 18 miles from Millinocket. Just beyond the gatehouse, take the dirt perimeter road's right fork and drive 8.1 miles to Roaring Brook Campground, and leave a vehicle in the parking lot. The Chimney Pond Trail—where you will end this hike—begins beside the ranger station. Drive a second vehicle back to the fork in the perimeter road, turn right and drive eight miles to Katahdin Stream Campground. Turn right onto the campground road and continue a tenth of a mile to the day-use parking area. The Hunt Trail begins there.

Maps: For a map of trails in the park, get the excellent "Baxter State Park and Katahdin" map for $4.95 from the DeLorme Mapping Company, (800) 253-5081; or the "Baxter Park–Katahdin" map for $2.95 from the Appalachian Mountain Club, (800)

262-4455. For topographic maps of the area, request Mount Katahdin and Katahdin Lake from the USGS.

Contact: Baxter State Park, 64 Balsam Drive, Millinocket, ME 04462-2190; (207) 723-5140.

Trail notes: If my one lament about hiking the Knife Edge Loop (hike number 8) is that you miss the Hunt Trail (hike number 12), this traverse of Katahdin remedies that dilemma. While this hike could be accomplished in a very long day (its length is compounded by the necessity of shuttling vehicles between Katahdin Stream and Roaring Brook Campgrounds), it's best spread over two days, with an overnight at Chimney Pond Campground. On the second day, you may have time to make an early morning scramble up the Cathedral Trail (hike number 8) to catch Katahdin's summit free of the afternoon crowds, or to hike up onto the spectacular Hamlin Ridge (hike number 7).

From Katahdin Stream Campground, follow the white-blazed Hunt Trail for 5.2 miles to Katahdin's main summit, 5,267-foot Baxter Peak. (See hike number 12 for a detailed description of the Hunt Trail.) Turn right (east) on the Knife Edge Trail, which continues for a mile over South Peak and the narrow crest of the Knife Edge to Chimney Peak, then drops very steeply into a col and climbs a few hundred feet up onto Pamola Peak (see hike number 8, Knife Edge Loop). From there, the Dudley Trail drops steeply 1.3 miles to Chimney Pond. On day two, the 3.3-mile hike out to Roaring Brook Campground is an easy couple of hours.

⑩ Mount Katahdin: the Abol Trail

7.6 mi/7.0 hrs 

Location: In southern Baxter State Park; Northern Maine map page 2, grid c4.

User groups: Hikers only. No wheelchair facilities. This trail may be difficult to snowshoe because of severe winter weather, and is not suitable for skis. Bikes, dogs, and hunting are prohibited.

Access, fees: An entrance fee of $8 per vehicle is charged at the gatehouse, except to vehicles bearing a Maine registration, which enter for free. The park's entrance closes at 8:30 P.M.

Directions: Take Interstate 95 in Maine to exit 56 for Medway/Millinocket. Drive on Route 157 west through East Millinocket to Millinocket. Follow signs for Baxter State Park; the park's Togue Pond gatehouse is 18 miles from Millinocket. Just beyond the gatehouse, take the dirt perimeter road's right fork and drive 5.7 miles to Abol Campground and day-use parking on the left, opposite the campground entrance.

Maps: For a map of trails in the park, get the excellent "Baxter State Park and Katahdin" map for $4.95 from the DeLorme Mapping Company, (800) 253-5081; or the "Baxter Park–Katahdin" map for $2.95 from the Appalachian Mountain Club, (800) 262-4455. For topographic maps of the area, request Mount Katahdin and Katahdin Lake from the USGS.

Contact: Baxter State Park, 64 Balsam Drive, Millinocket, ME 04462-2190; (207) 723-5140.

Trail notes: This trail follows the path of the Abol landslide of 1816, and may be the oldest existing route up the 5,267-foot Katahdin. It's the shortest way to Katahdin's main summit, Baxter Peak, but by no means easy: the slide's steepness and loose rock make for an arduous ascent, complicated by the possibility of falling rock. Descending this way is extremely difficult, though not impossible (but believe me, it's rough on the knees).

From the day-use parking area on the perimeter road, walk to the back of the campground loop and pick up the Abol Trail. The trail leads through woods for more than a mile to the base of the broad slide. Pick your way carefully up the slide; avoid hiking directly below another hiker. At 2.6 miles, the trail reaches the level ground of the Tableland, and two-tenths of a mile farther it connects with the Hunt Trail near Thoreau Spring. Turn right on the Hunt Trail for the final mile to Baxter Peak, the northern terminus of the Appalachian Trail. By shuttling vehicles between Abol and Katahdin Stream Campgrounds, you could ascend the Abol and descend the Hunt Trail, a nine-mile hike if you go to Baxter Peak.

⑪ Little Abol Falls

1.6 mi/1.0 hr 

Location: In southern Baxter State Park; Northern Maine map page 2, grid c4.

User groups: Hikers only. No wheelchair facilities. This trail may be difficult to snowshoe because of severe winter weather, and is not suitable for skis. Bikes, dogs, and hunting are prohibited.

Access, fees: An entrance fee of $8 per vehicle is charged at the gatehouse, except to vehicles bearing a Maine registration, which enter for free. The park's entrance closes at 8:30 P.M.

Directions: Take Interstate 95 in Maine to exit 56 for Medway/Millinocket. Drive on Route 157 west through East Millinocket to Millinocket. Follow signs for Baxter State Park; the park's Togue Pond gatehouse is 18 miles from Millinocket. Just beyond the gatehouse, take the dirt perimeter road's left fork and drive 5.7 miles to the day-use parking are on the left, opposite the entrance to Abol Campground.

Maps: For a map of trails in the park, get the excellent "Baxter State Park and Katahdin" map for $4.95 from the DeLorme Mapping Co., (800) 253-5081; or the "Baxter Park-Katahdin" map for $2.95 from the Appalachian Mountain Club, (800) 262-4455. For topographic maps of the area, request Doubletop Mountain and Mount Katahdin from the USGS.

Contact: Baxter State Park, 64 Balsam Drive, Millinocket, ME 04462-2190; (207) 723-5140.

Trail notes: This easy walk along a path of packed dirt and gravel ascends gently for eight-tenths of a mile to where one of the branches of Abol Stream drops over a 12-foot falls into a pleasant little pool. This can be a popular hike, so if you want some solitude, start out in the early morning. From the parking area, walk up the campground road. The Little Abol Falls Trail begins at the rear of the campground, just to the right of the Abol Trail.

⑫ Mount Katahdin: the Hunt Trail

10.0 mi/8.0 hrs 

Location: In southern Baxter State Park; Northern Maine map page 2, grid c4.

User groups: Hikers only. No wheelchair facilities. This trail may be difficult to snowshoe because of severe winter weather, and is not suitable for skis. Bikes, dogs, and hunting are prohibited.

Access, fees: An entrance fee of $8 per vehicle is charged at the gatehouse, except to vehicles bearing a Maine registration, which enter for free. The park's entrance closes at 8:30 P.M.

Directions: Take Interstate 95 in Maine to exit 56 for Medway/Millinocket. Drive on Route 157 west through East Millinocket to Millinocket. Follow signs for Baxter State Park; the park's Togue Pond gatehouse is 18 miles from Millinocket. Just beyond the gatehouse, take the left fork of the dirt perimeter road and drive eight miles to Katahdin Stream Campground. Turn right onto the campground road and continue a tenth of a mile to the day-use parking area, where the Hunt Trail begins.

Maps: For a map of trails in the park, get the excellent "Baxter State Park and Katahdin" map for $4.95 from the DeLorme Mapping Company, (800) 253-5081; or the "Baxter Park–Katahdin" map for $2.95 from the Appalachian Mountain Club, (800) 262-4455. For topographic maps of the area, request Mount Katahdin and Katahdin Lake from the USGS.

Contact: Baxter State Park, 64 Balsam Drive, Millinocket, ME 04462-2190; (207) 723-5140.

Trail notes: This is the trail I followed on my first hike of the 5,267-foot Katahdin, when I fell in love with this magnificent mountain. Were it not for the Knife Edge, I'd describe the Hunt Trail as the most interesting route up the mountain. The trail is rugged, gains nearly 5,000 feet of elevation, and traverses a substantial area above timberline; it's not uncommon for people to spend a very long day on this hike.

From the campground, follow the white-blazed Hunt Trail (it's the final stretch of the Appalachian Trail, so in the fall you may see some through-hikers finishing their 2,158-mile journey). Just over a mile from the campground, a side trail leads left to roaring Katahdin Stream Falls. The trail continues upward through the woods, with occasional views. It abruptly breaks out above the trees, where you'll use iron rungs drilled into the stone to scale a short but vertical rock face.

The trail ascends the crest of the rocky, open ridge to the Tableland, a mile-wide plateau at about 4,500 feet, a tundra littered with rocks. The trail passes Thoreau Spring near the Abol Trail junction before ascending the summit cone to the main summit, Baxter Peak, where on a clear day you will enjoy one of the finest mountain views in New England. A large sign marks the northern terminus of the Appalachian Trail. Some 2,000 feet below is the blue dot of Chimney Pond. To the right (east) is the serrated crest of the Knife Edge, and to the north lie Hamlin Peak, the Howe Peaks, and the vast wilderness of Baxter Park. Return via the Hunt Trail.

13 Katahdin Stream Falls

2.4 mi/1.5 hrs 

Location: In southern Baxter State Park; Northern Maine map page 2, grid c4.

User groups: Hikers only. No wheelchair facilities. This trail may be difficult to snowshoe because of severe winter weather, and is not suitable for skis. Bikes, dogs, and hunting are prohibited.

Access, fees: An entrance fee of $8 per vehicle is charged at the gatehouse, except to vehicles bearing a Maine registration, which enter for free. The park's entrance closes at 8:30 P.M.

Directions: Take Interstate 95 in Maine to exit 56 for Medway/Millinocket. Drive one Route 157 west through East Millinocket to Millinocket. Follow signs for Baxter State Park; the park's Togue Pond gatehouse is 18 miles from Millinocket. Just beyond the gatehouse, take the dirt perimeter road's left fork and drive eight miles. Turn right into the Katahdin Stream Campground and continue a tenth of a mile to the day-use parking area.

Maps: For a map of trails in the park, get the excellent "Baxter State Park and Katahdin" map for $4.95 from the DeLorme Mapping Company, (800) 253-5081; or the "Baxter Park-Katahdin" map for $2.95 from the Appalachian Mountain Club, (800) 262-4455). For topographic maps of the area, request Doubletop Mountain and Mount Katahdin from the USGS.

Contact: Baxter State Park, 64 Balsam

Drive, Millinocket, ME 04462-2190; (207) 723-5140.

Trail notes: Katahdin Stream Falls tumbles about 50 feet, and is visible from the trail after an easy walk of just over a mile. From the parking area, follow the white blazes of the Hunt Trail, which is the final stretch of the Appalachian Trail. It ascends easily through the woods. After passing the Owl Trail one mile out, continue a tenth of a mile on the Hunt Trail and cross Katahdin Stream on a wooden bridge. Just a tenth of a mile farther, side paths lead to the waterfall. After enjoying the falls, head back the way you came.

14 North Brother

8.5 mi/6.0 hrs 

Location: In southern Baxter State Park; Northern Maine map page 2, grid c4.

User groups: Hikers only. No wheelchair facilities. This trail may be difficult to snowshoe because of severe winter weather, and is not suitable for skis. Bikes, dogs, and hunting are prohibited.

Access, fees: An entrance fee of $8 per vehicle is charged at the gatehouse, except to vehicles bearing a Maine registration, which enter for free. The park's entrance closes at 8:30 P.M.

Directions: Take Interstate 95 in Maine to exit 56 for Medway/Millinocket. Drive on Route 157 west through East Millinocket to Millinocket. Follow signs for Baxter State Park; the park's Togue Pond gatehouse is 18 miles from Millinocket. Just beyond the gatehouse, take the dirt perimeter road's left fork and drive 13.5 miles to a parking area on the right for the Marston Trail.

Maps: For a map of trails in the park, get the excellent "Baxter State Park and Katahdin" map for $4.95 from the DeLorme Mapping Company, (800) 253-5081; or the "Baxter Park-Katahdin" map for $2.95 from the Appalachian Mountain Club, (800) 262-4455. For topographic maps of the area, request Doubletop Mountain and Mount Katahdin from the USGS.

Contact: Baxter State Park, 64 Balsam Drive, Millinocket, ME 04462-2190; (207) 723-5140.

Trail notes: At 4,143 feet, Maine's seventh-highest mountain has a fairly extensive area above tree line around its summit, and the excellent views from the peak encompass Mount Katahdin to the southeast, the remote Northwest Plateau and Basin to the east, Fort and Traveler Mountains to the north, Doubletop to the west, and the wild, trailless area known as The Klondike to the immediate south.

From the parking lot, pick up the Marston Trail. At 1.2 miles, the Mount Coe Trail branches right; bear left with the Marston Trail. At two miles the trail passes a small pond, and at 3.4 miles it reaches a second junction with the Mount Coe Trail. To reach the open summit of South Brother (3,930 feet), which has views comparable to North Brother for somewhat less effort, turn right at this junction and follow the Mount Coe Trail over fairly flat terrain for seven-tenths of a mile to a side path leading left three-tenths of a mile to the top of South Brother. (That detour adds two miles to this hike's distance.) A good example of Baxter's famous "striped forest" is visible between South and North Brother. For this hike, however, turn left and climb eight-tenths of a mile to North Brother's summit. Return the same way you hiked up.

Special note: You can combine this hike with the hike up Mount Coe, and bag South Brother as well, in a loop of 9.4 miles. The best route is to ascend the Mount Coe slide, hitting Coe first, then South Brother, and finally North Brother, and descending the Marston Trail. See hike number 16 for more information.

⑮ The Owl

6.0 mi/6.0 hrs 

Location: In southern Baxter State Park; Northern Maine map page 2, grid c4.

User groups: Hikers only. No wheelchair facilities. This trail may be difficult to snowshoe because of severe winter weather, and is not suitable for skis. Bikes, dogs, and hunting are prohibited.

Access, fees: An entrance fee of $8 per vehicle is charged at the gatehouse, except to vehicles bearing a Maine registration, which enter for free. The park's entrance closes at 8:30 P.M.

Directions: Take Interstate 95 in Maine to exit 56 for Medway/Millinocket. Drive on Route 157 west through East Millinocket to Millinocket. Follow signs for Baxter State Park; the park's Togue Pond gatehouse is 18 miles from Millinocket. Just beyond the gatehouse, take the dirt perimeter road's left fork and drive eight miles. Turn right into the Katahdin Stream Campground and continue a tenth of a mile to the day-use parking area.

Maps: For a map of trails in the park, get the excellent "Baxter State Park and Katahdin" map for $4.95 from the DeLorme Mapping Company, (800) 253-5081; or the "Baxter Park-Katahdin" map for $2.95, from the Appalachian Mountain Club, (800) 262-4455. For topographic maps of the area, request Doubletop Mountain and Mount Katahdin from the USGS.

Contact: Baxter State Park, 64 Balsam Drive, Millinocket, ME 04462-2190; (207) 723-5140.

Trail notes: One of the most arduous hikes in Baxter State Park, and one of its best-kept secrets, this six-mile round-tripper leads to the 3,736-foot summit of The Owl, whose cliffs are visible from the Hunt Trail (Appalachian Trail) ridge on neighboring Mount Katahdin. On the Thursday of a busy Labor Day weekend which saw hundreds of hikers on Katahdin, I encountered just seven other people on The Owl, and spent a half hour at the summit completely alone.

From the parking area, follow the white blazes of the Hunt Trail, which is the final stretch of the Appalachian Trail, ascending easily through the woods. After one mile, turn left at the sign for The Owl Trail, which you will find lined with ripe blueberries in late August and early September. Within a mile from the Hunt Trail, you will pass huge boulders. About two-tenths of a mile below the summit, you emerge onto an open ledge with a great view down into the ravine of Katahdin Stream and across it to Katahdin. Some hikers may want to turn around from here, because the trail grows increasingly difficult and exposed.

If you decide to persevere, scramble up rocks to a second ledge, where a boulder perches at the brink of a precipice. After another short scramble, you will reach the level shoulder of The Owl. The trail follows the crest of that narrow ridge, ducking briefly through a subalpine forest and ascending slightly to the bare ledges at the summit, where there are sweeping views in every direction. An example of Baxter's famed "striped forest" is visible to the west. Katahdin dominates the skyline to the east, the Northwest Plateau lies to the northeast, the Brothers, Coe, and O-J-I to the west, and the wilderness lakes along the Appalachian Trail to the south. Descend along the same route.

⑯ Mount Coe

6.6 mi/6.0 hrs 

Location: In southern Baxter State Park; Northern Maine map page 2, grid c4.

User groups: Hikers only. No wheelchair

facilities. This trail may be difficult to snowshoe because of severe winter weather, and is not suitable for skis. Bikes, dogs, and hunting are prohibited.

Access, fees: An entrance fee of $8 per vehicle is charged at the gatehouse, except to vehicles bearing a Maine registration, which enter for free. The park's entrance closes at 8:30 P.M.

Directions: Take Interstate 95 in Maine to exit 56 for Medway/Millinocket. Drive on Route 157 west through East Millinocket to Millinocket. Follow signs for Baxter State Park; the park's Togue Pond gatehouse is 18 miles from Millinocket. Just beyond the gatehouse, take the dirt perimeter road's left fork and drive 13.5 miles to a parking area on the right for the Marston Trail.

Maps: For a map of trails in the park, get the excellent "Baxter State Park and Katahdin" map for $4.95 from the DeLorme Mapping Co., (800) 253-5081; or the "Baxter Park-Katahdin" map for $2.95 from the Appalachian Mountain Club, (800) 262-4455. For topographic maps of the area, request Doubletop Mountain and Mount Katahdin from the USGS.

Contact: Baxter State Park, 64 Balsam Drive, Millinocket, ME 04462-2190; (207) 723-5140.

Trail notes: Mount Coe's 3,764-foot summit has very nice views in every direction, particularly east over The Klondike and toward Katahdin and the Northwest Plateau. From the parking area, follow the Marston Trail for 1.2 miles, then bear right onto the Mount Coe Trail. It ascends easily at first, reaching the foot of the Mount Coe rockslide, still in the forest, within a quarter of a mile. The trail emerges about a mile farther onto the open, broad scar of the slide, and for the next half mile climbs the steep slabs and loose stone of the slide; this section becomes treacherous when wet, with the potential for long falls. Watch closely for the blazes and rock cairns, because the trail zigzags several times across the slide.

Near the top of the slide, a side trail—easy to overlook—branches right, leading seven-tenths of a mile to the summit of Mount O-J-I. This hike continues straight up the slide, enters the scrub forest, and reaches the summit of Mount Coe 3.3 miles from the trailhead. It's possible to continue over Coe toward the Brothers (see hike number 14). This hike descends the same way you came up.

---

⑰ Mount O-J-I

6.2 mi/6.0 hrs 

Location: In southern Baxter State Park; Northern Maine map page 2, grid c4.

User groups: Hikers only. No wheelchair facilities. This trail may be difficult to snowshoe because of severe winter weather, and is not suitable for skis. Bikes, dogs, and hunting are prohibited.

Access, fees: An entrance fee of $8 per vehicle is charged at the gatehouse, except to vehicles bearing a Maine registration, which enter for free. The park's entrance closes at 8:30 P.M.

Directions: Take Interstate 95 in Maine to exit 56 for Medway/Millinocket. Drive on Route 157 west through East Millinocket to Millinocket. Follow signs for Baxter State Park; the park's Togue Pond gatehouse is 18 miles from Millinocket. Just beyond the gatehouse, take the dirt perimeter road's left fork and drive 10.5 miles to a parking area on the right for the Mount O-J-I Loop, just before Foster Field.

Maps: For a map of trails in the park, get the excellent "Baxter State Park and Katahdin" map for $4.95 from the DeLorme Mapping Company, (800) 253-5081; or the "Baxter Park-Katahdin" map for $2.95 from the Appalachian Mountain Club, (800) 262-4455. For topographic maps of the area, request Doubletop Mountain and Mount Katahdin from the USGS.

Contact: Baxter State Park, 64 Balsam Drive, Millinocket, ME 04462-2190; (207) 723-5140.

Trail notes: This 6.2-mile loop up 3,410-foot Mount O-J-I is one of the most arduous hikes in Baxter State Park off Mount Katahdin. It climbs the mountain's north rockslide—the logical ascent route, being the more difficult of the two slides—and descends the south slide. Both slides are steep, with lots of loose rock and slabs which are hazardous when wet. Hiking time can vary greatly depending upon your comfort level on exposed rock. But you will enjoy extensive views from the slides to the west and south, and excellent views from points near the summit. By the way, O-J-I takes its name from the shapes of three slides visible from the southwest, although the slides have expanded and the letters have become obscured in recent decades.

From the parking area, walk the road toward Foster Field for about 50 feet, and turn right onto the O-J-I Trail. For the first four-tenths of a mile, the terrain is flat, crossing wet areas. Then bear left onto the North Slide Trail, climbing steadily. The trail reaches an often dry streambed at 1.1 miles; turn left and follow it upward for a tenth of a mile to the base of the north slide. Follow the cairns and blazes of the trail, snaking up the slide for about a mile. The trail then re-enters the woods; at 2.5 miles, turn left onto the Old Jay Eye Rock Trail, which leads four-tenths of a mile down a ridge to Old Jay Eye Rock, a boulder perched on the crest of the open ridge where there are long views in every direction. (Skipping this side trail cuts eight-tenths of a mile from this hike's distance.) Double back to the main trail and follow it another two-tenths of a mile to the largely wooded summit, where you get a view toward Mount Coe. Continuing over the summit, the ridge opens up more, with sweeping views of Coe, Katahdin, Doubletop Mountain, and the wilderness lakes to the south. Turn right and descend the south slide, which re-enters the forest within a mile and reaches the junction with the North Slide Trail 2.5 miles below O-J-I's summit. Turn left for the flat walk of four-tenths of a mile back to the road.

18 Doubletop Mountain

6.0 mi/5.5 hrs 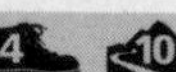

Location: In southern Baxter State Park; Northern Maine map page 2, grid c4.

User groups: Hikers only. No wheelchair facilities. This trail may be difficult to snowshoe because of severe winter weather, and is not suitable for skis. Bikes, dogs, and hunting are prohibited.

Access, fees: An entrance fee of $8 per vehicle is charged at the gatehouse, except to vehicles bearing a Maine registration, which enter for free. The park's entrance closes at 8:30 P.M.

Directions: Take Interstate 95 in Maine to exit 56 for Medway/Millinocket. Drive on Route 157 west through East Millinocket to Millinocket. Follow signs for Baxter State Park; the park's Togue Pond gatehouse is 18 miles from Millinocket. Just beyond the gatehouse, take the dirt perimeter road's left fork and drive 16.9 miles, then turn left into the Nesowadnehunk Field Campground. Drive three-tenths of a mile to the parking area on the right.

Maps: For a map of trails in the park, get the excellent "Baxter State Park and Katahdin" map for $4.95 from the DeLorme Mapping Company, (800) 253-5081; or the "Baxter Park-Katahdin" map for $2.95 from the Appalachian Mountain Club, (800) 262-4455. For a topographic map of the area, request Doubletop Mountain from the USGS.

Contact: Baxter State Park, 64 Balsam Drive, Millinocket, ME 04462-2190; (207) 723-5140.

Trail notes: Measuring in at 3,488 feet, Doubletop Mountain's distinctive high ridge stands out prominently when seen from various points around the south end of Baxter State Park, rising like an upturned ax blade above the narrow valley of Nesowadnehunk Stream. Much of the quarter mile of ridge connecting the North and South peaks lies above tree line, affording some of the best views in the park, from Katahdin to the east, to the cluster of peaks immediately north that includes the Brothers, Coe, and O-J-I, and the wilderness lakes to the south.

From the parking area, cross the road onto a second road leading past campsites. At half a mile, the road ends at the start of the Doubletop Trail. The trail begins relatively flat, until crossing a stream at 1.2 miles, where it begins a very steep climb. It levels out briefly on the mountain's north shoulder, then ascends again. After climbing a short iron ladder, you emerge above the forest a few steps from the North Peak of Doubletop, which is marked by a sign, at 3.1 miles. The trail drops off that summit to the west, then turns south and follows the ridge for two-tenths of a mile to the South Peak. Return the same way you hiked up.

⑲ Kidney Pond Loop

3.1 mi/1.5 hrs 

Location: In southern Baxter State Park; Northern Maine map page 2, grid c4.

User groups: Hikers only. No wheelchair facilities. This trail may be difficult to snowshoe because of severe winter weather, and is not suitable for skis. Bikes, dogs, and hunting are prohibited.

Access, fees: An entrance fee of $8 per vehicle is charged at the gatehouse, except to vehicles bearing a Maine registration, which enter for free. The park's entrance closes at 8:30 P.M.

Directions: Take Interstate 95 in Maine to exit 56 for Medway/Millinocket. Drive on Route 157 west through East Millinocket to Millinocket. Follow signs for Baxter State Park; the park's Togue Pond gatehouse is 18 miles from Millinocket. Just beyond the gatehouse, take the dirt perimeter road's left fork and drive 10.6 miles, then turn left at a sign for Kidney Pond Camps. Drive 1.1 miles to the parking area at the end of the road.

Maps: For a map of trails in the park, get the excellent "Baxter State Park and Katahdin" map for $4.95 from the DeLorme Mapping Company, (800) 253-5081; or the "Baxter Park-Katahdin" map for $2.95 from the Appalachian Mountain Club, (800) 262-4455. For a topographic map of the area, request Doubletop Mountain from the USGS.

Contact: Baxter State Park, 64 Balsam Drive, Millinocket, ME 04462-2190; (207) 723-5140.

Trail notes: This easy, 3.1-mile loop around lovely Kidney Pond offers a chance at seeing moose or other wildlife and good views across the pond toward Katahdin, Doubletop, and O-J-I. Side paths lead to such lakeshore views as Colt's Point, a peninsula jutting into the pond. Paths radiate outward from the loop trail like spokes from a wheel's center, leading to Rocky Pond and other nearby ponds. You could spend hours exploring the various little water bodies in this corner of Baxter State Park.

This hike follows the loop trail around the pond. From the rear of the parking area, pick up the trail at a sign for the Kidney Pond Loop. The trail follows the pond's shore at first, then skirts wide of it into the woods at its southern end. Where a trail bears right toward Daicey Pond about halfway through the hike, go left, passing through woods, following and crossing a stream, and eventually reaching the campground road. Turn left on the road and walk the quarter mile back to the parking area.

⓴ 100-Mile Wilderness

99.4 mi. one way/
9–10 days

Location: Between Monson and Baxter State Park; Northern Maine map page 2, grid d3.

User groups: Hikers only. No wheelchair facilities. Dogs are discouraged along the Appalachian Trail in Maine. Portions of this trail are difficult to ski or snowshoe. Bikes, horses, and hunting are prohibited.

Access, fees: A fee is charged for access to privately owned Golden Road; it has been $8 per vehicle. There are numerous shelters along the Appalachian Trail, and it's legal to camp anywhere along the AT in the 100-Mile Wilderness; low-impact camping is encouraged. A fee-based shuttle to road crossings along the Appalachian Trail, as well as other hiker services, is offered by Shaw's Boarding House, P.O. Box 157, Pleasant Street, Monson, ME 04464; (207) 997-2908 or (207) 997-3597.

Directions: You need to shuttle two vehicles for this trip. Take Interstate 95 in Maine to exit 56 for Medway/Millinocket. Drive on Route 157 west through East Millinocket to Millinocket. Follow signs for Baxter State Park. About a mile beyond the North Woods Trading Post (before the park entrance), bear left onto Golden Road, a private logging road where you will pass through a gate and pay a toll. Continue about seven miles to the private campground at Abol Bridge. Drive over the bridge and park in the dirt lot on the left, about a tenth of a mile east of where the Appalachian Trail emerges at the road. Drive a second vehicle to Monson, and pick up Route 15 north for 3.5 miles to a large turnout on the right and the trailhead for the Appalachian Trail.

Maps: For a trail map, refer to maps 1, 2, and 3 in the "Map and Guide to the Appalachian Trail in Maine," a set of seven maps and a guidebook for $19.95 from the Maine Appalachian Trail Club or the Appalachian Trail Conference (see addresses below). For topographic maps of the area, request Rainbow Lake East, Rainbow Lake West, Wadleigh Mountain, Nahmakanta Stream, Pemadumcook Lake, Jo-Mary Mountain, Big Shanty Mountain, Silver Lake, Barren Mountain East, Barren Mountain West, Monson East, and Monson West from the USGS.

Contact: Maine Appalachian Trail Club, Box 283, Augusta, ME 04332. Appalachian Trail Conference, P.O. Box 807, Harpers Ferry, WV 25425; (304) 535-6331.

Trail notes: The 100-Mile Wilderness is a stretch of the Appalachian Trail in northern Maine which runs for 99.4 miles without crossing a paved or public road. It starts just north of Monson on Route 15 and then is routed to the West Branch of the Penobscot River at Abol Bridge on the Golden Road, a private logging road just outside the southern boundary of Baxter State Park. The trail, however, does cross a few logging roads which provide access to it. While it has grown more popular in recent years, the 100-Mile Wilderness still constitutes one of the most remote backpacking experiences possible in New England. On an August trip, my companions and I spent evenings by ourselves on the shores of vast wilderness lakes, listening to the hysterical song of loons, enjoying wonderful sunsets and sunrises. We swam in chilly streams and walked hours at a time some days without encountering another hiker. This stretch of trail is busiest in August and early September, when the weather is warm and drier, the mosquitoes have dissipated somewhat (though certainly not disappeared), and AT through-hikers are passing through on their way to Katahdin. This far north, the prime hiking season is short, usually commencing once the ground has dried out in July and lasting to early October, when the cooler temperatures start to feel like winter. Remember that there is no place to obtain supplies along this route, so carry everything you will need. The number of days spent on this trail can vary greatly; but generally, the southern half, below Crawford Pond, is more mountainous and rugged, and from Crawford north the trail covers easier, flatter terrain around several vast wilderness lakes. The trail is well marked with the white blazes of the AT, and there are signs at many junctions. Because this is such a long hike, I will describe it in mileage distances beginning at Route 15 and finishing at Abol Bridge.

From Route 15 (mile 0), the AT enters the woods at a trail sign; there is ample parking at a turnout. Traversing relatively easy terrain, the trail passes a series of ponds: the east shore of Spectacle Pond (mile 0.1), the south shore of Bell Pond (1.2), and then a short side path leading right to the west shore of Lily Pond (1.9). With relatively easy hiking from the highway, you reach the Leeman Brook lean-to (3.0), which sleeps six and sits above a small gorge and falls with reliable water. Continuing north, the trail crosses a gravel road (4.2), then passes the west and north shores of Mud Pond (5.2). It crosses a gravel road (6.5), then reaches the top of 60-foot Little Wilson Falls (6.6), one of the highest waterfalls along the AT. The trail turns sharply right, following the rim of the long, deep gorge below the falls, then descends steeply, eventually fording Little Wilson Stream (6.8) at a good view upstream into the gorge. Turn left onto a gravel road (7.2) and follow it for 100 yards, then turn right into the woods. At mile 7.4, the trail reaches a half-mile-long ridge of exposed slate with good views to the east. At the Big Wilson tote road (9.1), turn left, follow it for six-tenths of a mile, then turn right off the road (9.7) and ford Big Wilson Stream, which can be difficult in high water. There is a bridge across the stream 1.5 miles downstream. At mile 10, cross the Canadian Pacific Railroad line.

Less than a half mile from the railroad right-of-way, a short side path leads right to the Wilson Valley lean-to (10.4), which sleeps six; there is water at a nearby spring. At mile 11.6, cross open ledges with views of Barren Mountain. The trail fords Wilbur Brook (13.6) and Vaughn Stream (13.7) above a spectacular 20-foot waterfall that drops into a broad pool. At a tote road (14.2), turn right for 100 yards, then left again into the woods. (That road continues another 1.6 miles southwest to the old Bodfish Farm site, from which it's nearly 12 miles to Monson on Elliotsville Road.) Ford Long Pond Stream (14.3), walk alongside nice pools and flumes, then reach a short side path at 15 miles which leads left to Slu-gundy Gorge, a scenic gorge and falls. Just beyond, another side path leads left 150 yards to the Long Pond Stream lean-to, which sleeps eight; get water from the nearby brook.

Beyond the shelter, the AT begins the steep climb of Barren Mountain. At mile 16.2, a side path leads to the right about 250 feet to the top of the Barren Slide, from which there are excellent views south of Lake Onawa and Boarstone Mountain. Following the ridge, the trail reaches the 2,670-foot summit of Barren Mountain (18.2), which offers sweeping views, particularly south and west; also here is an abandoned fire tower, no longer open. Dropping back into the woods, you pass a side trail (19.1) leading right three-tenths of a mile to the beautiful tarn called Cloud Pond and the nearby lean-to, which sleeps six; water can be obtained from a spring or the pond.

Continuing along the Barren-Chairback Ridge, the trail bounces like a yo-yo over

Southern Maine Map—page 3

rugged terrain, passing over the wooded, 2,383-foot summit of Fourth Mountain (21.2), cliffs on Third Mountain which offer some views (23.7), and a side path leading right two-tenths of a mile to West Chairback Pond (24.3). Just beyond that path, the AT crosses a good stream where you may want to load up on water if you're planning to stay at the Chairback Gap lean-to, where the spring may run dry in late summer. The trail climbs steeply over Columbus Mountain, then drops into Chairback Gap, passing in front of the lean-to there, which sleeps six; the spring is about 200 yards downhill along the trail. The trail then ascends to the top of 2,219-foot Chairback Mountain (26.5), traversing its long, open crest with excellent views west and north. At the end of the ridge, the trail descends a very steep slope of loose talus (26.6), trending left near its bottom. It passes over open ledges (26.9) with views back to Chairback Mountain, then a side path (28.7)—the sign for which is easily overlooked—leading left two-tenths of a mile to East Chairback Pond. At mile 29.9, cross a wide logging road; half a mile to the right (east) is a parking area heavily used by day visitors to Gulf Hagas. The road continues east for 7.1 miles to the Katahdin Iron Works Museum.

Crossing the road, the AT passes through woods to the West Branch of the Pleasant River (30.4), a wide channel that was knee-deep during our August trip, but could be dangerous at high water. (Before fording the river, you will notice a blue-blazed trail leading back to the parking area on the logging road.) After crossing the river, the AT follows easy ground through a forest of tall white pines; a short side path (30.7) leads right to the Hermitage, a stand of white pines up to 130 feet tall. At mile 32, the AT hooks right and a blue-blazed trail leads straight ahead to the 5.2-mile loop through Gulf Hagas, one of the most scenic areas along the AT corridor through Maine and a very worthwhile (and packless!) detour if you have the time (see hike number 25). The AT ascends steadily northward for 4.2 miles, through dense forest where campsites are difficult to find, following Gulf Hagas Brook to the Carl A. Newhall lean-to and tentsites; the lean-to, accessed by a short side path off the AT (35.9), sleeps six and water is available from the brook. Climbing steeply, the trail passes over the 2,683-foot summit of Gulf Hagas Mountain (36.8), where there are limited views to the west from just north of the true summit, then descends to the Sidney Tappen campsite (37.7), for tents only; a spring nearby provides water. It continues north along the arduous ridge, over 3,178-foot West Peak (38.4), with limited views, and the wooded summit of 3,244-foot Hay Mountain (40.0).

At mile 40.6, the White Brook Trail departs to the right (east), descending 1.9 miles to logging roads which eventually link with the road to Katahdin Iron Works. The AT then climbs to the highest point on the ridge and one of the finest views along the 100-Mile Wilderness, the 3,654-foot summit of White Cap Mountain (41.7), where you get your first view on this hike of Mount Katahdin to the north. White Cap is the last big peak in the 100-Mile Wilderness. Descending north off White Cap, passing an open ledge with another good view toward Katahdin (42.5), the trail reaches the Logan Brook lean-to (43.1), which sleeps six and has marginal tentsites and a good stream nearby. Cross a gravel road (44.7), then reach a nice lean-to (46.8) which just opened in 1996 and sleeps at least six. The trail fords the East Branch of the Pleasant River (47.0), which could be difficult at high water, then climbs over 2,017-foot Little Boardman Mountain (50.2); just a tenth of a mile south of the summit are good views from open ledges.

Descending easily, the AT crosses the dirt Kokadjo-B Pond Road (51.6); to reach Route 11, you would turn right (east), continue 8.4 miles to Jo-Mary Road, then bear right and continue another 6.2 miles to Route 11. This hike crosses Kokadjo-B Pond Road, entering the woods and soon reaching the east shore of Crawford Pond (51.7), then a side path (51.9), marked by a sign, leading left about 200 feet to Sand Beach, a beautiful little beach of crushed pebbles. Descending very slightly northward along an old woods road, the AT reaches a side path (54.8) leading 150 feet to the right to the Cooper Brook Falls lean-to and the spectacular cascades along Cooper Brook. Continuing along that flat woods road, the trail crosses the dirt Jo-Mary Road (58.5) beside a bridge over Cooper Brook; to reach Route 11, turn right (east) and follow Jo-Mary Road for 12 miles. This hike crosses the road and re-enters the woods. The trail passes a side path (59.8) leading right two-tenths of a mile to the shore of Cooper Pond.

Continuing north on flat, easy terrain, the AT crosses a gravel road (61.4), fords several streams in succession (61.5), crosses another old logging road (62.0), and reaches a short side path (62.7) veering right to the Antlers campsite, a tenting area set amid red pines on a point of land jutting into vast Lower Jo-Mary Lake. From that junction, the AT hooks left and swings around the west shore of the lake to a junction with the Potaywadjo Ridge Trail (64.2), which leads left and ascends steadily for one mile to broad, open ledges on Potaywadjo Ridge, with sweeping views of the lakes and mountains to the south and east. This is one of the finest viewpoints in the northern half of the 100-Mile Wilderness, and a great place for picking blueberries in late August. From that junction, the AT ascends the wooded end of the ridge, then drops to the Potaywadjo Spring lean-to (66.2), which sleeps six; nearby is a large, reliable spring. Following easy terrain again, the AT crosses Twitchell Brook (66.7) and passes a junction with a side path (66.8) leading a short distance to the right to the shore of Pemadumcook Lake, where you get an excellent view across the water to Katahdin. Cross Deer Brook (68.0), an old logging road (68.8) which leads two-tenths of a mile to the right to a cove on Pemadumcook, then ford a tributary of Nahmakanta Stream (68.9). A high-water bypass trail two-tenths of a mile long diverges from the AT (69.3), then rejoins it (69.4). At mile 70.0, you will ford Tumbledown Dick Stream.

The AT parallels Nahmakanta Stream, where footing grows difficult over many rocks and roots, then crosses a gravel road (73.4); to reach Route 11, you would turn left (southwest) and continue 24 miles via this gravel road to the Jo-Mary Road. This hike crosses the gravel road and re-enters the woods. At mile 73.8, the AT reaches the south shore of Nahmakanta Lake near a short side path leading to a gravel beach. It follows along the lakeshore, skirting into the woods and out onto the rocky shore, to a short side path (76.0) leading right to a sandy beach; the path emerges at one end of the beach, near a small spring. From there the AT crosses Wadleigh Stream (76.3) and then reaches the Wadleigh Stream lean-to (76.4), which sleeps six; the nearby stream provides water. The trail then makes a steep ascent up Nesuntabunt Mountain; from its north summit (78.3), a short side path leads to an open ledge with an excellent view from high above Nahmakanta Lake toward Katahdin. Descending somewhat more moderately off Nesuntabunt, the AT crosses a logging road (79.5); to the right (north), it's 1.2 miles to Pollywog Bridge, and to the left (south) it's 25.2 miles to Route 11. This hike crosses the logging road and re-enters the woods.

After circling Crescent Pond (80.1), the AT passes a short side path (81.1) leading left to a rather exposed ledge high above Pollywog Gorge. It then parallels Pollywog Stream to a logging road (82.1); to reach Route 11, you would turn south and follow the road 26.4 miles. This hike turns left and crosses the stream on a bridge. Walk past a dirt road branching right, and re-enter the woods to the right. The trail follows a picturesque gorge along Rainbow Stream for about two miles, then reaches the Rainbow Stream lean-to (84.5), which sleeps six; water is available from the stream. After crossing the stream, the trail follows the Rainbow Deadwaters for 1.6 miles to the west end of Rainbow Lake (86.5). From here easy terrain leads to a small clearing (89.8); to the right, a short path leads to tentsites at the Rainbow Spring Campsite, and to the left it's just a short walk to the spring and the lakeshore. Continuing along the big lake's shore, the AT reaches the Rainbow Mountain Trail at mile 90.0, which bears right and climbs a fairly easy 1.1 miles to the bare summit of Rainbow Mountain and excellent views, especially toward Katahdin.

The AT continues to the east end of Rainbow Lake (91.7), passes a side path (91.8) leading right a tenth of a mile to Little Beaver Pond and four-tenths of a mile to Big Beaver Pond, then ascends to Rainbow Ledges (93.5); from various points along the ledges you get long views south and northeast to Katahdin. Descending easily, the AT fords Hurd Brook (96.0), which can be difficult when the water is high, and reaches the Hurd Brook lean-to on the other side of the brook; it sleeps six, and water is available from the brook. From there, the trail rolls through fairly easy terrain to Golden Road (99.3). Turn right and follow the road to Abol Bridge (99.4), the terminus of this momentous trek.

21 Half a 100-Mile Wilderness

47.8 or 51.6 mi. one way/ 4 10
4–6 days

Location: Between Monson and Baxter State Park; Northern Maine map page 2, grid d3.

User groups: Hikers only. No wheelchair facilities. Dogs are discouraged along the Appalachian Trail in Maine. Portions of this trail are difficult to ski or snowshoe. Bikes, horses, and hunting are prohibited.

Access, fees: A vehicle toll (most recently $8) is charged for access to privately owned Golden Road and Jo-Mary Road, which isn't passable at certain times of year due to snow or muddy conditions. There are numerous shelters along the Appalachian Trail, and it's legal to camp anywhere along the AT in the 100-Mile Wilderness; low-impact camping is encouraged. A fee-based shuttle to road crossings along the Appalachian Trail, as well as other hiker services, is offered by Shaw's Boarding House, P.O. Box 157, Pleasant Street, Monson, ME 04464; (207) 997-2908 or (207) 997-3597.

Directions: You need to shuttle two vehicles for this trip. To backpack the northern half of the 100-Mile Wilderness, take Interstate 95 in Maine to exit 56 for Medway/Millinocket. Drive on Route 157 west through East Millinocket to Millinocket. Follow signs for Baxter State Park. About a mile beyond the North Woods Trading Post (before the park entrance), bear left onto Golden Road, a private logging road where you will pass through a gate and pay a toll. Continue about seven miles to the private campground at the Abol Bridge over the West Branch of the Penobscot River. Drive over the bridge and park in the dirt lot on the left, about a tenth of a mile east of where the Appalachian Trail emerges at the road. Drive a second vehicle back to Millinocket. From the junction of Routes 11 and 157, go south on Route 11 for 15.5 miles and turn right (west) onto gravel Jo-Mary Road. Continue two-tenths of a mile and pass through a gate where a vehicle toll is collected. Proceed another six miles and bear left at a fork, following the sign for Gauntlet Falls/B-Pond (ignore the sign for the Appalachian Trail, which is also reached via the right fork). Continuing another 2.6 miles, bear right where the B-Pond Road branches left. At 14.6 miles from Route 11, the AT crosses the road a tenth of a mile south of Crawford Pond; park off the road. To backpack the southern half of the 100-Mile Wilderness, leave one car at the AT crossing of the above-mentioned logging road near Crawford Pond, then return to Route 11 and drive south to Monson. Pick up Route 15 north for 3.5 miles to a large turnout on the right and the trailhead for the Appalachian Trail at the southern end of the 100-Mile Wilderness.

Maps: For a trail map, refer to maps 1, 2, and 3 in the "Map and Guide to the Appalachian Trail in Maine," a set of seven maps and a guidebook for $19.95 from the Maine Appalachian Trail Club or the Appalachian Trail Conference (see addresses below). For topographic maps of the area, request Rainbow Lake East, Rainbow Lake West, Wadleigh Mountain, Nahmakanta Stream, Pemadumcook Lake, Jo-Mary Mountain, Big Shanty Mountain, Silver Lake, Barren Mountain East, Barren Mountain West, Monson East, and Monson West from the USGS.

Contact: Maine Appalachian Trail Club, Box 283, Augusta, ME 04332. Appalachian Trail Conference, P.O. Box 807, Harpers Ferry, WV 25425; (304) 535-6331.

Trail notes: Backpackers seeking one of the most remote experiences possible in New England, but who don't have the time to hike the entire 100-Mile Wilderness—the stretch of the Appalachian Trail in northern Maine which crosses no paved or public road for 99.4 miles—can instead backpack "half a wilderness." The AT crosses the dirt Kokadjo-B Pond Road, identified on some maps as Johnson Pond Road, at a logical place to begin or conclude a trek of either the northern or southern half of the 100-Mile Wilderness. The 51.6 trail miles from this logging road south to Route 15 are characterized by rugged hiking over a landscape dominated by low mountains boasting nice, if sporadic, views. The 47.8 miles of trail north to Golden Road at Abol Bridge have an entirely different personality, traversing mostly flat, low terrain around sprawling wilderness lakes. The southern portion can take five days or more; the northern is easier and can be done in four days by fit hikers. See the trail notes on the 100-Mile Wilderness (hike number 20) for a detailed description of both options.

22 Pollywog Gorge

3.8 mi/2.5 hrs 

Location: Southwest of Baxter State Park; Northern Maine map page 2, grid c3.

User groups: Hikers only. No wheelchair facilities. Dogs are discouraged along the Appalachian Trail in Maine. Portions of this trail are difficult to ski or snowshoe. Bikes, horses, and hunting are prohibited.

Access, fees: A toll is charged on private Jo-Mary Road, which isn't passable at certain times of year due to snow or muddy conditions. The Rainbow Stream lean-to is located 2.4 miles north on the AT from the Pollywog Stream bridge (not along this hike). It's legal to camp anywhere along the AT in the 100-Mile Wilderness; low-impact camping is encouraged.

Directions: From Route 11, 15.5 miles south of the junction of Routes 11 and 157 in Millinocket, and near where Route 11 crosses over Bear Brook, turn west onto private, gravel Jo-Mary Road. In two-tenths of a mile, pass through a gate and pay a vehicle toll. Continue six miles from the gate and bear right at a sign for the Appalachian Trail. Follow that road another 20.2 miles (ignoring unimproved roads diverging from it) to where the AT crosses Pollywog Stream on a bridge, and park at the roadside.

Maps: For a trail map, refer to map 1 in the "Map and Guide to the Appalachian Trail in Maine," a set of seven maps and a guidebook for $19.95 from the Maine Appalachian Trail Club or the Appalachian Trail Conference (see addresses below). For a topographic map of the area, request Rainbow Lake West from the USGS.

Contact: Maine Appalachian Trail Club, Box 283, Augusta, ME 04332. Appalachian Trail Conference, P.O. Box 807, Harpers Ferry, WV 25425; (304) 535-6331.

Trail notes: This hike makes a 3.8-mile loop mostly along the Appalachian Trail through scenic Pollywog Gorge, finishing on a 1.2-mile stretch of the logging road. From a small ledge high above the stream, you peer down a precipitous cliff into the gorge. Day hikers could easily combine this with the hike of Nesuntabunt Mountain (hike number 23). Immediately before the bridge over Pollywog Stream, turn left (southbound) on the AT and follow it one mile to a side path leading about 150 feet to the gorge overlook. Continue south on the AT through woods and around Crescent Pond to the logging road, 2.6 miles from the hike's start. Turn left and follow the road 1.2 miles back to the bridge.

---

23 Nesuntabunt Mountain

2.4 mi/1.5 hrs 

Location: Southwest of Baxter State Park; Northern Maine map page 2, grid c3.

User groups: Hikers only. No wheelchair facilities. Dogs are discouraged along the Appalachian Trail in Maine. Portions of this trail are difficult to ski or snowshoe. Bikes, horses, and hunting are prohibited.

Access, fees: A toll is charged on private Jo-Mary Road, which isn't passable at certain times of year due to snow or muddy conditions. The Wadleigh Stream lean-to is located 3.1 miles south on the AT from the access road, and 1.9 miles south of the summit of Nesuntabunt Mountain. It's legal to camp anywhere along the AT in the 100-Mile Wilderness; low-impact camping is encouraged.

Directions: From Route 11, 15.5 miles south of the junction of Routes 11 and 157 in Millinocket, and near where Route 11 crosses over Bear Brook, turn west onto the private, gravel Jo-Mary Road. In two-tenths of a mile, pass through a gate and pay a vehicle toll. Continue six miles from the gate and bear right at a sign for the Appalachian Trail. Follow that road another 19 miles (ignoring unimproved roads diverging from it) to the AT crossing, and park at the roadside.

Maps: For a trail map, refer to map 1 in the "Map and Guide to the Appalachian Trail in Maine," a set of seven maps and a guidebook for $19.95 from the Maine Appalachian Trail Club or the Appalachian Trail Conference (see addresses below). For a topographic map of the area, request Rainbow Lake West from the USGS.

Contact: Maine Appalachian Trail Club, Box 283, Augusta, ME 04332. Appalachian Trail Conference, P.O. Box 807, Harpers Ferry, WV 25425; (304) 535-6331.

Trail notes: At barely more than 1,500 feet, tiny Nesuntabunt Mountain merits notice only here in the relatively flat, low terrain around the wilderness lakes along the northern reaches of the Appalachian Trail. From an open ledge down a short side path off the AT at Nesuntabunt's summit, hikers get a sweeping view of vast Nahmakanta Lake and Mount Katahdin when clouds aren't smothering Maine's highest peak. You can turn this 2.4-mile hike into an overnight trip by pushing 1.9 miles beyond Nesuntabunt to the Wadleigh Stream lean-to, and continuing south along Nahmakanta's isolated shore. (From Wadleigh Stream, it's 2.6 miles south along the AT to the lake's southern tip.) Or you might want to combine this hike with nearby Pollywog Gorge (hike number 22). From the logging road, walk southbound (to the right) along the white-blazed AT for 1.2 miles to Nesuntabunt's summit. Turn left onto a side path to the open ledge. Retrace your steps back to the beginning of the hike.

24 White Cap Mountain

23.0 mi/2–3 days 

Location: Between Monson and Baxter State Park; Northern Maine map page 2, grid d3.

User groups: Hikers only. No wheelchair facilities. Dogs are discouraged along the Appalachian Trail in Maine. Portions of this trail are difficult to ski or snowshoe. Bikes, horses, and hunting are prohibited.

Access, fees: This section of the Appalachian Trail is reached via a private logging road, and a daily toll of $4 per person is collected; children under 15 enter free. The access road isn't passable at certain times of year due to snow or muddy conditions. The Carl A. Newhall lean-to, with tentsites, is located 5.7 miles north on the AT from the parking area, and the Sidney Tappan campsite, for tents only, lies 1.8 miles farther north. It's legal to camp anywhere along the AT in the 100-Mile Wilderness; low-impact camping is encouraged.

Directions: From Route 11, 5.5 miles north of Brownville Junction and 25.6 miles south of Millinocket, turn west onto a gravel road at a sign for Katahdin Iron Works. Follow it nearly seven miles to a gate where an entrance fee is collected. Beyond the gate, cross the bridge and turn right. Drive three miles, bear left at a fork, then continue another 3.7 miles to a parking area (half a mile before the road's crossing of the Appalachian Trail).

Maps: For a trail map, refer to map 2 in the "Map and Guide to the Appalachian Trail in Maine," a set of seven maps and a guidebook for $19.95 available from the Maine Appalachian Trail Club or the Appalachian Trail Conference (see addresses below). For topographic maps of the area, request Hay Mountain, Big Shanty Mountain, Barren Mountain East, and Silver Lake from the USGS.

Contact: Maine Appalachian Trail Club, Box 283, Augusta, ME 04332. Appalachian Trail Conference, P.O. Box 807, Harpers Ferry, WV 25425; (304) 535-6331.

Trail notes: At 3,654 feet, White Cap Mountain is the tallest peak in the 100-Mile Wilderness, the 99.4-mile stretch of the Appalachian Trail through northern Maine which isn't crossed by a paved or public road. White Cap is also the last big peak in the Wilderness for northbound hikers, and offers excellent views, especially toward Mount Katahdin. A remote summit, White Cap can be reached on a two- or three-day trek via the logging road which accesses the AT near Gulf Hagas.

From the parking area, follow the blue-blazed trail two-tenths of a mile to the white-blazed Appalachian Trail at the West Branch of the Pleasant River, a normally knee-deep channel about 80 feet across which you must ford (bringing a pair of sandals or old sneakers for this stony crossing makes it much easier on the feet). Continuing along the wide, flat AT, pass a side trail two-tenths of a mile from the river which leads to campsites at Hay Brook. At three tenths of a mile, another side path leads about 200 feet into the Hermitage, a grove of ancient white pine trees, some as tall as

130 feet. The AT continues over easy ground among other giant pines to the junction with the Gulf Hagas Trail, 1.3 miles from the river (a worthwhile detour from this hike; see hike number 25). The AT turns sharply right and ascends steadily northward for 4.2 miles, following Gulf Hagas Brook through dense forest to the Carl A. Newhall lean-to and tentsites, reached by a short side path off the AT; the lean-to sleeps six and water is available from the brook. Climbing steeply, the trail passes over the 2,683-foot summit of Gulf Hagas Mountain 6.6 miles from the road, where there are limited views to the west from just north of the true summit. After descending to the Sidney Tappen campsite, the AT yo-yos north along the arduous ridge, over 3,178-foot West Peak (8.2 miles), with limited views, and the wooded summit of 3,244-foot Hay Mountain (9.8 miles). The trail dips again, passing a junction at 10.4 miles with the White Brook Trail (which descends east 1.9 miles to logging roads that eventually link with the road to Katahdin Iron Works). The AT then climbs to the summit of White Cap. Return the way you came.

25 Gulf Hagas

8.0 mi/5.5 hrs 

Location: Between Monson and Baxter State Park; Northern Maine map page 2, grid d3.

User groups: Hikers only. No wheelchair facilities. Dogs are discouraged along the Appalachian Trail in Maine. Portions of this trail are difficult to ski or snowshoe. Bikes, horses, and hunting are prohibited.

Access, fees: Gulf Hagas is reached via a private logging road, and a daily toll of $4 per person is collected; children under 15 enter free. The access roads are not passable at certain times of year due to snow or muddy conditions.

Directions: From Route 11, 5.5 miles north of Brownville Junction and 25.6 miles south of Millinocket, turn west onto a gravel road at a sign for Katahdin Iron Works. Follow it nearly seven miles to a gate where an entrance fee is collected. Beyond the gate, cross the bridge and turn right. Drive three miles, bear left at a fork, then continue another 3.7 miles to a parking area (half a mile before the road crosses the Appalachian Trail).

Maps: For a trail map, refer to map 2 in the "Map and Guide to the Appalachian Trail in Maine," a set of seven maps and a guidebook for $19.95 available from the Maine Appalachian Trail Club or the Appalachian Trail Conference (see addresses below). For topographic maps of the area, request Barren Mountain East and Silver Lake from the USGS.

Contact: Maine Appalachian Trail Club, Box 283, Augusta, ME 04332. Appalachian Trail Conference, P.O. Box 807, Harpers Ferry, WV 25425; (304) 535-6331.

Trail notes: Known as "Maine's Little Grand Canyon," Gulf Hagas is a deep, narrow canyon along the West Branch of the Pleasant River that inspired a friend and me to ooh and aah nonstop throughout our hike along its rim. At every turn we'd think we had seen a view without comparison in New England, then we'd reach another lookout that completely blew us away again. Admiring its sheer walls which drop right into a boulder-choked, impassable river, it's easy to understand why the Abenaki gave it the name "hagas," their word for "evil place." The blue-blazed loop trail through the gulf is a 5.2-mile detour off the Appalachian Trail, but the round-trip hike from the parking area is eight miles. This trail goes through very little elevation gain or loss, but runs constantly up and down over rugged, rocky terrain; your hike could easily take more than the estimated

5.5 hours, especially when you start hanging out at the many waterfalls and clifftop viewpoints.

From the parking area, follow the blue-blazed trail two-tenths of a mile to the white-blazed Appalachian Trail at the West Branch of the Pleasant River, a normally knee-deep channel about 80 feet across which you must ford (bringing a pair of sandals or old sneakers for this stony crossing makes it much easier on the feet). Continuing along the wide, flat AT, pass a side trail two-tenths of a mile from the river which leads to campsites at Hay Brook. At three-tenths of a mile, another side path leads about 200 feet into the Hermitage, a grove of ancient white pine trees, some as tall as 130 feet. The AT continues over easy ground among other giant pines to the junction with the Gulf Hagas Trail, 1.3 miles from the river. The AT turns sharply right, but continue straight onto the blue-blazed trail, immediately crossing Gulf Hagas Brook. Bear left onto the loop trail. At a tenth of a mile, a side path leads left to beautiful Screw Auger Falls on Gulf Hagas Brook. At two-tenths of a mile, another side path leads to the bottom of Screw Auger. (The brook continues down through a series of cascades and pools, including some spots ideal for swimming.)

The Gulf Hagas Trail continues down to the rim of the canyon, weaving in and out of the forest to views from the canyon rim and dropping down to the riverbank in places. Significant features along the rim include Hammond Street Pitch, a view high above the river reached on a short path at seven-tenths of a mile; the Jaws Cascades (seen from side paths or views at 1.2, 1.4, and 1.5 miles); Buttermilk Falls at 1.8 miles; Stair Falls at 1.9 miles; Billings Falls at 2.7 miles; and a view down the gulf from its head at 2.9 miles. Three miles into the loop, turn right onto the Pleasant River Road, an old logging road which is at first a footpath, but widens over the 2.2 miles back to the start of this loop. The logging road provides much easier walking and a faster return route than doubling back along the gulf rim.

26 Barren Mountain and Slugundy Gorge

8.0 mi/6.0 hrs 

Location: Northeast of Monson; Northern Maine map page 2, grid d3.

User groups: Hikers only. No wheelchair facilities. Dogs are discouraged along the Appalachian Trail in Maine. Portions of this trail are difficult to ski or snowshoe. Bikes, horses, and hunting are prohibited.

Access, fees: Parking and access are free. The dirt roads from Monson aren't passable at certain times of year due to snow or muddy conditions. The Long Pond Stream lean-to is along the Appalachian Trail, nine-tenths of a mile into this hike, and the Cloud Pond lean-to lies 1.2 miles beyond the summit of Barren Mountain. It's legal to camp anywhere along the AT in the 100-Mile Wilderness; low-impact camping is encouraged.

Directions: From the center of Monson, drive half a mile north on Route 15 and turn right onto Elliottsville Road. Continue 7.8 miles to Big Wilson Stream, cross the bridge, then turn left onto a dirt road. Drive another 2.8 miles to the Bodfish Farm, bear left at a fork, then go 2.9 miles farther to where the white-blazed Appalachian Trail crosses the dirt road, known as the Bodfish Farm–Long Pond tote road; park at the roadside.

Maps: For a trail map, refer to map 3 in the "Map and Guide to the Appalachian Trail in Maine," a set of seven maps and a guidebook for $19.95 from the Maine Appalachian Trail Club or the Appalachian Trail Conference (see addresses below). For topographic maps of the area, request Monson East, Barren Mountain West, and Barren Mountain East from the USGS.

Contact: Maine Appalachian Trail Club, Box 283, Augusta, ME 04332. Appalachian Trail Conference, P.O. Box 807, Harpers Ferry, WV 25425; (304) 535-6331.

Trail notes: By employing dirt logging roads to access this stretch of the Appalachian Trail, you can make a one-day or an overnight hike into this picturesque and varied area of the 100-Mile Wilderness. The round-trip hike to the summit of Barren Mountain is eight demanding miles, but it's just 1.6 miles round-trip to Slugundy Gorge. Barren and Slugundy are reached by walking north on the AT, but just half a mile south on the trail lies a broad, 20-foot-high waterfall along Vaughn Stream (an easy detour not figured into this hike's distance).

From the dirt road, turn right (north) onto the AT. Within a tenth of a mile, ford Long Pond Stream. The trail then parallels nice pools and flumes in the stream for more than half a mile; after it turns uphill, a short side path leads left to Slugundy Gorge, a scenic gorge and falls. Just beyond, another side path leads left 150 yards to the Long Pond Stream lean-to. Beyond the shelter, the AT begins the steep climb of Barren Mountain. At two miles, a side path leads right about 250 feet to the top of the Barren Slide, from which there are excellent views south of Lake Onawa and Boarstone Mountain. Following the ridge, the trail reaches the aptly named, 2,670-foot summit of Barren Mountain two miles beyond the slide, where there are sweeping views, particularly south and west; an abandoned fire tower stands at the summit. Continuing north on the AT for nine-tenths of a mile brings you to a side trail leading right three-tenths of a mile to the beautiful tarn called Cloud Pond and the nearby lean-to, but to finish this hike, turn around and hike back the way you came.

27 Isle au Haut: Eben's Head

1.0 mi/0.75 hr 

Location: In Acadia National Park on Isle au Haut; Southern Maine map page 3, grid c4.

User groups: Hikers and dogs. No wheelchair facilities. Dogs must be on a leash. The island rarely gets enough snow for winter activities. Bikes, horses, and hunting are prohibited.

Access, fees: Isle au Haut is reached via mailboat/ferry from Stonington, at a round-trip cost of $20 per adult and $10 per child. Refer to the Isle au Haut description at the beginning of this chapter for more information.

Directions: To reach the dock where the ferry departs for Isle au Haut, take Route 15 to Main Street in Stonington and turn left at Bartlett's Market; the ferry landing is past the firehouse, at the end of the pier.

Maps: A basic map of trails and roads on the island is issued free to visitors on the ferry or with camping reservations. Two good trail and contour maps of the area are the waterproof "Acadia National Park, Mount Desert Island, Isle au Haut" map 212 for $8.99 from Trails Illustrated, (800) 962-1643; and the "Map of Acadia National Park/Mount Desert Island" for $5.95 (paper) from the Appalachian Mountain Club, (800) 262-4455. For topographic maps of the island, request Isle au Haut West and Isle au Haut East from the USGS.

Contact: Acadia National Park, P.O. Box 177, Bar Harbor, ME 04609; (207) 288-3338. For ferry information, contact the Isle au Haut Ferry Company, Stonington, ME 04681; (207) 367-5193.

Trail notes: Eben's Head is the rocky bluff jutting into the ocean at the mouth of Duck Harbor opposite the boat landing.

I watched the sunset behind Eben's Head two nights straight before getting up early one morning and walking the trail out onto the head. There, I stood atop cliffs above the pounding surf, watching morning fog slowly lift off the ocean. I highly recommend walking out here to catch the sunset some evening.

From the boat landing at Duck Harbor, turn left on the trail toward the water pump. Pass the trail branching right for the campground, and continue straight onto Western Head Road. Follow it past the water pump and out to the main road. Turn left and follow the dirt main road around Duck Harbor. About 0.1 mile after the main road turns inland, you'll pass the Duck Harbor Trail on the right, then turn left onto the Eben's Head Trail, which leads through woods out to that rocky bluff visible from the boat landing. I spent some time exploring the cove on the other side of Eben's Head before returning the same way I hiked in.

28 Isle Au Haut: Western Head Loop

5.0 mi/3.0 hrs 

Location: In Acadia National Park on Isle au Haut; Southern Maine map page 3, grid c4.

User groups: Hikers and dogs. No wheelchair facilities. Dogs must be on a leash. The island rarely gets enough snow for winter activities. Bikes, horses, and hunting are prohibited.

Access, fees: Isle au Haut is reached via mailboat/ferry from Stonington, at a round-trip cost of $20 per adult and $10 per child. Refer to the Isle au Haut description at the beginning of this chapter for more information.

Directions: To reach the dock where the ferry departs for Isle au Haut, drive Route 15 to Main Street in Stonington and turn left at Bartlett's Market; the ferry landing is past the firehouse, at the end of the pier.

Maps: A basic map of trails and roads on the island is issued free to visitors on the ferry or with camping reservations. Two good trail and contour maps of the area are the waterproof "Acadia National Park, Mount Desert Island, Isle au Haut" map 212 for $8.99 from Trails Illustrated, (800) 962-1643; and the "Map of Acadia National Park/ Mount Desert Island" for $5.95 (paper) from the Appalachian Mountain Club, (800) 262-4455. For topographic maps of the island, request Isle au Haut West and Isle au Haut East from the USGS.

Contact: Acadia National Park, P.O. Box 177, Bar Harbor, ME 04609; (207) 288-3338. For ferry information, contact the Isle au Haut Ferry Company, Stonington, ME 04681; (207) 367-5193.

Trail notes: If you have time for just one hike on Isle au Haut, this is the one to take. It follows the stunning, rocky coast around Western Head, offers the opportunity at low tide to wander onto the tiny island known as Western Ear, and climbs over 314-foot Duck Harbor Mountain, which boasts the most sweeping views on the island. Although much of the hike is relatively flat, the trail is fairly rugged in places. My companions on this hike ranged in age from 11 to 71, and we all equally enjoyed exploring the shore and woods—as well as receiving a surprise visit from a seal.

From the boat landing at Duck Harbor, follow the trail leading left toward the water pump. Pass the trail branching right for the campground, and continue straight until reaching Western Head Road. Bearing left along the road, it's about 200 yards to the water pump (if you need water). For this hike, take the grassy road to the right and follow it for less than a mile. Turn right onto the Western Head Trail, which reaches the coast within about a half mile. The trail turns left (south) and follows the rugged coast out to the point at Western Head, where that trail ends and the Cliff Trail begins. (At low tide, you can walk across the narrow channel out to Western Ear. Be careful not to get trapped out there, or you'll have to wait hours for the tide to go out again.)

The Cliff Trail heads northward into the woods, alternately following more rugged coastline and turning back into the forest to skirt steep cliffs. It reaches the end of Western Head Road in less than a mile. Turn left and follow the road about a quarter mile. When you see a cove on your right, turn right (watch for the trail sign, which is somewhat hidden) onto the Goat Trail. (The Western Head Road leads directly back to Duck Harbor landing, a hike of less than two miles, and is a good option for hikers who want to avoid the steep rock scrambling on Duck Harbor Mountain.) Follow the Goat Trail along the coast for less than a half mile. At scenic Squeaker Cove, turn left onto the Duck Harbor Mountain Trail; from here, it's a bit more than a mile back to Duck Harbor landing. The trail grows steep, involving somewhat exposed scrambling up rock slabs, and traverses several open ledges on Duck Harbor Mountain with terrific long views of Isle au Haut Bay to the west (including Vinalhaven Island, the nearest piece of land across Isle au Haut Bay), and the islands and peninsulas of Penobscot Bay to the north. The trail then descends to Western Head Road; turn right for Duck Harbor.

29 Isle Au Haut: Duck Harbor Mountain/ Merchant Point Loop

4.5 mi/2.5 hrs 

Location: In Acadia National Park on Isle au Haut; Southern Maine map page 3, grid c4.

User groups: Hikers and dogs. No wheelchair facilities. Dogs must be on a leash. The island rarely gets enough snow for winter activities. Bikes, horses, and hunting are prohibited.

Access, fees: Isle au Haut is reached via mailboat/ferry from Stonington, at a round-trip cost of $20 per adult and $10 per child. Refer to the Isle au Haut description at the beginning of this chapter for more information.

Directions: To reach the dock where the ferry departs for Isle au Haut, take Route 15 to Main Street in Stonington and turn left at Bartlett's Market; the ferry landing is past the firehouse, at the end of the pier.

Maps: A basic map of trails and roads on the island is issued free to visitors on the ferry or with camping reservations. Two good trail and contour maps of the area are the waterproof "Acadia National Park, Mount Desert Island, Isle au Haut" map 212 for $8.99 from Trails Illustrated, (800) 962-1643; and the "Map of Acadia National Park/ Mount Desert Island" for $5.95 (paper) from the Appalachian Mountain Club, (800) 262-4455. For topographic maps of the island, request Isle au Haut West and Isle au Haut East from the USGS.

Contact: Acadia National Park, P.O. Box 177, Bar Harbor, ME 04609; (207) 288-3338. For ferry information, contact the Isle au Haut Ferry Company, Stonington, ME 04681; (207) 367-5193.

Trail notes: This loop offers another way of hiking Duck Harbor Mountain and takes you out to rugged coastline, scenic coves, and Merchant Point. My companions and I saw few other people on these trails one June day—but we did see a seal, ducks, and cormorants, and we explored a wonderful cove littered with smooth stones. This hike traverses the mountain in the opposite direction from the Western Head Loop (hike number 28). It's easier going up the

Northern Maine Map—page 2

mountain from this side, so hikers squeamish about the rock scrambling on the other side can hike up this way for the views, then just double back to Duck Harbor.

From the boat landing at Duck Harbor, turn left on the trail toward the water pump. Pass the trail branching right for the campground, and continue straight until reaching Western Head Road. Bearing left along the road, it's about 200 yards to the water pump (if you need water). For this hike, take the grassy road to the right and follow it about a quarter mile, then turn left onto the Duck Harbor Mountain Trail. Follow it a little more than a mile, over several open ledges with commanding views of the southern end of Isle au Haut. Reaching the trail's terminus at Squeaker Cove, turn left onto the Goat Trail, which moves in and out between woods and the coast. In less than a mile you'll reach a trail junction; left leads back to the dirt main road (where you would turn left for Duck Harbor), and this hike bears right on a trail out to the rocky protrusion of Merchant Point (a great lunch spot). From the point, the trail turns back into the forest, crosses a marshy area, and reaches the main road. Turn left and follow the road a bit more than a mile to the head of Duck Harbor. Turn left onto Western Head Road, passing the water pump on the way back to the landing.

30 Isle Au Haut Eastern Head

6.5 mi/3.5 hrs 

Location: In Acadia National Park on Isle au Haut; Southern Maine map page 3, grid c4.

User groups: Hikers and dogs. No wheelchair facilities. Dogs must be on a leash. The island rarely gets enough snow for winter activities. Bikes, horses, and hunting are prohibited.

Access, fees: Isle au Haut is reached via mailboat/ferry from Stonington, at a round-trip cost of $20 per adult and $10 per child. Refer to the Isle au Haut description at the beginning of this chapter for more information.

Directions: To reach the dock where the ferry departs for Isle au Haut, drive on Route 15 to Main Street in Stonington and turn left at Bartlett's Market; the ferry landing is past the firehouse, at the end of the pier.

Maps: A basic map of trails and roads on the island is issued free to visitors on the ferry or with camping reservations. Two good trail and contour maps of the area are the waterproof "Acadia National Park, Mount Desert Island, Isle au Haut" map 212 for $8.99 from Trails Illustrated, (800) 962-1643; and the "Map of Acadia National Park/ Mount Desert Island" for $5.95 (paper) from the Appalachian Mountain Club, (800) 262-4455. For topographic maps of the island, request Isle au Haut West and Isle au Haut East from the USGS.

Contact: Acadia National Park, P.O. Box 177, Bar Harbor, ME 04609; (207) 288-3338. For ferry information, contact the Isle au Haut Ferry Company, Stonington, ME 04681; (207) 367-5193.

Trail notes: The Eastern Head of Isle au Haut attracts few hikers, probably for a variety of reasons, none of which reflect how nice a spot this is. It is not connected to the rest of the national parkland on the island. It is fairly distant from Duck Harbor. And the trail out to Eastern Head is not marked or easy to find. All of which help explain why my companion and I had this stretch of battered shoreline all to ourselves for an entire afternoon.

I'll describe here the most direct route to Eastern Head, but the best way to take this hike is to combine it with the Duck Harbor Mountain/Merchant Point Loop (hike number 29). From the boat landing at Duck

Harbor, turn left on the trail toward the water pump. Upon reaching Western Head Road, continue straight, passing the water pump, out to the main road. Turn right, and follow the dirt main road for more than two miles (passing the trail coming from Merchant Point on the right) to a cove on Head Harbor where there are several small homes. Respect the fact that this is private land along the town road. The road bends to the left and becomes pavement. Less than a tenth of a mile after the pavement begins, turn right onto an unmarked dirt road; a yellow house lies a short distance down this road on the left. Follow the road for about a half mile to its end, where it becomes a little-used, grassy lane and terminates at a red house. An old car sits in the yard, as a ranger described it to me, "melting into the ground." The unmarked but obvious trail begins here, and continues nearly a mile out to the coast at Thunder Gulch, a deep chop reaching about 100 feet back into the oceanside cliffs. You can wander around the clifftops here, and enjoy a view of ocean and the tiny island called Eastern Ear (which cannot be reached on foot). Return the way you came.

31 Bernard and Mansell Mountains

3.7 mi/2.5 hrs 

Location: In Acadia National Park; Southern Maine map page 3, grid b4.

User groups: Hikers, dogs, and snowshoers. No wheelchair facilities. Dogs must be on a leash. This trail is not suitable for skis. Bikes, horses, and hunting are prohibited.

Access, fees: Parking and access are free.

Directions: From Route 102 in Southwest Harbor, turn west onto Seal Cove Road. Take a right onto Long Pond Road and follow it to the parking area at the south end of Long Pond (and a great view of the pond). The park visitors center is located north of Bar Harbor, at the junction of Route 3 and the start of the Park Loop Road.

Maps: A basic park map is available at the visitors center. Three good trail and contour maps of the area are the waterproof "Acadia National Park, Mount Desert Island, Isle au Haut" map 212 for $8.99 from Trails Illustrated, (800) 962-1643; the waterproof "Mount Desert Island and Acadia National Park" map for $7.95 from the DeLorme Mapping Company, (800) 253-5081; and the "Map of Acadia National Park/Mount Desert Island" for $5.95 (paper) from the Appalachian Mountain Club, (800) 262-4455. For a topographic map of the area, request Southwest Harbor from the USGS.

Contact: Acadia National Park, P.O. Box 177, Bar Harbor, ME 04609; (207) 288-3338. Friends of Acadia, P.O. Box 725, Bar Harbor, ME 04609; (207) 288-3340.

Trail notes: While Bernard (1,071 feet) and Mansell (949 feet) are the two highest mountains on the west side of Mount Desert Island, their summits are wooded, so these trails lack the spectacular views of other peaks in Acadia National Park. Still, this loop offers a scenic walk through the woods, is fairly challenging, and does take you past a few good views of the bays and Long Pond.

From the parking area, hike west on the Long Pond Trail, soon branching left onto the Cold Brook Trail. In less than a half mile, cross Gilley Field and follow a road a short distance to the Sluiceway Trail on the right. It climbs fairly steeply to the South Face Trail, where you turn left for the summit of Bernard Mountain, a few minutes' walk away. Backtrack and follow the trail down into Great Notch and straight ahead to the summit of Mansell Mountain. Continue over the summit, picking up the Perpendicular Trail, which descends the rugged east face of Mansell, often passing below

low cliffs, to the Long Pond Trail. Turn right for the parking area.

㉜ Beech Mountain

1.2 mi/1.0 hr 

Location: In Acadia National Park; Southern Maine map page 3, grid b4.

User groups: Hikers, dogs, and snowshoers. No wheelchair facilities. Dogs must be on a leash. This trail is not suitable for skis. Bikes, horses, and hunting are prohibited.

Access, fees: Parking and access are free.

Directions: From the junction of Routes 198 and 102 in Somesville, drive south on Route 102 for eight-tenths of a mile and turn right onto Pretty Marsh Road at the sign for Beech Mountain and the Beech Cliffs. Drive two-tenths of a mile and turn left onto Beech Hill Road, then 3.1 miles to the parking lot at the end of the road. The trailhead is on the right as you enter. The park visitors center is located north of Bar Harbor, at the junction of Route 3 and the start of the Park Loop Road.

Maps: A basic park map is available at the visitors center. Three good trail and contour maps of the area are the waterproof "Acadia National Park, Mount Desert Island, Isle au Haut" map 212 for $8.99 from Trails Illustrated, (800) 962-1643; the waterproof "Mount Desert Island and Acadia National Park" map for $7.95 from the DeLorme Mapping Company, (800) 253-5081; and the "Map of Acadia National Park/Mount Desert Island" for $5.95 (paper) from the Appalachian Mountain Club, (800) 262-4455. For a topographic map of the area, request Southwest Harbor from the USGS.

Contact: Acadia National Park, P.O. Box 177, Bar Harbor, ME 04609; (207) 288-3338. Friends of Acadia, P.O. Box 725, Bar Harbor, ME 04609; (207) 288-3340.

Trail notes: Want a nice hike that avoids the crowds common on the east side of Acadia? This is the one. Soon after leaving the parking lot the trail forks; the loop can be hiked in either direction, but I recommend bearing left. You soon emerge onto an open ledge with a terrific view east and north: from the islands south of Mount Desert, to Acadia, Sargent, and Penobscot Mountains, to the myriad waterways to the north. A short distance farther up the trail is the summit, where trees block any view, but you can climb one flight of stairs on the closed fire tower for a 360-degree view. Beyond the summit, bear right onto the descent trail, which offers magnificent views over Long Pond and all the way to Camden Hills.

㉝ Beech and Canada Cliffs

0.7 mi/0.75 hr 

Location: In Acadia National Park; Southern Maine map page 3, grid b5.

User groups: Hikers, dogs, and snowshoers. No wheelchair facilities. Dogs must be on a leash. This trail is not suitable for skis. Bikes, horses, and hunting are prohibited.

Access, fees: Parking and access are free.

Directions: From the junction of Routes 198 and 102 in Somesville, drive south on Route 102 for eight-tenths of a mile and turn right onto Pretty Marsh Road at the sign for Beech Mountain and the Beech Cliffs. Continue two-tenths of a mile and turn left onto Beech Hill Road, then 3.1 miles to the parking lot at the end of the road; the trailhead is on the left as you enter. The park visitors center is located north of Bar Harbor, at the junction of Route 3 and the start of the Park Loop Road.

Maps: A basic park map is available at the visitors center. Three good trail and contour maps of the area are the waterproof "Acadia National Park, Mount Desert Island, Isle au Haut" map 212 for $8.99 from Trails Illustrated, (800) 962-1643; the waterproof "Mount Desert Island and Acadia National Park" map for $7.95 from the DeLorme Mapping Company, (800) 253-5081; and the "Map of Acadia National Park/Mount Desert Island" for $5.95 (paper) from the Appalachian Mountain Club, (800) 262-4455. For a topographic map of the area, request Southwest Harbor from the USGS.

Contact: Acadia National Park, P.O. Box 177, Bar Harbor, ME 04609; (207) 288-3338. Friends of Acadia, P.O. Box 725, Bar Harbor, ME 04609; (207) 288-3340.

Trail notes: From the parking lot, this almost flat, short hike leads to the crest of cliffs high above Echo Lake. A quarter mile up the trail you reach a junction: to the right is the trail to the Canada Cliffs, to the left the trail to the Beech Cliffs. Both entail a short walk to nice views, but the Beech Cliffs may be closed in late spring and early summer to protect nesting peregrine falcons. The Canada Cliffs should be open all year.

34 Acadia Mountain

2.5 mi/1.5 hrs

Location: In Acadia National Park; Southern Maine map page 3, grid b5.

User groups: Hikers, dogs, and snowshoers. No wheelchair facilities. Dogs must be on a leash. This trail is not suitable for skis. Bikes, horses, and hunting are prohibited.

Access, fees: Parking and access are free.

Directions: From the junction of Routes 198 and 102 in Somesville, drive south on Route 102 for 3.4 miles to a turnout on the right (there is a sign) at the trailhead for Acadia Mountain. The park visitors center is located north of Bar Harbor, at the junction of Route 3 and the start of the Park Loop Road.

Maps: A basic park map is available at the visitors center. Three good trail and contour maps of the area are the waterproof "Acadia National Park, Mount Desert Island, Isle au Haut" map 212 for $8.99 from Trails Illustrated, (800) 962-1643; the waterproof "Mount Desert Island and Acadia National Park" map for $7.95 from the DeLorme Mapping Company, (800) 253-5081; and the "Map of Acadia National Park/Mount Desert Island" for $5.95 (paper) from the Appalachian Mountain Club, (800) 262-4455. For a topographic map of the area, request Southwest Harbor from the USGS.

Contact: Acadia National Park, P.O. Box 177, Bar Harbor, ME 04609; (207) 288-3338. Friends of Acadia, P.O. Box 725, Bar Harbor, ME 04609; (207) 288-3340.

Trail notes: At 681 feet, Acadia Mountain is the biggest hill on the west side of Somes Sound—the only true fjord in the eastern United States—and offers excellent views of the sound, the towns of Northeast Harbor and Southwest Harbor, and the islands south of Mount Desert. Although you scramble up rocks a little on the way up, this easy hike is a good one for young children.

From the turnout, cross the highway to the trail. It soon branches; stay left, cross a fire road (your route of descent), and proceed to the open ledges at the summit. The trail continues past the summit to even better views from ledges atop the mountain's east face. The trail then turns right, descending steep ledges with good views, and reaches a junction with the fire road (which more resembles a trail here). Turn right, and the road soon widens. Just before reaching the highway, turn left onto the Acadia Mountain Trail, which leads back to the start.

35 Flying Mountain

0.6 mi/0.5 hr

Location: In Acadia National Park; Southern Maine map page 3, grid b5.

User groups: Hikers, dogs, and snowshoers. No wheelchair facilities. Dogs must

be on a leash. This trail is not suitable for skis. Bikes, horses, and hunting are prohibited.

Access, fees: Parking and access are free.

Directions: From the junction of Routes 198 and 102 in Somesville, go south on Route 102 for 5.4 miles and turn left on Fernald Point Road. Drive one mile to parking on the left at Valley Road. The park visitors center is north of Bar Harbor, at the junction of Route 3 and Park Loop Road.

Maps: A basic park map is available at the visitors center. Three good trail and contour maps of the area are the waterproof "Acadia National Park, Mount Desert Island, Isle au Haut" map 212 for $8.99 from Trails Illustrated, (800) 962-1643; the waterproof "Mount Desert Island and Acadia National Park" map for $7.95 from the DeLorme Mapping Company, (800) 253-5081; and the "Map of Acadia National Park/Mount Desert Island" for $5.95 (paper) from the Appalachian Mountain Club, (800) 262-4455. For a topographic map of the area, request Southwest Harbor from the USGS.

Contact: Acadia National Park, P.O. Box 177, Bar Harbor, ME 04609; (207) 288-3338. Friends of Acadia, P.O. Box 725, Bar Harbor, ME 04609; (207) 288-3340.

Trail notes: This is a short hike up a hill that rises just 284 feet above Somes Sound but that offers nice views of the fjord from open ledges. The trail begins at the parking area and ascends steadily; the last stretch is a bit steep. Once on the ledges, be sure to continue over them to the true summit, marked by a signpost, where the views are even better than those you see when you first reach the ledges.

36 Penobscot and Sargent Mountains

4.5 mi/3.0 hrs 

Location: In Acadia National Park; Southern Maine map page 3, grid b5.

User groups: Hikers, dogs, and snowshoers. No wheelchair facilities. Dogs must be on a leash. This trail is not suitable for skis. Bikes, horses, and hunting are prohibited.

Access, fees: Parking and access are free.

Directions: Take Route 3 south from Bar Harbor to Seal Harbor. Turn right at the Acadia National Park entrance and left on the Park Loop Road, following it to the Jordan Pond parking area. Or, from the park visitors center, follow the Park Loop Road south. Where it splits, turn right and continue to the Jordan Pond parking area. The park visitors center is located north of Bar Harbor, at the junction of Route 3 and the start of the Park Loop Road.

Maps: A basic park map is available at the visitors center. Three good trail and contour maps of the area are the waterproof "Acadia National Park, Mount Desert Island, Isle au Haut" map 212 for $8.99 from Trails Illustrated, (800) 962-1643; the waterproof "Mount Desert Island and Acadia National Park" map for $7.95 from the DeLorme Mapping Company, (800) 253-5081; and the "Map of Acadia National Park/Mount Desert Island" for $5.95 (paper) from the Appalachian Mountain Club, (800) 262-4455. For a topographic map of the area, request Southwest Harbor from the USGS.

Contact: Acadia National Park, P.O. Box 177, Bar Harbor, ME 04609; (207) 288-3338. Friends of Acadia, P.O. Box 725, Bar Harbor, ME 04609; (207) 288-3340.

Trail notes: While nearly everyone who comes to Acadia National Park knows of Cadillac Mountain, few have heard of—and even fewer will actually hike—Penobscot and Sargent Mountains, which rise abruptly to the west of Jordan Pond. Yet Sargent's 1,373-foot elevation and Penobscot's 1,194 feet rank them as the second- and fifth-highest peaks on Mount Desert Island. And the ridge connecting them pushes nearly as much area above the trees as

Cadillac's scenic South Ridge. For much of this hike, you enjoy long views east to the Pemetic and Cadillac Mountains, south to the many offshore islands, and west across Somes Sound and Penobscot Bay to the Camden Hills.

From the parking area, head down the dirt access road toward Jordan Pond, and turn left onto a trail leading to the Jordan Pond House. The Penobscot Mountain Trail begins behind the Jordan Pond House, soon ascending steep ledges that require some scrambling. Up on the ridge the hiking gets much easier. Beyond Penobscot's summit, the trail dips into a small saddle between the mountains. Turn left onto the Sargent Pond Trail, passing the small pond in the woods. Turn right onto the Sargent Mountain South Ridge Trail, ascending the long slope to the summit, marked by a pile of rocks. Just beyond the summit, turn right onto the Jordan Cliffs Trail, which traverses above the cliffs visible from Jordan Pond. Cross a carriage road and turn left onto the Penobscot Mountain Trail to return.

37 Jordan Pond/Sargent Mountain Carriage Road Loop

16.0 mi/8.0 hrs 

Location: In Acadia National Park; Southern Maine map page 3, grid b5.

User groups: Hikers, bikes, dogs, horses, skiers, and snowshoers. No wheelchair facilities. Dogs must be on a leash. Hunting is prohibited.

Access, fees: Parking and access are free.

Directions: Drive Route 3 south from Bar Harbor to Seal Harbor. Turn right at the Acadia National Park entrance and left on the Park Loop Road, following it to the Jordan Pond parking area. You can bike to the start from Blackwoods Campground, adding about seven miles round-trip: bike Route 3 toward Seal Harbor; where the highway crosses a bridge over the Park Loop Road, carry your bike down a footpath to the Loop Road, then follow it north and turn left onto a carriage path just before the Jordan Pond House. The park visitors center is located north of Bar Harbor, at the junction of Route 3 and the start of the Park Loop Road.

Maps: A basic park map is available at the visitors center. Three good trail and contour maps—all of which show the carriage roads in detail—are the waterproof "Acadia National Park, Mount Desert Island, Isle au Haut" map 212 for $8.99 from Trails Illustrated, (800) 962-1643; the waterproof "Mount Desert Island and Acadia National Park" map for $7.95 from the DeLorme Mapping Company, (800) 253-5081; and the "Map of Acadia National Park/Mount Desert Island" for $5.95 (paper) from the Appalachian Mountain Club, (800) 262-4455. For topographic maps of the area, request Seal Harbor and Southwest Harbor from the USGS.

Contact: Acadia National Park, P.O. Box 177, Bar Harbor, ME 04609; (207) 288-3338. Friends of Acadia, P.O. Box 725, Bar Harbor, ME 04609; (207) 288-3340.

Trail notes: While the Jordan Pond area is popular with bicyclists, the farther you wander from the pond, the fewer people you'll see on the carriage roads. This loop makes for a pleasant ride over the gravel roadways traveled by the country's upper crust decades ago. As with the Jordan Pond/Eagle Lake/Bubble Pond Carriage Road Loop (hike number 40), I would recommend doing this on a bike or skis rather than hiking; on a bike, it would take about three hours.

From the Jordan Pond parking area, go south on the Park Loop Road a short distance and turn right onto a carriage road. Stay right, soon ascending a gradual slope above Jordan Pond. Turn right, then left, and follow the northwest shoreline of Eagle Lake. At the lake's northwest corner, turn left. After passing Aunt Betty Pond—where there's a nice view across the pond toward Sargent Mountain—turn right and contour around Sargent. After passing Upper Hadlock Pond on the right, the carriage road makes a U-turn; take the first right after that. Stay left all the way back to Jordan Pond.

38 The Bubbles/ Eagle Lake Loop

4.2 mi/2.0 hrs 

Location: In Acadia National Park; Southern Maine map page 3, grid b5.

User groups: Hikers, dogs, skiers, and snowshoers. No wheelchair facilities. Dogs must be on a leash. Bikes, horses, and hunting are prohibited.

Access, fees: Parking and access are free.

Directions: Drive on Route 3 south from Bar Harbor to Seal Harbor. Turn right at the Acadia National Park entrance and left on the Park Loop Road, following it to the Bubble Rock parking area, 1.6 miles past the Jordan Pond parking area. Or, from the park visitors center, follow the Park Loop Road south. Where it splits, turn right for the Bubble Rock parking area. The park visitors center is located north of Bar Harbor, at the junction of Route 3 and the start of the Park Loop Road.

Maps: A basic park map is available at the visitors center. Three good trail and contour maps of the area are the waterproof "Acadia National Park, Mount Desert Island, Isle au Haut" map 212 for $8.99 from Trails Illustrated, (800) 962-1643; the waterproof "Mount Desert Island and Acadia National Park" map for $7.95 from the DeLorme Mapping Company, (800) 253-5081; and the "Map of Acadia National Park/Mount Desert Island" for $5.95 (paper) from the Appalachian Mountain Club, (800) 262-4455. For topographic maps of the area, request Seal Harbor and Southwest Harbor from the USGS.

Contact: Acadia National Park, P.O. Box 177, Bar Harbor, ME 04609; (207) 288-3338. Friends of Acadia, P.O. Box 725, Bar Harbor, ME 04609; (207) 288-3340.

Trail notes: If the view of the Bubbles from the south end of Jordan Pond is one of Acadia's most famous, then the views of Jordan Pond and the steep hills enclosing it from the open ledges atop North and South Bubble rival any in the national park. Best of all, they are reached with little effort.

This loop takes in Conners Nubble—a commanding overlook above Eagle Lake—and finishes with a walk along the rocky shore of Eagle Lake. For a shorter walk, the round-trip hike to the summit of North Bubble alone is 1.2 miles. From the Bubble Rock parking area, the Bubble-Pemetic Trail heads west, then northwest through the woods, then turns sharply left and climbs to the saddle between North and South Bubble. Turn left to reach the summit of South Bubble. Backtrack and ascend the North Bubble Trail to that summit, which is higher than the South. Continue over North Bubble, crossing a carriage road, to Conners Nubble. Descend and turn right onto the Eagle Lake Trail, and right again on the Jordan Pond Carry Trail and left on the Bubble-Pemetic Trail to return to the parking area.

39 Jordan Pond Loop

3.3 mi/1.5 hrs 

Location: In Acadia National Park; Southern Maine map page 3, grid b5.

User groups: Hikers, dogs, skiers, and snowshoers. No wheelchair facilities. Dogs must be on a leash. Bikes, horses, and hunting are prohibited.

Access, fees: Parking and access are free.

Directions: Take Route 3 south from Bar Harbor to Seal Harbor. Turn right at the Acadia National Park entrance and left on the Park Loop Road, following it to the Jordan Pond parking area. Or, from the park visitors center, follow the Park Loop Road south. Where it splits, turn right for the Jordan Pond parking area. The park visitors center is located north of Bar Harbor, at the junction of Route 3 and the start of the Park Loop Road.

Maps: A basic park map is available at the visitors center. Three good trail and contour maps of the area are the waterproof "Acadia National Park, Mount Desert Island, Isle au Haut" map 212 for $8.99 from Trails Illustrated, (800) 962-1643; the waterproof "Mount Desert Island and Acadia National Park" map for $7.95 from the DeLorme Mapping Company, (800) 253-5081; and the "Map of Acadia National Park/Mount Desert Island" for $5.95 (paper) from the Appalachian Mountain Club, (800) 262-4455. For topographic maps of the area, request Seal Harbor and Southwest Harbor from the USGS.

Contact: Acadia National Park, P.O. Box 177, Bar Harbor, ME 04609; (207) 288-3338. Friends of Acadia, P.O. Box 725, Bar Harbor, ME 04609; (207) 288-3340.

Trail notes: This fairly easy, flat trail loops around scenic Jordan Pond. You're constantly gazing across the water to the steep mountainsides surrounding it—from the cliffs and rounded humps of the Bubbles to the wooded slopes of Penobscot and Pemetic Mountains. The easiest walking is along the east shore of the pond; on the northeast and especially the northwest shores, the trail crosses areas of boulders that require some scrambling and rock-hopping. While these patches are not too difficult to navigate, you can avoid them altogether by hiking in a counter-clockwise direction and turning back upon reaching these sections.

From the Jordan Pond parking area, continue down the dirt road to the shore and turn right onto the wide gravel path of the Jordan Pond Shore Trail. At the pond's southwest corner, the trail reaches a carriage road; turn left over a bridge, then immediately left onto the trail again, soon reaching the famous view of the Bubbles from the pond's south end. Just beyond that, the trail completes the loop at the dirt access road. Turn right for the parking lot.

40 Jordan Pond/Eagle Lake/Bubble Pond Carriage Road Loop

11.5 mi/6.0 hrs 

Location: In Acadia National Park; Southern Maine map page 3, grid b5.

User groups: Hikers, bikes, dogs, skiers, and snowshoers. No wheelchair facilities. Dogs must be on a leash. Horses and hunting are prohibited.

Access, fees: Parking and access are free.

Directions: Drive on Route 3 south from Bar Harbor to Seal Harbor. Turn right at the Acadia National Park entrance and left on the Park Loop Road, following it 2.6 miles past the Jordan Pond parking area to the Bubble Pond parking area. From the park visitors center, follow the Park Loop Road south. Where it splits, turn right for the Bubble Pond parking area. You can bike to the start from Blackwoods Campground, adding about seven miles round-trip: bike Route 3 toward Seal Harbor; where the highway crosses a bridge over the Park Loop Road, carry your bike down a footpath to the Loop Road, then follow it north. Just before the Jordan Pond House, turn right onto this carriage road loop. The park visitors center is north of Bar Harbor, at the junction of Route 3 and Park Loop Road.

Maps: A basic park map is available at the visitors center. Three good trail and contour maps—all of which show the carriage roads in detail—are the waterproof "Acadia National Park, Mount Desert Island, Isle au Haut" map 212 for $8.99 from Trails Illustrated, (800) 962-1643; the waterproof "Mount Desert Island and Acadia National Park" map for $7.95 from the DeLorme Mapping Company, (800) 253-5081; and the "Map of Acadia National Park/Mount Desert Island" for $5.95 (paper) from the Appalachian Mountain Club, (800) 262-4455. For a topographic map of the area, request Seal Harbor and Southwest Harbor from the USGS.

Contact: Acadia National Park, P.O. Box 177, Bar Harbor, ME 04609; (207) 288-3338. Friends of Acadia, P.O. Box 725, Bar Harbor, ME 04609; (207) 288-3340.

Trail notes: This moderate loop is one of the nicest carriage road trails in the park, passing high above Jordan Pond, circling Eagle Lake, and cruising along the western shore of Bubble Pond. Although hiking is permitted, it's more interesting on a bike—or cross-country skis in winter.

From the Bubble Pond parking area, follow the carriage road north along Eagle Lake. At the lake's northwest corner, turn left and follow the carriage road along the lake's western shore. After angling away from the lake (around Conners Nubble), turn right, then left, soon passing above Jordan Pond. At the pond's south end, turn left and cross the Park Loop Road. Follow this carriage road all the way back to Bubble Pond. Along the way, you will pass a carriage road leading to the right across a bridge over the Loop Road; the loop beginning across the bridge climbs Day Mountain, a fun if challenging ride up and a fast ride down for mountain bikers who have the time and energy for adding a few miles to this trail's distance.

41 Pemetic Mountain

3.3 mi/2.5 hrs

Location: In Acadia National Park; Southern Maine map page 3, grid b5.

User groups: Hikers, dogs, skiers, and snowshoers. No wheelchair facilities. Dogs must be on a leash. Bikes, horses, and hunting are prohibited.

Access, fees: Parking and access are free.

Directions: Take Route 3 south from Bar Harbor to Seal Harbor. Turn right at the Acadia National Park entrance and left on the Park Loop Road, following it to the Jordan Pond parking area. Or, from the park visitors center, follow the Park Loop Road south. Where it splits, turn right and continue to the Jordan Pond parking area. The park visitors center is located north of Bar Harbor, at the junction of Route 3 and the start of the Park Loop Road.

Maps: A basic park map is available at the visitors center. Three good trail and contour maps of the area are the waterproof "Acadia National Park, Mount Desert Island, Isle au Haut" map 212 for $8.99 from Trails Illustrated, (800) 962-1643; the waterproof "Mount Desert Island and Acadia National Park" map for $7.95 from the DeLorme Mapping Company, (800) 253-5081; and the "Map of Acadia National Park/Mount Desert Island" for $5.95 (paper) from the Appalachian Mountain Club, (800) 262-4455. For topographic maps of the area, request Seal Harbor and Southwest Harbor from the USGS.

Contact: Acadia National Park, P.O. Box 177, Bar Harbor, ME 04609; (207) 288-3338. Friends of Acadia, P.O. Box 725, Bar Harbor, ME 04609; (207) 288-3340.

Trail notes: Pemetic Mountain, situated between Jordan Pond on the west and Bubble Pond and Cadillac Mountain on the east, thrusts a long, open ridge of rock into the sky. Its summit, at 1,284 feet, is one of the nicest on the island—but it's the walk along the ridge that makes this hike memorable. The views take in Cadillac, Penobscot, and Sargent Mountains, the islands south of Mount Desert, and Jordan Pond and a unique perspective on the Bubbles.

From the Jordan Pond parking area, follow the dirt access road to the southeast shore of Jordan Pond. Turn left and follow the Jordan Pond Shore Trail a short distance, then turn left onto the Pond Trail. Cross the Park Loop Road and, in less than a half mile, turn left onto the Pemetic Mountain West Cliff Trail, ascending the ridge. At the junction with the Pemetic Mountain Trail, turn left (north) and proceed to the summit. Double back and follow the Pemetic Mountain Trail all the way to the Pond Trail, then turn right to go back the way you came.

42 Cadillac Mountain: West Face Trail

2.8 mi/2.5 hrs 5 9

Location: In Acadia National Park; Southern Maine map page 3, grid b5.

User groups: Hikers and dogs. No wheelchair facilities. Dogs must be on a leash. This trail is not suitable for skis or snowshoes. Bikes, horses, and hunting are prohibited.

Access, fees: Parking and access are free.

Directions: Take Route 3 south from Bar Harbor to Seal Harbor. Turn right at the Acadia National Park entrance and left on the Park Loop Road, following it 2.6 miles past the Jordan Pond parking area to the Bubble Pond parking area. Or, from the park visitors center, follow the Park Loop Road south. Where it splits, turn right for the Bubble Pond parking area. The park visitors center is located north of Bar Harbor, at the junction of Route 3 and Park Loop Road.

Maps: A basic park map is available at the visitors center. Three good trail and contour maps of the area are the waterproof "Acadia National Park, Mount Desert Island, Isle au Haut" map 212 for $8.99 from Trails Illustrated, (800) 962-1643; the waterproof "Mount Desert Island and Acadia National Park" map for $7.95 from the DeLorme Mapping Company, (800) 253-5081; and the "Map of Acadia National Park/Mount Desert Island" for $5.95 (paper) from the Appalachian Mountain Club, (800) 262-4455. For topographic maps of the area, request Seal Harbor and Southwest Harbor from the USGS.

Contact: Acadia National Park, P.O. Box 177, Bar Harbor, ME 04609; (207) 288-3338. Friends of Acadia, P.O. Box 725, Bar Harbor, ME 04609; (207) 288-3340.

Trail notes: This trail offers the most direct and difficult route up Mount Desert Island's highest peak. It involves a great deal of scrambling over steep slabs of open rock and relentlessly strenuous hiking. Descending may be more difficult than hiking up. Much of the trail lies in the woods, but the occasional views—which become more frequent as you climb higher—down to Bubble Pond and of the deep cleft separating the Cadillac and Pemetic Mountains are spectacular. I like this trail for its challenge and relative solitude.

From the parking area, cross the carriage road and pick up the Cadillac Mountain West Face Trail at the north end of Bubble Pond. In just under a mile of steep climbing, you'll top out on the South Ridge of the mountain. Turn left onto the Cadillac Mountain South Ridge Trail and follow it to the summit. Head back along the same route.

43 Cadillac Mountain: South Ridge Trail

7.0 mi/4.0 hrs

Location: In Acadia National Park; Southern Maine map page 3, grid b5.

User groups: Hikers, dogs, and snowshoers. No wheelchair facilities. Dogs must be on a leash. This trail is not suitable for skis. Bikes, horses, and hunting are prohibited.

Access, fees: Parking and access are free.

Directions: Drive Route 3 south from Bar Harbor to the entrance to Blackwoods Campground. The Cadillac Mountain South Ridge Trail enters the woods on the right about 50 yards past the campground entrance road; there is parking at the roadside. Campers in Blackwoods can pick up the trail at the west end of the campground's south loop (adding 1.4 miles to the round-trip distance of this hike). The park visitors center is located north of Bar Harbor, at the junction of Route 3 and the start of the Park Loop Road.

Maps: A basic park map is available at the visitors center. Three good trail and contour maps of the area are the waterproof "Acadia National Park, Mount Desert Island, Isle au Haut" map 212 for $8.99 from Trails Illustrated, (800) 962-1643; the waterproof "Mount Desert Island and Acadia National Park" map for $7.95 from the DeLorme Mapping Company, (800) 253-5081; and the "Map of Acadia National Park/Mount Desert Island" for $5.95 (paper) from the Appalachian Mountain Club, (800) 262-4455. For a topographic map of the area, request Seal Harbor from the USGS.

Contact: Acadia National Park, P.O. Box 177, Bar Harbor, ME 04609; (207) 288-3338. Friends of Acadia, P.O. Box 725, Bar Harbor, ME 04609; (207) 288-3340.

Trail notes: The long, spectacular, wide-open South Ridge of the highest "peak" on Mount Desert Island—1,530-foot Cadillac Mountain—affords one of the longest and most scenic hikes in Acadia National Park. How many mountain ridges offer views not only of surrounding hills, but also of the ocean and a profusion of islands?

One of my first hikes ever in Acadia, it remains one of my favorites. A relatively short, if somewhat steep, hike through the woods brings you onto the broad ridge; then you'll have an easy walk and sweeping views all the way to the summit. About a mile from Route 3, take the loop trail out to Eagle Crag, which offers nice views to the east; the loop trail rejoins the South Ridge Trail in two-tenths of a mile. Continuing up the South Ridge, you break out above the trees to views west to Pemetic and Sargent Mountains, and east and south to Frenchman Bay and numerous islands. At three miles, the trail passes a junction with the Cadillac Mountain West Face Trail (which descends left, or west), reaches a switchback in the paved summit road, and veers right, winding another half mile to the summit. Return the same way you came.

44 Dorr and Cadillac Mountains

3.0 mi/2.0 hrs 

Location: In Acadia National Park; Southern Maine map page 3, grid b5.

User groups: Hikers and dogs. No wheelchair facilities. Dogs must be on a leash. The trail would be very difficult to snowshoe and is not suitable for skis. Bikes, horses, and hunting are prohibited.

Access, fees: Parking and access are free.

Directions: Take Route 3 south from Bar Harbor or north from Blackwoods Campground and turn into the parking area at the Tarn, just south of the Sieur de Monts entrance to the Park Loop Road. The park visitors center is located north of Bar Harbor, at the junction of Route 3 and the start of the Park Loop Road.

Maps: A basic park map is available at the visitors center. Three good trail and contour maps of the area are the waterproof "Acadia National Park, Mount Desert Island, Isle au Haut" map 212 for $8.99 from Trails

Illustrated, (800) 962-1643; the waterproof "Mount Desert Island and Acadia National Park" map for $7.95 from the DeLorme Mapping Company, (800) 253-5081; and the "Map of Acadia National Park/Mount Desert Island" for $5.95 (paper) from the Appalachian Mountain Club, (800) 262-4455. For a topographic map of the area, request Seal Harbor from the USGS.

Contact: Acadia National Park, P.O. Box 177, Bar Harbor, ME 04609; (207) 288-3338. Friends of Acadia, P.O. Box 725, Bar Harbor, ME 04609; (207) 288-3340.

Trail notes: This moderate hike combines the highest peak on Mount Desert Island, 1,530-foot Cadillac Mountain, with its neighbor to the east, 1,270-foot Dorr, a mountain just as scenic and far less crowded. For much of this hike, you'll enjoy continuous views that take in Champlain Mountain, the islands of Frenchman Bay, and the rugged terrain atop Dorr and Cadillac.

From the parking area, turn left onto the Jessup Path and right onto the Dorr Mountain East Face Trail, which ascends numerous switchbacks up the steep flank of the mountain. Turn left onto the Dorr Mountain Trail; the trail actually passes just north of Dorr's true summit, which is reached by walking a nearly flat tenth of a mile south on the Dorr Mountain South Ridge Trail. Double back and turn left (west) onto the Dorr Mountain Notch Trail, which drops into the rugged—though not very deep—notch between Dorr and Cadillac. (This distinctive notch is visible from Route 3 south of the Tarn.) Follow the trail up the open east slope of Cadillac to the summit. Descend the way you came, but instead of turning right onto the Dorr Mountain East Face Trail, continue straight on the somewhat more forgiving Dorr Mountain Trail, then turn right onto the Jessup Path for the parking area.

45 Acadia Traverse

13.5 mi. one way/ 10.0 hrs

Location: In Acadia National Park; Southern Maine map page 3, grid b5.

User groups: Hikers, dogs, and skiers. No wheelchair facilities. Dogs must be on a leash. The trail would be very difficult to snowshoe. Bikes, horses, and hunting are prohibited.

Access, fees: A $5 fee is charged per vehicle at an entrance station beyond the Sieur de Monts entrance on the one-way Park Loop Road, through which you must pass after this hike.

Directions: Two vehicles are needed for this traverse. Leave one vehicle at the northernmost of the two parking areas north of Upper Hadlock Pond along Route 198 in Northeast Harbor. Then drive to the hike's start, a turnout on the Park Loop Road at the Bear Brook Trail, two-tenths of a mile past a picnic area. If you're traveling with a group of friends, you might leave a third vehicle roughly halfway through the hike, at either the Bubble Pond or Jordan Pond parking areas, in case you can't finish the hike. The park visitors center is located north of Bar Harbor, at the junction of Route 3 and the start of the Park Loop Road.

Maps: A basic park map is available at the visitors center. Three good trail and contour maps of the area are the waterproof "Acadia National Park, Mount Desert Island, Isle au Haut" map 212 for $8.99 from Trails Illustrated, (800) 962-1643; the waterproof "Mount Desert Island and Acadia National Park" map for $7.95 from the DeLorme Mapping Company, (800) 253-5081; and the "Map of Acadia National Park/Mount Desert Island" for $5.95 (paper) from the Appalachian Mountain Club, (800) 262-4455. For a topographic map of the area, request Seal Harbor from the USGS.

Contact: Acadia National Park, P.O. Box 177, Bar Harbor, ME 04609; (207) 288-3338. Friends of Acadia, P.O. Box 725, Bar Harbor, ME 04609; (207) 288-3340.

Trail notes: While poring over my maps of Acadia National Park one evening (my idea of a wild night), I noticed that you could link trails and create a traverse of the east side of Mount Desert Island—hitting the park's six major peaks and using no roads. At roughly 13 miles, the traverse would be an ambitious but feasible day hike. So I recruited five guinea pigs—um, fellow intrepid adventurers—including my girlfriend's 13-year-old nephew, Brendan, and we embarked on a hike that far exceeded our expectations.

On this Acadia Traverse, you'll hit the national park's nicest peaks and ponds and spend much of the day above the trees, with sweeping views from a succession of long, open ridges. And it's a long day: including time spent on short rest stops (but not including time spent shuttling vehicles), we were out for 10 hours, finishing just before sunset. The cumulative elevation gain is about 4,700 feet—more than hiking up Mount Washington. And many of these trails—particularly the Beechcroft, the Cadillac Mountain West Face, and a section of the Penobscot Mountain Trail—are very steep. There are water sources on top of Cadillac Mountain and at the Jordan Pond House for refilling bottles. An exciting alternative start would be on the Precipice Trail of Champlain Mountain (which is often closed in late spring and early summer to protect nesting peregrine falcons).

Follow the Bear Brook Trail south to the summit of Champlain Mountain; within minutes of setting out, you'll enjoy views of the islands of Frenchman Bay. Turn right (west) and descend the Beechcroft Trail eight-tenths of a mile to the small pond called the Tarn (crossing Route 3). Ascend the Dorr Mountain East Face Trail, then turn left (south) onto the Dorr Mountain Trail and take it to the top of Dorr Mountain, one mile from the Tarn. (To reach the true summit, turn left, or south, on the Dorr Mountain South Ridge Trail for a flat tenth of a mile, then double back.) The Dorr Mountain Notch Trail dips four-tenths of a mile into the shallow but spectacular notch between Dorr and Cadillac, then climbs the open slope for half a mile to the summit of Cadillac Mountain.

Descend the Cadillac Mountain South Ridge Trail for half a mile to the Cadillac Mountain West Face Trail, which drops very steeply for nearly a mile to a parking lot at the north end of Bubble Pond. Follow the carriage road south a tenth of a mile or less, then turn right onto the Pemetic Mountain Trail and take it over Pemetic's summit, 1.3 miles from Bubble Pond. Continue south over the long, rocky ridge for just over half a mile, then bear right onto the Pemetic West Cliff Trail. That trail descends six-tenths of a mile to the Pond Trail; turn right, and descend easily another four-tenths of a mile to the Park Loop Road. Cross the road, enter the woods, and turn left on a trail to the Jordan Pond House. The Penobscot Mountain Trail begins behind the Jordan Pond House and leads 1.5 miles to the summit of Penobscot, at one point going straight up steep, rocky terrain. Pick up the Sargent Pond Trail north and west—passing the tiny alpine pond nestled in conifers—then turn right (north) onto the Sargent Mountain South Ridge Trail, gradually climbing the long ridge to the 1,373-foot summit, a mile beyond Penobscot's, for the final panoramic view of this hike.

Descend west on the Grandgent Trail (be careful not to confuse it with the Sargent Mountain North Ridge Trail, which will add mileage to your hike at a time when you don't want it) for just over a mile to the top of little Parkman Mountain. Turn left onto the Parkman Mountain Trail, descending southward. You will cross two carriage roads; at the second crossing, turn right and follow that carriage road a short distance to a connector leading left to the parking area on Route 198, a mile from the Parkman summit. Then take off your boots and vigorously massage your feet.

46 The Beehive

1.3 mi/1.5 hrs 

Location: In Acadia National Park; Southern Maine map page 3, grid b5.

User groups: Hikers and dogs. No wheelchair facilities. Dogs must be on a leash. The trail would be very difficult to snowshoe and is not suitable for skis. Bikes, horses, and hunting are prohibited.

Access, fees: A $5 fee is charged per vehicle at an entrance station beyond the Sieur de Monts entrance on the one-way Park Loop Road.

Directions: Drive the Park Loop Road to the east side of Mount Desert Island and the large parking area at Sand Beach, half a mile south of the entrance station. The park visitors center is located north of Bar Harbor, at the junction of Route 3 and the start of the Park Loop Road.

Maps: A basic park map is available at the visitors center. Three good trail and contour maps of the area are the waterproof "Acadia National Park, Mount Desert Island, Isle au Haut" map 212 for $8.99 from Trails Illustrated, (800) 962-1643; the waterproof "Mount Desert Island and Acadia National Park" map for $7.95 from the DeLorme Mapping Company, (800) 253-5081; and the "Map of Acadia National Park/Mount Desert Island" for $5.95 (paper) from the Appalachian Mountain Club, (800) 262-4455. For a topographic map of the area, request Seal Harbor from the USGS.

Contact: Acadia National Park, P.O. Box 177, Bar Harbor, ME 04609; (207) 288-3338. Friends of Acadia, P.O. Box 725, Bar Harbor, ME 04609; (207) 288-3340.

Trail notes: The climb up the cliffs on the east face of the Beehive may look as if it's strictly for technical rock climbers when you stare up at it from the Sand Beach parking lot. The trail zigs and zags up ledges on the nearly vertical face, requiring hand-and-foot scrambling and the use of iron ladder rungs drilled into the rock. Though it's a fairly short climb in terms of elevation, and just a half-mile walk uphill, this trail is not for anyone in poor physical condition or uncomfortable with exposure and heights. On the other hand, it's a wonderful trail for hikers looking for a little adventure—and for children old enough to know not to wander off a precipice. All the way up, you're treated to unimpeded views over Frenchman Bay and the coast from Sand Beach and Great Head south to Otter Cliffs. On the summit, you'll look north to Champlain Mountain and northwest to Dorr and Cadillac Mountains.

From the parking area, cross the Loop Road and walk a few steps to the right, to the Bowl Trail. You will soon turn onto the Beehive Trail and follow it to the summit. Continuing over the summit, turn left onto the Bowl Trail and make the easy descent back to the Loop Road. A very nice 3.7-mile loop links this with the Gorham Mountain Trail (hike number 47) and Ocean Path (hike number 49).

47 Gorham Mountain/ Cadillac Cliffs

2.0 mi/1.5 hrs 

Location: In Acadia National Park; Southern Maine map page 3, grid b5.

User groups: Hikers, dogs, skiers, and snowshoers. No wheelchair facilities. Dogs must be on a leash. Bikes, horses, and hunting are prohibited.

Access, fees: A $5 fee is charged per vehicle at an entrance station beyond the Sieur de Monts entrance on the one-way Park Loop Road.

Directions: Take the Park Loop Road to the east side of Mount Desert Island and the parking area at the Gorham Mountain Trail and Monument Cove, south of Sand Beach and north of Otter Cliffs. The park visitors center is located north of Bar Harbor, at the junction of Route 3 and the start of the Park Loop Road.

Maps: A basic park map is available at the visitors center. Three good trail and contour maps of the area are the waterproof "Acadia National Park, Mount Desert Island, Isle au Haut" map 212 for $8.99 from Trails Illustrated, (800) 962-1643; the waterproof "Mount Desert Island and Acadia National Park" map for $7.95 from the DeLorme Mapping Company, (800) 253-5081; and the "Map of Acadia National Park/Mount Desert Island" for $5.95 (paper) from the Appalachian Mountain Club, (800) 262-4455. For a topographic map of the area, request Seal Harbor from the USGS.

Contact: Acadia National Park, P.O. Box 177, Bar Harbor, ME 04609; (207) 288-3338. Friends of Acadia, P.O. Box 725, Bar Harbor, ME 04609; (207) 288-3340.

Trail notes: I hiked over Gorham Mountain after making the climb of the Beehive and thinking nothing could match that experience. But I had to change my mind after walking along Gorham's long, open ridge, enjoying views of Acadia's coast and countless islands. At just 525 feet high, Gorham's rocky crown is easily reached. Only the Cadillac Cliffs Trail entails some scrambling, and that can be avoided. From the parking area, follow the Gorham Mountain Trail, then turn right onto the Cadillac Cliffs Trail, which passes below the cliffs and rejoins the Gorham Mountain Trail just below the summit. Descend the Gorham Mountain Trail. A nice 3.7-mile loop links this with the Beehive Trail (hike number 46) and Ocean Path (hike number 49).

48 Great Head

1.6 mi/1.0 hr

Location: In Acadia National Park; Southern Maine map page 3, grid b5.

User groups: Hikers, dogs, skiers, and snowshoers. No wheelchair facilities. Dogs must be on a leash. Bikes, horses, and hunting are prohibited.

Access, fees: A $5 fee is charged per vehicle at an entrance station beyond the Sieur de Monts entrance on the one-way Park Loop Road, through which you must pass after this hike.

Directions: Drive on the Park Loop Road to the east side of Mount Desert Island, past the Precipice parking area. Immediately before the Loop Road entrance station (fee charged), turn left onto an unmarked road. Drive two-tenths of a mile, then turn right, drive another four-tenths of a mile, and pull into a parking area on the left. The park visitors center is located north of Bar Harbor, at the junction of Route 3 and the start of Park Loop Road.

Maps: A basic park map is available at the visitors center. Three good trail and contour maps of the area are the waterproof "Acadia National Park, Mount Desert Island, Isle au Haut" map 212 for $8.99 from Trails Illustrated, (800) 962-1643; the waterproof "Mount Desert Island and Acadia National Park" map for $7.95 from the DeLorme Mapping Company, (800) 253-5081; and the "Map of Acadia National Park/Mount Desert Island" for $5.95 (paper) from the Appalachian Mountain Club, (800) 262-4455. For a topographic map of the area, request Seal Harbor from the USGS.

Contact: Acadia National Park, P.O. Box 177, Bar Harbor, ME 04609; (207) 288-3338. Friends of Acadia, P.O. Box 725, Bar Harbor, ME 04609; (207) 288-3340.

Trail notes: This short, easy walk leads out to the top of tall cliffs rising virtually out of the ocean, and spectacular views stretching from the islands of Frenchman Bay to Otter Cliffs. It's a popular hike, but like many popular hikes, it tends to attract most folks during the day. Two friends and I found solitude out here one sunny late afternoon in early June.

From the parking area, follow the wide gravel path into the woods, soon reaching a trail entering from the left—the way this loop returns. Continue straight ahead, passing above Sand Beach (a trail leads down to the beach), then ascending slightly. Where the trail forks, be sure to stay to the right (the left fork cuts off the walk along the cliffs), soon emerging at the cliffs. To return, follow the blue blazes north back to the gravel path, then turn right to head back to the parking area.

---

49 Ocean Path

3.6 mi/2.0 hrs 

Location: In Acadia National Park; Southern Maine map page 3, grid b5.

User groups: Hikers and dogs. No wheelchair facilities. Dogs must be on a leash. This trail rarely receives enough snow for skis or snowshoes. Bikes, horses, and hunting are prohibited.

Access, fees: A $5 fee is charged per vehicle at an entrance station beyond the Sieur de Monts entrance on the one-way Park Loop Road (reached via Route 3 south of Bar Harbor and north of Blackwoods Campground).

Directions: Drive on the Park Loop Road to the east side of Mount Desert Island and the large parking area at Sand Beach, half a mile south of the entrance station. The park visitors center is located north of Bar Harbor, at the junction of Route 3 and the start of the Park Loop Road.

Maps: A basic park map is available at the visitors center. Three good trail and contour maps of the area are the waterproof "Acadia National Park, Mount Desert Island, Isle au Haut" map 212 for $8.99 from Trails Illustrated, (800) 962-1643; the waterproof "Mount Desert Island and Acadia National Park" map for $7.95 from the DeLorme Mapping Company, (800) 253-5081; and the "Map of Acadia National Park/Mount Desert Island" for $5.95 (paper) from the Appalachian Mountain Club, (800) 262-4455. For a topographic map of the area, request Seal Harbor from the USGS.

Contact: Acadia National Park, P.O. Box 177, Bar Harbor, ME 04609; (207) 288-3338. Friends of Acadia, P.O. Box 725, Bar Harbor, ME 04609; (207) 288-3340.

Trail notes: This is one of the most popular hikes in the national park—and for good reason. The Ocean Path follows the rugged shoreline from Sand Beach to Otter Cliffs, the island's tallest cliffs and a haven for rock climbers. About midway along this trail is the famous Thunder Hole, where incoming waves crash into a channel-like pocket in the rocks, trapping air to create a loud and deep popping noise; it's most impressive near high tide.

From the parking area, the trail veers right. The shore here is mostly rocky, but constantly changes character over the course of this trail—some beaches are covered exclusively with small, round stones, others only with large rocks. As it approaches Otter Cliffs, the trail enters a small woods (across the road from another parking lot) and emerges atop Otter Cliffs. Hike back along the same route.

50 Maiden Cliff

2.0 mi/1.5 hrs 

Location: In Camden Hills State Park; Southern Maine map page 3, grid b3.

User groups: Hikers, dogs, and snowshoers. No wheelchair facilities. Dogs must be on a leash. This trail is not suitable for skis. Bikes and horses are prohibited. Hunting is allowed in season.

Access, fees: Parking and access are free at the Maiden Cliff Trailhead. A fee of $2 per person (age 12 and over) is charged at the state park entrance.

Directions: From the junction of Route 52 and U.S. 1 in Camden, drive west on Route 52 for three miles to a parking area on the right (just before Megunticook Lake). The Maiden Cliff Trail begins at the back of the lot.

Maps: A basic map of the trail system is available at the state park entrance on U.S. 1, two miles north of the Route 52 junction in Camden. For a trail map, get the Camden Hills/Pleasant Mountain map for $2.95 from the Appalachian Mountain Club, (800) 262-4455. For topographic maps of the area, request Camden and Lincolnville from the USGS.

Contact: Camden Hills State Park, HCR 60, Box 3110, Camden, ME 04843; (207) 236-3109. Maine Bureau of Parks and Lands, Department of Conservation, 22 State House Station, Augusta, ME 04333; (207) 287-3821.

Trail notes: This is my favorite hike in Camden Hills State Park. The Scenic Trail follows the open top of cliffs high above sprawling Megunticook Lake, with extensive views of the hills to the west. It is a great hike for late in the day, when the sun is sinking toward those hills and sparkling off the lake.

From the parking lot, follow the wide Maiden Cliff Trail, which ascends steadily through the woods for a half mile. Bear right on the Ridge Trail, reaching an open area and the junction with the Scenic Trail in three-tenths of a mile. Turn left (northwest) on the Scenic Trail, following the top of cliffs with outstanding views for a quarter mile, then descending into the woods again to reach the junction with the Maiden Cliff Trail (marked by a sign) a half mile from the Ridge Trail. Before descending the Maiden Cliff Trail back to your car, continue ahead 100 feet to the Maiden Cliff; here a large wooden cross marks the spot where a young girl named Elenora French fell to her death in 1864. The cliffs seem to drop almost straight down into the lake. Double back and descend the Maiden Cliff Trail for nearly a mile to the parking lot.

51 Mount Megunticook Traverse

5.3 mi. one way/3.0 hrs 

Location: In Camden Hills State Park; Southern Maine map page 3, grid b3.

User groups: Hikers, dogs, and snowshoers. No wheelchair facilities. Dogs must be on a leash. This trail is not suitable for skis. Bikes and horses are prohibited. Hunting is allowed in season.

Access, fees: Parking and access are free at the Maiden Cliff Trailhead. A fee of $2 per person (age 12 and over) is charged at the state park entrance.

Directions: Two vehicles must be shuttled at either end of this hike. From the junction of Route 52 and U.S. 1 in Camden, drive west on Route 52 for three miles to a parking area on the right (just before Megunticook Lake). The Maiden Cliff Trail begins at the back of the lot. Leave one vehicle there. Then drive back to Camden and head north on U.S. 1 for two miles to the state park entrance on the left. Past the entrance gate, turn left on the Mount Battie Road, then right into a parking lot marked with a sign reading "Hikers Parking." The Mount Megunticook Trail begins at the back of the lot.

Maps: A basic map of the trail system is available at the state park entrance. For a more detailed trail map, get the Camden Hills/Pleasant Mountain map for $2.95 from the Appalachian Mountain Club, (800) 262-4455. For topographic maps of the area, request Camden and Lincolnville from the USGS.

Contact: Camden Hills State Park, HCR 60, Box 3110, Camden, ME 04843; (207) 236-3109. Maine Bureau of Parks and Lands, Department of Conservation, 22 State House Station, Augusta, ME 04333; (207) 287-3821.

Trail notes: This fairly easy traverse of the highest mountain in Camden Hills State Park combines the good views of hike numbers 50 and 52 with a pleasant walk along the mostly wooded ridge—though this ridge has its own nice views as well.

From the parking area on Mount Battie Road, follow the Mount Megunticook Trail for a mile to Ocean Lookout, where you'll get terrific views south and east of the Camden area and the islands of Penobscot Bay. Continue northwest on the Ridge Trail, passing over the wooded 1,380-foot summit of Megunticook a half mile beyond Ocean Lookout. A mile past the summit, stay left on the Ridge Trail where Zeke's Trail branches right; then, a half mile farther, stay right where the Jack Williams Trail enters from the left. Two miles past the summit, walk straight onto the Scenic Trail, following the top of open cliffs with views of Megunticook Lake and the hills to the west. Descending into the woods again, you'll reach the Maiden Cliff Trail (marked by a sign) a half mile from the Ridge Trail. Before heading down, though, continue ahead 100 feet to the Maiden Cliff; here a large wooden cross marks the spot where a young girl named Elenora French fell to her death in 1864. The cliffs seem to drop almost straight down into the lake. Double back and descend the Maiden Cliff Trail for nearly a mile to the parking lot on Route 52.

52 Ocean Lookout

2.0 mi/1.5 hrs 

Location: In Camden Hills State Park; Southern Maine map page 3, grid b3.

User groups: Hikers, dogs, and snowshoers. No wheelchair facilities. Dogs must be on a leash. This trail is not suitable for skis. Bikes and horses are prohibited. Hunting is allowed in season.

Access, fees: Admission to the state park is $2 per person (age 12 and over). The entrance gate closes at 8 P.M. and is not staffed in winter.

Directions: The entrance to Camden Hills State Park is along U.S. 1, two miles north of the Route 52 junction in Camden. After passing through the entrance gate, turn left on Mount Battie Road, then right into a parking lot marked with a sign reading "Hikers Parking." The Mount Megunticook Trail begins at the back of the lot.

Maps: A basic map of the trail system is available at the state park entrance. For a more detailed trail map, get the Camden Hills/Pleasant Mountain map for $2.95 from the Appalachian Mountain Club, (800) 262-4455. For topographic maps of the area, request Camden and Lincolnville from the USGS.

Contact: Camden Hills State Park, HCR 60, Box 3110, Camden, ME 04843; (207) 236-3109. Maine Bureau of Parks and Lands, Department of Conservation, 22 State House Station, Augusta, ME 04333; (207) 287-3821.

Trail notes: This relatively easy hike to the best viewpoint on Mount Megunticook—which is the biggest hill in Camden Hills State Park—is very popular because it offers a wide view to the south and east of the Camden area and the islands of Penobscot Bay. A companion and I hiked up here on a weekday afternoon and had the view to ourselves for a little while: Mount Battie was visible below us, and a bank of clouds rolling in off the ocean crested like a wave over Camden.

Follow the Mount Megunticook Trail for one mile to Ocean Lookout, 1,300 feet above the sea. The wooded summit of 1,380-foot Mount Megunticook lies a half mile farther north on the Ridge Trail (hike number 51), but this hike ends at the lookout. After you've looked out, return the same way you came up.

53 Bigelow Range

16.7 mi. one way/ 2.0 days

Location: East of Stratton; Southern Maine map page 3, grid a2.

User groups: Hikers only. No wheelchair facilities. Dogs are discouraged along the Appalachian Trail in Maine. Bikes and horses are prohibited. Hunting is allowed in season in the Bigelow Preserve, but not on or near trails.

Access, fees: Parking and access are free. Camp at existing camping areas and shelters: Little Bigelow lean-to at 1.4 miles south of East Flagstaff Road; Safford Notch campsite at 6.3 miles; Avery tenting area at 8.7 miles; Horns Pond lean-tos and tentsites at 11.6 miles; and the Cranberry Stream campsite at 14.8 miles. Stephen Martelli of Stratton runs a fee-based hiker shuttle service to road crossings along the Appalachian Trail between Grafton Notch and Monson; call (207) 246-4642.

Directions: You need to shuttle two vehicles for this trip. To do the hike from north to south, as described below, leave one vehicle at the junction of the Appalachian Trail and Routes 27 and 16, 5.3 miles south of where Routes 27 and 16 split in Stratton and 16 miles north of where Routes 27 and 16 split in Kingfield. Then drive on Route 16 east to North New Portland. Turn left (north) in front of the country store onto Long Falls Dam Road and follow it for 17.4 miles. Bear left onto the dirt Bog Brook Road. Drive seven-tenths of a mile, bear left onto the dirt East Flagstaff Road, and drive a tenth of a mile. Park either in the gravel pit on the right, or at the roadside where the Appalachian Trail crosses the road just beyond the pit.

Maps: A free contour map of trails in the Bigelow Preserve is available at some trailheads and from the Maine Bureau of Public Lands (see address below). For a trail map, refer to map 5 in the "Map and Guide to the Appalachian Trail in Maine," a set of seven maps and a guidebook for $19.95 from the Maine Appalachian Trail Club or the Appalachian Trail Conference (see addresses below). Also available is the "Carter-Mahoosuc/Rangeley-Stratton" map for $2.95 from the Appalachian Mountain Club, (800) 262-4455. For topographic maps of the area, request Little Bigelow Mountain, The Horns, Sugarloaf Mountain, and Poplar Mountain from the USGS.

Contact: Maine Bureau of Parks and Lands, 25 Main Street, P.O. Box 327, Farmington, ME 04938; (207) 778-8231. Bureau of Land Management, Main Office, 22 State House Station, Augusta, ME 04333; (207) 287-3821. Maine Appalachian Trail Club, P.O. Box 283, Augusta, ME 04332. Appalachian Trail Conference, P.O. Box 807, Harpers Ferry, WV 25425; (304) 535-6331.

Trail notes: A darling of Maine hikers, Bigelow Mountain is unquestionably one of the two or three most spectacular peaks in the state; only Katahdin and Bigelow's neighbor to the south, the Saddleback Range, warrant comparison. Reflecting the state's affection for this range, its voters supported a grassroots movement, and in 1976 created the Bigelow Preserve, a 35,000-acre park encompassing the entire Bigelow Range—including about 17 miles of the Appalachian Trail—and 21 miles of shoreline on sprawling Flagstaff Lake. Both of Bigelow's summits rise well above tree line, affording long views in every direction. Perhaps the best view is north to Flagstaff Lake and the vast wilderness of Maine's North Woods (though a few logging clear-cuts tarnish that view). On rare clear days, you can see north to Katahdin and south-west to Mount Washington.

This 16.7-mile, two-day backpacking trip traverses the entire range along the Appalachian Trail. The distance is moderate for two days, but don't underestimate the trail's ruggedness. From East Flagstaff Road, follow the white blazes of the AT south-bound, passing a blue-blazed side trail at 1.4 miles which leads a tenth of a mile to the Little Bigelow lean-to, where there is a good spring and space for tents. From there, the AT climbs steadily until cresting the eastern end of the long, low ridge of Little Bigelow Mountain three miles from the road. There are excellent views from open ledges west toward Bigelow Mountain and, across the Carrabassett Valley, the ski area at Sugarloaf Mountain. The trail follows the relatively flat, wooded ridgetop, passing another open ledge with a view of Bigelow and Flagstaff Lake at 4.5 miles. It then descends about 1,000 feet over less than two miles into Safford Notch, the forested floor of which is littered with giant boulders, some of them stacked dramatically atop one another.

At 6.3 miles from East Flagstaff Road, a side trail leads left (southwest) three-tenths of a mile to tent platforms at the Safford Notch campsite. Just a tenth of a mile farther down the AT, the Safford Brook Trail exits right (north), leading 2.2 miles to East Flagstaff Road (and 2.5 miles to Flagstaff Lake). The AT climbs steeply out of Safford Notch, over and around boulders, gaining about 2,000 feet of elevation over two miles to Bigelow's east summit, 4,088-foot Avery Peak. On the way up Avery, the trail passes a side path at 7.5 miles which leads a tenth of a mile to an excellent view east and north from atop the cliff called the "Old Man's Head." Beyond that side path, the AT ascends the crest of a narrow, wooded ridge, breaking out of the trees for the final tenth of a mile up Avery Peak. Passing over Avery, the trail descends into the wooded col between the summits, reaching the Avery tenting area at 8.7 miles.

The ascent grows fairly steep up West Peak, the true summit at 4,145 feet, seven-tenths of a mile from Avery Peak. The AT descends to and follows the up-and-down ridge connecting Bigelow to the 3,805-foot summit of South Horn, where you'll get a good view to the west from directly above Horns Pond. Just a tenth of a mile farther, a side trail leads two-tenths of a mile to the summit of North Horn (3,792 feet). Continue steeply downhill on the AT, reaching the Horns Pond lean-tos and tentsites at 11.6 miles from East Flagstaff Road and half a mile from South Horn. Horns Pond is a scenic tarn nestled in a tiny bowl at about 3,200 feet on the west slope of Bigelow. From there, the AT climbs slightly out of that bowl, passing the junction with the Horns Pond Trail two-tenths of a mile south of Horns Pond and a short side path to an overlook of the pond at three-tenths of a mile. The trail then descends steadily, swinging south and passing the Bigelow Range Trail junction nearly two miles from Horns Pond, to the Cranberry Stream campsite at 14.8 miles (3.2 miles

Northern Maine Map—page 2

south of Horns Pond and 1.9 miles north of Route 27/16). At 15.8 miles, the AT crosses Stratton Brook on a bridge, before reaching Route 27/16 at mile 16.7 of this trip, 5.1 miles from Horns Pond.

Special note: The traverse of this range ranks among the most popular backpacking treks in New England. Especially during the warmer months, the campsites and shelters fill quickly, even during the week. Bringing a tent is recommended. Also, take care to walk only on the trail above tree line, where fragile alpine vegetation is easily trampled.

54 Bigelow Mountain

13.8 mi/
10.5 hrs or 1–2 days 

Location: East of Stratton; Southern Maine map page 3, grid a2.

User groups: Hikers only. No wheelchair facilities. Dogs are discouraged along the Appalachian Trail in Maine. This trail may be difficult to snowshoe and is not suitable for skis. Bikes and horses are prohibited. Hunting is allowed in season in the Bigelow Preserve, but not on or near trails.

Access, fees: Parking and access are free. Camp at existing camping areas and shelters, which along this route include the Cranberry Stream campsite 1.1 miles from Stratton Brook Pond Road, the Horns Pond lean-tos and tentsites at 4.3 miles, and the Avery tenting area at 7.2 miles.

Directions: From Route 27/16, turn north onto Stratton Brook Pond Road, five miles east of where Routes 27 and 16 split in Stratton and about 16.3 miles west of where Routes 27 and 16 split in Kingfield (and about three-tenths of a mile west of where the Appalachian Trail crosses Route 27/16). Drive 1.4 miles to where the AT crosses the dirt road and park at the roadside.

Maps: A free contour map of trails in the Bigelow Preserve is available at some trailheads and from the Maine Bureau of Public Lands (see address below). For a trail map, refer to map 5 in the "Map and Guide to the Appalachian Trail in Maine," a set of seven maps and a guidebook for $19.95 from the Maine Appalachian Trail Club or the Appalachian Trail Conference (see addresses below). Also available is the "Carter-Mahoosuc/Rangeley-Stratton" map for $2.95 from the Appalachian Mountain Club, (800) 262-4455. For topographic maps of the area, request Horns and Sugarloaf Mountain from the USGS.

Contact: Maine Bureau of Parks and Lands, 25 Main Street, P.O. Box 327, Farmington, ME 04938; (207) 778-8231. Bureau of Land Management, Main Office, 22 State House Station, Augusta, ME 04333; (207) 287-3821. Maine Appalachian Trail Club, P.O. Box 283, Augusta, ME 04332. Appalachian Trail Conference, P.O. Box 807, Harpers Ferry, WV 25425; (304) 535-6331.

Trail notes: This hike up one of Maine's most spectacular and popular mountains, Bigelow, can be accomplished in a single long day by fit hikers getting an early start. But there are two camping areas along the trail which offer the option of a two-day trip, leaving your heavy pack behind for the day hike to Bigelow's summits. From Stratton Brook Pond Road, follow the white blazes of the Appalachian Trail northbound into the woods. Within a quarter of a mile you will cross a logging road and Stratton Brook on a bridge. The AT ascends steadily, passing a junction with the Bigelow Range Trail at 2.4 miles. Stay on the AT, which swings east and climbs to a short side trail out to ledges above Horns Pond at four miles, then passes the Horns Pond Trail junction a tenth of a mile farther. The trail drops slightly into the bowl, home to the tiny mountain tarn called Horns Pond and a camping area with two lean-tos and tentsites, at 4.3 miles.

The AT climbs steeply for the next half mile, passing a side trail leading two-tenths of a mile to North Horn (3,792 feet) at 4.7 miles and reaching the 3,805-foot summit of South Horn at 4.8 miles, with a good view over Horns Pond and north to Flagstaff Lake. Descending steeply off South Horn, you will follow an up-and-down ridge for more than a mile, then climb steeply to West Peak, Bigelow's true summit at 4,145 feet, 6.9 miles from the road. The rocky, open summit affords views in every direction: north over Flagstaff Lake and the wilderness of the North Woods, all the way to Katahdin on a clear day, and southwest to Washington when conditions are right. For this hike, turn around and descend the same way you came up. To reach 4,088-foot Avery Peak, continue northbound on the AT, dropping into the saddle between Bigelow's two summits, passing the Avery tenting area at 7.2 miles, then climbing to the open summit of Avery Peak. Hiking to Avery and back adds 1.4 miles and an hour (possibly more) to this hike's distance.

Special note: Bigelow Mountain ranks among the most popular peaks in New England. Especially during the warmer months, the campsites and shelters fill quickly, even during the week. Bringing a tent is recommended. Also, take care to walk only on the trail above tree line, where fragile alpine vegetation is easily trampled.

55 North Crocker Mountain

10.4 mi/7.0 hrs 

Location: South of Stratton; Southern Maine map page 3, grid a2.

User groups: Hikers and snowshoers. No wheelchair facilities. Dogs are discouraged along the Appalachian Trail in Maine. This trail is not suitable for skis. Bikes, horses, and hunting are prohibited.

Access, fees: Parking and access are free.

Directions: Park where the Appalachian Trail crosses Route 27/16, 5.3 miles south of where Routes 27 and 16 split in Stratton and 16 miles north of where Routes 27 and 16 split in Kingfield.

Maps: For a trail map, refer to map 6 in the "Map and Guide to the Appalachian Trail in Maine," a set of seven maps and a guidebook for $19.95 available from the Maine Appalachian Trail Club or the Appalachian Trail Conference (see addresses below). Also available is the "Carter-Mahoosuc/Rangeley-Stratton" map for $2.95 from the Appalachian Mountain Club, (800) 262-4455. For topographic maps of the area, request Sugarloaf Mountain and Black Nubble from the USGS.

Contact: Maine Appalachian Trail Club, P.O. Box 283, Augusta, ME 04332. Appalachian Trail Conference, P.O. Box 807, Harpers Ferry, WV 25425; (304) 535-6331.

Trail notes: Despite North Crocker Mountain's 4,168-foot elevation, Maine's fifth-highest summit does little to distinguish itself in the area of visual spectacle. The low spruce trees that grow right to the top of the peak obscure the views; I tried standing on the summit cairn to see over the trees, but it didn't help much. There is actually a decent view toward Sugarloaf Mountain and Mount Abraham just beyond the summit, heading south on the AT. But for someone looking to tick off a 4,000-footer, or for a quiet and fairly easy hike up a wooded ridge, this 10.4-mile trip is a fine day's outing. In winter, with a snowpack at the summit, you might actually be able to see over the trees; but bear in mind that this could be a very long hike if you have to break trail in snowshoes all the way. Although hike number 56 provides a shorter route over both Crocker peaks, this hike is the only route to them when Caribou Valley Road is impassable to motor vehicles.

From Route 16/27, follow the white blazes of the AT southbound. It rises gently at first, and never grows more than moderately steep before reaching the wooded summit of North Crocker, 5.2 miles from the highway. Continuing south on the AT to the summit of South Crocker (4,010 feet) adds two miles round-trip to this hike's distance. Retrace your steps to return to your car.

---

56 North and South Crocker Mountain

6.2 mi/4.5 hrs 

Location: South of Stratton; Southern Maine map page 3, grid a2.

User groups: Hikers only. No wheelchair facilities. Dogs are discouraged along the Appalachian Trail in Maine. This trail may be difficult to snowshoe and is not suitable for skis. Bikes, horses, and hunting are prohibited.

Access, fees: Parking and access are free. The condition of the dirt Caribou Valley Road varies, and it may not be entirely passable by car. The Crocker Cirque campsite, with three tent platforms, lies a tenth of a mile down a side path off the AT, one mile north of Caribou Valley Road.

Directions: From Route 27/16, about a mile west of the entrance to the Sugarloaf USA ski resort in Carrabassett, turn south onto the dirt Caribou Valley Road. Drive 4.3 miles to the Appalachian Trail crossing and park at the roadside.

Maps: For a trail map, refer to map 6 in the "Map and Guide to the Appalachian Trail in Maine," a set of seven maps and a guidebook for $19.95 from the Maine Appalachian Trail Club or the Appalachian Trail Conference (see addresses below). Also available is the "Carter-Mahoosuc/Rangeley-Stratton" map for $2.95 from the Appalachian Mountain Club, (800) 262-4455. For a topographic map of the area, request Sugarloaf Mountain from the USGS.

Contact: Maine Appalachian Trail Club, Box 283, Augusta, ME 04332. Appalachian Trail Conference, P.O. Box 807, Harpers Ferry, WV 25425; (304) 535-6331.

Trail notes: When the dirt Caribou Valley Road is passable to motor vehicles, this 6.2-mile hike offers the most direct route up Maine's fifth- and 12th-highest peaks, the 4,000-footers North and South Crocker. Their wooded summits, unfortunately, offer only very limited views. South Crocker has the better view of the two, toward Sugarloaf Mountain and Mount Abraham from a small ledge. The best view on North Crocker is actually from the trail just shy of the actual summit, but it essentially mirrors the perspective from the south summit. The hike up South Crocker, however, does cross open slopes with pretty good views to the north and east.

From the road, turn right onto the Appalachian Trail northbound. It climbs steadily, and in one mile reaches a side path leading a tenth of a mile to the Crocker Cirque campsite. Above the campsite, the AT heads straight up a very steep and loose slope of broken slate, which can be treacherous when wet and very difficult to descend even when dry; there are views from here of Crocker Cirque. The trail enters the woods again, then traverses an old rockslide, with views out toward the Bigelow Range. Climbing steadily from there, the Appalachian Trail reaches a side path 2.1 miles from Caribou Valley Road which leads about 150 feet to the summit ledge of South Crocker. Continuing north, the AT drops down into the saddle between the two summits, then climbs to the higher of the two mountains, North Crocker, 3.1 miles from the road. Head back to your vehicle the same way you hiked up.

57 Sugarloaf Mountain

5.8 mi/4.5 hrs

Location: South of Stratton; Southern Maine map page 3, grid a2.

User groups: Hikers only. No wheelchair facilities. Dogs are discouraged along the Appalachian Trail in Maine. This trail may be difficult to snowshoe and is not suitable for skis. Bikes, horses, and hunting are prohibited.

Access, fees: Parking and access are free. The condition of the dirt Caribou Valley Road varies, and it may not be entirely passable by car.

Directions: From Route 27/16, about a mile west of the entrance to the Sugarloaf USA ski resort in Carrabassett, turn south onto the dirt Caribou Valley Road. Drive 4.3 miles to the Appalachian Trail crossing and park at the roadside.

Maps: For a trail map, refer to map 6 in the "Map and Guide to the Appalachian Trail in Maine," a set of seven maps and a guidebook for $19.95 from the Maine Appalachian Trail Club or the Appalachian Trail Conference (see addresses below). Also available is the "Carter-Mahoosuc/Rangeley-Stratton" map for $2.95 from the Appalachian Mountain Club, (800) 262-4455. For a topographic map of the area, request Sugarloaf Mountain from the USGS.

Contact: Maine Appalachian Trail Club, Box 283, Augusta, ME 04332. Appalachian Trail Conference, P.O. Box 807, Harpers Ferry, WV 25425; (304) 535-6331.

Trail notes: Maine's third-highest peak at 4,237 feet, Sugarloaf's barren summit offers long views in every direction. On a clear day, you can see from Mount Washington in New Hampshire to the southwest, all the way to Katahdin in the far north. Like any high, exposed peak, this can be a rough place in foul weather: I trucked up here while on a four-day traverse of the Saddleback Range only to be greeted by swirling fog and a biting wind—in August—although those conditions made for some interesting views into the Carrabassett Valley. When Caribou Valley Road is passable by car, it makes a day hike of Sugarloaf via the Appalachian Trail feasible by this rugged, 5.8-mile route.

From the road, follow the white-blazed AT to the left (south), immediately crossing the South Branch of the Carrabassett River, which can be dangerous at times of high water. The AT then climbs very steeply up Sugarloaf Mountain, involving short stretches of tricky scrambling up a heavily eroded trail. The trail emerges from the woods high on the north slope of Sugarloaf, with views to South and North Crocker across the valley. It re-enters the woods, then reaches a junction with the Sugarloaf Mountain Trail 2.3 miles from Caribou Valley Road. Turn left onto that trail and follow its rocky path steeply uphill for six-tenths of a mile to the exposed summit of Sugarloaf, where there are ski area buildings and long views in every direction. Descend the same route back to the road.

Special note: Sugarloaf can be linked with Spaulding Mountain (hike number 59) by continuing on the AT southbound, a 10.2-mile round-trip from Caribou Valley Road. An ambitious hiker can continue on to Mount Abraham (hike number 58), making for a 17.4-mile day hike or two-day backpacking trip. See the listings for those hikes for more details.

58 Mount Abraham

16.0 mi/
12.0 hrs or 1–2 days

Location: South of Stratton; Southern Maine map page 3, grid a2.

User groups: Hikers only. No wheelchair

facilities. Dogs are discouraged along the Appalachian Trail in Maine. This trail may be difficult to snowshoe and is not suitable for skis. Bikes, horses, and hunting are prohibited.

Access, fees: Parking and access are free. The condition of the dirt Caribou Valley Road varies, and it may not be entirely passable by car. The Spaulding Mountain lean-to is located down a short side path off the AT, 5.2 miles south of Caribou Valley Road.

Directions: From Route 27/16, about a mile west of the entrance to the Sugarloaf USA ski resort in Carrabassett, turn south onto the dirt Caribou Valley Road. Drive 4.3 miles to the Appalachian Trail crossing and park at the roadside.

Maps: For a trail map, refer to map 6 in the "Map and Guide to the Appalachian Trail in Maine," a set of seven maps and a guidebook for $19.95 from the Maine Appalachian Trail Club or the Appalachian Trail Conference (see addresses below). Also available is the "Carter-Mahoosuc/Rangeley-Stratton" map for $2.95 from the Appalachian Mountain Club, (800) 262-4455. For topographic maps of the area, request Sugarloaf Mountain and Mount Abraham from the USGS.

Contact: Maine Appalachian Trail Club, Box 283, Augusta, ME 04332. Appalachian Trail Conference, P.O. Box 807, Harpers Ferry, WV 25425; (304) 535-6331.

Trail notes: Mount Abraham boasts one of the largest alpine areas—or areas above tree line—in Maine, plus excellent panoramic views from its summit and long ridge. But because Appalachian Trail hikers have to make a 3.4-mile detour to climb Abraham, it attracts fewer visitors than some peaks here in western Maine, such as neighboring Saddleback Mountain. I actually stood alone on this rocky summit one August morning, on a trip where I saw several other hikers every day. This 16-mile hike to bag one of Maine's dozen 4,000-footers is difficult and long—a conceivable one-day goal for fit hikers getting an early start at a time of year that affords lots of daylight, but also a nice two-day trip.

From Caribou Valley Road, turn left (south) on the AT, immediately crossing the South Branch of the Carrabassett River, which can be dangerous at times of high water. The trail then climbs very steeply up Sugarloaf Mountain, involving short stretches of tricky scrambling up a heavily eroded trail. The trail emerges from the woods high on the north slope of Sugarloaf, with views to South and North Crocker across the valley. It re-enters the woods, then reaches a junction with the Sugarloaf Mountain Trail 2.3 miles from Caribou Valley Road. (For a scenic 1.2-mile detour off this hike, follow that rocky trail steeply uphill to the exposed 4,237-foot summit of Sugarloaf, Maine's third-highest peak, where there are ski area buildings and long views in every direction.) From the Sugarloaf Mountain Trail junction, follow the AT along the fairly flat ridge connecting Sugarloaf to Spaulding Mountain—a quiet stretch of trail through lush forest of hemlock, ferns, and moss. About a tenth of a mile south of the Sugarloaf Mountain Trail junction, a side path leads some 40 feet to a good view. The AT continues along the wooded ridge to a junction with the Spaulding Mountain Trail, 4.4 miles from Caribou Valley Road. (That trail, which is not included in this hike's distance, leads a tenth of a mile uphill to Spaulding's 3,988-foot summit, where three short side paths lead to limited views toward Sugarloaf and Abraham.) From the Spaulding Mountain Trail junction, the AT descends eight-tenths of a mile to a side path leading 150 feet to the Spaulding Mountain lean-to, where there is also space for tents.

The AT follows moderate terrain south, reaching the Mount Abraham Trail 1.1 miles from the Spaulding lean-to. On that blue-blazed trail, it's 1.7 miles one way to the 4,043-foot summit of Abraham. Although it's relatively flat for the first half mile, after emerging from the woods the trail climbs over three bumps on a ridge, crossing rough talus slopes. From the summit, marked by the rusting remains of an old fire tower, The Horn and Saddleback Mountain are visible to the southwest, and the Bigelow Range can be seen to the north. About 30 feet from the tower, along the Fire Warden's Trail, there is a primitive stone shelter with a shingled roof and enough space under its very low ceiling for a few people to crawl inside (not a place I'd want to spend a night). About 100 feet beyond the summit stand several tall cairns. For this hike, return to Caribou Valley Road via the same route you took up.

Special note: Abraham can be linked with Sugarloaf (hike number 57) and Spaulding Mountains (hike number 59) on a marathon 17.4-mile day hike or a more moderate two-day backpacking trip, adding just 1.4 miles to this hike.

59 Spaulding Mountain

9.0 mi/7.0 hrs 

Location: South of Stratton; Southern Maine map page 3, grid a2.

User groups: Hikers only. No wheelchair facilities. Dogs are discouraged along the Appalachian Trail in Maine. This trail may be difficult to snowshoe and is not suitable for skis. Bikes, horses, and hunting are prohibited.

Access, fees: Parking and access are free. The condition of the dirt Caribou Valley Road varies, and it may not be entirely passable by car. The Spaulding Mountain lean-to is located down a short side path off the AT, 5.2 miles south of Caribou Valley Road and eight-tenths of a mile south of the Spaulding Mountain Trail/Appalachian Trail junction.

Directions: From Route 27/16, about a mile west of the entrance to the Sugarloaf USA ski resort in Carrabassett, turn south onto the dirt Caribou Valley Road. Drive 4.3 miles to the Appalachian Trail crossing and park at the roadside.

Maps: For a trail map, refer to map 6 in the "Map and Guide to the Appalachian Trail in Maine," a set of seven maps and a guidebook for $19.95 from the Maine Appalachian Trail Club or the Appalachian Trail Conference (see addresses below). Also available is the "Carter-Mahoosuc/Rangeley-Stratton" map for $2.95 from the Appalachian Mountain Club, (800) 262-4455. For a topographic map of the area, request Sugarloaf Mountain from the USGS.

Contact: Maine Appalachian Trail Club, Box 283, Augusta, ME 04332. Appalachian Trail Conference, P.O. Box 807, Harpers Ferry, WV 25425; (304) 535-6331.

Trail notes: Just 12 feet short of 4,000 feet high, Spaulding Mountain offers better summit views—if not spectacular—than a pair of 4,000-footers to the north, the Crockers. Just a two-tenths-of-a-mile detour off the Appalachian Trail, its summit has three short side paths which lead to views toward Sugarloaf Mountain and Mount Abraham. One of the features I enjoy most about this hike is walking the fairly flat ridge from Sugarloaf to Spaulding, a quiet stretch of trail through a lush forest of hemlock, ferns, and moss.

From Caribou Valley Road, turn left (south) on the AT, immediately crossing the South Branch of the Carrabassett River, which can be dangerous at times of high water. The trail climbs very steeply up Sugarloaf Mountain, involving short stretches of tricky scrambling on a heavily eroded trail. It breaks out of the woods high on the north slope of Sugarloaf, with views to South and

North Crocker across the valley. It re-enters the woods, then reaches a junction with the Sugarloaf Mountain Trail, 2.3 miles from Caribou Valley Road. (See the special note below.) From the Sugarloaf Mountain Trail junction, follow the AT along the fairly flat ridge from Sugarloaf to Spaulding. About a tenth of a mile south of the Sugarloaf Mountain Trail junction, a side path leads about 40 feet to a good view. The AT continues along the wooded ridge to a junction with the Spaulding Mountain Trail, 4.4 miles from Caribou Valley Road. That trail leads a tenth of a mile uphill to Spaulding's 3,988-foot summit. Return the way you came up.

Special note: Spaulding can be linked with Sugarloaf Mountain (hike number 57)—Maine's third-highest peak, whose craggy summit allows views in every direction—for a 10.2-mile round-trip from Caribou Valley Road. An ambitious hiker can continue on to Mount Abraham (hike number 58)—making for a 17.4-mile day hike or two-day backpacking trip. See the listings for those hikes for more details.

60 Saddleback Range

32.2 mi. one way/
3–4 days

Location: East of Rangeley; Southern Maine map page 3, grid a2.

User groups: Hikers only. No wheelchair facilities. Dogs are discouraged along the Appalachian Trail in Maine. This trail may be difficult to snowshoe and is not suitable for skis. Bikes, horses, and hunting are prohibited.

Access, fees: Parking and access are free. There are three lean-to shelters and one campsite along this section of the Appalachian Trail: the Crocker Cirque campsite, with three tent platforms, lies a tenth of a mile down a side path off the AT, 7.3 miles south of Route 27/16; the Spaulding Mountain lean-to is located down a short side path off the AT, 6.2 miles south of the Crocker Cirque campsite; the Poplar Ridge lean-to sits along the AT, eight miles south of the Spaulding Mountain lean-to; and the Piazza Rock lean-to lies on a short side path off the AT, 8.9 miles south of the Poplar Ridge lean-to. Stephen Martelli of Stratton runs a hiker shuttle service to road crossings along the Appalachian Trail between Grafton Notch and Monson; call (207) 246-4642.

Directions: You need to shuttle two vehicles for this backpacking trip. To do the hike from north to south, as described below, leave one vehicle where the Appalachian Trail crosses Route 4, about 12 miles north of the junction of Routes 4 and 142 in Phillips and 10.1 miles south of the junction of Routes 4 and 16. Then drive to the hike's start, where the AT crosses Route 27/16, 5.3 miles south of where Routes 27 and 16 split in Stratton and 16 miles north of where Routes 27 and 16 split in Kingfield.

Maps: For a trail map, refer to map 6 in the "Map and Guide to the Appalachian Trail in Maine," a set of seven maps and a guidebook for $19.95 from the Maine Appalachian Trail Club or the Appalachian Trail Conference (see addresses below). Also available is the "Carter-Mahoosuc/Rangeley-Stratton" map for $2.95 from the Appalachian Mountain Club, (800) 262-4455. For topographic maps of the area, request Sugarloaf Mountain, Black Nubble, Mount Abraham, Redington, and Saddleback Mountain from the USGS.

Contact: Maine Appalachian Trail Club, Box 283, Augusta, ME 04332. Appalachian Trail Conference, P.O. Box 807, Harpers Ferry, WV 25425; (304) 535-6331.

Trail notes: The Saddleback Range stands out as one of the three premier mountain ranges in Maine—the other two being the greater Katahdin region and the Bigelow

Range—and a multi-day traverse of its peaks is as rugged, varied, and scenic a mountain experience as can be had anywhere in New England. Six of the eight summits rise above 4,000 feet, and four of them thrust extensive areas above tree line, offering long, panoramic views. Three miles of ridge above the trees extend from Saddleback Mountain to The Horn. Wintry storms with dangerously high winds occur year-round, so avoid this exposed ground if bad weather threatens. (On my own traverse of this range, I had overcast weather until my final day, hiking over Saddleback Junior, The Horn, and Saddleback.) This traverse could be accomplished in three days, but I took four, allowing me to make the side trips to Sugarloaf Mountain and Mount Abraham and maintain only a moderate pace.

From Route 16/27, follow the white blazes of the Appalachian Trail southbound. It rises gently at first, and never grows more than moderately steep before reaching the wooded summit of North Crocker Mountain (4,168 feet), 5.2 miles from the highway. There are limited views over the tops of low spruce trees. A better view is along the AT just south of the summit, looking toward Sugarloaf Mountain and Mount Abraham. Continuing south on the AT, you drop into the shallow col between the two summits of Crocker, then climb to the top of South Crocker (4,010 feet), a mile away from North Crocker. The actual summit is reached via a 100-foot side path off the AT. An open ledge there affords a limited view toward Sugarloaf and Abraham.

Descending south, the AT crosses an open slope of loose, broken rocks with views north and east toward the Bigelow Range. Footing becomes difficult descending the steep and very loose final half mile to Crocker Cirque campsite, just over a mile from South Crocker's summit and 7.3 miles from Route 27/16. One mile farther south, the AT crosses the dirt Caribou Valley Road (which may be passable by car, providing another access to the AT; Route 27/16 is 4.3 miles down Caribou Valley Road). From the road, the AT immediately crosses the South Branch of the Carrabassett River—which can be dangerous at times of high water—then climbs very steeply up Sugarloaf Mountain, involving short stretches of tricky scrambling. The trail emerges from the woods high on the north slope of Sugarloaf, with views of the Crockers across the valley. It re-enters the woods, then reaches a junction with the Sugarloaf Mountain Trail 3.3 miles south of Crocker Cirque campsite (and 2.3 miles from Caribou Valley Road); that rocky trail leads steeply uphill six-tenths of a mile to the exposed 4,237-foot summit of Sugarloaf, Maine's third-highest peak, where there are ski area buildings and long views in every direction. From the Sugarloaf Mountain Trail junction, the AT follows the fairly flat ridge connecting Sugarloaf to Spaulding Mountain—a quiet stretch of trail through a lush forest of hemlock, ferns, and moss. About a tenth of a mile south of the Sugarloaf Mountain Trail junction, a side path leads about 40 feet to a good view. The AT continues along the wooded ridge to a junction with the Spaulding Mountain Trail, 5.4 miles from Crocker Cirque campsite; that trail leads a tenth of a mile uphill to Spaulding's 3,988-foot summit, where three short side paths lead to limited views toward Sugarloaf and Abraham.

From the Spaulding Mountain Trail junction, the AT descends eight-tenths of a mile to a side path leading 150 feet to the Spaulding Mountain lean-to, where there is also space for tents. The AT follows moderate terrain south, reaching the Mount Abraham Trail 1.1 miles from the Spaulding lean-to. On that blue-blazed trail, it's 1.7 miles one way to the 4,043-foot summit of

Abraham. Although it's relatively flat for the first half mile, after emerging from the woods the trail climbs over three bumps on a ridge, crossing talus slopes reminiscent of bigger mountains like Washington or Katahdin. But the views from Abraham are among the best in the range. From the Mount Abraham Trail junction, the AT southbound passes a view toward Abraham within two-tenths of a mile, then over the wooded top of Lone Mountain in a mile.

Descending, the trail follows and then crosses beautiful Perham Stream (immediately after crossing a logging road), its narrow current choked with moss-covered rocks. The AT crosses a second logging road, and 1.2 miles from Perham Stream crosses another gem, Sluice Brook, then parallels it for seven-tenths of a mile, the last 200 feet of which the brook pours through a narrow flume. The trail crosses a gravel road and descends very steeply to Orbeton Stream, 5.3 miles from the Spaulding lean-to. I crossed the wide stream on stones in August, but fording it could be difficult in high water. From Orbeton, the AT makes one of its steepest and most arduous ascents in this range, more than two miles to the open ledges of Poplar Ridge, where there are views to the south and east. A half mile beyond the ledges is the Poplar Ridge lean-to (a small brook provides the water, but I found it barely trickling in August).

From the shelter, the AT climbs steadily 1.4 miles to the open summit of Saddleback Junior (3,655 feet), with excellent views in all directions. I reached this summit at 7 A.M., early enough to see a cloud tail wave like a flag from the summit of Saddleback while fog still sat low in the valleys to the north. Follow white blazes and cairns across the top of Saddleback Junior, descend about 500 feet, then climb steeply 1,000 feet to the open, 4,041-foot summit of The Horn, two miles from Saddleback Junior. Again, the views are spectacular, encompassing the Rangeley Lake area and Saddleback Mountain to the west, and extending north to Katahdin and southwest to Washington on a clear day.

Descend south on the AT, crossing mostly open ground with nonstop views, then ascend the ledges of Saddleback to the lower of its two summits. Walk the easy ridge to the true summit, at 4,120 feet, 1.6 miles from The Horn's summit. Continuing south, the AT drops back into the woods a mile below the summit, then crosses a logging road nearly a mile below tree line. The trail crosses a good stream two-tenths of a mile beyond the logging road, and crosses Saddleback Stream six-tenths of a mile farther. At 3.7 miles from Saddleback's summit, a side path leads a short distance to The Caves, actually passageways through giant boulders which have cleaved from the cliff above over the eons. Just two-tenths of a mile past The Caves, the trail reaches the Piazza Rock lean-to area, a popular backcountry campsite less than two miles from Route 4. There are tentsites and a large shelter, but this place fills quickly on weekends. A side path off the AT leads about 200 yards uphill to Piazza Rock, an enormous horizontal slab protruding improbably from the cliff. You can follow the trail up onto the slab with a little scrambling. From the lean-to area, the AT descends south for 1.8 miles to Route 4, this hike's terminus.

61 Saddleback Mountain and The Horn

13.4 mi/8.5 hrs 

Location: Southeast of Rangeley; Southern Maine map page 3, grid a1.

User groups: Hikers only. No wheelchair facilities. Dogs are discouraged along the Appalachian Trail in Maine. This trail may be difficult to snowshoe and is not suitable for skis. Bikes, horses, and hunting are prohibited.

Access, fees: Parking and access are free. The Piazza Rock lean-to and camping area is reached via a short side path off the Appalachian Trail, 1.8 miles north of Route 4.

Directions: Park in the roadside turnout where the AT crosses Route 4, about 12 miles north of the junction of Routes 4 and 142 in Phillips and 10.1 miles south of the junction of Routes 4 and 16 in Rangeley.

Maps: For a trail map, refer to map 6 in the "Map and Guide to the Appalachian Trail in Maine," a set of seven maps and a guidebook for $19.95 from the Maine Appalachian Trail Club or the Appalachian Trail Conference (see addresses below). Also available is the "Carter-Mahoosuc/Rangeley-Stratton" map for $2.95 from the Appalachian Mountain Club, (800) 262-4455. For topographic maps of the area, request Redington and Saddleback Mountain from the USGS.

Contact: Maine Appalachian Trail Club, Box 283, Augusta, ME 04332. Appalachian Trail Conference, P.O. Box 807, Harpers Ferry, WV 25425; (304) 535-6331.

Trail notes: Saddleback Mountain rises to 4,120 feet, offering some of the best views in the state from its summit and the open, three-mile ridge linking it and its neighboring 4,000-footer, The Horn. A round-trip hike on the Appalachian Trail from Route 4 to the true summit of Saddleback—the first of its two summits reached from this direction—is a strenuous 10.2-mile day hike. Continuing to The Horn makes the round-trip distance a very committing 13.4 miles. While these are among the most sought-after summits in Maine, avoid this exposed ridge in inclement weather. Also, carry plenty of water, because there is no water source above the outlet to Moose and Deer Pond.

From Route 4, follow the white blazes of the AT northbound. Within a tenth of a mile, the trail crosses a bridge over Sandy River, then climbs steadily to the Piazza Rock lean-to and camping area, 1.8 miles from the road (a very popular destination among weekend backpackers). A side path off the AT leads about 200 yards uphill to Piazza Rock, an enormous horizontal slab protruding improbably from the cliff. You can follow the trail up onto the slab with a little scrambling. Following the AT two-tenths of a mile north of the camping area, pass another side path leading a short distance to The Caves, actually passageways through giant boulders which have cleaved from the cliff above over the eons. Just over a mile beyond The Caves, the AT crosses Saddleback Stream, and six-tenths of a mile farther it crosses the outlet of Moose and Deer Pond, the last water source on this hike. At 4.7 miles from Route 4, the trail emerges above tree line on Saddleback and ascends the open ridge another mile to the summit. Views here are spectacular, encompassing the Rangeley Lake area to the west, The Horn to the northeast, and extending north to Katahdin and southwest to Washington on a clear day. The AT continues down into the slight saddle which gives the mountain its name, over Saddleback's second summit, then drops more steeply over ledges for several hundred feet into the col between Saddleback and The Horn. It turns upward again, climbing gently to the 4,041-foot summit of The Horn, 1.6 miles from Saddleback's summit, where again the views are long in every direction. The AT continues north, but this hike returns via the same route you came up.

62 Piazza Rock and The Caves

4.0 mi/3.0 hrs 

Location: Southeast of Rangeley; Southern Maine map page 3, grid a1.

User groups: Hikers only. No wheelchair

facilities. Dogs are discouraged along the Appalachian Trail in Maine. This trail is not suitable for skis or snowshoes. Bikes, horses, and hunting are prohibited.

Access, fees: Parking and access are free. The Piazza Rock lean-to and camping area is reached via a short side path off the Appalachian Trail, 1.8 miles north of Route 4.

Directions: Park in the roadside turnout where the AT crosses Route 4, about 12 miles north of the junction of Routes 4 and 142 in Phillips and 10.1 miles south of the junction of Routes 4 and 16 in Rangeley.

Maps: For a trail map, refer to map 6 in the "Map and Guide to the Appalachian Trail in Maine," a set of seven maps and a guidebook for $19.95 from the Maine Appalachian Trail Club or the Appalachian Trail Conference (see addresses below). Also available is the "Carter-Mahoosuc/Rangeley-Stratton" map for $2.95 from the Appalachian Mountain Club, (800) 262-4455. For topographic maps of the area, request Redington and Saddleback Mountain from the USGS.

Contact: Maine Appalachian Trail Club, Box 283, Augusta, ME 04332. Appalachian Trail Conference, P.O. Box 807, Harpers Ferry, WV 25425; (304) 535-6331.

Trail notes: Many Appalachian Trail hikers continue beyond Piazza Rock and The Caves on their way to bag Saddleback Mountain and The Horn (hike number 61). But these two interesting geological formations just a couple miles from the road offer a wonderful destination for a short hike, especially with young children. Piazza Rock is an enormous horizontal slab protruding improbably from the cliff. The Caves are interesting passageways through giant boulders which have cleaved from the cliff above over the eons. The lean-to and camping area nearby provides the option of an overnight trip, though the area is very popular and fills quickly on summer and fall weekends.

From Route 4, follow the white blazes of the AT northbound. Within a tenth of a mile, the trail crosses a bridge over Sandy River, then climbs steadily to the Piazza Rock lean-to and camping area, 1.8 miles from the highway. Turn left on a side path which leads about 200 yards uphill to Piazza Rock. You can follow the trail up onto the slab with a little scrambling. Follow the AT two-tenths of a mile north of the camping area, and turn onto another side path leading a short distance to The Caves. Hike back to your vehicle the same way you came up.

63 Tumbledown Mountain Loop Trail

4.2 mi/4.0 hrs 

Location: Northwest of Weld; Southern Maine map page 3, grid b1.

User groups: Hikers only. No wheelchair facilities. A sign at the start of the Loop Trail advises against bringing children or dogs on this trail because of its difficulty. This trail would be very difficult to snowshoe and is not suitable for bikes, dogs, horses, or skis. Hunting is allowed in season.

Access, fees: Parking and access are free.

Directions: From the junction of Routes 142 and 156 in Weld, drive 2.4 miles north on Route 142 to Weld Corner. Turn left onto West Side Road at the sign for Mount Blue State Park. Continue a half mile and bear right on a dirt road. Drive 2.3 miles on that road, passing the Mountain View Cemetery; then bear right again on another dirt road (there's no sign), heading toward Byron Notch. From that intersection, it's 1.6 miles to the Brook Trail (park at the roadside) and 3 miles to the Loop Trail (park in a dirt lot on the left). For this hike, you will need to either leave vehicles at each trailhead, or park at the Loop Trail and walk the 1.4 miles on the dirt road between the two trailheads at the hike's end.

Maps: For a contour map of trails, obtain the "Weld Region" map, which appears on the flip side of the "Map of Acadia National Park/Mount Desert Island," and costs $5.95 (paper) from the Appalachian Mountain Club, (800) 262-4455. For topographic maps of the area, request Weld, Madrid, Roxbury, and Jackson Mountain from the USGS.

Contact: There is no contact agency for this hike.

Trail notes: With a 700-foot cliff on its south face, a pristine alpine pond, and more than a half mile of open, rocky ridge, Tumbledown Mountain seems far taller than 3,068 feet. The views from the ridge and the East and West Peaks take in a landscape of mountains and lakes offering few if any signs of human presence. As a pair of peregrine falcons circled overhead, I stood alone on the West Peak, enjoying a sunny July day and long views of mountains and lakes to the east, south, and west, all the way to Mount Washington and the White Mountains in New Hampshire (the tall ridge looming in the distance to the southwest). Of the two hikes up Tumbledown described in this guide, this 4.2-mile trek is far and away more difficult; some hikers will not feel comfortable climbing up through the wet, fallen boulders near the top of the Loop Trail. (See hike number 64 for an easier route up Tumbledown Mountain.) All trail junctions are marked with signs. There exists no trail to the North Peak, which along with Jackson Mountain blocks views to the north.

Begin on the Loop Trail, which enters the woods across from the dirt parking lot. The trail soon begins a very steep ascent of 1.3 miles to the Great Ledges, a flat, open shelf below the towering cliff of Tumbledown. The trail trends to the right along the ledges for nearly two-tenths of a mile, then turns steeply upward again. Just before reaching the saddle between the East and West Peaks—1.9 miles from the trailhead—you will have to scramble up through a passage between boulders that typically runs with water. In the saddle, turn left (west) on the Tumbledown Ridge Trail for the tenth-of-a-mile, moderate climb to West Peak, the true summit at 3,068 feet. Double back to the saddle, then follow the Tumbledown Ridge Trail two-tenths of a mile to East Peak. From there, it's nearly a half mile down the Tumbledown Ridge Trail to Tumbledown Pond and the junction with the Brook Trail. Turn right (south) on the Brook Trail, which leads 1.5 miles to the road; it descends steeply at first, but the last mile follows an old logging road.

64 Tumbledown Mountain Brook Trail

3.8 mi/3.0 hrs 

Location: Northwest of Weld; Southern Maine map page 3, grid b1.

User groups: Hikers and dogs. No wheelchair facilities. This trail would be very difficult to snowshoe and is not suitable for bikes, horses, or skis. Hunting is allowed in season.

Access, fees: Parking and access are free.

Directions: From the junction of Routes 142 and 156 in Weld, drive 2.4 miles north on Route 142 to Weld Corner. Turn left onto West Side Road at the sign for Mount Blue State Park. Continue a half mile and bear right on a dirt road. Drive 2.3 miles on that road, passing the Mountain View Cemetery, then bear right again on another dirt road, heading toward Byron Notch. From that intersection, it's 1.6 miles to the Brook Trail; park at the roadside.

Maps: For a contour map of trails, obtain the Weld Region map, which appears on the flip side of the "Map of Acadia National Park/Mount Desert Island" and costs $5.95 (paper) from the Appalachian Mountain Club, (800) 262-4455. For a topographic map of the area, request Weld, Madrid, Roxbury, and Jackson Mountain from the USGS.

Contact: There is no contact agency for this hike.

Trail notes: Of the two hikes up spectacular Tumbledown Mountain that are described in this guide, this one is significantly easier and more appropriate for children and casual hikers. (See hike number 63 for another option and more description of Tumbledown Mountain.) All trail junctions are marked with signs. The Brook Trail follows an old logging road for its first mile, then climbs more steeply for the next half mile to Tumbledown Pond, a scenic alpine tarn tucked amid Tumbledown's three summits. From the pond, turn left (west) on the Tumbledown Ridge Trail and hike up a moderately steep, open ridge of rock for four-tenths of a mile to East Peak, where there are sweeping views of the mountains to the east, south, and west, all the way to Mount Washington in New Hampshire.

This hike ends here and returns the way you came. But to reach the West Peak—the true summit at 3,068 feet—follow the Tumbledown Ridge Trail another three-tenths of a mile west; it drops down into the saddle between the peaks, then climbs the rocky ridge to West Peak (adding six-tenths of a mile to this hike's distance).

65 Old Blue Mountain

5.6 mi/4.0 hrs 

Location: North of Andover; Southern Maine map page 3, grid b1.

User groups: Hikers and snowshoers. No wheelchair facilities. Dogs are discouraged along the Appalachian Trail in Maine. The hike requires advanced skills to snowshoe and is not suitable for skis. Bikes, horses, and hunting are prohibited.

Access, fees: Parking and access are free.

Directions: From the junction of Routes 5 and 120 in Andover, head east on Route 120 for half a mile, then turn left onto South Arm Road. Drive another 7.7 miles into Black Brook Notch to where the AT crosses the road. Park at the roadside.

Maps: For a trail map, refer to map 7 in the "Map and Guide to the Appalachian Trail in Maine," a set of seven maps and a guidebook for $19.95 from the Maine Appalachian Trail Club or the Appalachian Trail Conference (see addresses below). For topographic maps of the area, request Metallak Mountain and Andover from the USGS.

Contact: Maine Appalachian Trail Club, Box 283, Augusta, ME 04332. Appalachian Trail Conference, P.O. Box 807, Harpers Ferry, WV 25425; (304) 535-6331.

Trail notes: From the first steps up this remote stretch of the Appalachian Trail to the 3,600-foot summit of Old Blue Mountain, this is a hike without a dull moment. I made this trek on the first weekend of spring—which retains a decidedly wintry feel in the northern mountains—and enjoyed a wilderness experience on a trail that had seen few if any hikers all winter. We broke trail through drifted snow deep enough at times to bury the blazes on trees, climbed around and over blown-down trees, and took four hours to hike less than three miles up. For a more moderate yet still fairly remote hiking experience, day hike Old Blue between July and early October—but be prepared for any weather.

The AT leaves South Arm Road (look for a sign a few steps in from the road) and climbs steeply above spectacular Black Brook Notch. Atop the cliffs, watch for an open ledge to the right of the trail with an unobstructed view of the notch. The AT then meanders through dense woods, once offering a good view toward Old Blue's summit. The summit itself is a broad plateau covered with scrub trees and offering views in all directions. Visible to the south are the Mahoosucs and the slopes of the Sunday River Ski Area, and to the northeast are the Saddleback Range and Bigelow Mountain. Descend the same way you came up.

66 Table Rock: Grafton Notch

2.5 mi/1.5 hrs 

Location: In Grafton Notch State Park; Southern Maine map page 3, grid b1.

User groups: Hikers only. No wheelchair facilities. Dogs are discouraged along the Appalachian Trail in Maine. This trail would be difficult to snowshoe and is not suitable for skis. Bikes, horses, and hunting are prohibited.

Access, fees: Visitors using the parking lot at this trailhead are asked to pay a self-service fee of $1 per adult and 50 cents per child. There is a box beside the parking lot.

Directions: This hike begins from a large parking lot (marked by a sign reading "Hiking Trail") where the Appalachian Trail crosses Route 26 in Grafton Notch State Park, 6.7 miles north of the sign at the state park's southern entrance, and 1.8 miles south of the sign at the state park's northern entrance.

Maps: A very basic map of trails in Grafton Notch State Park is available from park rangers, who are usually on duty at high-traffic areas such as Screw Auger Falls (hike number 68); it can also be obtained through the park office or the state Bureau of Parks and Lands (see addresses below). For a contour map of trails, refer to map 7 in the "Map and Guide to the Appalachian Trail in Maine," a set of seven maps and a guidebook for $19.95 from the Maine Appalachian Trail Club or the Appalachian Trail Conference (see addresses below). For a topographic map of the area, request Old Speck Mountain from the USGS.

Contact: Grafton Notch State Park, HCR 61, Box 330, Newry, ME 04261; (207) 824-2912. Maine Bureau of Parks and Lands, Department of Conservation, 22 State House Station, Augusta, ME 04333; (207) 287-3821. Maine Appalachian Trail Club, P.O. Box 283, Augusta, ME 04332-0283. Appalachian Trail Conference, P.O. Box 807, Harpers Ferry, WV 25425; (304) 535-6331.

Trail notes: Flanked to the south by Old Speck Mountain and to the north by Baldpate Mountain, Grafton Notch takes a deep bite out of this western Maine stretch of the Appalachians and marks the northern terminus of the Mahoosuc Range. Perched hundreds of feet up Baldpate Mountain, the broad, flat Table Rock overlooks the notch. Visible from Route 26, it affords commanding views of the notch and Old Speck. This 2.4-mile loop over Table Rock employs the orange-blazed Table Rock Trail, which ascends very steeply and relentlessly for a mile. The difficult section can be avoided by hiking the more moderate Appalachian Trail and the upper part of the Table Rock Trail both ways, instead of just on the descent as described here. But while it was physically demanding, I enjoyed the steep stretch of trail, particularly when it emerged at the slab caves below Table Rock.

From the parking lot, pick up the white-blazed Appalachian Trail heading north, crossing the highway. After re-entering the woods, follow the AT for a tenth of a mile, then turn right at the sign for Table Rock. The trail almost immediately grows steep, emerging a mile later at the so-called slab caves, which are actually intriguing cavities amid boulders rather than true caves. The trail turns right and circles around and up onto Table Rock. To descend, walk off the back of Table Rock, following the blue-blazed trail for a half mile to the left until reaching the AT. Turn left (south), and follow the AT nearly a mile back to Route 26. Cross the highway to the parking lot.

67 Mother Walker Falls

0.2 mi/0.25 hr 

Location: In Grafton Notch State Park; Southern Maine map page 3, grid b1.

User groups: Hikers, dogs, and snowshoers. No wheelchair facilities. Dogs must be on a leash. This trail is not suitable for bikes, horses, or skis. Hunting is allowed in season.

Access, fees: Parking and access are free.

Directions: This hike begins from a roadside turnout marked by a sign for Mother Walker Falls, on Route 26 in Grafton Notch State Park, 2.2 miles north of the sign at the state park's southern entrance, and 6.3 miles south of the sign at the state park's northern entrance.

Maps: Although no map is needed for this walk, a very basic map of trails in Grafton Notch State Park is available from park rangers, who are usually on duty at Screw Auger Falls (hike number 68); it can also be obtained through the park office or the state Bureau of Parks and Lands (see addresses below). For a topographic map of the area, request Old Speck Mountain from the USGS.

Contact: Grafton Notch State Park, HCR 61, Box 330, Newry, ME 04261; (207) 824-2912. Maine Bureau of Parks and Lands, Department of Conservation, 22 State House Station, Augusta, ME 04333; (207) 287-3821.

Trail notes: This short walk on an easy, wide path leads to a couple of viewpoints above what is more of a gorge than falls. From the turnout, walk down the stairs. A gravel path leads both to the right and to the left, and both directions lead a short distance to views into the narrow gorge, in which the stream drops through several short steps for 100 yards or more. To the right, the walkway ends at a fence. If you go left, you have greater liberty to explore the stream and gorge. It can be difficult to get a good view into the gorge because of the denseness of the forest and rugged nature of the terrain along the stream.

68 Screw Auger Falls

0.1 mi/0.25 hr 

Location: In Grafton Notch State Park; Southern Maine map page 3, grid b1.

User groups: Hikers, dogs, and wheelchair users. Dogs must be on a leash. This trail is not suitable for bikes, horses, or skis. Hunting is allowed in season.

Access, fees: Parking and access are free.

Directions: This hike begins from a large parking lot marked by a sign for Screw Auger Falls, on Route 26 in Grafton Notch State Park, one mile north of the sign at the state park's southern entrance, and 7.5 miles south of the sign at the state park's northern entrance.

Maps: Although no map is needed for this walk, a very basic map of trails in Grafton Notch State Park is available from park rangers, who are usually on duty at Screw Auger Falls; it can also be obtained through the park office or the state Bureau of Parks and Lands (see addresses below). For a topographic map of the area, request Old Speck Mountain from the USGS.

Contact: Grafton Notch State Park, HCR 61, Box 330, Newry, ME 04261; (207) 824-2912. Maine Bureau of Parks and Lands, Department of Conservation, 22 State House Station, Augusta, ME 04333; (207) 287-3821.

Trail notes: A popular swimming hole for families and scenic attraction for tourists, Screw Auger Falls lies just a few minutes' stroll down a flat walkway from the parking lot. The Bear River pours over smooth slabs of stone, tumbling through the impressive waterfall and a tight gorge of water-sculpted rock reminiscent of some Southwestern slot canyons (albeit on a smaller scale). While today it sits in the heart of 3,192-acre Grafton Notch State Park, the falls once sported a water-powered log saw. Up until the early twentieth century, the logging community of Grafton, with a population of more than 100, sprawled up through the notch. Interestingly, the town's children attended school during the summer because the notch road was often impassable in winter.

69 Step Falls

1.0 mi/0.5 hr 

Location: South of Grafton Notch State Park; Southern Maine map page 3, grid b1.

User groups: Hikers and snowshoers. No wheelchair facilities. This trail is not suitable for bikes, dogs, horses, or skis. Hunting is prohibited.

Access, fees: Parking and access are free. The preserve is closed from dusk to dawn.

Directions: This hike begins from a large dirt parking lot off Route 26, 0.6 mile south of the southern entrance to Grafton Notch State Park. Watch for a dirt road, marked by a small sign, on the south side of a small bridge over Wight Brook; it leads 100 feet to the parking area.

Maps: No map is needed for this easy walk. But for a topographic map of the area, request Old Speck Mountain from the USGS.

Contact: Maine Chapter of the Nature Conservancy, (207) 729-5181.

Trail notes: On a typical, stiflingly hot and humid July day, I walked these cool hemlock woods to the lower part of Step Falls. Seeing it for the first time, I thought, "Nice." Then I rounded a bend in Wight Brook for my first glimpse of the upper falls, and thought, "Wow!" I won't try to build up these falls with some verbose description—this is the sort of place you should discover without expectations.

From the parking lot, follow the obvious, white-blazed trail for a half mile to the falls. The trail is an easy, flat walk; take care not to wander off it onto false trails, because such roaming contributes to erosion of the surrounding woods. Return the same way.

70 Old Speck Mountain

7.6 mi/5.0 hrs 

Location: In Grafton Notch State Park; Southern Maine map page 3, grid b1.

User groups: Hikers only. No wheelchair facilities. Dogs are discouraged along the Appalachian Trail in Maine. This trail may be difficult to snowshoe and is not suitable for skis. Bikes, horses, and hunting are prohibited.

Access, fees: Visitors using the parking lot at this trailhead are asked to pay a self-service fee of $1 per adult and 50 cents per child. There is a box beside the parking lot. The summit and northeast slopes of Old Speck are within Grafton Notch State Park in Maine.

Directions: Park in the large parking lot located where the white-blazed Appalachian Trail crosses Route 26, 1.8 miles south of the sign marking the northern boundary of Grafton Notch State Park in Maine.

Maps: Map 1 in the "Map and Guide to the Appalachian Trail in New Hampshire and Vermont," an eight-map set for $10.95 from the Appalachian Trail Conference (see address below), covers the entire Mahoosuc Range, as does the "Carter-Mahoosuc/Rangeley-Stratton" map for $2.95 from the Appalachian Mountain Club, (800) 262-4455. Map 7 in the "Map and Guide to the Appalachian Trail in Maine," a set of seven maps and a guidebook for $19.95 from the ATC, covers just the AT in Maine (including this hike). For a topographic map of the area, request Old Speck Mountain from the USGS.

Contact: Appalachian Mountain Club, P.O. Box 298, Gorham, NH 03581; (603) 466-2721. Appalachian Trail Conference, P.O. Box 807, Harpers Ferry, WV 25425; (304) 535-6331. Grafton Notch State Park, HCR 61, Box 330, Newry, ME 04261; (207) 824-2912. Maine Bureau of Parks and Lands, 22 State House Station, Augusta, ME 04333; (207) 287-3821.

Trail notes: This 7.6-mile round-trip hike brings you to the summit of Maine's fourth-highest peak and one of the state's dozen 4,000-footers (4,180 feet)—yet, a summit that lacks views. Only an abandoned fire tower, unsafe to climb, stands there. There are some views along the Old Speck Trail, which coincides with the Appalachian Trail, from the shoulder of Old Speck out over the vast sweep of woodlands to the north. Otherwise, the greatest attractions of this hike are bagging one of Maine's bigger hills, and perhaps the cascades in brooks which the trail parallels lower on the mountain.

From the parking lot in Grafton Notch, follow the white blazes of the AT/Old Speck Trail southbound. At 3.5 miles, the trail reaches a junction with the Mahoosuc Trail. Turn left for the easy, final three-tenths-of-a-mile climb to Old Speck's summit. Head back along the same route.

71 Mahoosuc Notch

6.5 mi/6.0 hrs 

Location: South of Grafton Notch State Park; Southern Maine map page 3, grid b1.

User groups: Hikers only. No wheelchair facilities. Dogs are discouraged along the Appalachian Trail in Maine. This trail would be very difficult to snowshoe and is not suitable for skis. Bikes, horses, and hunting are prohibited.

Access, fees: Parking and access are free. Success Pond Road, a private logging road which parallels the Mahoosuc Range on its west side, isn't maintained in winter and may not be passable due to mud in spring; it may also be difficult to follow because side roads branch from it.

Directions: The Mahoosuc Notch Trail begins on the dirt Success Pond Road, which runs south from Route 26, 2.8 miles north of where the white-blazed Appalachian Trail crosses the highway in Grafton Notch State Park. To access Success Pond Road from the south, drive north on Route 16 from its southern junction with U.S. 2 in Gorham for about 4.5 miles, and turn east on the Cleveland Bridge across the Androscoggin River in Berlin. Bear left onto Unity Street; go through traffic lights seven-tenths of a mile from Route 16, then continue a tenth of a mile and bear right onto Hutchins Street. Drive eight-tenths of a mile farther and turn sharply left, passing the paper company millyard. Just three-tenths of a mile farther, turn right onto Success Pond Road. From Hutchins Street, follow Success Pond Road about 11 miles to the trailhead parking area on the right at a sign for the Notch Trail.

Maps: Map 1 in the "Map and Guide to the Appalachian Trail in New Hampshire and Vermont," an eight-map set for $10.95 from the Appalachian Trail Conference (see address below), covers the entire Mahoosuc Range, including the notch, as does the "Carter-Mahoosuc/Rangeley-Stratton" map for $2.95 from the Appalachian Mountain Club, (800) 262-4455. For topographic maps of the area, request Success Pond and Old Speck Mountain from the USGS.

Contact: Appalachian Mountain Club, P.O. Box 298, Gorham, NH 03581; (603) 466-2721. Appalachian Trail Conference, P.O. Box 807, Harpers Ferry, WV 25425; (304) 535-6331.

Trail notes: Backpacking the northern Mahoosuc Range with a friend a few years back, we were descending toward our introduction to Mahoosuc Notch—which bears a reputation as "the hardest mile on the Appalachian Trail"—when we encountered another backpacker. He had just come through the notch, so we curiously inquired about it. He smiled wickedly and said, "The notch was full of surprises this morning." Indeed. On a 70-degree Indian summer day, we dropped into the notch and immediately the temperature plummeted about 20 degrees. Giant boulders which over the eons have toppled off the towering cliffs that embrace the notch lay strewn about its floor, a maze of stone through which we picked our careful way, crawling through cave-like passages, constantly scrambling over and around obstacles.

Mahoosuc Notch can be day hiked via the Notch Trail from Success Pond Road when the road is passable, a 6.5-mile round-trip which can easily take several hours. Follow the white blazes of the AT carefully through the notch. From Success Pond Road, the trail ascends gently eastward. At 2.2 miles, it reaches a junction with the Mahoosuc Trail, which coincides with the AT. Continue straight ahead (northbound) on the AT, soon entering the bouldery realm of the notch. Upon reaching the opposite end—you will know when you're through it—turn around and return the way you came. For a two- or three-day loop that incorporates the notch and allows you to avoid backtracking, see the description of the Mahoosuc Range (hike number 72).

72 The Mahoosuc Range

30.6 mi. one way/
5.0 days

Location: Between Shelburne, New Hampshire, and Grafton Notch State Park; Southern Maine map page 3, grid b1.

User groups: Hikers only. No wheelchair facilities. Dogs are discouraged along the Appalachian Trail in Maine. This trail would be very difficult to snowshoe and is not suitable for skis. Bikes, horses, and hunting are prohibited.

Access, fees: Parking and access are free. The dirt Success Pond Road, a private logging road which parallels the Mahoosuc Range on its west side, provides a shorter drive between both ends of this hike than taking state highways, but it's not maintained in winter and may not be passable due to mud in spring; it may also be difficult to follow because side roads branch from it. Trails into the Mahoosucs which begin on Success Pond Road are marked by signs. Camping is permitted only at the five backcountry campsites/shelters along the Appalachian Trail through the Mahoosuc Range. The summit and northeast slopes of Old Speck are within Grafton Notch State Park in Maine, but the rest of the Mahoosucs are on private property, and not a part of the White Mountain National Forest.

Directions: You will need to shuttle two vehicles for this backpacking trip. To hike the range from south to north, as described here, leave one vehicle in the large parking lot located where the white-blazed Appalachian Trail crosses Route 26, 1.8 miles south of the sign marking the northern boundary of Grafton Notch State Park in Maine. From that parking lot, it's 2.8 miles north on Route 26 to Success Pond Road. To reach the start of this hike, turn north off U.S. 2 onto North Road in Shelburne, NH, about 3.2 miles east of the southern junction of U.S. 2 and Route 16 in Gorham. Cross the Androscoggin River, then turn left onto Hogan Road and continue two-tenths of a mile to a small parking area for the Centennial Trail. You can also park at the junction of North and Hogan Roads, but don't block the road. To reach the southern end of Success Pond Road, drive north on Route 16 from its southern junction with U.S. 2 in Gorham for about 4.5 miles and turn east on the Cleveland Bridge across the Androscoggin River in Berlin. Bear left onto Unity Street; go through traffic lights seven-tenths of a mile from Route 16, then continue a tenth of a mile and bear right onto Hutchins Street. Drive eight-tenths of a mile farther and turn sharply left, passing the paper company millyard. Just three-tenths of a mile farther, turn right onto Success Pond Road.

Maps: Map 1 in the "Map and Guide to the Appalachian Trail in New Hampshire and Vermont," an eight-map set for $10.95 from the Appalachian Trail Conference (see address below), covers the entire Mahoosuc Range, as does the "Carter-Mahoosuc/Rangeley-Stratton" map for $2.95 from the Appalachian Mountain Club, (800) 262-4455. Map 7 in the "Map and Guide to the Appalachian Trail in Maine," a set of seven maps and a guidebook for $19.95 from the ATC, covers just the AT in Maine (roughly the northern half of the Mahoosuc Range). For topographic maps of the area, request Berlin, Shelburne, Success Pond, Gilead, and Old Speck Mountain from the USGS.

Contact: Appalachian Mountain Club, P.O. Box 298, Gorham, NH 03581; (603) 466-2721. Appalachian Trail Conference, P.O. Box 807, Harpers Ferry, WV 25425; (304) 535-6331. Grafton Notch State Park, HCR 61, Box 330, Newry, ME 04261; (207) 824-2912. Maine Bureau of Parks and Lands, 22 State House Station, Augusta, ME 04333; (207) 287-3821.

Trail notes: I've considered the Mahoosucs one of my favorite mountain ranges in New England since my first foray into this wild, remote string of rugged hills one March weekend several years ago. A friend and I spent three days here and saw no one else; and the log in our shelter indicated no more than a half-dozen people had visited since November. On an autumn trip here, I enjoyed one of my finest sunrises ever from the open south summit of Fulling Mill Mountain. Among the many highlights of this trek are the ridge walk over Goose Eye Mountain, and Mahoosuc Notch, a boulder-strewn cleft in the range often referred to as "the hardest mile on the Appalachian Trail." The Mahoosucs grow much busier from July through October than they are in March, of course, and their popularity has mushroomed in recent years. Still, they are far enough removed from population centers that fewer people wander onto these trails than onto many trails just a bit south of here, in the White Mountains. Only one peak, Old Speck, rises above 4,000 feet, but there's nary a flat piece of earth through the entire range. Read: very tough hiking. This trek traverses the Mahoosucs on the Appalachian Trail from U.S. 2 in Shelburne, New Hampshire, to Grafton Notch, Maine, a 30.6-mile outing that can easily take five days. For a shorter trip, you should consider a two- or three-day hike from Grafton Notch to either the Mahoosuc Notch Trail or the Carlo Col Trail (both of which begin on Success Pond Road).

Beginning on an old woods road, the Centennial Trail ascends steadily, and steeply at times, to the eastern summit of Mount Hayes at 2.8 miles, which offers good views of the Carter-Moriah Range and Northern Presidentials to the south and southwest. At 3.1 miles, turn right (north) on the Mahoosuc Trail, which coincides with the AT. (Just two-tenths of a mile to the left is a good view from the summit of Mount Hayes.) At 4.9 miles, the AT passes over the open summit of Cascade Mountain, and at 6.1 miles a side path leads two-tenths of a mile to the Trident Col campsite. It skirts Page Pond at 7.1 miles, and at 7.7 miles a side path leads to views from Wocket Ledge. At 8.8 miles, the trail runs along the north shore of Dream Lake; at the lake's far end, the Peabody Brook Trail diverges right, leading 3.1 miles south to North Road. (The Dryad Falls Trail branches east from the Peabody Brook Trail a tenth of a mile from the AT and leads 1.8 miles to the Austin Brook Trail.) At 11 miles, the AT descends to Gentian Pond and a lean-to near its shore.

Continuing northbound, the trail climbs steeply up Mount Success, reaching the summit at 13.8 miles. After the Success Trail diverges left (west) at 14.4 miles (leading 2.4 miles to Success Pond Road), the AT descends steeply, then climbs to the Carlo Col Trail junction at 16.2 miles. (That trail leads two-tenths of a mile to the Carlo Col shelter and 2.6 miles west to Success Pond Road.) At 16.6 miles it passes over the open summit of Mount Carlo, descends, then climbs—very steeply near the top—to the high ridge of Goose Eye Mountain at 18 miles. Walk the open ridge to the left a short distance for the terrific view from the West Peak, where the Goose Eye Trail diverges left (west), leading 3.1 miles to Success Pond Road. Then turn north again on the AT, descend, then climb to the 3,794-foot East Peak, which also offers sweeping views. (The two branches of the Wright Trail reach the AT immediately south and north of the East Peak, both leading east about four miles to the Sunday River Ski Area road in Ketchum, Maine.) Descend again, then climb over the summit of North Peak at 19.6 miles, and reach the Full Goose shelter at 20.6 miles. The AT climbs steeply north from the shelter to the barren summit of South Peak, with views in nearly every direction. It swings left, then descends steeply to the junction with the Mahoosuc Notch Trail at 22.1 miles (that trail leads 2.2 miles west to Success Pond Road).

The next mile of trail traverses the floor of Mahoosuc Notch, ringed with tall cliffs that usually leave the notch in cool shadow. Follow the white blazes carefully through the jumbled terrain of boulders, where carrying a backpack can be very difficult. At the far end of the notch, at 23.1 miles, the AT swings uphill for the sustained climb of Mahoosuc Arm, passes ledges with good views, then drops downhill to beautiful Speck Pond, at 3,430 feet one of the highest ponds in Maine. There is a lean-to just above the pond's shore, at 25.7 miles, near which the Speck Pond Trail descends west 3.6 miles to Success Pond Road. From the shelter, the AT ascends north up Old Speck Mountain, traversing open ledges with excellent views to the south, then re-entering the woods to reach a junction with the Old Speck Trail at 26.8 miles (where the Mahoosuc Trail ends). From that junction, the Old Speck Trail continues straight ahead three-tenths of a mile over easy ground to the wooded 4,180-foot summit of Old Speck, where an abandoned fire tower stands; and the AT coincides with the Old Speck Trail for the circuitous, 3.5-mile descent to Grafton Notch, culminating at the parking lot.

73 The Roost

1.0 mi/0.75 hr 

Location: South of Gilead; Southern Maine map page 3, grid b1.

User groups: Hikers, dogs, and snowshoers. No wheelchair facilities. This trail is not suitable for bikes, horses, or skis. Hunting is allowed in season.

Access, fees: Parking and access are free. Route 113 through Evans Notch is not maintained in winter, and gates are used to close off a 9.1-mile stretch of the highway. But you can drive to parking areas near the gates, and ski or snowshoe the road beyond the gates to access this area. The northern gate on Route 113 is 1.6 miles south of the junction of U.S. 2 and Route 133 in Gilead. The southern gate sits on the Maine–New Hampshire line, two-tenths of a mile south of Brickett Place in North Chatham and immediately north of the entrance to the White Mountain National Forest Basin Recreation Area. The distance given for this hike is from the trailhead.

Directions: Drive to a turnout just north of the bridge over Evans Brook on Route 113, 3.7 miles south of the junction of Route 113 and U.S. 2 in Gilead and seven miles north of where Route 113 crosses the Maine–New Hampshire border.

Maps: For a contour map of trails, obtain the "Map of Cold River Valley and Evans Notch" for $5 from the Chatham Trails Association, P.O. Box 605, Center Conway, NH 03813; the "Carter-Mahoosuc/Rangeley-Stratton" map for $2.95 from the Appalachian Mountain Club, (800) 262-4455; or the "Trail Map and Guide to the White Mountain National Forest" for $4.95 from the DeLorme Mapping Company, (800) 253-5081. For a topographic map of the area, request Speckled Mountain from the USGS.

Contact: White Mountain National Forest Supervisor, 719 North Main Street, Laconia, NH 03246; (603) 528-8721, TDD for hearing impaired (603) 528-8722.

Trail notes: From the turnout, walk south across the bridge and turn left (east) on the Roost Trail. Cross two small brooks within the first quarter mile, then walk an old woods road. Less than a half mile from the trailhead, turn left (where indicated by an arrow and yellow blazes). Cross a brook and climb steeply uphill for the final two-tenths of a mile to the rocky knob of a summit, where the views are largely obscured by trees. Follow the "view" sign and trail downhill for a tenth of a mile to open ledges with a good view overlooking the Wild River Valley. Turn around and return the way you came.

74 Mount Caribou

7.3 mi/4.5 hrs 

Location: South of Gilead; Southern Maine map page 3, grid b1.

User groups: Hikers, dogs, and snowshoers. No wheelchair facilities. This trail is not suitable for bikes, horses, or skis. Hunting is allowed in season.

Access, fees: Parking and access are free. Route 113 through Evans Notch is not maintained in winter, and gates are used to close off a 9.1-mile stretch of the highway. But you can drive to parking areas near the gates, and ski or snowshoe the road beyond the gates to access this area. The northern gate on Route 113 is 1.6 miles south of the junction of U.S. 2 and Route 133 in Gilead. The southern gate sits on the Maine–New Hampshire line, two-tenths of a mile south of Brickett Place in North Chatham and immediately north of the entrance to the White Mountain National Forest Basin Recreation Area. The distance given for this hike is from the trailhead.

Directions: The hike begins from a parking lot on Route 113, 4.8 miles south of its junction with U.S. 2 in Gilead, and 5.9 miles north of where Route 113 crosses the Maine–New Hampshire border.

Maps: For a contour map of trails, obtain the "Map of Cold River Valley and Evans Notch" for $5 from the Chatham Trails Association, P.O. Box 605, Center Conway, NH 03813; the "Carter-Mahoosuc/Rangeley-Stratton" map for $2.95 from the Appalachian Mountain Club, (800) 262-4455; or the "Trail Map and Guide to the White Mountain National Forest" for $4.95 from the DeLorme Mapping Company, (800) 253-5081. For a topographic map of the area, request Speckled Mountain from the USGS.

Contact: White Mountain National Forest Supervisor, 719 North Main Street,

Laconia, NH 03246; (603) 528-8721, TDD for hearing impaired (603) 528-8722.

Trail notes: I first attempted this hike on a winter backpacking trip, when a friend and I had to walk the road for three miles to the trailhead, and ultimately never reached the summit because the trail became difficult to follow under a blanket of snow. Months later, in shorts and a T-shirt, I completed this scenic 7.3-mile loop over Mount Caribou, a hill with unusually excellent summit views for its 2,828-foot elevation. Caribou lies within the Caribou–Speckled Mountain Wilderness of the White Mountain National Forest, where the national forest pushes into western Maine.

The Caribou Trail–Mud Brook Trail loop begins and ends at the parking area; this 7.3-mile hike follows it clockwise. Yellow blazes mark both trails only sporadically, though the paths are well used and obvious (except in winter). Hike north (left from the parking area) on the Caribou Trail, crossing a wooden footbridge over a brook at three-tenths of a mile. About a half mile past the footbridge, the trail crosses Morrison Brook and trends in a more easterly direction—making several more stream crossings over the next two miles, some of which could be difficult at times of high water. One stretch of about a half mile makes five crossings near several waterfalls and cascades, including 25-foot Kees Falls. Three miles from the trailhead, the Caribou Trail reaches a junction with the Mud Brook Trail, marked by a sign. Turn right (south) on the Mud Brook Trail and follow it a half mile, climbing steadily, to the open ledges of the summit. From various spots on the ledges you'll enjoy views, in virtually every direction, of the low mountains and lakes of western Maine. Numerous false trails lead through the scrub brush of the summit, so take care to follow cairns and faint yellow blazes over the summit, continuing on the Mud Brook Trail. A half mile below the summit, the trail traverses the top of a cliff with a good view east. From the summit, it's nearly four miles back to the parking area. Along its lower two miles, the trail parallels and twice crosses Mud Brook.

75 East Royce

2.8 mi/2.0 hrs 

Location: South of Gilead; Southern Maine map page 3, grid b1.

User groups: Hikers, dogs, and snowshoers. No wheelchair facilities. This trail is not suitable for bikes, horses, or skis. Hunting is allowed in season.

Access, fees: Parking and access are free. Route 113 through Evans Notch is not maintained in winter, and gates are used to close off a 9.1-mile stretch of the highway. But you can drive to parking areas near the gates, and ski or snowshoe the road beyond the gates to access this area. The northern gate on Route 113 is 1.6 miles south of the junction of U.S. 2 and Route 133 in Gilead. The southern gate sits on the Maine–New Hampshire line, two-tenths of a mile south of Brickett Place in North Chatham and immediately north of the entrance to the White Mountain National Forest Basin Recreation Area. The distance given for this hike is from the trailhead.

Directions: The East Royce Trail begins at a parking lot on the west side of Route 113, 7.6 miles south of the junction of U.S. 2 and Route 113 in Gilead, and 3.1 miles north of where Route 113 crosses the Maine–New Hampshire border.

Maps: For a contour map of trails, obtain the "Map of Cold River Valley and Evans Notch" for $5 from the Chatham Trails Association, P.O. Box 605, Center Conway, NH 03813; the "Carter-Mahoosuc/Rangeley-Stratton" map for $2.95 from the Appalachian Mountain Club, (800) 262-4455; or the

"Trail Map and Guide to the White Mountain National Forest" for $4.95 from the DeLorme Mapping Company, (800) 253-5081. For a topographic map of the area, request Speckled Mountain from the USGS.

Contact: White Mountain National Forest Supervisor, 719 North Main Street, Laconia, NH 03246; (603) 528-8721, TDD for hearing impaired (603) 528-8722.

Trail notes: From the parking lot, the trail immediately crosses a braided stream and begins a steep climb—both portents of what lies ahead on this short but rigorous 2.8-mile hike. The hike up East Royce makes several stream crossings, passing picturesque waterfalls and cascades, and ascends a relentlessly steep mountainside. I hustled up here one morning after a day of heavy downpours, and found the streams swelled nearly to bursting. The summit proves worth the effort, with sweeping views that encompass the dramatic cliffs of West Royce, the peaks of South and North Baldface, and the lakes and lower hills of western Maine.

From the parking lot, follow the East Royce Trail a mile to where the Royce Connector Trail enters from the left. Turn right with the East Royce Trail, reaching open ledges that involve somewhat exposed scrambling within a quarter mile, and the summit just a tenth of a mile farther.

Special note: Across Route 113 from the parking area, the Spruce Hill Trail enters the woods beside a series of cascades worth checking out when the water is high.

76 Speckled and Blueberry Mountains

7.9 mi/5.0 hrs 

Location: South of Gilead; Southern Maine map page 3, grid b1.

User groups: Hikers, dogs, and snowshoers. No wheelchair facilities. This trail is not suitable for bikes, horses, or skis. Hunting is allowed in season.

Access, fees: Parking and access are free. Route 113 through Evans Notch is not maintained in winter, and gates are used to close off a 9.1-mile stretch of the highway. But you can drive to parking areas near the gates, and ski or snowshoe the road beyond the gates to access this area. The northern gate on Route 113 is 1.6 miles south of the junction of U.S. 2 and Route 133 in Gilead. The southern gate sits on the Maine–New Hampshire line, two-tenths of a mile south of Brickett Place in North Chatham and immediately north of the entrance to the White Mountain National Forest Basin Recreation Area. The distance given for this hike is from the trailhead.

Directions: This hike begins at Brickett Place, a parking area beside a brick building on Route 113 in North Chatham, two-tenths of a mile north of where Route 113 crosses the Maine–New Hampshire border, and 10.5 miles south of the junction of Route 113 and U.S. 2 in Gilead.

Maps: For a contour map of trails, obtain the "Map of Cold River Valley and Evans Notch" for $5 from the Chatham Trails Association, P.O. Box 605, Center Conway, NH 03813; the "Carter-Mahoosuc/Rangeley-Stratton" map for $2.95 from the Appalachian Mountain Club, (800) 262-4455; or the "Trail Map and Guide to the White Mountain National Forest" for $4.95 from the DeLorme Mapping Company, (800) 253-5081. For a topographic map of the area, request Speckled Mountain from the USGS.

Contact: White Mountain National Forest Supervisor, 719 North Main Street, Laconia, NH 03246; (603) 528-8721, TDD for hearing impaired (603) 528-8722.

Trail notes: The views from the barren summit of Speckled Mountain are among the best in the area. A companion and I had this summit and the cliffs of Blueberry

Mountain to ourselves one summer afternoon, when the wind blew hard enough to knock us around.

From the parking area, pick up the Bickford Brook Trail. At six-tenths of a mile, turn right at the sign for the Blueberry Ridge Trail. Immediately, the trail makes a stream crossing at a narrow gorge that definitely could be dangerous during high water. (If the stream is impassable, or if you would prefer a less strenuous hike to the summit of Speckled Mountain, skip this trail and follow the Bickford Brook Trail all the way to the summit, an 8.6-mile round-trip. That option would be the easier route on snowshoes as well.) Continue up the Blueberry Ridge Trail for seven-tenths of a mile to a junction with the Lookout Loop, a half-mile detour out to the cliffs of Blueberry Mountain and a great panoramic view of lakes and hills to the south and east, including Pleasant Mountain (hike number 79). The Lookout Loop rejoins the Blueberry Ridge Trail; follow it to the right. (Hikers seeking a shorter day can turn left and descend the Blueberry Ridge and Bickford Brook Trails, a round-trip of 3.1 miles.) It ascends the two-mile ridge, much of it open with wide views over your shoulder of the peaks across Evans Notch: East and West Royce, Meader, and North and South Baldface. At the upper junction with the Bickford Brook Trail, turn right (east) for the easy half-mile hike to the summit of Speckled Mountain, a bald crown of rock with great views in almost every direction. Descend the same way, except stay on the Bickford Brook Trail all the way (4.3 miles) back to the parking area.

77 Sabattus Mountain

1.5 mi/1.0 hr 

Location: Outside Center Lovell; Southern Maine map page 3, grid b1.

User groups: Hikers, dogs, and snowshoers. No wheelchair facilities. This trail is not suitable for bikes, horses, or skis. Hunting is allowed in season.

Access, fees: Parking and access are free.

Directions: From the Center Lovell Inn on Route 5 in Center Lovell, drive north for two-tenths of a mile on Route 5 and turn right on Sabattus Road. Continue for 1.5 miles, then bear right on the dirt Sabattus Mountain Road. Park in a small dirt lot or at the roadside 0.3 mile farther. The trail begins across the road from the lot.

Maps: For a topographic map of the area, request Center Lovell from the USGS.

Contact: There is no contact agency for this hike.

Trail notes: This short but popular local hike leads to the top of a sheer drop of hundreds of feet, providing wide views of nearly unbroken forest and mountains, including Pleasant Mountain (hike number 79) to the south and the White Mountains to the east. This is a great hike for young children and for foliage viewing. Follow the wide trail, which ascends steadily—and at times steeply—for three-quarters of a mile to the summit. Walk the clifftop to the right for the best views of the Whites. Return the same way.

78 Jockey Cap

0.4 mi/0.5 hr 

Location: East of Fryeburg; Southern Maine map page 3, grid c1.

User groups: Hikers, dogs, and snowshoers. No wheelchair facilities. This trail is not suitable for bikes, horses, or skis. Hunting is prohibited.

Access, fees: Parking and access are free. The trail is open to the public year-round.

Directions: From the junction of U.S. 302, Route 5, and Route 113 in Fryeburg, drive east on U.S. 302 for one mile and park at the Jockey Cap country store on the left. The Jockey Cap Trail begins at a gate between the store and the cabins to the right.

Maps: No map is needed for this short walk, but for a topographic map of the area, request Fryeburg from the USGS.

Contact: This trail crosses private land owned by the proprietors of the Jockey Cap country store, (207) 935-2306, and land owned by the town of Fryeburg and managed by its Recreation Department, (207) 935-3933.

Trail notes: This short walk in Fryeburg—just down the road from North Conway, New Hampshire—leads to the top of what a sign along the trail describes as "the largest boulder in the United States." While the veracity of that claim might be questionable, the hike does nonetheless provide a nice walk to a good view of the surrounding countryside, including Mounts Washington and Chocorua in the White Mountains.

Follow the wide and obvious trail into the woods. As the cliffs on the face of Jockey Cap come into view through the trees, the trail circles to the left around the boulder and emerges from the woods at a spot where you can safely walk up onto the cap. Return the same way.

79 Pleasant Mountain

5.7 mi/3.5 hrs 

Location: Between Fryeburg, Denmark, and Bridgeton; Southern Maine map page 3, grid c1.

User groups: Hikers, dogs, and snowshoers. No wheelchair facilities. This trail is not suitable for bikes, horses, or skis. Hunting is allowed in season.

Access, fees: Parking and access are free.

Directions: From the junction of U.S. 302 and Route 93, west of Bridgeton, drive 4.5 miles west on 302 and turn left onto Mountain Road (heading toward the Shawnee Peak Ski Area). Drive another 1.8 miles to a turnout at the Bald Peak Trailhead (marked by a sign on the right). If you have two vehicles, leave one at the Ledges Trailhead (marked by a sign) 1.5 miles farther down the road. Otherwise, you'll walk that stretch of road to finish this loop.

Maps: For a trail map, obtain the Camden Hills/Pleasant Mountain map for $2.95 from the Appalachian Mountain Club, (800) 262-4455. For a topographic map of the area, request Pleasant Mountain from the USGS.

Contact: There is no contact agency for this hike.

Trail notes: Rising barely more than 2,000 feet above sea level, Pleasant Mountain is probably one of the finest low-elevation ridge walks in New England. Walking the ridge brings you alternately through beautiful forest, over open ledges, and to several distinct summit humps with sweeping views. Big Bald Peak may be the nicest stretch of the ridge, though the views from the main summit are excellent also.

For a shorter hike, go to either the main summit via the Ledges Trail (3.6 miles, 2.5 hours round-trip), or to Big Bald Peak via the Bald Peak Trail (2.2 miles, 1.5 hours). For the full loop, begin on the Bald Peak Trail, ascending steadily beside a stream; watch for short waterfalls and a miniature flume. Where the Sue's Way Trail branches right, stay left and climb steeply to Big Bald Peak. Continue along the ridge on the Bald Peak Trail, which eventually joins the wide corridor of the Fire Warden's Trail. Turn left for the main summit. Continue over the summit to pick up the Ledges Trail, which descends along open ledges with terrific views to the south. The lower sections of this trail can be muddy and running with water. At the road, if you did not shuttle two vehicles, turn left and walk 1.5 miles to the Bald Peak Trailhead.

80 Burnt Meadow Mountain

2.4 mi/1.5 hrs 

Location: Outside Brownfield; Southern Maine map page 3, grid c1.

User groups: Hikers, dogs, and snowshoers. No wheelchair facilities. This trail is not suitable for bikes, horses, or skis. Hunting is allowed in season.

Access, fees: Parking and access are free.

Directions: From the junction of Route 5/113 and Route 160 in Brownfield, turn west on Route 160 and continue 1.1 miles. Turn left, staying on Route 160, and continue another three-tenths of a mile. Turn right onto the paved Fire Lane 32. The parking area is two-tenths of a mile farther.

Maps: For a topographic map of the area, request Brownfield from the USGS.

Contact: There is no contact agency for this hike.

Trail notes: A nice, short local hike, this hill in Brownfield, in southwestern Maine, has an open summit with views in almost every direction, from the White Mountains to the lakes of western Maine. When a companion and I hiked it in July, we found ripe blueberries to nibble on.

From the parking area, walk uphill to the old T-bar of a former ski area. Turn left and follow the T-bar and a worn footpath uphill. Ignore the sign with an arrow pointing to the right, which you encounter within the first half mile, and continue straight ahead under the T-bar. The trail grows quite steep, with lots of loose stones and dirt. Footing may become very tricky here in spring. Where the T-bar ends in a small clearing, turn left onto a trail marked by blue blazes, which leads at a more moderate angle to the summit. Watch for a good view from ledges on the left before reaching the summit. The broad top of Burnt Meadow Mountain offers views to the west, north, and south; continue over it and you'll get views to the south and east. Descend the way you came up.

81 Mount Cutler

2.6 mi/1.5 hrs 

Location: In Hiram; Southern Maine map page 3, grid c1.

User groups: Hikers, dogs, and snowshoers. No wheelchair facilities. This trail is not suitable for bikes, horses, or skis. Hunting is allowed in season.

Access, fees: Parking and access are free.

Directions: From the junction of Route 117 and Route 5/113, drive over the concrete bridge and take an immediate left, then a right onto Mountain View Avenue. Drive about a tenth of a mile and park at the roadside near the railroad tracks.

Maps: For topographic maps of the area, request Hiram and Cornish from the USGS.

Contact: There is no contact agency for this hike.

Trail notes: Mount Cutler rises abruptly from the valley of the Saco River in Hiram, and is quite a nice hike for a relatively small hill. Cross the railroad tracks and turn left, then enter the woods on the right at a wide trail. Soon you will branch right onto a red-blazed trail. The blazes appear sporadically at times, and on rocks rather than on trees higher up the mountain, making the trail potentially difficult to follow (particularly in winter). The trail ascends steep ledges overlooking the town of Hiram and grows narrow; care is needed over the ledges. But once you gain the ridge, the walking grows much easier as you pass through forests with a mix of hardwoods and hemlocks and traverse open areas with sweeping views. The east summit ledges, with views of the Saco Valley, are a good destination for a hike of about 1.5 miles. Continue on the trail along the ridge and into a saddle where there's a grove of birch trees. A faint footpath leads up the left side of the slope to the main summit, which is wooded. Just beyond it, however, and to the right is an open area with great views toward Pleasant Mountain and the White Mountains.

82 Douglas Hill

0.5 mi/0.5 hr 

Location: South of Sebago; Southern Maine map page 3, grid c1.

User groups: Hikers and snowshoers. No wheelchair facilities. This trail is not suitable for bikes, horses, or skis. Dogs are prohibited. Hunting is allowed in season.

Access, fees: Parking and access are free; just register at the trailhead. The preserve is open only during daylight hours. Large groups should contact the Nature Conservancy's Maine chapter (see address below) before visiting.

Directions: From the junction of Routes 107 and 114 in East Sebago, drive a half mile north on Route 107 and turn left onto Douglas Mountain Road (which is one mile south of Sebago center). Drive 0.8 mile to a hilltop and take a sharp left. In another half mile, turn left into a small parking area. The lot is surrounded by private land that is posted prohibiting parking.

Maps: A free guide and map to the Douglas Mountain Preserve is available at the trailhead registration box. For topographic maps of the area, request Steep Falls and North Sebago from the USGS.

Contact: The Nature Conservancy, Maine Chapter, Fort Andross, 14 Maine Street, Suite 401, Brunswick, ME 04011; (207) 729-5181.

Trail notes: By purchasing this 169-acre preserve in 1971, the Nature Conservancy saved for the public a scenic hill with expansive views. The open summit and its stone tower afford views of Sebago Lake, Pleasant Mountain, and the mountains to the northwest as far as Mount Washington.

From the registration box, walk through the stone pillars and follow the yellow-blazed Woods Trail a short distance, then bear left onto the Ledges Trail (also blazed yellow). This trail leads over interesting open ledges with good views, though they are slick when wet or icy. At the summit, climb the steps of the stone tower; on top is a diagram identifying the distant peaks. A Nature Trail, blazed orange, makes a three-quarter-mile loop off the summit and returns to it. Descend back to the parking lot via the Woods Trail.

83 Mount Agamenticus

1.0 mi/0.75 hr 

Location: West of Ogunquit; Southern Maine map page 3, grid d1.

User groups: Hikers, dogs, and snowshoers. No wheelchair facilities. This trail is not suitable for bikes, horses, or skis. Hunting is allowed in season.

Access, fees: Parking and access are free.

Directions: Take Interstate 95 to exit 4 in Ogunquit. At the end of the off-ramp, turn left, passing over the highway, then immediately turn right onto Mountain Road. Follow it for about 2.7 miles to the base of the Agamenticus summit road and a dirt parking area.

Maps: A rough map of Mount Agamenticus is available from the Maine Department of Inland Fisheries and Wildlife regional office (see address below). For topographic maps of the area, request York Harbor and North Berwick from the USGS.

Contact: Maine Department of Inland Fisheries and Wildlife, Regional Office, 358 Shaker Road, Gray, ME 04039; (207) 657-3258.

Trail notes: This one-mile hike up and

down tiny Agamenticus is an easy walk to a summit with a fire tower that offers 360-degree views of the Seacoast region and southern Maine and New Hampshire. From the parking area, follow the trail along an old woods road, soon climbing moderately. The trail ascends ledges, crosses the summit road, and emerges after half a mile at the summit. Return the way you came, or descend the summit road.

Northern Maine Map—page 2

New Hampshire

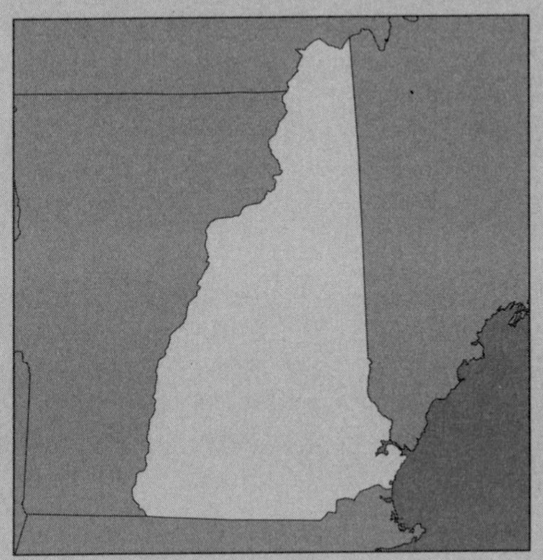

Overall Rating

1 2 3 4 5 6 7 8 9 10

Poor .... Fair .... Great

Difficulty

1 2 3 4 5

A stroll .... Moderate ...... A real butt-kicker!

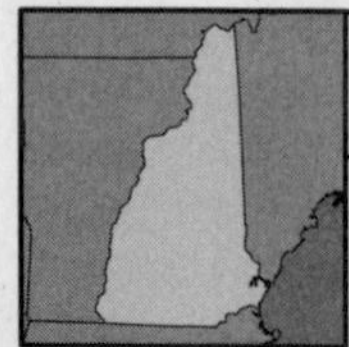

Northern New Hampshire

Adjoining Maps: East: Southern Maine .... *page* 3
West: Vermont .... *pages* 174-175
South: Southern New Hampshire .... *page* 87

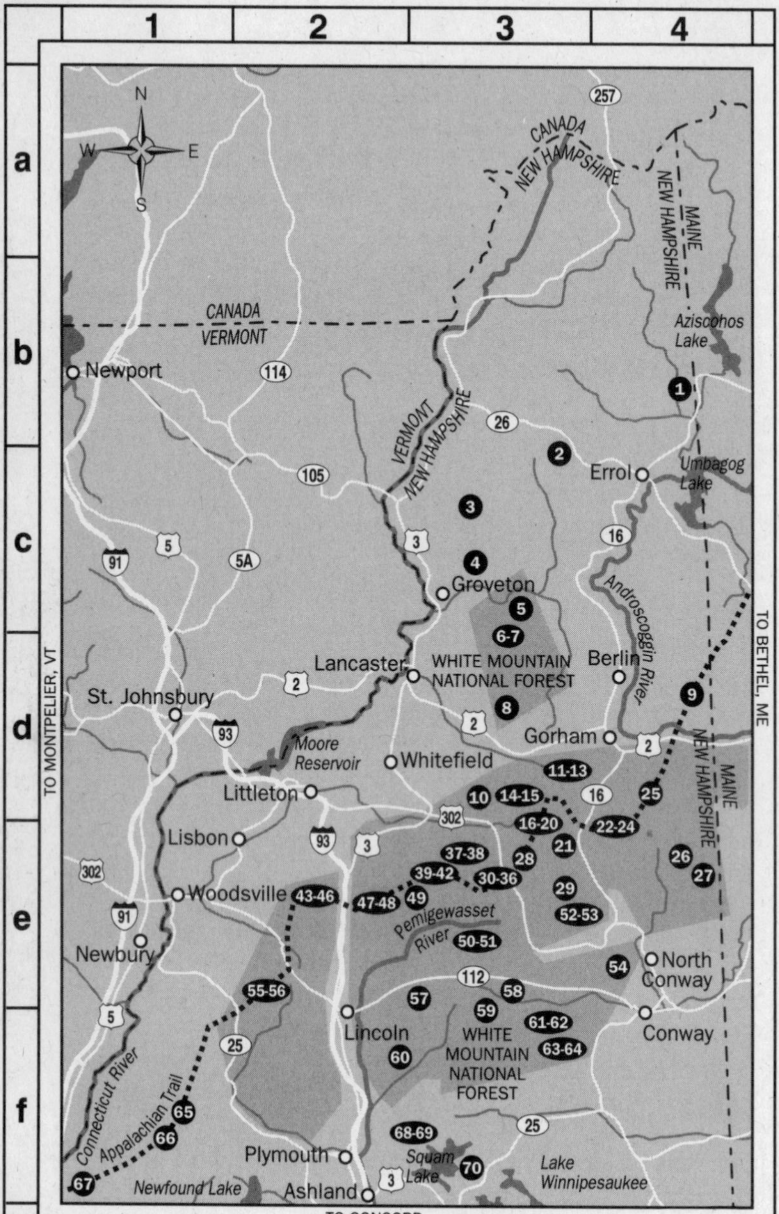

1 2 3 4

a
b
c
d
e
f

N
W
E
S
257
CANADA
NEW HAMPSHIRE
NEW HAMPSHIRE
MAINE
CANADA
VERMONT
Aziscohos Lake
Newport
114
1
VERMONT
NEW HAMPSHIRE
26
2
105
Errol
Umbagog Lake
3
16
5
91
5A
3
4
Groveton
5
6-7
Androscoggin River
Lancaster
WHITE MOUNTAIN NATIONAL FOREST
Berlin
2
St. Johnsbury
8
9
2
93
Gorham
2
Moore Reservoir
Whitefield
11-13
Littleton
10
14-15
16
25
302
16-20
22-24
Lisbon
93
3
37-38
28
21
26
302
39-42
30-36
27
Woodsville
43-46
47-48
49
29
91
Pemigewasset River
52-53
50-51
Newbury
North Conway
54
55-56
112
58
57
5
59
Conway
Lincoln
61-62
25
WHITE MOUNTAIN NATIONAL FOREST
60
63-64
Connecticut River
Appalachian Trail
65
66
68-69
25
Plymouth
Squam Lake
70
Lake Winnipesaukee
67
Newfound Lake
Ashland
3
TO MONTPELIER, VT
TO BETHEL, ME
TO CONCORD

Southern New Hampshire

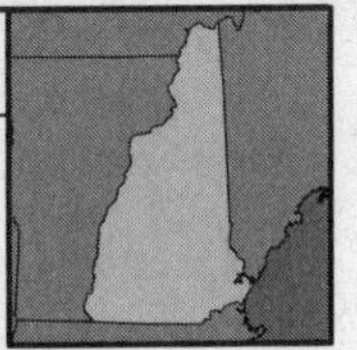

Adjoining Maps:

North: Northern New Hampshire .... *page* 86
East: Southern Maine .... *page* 3
West: Vermont .... *pages* 174-175
South: Massachusetts .... *pages* 238-239

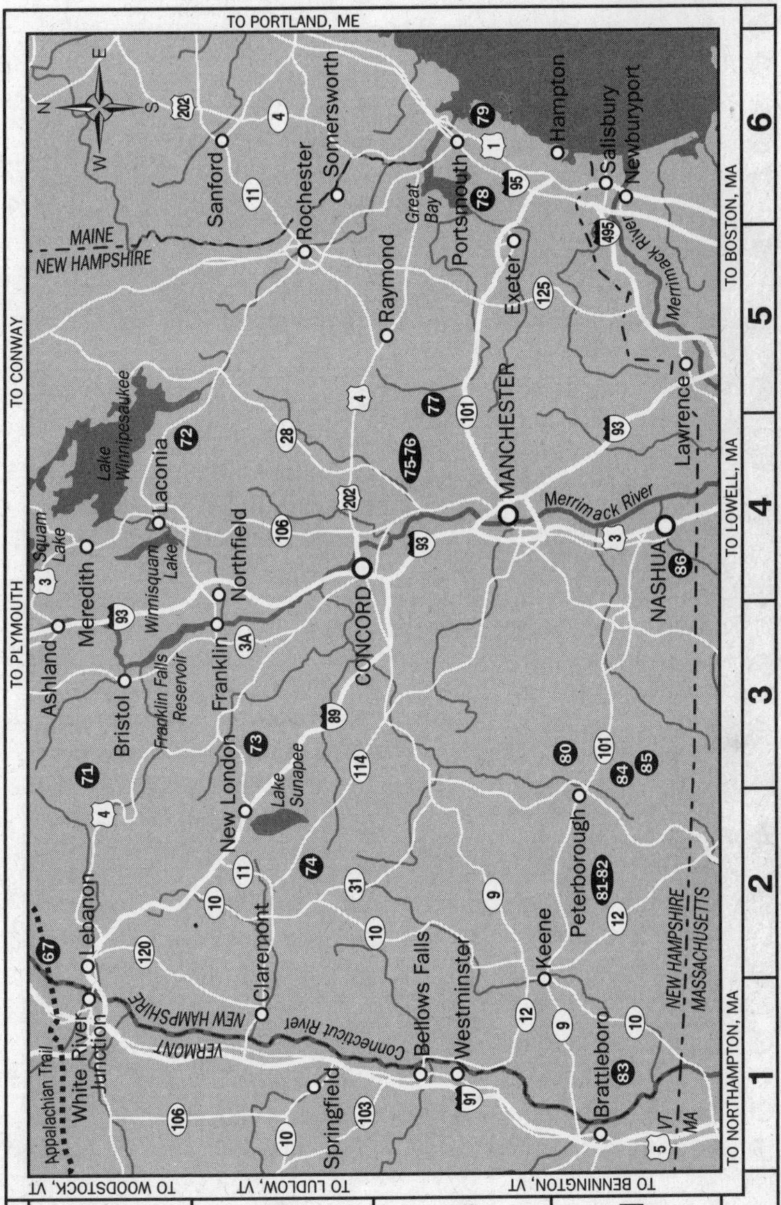

New Hampshire features:

Northern New Hampshire Map—page 86

NEW HAMPSHIRE

When hikers and backpackers think of New Hampshire, they think immediately of the White Mountains. With numerous summits that reach above tree line within a national forest encompassing about 800,000 acres and 1,200 miles of trails, the Whites are the most spectacular range east of the Rockies.

But the Granite State harbors much hiking beyond the Whites. The state manages 206 state parks and forests from the coast to the remote and wild North Country. Two long-distance trails in southern New Hampshire—the 21-mile Wapack Trail and the 50-mile Monadnock-Sunapee Greenway—offer scenic hiking over hills that see

Southern New Hampshire Map—page 87

far fewer boots than popular corners of the Whites. And the smaller mountains and hills scattered around the state reward hikers with sweeping views that demand less driving and hiking time than the big peaks in the northern reaches of the state.

Hikers in the White Mountain National Forest should be aware of certain regulations. Dogs must be under control at all times, and hunting is allowed in season. Backcountry camping permits are not required, but group size in any designated wilderness area should be kept to no more than 10 people (a good guideline to follow in nonwilderness areas as well, because large groups disproportionately affect the land and the experience of other hikers); contact the White Mountain National Forest (see address below) for information on permits for larger groups.

Fires are prohibited above timberline, and camping is prohibited within a quarter mile of any hut or shelter, except at authorized tent sites. Camping is permitted above timberline only where there exists a base of at least two feet of snow. Timberline is defined as that elevation at which trees are less than eight feet tall, and is often indicated by trailside signs. Stay on the trail in the so-called alpine zone above timberline, to avoid damaging fragile alpine vegetation.

The White Mountain National Forest maintains a list of Forest Protection Areas where camping may be prohibited, and periodically designates trails where no camping is allowed within 200 feet. For a current list, contact the White Mountain National Forest Supervisor, Box 638, Laconia, NH 03247; (603) 528-8721, TDD for the hearing impaired (603) 528-8722. The national forest office is on North Main Street in Laconia, across the railroad tracks from the downtown.

The Appalachian Trail extends for 158 miles through New Hampshire, from the Connecticut River in Hanover to the Mahoosuc Range on the Maine border. Along the trail, dogs must be kept under control, and horses, bikes, hunting, and possession of firearms are prohibited. Cross-country skiing and snowshoeing are allowed, though the trail is often too rugged for skiing.

In state parks and forests, dogs should remain under control, and many state lands post signs requiring leashes. Hunting is allowed in season in state parks and forests except Odiorne Point State Park and Shieling State Forest. Mountain bikes, cross-country skiing, and snowshoeing are allowed on trails unless otherwise posted.

Many of the state parks charge a day-use fee of $2.50 per person during a season that extends roughly from Memorial Day through Columbus Day. Children under 12 and New Hampshire residents age 65 and over enter free. Discount coupon books and summer season passes, as well as more information about state public lands, are available from the New Hampshire Division of Parks and Recreation, Bureau of Trails, P.O. Box 1856, Concord, NH 03302-1856; (603) 271-3254.

❶ Diamond Peaks

7.0 mi/4.5 hrs 

Location: In the Second College Grant; Northern New Hampshire map page 86, grid b4.

User groups: Hikers, dogs, and snowshoers. No wheelchair facilities. This trail may be difficult to ski and is not suitable for horses. Bikes are prohibited. Hunting is allowed in season.

Access, fees: The hike is on private land in the state's far north, within the Second College Grant, a township of nearly 27,000 acres owned by Dartmouth College in Hanover. The college uses gates to control access to the grant. A permit from the Outdoor Programs Office at Dartmouth College is required to park within the grant, and is available only to persons affiliated with the college or its Outing Club. However, day use by the public is allowed, provided you park outside the grant.

Directions: From the junction of Routes 16 and 26 in Errol, follow Route 16 north into Wentworths Location. Stop and ask about parking at the Mount Dustan Store in the village center. Or park at the turnout along Route 16 about two-tenths of a mile past the store (about 75 yards beyond a small cemetery and Dead Diamond Road).

Maps: The Outdoor Programs Office at Dartmouth College provides a waterproof contour trail map of the Second College Grant, available for $2 from the address below. To obtain a topographic map of the area, request Wilsons Mills from the USGS.

Contact: Outdoor Programs Office, 19 Robinson Hall, Dartmouth College, Hanover, NH 03755; (603) 646-2428.

Trail notes: Here's a wild seven-mile hike in the North Country—way above the White Mountains—that's too far from anything approaching civilization to ever become popular. You can mountain bike or cross-country ski the 2.5 miles of flat road to the trailhead to give this little adventure a mixed flavor.

About two-tenths of a mile past the Mount Dustan Store in the village center, turn left at a small cemetery onto Dead Diamond Road. Remember how far north you are—this road will be snow-covered from mid-autumn well into spring, and may be a mud bog until July. Follow it for 2.5 miles to the Management Center. The yellow-blazed trail up the Diamond Peaks begins at a sign on the right (east) side of the road, across from the Management Center. It rises gently through the woods at first (easy skiing, but bikes are prohibited), then makes a short but steep ascent of a rocky hillside. You will pass a short spur trail on the left, marked by a sign, which leads to Alice Ledge, with a good view of the valley of the Dead Diamond River. The grade becomes moderate again until the final push up to the first of the three Diamond Peaks. The trail ascends the ridge along the top of tall cliffs, with several good views of the valley below and the wooded hills across the valley. Just below the wooded summit of the first peak is an open ledge overlooking the precipitous cliffs. The trail ends atop the tall cliffs of the second peak. Follow the same route back.

❷ Table Rock: Dixville Notch

0.7 mi/1.5 hrs 

Location: In Dixville Notch State Park; Northern New Hampshire map page 86, grid b3.

User groups: Hikers only. No wheelchair facilities. This trail may be difficult to snowshoe and is not suitable for bikes, dogs, horses, or skis. Hunting is allowed in season.

Access, fees: Parking and access are free.

Directions: Park in the ample turnout along Route 26 in Dixville Notch, immediately west of the height-of-land, where a sign marks the start of the Dixville Notch Heritage Trail (behind the state park sign).

Maps: For a topographic map of the area, request Dixville Notch from the USGS.

Contact: New Hampshire Division of Parks and Recreation, P.O. Box 1856, Concord, NH 03302-1856; (603) 271-3254.

Trail notes: Scrambling up the steep, rocky trail to Table Rock, I'm stopped by an odd sound piercing the silence. Hearing it again, I realize the source—a bull moose. In late September the bellowing of a moose in rut is not an unusual sound in the North Country. The vibrant fall foliage, however, would be an unusual sight by this "late" in autumn: winter arrives sooner here than in the White Mountains farther south.

From the road, the trail climbs very steeply over difficult, rocky ground for three-tenths of a mile to the top of the cliffs flanking the notch. Turn right, walk uphill another 40 feet or so, then walk the long gangplank of Table Rock. This giant buttress of shattered rock thrusting well out from the main face of the cliff presents a rare perch hundreds of feet above the floor of one of New Hampshire's wildest notches. The precipitous drops off either side of the narrow walkway make it a rather unnerving adventure. With the notch being so far from population centers, you may have this place to yourself, as I did. While you can link other trails in the notch on a five-mile loop, this hike descends the way you came up—arguably more difficult and dangerous than the ascent, because of the steepness and the propensity for the rock to be wet.

3 Sugarloaf Mountain

3.5 mi/2.5 hrs 

Location: In Nash Stream State Forest; Northern New Hampshire map page 86, grid c3.

User groups: Hikers, dogs, and snowshoers. No wheelchair facilities. Dogs must be on a leash. This trail is not suitable for bikes, horses, or skis. Hunting is allowed in season.

Access, fees: Parking and access are free. Nash Stream Road is typically open from Memorial Day to early November, depending on weather, and can be cross-country skied in winter.

Directions: From Route 110, 2.6 miles east of the junction of Route 110 and U.S. 3 in Groveton, and 4.3 miles west of the Stark Union Church in Stark, turn north on Emerson Road. Drive 2.2 miles and turn left onto the dirt Nash Stream Road. Continue a half mile to an open area with an oversized locator map posted on a sign. From the map, follow Nash Stream Road another 4.6 miles, bear left, and continue 3.2 miles. Drive over a bridge and another 100 feet to a parking area on the left.

Maps: An oversized locator map is posted along the entrance road. For topographic maps of the area, request Tinkerville, Blue Mountain, Stratford, and Percy Peaks from the USGS.

Contact: New Hampshire Division of Forests and Lands, P.O. Box 1856, Concord, NH 03302-1856; (603) 271-3456.

Trail notes: The 39,601-acre Nash Stream State Forest in New Hampshire's quiet North Country offers some of the most remote and lonely hiking in the Granite State—and on some sizable hills, no less. Were 3,701-foot Sugarloaf just a few hundred feet taller, peak-baggers would flock here. As it is, the state forest sees few visitors. I stood alone on this summit one afternoon in late September, enjoying a 360-degree panorama of peaks stretching into Vermont, Maine, and Quebec which belies any suggestion that there aren't any mountains "north of the notches."

From the parking area, follow the old jeep

road past a cabin. Within three-tenths of a mile, a snowmobile trail diverges left, but continue straight ahead. The road ascends steeply without pause—a real calf-burner. But I felt no right to complain about its difficulty after seeing moose tracks following the same trail upward; he was carrying a lot more weight than I was. (I also found the angle perfect for letting my momentum carry me in a "run" on the descent.) The upper part of the trail eases somewhat, skirting left around a major blowdown just before reaching the craggy summit, about 1.7 miles from the trailhead. Hike back the same way.

4 North Percy Peak

4.0 mi/3.0 hrs 

Location: In Nash Stream State Forest; Northern New Hampshire map page 86, grid c3.

User groups: Hikers, dogs, and snowshoers. No wheelchair facilities. Dogs must be on a leash. This trail is not suitable for bikes, horses, or skis. Hunting is allowed in season.

Access, fees: Parking and access are free. Nash Stream Road is typically open from Memorial Day to early November, depending on weather, and can be cross-country skied in winter.

Directions: From Route 110, 2.6 miles east of the junction of Route 110 and U.S. 3 in Groveton, and 4.3 miles west of the Stark Union Church in Stark, turn north on Emerson Road. Drive 2.2 miles and turn left onto the dirt Nash Stream Road. Continue a half mile to an open area with an oversized locator map posted on a sign. From the map, follow the Nash Stream Road another 2.2 miles to a turnout on the right.

Maps: An oversized locator map is posted along the entrance road. For topographic maps of the area, request Tinkerville, Blue Mountain, Stratford, and Percy Peaks from the USGS.

Contact: New Hampshire Division of Forests and Lands, P.O. Box 1856, Concord, NH 03302-1856; (603) 271-3456.

Trail notes: More accessible than Sugarloaf Mountain (hike number 3) in the sprawling, 39,601-acre Nash Stream State Forest is this hike up 3,418-foot North Percy Peak, whose scrub-covered summit also offers long views in every direction. The Percy Peaks Trail follows the partially overgrown path of a rockslide, ascending exposed slabs that get dangerously slick when wet. The other risk on this hike is forgetting on your descent where the trail re-enters the woods at the tree line: The trail is only sporadically blazed and marked with cairns above tree line, and the landscape of scrub brush quickly becomes ubiquitous. Lose your way back to the trail and you'll be bushwhacking through viciously dense subalpine vegetation, or find yourself at the brink of a cliff with nowhere to go but to backtrack.

From the turnout, follow the Percy Peaks Trail's orange blazes. The rugged trail ascends the old slide, then emerges from the forest about 1.8 miles from the road. It zigzags, following occasional cairns, up the slabs to the rounded summit. Return the same way.

5 Rogers Ledge

10.0 mi/6.0 hrs 

Location: In the northern White Mountain National Forest, east of Lancaster and west of Berlin; Northern New Hampshire map page 86, grid c3.

User groups: Hikers, dogs, and snowshoers. No wheelchair facilities. This trail may be difficult to ski and is not suitable for bikes or horses. Hunting is allowed in season.

Access, fees: Parking and access are free. The entrance gate to the U.S. Fish Hatchery on York Pond Road is closed from 4 P.M. to 8 A.M., but not locked; close and pin the gate again after passing through if it is closed when you arrive. There is a backcountry campsite with a pit toilet on the Kilkenny Ridge Trail, one-tenth of a mile north of the Mill Brook Trail junction.

Directions: From the junction of Routes 16 and 110 in Berlin, drive north on Route 110 for about seven miles and turn left onto York Pond Road at a sign for the U.S. Fish Hatchery. Follow the paved road to the hatchery, then follow signs for the Mill Brook Trail to a small parking area at the end of a short dirt road behind the hatchery office.

Maps: For a contour map of hiking trails, obtain the "Pilot Range" map 8, which is $2.95 from the Appalachian Mountain Club, (800) 262-4455, and is also widely available in stores; the "Trail Map and Guide to the White Mountain National Forest," which is $4.95 from the DeLorme Mapping Company, (800) 253-5081; or the map of the national forest, available by sending a check for $4 to White Mountain National Forest main office (see address below). For topographic maps of the area, request West Milan, Milan, Pliny Range, and Berlin from the USGS.

Contact: White Mountain National Forest Supervisor, 719 North Main St., Laconia, NH 03246; (603) 528-8721, TDD for hearing impaired (603) 528-8722.

Trail notes: This fairly easy—although long, at 10 miles—hike leads into a relatively untrammeled area of the White Mountain National Forest to Rogers Ledge and its beautiful view of the mountains. From the parking lot, follow the Mill Brook Trail 3.8 easy miles to the Kilkenny Ridge Trail. Turn right (north) and walk this easy stretch of the Kilkenny six-tenths of a mile to Rogers Ledge. At 2,945 feet, this high ledge overlooks the Presidentials to the south, the Pilot Range to the southeast, and Berlin and the Mahoosuc Range to the southwest. After absorbing the views, follow the same route back.

6 Kilkenny Traverse

14.4 mi. one way/
2.0 days

Location: In the northern White Mountain National Forest, east of Lancaster and west of Berlin; Northern New Hampshire map page 86, grid c3.

User groups: Hikers, dogs, and snowshoers. No wheelchair facilities. This trail is not suitable for bikes, horses, or skis. Hunting is allowed in season.

Access, fees: Parking and access are free. The entrance gate to the U.S. Fish Hatchery on York Pond Road is closed from 4 P.M. to 8 A.M., but not locked; close and pin the gate again after passing through if it is closed when you arrive. There are two backcountry campsites with pit toilets on the Kilkenny Ridge Trail, one a tenth of a mile north of the Mill Brook Trail junction, the other at Unknown Pond; and a cabin with bunks on the Kilkenny Trail four-tenths of a mile south of the summit of Mount Cabot.

Directions: You will need to shuttle vehicles to either end of this hike. From the junction of U.S. 2 and Route 116 just west of Jefferson Village, drive west on U.S. 2 for two-tenths of a mile and turn right onto North Road. Drive 2.3 miles and turn right onto Gore Road. Continue 1.3 miles to the end of the road and turn left onto Garland Road. Just a half mile farther, turn right onto Pleasant Valley Road. Drive another seven-tenths of a mile, turn right onto Arthur White Road, and proceed a half mile to a parking area 50 yards before Heath's Gate, the end of this hike and the start of the Mount Cabot Trail. Leave one vehicle here.

To reach the start of this hike from the junction of Routes 16 and 110 in Berlin, drive north on Route 110 for about seven miles and turn left onto York Pond Road at a sign for the U.S. Fish Hatchery. Follow the paved road to the hatchery, then follow signs for the Mill Brook Trail to a small parking area at the end of a short dirt road behind the hatchery office.

Maps: For a contour map of hiking trails, obtain the "Pilot Range" map 8, which is $2.95 from the Appalachian Mountain Club, (800) 262-4455, and is also widely available in stores; the "Trail Map and Guide to the White Mountain National Forest," which is $4.95 from the DeLorme Mapping Company, (800) 253-5081; or the map of the national forest, available by sending a check for $4 to White Mountain National Forest main office (see address below). For topographic maps of the area, request West Milan, Milan, Pliny Range, and Berlin from the USGS.

Contact: White Mountain National Forest Supervisor, 719 North Main Street, Laconia, NH 03246; (603) 528-8721, TDD for hearing impaired (603) 528-8722.

Trail notes: Imagine, in a national forest as heavily used as the White Mountains, hiking a trail of pine-needle duff and moss that actually gives softly like a cushion underfoot. Or taking a two-day backpacking trip during the height of the foliage season and seeing just a few other people. That was the experience two friends and I had on this traverse of the Pilot Range, most of it on the Kilkenny Ridge Trail. This northernmost reach of the national forest lies far removed from population centers and boasts no giant peaks to attract hikers. Instead, you revel in the solitude and quiet, in a forest not yet loved to death, in a nice mountain pond, and in impressive, if sporadic, views. While fit hikers could do this traverse in a day, I would suggest making a leisurely, two-day outing of it. This hike includes the side trips to Rogers Ledge and The Horn, perhaps the two nicest views in the range.

Follow the gently rising Mill Brook Trail for 3.8 miles to the Kilkenny Ridge Trail, passing through an extensive area of birch forest. Drop your packs and turn right (north) for the side trip of 1.2 miles to Rogers Ledge, an open ledge atop cliffs with sweeping views south to the Presidentials, southwest of the unfolding Pilot Range, and southeast to Berlin's smokestacks and the Mahoosuc Range beyond. Double back to your packs and hike southwest on the Kilkenny Ridge Trail for 2.1 miles, much of it an easy walk, with a moderate hill climb just before you reach Unknown Pond and the intersection with the Unknown Pond Trail. Turn right at the pond, walk the trail paralleling its shore for less than a tenth of a mile, then turn left with the Kilkenny Ridge Trail. It climbs fairly steeply, gaining several hundred feet of elevation over 1.7 miles to a side trail leading left (east) three-tenths of a mile to the craggy, 3,905-foot summit of The Horn, with expansive views in every direction.

Back on the Kilkenny Ridge Trail, continue southwest over the wooded summit of The Bulge (3,920 feet) and on to the highest point on the ridge, 4,170-foot Mount Cabot, 2.8 miles from Unknown Pond. Cabot's summit is wooded, with no views, but a mile farther down the Kilkenny Ridge Trail lies Bunnell Rock, with a wide view to the south. From Cabot's summit, the Kilkenny Ridge Trail coincides with the Mount Cabot Trail for 1.4 miles; where they split, bear right (southwest) onto the Mount Cabot Trail and follow it easily downhill for 2.1 miles to a junction of forest roads and gates. Bear left onto the middle of three roads and walk a flat four-tenths of a mile to Heath's Gate and your second vehicle.

❼ Mount Cabot

7.8 mi/5.0 hrs 

Location: In the northern White Mountain National Forest, east of Lancaster and west of Berlin; Northern New Hampshire map page 86, grid c3.

User groups: Hikers, dogs, and snowshoers. No wheelchair facilities. This trail is not suitable for bikes, horses, or skis. Hunting is allowed in season.

Access, fees: Parking and access are free. There is a cabin with bunks on the Kilkenny Ridge Trail, four-tenths of a mile south of the summit of Mount Cabot.

Directions: From the junction of U.S. 2 and Route 116 just west of Jefferson Village, drive west on U.S. 2 for two-tenths of a mile and turn right onto North Road. Drive 2.3 miles and turn right onto Gore Road. Continue 1.3 miles to the end of the road and turn left onto Garland Road. Just a half mile farther, turn right onto Pleasant Valley Road. Drive another seven-tenths of a mile, turn right onto Arthur White Road, and proceed a half mile to a parking area 50 yards before Heath's Gate, the start of the Mount Cabot Trail.

Maps: For a contour map of hiking trails, obtain the "Pilot Range" map 8, which is $2.95 from the Appalachian Mountain Club, (800) 262-4455, and is also widely available in stores; the "Trail Map and Guide to the White Mountain National Forest," which is $4.95 from the DeLorme Mapping Company, (800) 253-5081; or the map of the national forest, available by sending a check for $4 to White Mountain National Forest main office (see address below). For topographic maps of the area, request Pliny Range and Stark from the USGS.

Contact: White Mountain National Forest Supervisor, 719 North Main Street, Laconia, NH 03246; (603) 528-8721, TDD for hearing impaired (603) 528-8722.

Trail notes: Mount Cabot (4,170 feet) has a wooded summit with no views. But the mountain nonetheless attracts hikers for its status as one of New Hampshire's 48 official 4,000-footers. Still, there are hardly the crowds up here that are found on peaks of comparable size to the south. And Bunnell Rock, an open ledge along this hike, offers a broad view of this corner of the Pilot Range.

From the parking area, walk around Heath's Gate onto the Mount Cabot Trail. In four-tenths of a mile, the trail bears right through a junction of woods roads (do not turn sharply right; that's the York Pond Trail). For the next 2.1 miles, the trail ascends steadily, then more steeply, to join with the Kilkenny Ridge Trail. Turn left (north) and follow the trail another four-tenths of a mile to Bunnell Rock, which lies just off the trail to the right. Continuing up the Mount Cabot Trail, you pass a cabin with bunks six-tenths of a mile from Bunnell Rock, and reach the wooded summit four-tenths of a mile beyond the cabin. Return the way you came.

❽ Mounts Starr King and Waumbek

7.2 mi/4.5 hrs  

Location: In the White Mountain National Forest near Jefferson; Northern New Hampshire map page 86, grid d3.

User groups: Hikers, dogs, and snowshoers. No wheelchair facilities. This trail is not suitable for bikes, horses, or skis. Hunting is allowed in season.

Access, fees: Parking and access are free.

Directions: From the junction of Route 115A and U.S. 2 in Jefferson, follow U.S. 2 east for two-tenths of mile. Turn left up a narrow road at a sign for the Starr King Trail. The road ends in about a tenth of a mile at a small parking area at the trailhead.

(The road is not maintained in winter; park at the Jefferson swimming pool on U.S. 2 near the town center, a short walk from the trailhead.)

Maps: For a contour map of hiking trails, obtain the "Pilot Range" map 8, which is $2.95 from the Appalachian Mountain Club, (800) 262-4455, and is also widely available in stores; "The Randolph Valley and the Northern Peaks of the Mount Washington Range" map, available by sending $3 to Treasurer, Randolph Mountain Club, RR 1, Box 1570, Randolph, NH 03570; or the map of the national forest, available for $4 from the White Mountain National Forest main office (see address below). For a topographic map of the area, request Pliny Range from the USGS.

Contact: White Mountain National Forest Supervisor, 719 North Main Street, Laconia, NH 03246; (603) 528-8721, TDD for the hearing impaired (603) 528-8722.

Trail notes: Just a 20-minute drive from the popular peaks of the Presidential Range, this underappreciated hike sees much less foot traffic. A friend and I hiked the trail one winter day when the clouds were building up around the Northern Presidentials just to the southeast, and we had clear weather on Starr King and Waumbek (elevation 4,006 feet). Plus, we saw no one else.

Ascending steadily but at a moderate grade, the trail leads 2.6 miles to the top of Starr King and a sweeping view of the Whites, from the Presidential Range (southeast) to the Pemigewasset Wilderness peaks (south) and Franconia Ridge (southwest). The trail continues another mile on easy terrain to the summit of one of New Hampshire's least-visited 4,000-footers, Mount Waumbek. This route is a good introduction to winter hiking because the trail is almost completely in the woods, and protected. For most of the year low trees obstruct the view from Waumbek, but when there's snow on the ground you'll get some views similar to those from Starr King. Watch for signs and arrows indicating turns in the trail early on. It's sporadically blazed, but not too difficult to follow. At the edge of an open area on Starr King's summit sits a fireplace from a former shelter. On Waumbek's summit, the Kilkenny Ridge Trail leads east and north into the Pilot Range, toward Mount Cabot, Unknown Pond, and Rogers Ledge (hike number 5). This hike descends the same way you came up.

9 Mahoosuc Range: Gentian Pond

7.0 mi/4.0 hrs 

Location: In Shelburne; Northern New Hampshire map page 86, grid d4.

User groups: Hikers, dogs, and snowshoers. No wheelchair facilities. The last steep stretch of this trail would be difficult to ski. This trail is not suitable for bikes or horses. Hunting is allowed in season.

Access, fees: Parking and access are free. The Mahoosuc Range is on private property, not within the White Mountain National Forest. Camping is only allowed at shelters and designated camping areas.

Directions: In Shelburne Village, New Hampshire, which lies between Gorham, New Hampshire, and Gilead, Maine, turn off U.S. 2 onto Meadow Road, crossing the Androscoggin River. At North Road, turn left. Immediately on the right you will see an old logging road that leads to the Austin Brook Trail; there may be limited roadside parking here. The trail begins a half mile farther west on North Road, where there is some additional parking.

Maps: For a map of hiking trails, obtain the "Carter-Mahoosuc" map 7, which is $2.95 from the Appalachian Mountain Club, (800) 262-4455, and is also widely available in stores; or map 7 in the "Map and Guide to the Appalachian Trail in New Hampshire and Vermont," an eight-map set for $10.95 from the Appalachian Trail Conference (see address below). For a topographic map of the area, request Shelburne from the USGS.

Contact: Appalachian Mountain Club Trails Program, AMC Pinkham Notch Visitors Center, AMC P.O. Box 298, Gorham, NH 03581, (603) 466-2721. Appalachian Trail Conference, P.O. Box 807, Harpers Ferry, WV 25425; (304) 535-6331.

Trail notes: While Gentian Pond may seem an unlikely destination for a hike, it's actually a picturesque big puddle tucked into an evergreen woods amid the steep and rugged Mahoosucs. The thing to do is load up a backpack for two or three days and stay in the shelter at Gentian Pond—the dusk view southward of the Androscoggin Valley and the Carter-Moriah Range is fantastic. The shelter is a good base for exploring this end of the Mahoosucs. A friend and I once spent three days in March here and saw no one else—and the shelter's register showed only a handful of visitors all winter. Expect more hiker traffic during the warmer months, of course, but not the level you'd see on many of the popular trails in the White Mountains.

The Austin Brook Trail follows old logging roads for more than two miles. After narrowing to a hiking trail, it skirts the edge of a swampy area, then gains much of its elevation in the last half-mile push up to the shelter, where it meets the Mahoosuc Trail, which is also the Appalachian Trail. To return to your vehicle, follow the Austin Brook Trail back out.

⑩ Cherry Mountain: Owl's Head Trail

3.8 mi/3.5 hrs 

Location: In the White Mountain National Forest south of Jefferson; Northern New Hampshire map page 86, grid d3.

User groups: Hikers and dogs. No wheelchair facilities. This trail may be difficult to snowshoe and is not suitable for bikes, horses, or skis. Hunting is allowed in season.

Access, fees: Parking and access are free.

Directions: The trailhead parking area is on Route 115, 5.8 miles north of the junction of Route 115 and U.S. 3 and four miles south of the junction of 115 and U.S. 2.

Maps: Several maps cover hiking trails in this area, including the "Pilot Range" map 8 from the Appalachian Mountain Club (800-262-4455), which is $2.95 and widely available in stores; "The Randolph Valley and the Northern Peaks of the Mount Washington Range," available by sending $3 to Treasurer, Randolph Mountain Club, RR1, Box 1570, Randolph, NH 03570; the "Trail Map and Guide to the White Mountain National Forest," which is $4.95 from the DeLorme Mapping Company, (800) 253-5081; and the map of the national forest, available by sending a check for $4 to White Mountain National Forest main office (see address below). For topographic maps of the area, request Bethlehem and Mount Washington from the USGS.

Contact: White Mountain National Forest Supervisor, 719 North Main Street, Laconia, NH 03246; (603) 528-8721, TDD for hearing impaired (603) 528-8722.

Trail notes: On the broad, open ledges of the Owl's Head on Cherry Mountain, you get an expansive view of the Presidential Range—and maybe a little solitude to boot in this quite corner of the White Mountains. I stood up here alone one cool, windy autumn day, not seeing another person until passing two hikers on my way back down again.

From the parking lot, the Owl's Head Trail enters a thin strip of woods, crosses a small brook, and emerges immediately into a cleared area. Head straight across the clearing to a post marker that reads, "path."

Watch for orange blazes. Follow a wide double-track for about 300 feet past the post, watching closely for where the trail enters the woods to the right (a spot I easily overlooked). The hiking is fairly easy at first, crossing some logged areas—watch for cairns and trail markers—then growing very steep and arduous ascending Cherry Mountain. Loose stones make footing difficult (even more so descending); I would avoid this hike in the muddy season, and avoid taking young children up here. About 1.8 miles from the road, the trail crests the ridge of Cherry Mountain; walk a relatively flat tenth of a mile to the ledges. To the south, the trail continues on to Mount Martha, eight-tenths of a mile farther, where there is a good view. This hike returns along the same route.

⓫ Mounts Adams and Madison: the Air Line

9.5 mi/8.0 hrs 

Location: In the White Mountain National Forest south of Randolph; Northern New Hampshire map page 86, grid d3.

User groups: Hikers and dogs. No wheelchair facilities. This trail may be difficult to snowshoe, in part because of severe winter weather, and is not suitable for bikes, horses, or skis. Hunting is allowed in season.

Access, fees: Parking and access are free.

Directions: Park in the large lot at the Appalachia Trailhead on U.S. 2 in Randolph, 2.1 miles west of the northern junction of U.S. 2 and Route 16 in Gorham, and 7.1 miles east of the junction of U.S. 2 and Route 115. The Air Line begins there.

Maps: Several maps cover hiking trails in this area, including Bradford Washburn's "Mount Washington and the Heart of the Presidential Range—New Hampshire," available for $4.95 from the Appalachian Mountain Club, (800) 262-4455; the "Mount Washington Range" map 6, which is $2.95 from the AMC and is also widely available in stores; "The Randolph Valley and the Northern Peaks of the Mount Washington Range," available by sending $3 to Treasurer, Randolph Mountain Club, RR 1, Box 1570, Randolph, NH 03570; the "Trail Map and Guide to the White Mountain National Forest," which is $4.95 from the DeLorme Mapping Company, (800) 253-5081; the map of the national forest, available for $4 from the White Mountain National Forest main office (see address below); and map 2 in the "Map and Guide to the Appalachian Trail in New Hampshire and Vermont," an eight-map set for $10.95 from the Appalachian Trail Conference (see address below). For a topographic map of the area, request Mount Washington from the USGS.

Contact: White Mountain National Forest Supervisor, 719 North Main Street, Laconia, NH 03246; (603) 528-8721, TDD for the hearing impaired (603) 528-8722. Appalachian Trail Conference, P.O. Box 807, Harpers Ferry, WV 25425; (304) 535-6331. The AMC's Pinkham Notch Visitors Center has up-to-date reports on weather in the Presidential Range; call (603) 466-2721.

Trail notes: This is the most direct route to the summit of the second-highest peak in New England, 5,774-foot Mount Adams, though not necessarily the fastest. It follows another of Adams' spectacular shoulders, the Durand Ridge, giving hikers extended views from atop high cliffs, down into King Ravine, west across the prominent ridges on the northern flanks of Mounts Adams and Jefferson, and north across the Randolph Valley to the more remote peaks of the Pilot Range. Some scrambling is necessary, and you'll need to be comfortable with exposure—there's an interesting little foot ledge traverse that gets your heart pumping. This route allows a fit hiker blessed with good weather the option of hitting both Adams and Madison in a day. On this hike, the Appalachian Trail coincides with the Osgood Trail up Mount Madison and with the Gulfside Trail, which this hike crosses on Mount Adams.

From the parking lot at Appalachia, the Air Line makes a 4.3-mile beeline to the summit of Adams, with the final 1.5 miles above the trees. Descend via the Air Line—or go for Madison's summit (5,367 feet). To reach Madison from Adams' summit, either backtrack eight-tenths of a mile on the Air Line to the Air Line cutoff leading two-tenths of a mile toward Madison hut, or take a somewhat more difficult but very scenic option, the less-traveled, mile-long Star Lake Trail, which descends southeast from Adams' summit, then turns left and traverses the steep northeast face of Adams. It passes beautiful Star Lake on the way to the hut. From the hut, follow the Osgood Trail a half mile to Madison's summit, then descend north via the Watson Path, Scar Trail, and the Valley Way back to Appalachia.

⓬ Mount Adams: Lowe's Path

9.5 mi/8.0 hrs 

Location: In the White Mountain National Forest south of Randolph; Northern New Hampshire map page 86, grid d3.

User groups: Hikers and dogs. No wheelchair facilities. This trail may be difficult to snowshoe, in part because of severe winter weather, and is not suitable for bikes, horses, or skis. Hunting is allowed in season.

Access, fees: Access is free. There is a parking fee of $1 per day per vehicle at Lowe's Store parking lot.

Directions: Park at Lowe's Store and gas station on U.S. 2, five miles east of the junction with Route 115 and 8.4 miles west of the north junction of U.S. 2 and Route 16 in Gorham. Cross U.S. 2, walking to the right (west), and turn up a dirt driveway that leads about 50 yards to Lowe's Path (on the right).

Maps: Several maps cover hiking trails in this area, including Bradford Washburn's "Mount Washington and the Heart of the Presidential Range—New Hampshire," available for $4.95 from the Appalachian Mountain Club, (800) 262-4455; the "Mount Washington Range" map 6, which is $2.95 from the AMC and is also widely available in stores; "The Randolph Valley and the Northern Peaks of the Mount Washington Range," available by sending $3 to Treasurer, Randolph Mountain Club, RR 1, Box 1570, Randolph, NH 03570; the "Trail Map and Guide to the White Mountain National Forest," which costs $4.95 from the DeLorme Mapping Company, (800) 253-5081; the map of the national forest, available for $4 from the White Mountain National Forest main office (see address below); and map 2 in the "Map and Guide to the Appalachian Trail in New Hampshire and Vermont," an eight-map set for $10.95 from the Appalachian Trail Conference (see address below). For a topographic map of the area, request Mount Washington from the USGS.

Contact: White Mountain National Forest Supervisor, 719 North Main Street, Laconia, NH 03246; (603) 528-8721, TDD for the hearing impaired (603) 528-8722. Randolph Mountain Club, RR 1, Box 1570, Randolph, NH 03570. Appalachian Trail Conference, P.O. Box 807, Harpers Ferry, WV 25425; (304) 535-6331. The AMC's Pinkham Notch Visitors Center has up-to-date reports on weather in the Presidential Range; call (603) 466-2721.

Trail notes: This is the easiest route to the summit of Mount Adams, which at 5,774 feet is the second-highest mountain in New England and one of the most interesting. I've hiked it several times, in summer, fall, and winter, and have never gotten bored with this peak. The trail has moderate grades and is well protected until timberline, but the last 1.5 miles are above the trees. It's also the oldest trail coming out of the Randolph Valley, cut in 1875–76.

Lowe's Path ascends gently at first, making several crossings of brooks through an area often wet and muddy. After 2.5 miles you reach the Log Cabin, a Randolph Mountain Club shelter where a caretaker collects the $3/person nightly fee. About seven-tenths of a mile farther, at timberline, a trail branching left leads a tenth of a mile to the RMC's Gray Knob cabin, which is winterized and costs $8/night per person. This trail junction offers the first sweeping views—with the Castellated Ridge on Mount Jefferson thrusting its craggy teeth skyward, and much of the White Mountains visible on a clear day. From there, Lowe's Path cuts through some krummholz (the dense stands of stunted and twisted conifers that grow at timberline), then ascends the barren talus, where finding cairns can be tricky. Nearly a mile from the Gray Knob Trail, you'll scramble over the mound of rocks known as Adams 4, then hike the final seven-tenths-of-a-mile stretch to the 5,774-foot summit, to be rewarded with some of the best views in these mountains. To the south are Mounts Jefferson, Clay, and Washington, and to the north lies Madison. This crescent-shaped ridge nearly encloses the largest glacial cirque in the region, the Great Gulf.

⓭ Mount Madison: Madison Gulf and Webster Trails

11.5 mi/10.0 hrs 

Location: In the White Mountain National Forest south of Randolph; Northern New Hampshire map page 86, grid d3.

User groups: Hikers and dogs. No wheelchair facilities. This trail may be difficult to snowshoe, in part because of severe winter weather, and is not suitable for bikes, horses, or skis. Hunting is allowed in season.

Access, fees: Parking and access are free.

Directions: From Gorham, drive south on Route 16 to the U.S. Forest Service's Dolly Copp Campground (entrance on right), which is operated on a first-come, first-served basis. Drive to the end of the campground road and park in the dirt lot at the start of the Great Gulf Link Trail. About a quarter mile before the parking lot, you will pass the start of the Daniel Webster (scout) Trail, which is where you will end this hike.

Maps: Several maps cover hiking trails in this area, including Bradford Washburn's "Mount Washington and the Heart of the Presidential Range—New Hampshire," available for $4.95 from the Appalachian Mountain Club, (800) 262-4455; the "Mount Washington Range" map 6, which is $2.95 from the AMC and is also widely available in stores; "The Randolph Valley and the Northern Peaks of the Mount Washington Range," available by sending $3 to Treasurer, Randolph Mountain Club, RR 1, Box 1570, Randolph, NH 03570; the "Trail Map and Guide to the White Mountain National Forest," which is $4.95 from the DeLorme Mapping Company, (800) 253-5081; the map of the national forest, available for $4 from the White Mountain National Forest main office (see address below); and map 2 in the "Map and Guide to the Appalachian Trail in New Hampshire and Vermont," an eight-map set for $10.95 from the Appalachian Trail Conference (see address below). For a topographic map of the area, request Mount Washington from the USGS.

Contact: White Mountain National Forest Supervisor, 719 North Main Street, Laconia, NH 03246; (603) 528-8721, TDD for the hearing impaired (603) 528-8722. Appalachian Trail Conference, P.O. Box 807, Harpers Ferry, WV 25425; (304) 535-6331. The

AMC's Pinkham Notch Visitors Center has up-to-date reports on weather in the Presidential Range; call (603) 466-2721.

Trail notes: The ascent of Madison's headwall on the Madison Gulf Trail is without question one of the most difficult hikes I have ever done in the White Mountains. But it also rates as one of the wildest hikes in these mountains—and you may well see no other hikers on Madison's headwall. On this hike, the Appalachian Trail coincides with the Madison Gulf Trail south of the Osgood Trail junction, and with the Osgood Trail from Madison hut over the summit of Madison to the Daniel Webster (scout) Trail.

From the parking area, follow the Great Gulf Link Trail a flat mile to the Great Gulf Trail. Turn right and continue about three easy miles (passing the Osgood Trail junction in less than two miles); soon after a jog left in the trail, turn right (north) onto the Madison Gulf Trail. You are in the Great Gulf, the enormous glacial cirque nearly enclosed by the high peaks of the Northern Presidentials, which loom around you. The Madison Gulf Trail grows increasingly steep, following Parapet Brook through a dense forest for about two miles to the base of the formidable headwall. Moss-covered glacial-erratic boulders fill the streambed; one huge boulder has a tall tree growing atop it. You cross a lush, boggy area in a shelf at the headwall's base, then attack the main headwall, which involves scrambling over steep, exposed rock ledges that can be hazardous in wet weather.

After a strenuous mile, the trail reaches the flat saddle between Mounts Madison and Adams, where you'll find the AMC's Madison hut and Star Lake, a beautiful little tarn and one of the few true alpine ponds in the Whites. From the hut, turn right (east) on the Osgood Trail leading to Madison's conical summit (elevation 5,367 feet)—which feels like a high pinhead compared to other peaks in this range. Continue over the summit and down the open Osgood Ridge for a half mile. The Daniel Webster Trail branches left (northeast) at Osgood Junction, heading diagonally down a vast talus slope to the woods, leading another 3.5 miles to the campground road in Dolly Copp. Turn right and walk two-tenths of a mile down the road to your car.

⑭ Mount Jefferson: the Castellated Ridge

10.0 mi/9.0 hrs 

Location: In the White Mountain National Forest south of Bowman; Northern New Hampshire map page 86, grid d3.

User groups: Hikers and dogs. No wheelchair facilities. This trail may be difficult to snowshoe, in part because of severe winter weather, and is not suitable for bikes, horses, or skis. Hunting is allowed in season.

Access, fees: Parking and access are free.

Directions: The parking area is on the south side of U.S. 2 in Randolph, 4.1 miles east of the junction of U.S. 2 and Route 115.

Maps: Several maps cover hiking trails in this area, including Bradford Washburn's "Mount Washington and the Heart of the Presidential Range—New Hampshire," available for $4.95 from the Appalachian Mountain Club, (800) 262-4455; the "Mount Washington Range" map 6, which is $2.95 from the AMC and is also widely available in stores; "The Randolph Valley and the Northern Peaks of the Mount Washington Range," available by sending $3 to Treasurer, Randolph Mountain Club, RR 1, Box 1570, Randolph, NH 03570; the "Trail Map and Guide to the White Mountain National Forest," which is $4.95 from the DeLorme Mapping Company, (800) 253-5081; the map of the national forest, available for $4 from the White Mountain National Forest main office (see address below); and map 2 in the "Map and Guide to the Appalachian Trail in New Hampshire and Vermont," an eight-map set for $10.95 from the Appalachian Trail Conference (see address below). For a topographic map of the area, request Mount Washington from the USGS.

Contact: White Mountain National Forest Supervisor, 719 North Main Street, Laconia, NH 03246; (603) 528-8721, TDD for the hearing impaired (603) 528-8722. Appalachian Trail Conference, P.O. Box 807, Harpers Ferry, WV 25425; (304) 535-6331. The AMC's Pinkham Notch Visitors Center has up-to-date reports on weather in the Presidential Range; call (603) 466-2721.

Trail notes: The stretch of the Castle Trail above timberline ranks among the most spectacular—and rigorous—ridge walks in New England. The Castellated Ridge narrows to a rocky spine jutting above the krummholz (the dense stands of stunted and twisted conifers that grow at timberline), with long, sharp drops off either side. The ridge acquired its name from the three "castles," or towers of barren rock you scramble over and around, which are visible from a distance. This can be a dangerous place in nasty weather. A friend and I once backpacked in early October as far as the first castle only to turn back in the face of ice, snow, and a looming whiteout—then returned a week later to hike the ridge in shorts and T-shirts. On a clear day, from Jefferson's summit (5,712 feet) you can see almost all of the Whites, and all the way to Vermont's Green Mountains and New York's Adirondacks to the west. You will walk briefly on the Appalachian Trail where it coincides with the Gulfside Trail north of Jefferson's summit.

From the parking area, follow the dirt driveway to the right for about 150 yards, until you reach a somewhat hidden marker on the right where the Castle Trail enters the woods. In the first half mile there's a bridgeless crossing of the Israel River, which can be difficult at high water. The hiking is fairly easy at first. Approximately one mile beyond the stream crossing, the trail passes the junction with the Israel Ridge Path on the left, on which you will return. The last certain water source is located at a brook a short distance up that path. The trail ascends the ridge, growing steep and passing through an interesting subalpine forest before reaching the Link's trail junction at 3.5 miles out.

The trail requires difficult scrambling from this point, reaching the first castle a quarter mile past the Link. Continue up the ridge to the vast talus field covering the upper flanks of Mount Jefferson, watching carefully for cairns. The trail follows a direct line to the summit, where twin mounds of rock sit nearly side by side; the first, or farthest west, is the true summit, five miles from the trailhead.

Descend to the trail junction between the two summits, and turn north on the Jefferson Loop Trail toward Mount Adams for four-tenths of a mile, then continue on the Gulfside Trail for another two-tenths of a mile into Edmands Col. Bear left onto the Randolph Path, which leads to the right (northeast) around the Castle Ravine headwall seven-tenths of a mile from Edmands Col to the Israel Ridge Path. The trails coincide briefly, then split; stay to the left on the Israel Ridge Path, continuing nearly a half mile to just beyond the Perch Path junction, where the Emerald Trail diverges left. If you have time, make the worthwhile 20-minute detour on the Emerald Trail out to Emerald Bluff, which offers a stunning view of Castle Ravine. The Israel Ridge Path continues down into the woods, eventually rejoining the Castle Trail 2.4 miles below the Perch Path junction. Turn right and continue to the trailhead parking area, 1.3 miles ahead.

⓯ Presidential Range Traverse

20.0 mi. one way/ 2.5 days 

Location: In the White Mountain National Forest, between Gorham and Crawford Notch; Northern New Hampshire map page 86, grid d3.

User groups: Hikers and dogs. No wheelchair facilities. This trail may be difficult to snowshoe, in part because of severe winter weather, and is not suitable for skis. Bikes, horses, and hunting are prohibited.

Access, fees: Parking and access are free. The Appalachian Mountain Club operates the Madison and Lakes of the Clouds huts, where a crew prepares meals and guests share bunkrooms and bathrooms; call (603) 466-2727 for reservation and rate information. The Randolph Mountain Club operates two cabins on Mount Adams, Crag Camp (capacity 20) and the winterized Gray Knob (capacity 15), which cost $7 per person per night and are run on a first-come, first-served basis; and two open-sided shelters on Adams, the Perch and the Log Cabin (each has a capacity of 10), which cost $3 per night, with the fee collected by a caretaker. There are also four tent platforms at the Perch.

Directions: From Gorham, drive south on Route 16 to the U.S. Forest Service's Dolly Copp Campground (entrance on right), which is operated on a first-come, first-served basis. Drive to the end of the campground road to a dirt parking lot at the Great Gulf Link Trailhead. About a quarter mile before the parking lot is the start of the Daniel Webster (scout) Trail, which is where you begin this hike. Leave a second vehicle at the other end of this traverse, just off U.S. 302 in Crawford Notch State Park. The Crawford Path Trailhead parking area is on Mount Clinton Road, opposite the Crawford House site and just north of Saco Lake.

Maps: Several maps cover hiking trails in this area, including the "Mount Washington Range" map 6, which is $2.95 from the Appalachian Mountain Club, (800) 262-4455, and is also widely available in stores; the "Trail Map and Guide to the White Mountain National Forest," which is $4.95 from the DeLorme Mapping Company, (800) 253-5081; the map of the national forest, available for $4 from the White Mountain National Forest main office (see address below); and map 2 in the "Map and Guide to the Appalachian Trail in New Hampshire and Vermont," an eight-map set for $10.95 from the Appalachian Trail Conference (see address below). For a topographic map of the area, request Mount Washington from the USGS.

Contact: White Mountain National Forest Supervisor, 719 North Main Street, Laconia, NH 03246; (603) 528-8721, TDD for the hearing impaired (603) 528-8722. Appalachian Trail Conference, P.O. Box 807, Harpers Ferry, WV 25425; (304) 535-6331. The AMC's Pinkham Notch Visitors Center has up-to-date reports on weather in the Presidential Range; call (603) 466-2721.

Trail notes: This is the premier backpacking trek in New England—in fact, nowhere else east of the Rockies can you hike a 15-mile ridge entirely above timberline. The route hits nine summits, seven of them higher than 5,000 feet—including New England's highest, 6,288-foot Mount Washington—and each with its own unique character. From the junction of the Osgood and Daniel Webster Trails to the junction of the Crawford Path and the Webster Cliff Trail, this hike coincides with the Appalachian Trail. The route also covers some very rugged terrain and requires a serious commitment. The task is complicated by the fact that the odds of drawing three straight sunny days in these peaks may be only slightly better than those of winning the lottery. Finding appropriate campsites can be difficult, too, because of the prohibition against camping above timberline (see detailed White Mountain National Forest regulations at the beginning of this chapter). Skipping the side paths to summits, though, will reduce the distance slightly and the elevation gain significantly. Some masochistic types have been known to attempt this traverse in a single day, a feat known in some circles as "The Death March" (two friends and I attempted it once, only to have to descend from Washington when gray clouds abruptly smothered the mountain, leaving us in a pea-soup fog). A winter traverse of the Presidentials is a mountaineering challenge considered by many to be good training for Alaskan peaks in summer.

My route here deviates a bit from the more common approach to this traverse, incorporating two scenic trails that see fewer hikers. The first, the Daniel Webster (scout) Trail, begins at the Dolly Copp Campground road and ascends moderately through the woods to a vast, open talus slope, where the climbing grows steeper. Upon reaching Osgood Ridge, you're treated to a stunning view of the Great Gulf Wilderness and the peaks of the Northern Presidentials. Follow the Osgood Trail to the top of Mount Madison, 4.1 miles from the trailhead, its 5,367-foot summit a small area atop a cone of boulders. Continue over the summit on the Osgood Trail a half mile down to Madison hut and turn left for the Star Lake Trail, a less-traveled footpath that passes the beautiful little tarn named Star Lake and winds a mile up the steep east side of 5,774-foot Mount Adams, the second-highest peak in New England. Adams has five distinct summits, several ridges and ravines, and excellent views. Descend via Lowe's Path nearly a half mile over an expansive talus field to the giant cairn at Thunderstorm Junction, where several trails meet.

From here, you can descend the Spur Trail a mile to the Randolph Mountain Club's Crag Camp cabin, or follow Lowe's Path for 1.3 miles to the Gray Knob cabin. This route turns left (southwest) onto the Gulfside Trail (which follows the ridge to Mount Washington while avoiding the summits). At six-tenths of a mile south of Thunderstorm Junction, you'll pass the Israel Ridge Path branching to the right toward the RMC's Perch camping area (one mile away via Israel Ridge, Randolph Path, and the Perch Path). From Edmands Col, the saddle 1.3 miles south of Thunderstorm Junction and six-tenths of a mile north of the summit of Mount Jefferson, hike two-tenths of a mile southwest and bear right onto the Jefferson Loop Trail, climbing four-tenths of a mile to the top of Mount Jefferson. Of its two summits, the westernmost (to your right from this direction) is the highest at 5,712 feet.

Continue between the two summits on the loop trail and rejoin the Gulfside. About a half mile farther, after dipping down through Sphinx Col, bear left onto the Mount Clay Loop Trail. On a day when you'll see two dozen hikers on Jefferson, you may have Clay to yourself. This is probably because Clay is considered a shoulder of Mount Washington rather than a distinct peak. Yet, on Clay's broad 5,541-foot summit, you can observe abundant alpine wildflowers (particularly in the second half of June) and peer down the sheer headwall of the Great Gulf. The Clay Loop rejoins the Gulfside in 1.2 miles, and then it's another mile to the roof of New England, Washington's 6,288-foot summit, finishing via the Crawford Path. The summit has a visitors center with a cafeteria and bathrooms.

From the summit, turn southwest onto the Crawford Path and follow it 1.4 miles down to Lakes of the Clouds, the location of another AMC hut. Just south of the hut, bear right off the Crawford onto the Mount Monroe Loop Trail for the steep half-mile climb to its 5,384-foot summit (a great place to catch the sunset if you're staying at the Lakes hut). The Monroe Loop rejoins the Crawford Path southbound three-tenths of a mile past the summit. The Crawford then traverses the bump on the ridge known as Mount Franklin (5,004 feet), also not considered a distinct summit. About two miles south of the Lakes hut, bear right for the loop over 4,761-foot Mount Eisenhower. A mile south of Eisenhower, follow the Webster Cliff Trail a tenth of a mile to the 4,312-foot summit of Mount Pierce, then double back and turn left on the Crawford Path, descending nearly three miles. Just before reaching U.S. 302 in Crawford Notch, turn right onto the Crawford Connector path leading two-tenths of a mile to the parking area on the Mount Clinton Road.

16 Mount Washington: Huntington Ravine and the Alpine Garden

8.0 mi/8.0 hrs 5 10

Location: In the White Mountain National Forest in Pinkham Notch; Northern New Hampshire map page 86, grid d3.

User groups: Hikers only. No wheelchair facilities. This trail is not suitable for bikes, dogs, horses, skis, or snowshoes. Hunting is prohibited.

Access, fees: Parking and access are free.

Directions: The hike begins from the Appalachian Mountain Club Visitors Center on Route 16 in Pinkham Notch, at the base of Mount Washington, 12 miles south of the junction of Route 16 and U.S. 2 in Gorham and about eight miles north of Jackson. The trailhead is behind the visitors center.

Maps: For a map of hiking trails, obtain Bradford Washburn's "Mount Washington and the Heart of the Presidential Range—New Hampshire," which is $4.95, or the "Mount Washington Range" map 6, which is $2.95, from the Appalachian Mountain Club, (800) 262-4455; the "Mount Washington" map, available for $4.50 from cartographer Ed Rolfe, (603) 788-3019; the "Trail Map and Guide to the White Mountain National Forest," which is $4.95 from the DeLorme Mapping Company, (800) 253-5081; the map of the national forest, available for $4 from the White Mountain National Forest main office (see address below); or map 2 in the "Map and Guide to the Appalachian Trail in New Hampshire and Vermont," an eight-map set for $10.95 from the Appalachian Trail Conference (see address below). For a topographic map of the area, request Mount Washington from the USGS.

Contact: White Mountain National Forest Supervisor, 719 North Main Street, Laconia, NH 03246; (603) 528-8721, TDD for the hearing impaired (603) 528-8722. Appalachian Trail Conference, P.O. Box 807, Harpers Ferry, WV 25425; (304) 535-6331. The AMC's Pinkham Notch Visitors Center has up-to-date reports on weather in the Presidential Range; call (603) 466-2721.

Trail notes: Discard all your preconceived notions of hard trails. Huntington Ravine has earned a reputation as the most difficult regular hiking trail in the White Mountains, for good reason. The trail ascends the ravine headwall, involving very exposed scrambling up steep slabs of rock with significant fall potential. Inexperienced scramblers should shy away from this route, and persons carrying a heavy pack may want to consider another way up the mountain. The ravine is strictly a summer and early fall hike, and even in those seasons snow can fall and treacherous ice can form. I've hiked this trail successfully in good August weather, but had to turn back from a technical rock climb up another section of the headwall when sleet fell in September. The headwall, the Alpine Garden, and the top of the Lion Head all lie above tree line and are exposed to the weather. From late fall through early spring, the headwall is draped with ice and snow, and is a prized destination for experienced ice climbers. For hikers comfortable with exposure and rugged scrambling, Huntington Ravine has no peer. And this loop will lead you through a variety of mountain terrain found on few other peaks east of the Rockies.

From the Appalachian Mountain Club Visitors Center, follow the wide Tuckerman Ravine Trail. Less than 1.5 miles up, the Huntington Ravine Trail diverges right (north); watch closely for it, because the sign may be partly hidden by trees and the path is narrow and easily overlooked. This trail climbs steeply in spots, and you'll get fleeting glimpses up at the ravine headwall. Within 1.5 miles from the Tuckerman Ravine Trail, you reach a flat, open area on the floor of Huntington Ravine—and your first sweeping view of the massive headwall, riven by several ominous gullies separating tall cliffs. Novice hikers can reach this point without any trouble, and the view of the ravine is worth it. Nearby is a first-aid cache bearing a plaque memorializing Albert Dow, a climber and mountain rescue volunteer killed by an avalanche in Huntington Ravine during a 1982 search for a pair of missing climbers.

The trail leads through a maze of giant boulders to the base of the headwall, then heads diagonally up the talus. On the headwall proper, the well-blazed trail ascends slabs, which may be wet, and sections of blocky rocks. Two miles from the Tuckerman Ravine Trail, you will reach the top of the ravine and the broad tableland known as the Alpine Garden, where colorful wildflowers bloom from mid-June (which is a little early to attempt the headwall, so hike up the Lion Head Trail) through August.

By following the Huntington Ravine Trail a short distance farther, you can pick up the Nelson Crag Trail for the final mile to Washington's summit, then descend the Tuckerman Ravine Trail to rejoin this loop at the other side of the Alpine Garden. But a finer hike—free from the tourists who flock to the summit via the auto road or cog railway—crosses the Alpine Garden to the Lion Head. For this, turn left (south) onto the Alpine Garden Trail, which traverses the mile-wide, tundralike plain. In a short distance, you will see to your left the top of a prominent cliff known as the Pinnacle, which is part of the Huntington Ravine headwall; the view from atop the Pinnacle merits the short detour, but take care to walk on rocks and not the fragile alpine vegetation. On your right rises the sprawling boulder pile of the mountain's upper cone.

Across the Alpine Garden, turn left (east) onto the Lion Head Trail. The flat trail follows the crest of a prominent buttress, above the cliffs that form the northern, or right-hand, wall of Tuckerman Ravine. There are numerous good views down into the ravine before the trail drops back into the woods again, descending steeply and eventually rejoining the Tuckerman Ravine Trail about two miles from the AMC visitors center. Turn left (east) and head down.

17 Mount Washington: Tuckerman Ravine

8.4 mi/7.0 hrs 

Location: In the White Mountain National Forest in Pinkham Notch; Northern New Hampshire map page 86, grid d3.

User groups: Hikers only. No wheelchair facilities. This trail is not suitable for bikes, dogs, horses, skis, or snowshoes. Hunting is prohibited.

Access, fees: Parking and access are free.

Directions: The hike begins from the Appalachian Mountain Club Visitors Center on Route 16 in Pinkham Notch, at the base of Mount Washington, 12 miles south of the junction of Route 16 and U.S. 2 in Gorham and about eight miles north of Jackson. The trailhead is behind the visitors center.

Maps: Several maps cover hiking trails in this area, including Bradford Washburn's "Mount Washington and the Heart of the Presidential Range—New Hampshire," which is $4.95, and the "Mount Washington Range" map 6, which is $2.95 from the Appalachian Mountain Club, (800) 262-4455; the "Mount Washington" map, available for $4.50 from cartographer Ed Rolfe, (603) 788-3019; the "Trail Map and Guide to the White Mountain National Forest," which is $4.95 from the DeLorme Mapping Company, (800) 253-5081; the map of the national forest, available for $4 from the White Mountain National Forest main office (see address below); and map 2 in the "Map and Guide to the Appalachian Trail in New Hampshire and Vermont," an eight-map set for $10.95 from the Appalachian Trail Conference (see address below). For a topographic map of the area, request Mount Washington from the USGS.

Contact: White Mountain National Forest Supervisor, 719 North Main Street, Laconia, NH 03246; (603) 528-8721, TDD for the hearing impaired (603) 528-8722. Appalachian Trail Conference, P.O. Box 807, Harpers Ferry, WV 25425; (304) 535-6331. The AMC's Pinkham Notch Visitors Center has up-to-date reports on weather in the Presidential Range; call (603) 466-2721.

Trail notes: This trail is the "trade route" and most direct way up the 6,288-foot Mount Washington, the Northeast's highest peak, so it typically sees hundreds of hikers on nice weekends in summer and autumn. It's also a busy place in spring, when skiers make the hike up into Tuckerman Ravine to ski its formidable headwall. While the crowds can diminish the mountain experience, the ravine is spectacular, an ascent of its headwall is a serious challenge, and reaching Washington's summit is an accomplishment sought by many. This is the common route for first-time hikers of Washington. The trail on the ravine headwall is sometimes closed due to ice; check on weather and conditions at the visitors center. While hiking the headwall, watch out for rocks kicked loose by hikers above you and be careful not to dislodge any rocks yourself. When you pass over the summit of Mount Washington, you'll be walking on the Appalachian Trail.

From behind the visitors center, the wide Tuckerman Ravine Trail ascends at a moderate grade, passing the short side path to Crystal Cascade within a half mile. Several trails branch from it. At 2.5 miles it reaches the floor of the ravine, a worthwhile destination in itself; to the right is the Lion Head, and to the left the cliffs of Boott Spur. (From the Hermit Lake shelter, walk to the right less than a quarter mile for a striking reflection of Boott Spur in Hermit Lake.) The trail then climbs the headwall, reaching its lip a mile from Hermit Lake, and follows rock cairns nearly another mile to the summit. While many hikers descend Tuckerman's headwall, an easier way down is via the Lion Head Trail, which diverges left from the Tuckerman Ravine Trail just below the summit, then rejoins it a tenth of a mile below Hermit Lake.

18 Mount Washington: Ammonoosuc-Jewell Loop

9.6 mi/7.5 hrs 

Location: In the White Mountain National Forest north of Crawford Notch; Northern New Hampshire map page 86, grid d3.

User groups: Hikers and dogs. No wheelchair facilities. This trail may be difficult to snowshoe, in part because of severe winter weather, and is not suitable for skis. Bikes, horses, and hunting are prohibited.

Access, fees: Parking and access are free. Mount Clinton Road is not maintained in winter. The Appalachian Mountain Club operates the Lakes of the Clouds hut, where a crew prepares meals and guests share bunkrooms and bathrooms; call (603) 466-2727 for reservation and rate information.

Directions: From the junction of U.S. 302 and U.S. 3 in Twin Mountain, drive east on U.S. 302 for 4.6 miles and turn left at signs for the Mount Washington Cog Railway. Continue 6.7 miles to a large parking lot on the right. Or from U.S. 302 in Crawford Notch, two-tenths of a mile north of the visitor information center, turn onto Mount Clinton Road. Follow it 3.7 miles and turn right. Continue 1.1 miles and turn right into the parking lot.

Maps: For a map of hiking trails, obtain Bradford Washburn's "Mount Washington and the Heart of the Presidential Range—New Hampshire," which is $4.95, or the "Mount Washington Range" map 6, which is $2.95, from the Appalachian Mountain Club, (800) 262-4455; the "Trail Map and Guide to the White Mountain National Forest," which is $4.95 from the DeLorme Mapping Company, (800) 253-5081; the map of the national forest, available for $4 from the White Mountain National Forest main office (see address below); or map 2 in the "Map and Guide to the Appalachian Trail in New Hampshire and Vermont," an eight-map set for $10.95 from the Appalachian Trail Conference (see address below). For a topographic map of the area, request Mount Washington from the USGS.

Contact: White Mountain National Forest Supervisor, 719 North Main Street, Laconia, NH 03246; (603) 528-8721, TDD for the hearing impaired (603) 528-8722. Appalachian Trail Conference, P.O. Box 807, Harpers Ferry, WV 25425; (304) 535-6331. The AMC's Pinkham Notch Visitors Center has up-to-date reports on weather in the Presidential Range; call (603) 466-2721.

Trail notes: Like any route up the Northeast's biggest hill, this hike offers great views and rough terrain. Like most others, it is also a fairly popular loop. And like any other way to the 6,288-foot summit of Mount Washington, this one can run you into some nasty weather. One September day not long ago I left behind a sun-splashed valley and ventured up here, only to reach the Lakes of the Clouds hut and find fog engulfing the mountain and a bitterly cold wind raking across the alpine zone. Dressed warmly and waiting patiently, I watched the clouds slowly dissipate under a warm sun—and made my way to the summit. This hike traverses exposed ground from just below the Lakes hut until you have descended more than a half mile down the Jewell Trail. The Ammonoosuc Ravine Trail provides the most direct route—3.1 miles—to the AMC's Lakes of the Clouds hut, in the saddle between Mounts Washington and Monroe. There are tricky stretches on the ravine's steep upper headwall, which can be slick with water, and several brook crossings, some of which would be impossible in times of high water.

From the parking lot, follow the Ammonoosuc Ravine Trail, which climbs moderately, passing picturesque Gem Pool about two miles out. For the next half mile, the trail makes a steep ascent of the headwall, passing several cascades and pools and good views back into Ammonoosuc Ravine. At three miles, you leave the last scrub vegetation behind and enter the alpine zone; take care to walk on rocks and not the fragile plant life. From the Lakes hut (reached at 3.1 miles), the detour south to the 5,384-foot summit of Monroe adds a relatively easy one-mile round-trip to this hike's distance. From the Lakes hut to the junction of the Jewell and Gulfside Trails, this hike follows the route of the Appalachian Trail.

To continue the hike, from the hut turn left (north) onto the Crawford Path, which passes by the two tiny tarns that give the hut its name and ascends more than 1,000 vertical feet over 1.4 miles to the top of Washington, where there is a visitors center, private weather observatory, and other buildings. Descend the Crawford Path from the summit for two-tenths of a mile, then bear right onto the Gulfside Trail heading north. Follow it 1.4 miles, walking the crest of the exposed ridge, passing the loop trail up Mount Clay, to the Jewell Trail. Turn left and descend the Jewell for 3.7 miles to the parking lot. It descends steep ground through several switchbacks at first, then proceeds at a more moderate grade.

⑲ Mounts Washington and Monroe: Crawford Path

16.4 mi/11.0 hrs 

Location: In the White Mountain National Forest in Crawford Notch State Park; Northern New Hampshire map page 86, grid d3.

User groups: Hikers and dogs. No wheelchair facilities. This trail may be difficult to snowshoe, in part because of severe winter weather, and is not suitable for skis. Bikes, horses, and hunting are prohibited.

Access, fees: Parking and access are free. The Appalachian Mountain Club operates the Lakes of the Clouds hut, where a crew prepares meals and guests share bunkrooms and bathrooms; call (603) 466-2727 for reservation and rate information.

Directions: Drive on U.S. 302 into Crawford Notch. The trailhead parking area is a tenth of a mile up Mount Clinton Road, which begins opposite the Crawford House site and just north of Saco Lake.

Maps: For a map of hiking trails, obtain Bradford Washburn's "Mount Washington and the Heart of the Presidential Range—New Hampshire," which is $4.95, or the "Mount Washington Range" map 6, which is $2.95, from the Appalachian Mountain Club, (800) 262-4455; the "Trail Map and Guide to the White Mountain National Forest," which is $4.95 from the DeLorme Mapping Company, (800) 253-5081; the map of the national forest, available for $4 from the White Mountain National Forest main office (see address below); or map 2 in the "Map and Guide to the Appalachian Trail in New Hampshire and Vermont," an eight-map set for $10.95 from the Appalachian Trail Conference (see address below). For a topographic map of the area, request Mount Washington from the USGS.

Contact: White Mountain National Forest Supervisor, 719 North Main Street, Laconia, NH 03246; (603) 528-8721, TDD for the hearing impaired (603) 528-8722. Appalachian Trail Conference, P.O. Box 807, Harpers Ferry, WV 25425; (304) 535-6331. The AMC's Pinkham Notch Visitors Center has up-to-date reports on weather in the Presidential Range; call (603) 466-2721.

Trail notes: This is a hike typically covered in two days, with a stay at the AMC's Lakes of the Clouds hut, but the gentle nature of the Crawford Path allows very fit hikers to cover this in a day. The southern ridge of the Presidentials is far less rugged than the northern ridge, yet the views surpass those of most hikes in New England. The Lakes of the Clouds are among the few true alpine tarns in the White Mountains. The 5,384-foot Mount Monroe rolls like a wave south from the 6,288-foot Mount Washington—and if you do spend a night at the hut, make the short walk up onto

Monroe to watch the sunset. Remember that weather changes quickly on these peaks, and may even be radically different atop Washington than on the other summits. I once hiked up the Crawford Path in early September, leaving a valley enjoying 65-degree temperatures, to find fresh snow on Mount Pierce—and to hear that Washington's summit was under bombardment by 100-mile-an-hour winds.

From the parking area, follow the Crawford Connector two-tenths of a mile to the Crawford Path, considered the oldest continuously maintained footpath in the country. (Nearby, a side path leads left for four-tenths of a mile over rough ground to Crawford Cliff, with a good view of Crawford Notch.) From the connector trail junction, the Crawford Path ascends steadily, passing a short side path in four-tenths of a mile that leads to Gibbs Falls. Less than three miles from U.S. 302, the trail emerges from the forest and meets the Webster Cliff Trail. From this point to Washington's summit, this hike follows the Appalachian Trail. Turn left, following the Crawford Path over more level ground, with views in all directions. A bit more than a mile from the Webster Cliff Trail junction, the Mount Eisenhower loop trail diverges for the four-tenths-of-a-mile climb to that 4,761-foot summit, rejoining the Crawford Path at a point eight-tenths of a mile north via the loop trail and a half mile via the Crawford Path. The trail continues to ascend at a very gentle grade until, six miles from U.S. 302, the Mount Monroe Loop branches left for its two summits (from this direction, the second, or northernmost, summit is the highest).

It's the same distance, seven-tenths of a mile, via either the Crawford Path or the Monroe Loop to where the two trails meet again north of Monroe, but the Monroe Loop involves another 350 feet of elevation gain and is much more exposed. From the northern junction of the trails, the Crawford Path leads a flat tenth of a mile to the Lakes of the Clouds hut. From there, it's a steady climb for 1.4 miles over very rocky terrain up the barren summit cone of Washington to the roof of New England. Return via the same route.

20 Mount Washington: Boott Spur/ Gulf of Slides

7.2 mi/5.0 hrs 

Location: In the White Mountain National Forest in Pinkham Notch; Northern New Hampshire map page 86, grid d3.

User groups: Hikers only. No wheelchair facilities. This trail may be difficult to snowshoe, in part because of severe winter weather, and is not suitable for bikes, dogs, horses, or skis. Hunting is prohibited.

Access, fees: Parking and access are free.

Directions: The hike begins from the Appalachian Mountain Club Visitors Center on Route 16 in Pinkham Notch, at the base of Mount Washington, 12 miles south of the junction of Route 16 and U.S. 2 in Gorham and about eight miles north of Jackson. The trailhead is behind the visitors center.

Maps: For a map of hiking trails, obtain Bradford Washburn's "Mount Washington and the Heart of the Presidential Range—New Hampshire," which is $4.95, or the "Mount Washington Range" map 6, which is $2.95, from the Appalachian Mountain Club, (800) 262-4455; the "Mount Washington" map, available for $4.50 from cartographer Ed Rolfe, (603) 788-3019; the "Trail Map and Guide to the White Mountain National Forest," which is $4.95 from the DeLorme Mapping Company, (800) 253-5081; or the map of the national forest, available for $4 from the White Mountain National Forest main office (see address below). For a topographic map of the area, request Mount Washington from the USGS.

Contact: White Mountain National Forest Supervisor, 719 North Main Street, Laconia, NH 03246; (603) 528-8721, TDD for the hearing impaired (603) 528-8722. The AMC's Pinkham Notch Visitors Center has up-to-date reports on weather in the Presidential Range; call (603) 466-2721.

Trail notes: The summit of 6,288-foot Mount Washington, with its commercial development and access by road and cog railway, is one of the least appealing features of this sprawling mountain—which is why I sometimes prefer a hike like this one, with its stiff climb onto a high shoulder of Washington and views down into two of its ravines.

From the Appalachian Mountain Club Visitors Center, follow the Tuckerman Ravine Trail for nearly a half mile. Shortly after passing the side path to Crystal Cascade, turn left onto the Boott Spur Trail. In another 1.7 miles, a side path leads a short distance right to Ravine Outlook, high above Tuckerman Ravine. The trail emerges from the woods nearly two miles from the Tuckerman Ravine Trail, and passes between the halves of Split Rock at 2.2 miles. It then ascends the open ridge known as Boott Spur, with excellent views down into Tuckerman Ravine. Although the grade is moderate, a few "false summits" along the steplike ridge deceive many hikers. Once atop the shoulder, three miles from the Tuckerman Ravine Trail, turn left (south) onto the Davis Path and follow it for a half mile. Then turn left again (southeast) onto the Glen Boulder Trail, which circles around the rim of the Gulf of Slides, a popular destination for backcountry skiers in winter and spring. At 1.5 miles from the Davis Path, you'll pass the Glen Boulder, an enormous glacial erratic set precariously on the mountainside. A bit more than a mile past the boulder, back down in the woods, turn left onto the Direttissima, the trail heading back to the visitors center parking lot.

21 Glen Ellis Falls

0.3 mi/0.75 hr 

Location: In the White Mountain National Forest south of Pinkham Notch; Northern New Hampshire map page 86, grid e3.

User groups: Hikers and dogs. No wheelchair facilities. This trail would be difficult to snowshoe and is not suitable for bikes, horses, or skis. Hunting is allowed in season.

Access, fees: Parking and access are free.

Directions: The trail begins at a parking lot for Glen Ellis Falls off Route 16, less than a mile south of the Appalachian Mountain Club Visitors Center in Pinkham Notch.

Maps: Although no map is needed for this hike, hiking trails in the area are shown on several maps, including three that are widely available in stores or from the Appalachian Mountain Club, (800) 262-4455: Bradford Washburn's "Mount Washington and the Heart of the Presidential Range—New Hampshire," which is $4.95, or the "Mount Washington Range" map 6 and the "Carter-Mahoosuc" map 7, which are $2.95 each. Other maps of the area include the "Trail Map and Guide to the White Mountain National Forest," which is $4.95 from the DeLorme Mapping Company, (800) 253-5081; and map 2 in the "Map and Guide to the Appalachian Trail in New Hampshire and Vermont," an eight-map set for $10.95 from the Appalachian Trail Conference (see address below). For topographic maps of the area, request Mount Washington, Carter Dome, Jackson, and Stairs Mountain from the USGS.

Contact: White Mountain National Forest Supervisor, 719 North Main Street, Laconia, NH 03246; (603) 528-8721, TDD for the hearing impaired (603) 528-8722.

Trail notes: Here's a scenic, short walk that's ideal for young children and enjoyable for adults—though it could be troublesome for people who have difficulty climbing steep steps. Follow the wide gravel trail through a tunnel under Route 16. It descends steeply at times, but there are rock steps and a handrail. The waterfall is less than a half-mile walk from the parking area, and more than worth the effort: a 70-foot wall of water makes a sheer drop into a small pool at its base. This is a popular walk with tourists, and it's especially spectacular in late spring, when water flow is heaviest.

22 Lost Pond

2.0 mi/1.0 hr 

Location: In the White Mountain National Forest in Pinkham Notch; Northern New Hampshire map page 86, grid d4.

User groups: Hikers, dogs, skiers, and snowshoers. No wheelchair facilities. Bikes, horses, and hunting are prohibited.

Access, fees: Parking and access are free.

Directions: The trail begins across Route 16 from the Appalachian Mountain Club Visitors Center in Pinkham Notch.

Maps: Several contour maps of hiking trails cover this area, including three that are widely available in stores or from the Appalachian Mountain Club, (800) 262-4455: Bradford Washburn's "Mount Washington and the Heart of the Presidential Range—New Hampshire," which is $4.95, or the "Mount Washington Range" map 6 and the "Carter-Mahoosuc" map 7, which are $2.95 each. Other maps of the area include the "Trail Map and Guide to the White Mountain National Forest," which is $4.95 from the DeLorme Mapping Company, (800) 253-5081; and map 2 in the "Map and Guide to the Appalachian Trail in New Hampshire and Vermont," an eight-map set for $10.95 from the Appalachian Trail Conference (see address below). For topographic maps of the area, request Mount Washington, Carter Dome, Jackson, and Stairs Mountain from the USGS.

Contact: White Mountain National Forest Supervisor, 719 North Main Street, Laconia, NH 03246; (603) 528-8721, TDD for the hearing impaired (603) 528-8722.

Trail notes: While this pond is no more "lost" than the popular Lonesome Lake on the other side of the Whites is "lonesome," this is a nice short hike that's flat and offers opportunities for wildlife viewing and a unique angle on Mount Washington. Cross Route 16 from the Appalachian Mountain Club center and follow the Lost Pond Trail, a section of the Appalachian Trail, around the pond. Immediately you will see signs of beaver activity—probably dams and a lodge—and if you're lucky, a moose will be grazing in the swampy area to the left. About halfway around the pond, look across it to a fine view up at Washington above the still water. The trail ends at the Wildcat Ridge Trail, just minutes from the Glen Ellis Falls (hike number 21), which can be reached by turning right (west) toward Route 16. Otherwise, return the way you came.

23 Wildcat Mountain

8.5 mi/5.5 hrs 

Location: In the White Mountain National Forest in Pinkham Notch; Northern New Hampshire map page 86, grid d4.

User groups: Hikers, dogs, and snowshoers. No wheelchair facilities. This trail is not suitable for skis. Bikes, horses, and hunting are prohibited.

Access, fees: Parking and access are free.

Directions: The Nineteen-Mile Brook Trail begins at a turnout on Route 16, a mile north of the Mount Washington Auto Road.

Maps: For a map of hiking trails, obtain the "Carter-Mahoosuc" map 7, which is $2.95 from the Appalachian Mountain Club, (800) 262-4455, and is also widely available in stores; the "Trail Map and Guide to the White Mountain National Forest," which is

$4.95 from the DeLorme Mapping Company, (800) 253-5081; or map 2 in the "Map and Guide to the Appalachian Trail in New Hampshire and Vermont," an eight-map set for $10.95 from the Appalachian Trail Conference (see address below). For a topographic map of the area, request Carter Dome from the USGS.

Contact: White Mountain National Forest Supervisor, 719 North Main Street, Laconia, NH 03246; (603) 528-8721, TDD for the hearing impaired (603) 528-8722. Appalachian Trail Conference, P.O. Box 807, Harpers Ferry, WV 25425; (304) 535-6331.

Trail notes: The summit of this 4,000-foot peak is wooded and uninteresting, but the walk along Nineteen-Mile Brook and the view from the top of cliffs overlooking Carter Notch and the Carter Range—reached via a short spur trail just below Wildcat Mountain's 4,422-foot summit—make this hike very worthwhile. Because this end of Wildcat Mountain does not tend to lure many hikers, you might have that viewpoint to yourself (as a friend and I once did on a backpacking trip through the Carter Range).

The Nineteen-Mile Brook Trail ascends very gently toward Carter Notch, paralleling the wide, rock-strewn streambed and crossing two tributaries. Just two-tenths of a mile before the trail drops down into the notch—and 3.5 miles from Route 16—the Wildcat Ridge Trail leads to the right and then climbs steeply up the sometimes eroded east face of Wildcat Mountain (the Wildcat Ridge Trail is part of the Appalachian Trail). Upon reaching more level ground, shortly before topping the summit, watch for the spur trail branching to the left about 30 feet to the cliffs. Return to the parking area the way you came—and on the descent, I highly recommend the half-mile detour down into Carter Notch on the Nineteen-Mile Brook Trail.

24 Mount Hight/Carter Dome/Carter Notch

10.0 mi/7.5 hrs 

Location: In the White Mountain National Forest north of Pinkham Notch; Northern New Hampshire map page 86, grid d4.

User groups: Hikers and dogs. No wheelchair facilities. This trail would be difficult to snowshoe and is not suitable for skis. Bikes, horses, and hunting are prohibited.

Access, fees: Parking and access are free.

Directions: The Nineteen-Mile Brook Trail begins at a turnout on Route 16, a mile north of the Mount Washington Auto Road.

Maps: For a map of hiking trails, obtain the "Carter-Mahoosuc" map 7, which is $2.95 from the Appalachian Mountain Club, (800) 262-4455, and is also widely available in stores; the "Trail Map and Guide to the White Mountain National Forest," which is $4.95 from the DeLorme Mapping Company, (800) 253-5081; or map 2 in the "Map and Guide to the Appalachian Trail in New Hampshire and Vermont," an eight-map set for $10.95 from the Appalachian Trail Conference (see address below). For a topographic map of the area, request Carter Dome from the USGS.

Contact: White Mountain National Forest Supervisor, 719 North Main Street, Laconia, NH 03246; (603) 528-8721, TDD for the hearing impaired (603) 528-8722. Appalachian Trail Conference, P.O. Box 807, Harpers Ferry, WV 25425; (304) 535-6331.

Trail notes: This very scenic 10-mile loop takes you over the nicest summit in the Carter Range, Mount Hight, onto the ninth-highest peak in the Granite State, 4,832-foot Carter Dome, and into a boulder-strewn mountain notch where towering cliffs flank a pair of tiny ponds.

From the trailhead, hike the Nineteen-Mile Brook Trail for nearly two miles, and turn left (east) onto the Carter Dome Trail. In about two miles, at Zeta Pass, you might exercise the option of exploring 4,430-foot South Carter (adding 1.5 miles to this hike) by heading north (left) on the Carter-Moriah Trail; then double back to Zeta Pass. This hike picks up the Carter-Moriah Trail south (right); from Zeta Pass to the junction of the Nineteen-Mile Brook and Wildcat Ridge Trails, this route follows the Appalachian Trail. The trail climbs steeply, requiring some scrambling over rocks, to the bare summit of 4,675-foot Mount Hight. There you have a 360-degree panorama of the Presidential Range dominating the skyline to the west, the Carters running north, and the lower hills of eastern New Hampshire and western Maine to the south and east. Continue south on the Carter-Moriah Trail, over the viewless summit of Carter Dome, and descend into Carter Notch. There's a great view of the notch from open ledges before you start the knee-pounding drop. At the larger of the two Carter Lakes in the notch, two miles from Mount Hight, turn right (northwest) onto the Nineteen-Mile Brook Trail for the nearly four-mile walk back to the parking area.

25 The Carter-Moriah Range

20.0 mi. one way/
3.0 days

Location: In the White Mountain National Forest, between Pinkham Notch and Shel-burne; Northern New Hampshire map page 86, grid d4.

User groups: Hikers and dogs. No wheelchair facilities. This trail would be difficult to snowshoe and is not suitable for skis. Bikes, horses, and hunting are prohibited.

Access, fees: Parking and access are free. Although backcountry campsites can be found along this route, they are scarce, and camping is prohibited along much of the high ridge. Carry cash for camping overnight at the Appalachian Mountain Club hut in Carter Notch or the AMC's Imp campsite. The hut costs $12/night for AMC members or $18/night for nonmembers, and is self service.

Directions: You will need to shuttle two vehicles for this traverse. Leave one at the hike's terminus, a parking area where the Appalachian Trail crosses U.S. 2, 3.6 miles east of the southern junction of U.S. 2 and Route 16 in Gorham. The hike begins from the Appalachian Mountain Club Visitors Center on Route 16 in Pinkham Notch, at the base of Mount Washington, 12 miles south of the junction with U.S. 2 in Gorham and about eight miles north of Jackson.

Maps: For a contour map of hiking trails, obtain the "Carter-Mahoosuc" map 7, which is $2.95 from the Appalachian Mountain Club, (800) 262-4455, and is also widely available in stores; or the "Trail Map and Guide to the White Mountain National Forest," which is $4.95 from the DeLorme Mapping Company, (800) 253-5081. For a topographic map of the area, request Carter Dome from the USGS.

Contact: White Mountain National Forest Supervisor, 719 North Main Street, Laconia, NH 03246; (603) 528-8721, TDD for the hearing impaired (603) 528-8722. Appalachian Trail Conference, P.O. Box 807, Harpers Ferry, WV 25425; (304) 535-6331.

Trail notes: This section of the Appalachian Trail just might have you cursing one moment, then uttering expressions of awe the next. This is a great three-day ridge walk on the AT with excellent views of the Presidential Range to the west and the Wild River Valley to the east.

From the Appalachian Mountain Club Visitors Center, follow the Lost Pond Trail to the Wildcat Ridge Trail; turn left (east), and you will soon begin the steep climb to the ridge, passing over open ledges with commanding views of Mount Washington—a good destination for a short day hike. The first of Wildcat's five summits that you'll encounter—Peak E, 4,041 feet high and one of New Hampshire's official 4,000-footers—is a 3.8-mile round-trip hike of about three hours. The trail traverses the roller-coaster Wildcat Ridge, up and down five humped summits with few views. Just beyond the final peak—Wildcat's true summit at 4,422 feet—is a short spur trail to a view atop cliffs overlooking Carter Notch and the Carter Range that will make you eat all your nasty comments about this trail. Descend north a steep mile, turning right (east) onto the Nineteen-Mile Brook Trail for the final two-tenths of a mile into the notch and circling around the larger of two ponds there. Tent sites can be found near the junction of the Wildcat Ridge and Nineteen-Mile Brook Trails, or ask a caretaker at the AMC hut in Carter Notch about nearby sites.

From the notch, hike north, climbing steeply on the Carter-Moriah Trail, which has one particularly nice overlook high above the notch. You'll pass a side trail leading to a good spring. A bit more than a mile from the notch, the trail passes over the highest point on this ridge, Carter Dome, at 4,832 feet. Unfortunately, trees block any views. The trail continues nearly a mile to the rocky summit of Mount Hight (4,675 feet)—the nicest summit in the range, with 360-degree views of the Presidentials and far into Maine to the east. From Hight, the Carter-Moriah Trail turns sharply left (west) a short distance, drops north down a steep slope into the forest for a half mile to Zeta Pass, then continues north over the wooded summits of South Carter and Middle Carter (2.7 miles from Mount Hight). As the ridge ascends gradually again toward North Carter, you break into the alpine zone and some of the best views on this hike, particularly west to Mount Washington. From the viewless summit of North Carter, the trail drops several hundred feet over rock ledges that require scrambling, passes over the hump known as Imp Mountain, and reaches the spur trail to the Imp campsite in two miles. Check out the view at sunset from the ledge just below the shelter.

Continuing north on the Carter-Moriah Trail, you cross over some open ledges on Imp Mountain before the trail ascends steadily onto the open southern ledges of Mount Moriah two miles from the shelter. A short distance farther, the Carter-Moriah Trail peels off left toward the town of Gorham, and the AT follows the Kenduskeag Trail; but drop your pack and make the short detour on the Carter-Moriah for the rocky scramble up the spur trail to Moriah's summit. Backtrack to the Kenduskeag—an Abenaki word meaning "a pleasant walk"—and follow its often wet path 1.5 miles to the Rattle River Trail; turn left (north). This descends steeply at first, through a dense, damp forest, then levels out before reaching the Rattle River shelter in 2.5 miles. From there, it's less than two miles to a parking lot on U.S. 2 in Shelburne, the terminus of this traverse.

26 The Baldies Loop

9.7 mi/7.0 hrs 

Location: In the White Mountain National Forest near North Chatham; Northern New Hampshire map page 86, grid e4.

User groups: Hikers and dogs. No wheelchair facilities. This trail is not suitable for bikes, horses, skis, or snowshoes. Hunting is allowed in season.

Access, fees: Parking and access are free.

Directions: The trail begins near a large parking lot on the east side of Route 113, 2.7 miles north of the northern junction of Routes 113 and 113B, and 13 miles south of the junction of U.S. 2 and Route 113.

Maps: For a contour map of trails,e obtain the "Map of Cold River Valley and Evans Notch," which is $5 from the Chatham Trails Association, P.O. Box 605, Center Conway, NH 03813; the "Carter-Mahoosuc" map 7, which is $2.95 from the Appalachian Mountain Club, (800) 262-4455; or the "Trail Map and Guide to the White Mountain National Forest," which is $4.95 from the DeLorme Mapping Company, (800) 253-5081. For a topographic map of the area, request Chatham from the USGS.

Contact: White Mountain National Forest Supervisor, 719 North Main Street, Laconia, NH 03246; (603) 528-8721, TDD for the hearing impaired (603) 528-8722.

Trail notes: As their names suggest, the pair of 3,500-foot peaks called the Baldies mimic higher mountains with their craggy summits, four miles of open ridge, and some of the best views this side of Mount Washington. This rugged hike of almost 10 miles is not to be underestimated, both for difficulty and for the propensity of the Baldies to attract harsh conditions: I've encountered winds up here strong enough to knock me around. Although it's probably the most popular hike in the Evans Notch area, I've done this loop without passing more than 10 other hikers—Evans Notch lies far enough from population centers that it attracts far fewer people than other areas of the Whites.

From the parking area, walk 50 yards north on Route 113 and cross the road to the start of the Baldface Circle Trail. It's a wide, easy trail for seven-tenths of a mile to Circle Junction, where a side trail leads right a tenth of a mile to Emerald Pool, a worthwhile detour (adding two-tenths of a mile to this hike) to a deep pool below a narrow gorge and a short falls along Charles Brook. From Circle Junction, bear left at a sign for South Baldface, following the loop clockwise. At 1.2 miles from the road, a side path marked by a sign leads a half mile to Chandler Gorge (adding a mile to this hike's distance).

Climbing steadily, the trail reaches the South Baldface shelter 2.5 miles from the road. Beyond the lean-to, the trail hits all the prominent ledges visible from the road, and for nearly a half mile winds up them, requiring steep, exposed scrambling that might discomfit inexperienced hikers. A bit more than three miles from the road, the trail reaches the level shoulder of South Baldface, where the Baldface Knob Trail leads left (south) to Baldface Knob and Eastman Mountain. From here, you'll get your first view into the broad glacial cirque, or ravine, bounded by North and South Baldface and the Bicknell Ridge. The Circle Trail continues a half mile west—and 500 feet up—to the 3,569-foot summit of South Baldface. The summit views extend to much of the White Mountains to the west and south, including Mounts Washington, Carrigain, and Chocorua, the triplet peaks of the Tripyramids above Waterville Valley, the distant Franconia Ridge, and the cliffs of Cathedral Ledge and Whitehorse Ledge near North Conway. To the north rise the Mahoosuc Range and a long chain of mountains reaching far into Maine. East lies a landscape of lakes and low hills, most prominently the long, low ridge of Pleasant Mountain.

Continue northwest on the Circle Trail another 1.2 miles, dropping into the woods and then ascending to the 3,591-foot summit of North Baldface, where the views are equally awesome. Descend north off North Baldy via the Circle Trail, and continue nearly a mile to the junction at a sign with the Bicknell Ridge Trail. Turn right (east) on this path, a scenic alternative to completing the Circle Trail loop. The Bicknell descends an open ridge for about a mile before entering the forest and reaching its lower junction with the Circle Trail in 2.5 miles, at a stream crossing. Follow the Circle Trail another seven-tenths of a mile to Circle Junction, from which it's seven-tenths of a mile farther to the road.

27 Emerald Pool

1.6 mi/1.0 hr 

Location: In the White Mountain National Forest near North Chatham; Northern New Hampshire map page 86, grid e4.

User groups: Hikers, dogs, and snowshoers. No wheelchair facilities. This trail is not suitable for bikes, horses, or skis. Hunting is allowed in season.

Access, fees: Parking and access are free.

Directions: The trail begins near a large parking lot on the east side of Route 113, 2.7 miles north of the northern junction of Routes 113 and 113B, and 13 miles south of the junction of U.S. 2 and Route 113.

Maps: For a contour map of trails, obtain the "Map of Cold River Valley and Evans Notch," which is $5 from the Chatham Trails Association, P.O. Box 605, Center Conway, NH 03813; the "Carter-Mahoosuc" map 7, which is $2.95 from the Appalachian Mountain Club, (800) 262-4455; or the "Trail Map and Guide to the White Mountain National Forest," which is $4.95 from the DeLorme Mapping Company, (800) 253-5081. For a topographic map of the area, request Chatham from the USGS.

Contact: White Mountain National Forest Supervisor, 719 North Main Street, Laconia, NH 03246; (603) 528-8721, TDD for the hearing impaired (603) 528-8722.

Trail notes: The aptly named Emerald Pool is a deep hole, below a narrow flume and gorge and a short falls, along Charles Brook. It's a flat, easy walk to the pool, making this a good hike for young children. From the parking area, walk 50 yards north on Route 113 and cross the road to the start of the Baldface Circle Trail. Follow the wide, easy trail for seven-tenths of a mile to Circle Junction, where a side trail leads right a tenth of a mile to Emerald Pool. Return the same way you came in.

28 Mounts Pierce and Eisenhower

10.8 mi/6.5 hrs 

Location: In the White Mountain National Forest and Crawford Notch State Park; Northern New Hampshire map page 86, grid e3.

User groups: Hikers and dogs. No wheelchair facilities. This trail may be difficult to snowshoe because of severe winter weather, and is not suitable for skis. Bikes, horses, and hunting are prohibited.

Access, fees: Parking and access are free.

Directions: From U.S. 302 in Crawford Notch, turn onto Mount Clinton Road opposite the Crawford House site, just north of Saco Lake. The trail begins at a parking area on the right within a tenth of a mile from U.S. 302.

Maps: For a map of hiking trails, obtain the "Mount Washington Range" map 6, which is $2.95 from the Appalachian Mountain Club, (800) 262-4455, and is also widely available in stores; the "Trail Map and Guide to the White Mountain National Forest," which is $4.95 from the DeLorme Mapping Company, (800) 253-5081; or map 2 in the "Map and Guide to the Appalachian Trail in New Hampshire and Vermont," an eight-map set for $10.95 from the Appalachian Trail Conference (see address below). For topographic maps of the area, request Crawford Notch and Stairs Mountain from the USGS.

Contact: White Mountain National Forest Supervisor, 719 North Main Street, Laconia, NH 03246; (603) 528-8721, TDD for the hearing impaired (603) 528-8722. Appalachian Trail Conference, P.O. Box 807,

Harpers Ferry, WV 25425; (304) 535-6331. The AMC's Pinkham Notch Visitors Center has up-to-date reports on weather in the Presidential Range; call (603) 466-2721.

Trail notes: The Crawford Path is reputedly the oldest continuously maintained footpath in the country, dating back to 1819, when Abel Crawford and his son Ethan Allen Crawford cut the first section. It's also the easiest route onto the high ridge of the Presidential Range—the road sits at 2,000 feet, and the trail breaks out above the trees in less than three miles. Once on the ridge, you'll have sweeping views of the Whites; the 4,761-foot Mount Eisenhower itself is one of the more distinctive summits in the Southern Presidentials. This can, however, be a difficult trail to follow down in foul weather, particularly when it comes to finding your way into the woods on Mount Pierce.

From the parking lot, the Crawford Connector spur leads two-tenths of a mile to the Crawford Path. (From there, a 45-minute, eight-tenths-of-a-mile detour on the Crawford Cliff Trail leads to a good view of the notch.) Less than a half mile up the Crawford Path, watch for a short side trail to Gibbs Falls. After emerging from the woods, nearly three miles from the trailhead, the Crawford Path meets the Webster Cliff Trail, which leads south a tenth of a mile to the summit of 4,312-foot Mount Pierce. (The Webster Cliff Trail and the Crawford Path from this junction north are part of the Appalachian Trail.) Turning back down the Crawford Path from Pierce makes for a six-mile round-trip. This hike follows the Crawford Path—which from here coincides with the Appalachian Trail—north another two miles to the Eisenhower Loop Trail, then four-tenths of a mile up the loop trail to that summit, which has excellent views in every direction. To the north rises the Northeast's tallest peak, 6,288-foot Mount Washington. Stretching northwest from Washington are the Northern Presidentials. The distinct hump in the ridge between Eisenhower and Washington is Mount Monroe. To the east you can see the Montalban Ridge running south from Washington—which includes Mount Isolation, a rocky high point about midway along that ridge—and beyond the ridge into western Maine. To the southwest are the peaks and valleys of the Pemigewasset Wilderness, with Mount Carrigain the tallest among them. And in the distance, more west than south, rises Franconia Ridge, including Mounts Lafayette and Lincoln as well as Liberty and Flume. Hike back along the same route.

29 Mount Isolation

20.0 mi. one way/
2.0 days

Location: In the White Mountain National Forest, north of Jackson and east of Crawford Notch State Park; Northern New Hampshire map page 86, grid e3.

User groups: Hikers and dogs. No wheelchair facilities. This trail may be difficult to snowshoe because of severe winter weather, and is not suitable for bikes, horses, or skis. Hunting is allowed in season.

Access, fees: Parking and access are free. In the Dry River Wilderness, two shelters along the Rocky Branch Trail are slated to be dismantled as soon as they need major maintenance, so don't count on them.

Directions: You will need to shuttle two vehicles. Leave one at the roadside turnout at the Dry River Trailhead on U.S. 302, three-tenths of a mile north of the Dry River Campground and 4.5 miles south of the Crawford Notch hostel. Then drive south on U.S. 302 to Glen, turn left onto Route 16 north, and drive 8.1 miles to a large parking lot on the left for the Rocky Branch Trail.

Maps: For a map of hiking trails, obtain the

"Mount Washington Range" map 6, which is $2.95 from the Appalachian Mountain Club, (800) 262-4455, and is also widely available in stores; or the "Trail Map and Guide to the White Mountain National Forest," which is $4.95 from the DeLorme Mapping Company, (800) 253-5081. For topographic maps of the area, request Jackson and Stairs Mountain from the USGS.

Contact: White Mountain National Forest Supervisor, 719 North Main Street, Laconia, NH 03246; (603) 528-8721, TDD for the hearing impaired (603) 528-8722.

Trail notes: In the heart of the Dry River Wilderness, south of Mount Washington, Mount Isolation's bald pate lies too far from any road for most day hikers—which translates into a true sense of isolation. A friend and I made this two-day traverse once in late spring and saw only four other backpackers in two days.

Follow the Rocky Branch Trail west for 3.7 miles to the Rocky Branch, an aptly named tributary of the Saco River. Cross the stream and turn right (north) on the Isolation Trail, which eventually swings west in its 2.5-mile climb onto the Montalban Ridge, where it meets the Davis Path. Find a place to camp well off the trail, and leave your backpacks behind for the one-mile hike south on the Davis Path to the short but steep spur trail to Mount Isolation's barren summit (4,005 feet). You'll have terrific views west and north to the Southern Presidentials and Mount Washington, and to the southwest and south of the sprawling Whites. Return to your campsite.

On day two, hike north three-tenths of a mile on the Davis Path to where the Isolation Trail turns west (left) toward the valley of the Dry River; be careful, because this trail junction is easily overlooked—especially, I can tell you, when it lies under four feet of snow. In about 2.5 miles, turn left (south) on the Dry River Trail, paralleling the broad, boulder-choked river and crossing countless mountain brooks feeding into it. When the trees are bare, you get some fine views, directly upriver, of Mount Washington. It's nearly five miles from the Isolation Trail junction to U.S. 302.

30 Elephant Head

0.6 mi/0.5 hr 

Location: In Crawford Notch State Park; Northern New Hampshire map page 86, grid e3.

User groups: Hikers and snowshoers. No wheelchair facilities. Dogs must be on a leash. This trail is not suitable for bikes, horses, or skis. Hunting is allowed in season.

Access, fees: Parking and access are free.

Directions: Park in the turnout on the west side of U.S. 302, three-tenths of a mile south of the Crawford Notch hostel.

Maps: Several maps cover hiking trails in this area, including the "Mount Washington Range" map 6 from the Appalachian Mountain Club, (800) 262-4455, which is $2.95 and widely available in stores; the "Crawford Notch" map available for $4.50 from Ed Rolfe, Cartographer, P.O. Box 349, Twin Mountain, NH 03595, (603) 788-3019; the "Trail Map and Guide to the White Mountain National Forest," which is $4.95, from the DeLorme Mapping Company, (800) 253-5081; and the map of the national forest, available by sending a check for $4 to White Mountain National Forest main office (see address below). For a topographic map of the area, request Crawford Notch from the USGS.

Contact: White Mountain National Forest Supervisor, 719 North Main Street, Laconia, NH 03246; (603) 528-8721, TDD for hearing impaired (603) 528-8722. New Hampshire Division of Parks and Recreation, Bureau of Trails, P.O. Box 1856, Concord, NH 03302-1856; (603) 271-3254.

Trail notes: From the north end of Saco Lake in Crawford Notch, gaze south toward the short but prominent cliff at the far end of the pond; it resembles the head and trunk of an elephant. To hike an easy trail to the top of that cliff and a good view of the notch, cross U.S. 302 from the parking area to the Webster-Jackson Trail. After just a tenth of a mile, turn right onto the Elephant Head Trail, and continue two-tenths of a mile to the top of the cliff. Return the way you came.

31 Mount Avalon

3.6 mi/2.5 hrs 

Location: In the White Mountain National Forest and Crawford Notch State Park, north of Bartlett and south of Twin Mountain; Northern New Hampshire map page 86, grid e3.

User groups: Hikers and dogs. No wheelchair facilities. Dogs must be on a leash. This trail is not suitable for bikes, horses, or skis. Hunting is allowed in season.

Access, fees: Parking and access are free.

Directions: Park at the visitors center on U.S. 302 in Crawford Notch.

Maps: Several maps cover hiking trails in this area, including the "Mount Washington Range" map 6 and the "Franconia" map 5 from the Appalachian Mountain Club (800-262-4455), which are $2.95 each and are widely available in stores; the "Crawford Notch" map available for $4.50 from Ed Rolfe, Cartographer, P.O. Box 349, Twin Mountain, NH 03595, (603) 788-3019; the "Trail Map and Guide to the White Mountain National Forest," which is $4.95 from the DeLorme Mapping Company, (800) 253-5081; the map of the national forest, available by sending a check for $4 to the White Mountain National Forest main office (see address below); and map 3 in the "Map and Guide to the Appalachian Trail in New Hampshire and Vermont," an eight-map set for $10.95 from the Appalachian Trail Conference (see address below). For a topographic map of the area, request Crawford Notch from the USGS.

Contact: White Mountain National Forest Supervisor, 719 North Main Street, Laconia, NH 03246; (603) 528-8721, TDD for hearing impaired (603) 528-8722. Appalachian Trail Conference, P.O. Box 807, Harpers Ferry, WV 25425; (304) 535-6331. New Hampshire Division of Parks and Recreation, P.O. Box 1856, Concord, NH 03302-1856; (603) 271-3254.

Trail notes: From the parking area, cross the railroad tracks behind the visitors center and pick up the Avalon Trail. At about two-tenths of a mile, turn left onto the Cascade Loop Trail, which passes scenic Beecher and Pearl Cascades and rejoins the Avalon Trail about a half mile from the parking lot. (In fact, the cascades are a worthy destination on an easy hike of a mile; Beecher, an impressive flume-like cascade above a gorge, lies just three-tenths of a mile from the trailhead, and Pearl a short distance farther.) Turning left on the Avalon Trail, follow it another eight-tenths of a mile to a junction with the A-Z Trail; bear left, staying on the Avalon, which grows very steep and rocky for the next half mile. Then turn left onto a spur trail which climbs 100 yards to Avalon's craggy summit, where from various spots you get views in virtually every direction of the Whites. Follow the same route back.

32 Mount Willard

2.8 mi/2.0 hrs 

Location: In Crawford Notch State Park, north of Bartlett and south of Twin Mountain; Northern New Hampshire map page 86, grid e3.

User groups: Hikers, dogs, and snowshoers. No wheelchair facilities. Dogs must

be on a leash. This trail is not suitable for bikes, horses, or skis. Hunting is allowed in season.

Access, fees: Parking and access are free.

Directions: Park at the visitors center on U.S. 302 in Crawford Notch.

Maps: Several maps cover hiking trails in this area, including the "Mount Washington Range" map 6 and the "Franconia" map 5 from the Appalachian Mountain Club (800-262-4455, which are $2.95 each and are widely available in stores; the "Crawford Notch" map available for $4.50 from Ed Rolfe, Cartographer, P.O. Box 349, Twin Mountain, NH 03595, (603) 788-3019; the "Trail Map and Guide to the White Mountain National Forest," which is $4.95 from the DeLorme Mapping Company, (800) 253-5081; the map of the national forest, available by sending a check for $4 to the White Mountain National Forest main office (see address below); and map 3 in the "Map and Guide to the Appalachian Trail in New Hampshire and Vermont," an eight-map set for $10.95 from the Appalachian Trail Conference (see address below). For a topographic map of the area, request Crawford Notch from the USGS.

Contact: White Mountain National Forest Supervisor, 719 North Main Street, Laconia, NH 03246; (603) 528-8721, TDD for hearing impaired (603) 528-8722. Appalachian Trail Conference, P.O. Box 807, Harpers Ferry, WV 25425; (304) 535-6331. New Hampshire Division of Parks and Recreation, P.O. Box 1856, Concord, NH 03302-1856; (603) 271-3254.

Trail notes: The view from the cliffs of Mount Willard is widely considered one of the best in the White Mountains for the relatively minor effort needed to reach it. From the parking area, cross the railroad tracks behind the visitors center and pick up the Avalon Trail. Within 100 yards, turn left onto the Mount Willard Trail, which ascends at a moderate grade. At 1.2 miles, a side path on the left leads two-tenths of a mile downhill to the Hitchcock Flume, a dramatic gorge worn into the mountainside by erosion. From that trail junction, it's just another two-tenths of a mile of flat walking on the Mount Willard Trail to Willard's summit. Its open ledges afford an excellent view from high above the notch, with the Webster Cliffs to the east (left), and the Willey Slide directly south (straight ahead). Hike back the same way.

33 Webster Cliffs

9.4 mi/6.5 hrs 

Location: In the White Mountain National Forest and Crawford Notch State Park, north of Bartlett and south of Twin Mountain; Northern New Hampshire map page 86, grid e3.

User groups: Hikers and dogs. No wheelchair facilities. This trail may be difficult to snowshoe because of severe winter weather, and is not suitable for skis. Bikes, horses, and hunting are prohibited.

Access, fees: Parking and access are free.

Directions: Park in the turnout on the west side of U.S. 302, 3.9 miles south of the Crawford Notch hostel, at the access road to the Ripley Falls Trail, and 1.3 miles north of the access road for Arethusa Falls.

Maps: Several maps cover hiking trails in this area, including the "Mount Washington Range" map 6 and the "Franconia" map 5 from the Appalachian Mountain Club (800-262-4455), which are $2.95 each and are widely available in stores; the "Crawford Notch" map available for $4.50 from Ed Rolfe, Cartographer, P.O. Box 349, Twin Mountain, NH 03595, (603) 788-3019; the "Trail Map and Guide to the White Mountain National Forest," which is $4.95 from the DeLorme Mapping Company, (800) 253-5081; the map of the national forest, available by sending a check for $4 to White Mountain National Forest main office (see address below); and map 2 in the "Map and Guide to the Appalachian Trail in New Hampshire and Vermont," an eight-map set for $10.95 from the Appalachian Trail Conference (see address below). For a topographic map of the area, request Crawford Notch from the USGS.

Contact: White Mountain National Forest Supervisor, 719 North Main Street, Laconia, NH 03246; (603) 528-8721, TDD for hearing impaired (603) 528-8722. Appalachian Trail Conference, P.O. Box 807, Harpers Ferry, WV 25425; (304) 535-6331. New Hampshire Division of Parks and Recreation, Bureau of Trails, P.O. Box 1856, Concord, NH 03302-1856; (603) 271-3254.

Trail notes: This rugged, 9.4-mile hike along a spectacular stretch of the Appalachian Trail follows the brink of the Webster Cliffs high above Crawford Notch, and goes to 4,052-foot Mount Jackson, whose open summit gives views in every direction. From the parking area, cross U.S. 302 to a sign for the Webster Cliffs Trail/Appalachian Trail. The white-blazed trail ascends steadily with good footing at first, then grows steeper and rockier. The first good view comes within two miles, from a wide, flat ledge overlooking the notch and White Mountains to the south and west. (Just before that ledge is a smaller ledge with less-expansive views.)

For a round-trip hike of just four miles, this ledge makes a worthwhile destination. But from there, you can see the next open ledge just two-tenths of a mile farther and a little higher along the ridge, beckoning you onward. The trail continues past several outlooks along the cliffs with sweeping views of the Whites, including the Willey Range across Crawford Notch and Mount Chocorua, the prominent horned peak to the southeast. At 3.3 miles, the AT passes over Mount Webster's 3,910-foot, partly wooded but craggy summit, with excellent views of the notch and mountains from Chocorua to Carrigain—the largest peak in the middle distance to the south—and the Saco River Valley. Descending slightly off Webster, the trail crosses relatively flat and boggy terrain, then slabs up to the open summit of Jackson, 4.7 miles from the trailhead. In my opinion, only one other summit offers a better view of the Southern Presidentials and Mount Washington, and that's Mount Isolation (hike number 29). Head back the same way.

34 Arethusa Falls and Frankenstein Cliff

4.7 mi/3.0 hrs 

Location: In Crawford Notch State Park, north of Bartlett and south of Twin Mountain; Northern New Hampshire map page 86, grid e3.

User groups: Hikers, dogs, and snowshoers. No wheelchair facilities. Dogs must be on a leash. This trail is not suitable for bikes, horses, or skis. Hunting is allowed in season.

Access, fees: Parking and access are free.

Directions: From U.S. 302, 5.2 miles south of the Crawford Notch hostel, turn west onto a paved road at a sign for Arethusa Falls. You can park in the lower lot immediately on the right, or drive two-tenths of a mile and park at the end of the road.

Maps: Several maps cover hiking trails in this area, including the "Mount Washington Range" map 6 and the "Franconia" map 5 from the Appalachian Mountain Club (800-262-4455), which are $2.95 each and are widely available in stores; the "Crawford Notch" map available for $4.50 from Ed Rolfe, Cartographer, P.O. Box 349, Twin Mountain, NH 03595, (603) 788-3019; the "Trail Map and Guide to the White Mountain National Forest," which is $4.95 from the DeLorme Mapping Company, (800) 253-5081; and the map of the national forest, available by sending a check for $4 to White Mountain National Forest main office (see address below). For topographic maps of the area, request Crawford Notch and Stairs Mountain from the USGS.

Contact: White Mountain National Forest Supervisor, 719 North Main Street, Laconia, NH 03246; (603) 528-8721, TDD for hearing impaired (603) 528-8722. New Hampshire Division of Parks and Recreation, P.O. Box 1856, Concord, NH 03302-1856; (603) 271-3254.

Trail notes: This fairly easy loop of 4.7 miles takes in both New Hampshire's highest waterfall and the nice view from the top of Frankenstein Cliff. From the far end of the lower parking lot, you can pick up a connector trail to the upper lot. There, follow the Arethusa Falls Trail for a tenth of a mile, then turn left onto the Bemis Brook Trail, which parallels the Arethusa Trail for a half mile and eventually rejoins it, but is more interesting for the short cascades it passes—Bemis Falls and Colesium Falls—as well as Fawn Pool. After reaching the Arethusa Trail again, turn left and continue uphill another eight-tenths of a mile to the base of the magnificent falls, more than 200 feet tall.

Many hikers return the same way, making for a 2.8-mile round-trip. But this hike crosses the stream below the falls on rocks, following the Arethusa-Ripley Falls Trail, which crosses another stream on rocks within three-tenths of a mile (which could be difficult in high water). At 1.3 miles from Arethusa Falls, bear right onto the Frankenstein Cliff Trail and continue eight-tenths of a mile to a ledge atop the cliffs with a view south of the lower end of Crawford Notch and the Saco Valley. Descend steeply another 1.3 miles on the Frankenstein Cliff Trail to the parking area. See the special note in the trail notes for Ripley Falls (hike number 35) for a loop hike incorporating both waterfalls.

35 Ripley Falls

1.0 mi/0.75 hr 

Location: In Crawford Notch State Park, north of Bartlett and south of Twin Mountain; Northern New Hampshire map page 86, grid e3.

User groups: Hikers, dogs, and snowshoers. No wheelchair facilities. This trail is not suitable for skis. Bikes, horses, and hunting are prohibited.

Access, fees: Parking and access are free.

Directions: From U.S. 302, 3.9 miles south of the Crawford Notch hostel, turn south onto a paved road at a sign for Ripley Falls. Drive three-tenths of a mile and park at the end of the road.

Maps: Several maps cover hiking trails in this area, including the "Mount Washington Range" map 6 and the "Franconia" map 5 from the Appalachian Mountain Club (800-262-4455), which are $2.95 each and are widely available in stores; the "Crawford Notch" map available for $4.50 from Ed Rolfe, Cartographer, P.O. Box 349, Twin Mountain, NH 03595, (603) 788-3019; the "Trail Map and Guide to the White Mountain National Forest," which is $4.95 from the DeLorme Mapping Company, (800) 253-5081; the map of the national forest, available by sending a check for $4 to White Mountain National Forest main office (see address below); and map 3 in the "Map and Guide to the Appalachian Trail in New Hampshire and Vermont," an eight-map set for $10.95 from the Appalachian Trail Conference (see address below). For a topographic map of the area, request Crawford Notch from the USGS.

Contact: White Mountain National Forest Supervisor, 719 North Main Street, Laconia,

NH 03246; (603) 528-8721, TDD for hearing impaired (603) 528-8722. Appalachian Trail Conference, P.O. Box 807, Harpers Ferry, WV 25425; (304) 535-6331. New Hampshire Division of Parks and Recreation, P.O. Box 1856, Concord, NH 03302-1856; (603) 271-3254.

Trail notes: This hike in Crawford Notch State Park begins on the Ethan Pond Trail, which coincides with the Appalachian Trail. Within 100 feet of the parking lot, cross railroad tracks and climb steadily uphill on an easy, wide trail. It passes through an area of tall birch trees at two-tenths of a mile, and then forks; the Ethan Pond Trail/AT bears right, but go left onto the Ripley Falls Trail. Continue three-tenths of a mile to the beautiful, cascading falls which tumble from a height of more than 100 feet and are most impressive in late spring and early summer. Return the way you came.

Special note: You can combine this hike with the hike of Arethusa Falls (hike number 34) on a loop of 4.3 miles (about three hours); shuttling vehicles is necessary. Start by hiking to Arethusa. After passing that waterfall, bear left onto the Arethusa-Ripley Falls Trail (instead of right onto the Frankenstein Cliff Trail, as that hike describes) and follow it to Ripley Falls, then descend the Ripley Falls Trail.

36 Ethan Pond/ Thoreau Falls

10.4 mi/7.0 hrs 

Location: In the White Mountain National Forest, between Zealand Notch and Crawford Notch; Northern New Hampshire map page 86, grid e3.

User groups: Hikers, dogs, skiers, and snowshoers. No wheelchair facilities. Bikes, horses, and hunting are prohibited.

Access, fees: Parking and access are free. The Appalachian Mountain Club operates the Ethan Pond shelter, located just off the Ethan Pond Trail, 2.6 miles from U.S. 302 in Crawford Notch. A caretaker collects the $5 nightly fee from late spring through fall.

Directions: From U.S. 302, 3.9 miles south of the Crawford Notch hostel, turn south onto a paved road at a sign for Ripley Falls. Drive three-tenths of a mile and park at the end of the road.

Maps: Several maps cover hiking trails in this area, including the "Franconia" map 5 from the Appalachian Mountain Club (800-262-4455), which is $2.95 and widely available in stores; the "Trail Map and Guide to the White Mountain National Forest," which is $4.95 from the DeLorme Mapping Company, (800) 253-5081; the map of the national forest, available by sending a check for $4 to White Mountain National Forest main office (see address below); and map 3 in the "Map and Guide to the Appalachian Trail in New Hampshire and Vermont," an eight-map set for $10.95 from the Appalachian Trail Conference (see address below). For a topographic map of the area, request Crawford Notch from the USGS.

Contact: White Mountain National Forest Supervisor, 719 North Main Street, Laconia, NH 03246; (603) 528-8721, TDD for hearing impaired (603) 528-8722. Appalachian Trail Conference, P.O. Box 807, Harpers Ferry, WV 25425; (304) 535-6331. New Hampshire Division of Parks and Recreation, P.O. Box 1856, Concord, NH 03302-1856; (603) 271-3254.

Trail notes: This moderate day hike—much of it following a flat section of the Appalachian Trail—begins at one of New Hampshire's most spectacular notches, and takes in a popular backcountry pond and towering waterfall. With a short, easy detour off this route, you can also take in a second notch. I like doing this hike on snowshoes in winter, when Thoreau Falls transforms into a giant staircase of ice; the trail may even be sufficiently packed down by other hikers that you won't need snowshoes.

From the parking area in Crawford Notch State Park, follow the white blazes of the Appalachian Trail, which coincides here with the Ethan Pond Trail. After crossing railroad tracks, the trail climbs steadily. At two-tenths of a mile, in a stand of tall birch trees, the trail to Ripley Falls (a worthwhile side trip of two-tenths of a mile; see hike number 35) branches left. But this hike veers right, toward Ethan Pond. At 1.6 miles, the Willey Range Trail continues north; turn left (west) with the Ethan Pond Trail/AT, which soon flattens out. A mile farther, turn right onto the side path leading about a tenth of a mile to scenic Ethan Pond. (You can cross the pond on stones to the AMC's Ethan Pond shelter.) Back on the Ethan Pond Trail, continue west on flat ground another 2.5 miles, then turn left onto the Thoreau Falls Trail for the tenth-of-a-mile walk to the waterfall. On the way back, you might want to add about a half mile to this hike by following the Ethan Pond Trail into the southern end of spectacular Zealand Notch. Hike back along the same route.

37 Zealand Notch/ Willey Range

17.0 mi/2–3 days 

Location: In the White Mountain National Forest southeast of Twin Mountain; Northern New Hampshire map page 86, grid e3.

User groups: Hikers and dogs. No wheelchair facilities. This trail may be difficult to snowshoe because of severe winter weather, and is not suitable for bikes, horses, or skis. Hunting is allowed in season, except along the Appalachian Trail, which coincides with the Twinway and the Ethan Pond Trail.

Access, fees: Parking and access are free. Zealand Road is not maintained in winter; the winter parking lot is on U.S. 302, immediately east of Zealand Road. The Appalachian Mountain Club operates the Zealand Falls hut year-round; it is on the Twinway, two-tenths of a mile from the junction of the Zealand, Twinway, and Ethan Pond Trails, and 2.7 miles from the end of Zealand Road. Contact the AMC (see address below) for information on cost and reservations. The AMC also operates the first-come, first-served Ethan Pond shelter, located just off the Ethan Pond Trail, 7.3 miles from the Zealand Road parking lot along this hike's route. A caretaker collects the $5 nightly fee from late spring through fall.

Directions: From the junction of U.S. 3 and U.S. 302 in Twin Mountain, drive east on U.S. 302 for 2.3 miles and turn right onto Zealand Road. Continue 3.5 miles to a parking lot at the end of the road.

Maps: Several maps cover hiking trails in this area, including the "Franconia" map 5 from the Appalachian Mountain Club (800-262-4455), which is $2.95 and widely available in stores; the "Trail Map and Guide to the White Mountain National Forest," which is $4.95 from the DeLorme Mapping Company, (800) 253-5081; the map of the national forest, available by sending a check for $4 to White Mountain National Forest main office (see address below); and map 3 in the "Map and Guide to the Appalachian Trail in New Hampshire and Vermont," an eight-map set for $10.95 from the Appalachian Trail Conference (see address below). For a topographic map of the area, request Crawford Notch from the USGS.

Contact: White Mountain National Forest Supervisor, 719 North Main Street, Laconia, NH 03246; (603) 528-8721, TDD for hearing impaired (603) 528-8722. Appalachian Mountain Club, P.O. Box 298, Gorham, NH 03581; (603) 466-2721. Appalachian Trail

Conference, P.O. Box 807, Harpers Ferry, WV 25425; (304) 535-6331.

Trail notes: This 17-mile loop, best spread over two to three days, passes through spectacular Zealand Notch and traverses the Willey Range, a less well-known corner of the Whites with a pair of 4,000-foot peaks and rugged terrain, if limited views. Two friends and I made this trip one Thanksgiving weekend, hiking through the notch on a chilly but calm night under a full moon, and enjoying views from Mount Willey of clouds swirling around the Presidentials before a storm blew in and "dampened" our spirits with a cold, driving rain.

From the Zealand Road parking lot, follow the Zealand Trail south, paralleling the Zealand River. At 2.3 miles, the A-Z Trail enters from the left; you will return on that trail. The Zealand Trail reaches a junction with the Twinway and the Ethan Pond Trail at 2.5 miles. The AMC's Zealand Falls hut lies two-tenths of a mile uphill on the Twinway; on the way, you pass a short side path to a view of Zealand Falls, and there are views of the notch from the hut. This hike bears left onto the Ethan Pond Trail, which runs for two miles to the opposite end of the notch, passing numerous overlooks through the trees. Reaching the Thoreau Falls Trail at 4.6 miles, bear right and follow it for a tenth of a mile to Thoreau Falls, which tumbles more than 100 feet down through several steps. Backtrack and turn right (east) on the Ethan Pond Trail, which follows level ground for 2.5 miles to the side path leading left less than a tenth of a mile to Ethan Pond and the shelter just above the pond.

A mile beyond that junction, turn left (north) onto the Willey Range Trail, which soon begins a steep and sustained climb—employing wooden ladders in spots—of 1.1 miles up 4,302-foot Mount Willey, where there are some views from just below the summit. The trail continues north, dropping into a saddle, then ascending to the 4,326-foot summit of Mount Field—named for Darby Field, the first person known to climb Mount Washington—1.4 miles from Willey's summit. Field is wooded, with no views. Just beyond the summit, the Avalon Trail branches right, but stay left with the Willey Range Trail, descending steadily to the A-Z Trail, nine-tenths of a mile from the summit of Field. Turn left (west), descending easily for 2.7 miles to the Zealand Trail. Turn right (north) and walk 2.5 miles back to the Zealand Road parking lot.

38 Zealand Notch

7.6 mi/5.0 hrs 

Location: In the White Mountain National Forest southeast of Twin Mountain; Northern New Hampshire map page 86, grid e3.

User groups: Hikers, dogs, skiers, and snowshoers. No wheelchair facilities. Bikes and horses are prohibited. Hunting is allowed in season, except along the Appalachian Trail, which coincides with the Twinway and the Ethan Pond Trail.

Access, fees: Parking and access are free. Zealand Road is not maintained in winter. The Appalachian Mountain Club operates the Zealand Falls hut year-round; it is on the Twinway, two-tenths of a mile from the junction of the Zealand, Twinway, and Ethan Pond Trails, and 2.7 miles from the end of Zealand Road. Contact the AMC (see address below) for information on cost and reservations.

Directions: From the junction of U.S. 3 and U.S. 302 in Twin Mountain, drive east on U.S. 302 for 2.3 miles and turn right onto Zealand Road. Continue 3.5 miles to a parking lot at the end of the road. The winter parking lot is on U.S. 302, a tenth of a mile east of Zealand Road.

Maps: Several maps cover hiking trails in this area, including the "Franconia" map 5 from the Appalachian Mountain Club (800-262-4455), which is $2.95 and widely available in stores; the "Trail Map and Guide to the White Mountain National Forest," which is $4.95 from the DeLorme Mapping Company, (800) 253-5081; the map of the national forest, available by sending a check for $4 to White Mountain National Forest main office (see address below); and map 3 in the "Map and Guide to the Appalachian Trail in New Hampshire and Vermont," an eight-map set for $10.95 from the Appalachian Trail Conference (see address below). For a topographic map of the area, request Crawford Notch from the USGS.

Contact: White Mountain National Forest Supervisor, 719 North Main Street, Laconia, NH 03246; (603) 528-8721, TDD for hearing impaired (603) 528-8722. Appalachian Mountain Club, P.O. Box 298, Gorham, NH 03581; (603) 466-2721. Appalachian Trail Conference, P.O. Box 807, Harpers Ferry, WV 25425; (304) 535-6331.

Trail notes: In part due to the convenience provided by the Appalachian Mountain Club's Zealand Falls hut, but also simply for its splendor, Zealand Notch ranks as one of the most visited spots in the White Mountains year-round. Although the trail tends to be muddy, this is a nice hike in summer and fall. On snowshoes or cross-country skis in winter, however, it's arguably even more beautiful. The Zealand Road is not maintained in winter—you have to ski or snowshoe up it—making the round-trip distance into the notch 14.6 miles, instead of 7.6 miles. On skis, the trail is easy to moderately difficult, though possible for an experienced cross-country skier to do in one day, without metal-edged skis. Two friends and I skied to the hut one bitterly cold December Sunday after a series of storms had dumped at least a few feet of dry powder in the mountains. The forest wore a thick comforter of white which smothered all sound, and the skiing was fabulous.

From the end of Zealand Road, follow the Zealand Trail south, paralleling the Zealand River. At 2.3 miles, the A-Z Trail diverges left. Continuing on the Zealand Trail, you reach the junction with the Twinway and the Ethan Pond Trail at 2.5 miles. The AMC's Zealand Falls hut lies two-tenths of a mile to the right on the Twinway (adding four-tenths of a mile to this hike's distance). Continue straight ahead onto the Ethan Pond Trail into Zealand Notch. After about a mile, the trail breaks out of the woods and traverses a shelf across the boulder field left behind by an old rockslide on the side of Whitewall Mountain, and the views of Zealand Notch are spectacular. Cross this open area to where the Ethan Pond Trail reenters the woods, near the junction with the Zeacliff Trail, 1.3 miles from the Twinway/Zealand Trail junction. Return the way you came.

Special note: For the ambitious, or those with more time because they are spending a night at the Zealand Falls hut, hiking all the way to Thoreau Falls would add 1.6 miles round-trip to this hike. Continue on the Ethan Pond Trail beyond the Zeacliff Trail junction for seven-tenths of a mile, then bear right onto the Thoreau Falls Trail. In another tenth of a mile, the trail reaches the top of the falls, which drops more than 100 feet through several steps and creates a very impressive cascade of ice in winter.

39 Zealand Notch: Twins Loop

16.1 mi. one way/
2.0 days

Location: In the White Mountain National Forest south of Twin Mountain; Northern New Hampshire map page 86, grid e3.

User groups: Hikers and dogs. No wheelchair facilities. This trail may be difficult to snowshoe because of severe winter weather, and is not suitable for bikes, horses, or skis. Hunting is allowed in season, except along the Appalachian Trail, which coincides with the Twinway.

Directions: You will need to shuttle two vehicles for this trip. To reach this hike's endpoint from the junction of U.S. 302 and U.S. 3 in Twin Mountain, drive south on U.S. 3 for 2.5 miles and turn left onto Haystack Road (Fire Road 304). Or, from Interstate 93 north of Franconia Notch State Park, take exit 35 for U.S. 3 north and continue about 7.5 miles, then turn right onto Fire Road 304. Follow Fire Road 304 to its end and a parking area at the trailhead. Leave one vehicle there. To reach the start of this hike from the junction of U.S. 3 and U.S. 302 in Twin Mountain, drive east on U.S. 302 for 2.3 miles and turn right onto Zealand Road. Continue 3.5 miles to a parking lot at the end of the road.

Access, fees: Parking and access are free. Zealand Road is not maintained in winter; the winter parking lot is on U.S. 302, immediately east of Zealand Road. The Appalachian Mountain Club operates the Zealand Falls hut year-round; it is on the Twinway, two-tenths of a mile from the junction of the Zealand, Twinway, and Ethan Pond Trails, and 2.7 miles from the end of Zealand Road. Contact the AMC (see address below) for information on cost and reservations. The AMC also operates the first-come, first-served Guyot campsite, with a shelter and several tent platforms, located just off the Bondcliff Trail eight-tenths of a mile from the Twinway on Mount Guyot. A caretaker collects the $5 nightly fee from late spring through fall.

Maps: Several maps cover hiking trails in this area, including the "Franconia" map 5 from the Appalachian Mountain Club (800-262-4455), which is $2.95 and widely available in stores; the "Trail Map and Guide to the White Mountain National Forest," which is $4.95 from the DeLorme Mapping Company, (800) 253-5081; and the map of the national forest, available by sending a check for $4 to White Mountain National Forest main office (see address below). For topographic maps of the area, request Mount Washington, Bethlehem, South Twin Mountain, and Crawford Notch from the USGS.

Contact: White Mountain National Forest Supervisor, 719 North Main Street, Laconia, NH 03246; (603) 528-8721, TDD for hearing impaired (603) 528-8722. Appalachian Mountain Club, P.O. Box 298, Gorham, NH 03581; (603) 466-2721.

Trail notes: This moderately difficult 16-mile trek was one of my first overnight trips in the White Mountains. With superb views, lots of relatively easy terrain, and a reasonable distance to cover in two days, it's a fairly popular weekend loop for backpackers. From the Zealand Road parking lot, follow the relatively easy Zealand Trail for 2.5 miles to its junction with the Ethan Pond Trail and the Twinway. Turn right onto the Twinway, which coincides with the Appalachian Trail, climbing two-tenths of a mile to the AMC's Zealand Falls hut.

Beyond the hut, the Twinway passes nice cascades and the Lend-a-Hand Trail junction, climbing high above Zealand Notch. Where the trail takes a right turn 3.9 miles into this trip, a short side path loops out to the Zeacliff overlook, with a spectacular view of Zealand Notch and mountains from Carrigain to the south, to Mount Washington and the Presidential Range to the northeast. Just a tenth of a mile farther up the Twinway, the Zeacliff Trail departs to the left, descending steeply into the notch. The Twinway traverses more level terrain on Zealand Mountain, passing a side path 4.4 miles into this hike which leads left a tenth of a mile to Zeacliff Pond; and, after a short climb above the pond, passes a side path at 5.6 miles which leads right a flat tenth of a mile to the summit of 4,260-foot Zealand Mountain. The Twinway then dips and climbs again to the flat, open summit of Mount Guyot, with views in every direction.

At 8.1 miles, the Twinway bears right and the Bondcliff Trail diverges left (south); the Guyot campsite, a logical stop for the night, is eight-tenths of a mile distant along that trail and a side path marked by a sign. (The 1.6 miles round-trip to the campsite is figured into this hike's total distance.) Following the Twinway, you will traverse easy terrain, then climb more steeply the final short stretch up South Twin Mountain, 8.9 miles into this trek, at 4,902 feet the highest point on this trip and the eighth-highest mountain in New Hampshire. The views span much of the Pemigewasset Wilderness and stretch to the Presidential Range. Turn north off the Twinway onto the North Twin Spur, descending into a saddle, then climbing to the wooded and viewless summit of North Twin Mountain (4,761 feet), 1.3 miles from South Twin's summit and 10.2 miles into this trek. Turn right onto the North Twin Trail, soon emerging from the trees onto open ledges with some of the nicest views on this trip. The trail descends, quite steeply for long stretches, for two miles to the Little River; it then swings left and follows an old railroad bed along the river for more than two miles to the parking area where your second vehicle awaits.

40 North Twin Mountain

8.6 mi/6.0 hrs 

Location: In the White Mountain National Forest south of Twin Mountain; Northern New Hampshire map page 86, grid e3.

User groups: Hikers and dogs. No wheelchair facilities. This trail may be difficult to snowshoe because of severe winter weather, and is not suitable for bikes, horses, or skis. Hunting is allowed in season.

Access, fees: Parking and access are free.

Directions: From the junction of U.S. 302 and U.S. 3 in Twin Mountain, drive south on U.S. 3 for 2.5 miles and turn left onto Haystack Road (Fire Road 304). Or, from Interstate 93 north of Franconia Notch State Park, take exit 35 for U.S. 3 north and continue about 7.5 miles, then turn right onto Fire Road 304. Follow Fire Road 304 to its end and a parking area at the trailhead for the North Twin Trail.

Maps: For a map of hiking trails, get the "Franconia" map 5, which is $2.95 from the Appalachian Mountain Club, (800) 262-4455, and is also widely available in stores. Or get the "Trail Map and Guide to the White Mountain National Forest," which is $4.95 from the DeLorme Mapping Company, (800) 253-5081. For topographic maps of the area, request Bethlehem and South Twin Mountain from the USGS.

Contact: White Mountain National Forest Supervisor, 719 North Main Street, Laconia, NH 03246; (603) 528-8721, TDD for the hearing impaired (603) 528-8722.

Trail notes: Although it is the 12th-highest mountain in New Hampshire at 4,761 feet, North Twin lies sufficiently out of the way and attracts far fewer hikers than its neighbors, such as Franconia Ridge and Zealand Notch. Every time I've stood atop this mountain, my only company was my own companions. But from open ledges just below its summit, you get a commanding view south over the Pemigewasset Wilderness, east toward the Presidential Range, and west to Franconia.

Take the North Twin Trail for 4.3 miles to the summit. It follows an old railroad bed along the Little River for more than two miles, then turns sharply west and makes a fairly steep and sustained ascent of the mountain's east side. The trail emerges abruptly from the scrub forest onto the ledges, more than four miles from the trailhead. Just a few hundred feet farther lies the summit, which is wooded, and the junction with the North Twin Spur Trail. Hike back the same way.

41 Galehead Mountain

10.2 mi/7.0 hrs 

Location: In the White Mountain National Forest south of Twin Mountain; Northern New Hampshire map page 86, grid e3.

User groups: Hikers and dogs. No wheelchair facilities. This trail may be difficult to snowshoe because of severe winter weather, and is not suitable for skis. Bikes, horses, and hunting are prohibited.

Access, fees: Parking and access are free. The Appalachian Mountain Club (see address below) operates the Galehead hut, where a crew prepares meals and guests share bunkrooms and bathrooms. The hut lies at the western end of the trail called the Twinway, about 100 feet from the junction of the Twinway and the Garfield Ridge Trail; contact the AMC (see address below) for reservation and rate information.

Directions: From Interstate 93 north of Franconia Notch State Park, take exit 35 for U.S. 3 north. Drive about 4.8 miles, and then turn right onto the dirt Fire Road 25 at a sign for the Gale River Trail. Or, from the junction of U.S. 3 and U.S. 302 in Twin Mountain, drive south on U.S. 3 for 5.3 miles and turn left on Fire Road 25. Follow Fire Road 25 for 1.3 miles and turn right onto Fire Road 92. Continue three-tenths of a mile to a parking area on the left for the Gale River Trail.

Maps: For a contour map of hiking trails, get the "Franconia" map 5, which is $2.95 from the Appalachian Mountain Club, (800) 262-4455, and is also widely available in stores. Or get the "Trail Map and Guide to the White Mountain National Forest," which is $4.95 from the DeLorme Mapping Company, (800) 253-5081. For topographic maps of the area, request South Twin Mountain and Bethlehem from the USGS.

Contact: White Mountain National Forest Supervisor, 719 North Main Street, Laconia, NH 03246; (603) 528-8721, TDD for the hearing impaired (603) 528-8722. Appalachian Mountain Club, P.O. Box 298, Gorham, NH 03581; (603) 466-2727. Appalachian Trail Conference, P.O. Box 807, Harpers Ferry, WV 25425; (304) 535-6331.

Trail notes: Galehead Mountain, despite being an "official" 4,000-footer, attracts few hikers because trees cover its 4,024-foot summit, blocking any views. There is a good view of the tight valley of Twin Brook and a ridge of South Twin Mountain, however, from an overlook halfway between the Galehead hut and the summit on the Frost Trail. For visitors to the Galehead hut, the summit demands no more than a fairly easy one-mile hike—one that promises an opportunity for some quiet.

From the parking area, follow the Gale River Trail, a wide and relatively flat path until right before it crosses the North Branch of the Gale River—over a wooden footbridge—at about 1.5 miles. For more than a mile beyond that bridge the trail parallels the river, one of this 10-mile hike's most appealing stretches. It then makes a second river crossing on rocks, which could be difficult in high water. Four miles from the trailhead, the Gale River Trail ends at a junction with the Garfield Ridge Trail, which coincides with the Appalachian Trail. Bear left on the Ridge Trail and follow it another six-tenths of a mile to its junction with the Twinway. Turn right for the Galehead hut. Behind the hut, pick up the Frost Trail, which leads a half mile to Galehead's summit. A short side path a quarter mile from the hut leads to the overlook described above. Descend the same way you came up. For a longer hike combining Galehead and Mount Garfield, see the special note in the trail notes for Mount Garfield (hike number 42).

42 Mount Garfield

10.0 mi/7.0 hrs 

Location: In the White Mountain National Forest south of Twin Mountain; Northern New Hampshire map page 86, grid e3.

User groups: Hikers and dogs. No wheelchair facilities. This trail may be difficult to snowshoe because of severe winter weather, and is not suitable for skis. Bikes, horses, and hunting are prohibited.

Access, fees: Parking and access are free. The Appalachian Mountain Club (see address below) operates the Garfield Ridge campsite (a shelter and seven tent platforms), reached via a 200-yard spur trail off the Garfield Ridge Trail two-tenths of a mile east of its junction with the Garfield Trail. A caretaker collects the $5-per-person nightly fee from late spring through fall.

Directions: From Interstate 93 north of Franconia Notch State Park, take exit 35 for U.S. 3 north and continue about 4.5 miles, then turn right on the dirt Fire Road 92. Or, from the junction of U.S. 3 and U.S. 302 in Twin Mountain, drive south on U.S. 3 for 5.6 miles and turn left on Fire Road 92. Follow Fire Road 92 for 1.3 miles to a parking area on the right for the Garfield Trail.

Maps: For a map of hiking trails, get the "Franconia" map 5, which is $2.95 from the Appalachian Mountain Club, (800) 262-4455, and is also widely available in stores. Or get the "Trail Map and Guide to the White Mountain National Forest," which is $4.95 from the DeLorme Mapping Company, (800) 253-5081. For topographic maps of the area, request South Twin Mountain and Bethlehem from the USGS.

Contact: White Mountain National Forest Supervisor, 719 North Main Street, Laconia, NH 03246; (603) 528-8721, TDD for the hearing impaired (603) 528-8722. Appalachian Mountain Club, P.O. Box 298, Gorham, NH 03581; (603) 466-2727. Appalachian Trail Conference, P.O. Box 807, Harpers Ferry, WV 25425; (304) 535-6331.

Trail notes: Holding down the northwest corner of the Pemigewasset Wilderness in the White Mountains, the craggy, 4,500-foot summit of Garfield gives views in all directions, taking in Franconia Ridge to the southwest, the wooded mound of Owl's Head directly south, the Bonds and Mount Carrigain to the southeast, the valley of the Ammonoosuc River to the north, and Galehead Mountain, as well as the long ridge comprising North and South Twin Mountains due east. When weather permits, you will see peaks of the Presidential Range poking above the Twins. The foundation of an old fire tower remains on Garfield's summit. I had been hiking for years in the Whites before finally hoofing it up Garfield—and discovered views as nice as many of my favorite summits in these mountains. The hike up the Garfield Trail, while fairly long and gaining nearly 3,000 feet in elevation, never gets oppressively steep.

From the parking area, follow the Garfield Trail, which for a short time parallels Spruce Brook on its steady ascent through woods. The path is wide and obvious. At 4.8 miles, the trail terminates at the Garfield Ridge Trail, which is part of the white-blazed Appalachian Trail. To the left (east) on the Garfield Ridge Trail, it's two-tenths of a mile to the spur trail to the Garfield Ridge campsite. The summit lies two-tenths of a mile to the right (west). Descend the same way you came up.

Special note: Mount Garfield and Galehead Mountain (hike number 41) can be combined on a loop of 13.5 miles, in which they are linked by hiking 2.7 miles along the Garfield Ridge Trail between the Garfield Trail and the Gale River Trail. The best way to do the loop is to begin on the Gale River Trail and descend the Garfield Trail; that way you will ascend, rather than descend, the often slick, steep, and rocky stretch of the Garfield Ridge Trail east of Mount Garfield. The Gale River Trail and Garfield Trail both begin on Fire Road 92, 1.6 miles apart (a distance not figured into the 13.5-mile loop).

43 Cannon Mountain

4.4 mi/3.0 hrs 

Location: In Franconia Notch State Park, north of Lincoln and south of Franconia; Northern New Hampshire map page 86, grid e2.

User groups: Hikers and dogs. No wheelchair facilities. Dogs must be on a leash. This trail may be difficult to snowshoe because of severe winter weather, and is not suitable for bikes, horses, or skis. Hunting is allowed in season, but not near trails.

Access, fees: Parking and access are free.

Directions: The hike begins from the tramway parking lot at exit 2 off Interstate 93, at the north end of Franconia Notch. Look for a sign for the Kinsman Ridge Trail.

Maps: Several maps cover hiking trails in this area, including the "Franconia" map 5 from the Appalachian Mountain Club, (800) 262-4455, which is $2.95 and widely available in stores; the "Franconia Notch" map available for $4.50 from Ed Rolfe, Cartographer, P.O. Box 349, Twin Mountain, NH 03595, (603) 788-3019; the "Trail Map and Guide to the White Mountain National Forest," which is $4.95 from the DeLorme Mapping Company, (800) 253-5081; the map of the national forest, available by sending a check for $4 to White Mountain National Forest main office (see address below); and map 3 in the "Map and Guide to the Appalachian Trail in New Hampshire and Vermont," an eight-map set for $10.95 from the Appalachian Trail Conference (see address below). For a topographic map of the area, request Franconia from the USGS.

Contact: Franconia Notch State Park, Franconia, NH 03580; (603) 823-5563. New Hampshire Division of Parks and Recreation, P.O. Box 1856, Concord, NH 03302-1856; (603) 271-3254. Appalachian Trail Conference, P.O. Box 807, Harpers Ferry, WV 25425; (304) 535-6331.

Trail notes: Cannon Mountain (4,077 feet) stands out at the north end of spectacular Franconia Notch because of the 1,000-foot cliff on its east face—a cliff famous for the Old Man of the Mountains, a stone profile visible from parking lots in the notch's north end. This moderate hike of 4.4 miles round-trip leads to the excellent views from Cannon's summit.

From the parking lot, follow the Kinsman Ridge Trail through a picnic area and briefly along a ski area trail before entering the woods. The trail ascends at a moderate grade, passing a short side path at 1.5 miles which leads to open ledges and a nice view across the notch to Franconia Ridge. The Kinsman Ridge Trail swings right, soon climbing more steeply to the summit, where there is an observation platform and the summit tramway station. To the east, the views extend to Mounts Lafayette and Lincoln. To the west, on a clear day, you can see Vermont's Green Mountains and New York's Adirondacks. Head back along the same route.

44 Lonesome Lake

3.2 mi/2.0 hrs 

Location: In Franconia Notch State Park, north of Lincoln and south of Franconia; Northern New Hampshire map page 86, grid e2.

User groups: Hikers and dogs. No wheelchair facilities. Dogs must be on a leash. This trail may be difficult to snowshoe because of severe winter weather, and is not suitable for bikes, horses, or skis. Hunting is allowed in season, but not near trails.

Access, fees: Parking and access are free. The Appalachian Mountain Club operates the Lonesome Lake hut on the Fishin' Jimmy Trail near Lonesome Lake; contact the AMC for reservation and rate information (see address below).

Directions: Drive to one of the large parking lots on the east and west side of Interstate 93 at the Lafayette Place Campground in Franconia Notch State Park. From the east side parking lot, hikers can cross under the highway to the Lafayette Place Campground on the west side, where the trail begins.

Maps: For a contour map of trails, obtain the "Franconia" map 5 from the Appalachian Mountain Club, (800) 262-4455, which is $2.95 and widely available in stores; the "Franconia Notch" map available for $4.50 from Ed Rolfe, Cartographer, P.O. Box 349, Twin Mountain, NH 03595, (603) 788-3019; or map 3 in the "Map and Guide to the Appalachian Trail in New Hampshire and Vermont," an eight-map set for $10.95 from the Appalachian Trail Conference (see address below). For a topographic map of the area, request Franconia from the USGS.

Contact: Franconia Notch State Park, Franconia, NH 03580; (603) 823-5563. New Hampshire Division of Parks and Recreation, P.O. Box 1856, Concord, NH 03302-1856; (603) 271-3254. Appalachian Mountain Club, P.O. Box 298, Gorham, NH 03581; (603) 466-2721. Appalachian Trail Conference, P.O. Box 807, Harpers Ferry, WV 25425; (304) 535-6331.

Trail notes: Lonesome Lake's name gives a newcomer to Franconia Notch no forewarning of the crowds that flock to this scenic mountain tarn; nonetheless, if you accept the likelihood of sharing this beautiful spot with dozens of other visitors, the view from the lake's southwest corner across its crystal waters to Mounts Lafayette and Lincoln on Franconia Ridge has no comparison. This trail passes through extensive boggy areas, which, combined with the heavy foot traffic it sees, can make for a muddy hike.

From the parking lot, pick up the Lonesome Lake Trail, which crosses Lafayette Place Campground, and ascends at a moderate grade for 1.2 miles to the northeast corner of the lake. Turn left (south) on the Cascade Brook Trail, following it nearly three-tenths of a mile to the south end of the lake. Turn right on the Fishin' Jimmy Trail, crossing the lake's outlet and reaching a small beach area where people often swim in the lake. The AMC hut lies a short distance off the lake, in the woods. Bear right off the Fishin' Jimmy Trail onto the Around-Lonesome-Lake Trail, which heads north along the lake's west shore, crossing boggy areas on boardwalks. In three-tenths of a mile, turn right (east) on the Lonesome Lake Trail and follow it 1.4 miles back to the campground.

45 North and South Kinsman

11.1 mi/8.0 hrs

Location: In the White Mountain National Forest and Franconia Notch State Park, north of Lincoln and south of Franconia; Northern New Hampshire map page 86, grid e2.

User groups: Hikers and dogs. No wheelchair facilities. This trail may be difficult to snowshoe because of severe winter weather, and is not suitable for skis. Bikes, horses, and hunting are prohibited.

Access, fees: Parking and access are free. This hike begins in Franconia Notch State Park, but much of it lies within the White

Mountain National Forest. The Appalachian Mountain Club operates the Kinsman Pond campsite, with a shelter and three tent platforms, located along the Kinsman Pond Trail, a tenth of a mile from Kinsman Junction and 4.5 miles from the Basin following this route. A caretaker collects the $5 nightly fee during the warmer months. The AMC also operates the Lonesome Lake hut, where a crew prepares meals and guests share bunkrooms and bathrooms; contact the AMC (see address below) for reservation and rate information.

Directions: From Interstate 93 in Franconia Notch, take the exit for the Basin. There are separate parking lots on the northbound and southbound sides of the highway; see trail notes below for details on locating the trailhead from each lot.

Maps: For a map of hiking trails, obtain the "Franconia" map 5, which is $2.95 from the Appalachian Mountain Club, (800) 262-4455, and is also widely available in stores; the "Trail Map and Guide to the White Mountain National Forest," which is $4.95 from the DeLorme Mapping Company, (800) 253-5081; or map 3 in the "Map and Guide to the Appalachian Trail in New Hampshire and Vermont," an eight-map set for $10.95 from the Appalachian Trail Conference (see address below). For topographic maps of the area, request Franconia and Lincoln from the USGS.

Contact: White Mountain National Forest Supervisor, 719 North Main Street, Laconia, NH 03246; (603) 528-8721, TDD for the hearing impaired (603) 528-8722. New Hampshire Department of Resources and Economic Development, Division of Parks and Recreation, Trails Bureau, P.O. Box 1856, Concord, NH 03302; (603) 271-3254. Appalachian Mountain Club, P.O. Box 298, Gorham, NH 03581; (603) 466-2727. Appalachian Trail Conference, P.O. Box 807, Harpers Ferry, WV 25425; (304) 535-6331.

Trail notes: Rising high above Franconia Notch, opposite the 5,000-foot peaks Lafayette and Lincoln, Kinsman Mountain's two distinct peaks offer good views of the notch. But the more popular attractions of this 11.1-mile hike are the 1.5 miles of falls and cascades along Cascade Brook, and the views across Lonesome Lake to Franconia Ridge. Many hikers, especially families with young children, explore only as far as the brook—a refreshing place on a hot summer day—but steer clear of the drops. Most of the stream crossings on this hike utilize rocks or downed trees, and can be difficult at times of high water. Also, the heavily used trails described here are often wet and muddy, making rocks and exposed roots slick and footing difficult.

Begin this hike at the Basin, a natural stone bowl carved out by the Pemigewasset River and a popular spot for tourists. From the parking lot on the northbound side of Interstate 93, follow the signs to the Basin, passing beneath Interstate 93 and crossing a footbridge over the Pemigewasset River. Beyond the bridge, the trail bends right; within 100 feet, bear left at a sign for the Basin-Cascades Trail. From the parking lot on the southbound sign, follow the walkway south to the Basin. Turn right on the bridge over the Pemigewasset and watch for the Basin-Cascades Trail branching left. Follow the Basin-Cascades Trail, where open ledges provide views to Franconia Ridge across the notch. Kinsman Falls lies a half mile up the trail, and Rocky Glen Falls is nine-tenths of a mile up, just a tenth of a mile before the Basin-Cascades Trail meets the Cascade Brook Trail.

From this junction to the summit of 4,356-foot South Kinsman, the hike follows the Appalachian Trail. Turn right (northwest) on the Cascade Brook Trail, immediately crossing the brook on stones or a downed tree. A half mile farther, the Kinsman Pond Trail bears left and crosses Cascade Brook; bear right and continue roughly north on the Cascade Brook Trail another mile to a junction with the Fishin' Jimmy Trail at the south end of Lonesome Lake. Turn left (west) on the Fishin' Jimmy, crossing a log bridge over the lake's outlet to a beachlike area popular for swimming. There's an outstanding view across Lonesome Lake to Franconia Ridge and Mounts Lafayette and Lincoln and Little Haystack (left to right). Stay on the Fishin' Jimmy, passing the AMC's Lonesome Lake hut, which sits back in the woods just above the beach area. The trail rises and falls, passing over the hump separating Lonesome Lake from the upper flanks of Kinsman Mountain. After crossing a feeder stream to Cascade Brook, the trail ascends steeply, often up rock slabs into which wooden steps have been drilled in places. Two miles from Lonesome Lake, the Fishin' Jimmy Trail terminates at Kinsman Junction, a confluence of three trails—and a point you will return to on the descent.

Walk straight (west) onto the Kinsman Ridge Trail, climbing steep rock. Within two-tenths of a mile from Kinsman Junction, you begin to see views back toward Franconia Ridge; you reach the wooded summit of 4,293-foot North Kinsman at four-tenths of a mile. A side path leads 20 feet from the summit cairn to an open ledge with a sweeping view eastward that takes in Cannon Mountain, Lonesome Lake, Franconia Ridge, and the mountains above Waterville Valley. Continue south on the Kinsman Ridge Trail, descending past two open areas with good views. The trail drops into the saddle between the two peaks, then ascends steadily to the broad, flat summit of South Kinsman, nearly a mile from North Kinsman's summit. From various spots on South Kinsman's summit, you have views toward Franconia Ridge, North Kinsman, and Moosilauke to the south.

Backtrack to North Kinsman and descend to Kinsman Junction. Turn right (south) on the Kinsman Pond Trail, reaching the AMC shelter at Kinsman Pond in a tenth of a mile. The trail follows the eastern shore of this scenic mountain tarn, below the summit cone of North Kinsman. It then hooks southeast into the forest, leading steadily downhill and making four stream crossings. It reaches the Cascade Brook Trail 2.5 miles from Kinsman Junction, right after crossing Cascade Brook. Bear right (southeast) onto the Cascade Brook Trail, following it a half mile. Immediately after crossing Cascade Brook again, turn left onto the Basin-Cascades Trail, which leads a mile back to the Basin.

Special note: Some hikers go just to the summit of North Kinsman, skipping the 1.8-mile round-trip hike from North to South Kinsman. This option creates a 9.3-mile hike along the route described here, reducing this hike's time by about 1.5 hours.

46 Franconia Notch: Pemi Trail

5.0 mi. one way/2.5 hrs 1 8

Location: In Franconia Notch State Park, north of Lincoln and south of Franconia; Northern New Hampshire map page 86, grid e2.

User groups: Hikers, dogs, and snowshoers. No wheelchair facilities. Dogs must be on a leash. This trail is not suitable for bikes, horses, or skis. Hunting is allowed in season, but not near trails.

Access, fees: Parking and access are free.

Directions: The trail's endpoints are at the parking area off Interstate 93 at the exit immediately north of The Flume near the south end of Franconia Notch State Park; and the parking area for the Kinsman Ridge Trail, reached via exit 2 at the north end of the notch.

Maps: Obtain the free map of Franconia Notch State Park, available from the state park or the New Hampshire Division of Parks and Recreation (see address below); or the "Franconia Notch" map available for $4.50 from Ed Rolfe, Cartographer, P.O. Box 349, Twin Mountain, NH 03595, (603) 788-3019. For topographic maps of the area, request Franconia and Lincoln from the USGS.

Contact: Franconia Notch State Park, Franconia, NH 03580; (603) 823-5563. New Hampshire Division of Parks and Recreation, P.O. Box 1856, Concord, NH 03302-1856; (603) 271-3254.

Trail notes: The Pemi Trail offers an easy and scenic five-mile, one-way walk through Franconia Notch, with periodic views of the cliffs and peaks flanking the notch. The trail follows the west shore of Profile Lake, with excellent views across the water to Eagle Cliff on Mount Lafayette. When the light is right, you can distinguish a free-standing rock pinnacle in a gully separating two major cliffs on this shoulder of Lafayette; known as the Eaglet, this pinnacle is a destination for rock climbers and has been a nesting site in spring for peregrine falcons. Reaching Lafayette Campground, the trail follows a campground road along the west bank of the Pemigewasset River, then leaves the campground and parallels the river all the way to the water-sculpted rock at the Basin. It crosses the Basin-Cascades Trail, then meets the Cascade Brook Trail before crossing east beneath Interstate 93 and finishing at the parking lot immediately north of the Flume.

47 Mounts Lincoln and Lafayette

8.8 mi/6.5 hrs 

Location: In the White Mountain National Forest and Franconia Notch State Park, north of Lincoln and south of Franconia; Northern New Hampshire map page 86, grid e2.

User groups: Hikers and dogs. No wheelchair facilities. Dogs must be on a leash. This trail may be difficult to snowshoe because of severe winter weather, and is not suitable for skis. Bikes, horses, and hunting are prohibited.

Access, fees: Parking and access are free. The Appalachian Mountain Club operates the Greenleaf hut at the junction of the Greenleaf Trail and Old Bridle Path; contact the AMC for reservation and rate information (see address below).

Directions: Drive to one of the large parking lots on the east and west side of Interstate 93 at the Lafayette Place Campground in Franconia Notch State Park. From the west side parking lot, hikers can walk under the highway to the east side, where the trails begin.

Maps: Several maps cover hiking trails in this area, including the "Franconia" map 5 from the Appalachian Mountain Club, (800) 262-4455, which is $2.95 and widely available in stores; the "Franconia Notch" map available for $4.50 from Ed Rolfe, Cartographer, P.O. Box 349, Twin Mountain, NH 03595, (603) 788-3019; the "Trail Map and Guide to the White Mountain National Forest," which is $4.95, from the DeLorme Mapping Company, (800) 253-5081; the map of the national forest, available by sending a check for $4 to White Mountain National Forest main office (see address below); and map 3 in the "Map and Guide to the Appalachian Trail in New Hampshire and Vermont," an eight-map set for $10.95 from the Appalachian Trail Conference (see address below). For a topographic map of the area, request Franconia from the USGS.

Contact: Franconia Notch State Park, Franconia, NH 03580; (603) 823-5563. White Mountain National Forest Supervisor, 719

North Main Street, Laconia, NH 03246; (603) 528-8721, TDD for hearing impaired (603) 528-8722. Appalachian Mountain Club, P.O. Box 298, Gorham, NH 03581; (603) 466-2721. Appalachian Trail Conference, P.O. Box 807, Harpers Ferry, WV 25425; (304) 535-6331. New Hampshire Division of Parks and Recreation, P.O. Box 1856, Concord, NH 03302-1856; (603) 271-3254.

Trail notes: For many New England hikers—myself included— this 8.8-mile loop over the sixth- and seventh-highest peaks in New Hampshire represented a dramatic introduction to the White Mountains, and has become a favorite hike revisited many times over the years. With nearly two miles of continuous, exposed ridgeline high above the forest connecting Mounts Lincoln (5,089 feet) and Lafayette (5,249 feet), this hike lures hundreds of people on warm weekends in summer and fall, and a surprising number of winter warriors as well. The views from Franconia Ridge encompass most of the White Mountains, spanning the peaks and valleys of the Pemigewasset Wilderness all the way to the Presidential Range, Vermont's Green Mountains, and, on a very clear day, New York's Adirondacks. The Falling Waters Trail passes several waterfalls and cascades, and the Old Bridle Path follows a long shoulder of Mount Lafayette over some open ledges which offer excellent views of Lincoln and Lafayette.

Because of the heavy foot traffic on Franconia Ridge and the fragility of the alpine flora, you should take care to walk only on the clearly marked trail or on bare rock. From the parking lot on the east side of Interstate 93, follow the Falling Waters Trail, which coincides for two-tenths of a mile with the Old Bridle Path, then turns sharply right and crosses Walker Brook on a bridge. The trail climbs steadily and steeply, crossing Dry Brook at seven-tenths of a mile, which could be difficult in high water. Over the ensuing mile, it passes several cascades and waterfalls, including Cloudland Falls, with a sheer drop of 80 feet, and makes two more crossings of the brook.

At 2.8 miles, a side path leads to the right a short distance to Shining Rock, a huge slab on the mountainside which appears to shimmer when viewed from the road far below. The views of the notch are excellent, but bear in mind that the "shining" is caused by running water, making it slippery and dangerous to scramble around on. Continue up the Falling Waters Trail, emerging above the trees about a tenth of a mile before reaching the Franconia Ridge Trail (which is part of the Appalachian Trail) at 3.2 miles, at the summit of Little Haystack Mountain. Turn left (north), following the cairns and white blazes of the Franconia Ridge Trail along the open ridge.

Among the peaks in view as you head over Lincoln and Lafayette are: the bald cap of Mount Garfield immediately northeast of Lafayette; North and South Twin Mountains, east of Garfield; Mount Washington and the high peaks of the Presidential Range in the more distant northeast; the wooded mound of Owl's Head, standing alone across the valley immediately east of Franconia Ridge; the Bonds and Bondcliff on the other side of Owl's Head; the towering mass of Mount Carrigain southeast of Owl's Head and the Bonds; the jumble of peaks above Waterville Valley farther south and east, including the three pointed summits of Mount Tripyramid; the distinct horn of Mount Chocorua in the distance between Carrigain and Waterville Valley; Cannon Cliff and Mountain to the west across Franconia Notch; south of and behind Cannon, the north and south peaks of Kinsman Mountain; and to the southwest, sprawling Mount Moosilauke.

From Haystack, the trail drops slightly but follows easy ground until climbing steeply to the summit of Lincoln, seven-tenths of a mile from Haystack. It passes over a subsidiary summit of Lincoln immediately to the north, then drops into a saddle with the tallest scrub vegetation on the ridge before making the long ascent of Mount Lafayette, nine-tenths of a mile from Lincoln's summit. This highest point on the ridge, predictably, tends to be the windiest and coldest spot as well, although there are sheltered places in the rocks on the summit's north side. Turn left (west) and descend the Greenleaf Trail, much of it over open terrain, for 1.1 miles to the AMC's Greenleaf hut. Just beyond the hut, bear left onto the Old Bridle Path, descending southwest over the crest of a long ridge, with occasional views, before re-entering the woods and eventually reaching the parking lot, 2.9 miles from the hut.

48 Mounts Flume and Liberty

9.8 mi/7.0 hrs 

Location: In the White Mountain National Forest and Franconia Notch State Park, north of Lincoln and south of Franconia; Northern New Hampshire map page 86, grid e2.

User groups: Hikers and dogs. No wheelchair facilities. Dogs must be on a leash. This trail may be difficult to snowshoe because of severe winter weather, and is not suitable for skis. Bikes, horses, and hunting are prohibited.

Access, fees: Parking and access are free. This hike begins in Franconia Notch State Park, but much of it lies within the White Mountain National Forest. The Appalachian Mountain Club (see address below) operates the Liberty Spring campsite, with 12 tent platforms, located along the Liberty Spring Trail, 2.6 miles from the Whitehouse Trail and three-tenths of a mile from the Franconia Ridge Trail. A caretaker collects the $5 nightly fee during the warmer months.

Directions: From Interstate 93 in Franconia Notch, take the exit for the Flume. Follow the sign to trailhead parking for the Whitehouse Trail and the Appalachian Trail, which coincides with the Liberty Spring Trail and is reached via the Whitehouse.

Maps: For a contour map of hiking trails, get the "Franconia" map 5, which is $2.95 from the Appalachian Mountain Club, (800) 262-4455, and is also widely available in stores; the "Trail Map and Guide to the White Mountain National Forest," which is $4.95 from the DeLorme Mapping Company, (800) 253-5081; or map 3 in the "Map and Guide to the Appalachian Trail in New Hampshire and Vermont," an eight-map set for $10.95 from the Appalachian Trail Conference (see address below). For topographic maps of the area, request Franconia and Lincoln from the USGS.

Contact: White Mountain National Forest Supervisor, 719 North Main Street, Laconia, NH 03246; (603) 528-8721, TDD for the hearing impaired (603) 528-8722. New Hampshire Division of Parks and Recreation, Trails Bureau, P.O. Box 1856, Concord, NH 03302; (603) 271-3254. Appalachian Mountain Club, P.O. Box 298, Gorham, NH 03581; (603) 466-2727. Appalachian Trail Conference, P.O. Box 807, Harpers Ferry, WV 25425; (304) 535-6331.

Trail notes: If these two summits were located virtually anywhere else, this loop hike would enjoy enormous popularity. But the 5,000-footers to the north, Lafayette and Lincoln, are what captures the attention of most hikers venturing onto spectacular Franconia Ridge. Many people who call the Lafayette-Lincoln Loop (hike number 47) their favorite hike in the Whites have never enjoyed the uninterrupted views from the rocky summits of 4,325-foot

Flume or 4,459-foot Liberty: Franconia Notch, west to Mount Moosilauke and the Green Mountains, and a grand sweep of peaks to the east all the way to the Presidential Range. I hiked this loop on a March day when the sun felt like July—although the notion of summer approaching was dispelled by the cool wind, snow, and ice.

From the parking lot, take the blue-blazed Whitehouse Trail north for nearly a mile (it coincides briefly with the Franconia Notch bike path). Pick up the white-blazed Liberty Spring Trail—a part of the Appalachian Trail—heading east. Within a half mile, signs mark where the Flume Slide Trail branches right. This trail is marked very sporadically with light-blue blazes and can be very difficult to follow. It grows steep on the upper part of the slide, and you will scramble over rocks that can be very slick when wet. (For these reasons, some hikers merely go up and down the Liberty Spring Trail to Mount Liberty.)

Where the Flume Slide Trail hits the ridge crest, 3.3 miles from the Liberty Spring Trail, turn left onto the Osseo Trail, which leads a short distance to Mount Flume's summit. Continue over the summit on the Franconia Ridge Trail, dipping into the saddle between the peaks, then climbing to Liberty's summit a mile from the top of Flume. Another three-tenths of a mile beyond the summit, turn left onto the Liberty Spring Trail and descend to the Whitehouse Trail, following it back to the parking lot.

49 Twins-Bonds Traverse

20.0 mi. one way/
2.5–3.0 days

Location: In the White Mountain National Forest, between Twin Mountain and the Kancamagus Highway; Northern New Hampshire map page 86, grid e2.

User groups: Hikers and dogs. No wheelchair facilities. The Wilderness Trail stretch of this hike is flat and is a popular day trip with skiers and snowshoers. Bikes and horses are prohibited. Hunting is allowed in season.

Access, fees: Parking and access are free. The Guyot campsite, operated by the Appalachian Mountain Club, (800) 262-4455, has a shelter and six tent platforms and is reached via a short spur trail (marked by a sign) off the Bondcliff Trail about a quarter mile south of the Twinway junction. A caretaker collects the $5-per-person nightly fee at Guyot from late spring through fall. The Franconia Brook campsite (16 tent platforms), operated by the White Mountain National Forest, is on the Wilderness Trail just west of the Franconia Brook Trail junction and 2.8 miles north of Route 112. Both campsites are popular and often full on weekends. The former Camp 16, at the junction of the Bondcliff and Wilderness Trails, is closed and camping there is illegal. Camping in the forest is legal provided you remain at least 200 feet from a trail and a quarter mile from established camping areas such as Guyot campsite. Well-used backcountry sites along the southern end of the Bondcliff Trail have attracted heavy black bear activity in recent summers.

Directions: You will need to shuttle two vehicles for this trek. Leave one in the large parking lot at Lincoln Woods, where there is a White Mountain National Forest ranger station. It is along the Kancamagus Highway (Route 112), five miles east of McDonald's in Lincoln and just east of the bridge where the Kancamagus crosses the East Branch of the Pemigewasset River. The Wilderness Trail—also known for its initial three miles as the Lincoln Woods Trail—begins here.

The other trailhead—where this hike begins—is off U.S. 3. From the junction of U.S. 302 and U.S. 3 in Twin Mountain, drive south on U.S. 3 for 2.5 miles and turn left onto Haystack Road (Fire Road 304). Or, from Interstate 93 north of Franconia Notch State Park, take exit 35 for U.S. 3 north and continue approximately 7.5 miles, then turn right onto Fire Road 304. Follow this road to its end and a parking area at the North Twin Trail.

Maps: For a map of hiking trails, get the "Franconia" map 5, which is $2.95 from the Appalachian Mountain Club, (800) 262-4455, and is also widely available in stores. Or get the "Trail Map and Guide to the White Mountain National Forest," which is $4.95 from the DeLorme Mapping Company, (800) 253-5081. For topographic maps of the area, request Bethlehem, South Twin Mountain, and Mount Osceola from the USGS.

Contact: White Mountain National Forest Supervisor, 719 North Main Street, Laconia, NH 03246; (603) 528-8721, TDD for the hearing impaired (603) 528-8722.

Trail notes: Of the several good routes to backpack across the Pemigewasset Wilderness—the vast roadless area in the heart of the White Mountains—this ranks as my favorite because it traverses the spectacular Bondcliff Ridge dividing the east and west sides of the Pemi. The views are great from the summits of all five "official" 4,000-footers along this trek: North (4,761 feet) and South Twin (4,902 feet), Bond (4,698 feet), Bondcliff (4,265 feet), and West Bond (4,540 feet), which is a wonderful knob of rock jutting above the dense scrub forest with terrific views of Franconia Ridge, Bondcliff, and the southern White Mountains. Two friends and I also caught a fabulous, burning red sunrise from the shelter at the Guyot campsite.

Hiking north to south, follow the North Twin Trail 4.3 miles to the summit of North Twin, and the North Twin Spur 1.3 miles to South Twin. Turn left (southeast) on the Twinway and follow it for two miles. Turn right (south) onto the Bondcliff Trail. Within a half mile—a short distance beyond the spur trail leading left to Guyot campsite—turn right onto a spur trail for the one-mile round-trip to the summit of West Bond. Return to the Bondcliff Trail, and turn right (south) and continue about a half mile to the summit of Mount Bond, with excellent views in all directions, including Mount Washington to the east and the spectacular Bondcliff Ridge immediately south. Continuing south, within a mile you'll reach that ridge and walk its open crest, above tall cliffs. From Bondcliff's summit, it's 4.4 miles down through the woods to the Wilderness Trail. Turn right (west) and follow the Wilderness Trail 1.8 miles to the Franconia Brook campsite, then another three miles to the parking area at Lincoln Woods.

---

50 Pemigewasset Wilderness Traverse

19.5 mi. one way/
10–12 hrs or 1–2 days

Location: In the White Mountain National Forest, between U.S. 302 near Twin Mountain and Route 112 east of Lincoln; Northern New Hampshire map page 86, grid e3.

User groups: Hikers, dogs, skiers, and snowshoers. No wheelchair facilities. Bikes and horses are prohibited. Hunting is allowed in season, except along the Appalachian Trail, which coincides with the Twinway and the Ethan Pond Trail.

Access, fees: Parking and access are free. Zealand Road is not maintained in winter. The Appalachian Mountain Club operates the Zealand Falls hut year-round; it is on the Twinway, two-tenths of a mile from the junction of the Zealand, Twinway, and Ethan Pond Trails and 2.7 miles from the end of Zealand Road. Contact the AMC (see address below) for information on cost and reservations.

Directions: You need to shuttle two vehicles for this one-way traverse. To go north to south, as described here, leave one vehicle in the large parking lot at Lincoln Woods, where there is a White Mountain National Forest ranger station. It is along the Kancamagus Highway (Route 112), five miles east of the McDonald's in Lincoln, New Hampshire, and just east of the bridge where the Kancamagus crosses the East Branch of the Pemigewasset River. The Wilderness Trail—also known for its initial three miles as the Lincoln Woods Trail—begins here. To reach the start of this hike, from the junction of U.S. 3 and U.S. 302 in Twin Mountain, drive east on U.S. 302 for 2.3 miles and turn right onto Zealand Road. (In winter, continue east on U.S. 302 for a tenth of a mile beyond Zealand Road and park in the winter lot on the left.) Continue 3.5 miles to a parking lot at the end of the road.

Maps: Several maps cover hiking trails in this area, including the "Franconia" map 5 from the Appalachian Mountain Club (800-262-4455), which is $2.95 and widely available in stores; map 3 in the "Map and Guide to the Appalachian Trail in New Hampshire and Vermont," an eight-map set for $10.95 from the Appalachian Trail Conference (see address below); the "Trail Map and Guide to the White Mountain National Forest," which is $4.95, from the DeLorme Mapping Company, (800) 253-5081; and the map of the national forest, available by sending a check for $4 to White Mountain National Forest main office (see address below). For topographic maps of the area, request Bethlehem, Mount Washington, South Twin Mountain, Crawford Notch, Mount Osceola, and Mount Carrigain from the USGS.

Contact: White Mountain National Forest Supervisor, 719 North Main St., Laconia, NH 03246; (603) 528-8721, TDD for hearing impaired (603) 528-8722. Appalachian Mountain Club, P.O. Box 298, Gorham, NH 03581; (603) 466-2721. Appalachian Trail Conference, P.O. Box 807, Harpers Ferry, WV 25425; (304) 535-6331.

Trail notes: The Pemigewasset Wilderness is the sprawling roadless area of mountains and wide, flat valleys in the heart of the White Mountains. A federally designated wilderness area, the "Pemi" harbors spectacular big-mountain hikes such as the Twins-Bonds Traverse (hike number 49) and Mount Carrigain (hike number 51). This traverse, however, follows the valleys of the Pemi, much of it relatively easy hiking along routes once followed by the railroads of 19th-century logging companies. It could be done in a two-day backpacking trip. But I've included this mainly because it's considered a classic ski tour, feasible to accomplish in a day for experienced cross-country skiers also skilled in winter mountain travel. For that reason, I've included in this hike's distance the 3.5 miles you have to ski up Zealand Road, which is not plowed in winter. This hike is thus 3.5 miles shorter in the warmer months. The route may follow lower elevations, but weather can change quickly in here, and 20 miles on skis is a long day. You may have to break trail through varied snow conditions much of the way, and not finish until after dark (which is what happened to three friends and I when we skied this route). Zealand Notch, in my opinion, is even more wild in winter than in the warmer months, and there's some nice skiing along these other trails. The Thoreau Falls Trail presents significant amounts of steeper terrain; you will have to carry skis and hike, intermittently, for a mile or more. Depending upon the amount of snowfall and how much freezing has occurred, numerous brooks crossing that trail may not be frozen, necessitating repeated removal of skis to cross the brooks. Do not underestimate how long or difficult a winter trip this can be.

From the winter parking lot, follow the

Northern New Hampshire Map—page 86

Zealand Road, climbing gradually for 3.5 miles to its end (where this hike begins in warmer months). Then pick up the blue-blazed Zealand Trail, winding through the forest on fairly flat ground, with some short, steep steps, for 2.5 miles to a trails junction. To the right, the Twinway leads two-tenths of a mile uphill to the AMC's Zealand Falls hut. This hike continues straight ahead onto the Ethan Pond Trail, which coincides with the Appalachian Trail. The Ethan Pond Trail contours along the west slope of Whitewall Mountain.

About 1.3 miles from the Zealand Trail, the Ethan Pond Trail emerges from the forest onto the open scar of an old rockslide on Whitewall, in the middle of Zealand Notch. Above loom the towering cliffs of the mountain; below, the rockslide's fallout, a broad boulder field. Across the notch rises Zealand Mountain, and straight ahead, to the south, stands Carrigain. The trail crosses the rockslide for about two-tenths of a mile, then re-enters the woods. At 2.1 miles from the Zealand Trail, bear right onto the Thoreau Falls Trail, following easy terrain for a tenth of a mile to Thoreau Falls, which tumbles more than 100 feet and forms an impressive cascade of ice in winter. The trail crosses the stream immediately above the brink of the falls: Be careful here in any season, but especially in winter do not assume that any snow or ice bridge is safe; two days before my friends and I skied through here in January 1997, someone had fallen through the ice.

Once across the stream, the trail climbs steeply, angling across a wooded hillside, then drops just as steeply down the other side. This trail may be difficult or impossible to ski for a mile or more, but eventually reaches more level ground. At 4.7 miles from the Ethan Pond Trail, this trail crosses a bridge over the East Branch of the Pemigewasset River. Just four-tenths of a mile past the bridge, turn right (west) onto the Wilderness Trail, which is the easiest trail on this route (making it the preferred way to finish if there's a chance of finishing after dark). The Wilderness Trail crosses the river again in nine-tenths of a mile, on a 180-foot suspension bridge, then parallels the East Branch for the remaining 5.4 flat miles to the Lincoln Woods parking lot on the Kancamagus Highway.

Special note: Skiers who do not want to wrestle their skis up and down the steep sections of the Thoreau Falls Trail might consider another option, two miles longer but easier. After passing through Zealand Notch, instead of turning right onto the Thoreau Falls Trail, continue left with the Ethan Pond Trail for a half mile, then turn right (south) onto the Shoal Pond Trail. Follow it for four miles to a spot called Stillwater Junction, then turn right (west) onto the Wilderness Trail and follow it 8.9 miles to Lincoln Woods.

51 Mount Carrigain

10.0 mi/7.0 hrs 

Location: In the White Mountain National Forest southwest of Crawford Notch State Park; Northern New Hampshire map page 86, grid e3.

User groups: Hikers and dogs. No wheelchair facilities. This trail may be difficult to snowshoe because of severe winter weather, and is not suitable for bikes, horses, or skis. Hunting is allowed in season.

Access, fees: Parking and access are free. Sawyer River Road is usually closed to vehicles once the snow arrives.

Directions: From U.S. 302, 10.7 miles south of the visitor information center in Crawford Notch and 10.3 miles north of the junction of U.S. 302 and Route 16 in Glen, turn south onto Sawyer River Road (Fire Road 34). Follow it for two miles to the Signal Ridge Trail on the right, just before a bridge over Whiteface Brook. There is parking on the left, just past the brook.

Maps: For a map of hiking trails, get the "Mount Washington Range" map 6 or the "Franconia" map 5; each are $2.95 from the Appalachian Mountain Club, (800) 262-4455, and are also widely available in stores. Or get the "Trail Map and Guide to the White Mountain National Forest," which is $4.95 from the DeLorme Mapping Company, (800) 253-5081. For topographic maps of the area, request Mount Carrigain and Bartlett from the USGS.

Contact: White Mountain National Forest Supervisor, 719 North Main Street, Laconia, NH 03246; (603) 528-8721, TDD for the hearing impaired (603) 528-8722.

Trail notes: The tallest peak in this corner of the Whites, 4,680-foot Carrigain offers one of the finest—and unquestionably unique—views in these mountains from the observation tower on its summit. On a clear day, the panorama takes in Mount Washington and the Presidential Range, the vast sweep of peaks across the Pemigewasset Wilderness to Franconia Ridge, Moosilauke to the west, and the peaks above Waterville Valley and the distinctive horn of Chocorua to the south. Although fairly long, this hike grows steep only for the ascent to the crest of Signal Ridge, which itself has spectacular views, including one toward the cliffs of Mount Lowell to the east.

Follow the Signal Ridge Trail, which leads five miles to the summit. The trail follows Whiteface Brook at first, passing picturesque cascades. At 1.7 miles from the road, the Carrigain Notch Trail branches right; continue up the Signal Ridge Trail. Reaching the open terrain of Signal Ridge at about 4.5 miles, you enjoy excellent views, particularly east across Carrigain Notch to Mount Lowell's cliffs. The ridge ascends easily to the summit observation tower. Return the same way you came.

52 Stairs Mountain

9.2 mi/6.0 hrs 

Location: In the White Mountain National Forest north of Bartlett; Northern New Hampshire map page 86, grid e3.

User groups: Hikers, dogs, and snowshoers. No wheelchair facilities. The Rocky Branch Trail is fairly easy to ski as far as the Stairs Col Trail junction. Bikes and horses are prohibited. Hunting is allowed in season.

Access, fees: Parking and access are free. Rocky Branch Shelter 1 consists of an open lean-to and tent site, reached via a short spur trail just south of the junction of the Rocky Branch Trail and the Stairs Col Trail (just outside the boundary of the Dry River Wilderness).

Directions: From the junction of Route 16 and U.S. 302 in Glen, drive west on U.S. 302 for one mile and turn right onto Jericho Road (also called Rocky Branch Road). Follow that road, which is paved for about a mile and then becomes gravel (passable by car), for five miles to its end, where there is parking and the Rocky Branch Trail begins.

Maps: For a map of hiking trails, obtain the "Mount Washington Range" map 6, which is $2.95 from the Appalachian Mountain Club, (800) 262-4455, and is also widely available in stores; or the "Trail Map and Guide to the White Mountain National Forest," which is $4.95 from the DeLorme Mapping Company, (800) 253-5081. For topographic maps of the area, request North Conway West, Bartlett, and Stairs Mountain from the USGS.

Contact: White Mountain National Forest Supervisor, 719 North Main Street, Laconia, NH 03246; (603) 528-8721, TDD for the hearing impaired (603) 528-8722. The AMC's Pinkham Notch Visitors Center has up-to-date reports on weather in the Presidential Range (although primarily for Mount Washington, to the north of Stairs); call (603) 466-2721.

Trail notes: This hike can be done in a day, or can be split up over a couple of days with a stay at the shelter. Stairs Mountain is so named because of the Giant Stairs, a pair of steplike ledges on the 3,460-foot mountain's south end. From the cliffs atop the Giant Stairs, you get wide views of the mountains to the south. Although the Rocky Branch Trail attracts backpackers to the shelters along it, many of those people are headed for the 4,000-foot peaks farther north; you might find a little piece of solitude on Stairs Mountain. I snowshoed up Stairs once with a group of friends right after back-to-back blizzards in March—we were walking on several feet of snow, and it was an adventure just staying with the unbroken trail.

From the end of Jericho Road, follow the Rocky Branch Trail north a flat two miles to the Rocky Branch shelter 1, where there is a lean-to and a tent site. Nearby, the Stairs Col Trail turns left (west) and ascends steadily for nearly two miles, passing below the Giant Stairs and through Stairs Col to the Davis Path. Turn right (north) on the Davis Path and follow it for a bit less than a half mile to a side path leading right for about two-tenths of a mile to the cliffs above the Giant Stairs. Return the way you came.

53 Mount Stanton

3.0 mi/2.0 hrs 

Location: In the White Mountain National Forest between Bartlett and Glen; Northern New Hampshire map page 86, grid e3.

User groups: Hikers, dogs, and snowshoers. No wheelchair facilities. This trail is not suitable for bikes, horses, or skis. Hunting is allowed in season.

Access, fees: Parking and access are free.

Directions: From the junction of U.S. 302 and Route 16 in Glen, drive north on U.S. 302 toward Bartlett for about two miles. Between the covered bridge and the Spaghetti Shed, turn right into a housing development; then take the first left, a road that may have no sign. Wind through the neighborhood looking for the trailhead on the left, near a sandy bend in the road. Parking is limited.

Maps: For a map of hiking trails, obtain the "Mount Washington Range" map 6, which is $2.95 from the Appalachian Mountain Club, (800) 262-4455, and is also widely available in stores; or the "Trail Map and Guide to the White Mountain National Forest," which is $4.95 from the DeLorme Mapping Company, (800) 253-5081. For a topographic map of the area, request North Conway West from the USGS.

Contact: White Mountain National Forest Supervisor, 719 North Main Street, Laconia, NH 03246; (603) 528-8721, TDD for the hearing impaired (603) 528-8722.

Trail notes: Here's a hike that offers spectacular views and the feel of a big mountain for relatively little work and a summit elevation of just 1,748 feet. These factors make it a good hike for children, or for a day when clouds descend upon the big mountains. The trail does have a few moderately steep stretches, but they are neither sustained nor very difficult; fit hikers could easily run up the path for a quick workout. Near Mount Stanton's summit, you will see open ledges to the left (south) worth exploring. Out on the ledges, you will find yourself on the brink of a 500-foot sheer drop, atop a cliff called White's Ledge (a wonderful technical rock climb for those with experience). You might see rock climbers reaching the top; be careful not to kick stones over the edge. The ledges offer broad views of the Saco River Valley. Follow the same route back.

54 Cathedral Ledge

0.1 mi/0.25 hr 

Location: In Echo Lake State Park west of North Conway; Northern New Hampshire map page 86, grid e4.

User groups: Hikers, bikes, dogs, skiers, and snowshoers. No wheelchair facilities. Skiers and snowshoers must begin at the base of the access road, which adds about one mile to the round-trip mileage listed above. Dogs must be on a leash. Hunting is allowed in season.

Access, fees: Parking and access are free. The access road is not maintained in winter and is blocked by a gate.

Directions: From Route 16 in North Conway, in front of the Eastern Slope Inn, turn west at traffic lights onto River Road. Continue 1.5 miles, and turn left at a sign for Cathedral Ledge. Follow the road, passing below the cliff, more than a mile to its end at a circle.

Maps: Although no map is necessary for this hike, for a topographic map of the area, request North Conway West from the USGS.

Contact: New Hampshire Division of Parks and Recreation, P.O. Box 1856, Concord, NH 03302-1856; (603) 271-3254.

Trail notes: This is less a hike than an easy, five-minute walk to the top of Cathedral Ledge, a sheer, 400-foot cliff overlooking the Mount Washington Valley. Popular with tourists when the access road is open, from late spring through autumn, the lookout is protected by a fence to keep visitors from wandering too close to the brink. Cathedral is one of New Hampshire's most popular rock-climbing areas, so you're likely to see climbers pulling over the top of the cliff right in front of you. Obviously, you should not throw anything off the cliff, given the likelihood of there being people below. From the circle, follow a wide, obvious path to the east a short distance through the woods to the top of the cliff. Return the same way.

55 Mount Moosilauke: Beaver Brook Trail

7.8 mi/5.5 hrs 

Location: West of North Woodstock; Northern New Hampshire map page 86, grid e2.

User groups: Hikers and dogs. No wheelchair facilities. This trail may be difficult to snowshoe because of severe winter weather, and is not suitable for skis. Bikes, horses, and hunting are prohibited.

Access, fees: Parking and access are free. The Dartmouth Outing Club maintains the Beaver Brook shelter, a newly reconstructed lean-to located on the Beaver Brook Trail three-tenths of a mile from Route 112 in Kinsman Notch.

Directions: The Beaver Brook Trail, which coincides with the Appalachian Trail, begins from a parking lot along Route 112 at the height-of-land in Kinsman Notch, 6.2 miles west of North Woodstock and 4.8 miles south of the junction of Routes 112 and 116.

Maps: Several maps cover hiking trails in this area, including the "Franconia" map 5 and the "Chocorua-Waterville" map 4 from the Appalachian Mountain Club, (800) 262-4455, which are $2.95 each and widely available in stores; the "Trail Map and Guide to the White Mountain National Forest," which is $4.95 from the DeLorme Mapping Company, (800) 253-5081; the map of the national forest, available by sending a check for $4 to White Mountain National Forest main office (see address below); and map 3 in the "Map and Guide to the Appalachian Trail in New Hampshire and Vermont," an eight-map set for $10.95 from the Appalachian Trail Conference (see address below). For a topographic map of the area, request Mount Moosilauke from the USGS.

Contact: White Mountain National Forest Supervisor, 719 North Main Street, Laconia, NH 03246; (603) 528-8721, TDD for hearing impaired (603) 528-8722. Appalachian Trail Conference, P.O. Box 807, Harpers Ferry, WV 25425; (304) 535-6331.

Trail notes: A number of years ago, a friend invited me to hike Mount Moosilauke with a group of people—my first of many trips up this 4,802-foot massif in the southwest corner of the White Mountains. We went up the Beaver Brook Trail, past its numerous cascades, and on to a summit with an extensive alpine area and views which span much of the White Mountains, and extend west to the Green Mountains in Vermont and New York's Adirondacks. Moosilauke is one of the most popular peaks in the Whites, and the Beaver Brook Trail a popular route up the mountain. But it is steep and rugged, and hikers seeking a more moderate route, especially on snowshoes in winter, might better consider the Glencliff Trail (hike number 56).

The Beaver Brook Trail, which coincides with the Appalachian Trail, leaves Route 112 and soon begins the steep, sustained climb up the narrow drainage of Beaver Brook. At three-tenths of a mile, a side path leads right a short distance to the Dartmouth Outing Club's Beaver Brook lean-to. The trail levels somewhat, and at 1.9 miles the Asquam-Ridge Trail branches left. The Beaver Brook Trail/AT then ascends over the wooded shoulder known as Mount Blue, and finally emerges above the trees for the nearly flat final two-tenths of a mile to the summit. Visible to the northeast are Franconia Ridge and, much farther to the northeast, the Presidential Range. Hike back the way you came up.

Special note: By shuttling two vehicles to the trailheads, this hike can be combined with the Glencliff Trail (hike number 56) for a traverse of Moosilauke via the Appalachian Trail. Hike up the Beaver Brook Trail and descend the Glencliff.

56 Mount Moosilauke: Glencliff Trail

7.8 mi/5.5 hrs 

Location: North of Warren; Northern New Hampshire map page 86, grid e2.

User groups: Hikers and dogs. No wheelchair facilities. This trail may be difficult to snowshoe because of severe winter weather, and is not suitable for skis. Bikes, horses, and hunting are prohibited.

Access, fees: Parking and access are free.

Directions: From Route 25 in Glencliff Village, turn onto Sanatorium Road (watch for signs for the New Hampshire Home for the Elderly). Drive 1.2 miles to a dirt parking lot on the right.

Maps: Several maps cover hiking trails in this area, including the "Franconia" map 5 and the "Chocorua-Waterville" map 4 from the Appalachian Mountain Club, (800) 262-4455, which are $2.95 each and widely available in stores; the "Trail Map and Guide to the White Mountain National Forest," which is $4.95 from the DeLorme Mapping Company, (800) 253-5081; the map of the national forest, available by sending a check for $4 to White Mountain National Forest main office (see address below); and map 3 in the "Map and Guide to the Appalachian Trail in New Hampshire and Vermont," an eight-map set for $10.95 from the Appalachian Trail Conference (see address below). For a topographic map of the area, request Mount Moosilauke from the USGS.

Contact: White Mountain National Forest Supervisor, 719 North Main St., Laconia, NH 03246; (603) 528-8721, TDD for hearing impaired (603) 528-8722. Appalachian Trail

Conference, P.O. Box 807, Harpers Ferry, WV 25425; (304) 535-6331.

Trail notes: The Glencliff Trail, a section of the white-blazed Appalachian Trail, offers a moderately difficult and very scenic route to the 4,802-foot summit of Mount Moosilauke, where an extensive alpine area offers panoramic views stretching across much of the White Mountains, and west to the Green Mountains in Vermont and New York's Adirondacks.

From the parking lot, follow the white blazes past a gate and along old farm roads through pastures before entering the woods at four-tenths of a mile, where a side path leads left to a Dartmouth College cabin (not open to the public) and the Hurricane Trail diverges right. The Glencliff Trail ascends steadily but at a moderate grade for the next two miles, then grows steeper as it rises into the mountain's krummholtz, the scrub conifers which grow in the subalpine zone. At three miles the trail hits the old carriage road on Moosilauke. A spur path leads right (south) to Moosilauke's craggy South Peak just two-tenths of a mile distant. This hike turns left (north) and follows the wide carriage road over easy ground along the open ridge—with great views—ascending gently to the summit at 3.9 miles. Return the way you came. For a full traverse of Moosilauke via the Appalachian Trail, see the special note in the trail notes for the Mount Moosilauke Beaver Brook Trail (hike number 55).

57 Mount Osceola

6.4 mi/4.0 hrs 

Location: In the White Mountain National Forest, north of Waterville Valley and east of Lincoln; Northern New Hampshire map page 86, grid f3.

User groups: Hikers and dogs. No wheelchair facilities. This trail may be difficult to snowshoe because of severe winter weather, and is not suitable for bikes, horses, or skis. Hunting is allowed in season.

Access, fees: Parking and access are free. Tripoli Road is not generally maintained in winter.

Directions: From Interstate 93, take exit 31 for Tripoli Road. Drive east on Tripoli Road for seven miles to a parking lot on the left for the Mount Osceola Trail.

Maps: For a contour map of trails, see the "Chocorua-Waterville" map 4 from the Appalachian Mountain Club (800-262-4455), which is $2.95 and widely available in stores; the "Trail Map and Guide to the White Mountain National Forest," which is $4.95 from the DeLorme Mapping Company, (800) 253-5081; or the map of the national forest, available by sending a check for $4 to White Mountain National Forest main office (see address below). For topographic maps of the area, request Mount Osceola and Waterville Valley from the USGS.

Contact: White Mountain National Forest Supervisor, 719 North Main Street, Laconia, NH 03246; (603) 528-8721, TDD for hearing impaired (603) 528-8722.

Trail notes: One of the easiest 4,000-footers in New Hampshire to hike, Osceola's summit ledges, rising 4,340 feet, give a sweeping view to the south and southeast of Waterville Valley and Mount Tripyramid, and northeast to the Pemigewasset Wilderness and the Presidential Range.

From the parking lot, follow the Mount Osceola Trail as it ascends at a moderate angle, through numerous switchbacks, and reaches the summit ledges at 3.2 miles. The trail continues one more mile to reach 4,156-foot East Osceola, which will add two miles and approximately 1.5 hours to this hike's distance and time. Hike back along the same route.

58 Sabbaday Falls

0.8 mi/0.75 hr 

Location: In the White Mountain National Forest, on the Kancamagus Highway (Route 112) between Lincoln and Conway; Northern New Hampshire map page 86, grid e3.

User groups: Hikers, dogs, skiers, and snowshoers. No wheelchair facilities. This trail is not suitable for bikes or horses. Hunting is allowed in season.

Access, fees: Parking and access are free.

Directions: The hike begins at the Sabbaday Falls parking area along the Kancamagus Highway (Route 112), 19.9 miles east of the McDonald's on Route 112 in Lincoln, 6.6 miles east of the sign at Kancamagus Pass, and 15.6 miles west of the junction of Routes 112 and 16 in Conway.

Maps: For a contour map of hiking trails, get the "Franconia" map 5, which is $2.95 from the Appalachian Mountain Club, (800) 262-4455, and is also widely available in stores. Or get the "Trail Map and Guide to the White Mountain National Forest," which is $4.95 from the DeLorme Mapping Company, (800) 253-5081. For a topographic map of the area, request Mount Tripyramid from the USGS.

Contact: White Mountain National Forest Supervisor, 719 North Main Street, Laconia, NH 03246; (603) 528-8721, TDD for the hearing impaired (603) 528-8722.

Trail notes: The early explorers of the Passaconaway Valley reached Sabbaday Falls on a Sunday, and thereafter the spectacular falls became a popular destination on the "Sabbath day." The falls drop twice through a narrow gorge so perfect in its geometry it seems the work of engineers. The gorge was formed from the gouging action of rocks and sand released by glacial melt-off 10,000 years ago. Below the gorge, Sabbaday Brook settles quietly, if briefly, in a clear pool. This easy hike is a great one for young children.

From the parking area, follow the wide gravel and dirt Sabbaday Brook Trail, which parallels the rocky brook. The trail ascends very little over its first three-tenths of a mile to where a side path leads left. This path loops past the lower pool and above the gorge and both falls before rejoining the Sabbaday Brook Trail. Turn right to return to the parking area.

59 Mount Tripyramid

11.0 mi/7.0 hrs 

Location: In the White Mountain National Forest east of Waterville Valley; Northern New Hampshire map page 86, grid e3.

User groups: Hikers and dogs on the Mount Tripyramid Trail; hikers, bikes, dogs, and skiers on the Livermore Trail. No wheelchair facilities. This trail may be difficult to snowshoe because of severe winter weather, and is not suitable for horses. Hunting is allowed in season.

Access, fees: Parking and access are free, except in the winter months, when skiers must pay a trail fee at the cross-country ski touring center in Waterville Valley to ski Livermore Road.

Directions: From Interstate 93, take exit 28 for Route 49 north. Drive about 11 miles into Waterville Valley. Before town, turn left onto Tripoli Road toward the Mount Tecumseh Ski Area. Follow it for about a half mile, then bear right (the left fork goes to the ski area). Continue about three-tenths of a mile and bear right, crossing the West Branch of the Mad River on a bridge, then drive straight ahead about 250 feet to a parking area at the start of the Greeley Ponds Trail and Livermore Road.

Maps: For a contour map of trails, see the "Chocorua-Waterville" map 4 from the

Appalachian Mountain Club (800-262-4455), which is $2.95 and widely available in stores; the "Trail Map and Guide to the White Mountain National Forest," which is $4.95, from the DeLorme Mapping Company, (800) 253-5081; or the map of the national forest, available by sending a check for $4 to White Mountain National Forest main office (see address below). For topographic maps of the area, request Mount Tripyramid and Waterville Valley from the USGS.

Contact: White Mountain National Forest Supervisor, 719 North Main Street, Laconia, NH 03246; (603) 528-8721, TDD for hearing impaired (603) 528-8722.

Trail notes: Tripyramid's three wooded summits offer little in the way of compelling views. But two friends and I spent a wonderful day mountain biking to the hiking trail loop and scrambling up and down Tripyramid's two rockslides. While you can hike this entire route, I suggest mountain biking the Livermore Trail, an old logging road, then stashing your bikes in the woods and hiking the Mount Tripyramid Trail. And two of the three summits along this route, the North and Middle Peaks, are both official 4,000-footers.

From the parking area, walk around the gate onto Livermore Road (also called the Livermore Trail), a rough road ascending gradually for 2.6 miles to the south end of the Tripyramid Trail, which loops over the mountain. If you have bikes, leave them here at the south end of the loop, and walk another mile up the Livermore Trail, then turn right onto the Mount Tripyramid Trail at its north end. The trail ascends the north slide, which is more exposed and steeper than the south slide (making this the preferred direction of travel of the loop), and dangerous when wet or icy. At 1.2 miles, the trail reaches the North Peak and true summit at 4,140 feet. There are limited views. Continue on the narrow path, passing a junction with the Sabbaday Brook Trail a half mile from North Peak, and reaching Middle Peak (4,110 feet) three-tenths of a mile farther. A pair of outlooks just off the trail offer decent views. The trail continues to the South Peak (4,090 feet), which is wooded. Just beyond that peak, bear right where the Sleeper Trail branches left and descend the steep south slide, which has lots of loose rock. The trail enters the woods again and follows Slide Brook past nice pools to the Livermore Trail, 2.5 miles from South Peak. Turn left and hike (or bike) the 2.6 miles back to the parking area.

60 Welch and Dickey

4.5 mi/3.0 hrs 

Location: In the White Mountain National Forest southwest of Waterville Valley; Northern New Hampshire map page 86, grid f2.

User groups: Hikers, dogs, and snowshoers. No wheelchair facilities. This trail is not suitable for bikes, horses, or skis. Hunting is allowed in season.

Access, fees: Parking and access are free.

Directions: From Interstate 93 in Campton, take exit 28 onto Route 49 north, toward Waterville Valley. After passing through the traffic lights in Campton, drive another 4.4 miles on Route 49, then turn left onto Upper Mad River Road, immediately crossing the Mad River on Six Mile Bridge. Continue seven-tenths of a mile from Route 49, then turn right at a sign reading "Welch Mountain Trail." Drive another seven-tenths of a mile to a parking area at the trailhead.

Maps: For a map of trails, obtain the "Chocorua-Waterville" map 4 from the Appalachian Mountain Club, (800) 262-4455, which is $2.95 and widely available in stores; the "Trail Map and Guide to the

White Mountain National Forest," which is $4.95 from the DeLorme Mapping Company, (800) 253-5081; or the map of the national forest, available by sending a check for $4 to White Mountain National Forest main office (see address below). For a topographic map of the area, request Waterville Valley from the USGS.

Contact: White Mountain National Forest Supervisor, 719 North Main Street, Laconia, NH 03246; (603) 528-8721, TDD for hearing impaired (603) 528-8722.

Trail notes: My mom, an avid hiker, and I hiked this 4.5-mile loop over Welch (2,605 feet) and Dickey (2,736 feet) Mountains at the peak of foliage on a day when the higher mountains were swathed in clouds. Yet, these lower summits remained clear, giving us colorful views from the many open ledges on this loop hike. Relatively easy, with just a few brief, steep stretches, it's a good hike for young children.

From the parking area, you can do the loop in either direction, but I recommend heading up the Welch Mountain Trail (hiking counter-clockwise). Within a mile, the trail emerges onto open ledges just below the summit of Welch Mountain, with a wide view across the Mad River Valley to Sandwich Mountain. The trail turns left and ascends another mile to the summit, with broad views in every direction, including of Dickey Mountain to the north. Continuing on the trail, you drop steeply into a shallow saddle, then climb up onto Dickey, a half mile from Welch. Watch for a sign pointing to nearby "Ledges," where there is a good view toward Franconia Notch. From Dickey's summit, follow an arrow onto an obvious trail north, which soon descends steeply to slab ledges above the cliffs of Dickey Mountain, overlooking a beautiful, narrow valley between Welch and Dickey that blazes with color during the peak of foliage. The Dickey Mountain Trail continues descending the ridge, re-entering the woods, then reaching the parking area, two miles from Dickey's summit.

61 Mount Whiteface

8.0 mi/5.5 hrs 

Location: In the southern White Mountain National Forest north of Wonalancet; Northern New Hampshire map page 86, grid f3.

User groups: Hikers only. No wheelchair facilities. This trail may be difficult to snowshoe because of severe winter weather, and is not suitable for bikes, dogs, horses, or skis. Hunting is allowed in season.

Access, fees: Parking and access are free. Trails in this part of the national forest are accessed through private land; be sure to stay on trails. The Camp Heermance shelter is 3.8 miles from the Ferncroft parking area via the Blueberry Ledge Trail. The Camp Shehadi shelter is a tenth of a mile north of Whiteface's south summit on the Rollins Path. Both shelters are free and open to the public.

Directions: From Route 113A in Wonalancet, turn north onto Ferncroft Road. Follow it for a half mile and bear right at a sign into the hiker parking lot.

Maps: For a contour map of trails, obtain the Tyvek map by sending a check for $5 to the Wonalancet Out Door Club (see address below); the map is also available in local stores. Or obtain the "Chocorua-Waterville" map from the Appalachian Mountain Club (800-262-4455), which is $2.95 and widely available in stores; the "Trail Map and Guide to the White Mountain National Forest," which is $4.95 from the DeLorme Mapping Company, (800) 253-5081; or the map of the national forest, available by sending a check for $4 to White Mountain National Forest main office (see address below). For topographic maps of the area, request

Mount Chocorua and Mount Tripyramid from the USGS.

Contact: Wonalancet Out Door Club, WODC, HCR 64 Box 5, Wonalancet, NH 03897. White Mountain National Forest Supervisor, 719 North Main St., Laconia, NH 03246; (603) 528-8721, TDD for hearing impaired (603) 528-8722.

Trail notes: While Whiteface, at 4,105 feet, is not among the best-known 4,000-footers in the Whites, the cliffs just below its summit offer dramatic views of the southern Whites, Mount Washington, and the lakes region to the south. The precipices along the upper Blueberry Ledge Trail are a great place to catch the fall foliage; I did one late September morning, and also saw my first snowflakes of the season. All trails here are blazed in blue.

From the parking lot, walk back to the road and turn right, following the road and signs for the trails for three-tenths of a mile. Turn left onto the Blueberry Ledge Trail, crossing over Wonalancet Brook on a bridge. Continue hiking on the single-lane dirt road to its end, where the Blueberry Ledge Trail enters the woods. The trail remains fairly easy at first, crossing slab ledges 1.5 miles from the parking lot.

At 3.2 miles, the Wiggin Trail diverges right (east), leading 1.1 miles to the Dicey's Mill Trail—the descent route for this hike. The best views begin at 3.6 miles, where the Blueberry Ledge Trail turns sharply right at a slab and the brink of a cliff which could be hazardous when wet or icy. To the south and southwest are the lakes of central New Hampshire and Sandwich Mountain. Continue up the Blueberry Ledge Trail for another three-tenths of a mile, employing a wooden ladder in one section of nearly vertical rock. You will pass ledges with terrific views down into the broad glacial cirque known as The Bowl, which is framed by Whiteface and neighboring Mount Passaconaway, east to Mount Chocorua, and north to Mount Washington. Bear right at a trail junction near open ledges onto the Rollins Trail, following it two-tenths of a mile to the wooded summit of Whiteface. To descend, return to the Wiggin Trail, turn left, and follow it to the Dicey's Mill Trail; turn right, and descend 1.9 miles to the parking area, the last half mile of hiking following Ferncroft Road. For a longer loop linking Whiteface with Passaconaway, see the special note in the trail notes for Mount Passaconaway (hike number 62).

---

62 Mount Passaconaway

9.5 mi/6.5 hrs 

Location: In the southern White Mountain National Forest north of Wonalancet; Northern New Hampshire map page 86, grid f3.

User groups: Hikers only. No wheelchair facilities. This trail could be difficult to snowshoe because of severe winter weather, and is not suitable for bikes, dogs, horses, or skis. Hunting is allowed in season.

Access, fees: Parking and access are free. Trails in this part of the national forest are accessed through private land; be sure to stay on trails. The Camp Rich shelter is along the Dicey's Mill Trail, 3.9 miles from the Ferncroft parking area. It is free and open to the public.

Directions: From Route 113A in Wonalancet, turn north onto Ferncroft Road. Follow it for a half mile and bear right at a sign into the hiker parking lot.

Maps: For a contour map of trails, obtain the Tyvek map by sending a check for $5 to the Wonalancet Out Door Club (see address below); the map is also available in local stores. Or obtain the "Chocorua-Waterville" map from the Appalachian Mountain Club (800-262-4455), which is $2.95 and widely available in stores; the "Trail Map and Guide to the White Mountain National Forest," which is $4.95 from the DeLorme Mapping Company, (800) 253-5081; or the map of the national forest, available by sending a check for $4 to White Mountain National Forest main office (see address below). For topographic maps of the area, request Mount Chocorua and Mount Tripyramid from the USGS.

Contact: Wonalancet Out Door Club, WODC, HCR 64 Box 5, Wonalancet, NH 03897. White Mountain National Forest Supervisor, 719 North Main Street, Laconia, NH 03246; (603) 528-8721, TDD for hearing impaired (603) 528-8722.

Trail notes: Probably one of the least-visited of New Hampshire's 4,000-foot summits, the top of Passaconaway (4,060 feet) is wooded, with no views (unless you're standing on a few feet of snow and can see over the low spruce trees). But there are two nice views near the summit. The trails are marked with blue blazes.

From the parking lot, walk back to the road and turn right, following the road for eight-tenths of a mile straight onto the Dicey's Mill Trail. Soon after entering the woods, the trail crosses into the national forest. It parallels and eventually crosses Wonalancet Brook at 2.3 miles (four-tenths of a mile beyond the Wiggin Trail junction), then begins ascending more steeply. The trail passes the junction with the Rollins Trail, coming in from the left (west) at 3.7 miles, then the East Loop Trail departing right (east) at 3.9 miles. At around 4.5 miles, you'll get a view toward the peaks above Waterville Valley to the northwest. The junction with the Walden Trail is reached at 4.6 miles; from there, a spur path leads to the right about 50 yards to Passaconaway's summit. Follow the Walden Trail around the summit cone about 100 yards to the best view on this hike, from a ledge overlooking Mount Chocorua to the east and Mount Washington to the north. Continue descending the Walden Trail, dropping steeply to the East Loop, six-tenths of a mile from the summit spur path. Turn right (west) on the East Loop, which leads two-tenths of a mile back to the Dicey's Mill Trail. Turn left (south) and follow that trail 3.9 miles back to the Ferncroft Road parking area.

Special note: You can combine Passaconaway and Mount Whiteface on a rugged loop of nearly 12 miles. Hike the Blueberry Ledge Trail up Whiteface, then the Rollins Trail for 2.3 miles over the high ridge connecting the two peaks; there are some views along the Rollins, though much of it is within the subalpine conifer forest. Turn left (north) on the Dicey's Mill Trail, then complete the Passaconaway hike described above.

63 Mount Chocorua: Brook-Liberty Loop

7.4 mi/5.0 hrs 3 10

Location: In the White Mountain National Forest, north of Tamworth and east of Wonalancet; Northern New Hampshire map page 86, grid f3.

User groups: Hikers and dogs. No wheelchair facilities. This trail may be difficult to snowshoe because of severe winter weather, and is not suitable for bikes, horses, or skis. Hunting is allowed in season.

Access, fees: Parking and access are free. The national forest maintains the Jim Liberty cabin (which has a capacity of nine) on the Liberty Trail, a half mile below Chocorua's summit; a fee is charged and the water source is unreliable in dry seasons. Contact the White Mountain National Forest (see address below) for rate and reservation information.

Directions: From the junction of Routes 113 and 113A in Tamworth, drive west on Route 113A for 3.4 miles and turn right onto the dirt Fowler's Mill Road. Continue for 1.2

miles and turn left (at trail signs) onto Paugus Road (Fire Road 68). The parking area and trailhead lie eight-tenths of a mile up the road.

Maps: For a contour map of hiking trails, get the "Chocorua-Waterville" map 4, which is $2.95 from the Appalachian Mountain Club, (800) 262-4455, and is also widely available in stores. Or get the "Trail Map and Guide to the White Mountain National Forest," which is $4.95 from the DeLorme Mapping Company, (800) 253-5081. For topographic maps of the area, request Mount Chocorua and Silver Lake from the USGS.

Contact: White Mountain National Forest Supervisor, 719 North Main Street, Laconia, NH 03246; (603) 528-8721, TDD for the hearing impaired (603) 528-8722.

Trail notes: Of the two routes described in this guide up the popular, 3,475-foot Mount Chocorua, this one is far less traveled—and, in my opinion, a better hike. Chocorua is a great place to bring children; I hiked this loop with my nephew Nicholas shortly before he turned seven, and he could not contain his excitement as we scrambled up the final slabs and ledges to the open, rocky summit. The summit attracts many dozens of hikers on clear weekend days in summer and fall, for good reason: the views north to Mount Washington, west across the White Mountains, south to the lakes region, and east over the hills and lakes of western Maine are among the finest attainable in the Whites without climbing a bigger peak. The foliage views are particularly striking.

On this loop, hike up the Brook Trail, which is steeper, and descend the Liberty Trail—the easiest route on Chocorua. (Hikers looking for a less demanding route could opt to go up and down the Liberty Trail.) From the parking area, walk past the gate and follow the gravel woods road, which the Brook Trail leaves within a half mile. The trail passes a small waterfall along Claybank Brook less than two miles up and, after some easy to moderately difficult hiking, emerges from the woods onto the bare rock of Chocorua's summit cone at three miles. The final six-tenths of a mile ascends steep slabs and ledges; the Liberty Trail coincides with the Brook Trail for the last two-tenths of a mile. To descend, follow the two trails down for that two-tenths of a mile, then bear left onto the Liberty Trail. It traverses somewhat rocky ground high on the mountain, passing the U.S. Forest Service's Jim Liberty cabin within a half mile. The descent grows more moderate, eventually following an old bridle path back to the parking area, 3.8 miles from the summit.

64 Mount Chocorua: Piper Trail

9.0 mi/6.5 hrs 

Location: In the White Mountain National Forest, north of Chocorua and west of Conway; Northern New Hampshire map page 86, grid f3.

User groups: Hikers and dogs. No wheelchair facilities. This trail may be difficult to snowshoe because of severe winter weather, and is not suitable for bikes, horses, or skis. Hunting is allowed in season.

Access, fees: A small fee is charged for parking at the Piper Trail Restaurant and Cabins, where the trail begins. The national forest maintains Camp Penacook, which consists of a lean-to shelter and four tent platforms, 3.1 miles up the Piper Trail and 1.4 miles below Chocorua's summit; there is no fee.

Directions: The Piper Trail begins behind the Piper Trail Restaurant and Cabins on Route 16 between the towns of Chocorua and Conway.

Maps: For a contour map of hiking trails, get the "Chocorua-Waterville" map 4, which is $2.95 from the Appalachian Mountain Club, (800) 262-4455, and is also widely available in stores. Or get the "Trail Map and Guide to the White Mountain National Forest," which is $4.95 from the DeLorme Mapping Company, (800) 253-5081. For topographic maps of the area, request Mount Chocorua and Silver Lake from the USGS.

Contact: White Mountain National Forest Supervisor, 719 North Main Street, Laconia, NH 03246; (603) 528-8721, TDD for the hearing impaired (603) 528-8722.

Trail notes: This is the most heavily used route up the popular, 3,475-foot Mount Chocorua, though at nine miles for the round-trip it is not the shortest; the trail suffers from erosion due to overuse, which can make the footing difficult in places.

From the parking area, the trail starts out on easy ground, entering the woods. About two miles out, it crosses the Chocorua River and ascends switchbacks up the steepening mountainside. At 3.1 miles, a short side path leads to the Camp Penacook shelter and tent sites. The final half mile of trail passes over open ledges, with sweeping views, to the summit, where the panoramic views take in Mount Washington to the north, New Hampshire's lakes region to the south, the hills and lakes of western Maine to the east, and the grand sweep of the White Mountains to the west and northwest. Descend the same trail.

65 Smarts Mountain

7.5 mi/4.5 hrs 

Location: In Lyme; Northern New Hampshire map page 86, grid f1.

User groups: Hikers, dogs, and snowshoers. No wheelchair facilities. This trail is not suitable for skis. Bikes, horses, and hunting are prohibited.

Access, fees: Parking and access are free. The Smarts tent platform is located about four miles up the Lambert Ridge (Appalachian Trail) and a tenth of a mile below the summit.

Directions: From Route 10 on the Green in Lyme, take Dorchester Road (at the white church), following signs for the Dartmouth Skiway. Two miles from the Green, pass through the village of Lyme Center. In another 1.3 miles, bear left onto the gravel Lyme-Dorchester Road (across from where the Appalachian Trail emerges from the woods on the right). In another 1.8 miles, just before an iron bridge over Grant Brook, park in a small lot on the left, at the trailhead.

Maps: A map of the Appalachian Trail between Pomfret, Vermont, and Kinsman Notch, New Hampshire, is available from the Dartmouth Outing Club (see address below). Map 4 in the "Map and Guide to the Appalachian Trail in New Hampshire and Vermont," an eight-map set for $10.95 from the Appalachian Trail Conference (see address below), also covers this hike. For a topographic map of the area, request Smarts Mountain from the USGS.

Contact: The Dartmouth Outing Club, P.O. Box 9, Hanover, NH 03755; (603) 646-2428. Appalachian Trail Conference, P.O. Box 807, Harpers Ferry, WV 25425; (304) 535-6331.

Trail notes: New England's topography and weather sometimes collaborate to make a smaller peak feel like a bigger mountain. At 3,240 feet, Smarts is one of those. This hike, not to be underestimated, blends nice walks in the woods and along the rocky crest of a ridge with a rigorous final push to the summit through the sort of evergreen forest usually found at higher elevations. A fire tower on the wooded summit offers a magnificent panorama of the upper Connecticut Valley, the Green Mountains, and the Whites on a clear day.

From the parking lot, pick up the Lambert Ridge Trail (there's a sign), which is also the

AT. (The unmarked but wide path at the end of the lot is the Ranger Trail, your route of descent.) Within the first 1.5 miles, the pleasant woods walk is enhanced with several views in various directions atop the rocky Lambert Ridge (itself a nice destination for a short hike). The trail then drops slightly, changes direction a few times—watch for white blazes—then ascends relentlessly the steep west slope of Smarts, passing the unmarked junction (on the right) with the Ranger Trail 3.5 miles from the parking lot. A half mile farther, a side trail leads right to the Smarts tent platform. Continuing on the AT about a tenth of a mile, watch on the left for a spur trail to the fire tower. Backtrack six-tenths of a mile and bear left to descend the Ranger Trail 3.5 miles to the trailhead. (The final 1.5 miles of the Ranger Trail, which ascends at a gentle angle, could be skied on an approach in winter, up to an abandoned garage where the trail crosses Grant Brook.)

66 Holt's Ledge

2.2 mi/1.5 hrs 

Location: In Lyme; Northern New Hampshire map page 86, grid f1.

User groups: Hikers, dogs, and snowshoers. No wheelchair facilities. This trail is not suitable for skis. Bikes, horses, and hunting are prohibited.

Access, fees: Parking and access are free. The Trapper John lean-to shelter is located two-tenths of a mile down a side path off the Appalachian Trail, a half mile south of this hike's start.

Directions: From Route 10 on the Green in Lyme, take Dorchester Road (at the white church), following signs for the Dartmouth Skiway. Two miles from the Green, you will pass through the village of Lyme Center. In another 1.3 miles, across from the gravel Lyme-Dorchester Road, the Appalachian Trail emerges from the woods on the right. Park either at the roadside or a short distance farther in the dirt lot for the Dartmouth Skiway.

Maps: A map of the Appalachian Trail between Pomfret, Vermont, and Kinsman Notch, New Hampshire, is available from the Dartmouth Outing Club (see address below). Map 4 in the "Map and Guide to the Appalachian Trail in New Hampshire and Vermont," an eight-map set for $10.95 from the Appalachian Trail Conference (see address below), covers this hike. For a topographic map of the area, request Smarts Mountain from the USGS.

Contact: The Dartmouth Outing Club, P.O. Box 9, Hanover, NH 03755; (603) 646-2428. Appalachian Trail Conference, P.O. Box 807, Harpers Ferry, WV 25425; (304) 535-6331.

Trail notes: Holt's Ledge, at the top of a tall, rugged cliff, lies at the end of a fairly easy walk through the woods along the Appalachian Trail. From Holt's Ledge you can see Smarts Mountain and Mount Cube (beyond and left of Smarts) to the north, Cardigan and Kearsarge to the east, and Ascutney in the distance to the south. Don't venture beyond the weathered fencing on the ledge, because the cliff's brink is quite crumbly and peregrine falcons nest below.

From the trailhead, follow the white-blazed AT. At a half mile, it passes a side trail leading two-tenths of a mile to the Trapper John shelter, where you'll find water and an outhouse. After crossing a stream, the trail climbs a hillside to the cliffs; the AT swings right, and a side trail leads left to the open ledges. Return the same way.

67 Moose Mountain

4.1 mi/3.0 hrs 

Location: In Hanover; Northern New Hampshire map page 86, grid f1.

User groups: Hikers, dogs, and snowshoers. No wheelchair facilities. This trail is not suitable for skis. Bikes, horses, and hunting are prohibited.

Access, fees: Parking and access are free. The Moose Mountain shelter is located two-tenths of a mile off this loop, 2.3 miles into the hike.

Directions: From Interstate 91, take exit 13 in Norwich. Head east, crossing the Connecticut River and driving up a long hill to the center of Hanover. Drive straight through the traffic lights (the Dartmouth College Green is to your left) onto East Wheelock Street, and follow it 4.3 miles into the Hanover village of Etna. Turn left onto Etna Road, proceed eight-tenths of a mile, then right onto Ruddsboro Road. Continue 1.5 miles, then turn left onto Three Mile Road. Drive another 1.3 miles to a turnout on the left, where the white-blazed Appalachian Trail crosses the road.

Maps: A map of the Appalachian Trail between Pomfret, Vermont, and Kinsman Notch, New Hampshire, is available from the Dartmouth Outing Club (see address below). Map 4 in the "Map and Guide to the Appalachian Trail in New Hampshire and Vermont," an eight-map set for $10.95 from the Appalachian Trail Conference (see address below), covers this hike. For topographic maps of the area, request Hanover and Canaan from the USGS.

Contact: Dartmouth Outing Club, P.O. Box 9, Hanover, NH 03755; (603) 646-2428. Appalachian Trail Conference, P.O. Box 807, Harpers Ferry, WV 25425; (304) 535-6331.

Trail notes: This loop, incorporating a stretch of the Appalachian Trail, passes over the South summit of Moose Mountain (2,290 feet), where a plane crashed in 1968. The ensuing rescue effort included a bulldozer clearing a route to the summit. The result is a lasting view east and southeast, taking in Goose Pond (in the foreground) and Clark Pond (in the distance) in the town of Canaan, and Mounts Cardigan and Kearsarge in the distance.

From the parking area, cross the road to the east, following the white-blazed AT northbound. The trail crosses a brook, then the wide, two-track Harris Trail at four-tenths of a mile. It then begins the ascent of Moose Mountain, climbing at a moderate angle at first, leveling somewhat, then climbing again to the South summit at 1.8 miles. Continue north across the clearing, following the white blazes another half mile to a junction with the Clark Pond Loop. To the right, the Clark Pond Loop leads two-tenths of a mile to the Moose Mountain shelter. Turn left (west) onto the Clark Loop and descend seven-tenths of a mile to the Harris Trail. Turn left again (south), following the Harris seven-tenths of a mile to the AT. Turn right and walk the AT four-tenths of a mile back to Three Mile Road.

68 Squam Mountains

5.1 mi/3.0 hrs 3 9

Location: Between Holderness and Center Sandwich; Northern New Hampshire map page 86, grid f2.

User groups: Hikers, dogs, and snowshoers. No wheelchair facilities. This trail is not suitable for bikes, horses, or skis. Hunting is allowed in season.

Access, fees: Parking and access are free.

Directions: The trailhead parking lot is on Route 113, 5.6 miles east of the junction of U.S. 3 and Route 113, and 6.3 miles west of the junction of Routes 109 and 113.

Maps: The Squam Lakes Association (see address below) sells a trail map for $7, and an area guidebook for $3.25, plus $1 shipping. For a topographic map of the area, request Squam Mountains from the USGS.

Contact: Squam Lakes Association, Main Street, Holderness, NH 03245.

Trail notes: This very popular hike leads

to views from the low peaks of the Squam Mountains range of Squam Lake and massive Lake Winnipesaukee. A friend and I made this loop on a sunny Saturday, the first weekend of October, when the fall foliage was at its peak. This is a fairly easy hike with only one short, difficult section—the cliffs on the Mount Morgan Trail—which can be avoided (described below).

From the parking lot, walk around the gate onto the Mount Morgan Trail. It ascends gently for more than a mile, then steepens somewhat. At 1.7 miles, the Crawford-Ridgepole Trail enters from the left and coincides with the Mount Morgan Trail for two-tenths of a mile. Where they split again, the Crawford-Ridgepole bears right for an easier route up Mount Morgan. This hike turns left with the Mount Morgan Trail, immediately scaling low cliffs on a wooden ladder, after which you crawl through a cavelike passage through rocks and emerge atop the cliffs with an excellent view of the big lakes to the south. Follow the blazes up the slabs to Morgan's open summit and extensive views south. Pick up the Crawford-Ridgepole Trail eastward along the Squam Mountains Ridge—with occasional views, including the distinctive horned summit of Mount Chocorua—another eight-tenths of a mile to the open summit of Mount Percival, which also has excellent views of the lakes. Turn right and descend the Mount Percival Trail (look for a small trail sign nailed to a tree at the base of the summit slabs). After a relatively easy descent of 1.9 miles to Route 113, turn right and walk the road for three-tenths of a mile back to the parking area.

69 West Rattlesnake

1.8 mi/1.0 hr 

Location: Between Holderness and Center Sandwich; Northern New Hampshire map page 86, grid f2.

User groups: Hikers, dogs, and snowshoers. No wheelchair facilities. This trail is not suitable for bikes, horses, or skis. Hunting is allowed in season.

Access, fees: Parking and access are free.

Directions: The trailhead parking lot is on Route 113, 5.6 miles east of the junction of U.S. 3 and Route 113, and 6.3 miles west of the junction of Routes 109 and 113.

Maps: The Squam Lakes Association (see address below) sells a trail map for $7, and an area guidebook for $3.25, plus $1 shipping. For a topographic map of the area, request Squam Mountains from the USGS.

Contact: Squam Lakes Association, Main Street, Holderness, NH 03245.

Trail notes: From the parking area for the Mount Morgan Trail, cross Route 113 and walk west about 100 feet to the Old Bridle Path. This easy hike, a good one for young children, follows a wide trail which rises gently for nine-tenths of a mile to clifftop views from several hundred feet above Squam Lake. Where the main trail turns left, follow a side path to the right about 100 feet to the cliffs. Return the way you came.

70 Eagle Cliff

1.2 mi/0.75 hr 

Location: North of Center Harbor; Northern New Hampshire map page 86, grid f3.

User groups: Hikers, dogs, and snowshoers. No wheelchair facilities. This trail is not suitable for bikes, horses, or skis. Hunting is allowed in season.

Access, fees: Parking and access are free.

Directions: In Center Harbor, immediately east of the junction of Routes 25 and 25B, turn north off Route 25 onto Bean Road. Follow it five miles to roadside parking; the trail is not marked, but it enters the woods across the road from a "Traffic turning and entering" sign (for southbound traffic).

Maps: The Squam Lakes Association (see address below) sells a trail map for $7, and an area guidebook for $3.25, plus $1 shipping. For a topographic map of the area, request Squam Mountains from the USGS.

Contact: Squam Lakes Association, Main Street, Holderness, NH 03245.

Trail notes: A few steps off the road on the trail, you pass a post marked with the name Eagle Cliff Trail. Rising moderately for much of its six-tenths-of-a-mile climb, the trail grows steep for the final two-tenths of a mile. Near the top, turn left to reach open ledges with a dramatic view from high above Squam Lake. Across the water rises the low ridge of the Squam Mountains. To the north lie the southern White Mountains; the most readily identifiable is the horn of Mount Chocorua to the northeast. Hike back along the same route.

---

71 Mount Cardigan: East Side Loop

5.2 mi/3.5 hrs 

Location: In Cardigan State Park west of Alexandria; Southern New Hampshire map page 87, grid a3.

User groups: Hikers and dogs. No wheelchair facilities. Dogs must be on a leash. This trail may be difficult to snowshoe, in part because of severe winter weather, and is not suitable for bikes, horses, or skis. Hunting is allowed in season unless otherwise posted.

Access, fees: Parking and access are free. The access road is maintained in winter.

Directions: From the junction of Routes 3A and 104 in Bristol, drive north on Route 3A for 2.1 miles and turn left at a stone church at the south end of Newfound Lake. Continue 1.9 miles and proceed straight through a crossroads. Reaching a fork in 1.2 miles, bear right, then turn left 3.2 miles farther. Continue another 1.1 miles, then turn right onto a dirt road; just a tenth of a mile farther, bear right at a red schoolhouse, then drive 1.4 miles to the end of that road, where parking is available near the Appalachian Mountain Club's Cardigan Lodge.

Maps: The Carter-Mahoosuc/Mount Monadnock/Mount Cardigan map is $2.95 from the Appalachian Mountain Club, (800) 262-4455, and is widely available in stores. For topographic maps of the area, request Mount Cardigan and Newfound Lake from the USGS.

Contact: New Hampshire Division of Parks and Recreation, P.O. Box 1856, Concord, NH 03302-1856; (603) 271-3254.

Trail notes: Left bare by a fire in 1855, the 3,121-foot crown of Mount Cardigan affords long views in a 360-degree panorama of the Green and White Mountains, and prominent hills to the south like Mounts Ascutney and Sunapee. It's a popular hike; hundreds of people, many of them children, will climb Cardigan on sunny weekends during the warm months. This steep hike up the east side of Cardigan provided quite a "big-mountain" adventure for my two nephews and niece, age 6 to 9 at the time of our climb on a sunny, blustery September Saturday. As we scaled the mountain's upper slabs to the summit, they called out comments like, "Wow, this is steep!" and "Wow, look how high we are!" The upper Holt Trail does grow quite steep, involving exposed scrambling on open slabs which become dangerous when wet or icy— and on which I watched the kids closely even though the rock was dry.

From the parking area, the Holt Trail at first follows a wide, nearly flat woods road for almost a mile. At 1.1 miles, the trail crosses Bailey Brook, then follows the brook (other trails branch left and right from the Holt). Growing steeper, the trail leaves the brook and ascends very steep, exposed rock slabs for the final three-tenths of a mile to the open summit, 2.2 miles from the parking area. Turn right (north) onto the Mowglis Trail and follow it off the summit, dropping sharply into the saddle between the main summit and Firescrew Mountain, a shoulder of Cardigan. The Mowglis Trail then climbs to the open top of Firescrew, with more long views, six-tenths of a mile from Cardigan's summit. Turn right (east) and follow the Manning Trail, descending steadily with good views for about two-tenths of a mile, then re-entering the woods and reaching the Holt Trail, nearly three miles from Cardigan's summit. Turn left and walk back to the parking lot.

72 Mount Major

3.0 mi/1.5 hrs 

Location: Between West Alton and Alton Bay; Southern New Hampshire map page 87, grid a4.

User groups: Hikers, dogs, and snowshoers. No wheelchair facilities. Dogs must be on a leash. This trail is not suitable for bikes, horses, or skis. Hunting is allowed in season.

Access, fees: Parking and access are free. The state owns the summit area and maintains the parking lot, but the trail crosses private property.

Directions: The Mount Major Trail begins from a large parking area on Route 11, 2.4 miles south of the intersection of Routes 11 and 11A in West Alton, and 4.2 miles north of the junction of Routes 11 and 28A in Alton Bay.

Maps: For a topographic map of the area, request Squam Mountains from the USGS.

Contact: New Hampshire Division of Parks and Recreation, P.O. Box 1856, Concord, NH 03302-1856; (603) 271-3254.

Trail notes: Perhaps the most popular hike in the lakes region, especially among families with young children, Mount Major has a bare summit which affords breathtaking views of Lake Winnipesaukee and north to the White Mountains on a clear day. From the parking lot, follow the wide, stone-littered trail climbing 1.5 miles to Major's summit. Descend the same way.

73 Mount Kearsarge

2.2 mi/2.0 hrs 

Location: In Winslow State Park in Wilmot; Southern New Hampshire map page 87, grid b3.

User groups: Hikers and dogs. No wheelchair facilities. Dogs must be on a leash. This trail may be difficult to snowshoe, in part because of severe winter weather, and is not suitable for bikes, horses, or skis. Hunting is allowed in season.

Access, fees: Winslow State Park is open from 9 A.M. to 8 P.M. from May 1 to mid-November. There is a $2.50-per-person park entrance fee levied daily during the season the park is open; children under 12 and New Hampshire residents 65 and older enter free. The last six-tenths of a mile of the entrance road is not maintained in winter (beyond the fork at the Dead End sign).

Directions: Take Interstate 89 to exit 10 and follow the signs to Winslow State Park. From the toll booth at the state park entrance, drive to the dirt parking lot at the end of the road.

Maps: A basic trail map of Winslow State Park is available at the park or from the New Hampshire Division of Parks and Recreation (see address below). For topographic maps of the area, request New London, Andover, Bradford, and Warner from the USGS.

Contact: Winslow State Park, P.O. Box 295, Newbury, NH 03255; (603) 526-6168. New Hampshire Division of Parks and Recreation, P.O. Box 1856, Concord, NH 03302-1856; (603) 271-3254.

Northern New Hampshire Map—page 86

Trail notes: The barren, 2,937-foot summit of Mount Kearsarge, offering views of the White Mountains, Green Mountains, and southern New Hampshire, makes this one of the finest short hikes in New England—and, while steep, a great adventure for young children. Walk to the upper end of the parking lot in Winslow State Park and pick up the red-blazed Wilmot Trail. The wide, well-beaten path rises quite steeply and relentlessly, and grows even more rugged the higher you go. At eight-tenths of a mile, a large boulder on the left gives a good view north. A short distance farther, you break out of the trees onto the bald summit, with views in every direction, including Monadnock to the south, Mount Sunapee and Lake Sunapee to the southwest, Mount Cardigan to the northwest, the Greens to the west, and the Whites to the north. This is also a wonderful hike during the height of the fall foliage colors. A fire tower stands at the summit, near which are a pair of picnic tables—although, on windy days, it can be hard to linger up here for very long. Hike back along the same route.

74 Mount Sunapee

4.0 mi/2.5 hrs 

Location: In Mount Sunapee State Park in Newbury; Southern New Hampshire map page 87, grid b2.

User groups: Hikers, dogs, and snowshoers. No wheelchair facilities. Dogs must be on a leash. This trail is not suitable for bikes, horses, or skis. Hunting is allowed in season unless otherwise posted.

Access, fees: Parking and access are free.

Directions: From Interstate 89 southbound, take exit 12A. Turn right, drive six-tenths of a mile, and turn right again onto Route 11 west. Continue 3.5 miles and turn left onto Route 103B. Or from Interstate 89 northbound, take exit 12, turn left, and follow Route 11 to the left onto Route 103B. Drive another 3.5 miles, halfway around a traffic circle, and bear right at a sign for the state park. Continue to the end of the road and a large parking area at the base of the ski area. Turn left and drive 5.1 miles on Route 11, then turn left onto Route 103B and follow the above directions from there.

Maps: A free map of trails is available at the state park or from the New Hampshire Division of Parks and Recreation (see address below). The Monadnock-Sunapee Greenway Club (see address below) publishes a guidebook, which includes maps, of the Monadnock-Sunapee Greenway, a trail stretching 50 miles from Mount Monadnock to Mount Sunapee. For a topographic map of the area, request Newport from the USGS.

Contact: Mount Sunapee State Park, P.O. Box 2021, Mount Sunapee, NH 03255; (603) 763-2356. New Hampshire Division of Parks and Recreation, P.O. Box 1856, Concord, NH 03302-1856; (603) 271-3254. Monadnock-Sunapee Greenway Trail Club (MSGTC), P.O. Box 164, Marlow, NH 03456.

Trail notes: The new Summit Trail up central New Hampshire's popular Mount Sunapee offers a fairly easy, four-mile round-trip route from the ski area parking lot to the 2,743-foot summit. Many hikers will be satisfied with that. But this description also covers the Monadnock-Sunapee Greenway Trail from Sunapee's summit to Lucia's Lookout on Sunapee's long southern ridge—an ambitious round-trip from the parking lot of 12.8 miles and about seven hours, but well worth the effort for the views along the ridge, particularly overlooking Lake Solitude. Walking this trail with an organizer of the Monadnock-Sunapee Greenway Trail Club one September afternoon, we spotted several moose tracks.

From the parking lot, walk behind the North Peak Lodge and to the right to pick up the Summit Trail, marked by a sign and red blazes. Ascending easily but steadily through the woods for two miles, the trail emerges onto an open meadow, where to the right (south) you get a view toward Mount Monadnock. Turn left and walk to the summit lodge a short distance ahead. Some of the best views on the mountain are from the decks at the lodge, with Mount Ascutney and the Green Mountains visible to the west, and Mounts Cardigan and Moosilauke and Franconia Ridge to the north. To complete this four-mile hike, return the way you came. To lengthen it with a walk along the somewhat rugged Sunapee Ridge, descend from the lodge toward the ski trails, following the Porky Trail and bearing right at the white blazes of the Monadnock-Sunapee Greenway. Watch for signs for Lake Solitude, also.

After re-entering the woods two-tenths of a mile from the summit, the greenway reaches the open White Ledges nine-tenths of a mile from the summit; the trail swings left, but walking to the right will lead you to an open ledge with an excellent view from atop a low cliff of beautiful Lake Solitude, a small tarn tucked into the mountain's shoulder. Monadnock is visible beyond the lake. Continuing south on the greenway, you skirt the lake's shore within two-tenths of a mile. The trail passes over an open ledge 2.7 miles from the summit before reaching Lucia's Lookout, 4.2 miles from the summit. Here, the views take in Monadnock and Lovewell Mountain to the south, the Green Mountains to the west, and Mount Kearsarge and the White Mountains to the north. Hike back the way you came.

75 Catamount Hill

2.2 mi/1.5 hrs 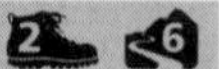

Location: In Bear Brook State Park in Allenstown; Southern New Hampshire map page 87, grid c4.

User groups: Hikers, dogs, and snowshoers. No wheelchair facilities. This trail is not suitable for bikes, horses, or skis. Hunting is allowed in season.

Access, fees: An entrance fee of $2.50 per person is collected at the state park entrance. Children under 12 and New Hampshire residents 65 and older enter state parks free.

Directions: The entrance to Bear Brook State Park is on Deerfield Road, off Route 28 in Allenstown, three miles north of the junction of Route 28 and U.S. 3. Turn left into a parking lot just past the entrance tollbooth on Deerfield Road.

Maps: A free trail map is available at the park entrance and several other points within the park. For topographic maps of the area, request Suncook and Gossville from the USGS.

Contact: Bear Brook State Park, 157 Deerfield Road, Allenstown, NH 03275; (603) 485-9874. New Hampshire Division of Parks and Recreation, P.O. Box 1856, Concord, NH 03302; (603) 271-3254.

Trail notes: This 2.2-mile hike ascends to one of the park's highest points, 721-foot Catamount Hill, where a largely wooded ridge offers limited views of the state park's rambling forest. From the parking lot, cross Deerfield Road and follow it briefly back toward Route 28. About 100 feet past the tollbooth, a trail marked One Mile Road enters the woods. Follow it for two-tenths of a mile, bearing left where another dirt road enters from the right. In a tenth of a mile from that junction, turn right onto the Catamount Hill Trail, which is marked by a sign. The trail climbs steadily, reaching a first lookout about six-tenths of a mile from the dirt road, just below the summit. Continue another two-tenths of a mile to the summit ridge, where another view is partially obscured by low trees. Return the way you came. At the bottom of the Catamount

Northern New Hampshire Map—page 86

Hill Trail, turn left on One Mile Road; do not take the first trail on the right, which leads quickly to a footbridge over Bear Brook. At the second junction, bear right to return to the tollbooth area.

76 Bear Brook State Park Bike Race Loop

12.0 mi/6.0 hrs 

Location: In Bear Brook State Park in Allenstown; Southern New Hampshire map page 87, grid c4.

User groups: Hikers, bikes, dogs, horses, skiers, and snowshoers No wheelchair facilities. Hunting is allowed in season.

Access, fees: An entrance fee of $2.50 per person is collected at the state park entrance. Children under 12 and New Hampshire residents 65 and older enter state parks free.

Directions: The entrance to Bear Brook State Park is on Deerfield Road, off Route 28 in Allenstown, three miles north of the junction of Route 28 and U.S. 3. From the entrance tollbooth on Deerfield Road, drive another 2.2 miles and turn right on Podunk Road (at signs for the Public Camping Area). Continue another three-tenths of a mile and turn right into a parking lot for hikers and mountain bikers.

Maps: A free trail map is available in a box in the parking lot at the start of this hike and at other points in the park. For topographic maps of the area, request Suncook and Gossville from the USGS.

Contact: Bear Brook State Park, 157 Deerfield Road, Allenstown, NH 03275; (603) 485-9874. New Hampshire Division of Parks and Recreation, P.O. Box 1856, Concord, NH 03302; (603) 271-3254.

Trail notes: Bear Brook—the largest developed state park in New Hampshire—comprises nearly 10,000 acres and 40 miles of trails. The mostly moderate terrain makes for excellent mountain biking and cross-country skiing, and the difficulty ranges from relatively easy gravel roads to technically demanding single-track trails.

This loop—originally mapped out for a mountain bike race the park hosted, but also excellent for skiing—provides a good introduction to Bear Brook's varied offerings. Trails and roads are generally well marked with signs at intersections. Biking the 12-mile trail takes about three hours.

From the parking lot, head across Podunk Road onto the narrow, winding Pitch Pine Trail. In a bit more than a mile, the trail crosses the paved Campground Road. About a quarter mile farther, merge straight onto the Broken Boulder Trail (entering from the right). It passes a side path to a shelter at Smith Pond, then crosses the gravel Spruce Pond Road a half mile past Smith Pond. Continue nearly another mile on the Broken Boulder Trail, then take a sharp right and run straight onto Podunk Road, which is gravel here. Follow the gravel road about a mile, turn right onto the gravel Spruce Road, and then take an immediate left onto the Chipmunk Trail.

This trail winds through the woods for nearly a mile; then you'll bear left onto the Bobcat Trail. Cross Podunk Road (gravel) and Hayes Field, then bear left at a fork onto the Carr Ridge Trail. Cross two trails within a half mile, then bear right about a mile beyond the second trail, crossing onto the Cascade Trail. Reaching a junction in less than a quarter mile, turn right on the Lane Trail, following it over rough ground along Bear Brook. It eventually turns away from the brook and a mile farther reaches a junction with the Hayes Farm Trail; turn left, then left again within a half mile (before reaching the gravel Podunk Road) on the Little Bear Trail. That leads in a mile back to the parking lot.

77 Pawtuckaway State Park

7.0 mi/3.5 hrs 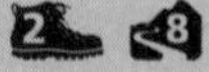

Location: In Raymond; Southern New Hampshire map page 87, grid c5.

User groups: Hikers, bikes, skiers, and snowshoers. No wheelchair facilities. Trails are closed to bikes during mud season, usually for the month of April. Dogs and horses are prohibited. Hunting is allowed in season.

Access, fees: A $2.50 entrance fee is charged to people age 12 and older at the park entrance on weekends from a week before Memorial Day until mid-June, and daily from then through Labor Day, except for New Hampshire residents 65 and older, who enter free. There is no fee the rest of the year.

Directions: From Route 101, take exit 5 for Raymond (there is a sign for Pawtuckaway). Follow Route 156 north and turn left onto Mountain Road at the sign for Pawtuckaway State Park. Follow the road to the entrance and a parking lot on the left.

Maps: A noncontour map of park trails is available at the park's main entrance. For a topographic map of the area, request Mount Pawtuckaway from the USGS.

Contact: Pawtuckaway State Park Manager, (603) 895-3031. New Hampshire Division of Parks and Recreation, Trails Bureau, P.O. Box 1856, Concord, NH 03302; (603) 271-3254.

Trail notes: Pawtuckaway is far and away the most diverse natural area in southeastern New Hampshire. Many of its trails are ideal for hiking, mountain biking, or cross-country skiing, and the extensive views from the ledges and fire tower atop South Mountain may surprise you. Besides this hike, there are numerous trails to explore (try stretching this hike into a 12-mile loop by combining Tower Road with the Shaw and Fundy Trails).

From the parking lot, follow the paved road around to the right for about a quarter mile. After passing a pond on your left, turn left at a sign onto the Mountain Trail. Where it forks, stay right. Almost three miles from the pond, you will reach junction 5 (marked by a sign); turn right and ascend the trail to the summit of South Mountain. (This trail is passable on bikes or skis until the steep final stretch.) Check out the views from the ledges to the left and right of the trail just below the summit; the east-facing trails to the right will be warmer on a sunny day when the breeze is cool.

78 Great Bay National Estuarine Reserve: Sandy Point Trail

1.0 mi/0.75 hr 

Location: In Stratham; Southern New Hampshire map page 87, grid c6.

User groups: Hikers only. The boardwalk is wheelchair accessible. This trail is not suitable for bikes, dogs, horses, skis, or snowshoes. Hunting is prohibited.

Access, fees: Parking and access are free. The Sandy Point Discovery Center is free and is open daily, although on an informal basis in the off-season.

Directions: From the Stratham traffic circle at the junction of Routes 108 and 33, drive 1.4 miles north on Route 33 and turn left onto Depot Road at a sign for the Sandy Point Discovery Center. At the end of Depot Road, turn left on Tidewater Farm Road. The Discovery Center is at the end of the road, and the trail begins behind the center.

Maps: An interpretive trail pamphlet available at the Sandy Point Discovery Center guides the visitor along a boardwalk at the estuary's edge and offers information about natural history and the local environment. The pamphlet and other information can also be obtained through the Great Bay Reserve Manager (see address below). For topographic maps of the area, re-quest Newmarket and Portsmouth from the USGS.

Contact: Great Bay Reserve Manager, New Hampshire Fish and Game Department, Marine Fisheries Division, 225 Main Street, Durham, NH 03824; (603) 868-1095.

Trail notes: The Great Bay National Estuarine Reserve comprises a 4,500-acre tidal estuary and 800 acres of coastal land that provide a refuge for 23 species of endangered or threatened plant and animal species. Bald eagles winter here, osprey nest, and cormorants and great blue herons, among other birds, can be seen. Ecosystems range from salt marshes to upland forests, mud flats to tidal creeks; three rivers empty into the bay. Great Bay also consistently has some of the finest sunsets I've ever seen. The Sandy Point Trail is one of two self-guided interpretive trails in the reserve; Adams Point in Durham, across the bay, also has an eagle-viewing platform. This trail largely follows a boardwalk for easy walking.

79 Odiorne Point State Park

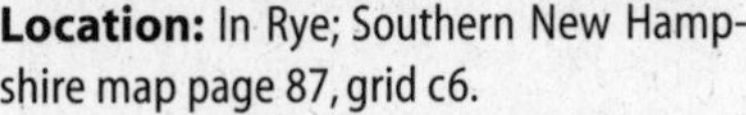

Location: In Rye; Southern New Hampshire map page 87, grid c6.

User groups: Hikers, bikes, skiers, and snowshoers. A portion of the trail is wheelchair accessible. Dogs, horses, and hunting are prohibited.

Access, fees: The park is open daily year-round. There is a $2.50-per-person park entrance fee levied daily from early May through late October and on weekends the rest of the year; children under 12 and New Hampshire residents 65 and older enter free. Admission to the Seacoast Science Center in the park is $1 per person.

Directions: The main entrance to Odiorne is on Route 1A, 1.6 miles north of Wallis Sands State Beach and three miles south of Portsmouth. Park in the lot to the right beyond the entrance gatehouse.

Maps: For a map with historical and natural information about Odiorne, contact the New Hampshire Division of Parks and Recreation, Box 856, Concord, NH 03301; (603) 271-3556. For a topographic map of the area, request Kittery from the USGS.

Contact: Seacoast Region Office, (603) 436-1552. The Seacoast Science Center, Audubon Society of New Hampshire; (603) 436-8043.

Trail notes: A relatively small park at 330 acres, Odiorne is still the largest tract of undeveloped land along New Hampshire's 18-mile shoreline. It has a rich history: beginning about 400 years ago, the Pennacook and Abenaki tribes frequented the area; later, several generations of descendants of settler John Odiorne farmed and fished here; and during World War II, the military acquired the property for the construction of Fort Dearborn. Ever since it became a state park in 1961, the public has been able to enjoy the rugged shore, a great place to catch an ocean sunrise or watch storm-fattened waves crash against the rocks.

Head to the far end of the parking lot and pick up the paved walkway; bear right where it forks. You'll walk past the small grove of low trees known as the Sunken Forest on your right, and continue out to Odiorne Point and a picnic area. The paved walkway leads through the picnic area to form a loop leading back to the parking lot. From the picnic area, walk the rocky shore or a path just above the beach to the Seacoast Science Center; a paved path leads left back to the parking lot. Or continue on either the beach or a trail past the center all the way out to the jetty at Frost Point for a broad shoreline view. Turn inland again along a wide trail. Turn left in front of a high military bunker, bear right onto a trail around a freshwater marsh, and follow the shoreline trail back to the science center and the parking lot.

80 North Pack Monadnock

3.2 mi/2.0 hrs 

Location: In Greenfield; Southern New Hampshire map page 87, grid d3.

User groups: Hikers, dogs, and snowshoers. No wheelchair facilities. This trail is not suitable for bikes, horses, or skis. Hunting is allowed in season.

Access, fees: Parking and access are free. Camping is allowed only at designated sites along the entire 21-mile Wapack Trail; neither of them are along this hike. Fires are prohibited.

Directions: The Wapack Trail begins at a parking area on Old Mountain Road in Greenfield, 2.6 miles west of Route 31, and 4.3 miles east of U.S. 202 in Peterborough (via Sand Hill Road).

Maps: For a contour map of hiking trails, obtain the Wapack Trail map available for $3 from the Friends of the Wapack (see address below). For topographic maps of the area, request Peterborough South, Peterborough North, Greenfield, and Greenville from the USGS.

Contact: Friends of the Wapack, P.O. Box 115, West Peterborough, NH 03468.

Trail notes: My nephews Stephen and Nicholas and niece Brittany were just 3, 4, and 6 years old when I took them on this fairly easy, 3.2-mile hike to the top of North Pack Monadnock. They gorged on the blueberries that lay ripened along the trail, and celebrated like mountaineers when they reached the summit, with its view west to Mount Monadnock.

From the parking area, walk south into the woods, following the yellow triangle blazes of the Wapack Trail. It ascends at an easy grade through the Wapack National Wildlife Refuge for a mile, then climbs steep ledges and passes over one open ledge with a view east before reaching the summit at 1.6 miles. The views from the 2,276-foot summit of southern New Hampshire's wooded hills and valleys are excellent, especially to the west and north. Return the way you came.

81 Mount Monadnock: White Arrow Trail

4.6 mi/3.0 hrs 

Location: In Monadnock State Park in Jaffrey; Southern New Hampshire map page 87, grid d2.

User groups: Hikers only. No wheelchair facilities. This trail may be difficult to snowshoe, in part because of severe winter weather, and is not suitable for bikes, horses, or skis. Dogs are prohibited. Hunting is allowed in season, but not near trails.

Access, fees: There is a parking fee of $2.50 per person, usually from April through November, and the parking lot is not maintained in winter.

Directions: This hike begins from a parking lot on the north side of Route 124, 7.1 miles east of the junction of Routes 101 and 124 in Marlborough, and 5.4 miles west of the junction of Route 124, Route 137, and U.S. 202 in Jaffrey.

Maps: A free map of trails is available from the state park or the New Hampshire Division of Parks and Recreation (see address below). The Carter-Mahoosuc/Mount Monadnock/Mount Cardigan map is available for $2.95 from the Appalachian Mountain Club, (800) 262-4455, and is widely avail-

Northern New Hampshire Map—page 86

able in stores. For topographic maps of the area, request Monadnock Mountain and Marlborough from the USGS.

Contact: Monadnock State Park, P.O. Box 181, Jaffrey, NH 03452-0181; (603) 532-8862. New Hampshire Division of Parks and Recreation, P.O. Box 1856, Concord, NH 03302-1856; (603) 271-3254.

Trail notes: Long one of my favorite mountains (see the trail notes in hike number 82), Monadnock is a peak I also hiked with my niece Brittany and nephew Stephen when they were just 6 and 5 years old—via this route. They loved scrambling up the rocky trail. From the parking lot, walk past the gate onto the old toll road; you can either follow the wide road or immediately bear left onto an obvious trail, which parallels the old carriage road for 1.2 miles to the meadow known as the Halfway House site. Cross the meadow to the White Arrow Trail, which ascends a rock-strewn but wide path for another 1.1 miles to the summit of Monadnock. Its final quarter mile is above the mountain's tree line, and very exposed to harsh weather. White blazes are painted on the rocks above the trees. Just below the summit, the trail makes a sharp right turn, then ascends slabs to the summit. Hike back the same way.

82 Mount Monadnock: White Dot–White Cross Loop

4.2 mi/3.0 hrs 

Location: In Monadnock State Park in Jaffrey; Southern New Hampshire map page 87, grid d2.

User groups: Hikers only. No wheelchair facilities. This trail may be difficult to snowshoe, in part because of severe winter weather, and is not suitable for bikes, horses, or skis. Dogs are prohibited. Hunting is allowed in season, but not near trails.

Access, fees: An entrance fee of $2.50 per person is charged at the state park's main entrance year-round.

Directions: From Route 124, 10.4 miles east of the junction of Routes 101 and 124 in Marlborough, and 2.1 miles west of the junction of Route 124, Route 137, and U.S. 202 in Jaffrey, turn north at a sign for Monadnock State Park. Follow the state park signs to the large parking lot at the park's main entrance.

Maps: A free map of trails is available from the state park or the New Hampshire Division of Parks and Recreation (see address below). The Carter-Mahoosuc/Mount Monadnock/Mount Cardigan map is available for $2.95 from the Appalachian Mountain Club, (800) 262-4455, and is widely available in stores. For topographic maps of the area, request Monadnock Mountain and Marlborough from the USGS.

Contact: Monadnock State Park, P.O. Box 181, Jaffrey, NH 03452-0181; (603) 532-8862. New Hampshire Division of Parks and Recreation, P.O. Box 1856, Concord, NH 03302-1856; (603) 271-3254.

Trail notes: At 3,165 feet high, majestic Mount Monadnock rises about 2,000 feet above the surrounding countryside of southern New Hampshire, making it prominently visible from many other lower peaks in the region. It was designated a National Natural Landmark in 1987. One of New England's most popular summits, it is said that Monadnock is hiked by more people than any peak in the world except Japan's Mount Fuji—although any ranger in the state park would tell you that's impossible to prove. Having grown up not far from here, Monadnock became early on one of my favorite mountains in New England. I would estimate I've hiked it 50 or 60 times, in every season (and conditions can be dangerous above tree line in winter). This can be a very crowded place from spring through fall, and this route may be the most commonly used on the mountain. Nonetheless, it's a scenic and moderately difficult 4.2-mile route to the summit.

From the parking lot, walk up the road past the bathrooms and state park headquarters onto the White Dot Trail. The wide path dips slightly, crosses a brook, then ascends gently. At a half mile, the Spruce Link bears left, leading in three-tenths of a mile to the White Cross Trail, but stay to the right on the White Dot. At seven-tenths of a mile, the White Cross turns left, leading a short distance to Falcon Spring, a good water source; this hike continues straight ahead on the White Dot. The trail climbs steeply for the next four-tenths of a mile, with some limited views, until emerging onto open ledges at 1.1 miles. It then follows more level terrain, enters a forest of low evergreens, and ascends again to its upper junction with the White Cross Trail at 1.7 miles. The trail then climbs the open, rocky terrain of the upper mountain for the final three-tenths of a mile to the summit. Descend the same way, except bear right onto the White Cross Trail, which descends steeply, with occasional views, for a mile. Continue straight ahead onto the Spruce Link Trail, which rejoins the White Dot in three-tenths of a mile. Turn right and walk a half mile back to the trailhead.

83 Mount Pisgah

5.0 mi/3.0 hrs 

Location: In Pisgah State Park, between Chesterfield and Hinsdale; Southern New Hampshire map page 87, grid d1.

User groups: Hikers, dogs, skiers, and snowshoers. No wheelchair facilities. Dogs must be on a leash. This trail may be difficult to snowshoe, in part because of severe winter weather, and is not suitable for bikes, horses, or skis. Hunting is allowed in season.

Access, fees: Parking and access are free.

Directions: From Interstate 91 in Brattleboro, Vermont, take exit 3 for Route 9 east. At Route 63, turn right (south), pass through Chesterfield, and continue three more miles to an entrance and parking area for Kilburn Road in Pisgah State Park.

Maps: For map of park trails, contact the state park or the New Hampshire Division of Parks and Recreation (see address below). For topographic maps of the area, request Winchester and Keene from the USGS.

Contact: Pisgah State Park, P.O. Box 242, Winchester, NH 03470-0242; (603) 239-8153. New Hampshire Division of Parks and Recreation, Box 856, Concord, NH 03301; (603) 271-3556.

Trail notes: Tucked away in the state's rural southwest corner, New Hampshire's largest state park includes this big hill called Mount Pisgah, whose open summit ledges afford nice views of the rolling countryside and Mount Monadnock to the east, and toward Massachusetts and Vermont to the southwest. Key trail junctions are marked with signs. From the trailhead, follow the Kilburn Road Trail, bearing left at junctions with the Kilburn Loop Trail, eventually turning onto the Pisgah Mountain Trail. Double back from the summit on the same trails. This is a wonderful intermediate ski tour, though you may have to carry skis up the steep stretch of trail below the summit. Though mountain bikes are permitted in much of the park, they are prohibited from these trails.

Special note: Want a little added adventure? For a challenging ski tour, continue over the summit of Mount Pisgah, following the sporadically blazed Pisgah Mountain Trail to the Reservoir Trail (which sees snowmobile use). Turn left (north), and keep bearing left at trail junctions until you reach a sign that reads "to Baker Trail." Turn left, and follow the Davis Hill Trail past the

Baker Trail and Baker Pond on the left; it eventually winds southwest to your starting point, completing a loop of about 10 miles. Bear in mind that snowmobilers use the Reservoir Trail and others in the park during winter, as do hunters in late fall.

84 Temple Mountain

5.8 mi/3.5 hrs 

Location: In Sharon; Southern New Hampshire map page 87, grid d3.

User groups: Hikers, dogs, and snowshoers. No wheelchair facilities. This trail is fairly difficult to ski and is not suitable for bikes or horses. Hunting is allowed in season unless otherwise posted.

Access, fees: Parking and access are free. Camping is allowed only at designated sites along the entire 21-mile Wapack Trail; there are no designated sites along this hike. Fires are illegal without landowner permission and a permit from the town forest-fire warden.

Directions: From the junction of Routes 101 and 123 (west of the Temple Mountain Ski Area), drive south four miles on Route 123 and turn left on Temple Road. Continue another seven-tenths of a mile to a small dirt parking area on the right. Or, from the junction where Routes 123 and 124 split, west of New Ipswich, drive north on Route 123 for a mile and turn right on Nashua Road. Continue another six-tenths of a mile and turn left on Temple Road. Drive three-tenths of a mile to the dirt parking area on the left.

Maps: For a contour map of hiking trails, obtain the map of the Wapack Trail available for $3 from the Friends of the Wapack (see address below). For topographic maps of the area, request Peterborough South and Greenville from the USGS.

Contact: Friends of the Wapack, P.O. Box 115, West Peterborough, NH 03468.

Trail notes: One of the more scenic stretches of a nice ridge trail, the Wapack, this hike traverses the long ridge of Temple Mountain all the way to the Temple Mountain Ledges, a 5.8-mile round-trip. But there are several nice views along the way that make worthwhile destinations for anyone seeking a shorter hike. I took my seven-year-old niece, Brittany, on this hike: She ran ahead much of the way and tasted her first wild blueberries (on the Sharon Ledges).

From the parking area, cross Temple Road and follow the yellow triangle blazes of the Wapack Trail into the woods. About a tenth of a mile from the road, the trail passes a dilapidated old house. At three-tenths of a mile, it reaches an open area at the start of the Sharon Ledges, and a view of Mount Monadnock. A sign points to an overlook 75 feet to the right with a view toward Mount Watatic. Continuing northeast, the Wapack follows the Sharon Ledges for three-quarters of a mile, with a series of views eastward of the hills and woods of southern New Hampshire. The trail enters the woods again, and 1.4 miles from the road passes over the wooded subsidiary summit known as Burton Peak. Nearly a half mile farther, a side path leads right to the top of cliffs and an unobstructed view to the east; on a clear day, the Boston skyline can be distinguished on the horizon. A short distance farther north on the Wapack lies an open ledge with a great view west to Monadnock—one of the nicest on this hike. The trail continues north seven-tenths of a mile to the wooded summit of Holt Peak, another significant bump on the ridge. A half mile beyond Holt, watch through the trees on the left for a glimpse of an unusually tall rock cairn—then a side path leading to a flat, broad rock ledge with several tall cairns and good views in almost every direction. You've reached the Temple Mountain Ledges. The Wapack continues over Temple Mountain to Route 101, but this hike returns the same way you came.

85 Kidder Mountain

3.0 mi/2.0 hrs 

Location: In New Ipswich; Southern New Hampshire map page 87, grid d3.

User groups: Hikers, dogs, and snowshoers. No wheelchair facilities. This trail is not suitable for horses or skis. Hunting is allowed in season unless otherwise posted.

Access, fees: Parking and access are free. Camping is allowed only at designated sites along the entire 21-mile Wapack Trail; there are no designated sites along this hike. Fires are illegal without landowner permission and a permit from the town forest-fire warden.

Directions: The trailhead parking area is on the north side of Route 123/124 in New Ipswich, 2.9 miles west of the junction with Route 123A and seven-tenths of a mile east of where Route 123 and Route 124 split.

Maps: For a contour map of hiking trails, obtain the map of the Wapack Trail available for $3 from the Friends of the Wapack (see address below). For topographic maps of the area, request Peterborough South and Greenville from the USGS.

Contact: Friends of the Wapack, P.O. Box 115, West Peterborough, NH 03468.

Trail notes: This easy, three-mile hike gains less than 400 feet in elevation, yet the views from the open meadow atop 1,800-foot Kidder Mountain take in a grand sweep of this rural corner of southern New Hampshire. To the south, the Wapack Range extends to Mount Watatic in Massachusetts; behind Watatic rises Mount Wachusett. Two of us relaxed up here one July afternoon, when there was just enough breeze to temper the heat and keep the bugs down, as we munched on the blueberries growing wild all over the meadow.

From the parking area, follow the yellow triangle blazes of the Wapack Trail into the woods, heading north. At three-tenths of a mile, the trail crosses a clearing and ascends a small hillside to the woods. At six-tenths of a mile from the road, the Wapack crosses a power line right-of-way. Turn right (east) at a sign onto the Kidder Mountain Trail. The trail follows a jeep road under the power line corridor for a tenth of a mile, then turns left, crossing under the lines and entering the woods. It gradually ascends Kidder Mountain, reaching the open summit meadow nearly a mile from the Wapack Trail. Follow the same route back.

86 Beaver Brook

2.5 mi/1.5 hrs 

Location: In Hollis; Southern New Hampshire map page 87, grid d4.

User groups: Hikers, dogs, skiers, and snowshoers. No wheelchair facilities. Dogs must be on a leash. This trail is not suitable for bikes or horses. Hunting is prohibited.

Access, fees: Parking and access are free.

Directions: From the junction of Routes 130 and 122 in Hollis, drive south on Route 122 for nine-tenths of a mile and turn right onto Ridge Road. Follow Ridge Road to the Maple Hill Farm and the office of the Beaver Brook Association. Once you become familiar with the trails here, another good access point to the Beaver Brook land is from the parking area off Route 130, west of the town center and across from the Diamond Casting and Machine Company.

Maps: A trail map is available at the Beaver Brook Association office. Office hours are weekdays, 9 A.M. to 4 P.M. For a topographic map of the area, request Pepperell from the USGS.

Contact: Beaver Brook Association, 117 Ridge Road, Hollis, NH 03049; (603) 465-7787.

Trail notes: Chartered in 1964 by the state as an educational nonprofit organization, the Beaver Brook Association manages about 1,700 acres of land and more than 30 miles of trails here at its "main campus" in Hollis. This place is a local jewel that attracts hikers, snowshoers, cross-country skiers, and mountain bikers from a wide radius. The terrain varies from flat wetlands, which cover at least one-third of the land, to abrupt little forested hills. Many of the trails are ideal for beginning skiers and bikers; some are appropriate for people with intermediate skills. This hike involves some trails that are closed to bikes and horses, but there are about 20 miles of trails here open to those activities. Also, do not overlook the trails on the north side of Route 130, in the area of Wildlife Pond; the Rocky Ridge and Mary Farley Trails also offer particularly nice hiking opportunities.

From the office, follow the wide woods road called Cow Lane. Turn onto the first trail on your left, Porcupine Trail, and follow it down to the wetlands. Turn right onto the Beaver Brook Trail, which parallels the broad marsh, a good place for bird-watching. Turn left and cross the boardwalk over the marsh, then continue straight onto Jason's Cutoff Trail. Turn right onto the wide forest road called Elkins Road, and follow it to a right turn where a woods road crosses Beaver Brook, leading to the Brown Lane barn. Walk Brown Lane a short distance, then turn right onto the Tepee Trail, which leads back to Cow Lane. Turn left to return to your car.

Vermont

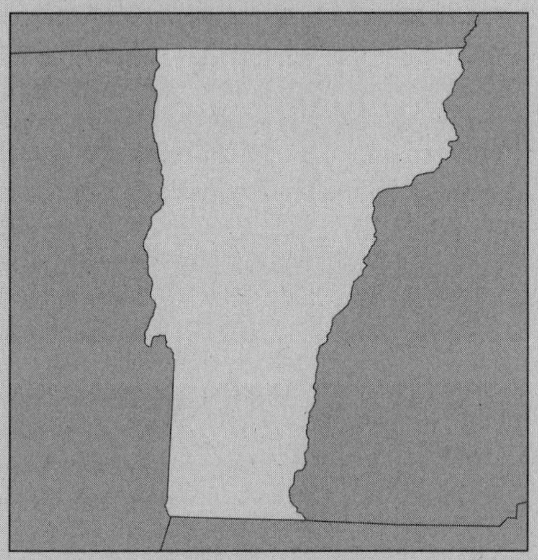

Overall Rating

1 2 3 4 5 6 7 8 9 10

Poor .... Fair .... Great

Difficulty

1 2 3 4 5

A stroll .... Moderate ...... A real butt-kicker!

Northern Vermont

Adjoining Maps: East: New Hampshire .... *pages* 86-87
South: Southern Vermont .... *page* 175

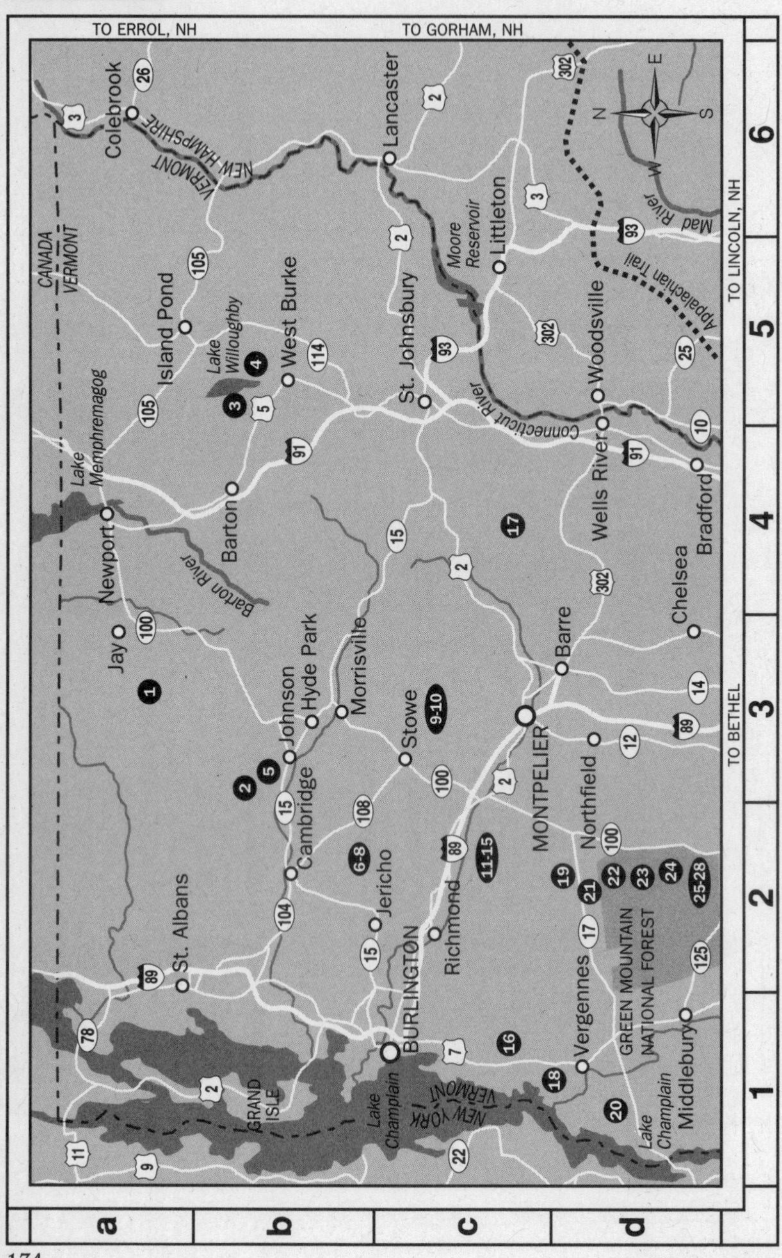

Southern Vermont

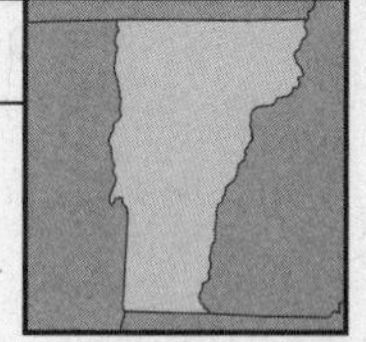

Adjoining Maps:

North: Northern Vermont .... *page* 174
East: New Hampshire .... *pages* 86-87
South: Western Massachusetts .... *page* 238

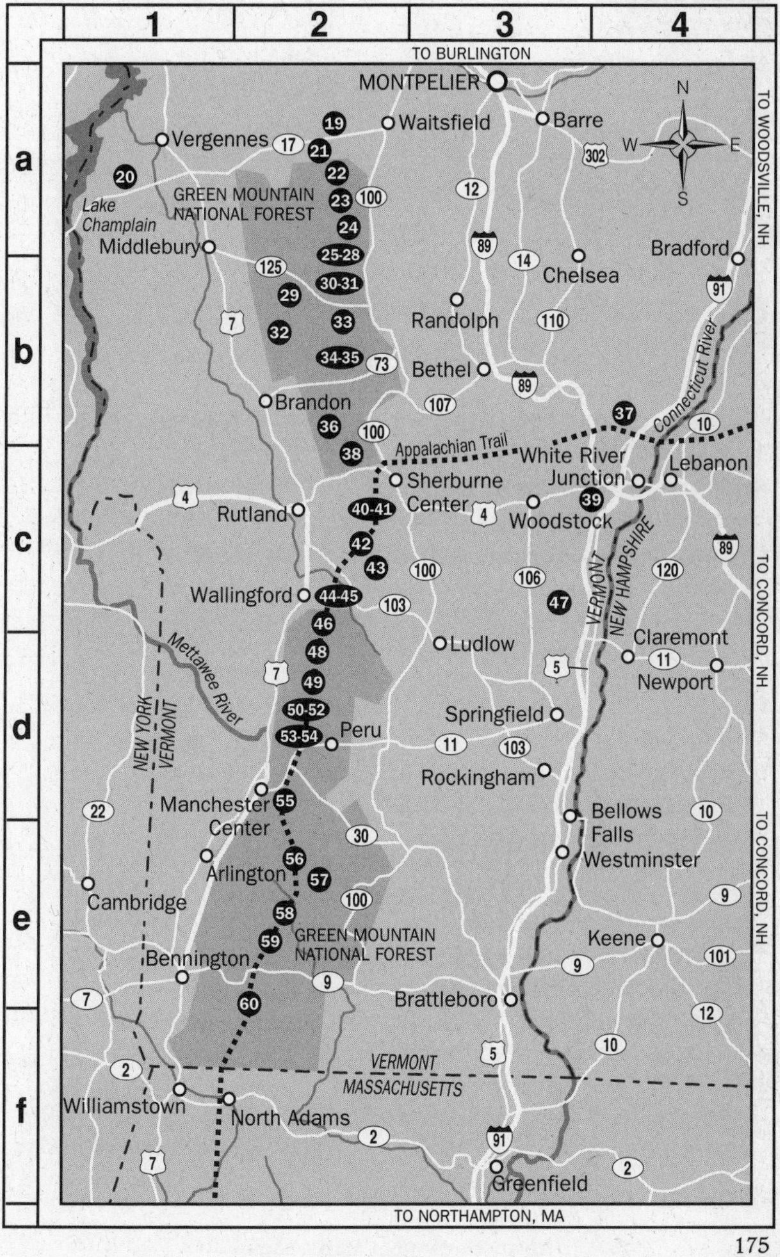

1 2 3 4

a b c d e f

TO BURLINGTON

MONTPELIER

Waitsfield

Barre

Vergennes

17

19

21

22

23

100

12

302

N W E S

20

Lake Champlain

GREEN MOUNTAIN NATIONAL FOREST

24

89

Middlebury

125

25-28

30-31

14

Chelsea

Bradford

91

29

Randolph

110

7

32

33

34-35

73

Bethel

89

Connecticut River

37

Brandon

107

36

100

10

38

Appalachian Trail

White River Junction

Lebanon

Sherburne Center

39

4

Rutland

40-41

4

Woodstock

42

VERMONT

NEW HAMPSHIRE

89

43

100

106

120

Wallingford

44-45

103

47

46

Mettawee River

Ludlow

Claremont

48

5

11

Newport

7

49

NEW YORK

VERMONT

50-52

Springfield

53-54

Peru

11

103

Rockingham

55

Manchester Center

22

Bellows Falls

10

30

56

Arlington

Westminster

57

Cambridge

100

9

58

59

GREEN MOUNTAIN NATIONAL FOREST

Keene

Bennington

9

101

7

9

Brattleboro

60

12

10

5

2

VERMONT

MASSACHUSETTS

Williamstown

North Adams

2

91

7

Greenfield

2

TO NORTHAMPTON, MA

TO WOODSVILLE, NH

TO CONCORD, NH

TO CONCORD, NH

Vermont features:

Northern Vermont Map—page 174

VERMONT

Like no other state in New England, Vermont is defined by its mountains. The Green Mountains run the length of the state, rolling up from round, forested hills in the south, to the taller, sometimes craggy peaks in the state's mid-section, and on to the rambling hills and occasional high peaks of the north country. The Green Mountains are the locus of much of the state's hiking. The 350,000-acre Green Mountain National Forest has 500 miles of hiking trails, but there are also many hikes on private or state-owned land in the Green Mountains.

The national forest enforces certain regulations. No-trace camping is permitted (see How to Use This Book, page **XX**). Dogs must be on a leash. Hunting is allowed in season, but not near trails. For more information, contact the Green Mountain National Forest Supervisor, 231 North Main Street, Rutland, VT 05701; (802) 747-6700.

Running for about 268 miles along the spine of the Green Mountains from the Massachusetts to the Canadian borders, the Long Trail (LT) is the nation's first long-distance hiking trail. While an estimated 60 to 80 people through-hike the Long Trail end to end every year, countless thousands access parts of the trail for day hikes.

The Green Mountain Club (GMC) maintains the Long Trail and the numerous shelters and camping areas along it, including lean-to structures with one open side similar to those found along the Appalachian Trail (referred to in this book simply as "shelters"), and the enclosed cabins, or lodges, most of which are on the trail's northern half. The water sources at most shelters and camping areas are usually reliable, though that is never guaranteed in a dry season.

To prevent erosion, parts of the Long Trail are closed to hiking during mud season, roughly mid-April through Memorial Day. Where the Long Trail crosses private land, camping is prohibited except at the Green Mountain Club cabins and shelters. Along the Appalachian National Scenic Trail—which coincides with the Long Trail for more than 100 miles from the Massachusetts line to a half mile north of U.S. 4 in Sherburne Pass—dogs must be kept under control and bikes, horses, hunting, and possession of firearms are prohibited.

The GMC sends a staff of caretakers into the mountains along the Long Trail at popular camping areas and summits between the Memorial Day and Columbus Day weekends; they provide information for hikers and collect an overnight fee at certain campsites and shelters of $4 ($3 for GMC members). The club sells sectional topographic maps of the Long Trail—either as a set of 21 for $7.95, or individually for $1 per map plus $1 postage. For information, contact the Green Mountain Club, Route 100, RR 1, Box 650, Waterbury Center, VT 05677; (802) 244-7037.

Vermont also harbors nice hiking beyond the Green Mountains. Several smaller peaks—such as Mounts Ascutney, Hunger, and Pisgah—offer fabulous views for comparatively less effort than required on many of the bigger hills in the Greens. On the Vermont side of massive Lake Champlain are a pair of small state parks with nice walking trails.

In Vermont state parks, dogs are not allowed on heavily used trails, but parks officials relax that rule on more remote trails. Trails are closed during the spring mud season, usually mid-April through mid-May. At all state park main entrances, an entrance fee of $2 is charged to persons 14 and older, and $1.50 for children age 4 to 13, from a week before Memorial Day through either Labor Day or Columbus Day, depending on the park. A free, basic trail map is available to virtually all state parks; and the Vermont State Parks Map Atlas can be purchased for $5 plus tax at any park when open, or from the Vermont Department of Forests, Parks, and Recreation, 103 South Main Street, Waterbury, VT 05671-0603; (802) 241-3655.

1 Jay Peak

3.4 mi/2.5 hrs 

Location: Between Jay and Montgomery Center; Northern Vermont map page 174, grid a3.

User groups: Hikers and dogs. No wheelchair facilities. Dogs must be on a leash. This trail may be difficult to snowshoe, in part because of severe winter weather, and is not suitable for bikes, horses, or skis. Hunting is allowed in season unless otherwise posted.

Access, fees: Parking and access are free. This section of the Long Trail is on private land. Camping is prohibited except at the Green Mountain Club cabins and shelters. The Jay Camp cabin is located three-tenths of a mile north of Route 242 and 2.5 miles south of the Jay Peak summit, two-tenths of a mile off the Long Trail. The Laura Woodward shelter lies 1.5 miles north of Jay Peak, on the LT. The Atlas Valley shelter is a small lean-to a few steps north of Route 242 on the LT; exposed to winds, it does not provide good overnight shelter.

Directions: Park in a large turnout where the Long Trail crosses Route 242, 6.5 miles east of the junction of Routes 242 and 118 in Montgomery Center, and 6.5 miles west of the junction of Routes 242 and101 in Jay.

Maps: The Green Mountain Club (see address below) sells sectional topographic maps of the Long Trail, either as a set of 21 for $7.95, or individually for $1 per map plus $1 postage. Jay Peak is within Division XII, Tillotson Camp to Canadian border. For a topographic map of the area, request Jay Peak from the USGS.

Contact: Green Mountain Club, Route 100, RR 1, Box 650, Waterbury Center, VT 05677; (802) 244-7037.

Trail notes: At 3,861 feet in elevation and just 10 trail miles from the Canadian border, Jay Peak is one of the more remote large mountains along the entire 268-mile length of the Long Trail. The views from the summit—where there are buildings belonging to the Jay Peak Ski Area—are of a vast North Country of mountains, endless forest, and few roads. And just about as much of what you see lies in Canada as in the United States. Remember that winter arrives earlier here than on peaks farther south. My girlfriend, her dad, and I hiked up here once in the first week of November to find lots of ice and a dusting of snow on the trail.

From the turnout, cross the highway and follow the white blazes of the Long Trail northbound. You immediately pass the small lean-to known as Atlas Valley shelter—not designed for overnight use. In a tenth of a mile, the Jay Loop Trail, also a part of the Catamount ski trail, branches left, leading two-tenths of a mile to the Jay Camp cabin. Just three-tenths of a mile farther up the LT, you pass the north end of the Jay Loop. The LT ascends steadily onto the mountain's southeast ridge. Just over a mile from the road, you start getting obstructed views to the south and west through the subalpine forest. The wooded, trailless peak to the west, connected to Jay by a high ridge, is Big Jay, at 3,800 feet one of New England's 100 highest summits and a destination for hikers seeking to tick off that list. At 1.5 miles from the highway, the LT crosses a ski trail, then climbs over open, rocky terrain the final two-tenths of a mile to the summit. Descend the way you came up.

❷ Laraway Lookout

3.6 mi/2.5 hrs 

Location: Between Waterville and Belvidere Junction; Northern Vermont map page 174, grid b3.

User groups: Hikers and dogs. No wheelchair facilities. Dogs must be on a leash. This trail may be difficult to snowshoe, in part because of severe winter weather, and is not suitable for bikes, horses, or skis. Hunting is allowed in season unless otherwise posted.

Access, fees: Parking and access are free. This section of the Long Trail is on private land. Camping is prohibited except at the Green Mountain Club cabins and shelters. The Corliss Camp is three miles north of Laraway Lookout on the Long Trail.

Directions: From Route 109, 1.8 miles north of the Waterville Market in the town center and 8.8 miles south of the junction of Routes 109 and 118 in Belvidere Corners, turn east onto Codding Hollow Road. Drive 1.4 miles and bear left at a fork and a sign for Long Trail parking. A mile farther, the road narrows to a two-track which may not be passable in mud season. Follow that two-track for two-tenths of a mile to a dirt parking lot on the left.

Maps: The Green Mountain Club (see address below) sells sectional topographic maps of the Long Trail, either as a set of 21 for $7.95, or individually for $1 per map plus $1 postage; Laraway Lookout is within Division XI, French Camp to Tillotson Camp. For a topographic map of the area, request Johnson from the USGS.

Contact: Green Mountain Club, Route 100, RR 1, Box 650, Waterbury Center, VT 05677; (802) 244-7037.

Trail notes: I hiked to Laraway Lookout on an early November day which felt decidedly wintry, with an inch of snow on the ground and icicles hanging from cliffs along the trail. At the lookout, clouds obscured any view for several minutes. But patience rewarded me, for the overcast separated, showing me the long view to the southwest and west of mountains and the Champlain Valley.

From the parking area, follow the white-blazed Long Trail northbound. The wide path crosses a brook in a tenth of a mile, then follows its opposite bank for about 200 yards, turning sharply left near picturesque cascades. The LT ascends gradually through woods, growing more rugged for the final three-tenths of a mile, passing beneath dramatically overhanging cliffs and climbing a narrow, rocky gully before reaching the open ledge at Laraway Lookout. The wooded summit of Laraway Mountain lies just four-tenths of a mile farther up the Long Trail, but this hike returns the way you came up.

3 Mount Hor

2.8 mi/1.5 hrs 

Location: In Willoughby State Forest; Northern Vermont map page 174, grid b5.

User groups: Hikers and snowshoers. No wheelchair facilities. This trail is not suitable for bikes, horses, or skis. Dogs are prohibited. Hunting is allowed in season.

Access, fees: Parking and access are free. Trails are closed during the spring mud season, usually mid-April through mid-May, and are posted when closed for peregrine falcon nesting, usually in spring.

Directions: Take Interstate 91 to exit 25 for Barton. Turn right off the ramp onto Route 16 east. Drive one mile into Barton and turn right, then two-tenths of a mile and turn left, staying on Route 16 east. Follow Route 16 for another 7.2 miles to the north end of Lake Willoughby and turn right onto Route 5A south. Drive 5.7 miles, beyond the foot of the lake, and turn right onto the gravel CCC Road beside a dirt parking lot. Follow that road for 1.8 miles to a parking area on the right.

Maps: For a free, basic map of hiking trails, or a copy of the Vermont State Parks Map Atlas (which costs $5 plus tax), contact the Vermont Department of Forests, Parks, and Recreation (see address below). For topographic maps of the area, request Sutton and Westmore from the USGS.

Contact: Vermont Department of Forests, Parks, and Recreation, St. Johnsbury District, 184 Portland Street, St. Johnsbury, VT 05819, (802) 748-8787; main office, 103 South Main Street, Waterbury, VT 05671-0603, (802) 241-3655.

Trail notes: Lake Willoughby is a long finger of water embraced on both sides by the sheer cliffs of Mount Hor to the west and Mount Pisgah to the east. Tucked away in Vermont's remote Northeast Kingdom, Willoughby's topography inspires images of a Norwegian fjord more than it does the bucolic farmland and forests surrounding Willoughby State Forest. It certainly evoked that image for me one raw, rainy day I spent hiking Mounts Hor and Pisgah (hike number 4). This is a great hike for viewing the fall foliage, which normally peaks by late September this far north. While the views from 2,656-foot Mount Hor are not as nice as they are from Mount Pisgah, Hor does have beautiful views and is easier to hike than Mount Pisgah because much of the elevation is gained while driving the CCC Road to the trailhead.

From the parking area, walk 40 feet farther up the road and turn right onto the Herbert Hawkes Trail. In another 30 feet, turn right with the trail onto an old logging road. The hike is easy and nearly flat for the first four-tenths of a mile, passing through several wet, muddy areas. The road eventually narrows to a trail, then swings left and ascends the mountainside. At seven-tenths of a mile you will reach a trail junction marked by signs: to the left it is three-tenths of a mile to the wooded, viewless summit of Mount Hor (not included in this hike's distance); for this hike, turn right and follow the fairly easy trail another half mile to the first overlook of Lake Willoughby and Mount Pisgah, and a tenth of a mile beyond that to the second overlook. After you've taken in the views, hike back along the same route to the parking area.

4 Mount Pisgah

3.8 mi/2.5 hrs 

Location: In Willoughby State Forest; Northern Vermont map page 174, grid b5.

User groups: Hikers and snowshoers. No wheelchair facilities. This trail is not suitable for bikes, horses, or skis. Dogs are prohibited. Hunting is allowed in season.

Access, fees: Parking and access are free. Trails are closed during the spring mud season, usually mid-April through mid-May, and are posted when closed for peregrine falcon nesting, usually in spring.

Directions: Take Interstate 91 to exit 25 for Barton. Turn right off the ramp onto Route 16 east. Drive one mile into Barton and turn right, then two-tenths of a mile and turn left, staying on Route 16 east. Follow Route 16 for another 7.2 miles to the north end of Lake Willoughby and turn right onto Route 5A south. Drive 5.7 miles, beyond the foot of the lake, to a dirt parking lot on the right.

Maps: For a free, basic map of hiking trails, or a copy of the Vermont State Parks Map Atlas (which costs $5 plus tax), contact the Vermont Department of Forests, Parks, and Recreation (see address below). For topographic maps of the area, request Sutton and Westmore from the USGS.

Contact: Vermont Department of Forests, Parks, and Recreation, St. Johnsbury District, 184 Portland Street, St. Johnsbury, VT 05819, (802) 748-8787; main office, 103 South Main Street, Waterbury, VT 05671-0603, (802) 241-3655.

Trail notes: See the Mount Hor trail notes (hike number 3) for more descriptive information about the Willoughby State Forest. From the parking area, cross the highway to the South Trail, which begins at a sign reading "Willoughby State Forest Trailhead." The trail soon crosses a swampy, flooded area on a boardwalk, then starts climbing a wide path well marked with blue blazes. After about seven-tenths of a mile, you pass the first of three successive lookouts on the left with partly obstructed views of Lake Willoughby and Mount Hor, the third being the best among them. At one mile, you reach a short side path leading left to Pulpit Rock, with an excellent view of the lake. Some hikers may choose to turn back from here, for a round-trip of two miles.

Continue up the trail, scrambling up rock slabs a half mile beyond Pulpit Rock, then watch for a side path leading to the right about 100 feet to a view southeast to New Hampshire's White Mountains. Return to the South Trail, turn right and continue to Mount Pisgah's 2,756-foot summit, 1.9 miles from the road. Three side paths around the wooded summit lead left to ledges atop tall cliffs with sweeping views of Lake Willoughby and Mount Hor. A sign points to the last side path, the north overlook. Head back the way you came up.

5 Prospect Rock

1.6 mi/1.0 hr 

Location: In Johnson; Northern Vermont map page 174, grid b3.

User groups: Hikers and dogs. No wheelchair facilities. Dogs must be on a leash. This trail may be difficult to snowshoe, in part because of severe winter weather, and is not suitable for bikes, horses, or skis. Hunting is allowed in season unless otherwise posted.

Access, fees: Parking and access are free. This section of the Long Trail is on private land. Camping is prohibited except at the Green Mountain Club cabins and shelters. The Roundtop shelter is located 1.8 miles north of Prospect Rock on the Long Trail.

Directions: From Route 15, two miles west of the junction of Routes 15 and 100C in Johnson, and immediately east of the Lamoille River bridge, turn north onto a secondary road at signs for the Long Trail and Waterville. Continue nine-tenths of a mile to a turnout on the right, across the road from the Ithiel Falls Camp Meeting Ground. You will see the LT's white blazes on rocks at the turnout. Do not block the dirt road with your vehicle.

Maps: The Green Mountain Club (see address below) sells sectional topographic maps of the Long Trail, either as a set of 21 for $7.95, or individually for $1 per map plus $1 postage; Prospect Rock is within Division XI, French Camp to Tillotson Camp. For a topographic map of the area, request Johnson from the USGS.

Contact: Green Mountain Club, Route 100, RR 1, Box 650, Waterbury Center, VT 05677; (802) 244-7037.

Trail notes: This relatively easy hike of less than a mile on a more remote stretch of the Long Trail leads to a bucolic view of a northern Vermont farming valley and its surrounding hills. From the turnout, follow the white blazes of the Long Trail northbound up the dirt road for about a tenth of a mile, then turn left with the trail into the woods. The LT follows an old woods road, then swings right onto a footpath winding uphill and reaching Prospect Rock, eight-tenths of a mile from the parking area. Its open ledges atop cliffs overlook the Lamoille River Valley and the Sterling Range to the south. Follow the same route back.

6 Smuggler's Notch

0.2 mi/0.25 hr 

Location: In Smuggler's Notch State Park, between Stowe and Jeffersonville; Northern Vermont map page 174, grid b2.

User groups: Hikers, bikes, skiers, and snowshoers. No wheelchair facilities. This trail is not suitable for horses. Dogs are prohibited. Hunting is allowed in season.

Access, fees: Parking and access are free. Trails are closed during the spring mud season, usually mid-April through mid-May. Route 108 is not maintained through Smuggler's Notch once the snow falls. But the road often has a packed-snow surface in winter, making it possible to drive up from the Jeffersonville side with a four-wheel-drive vehicle, or ski or hike up from either side.

Directions: Drive to the turnout immediately north of the height-of-land on Route 108 in Smuggler's Notch, south of Jeffersonville and north of Stowe.

Maps: The Green Mountain Club (see address below) sells a trail map to the Mount Mansfield region for $3.95. For a topographic map of the area, request Mount Mansfield from the USGS.

Contact: Smuggler's Notch State Park, Box 7248, Mountain Road, Stowe, VT 05672; (802) 253-4014. Vermont Department of Forests, Parks, and Recreation, 103 South

Main Street, Waterbury, VT 05671-0603; (802) 241-3655. Green Mountain Club, Route 100, RR 1, Box 650, Waterbury Center, VT 05677; (802) 244-7037.

Trail notes: During the warm months, this hike is an easy walk around the height-of-land in Smuggler's Notch, where massive boulders line the narrow, winding roadway and lie strewn throughout the woods. Tall cliffs flank the notch to either side, making it look more like the White Mountains than the usually more tame Green Mountains.

From the south end of the parking turnout, follow a short but obvious path about 200 feet back into the jumble of garage-sized boulders known as Smuggler's Cave, reputedly a stash for contraband during the War of 1812. Then wander around the notch; you will see the white blazes of the Long Trail enter the woods across the road a short distance uphill from the turnout. In winter, this hike transforms into a more involved outing, not to mention one typically accompanied by a frigid wind. With Route 108 not maintained through the notch, you have to hike or cross-country ski up to the height-of-land—about a mile at an easy to moderate grade from the Jeffersonville side, and about 2.3 miles from the Stowe side, which is much steeper. But the notch makes for a scenic ski tour, and a fun descent.

7 Mount Mansfield: Sunset Ridge and Laura Cowles Trails

6.4 mi/4.5 hrs 

Location: In Underhill State Park and Mount Mansfield State Forest in Underhill Center; Northern Vermont map page 174, grid b2.

User groups: Hikers and dogs. No wheelchair facilities. Dogs must be on a leash. This trail may be difficult to snowshoe above tree line because of severe winter weather, and is not suitable for bikes, horses, or skis. Hunting is allowed in season.

Access, fees: From Memorial Day through Columbus Day, an entrance fee of $2 per adult and $1 for children age 4 to 13 is collected at the ranger station. Once the snow falls, the CCC Road is maintained only to a point about half mile before the start of this hike, where winter visitors can park. Camping is prohibited except at the Green Mountain Club cabins and shelters.

Directions: From Route 15 in Underhill Flats, drive east on the road to Underhill Center. In Underhill Center, three miles from Route 15, continue straight past the Underhill Country Store for one mile and turn right (at a sign for Underhill State Park) onto Mountain Road (TH2). Drive approximately two miles farther to a large parking lot at the ranger station.

Maps: The Green Mountain Club (see address below) sells a trail map to the Mount Mansfield region for $3.95. For a topographic map of the area, request Mount Mansfield from the USGS.

Contact: Vermont Department of Forests, Parks, and Recreation Essex Junction District, 111 West Street, Essex Junction, VT 05452, (802) 879-6565; main office, 103 South Main Street, Waterbury, VT 05671-0603, (802) 241-3655. Green Mountain Club, Route 100, RR 1, Box 650, Waterbury Center, VT 05677; (802) 244-7037.

Trail notes: This 6.2-mile loop hike up Vermont's highest peak ascends the spectacular Sunset Ridge, much of it above the trees with long views and rugged terrain more reminiscent of a Mount Washington (New Hampshire chapter) or Mount Katahdin (Maine chapter) than of most peaks here in the Green Mountains, few of which have alpine terrain. About half of the two-mile ascent of the ridge is over exposed ground. The sweeping views from the ridge to the south and north of the Green Mountains—

including the prominent summit of Camel's Hump to the south—and west to Lake Champlain and the Adirondack Mountains are often accompanied by strong winds and harsh weather. Be prepared for wintry conditions any time of year. This hike passes over The Chin, Mansfield's true summit at 4,393 feet, with a 360-degree view encompassing the entire sweep of Vermont as well as New Hampshire's White Mountains to the east. As with virtually any trail up Mansfield, this is a popular hike in summer and fall, and even attracts winter climbers (who should have the proper gear and winter mountaineering skills). It gains about 2,500 feet in elevation from the state park to the summit. (See the trail notes in hike number 8 for more information about Mount Mansfield.)

From the parking lot at the ranger station, hike up the dirt CCC Road for about a mile; just beyond a sharp right bend in the road, the blue-blazed Sunset Ridge Trail, marked by a sign, enters the woods. Follow the trail over two wooden footbridges spanning brooks to a junction just a tenth of a mile from the road with the Laura Cowles Trail, branching right; you will descend that trail. Continuing up the Sunset Ridge Trail, ascending moderately, the first views through breaks in the forest begin within a half mile from the road. At seven-tenths of a mile, turn left onto the Cantilever Rock Trail and follow it a tenth of a mile to its namesake rock, a needlelike formation projecting horizontally about 40 feet from high up a cliff face. Backtrack to the Sunset Ridge Trail and continue climbing up through forest marked by occasional large boulders. About one mile from the road, the trail makes a short step up exposed rocks and emerges above tree line for the first broad views south and west. It then follows the ridge upward, over rocky terrain where scrub spruce grow close to the ground in places, to a junction at 1.9 miles where the Story Trail branches left, swinging around the north side of Mansfield's summit to join the Long Trail in four-tenths of a mile (two-tenths of a mile north of The Chin, providing an alternate route to the summit).

Just beyond the Story Trail, the Sunset Ridge Trail passes the Laura Cowles Trail, branching right—this hike's descent route. Continue another two-tenths of a mile up the Sunset Ridge Trail to its terminus at the Long Trail, on Mansfield's exposed summit ridge. Turn left (north) and follow the LT two-tenths of a mile to The Chin. Backtrack on the LT and Sunset Ridge Trail to the Laura Cowles Trail, and descend the Laura Cowles, re-entering the woods within a half mile of the Sunset Ridge Trail. It drops steadily for another nine-tenths of a mile to its lower junction with the Sunset Ridge Trail. Turn left and walk a tenth of a mile back to the CCC Road.

8 Mount Mansfield: the Long Trail

4.6 mi/3.5 hrs 3 10

Location: In Smuggler's Notch State Park in Stowe; Northern Vermont map page 174, grid b2.

User groups: Hikers and dogs. No wheelchair facilities. Dogs must be on a leash. This trail may be difficult to snowshoe above tree line because of severe winter weather, and is not suitable for bikes, horses, or skis. Hunting is allowed in season.

Access, fees: Parking and access are free. Route 108 is not maintained through Smuggler's Notch once the snow falls, only to a point about a half mile south of the start of this hike. Camping is prohibited except at the Green Mountain Club cabins and shelters. The Taft Lodge cabin is located on the Long Trail, 1.7 miles south of Route 108.

Directions: Drive to the roadside parking area immediately north of where the Long

Trail northbound from Mount Mansfield reaches Route 108, 8.5 miles west of the junction of Routes 108 and 100 in Stowe, and 1.7 miles east of the height-of-land in Smuggler's Notch.

Maps: The Green Mountain Club (see address below) sells a trail map to the Mount Mansfield region for $3.95. For a topographic map of the area, request Mount Mansfield from the USGS.

Contact: Smuggler's Notch State Park, Box 7248, Mountain Road, Stowe, VT 05672; (802) 253-4014. Vermont Department of Forests, Parks, and Recreation, 103 South Main Street, Waterbury, VT 05671-0603; (802) 241-3655. Green Mountain Club, Route 100, RR 1, Box 650, Waterbury Center, VT 05677; (802) 244-7037.

Trail notes: Probably the most commonly hiked route up Vermont's highest peak, 4,393-foot Mount Mansfield, the Long Trail is a good trail of only moderate difficulty. And just 2.3 miles from the road in Smuggler's Notch—after an elevation gain of nearly 2,800 feet—you are standing atop The Chin, Mansfield's true summit, with a 360-degree view taking in all of northern Vermont, including much of the Green Mountains, and stretching to New Hampshire's White Mountains, New York's Adirondacks, and Quebec. Predictably, this is a very popular hike that sees many boots on nice weekends in summer and fall. But I hiked up this trail on a bone-chilling November day, had Taft Lodge all to myself for a night, and then saw no one as I bagged the summit the next morning.

Numerous features on Mansfield's long, completely exposed ridge bear names which derive from the mountain's resemblance, especially from the east, to a man's profile: The Chin, The Nose, The Forehead, the Upper and Lower Lip, and the Adam's Apple. Mansfield is one of just two peaks in Vermont—the other being Camel's Hump (hike numbers 11 through 14)—with a significant alpine area, or area above the tree line. The rare plants which grow in this tundralike terrain are fragile, so take care to walk only on the trail or on rocks. Be aware, also, that alpine terrain signals frequent harsh weather: Mansfield can attract wintry weather in any month of the year, so come here prepared for the worst, and be willing to turn back whenever conditions turn threatening. A Green Mountain Club caretaker is on duty during the prime hiking season to assist hikers and ensure the protection of the alpine area. There are also TV and radio stations at the summit, a toll road up the mountain, and a ski area operating on its east side.

From the parking area, walk a short distance south on Route 108, then turn right (southbound) onto the white-blazed Long Trail. The trail climbs steadily, crossing a brook and changing direction a few times before reaching Taft Lodge at 1.7 miles. From the clearing at the lodge, you can see the imposing cliffs below the summit. Continue up the LT. The trail emerges from the trees within three-tenths of a mile of the lodge, then climbs steeply another three-tenths of a mile to the summit. Return the way you came.

9 Stowe Pinnacle

2.3 mi/1.5 hrs 

Location: In Putnam State Forest in Stowe; Northern Vermont map page 174, grid c3.

User groups: Hikers and snowshoers. No wheelchair facilities. This trail is not suitable for bikes, horses, or skis. Dogs are prohibited. Hunting is allowed in season.

Access, fees: Parking and access are free. Trails are closed during the spring mud season, usually mid-April through mid-May.

Directions: Take Interstate 89 to exit 10

and turn north onto Route 100. Continue about 10 miles and turn right onto School Street. Drive three-tenths of a mile and bear right onto Stowe Hollow Road. In another 1.5 miles, drive straight onto Upper Hollow Road, and continue seven-tenths of a mile to a parking area for the Pinnacle Trail on the left.

Maps: The Vermont State Parks Map Atlas can be purchased for $5 plus tax at any park when open, or from the Vermont Department of Forests, Parks, and Recreation (see address below). The "Map and Guide to the Mount Mansfield Region," which does not show contours, is $2.95 from Huntington Graphics, P.O. Box 163, Huntington, VT 05462. For a topographic map of the area, request Stowe from the USGS.

Contact: Vermont Department of Forests, Parks, and Recreation, Barre District, 324 North Main Street, Barre, VT 05641, (802) 479-3241; main office, 103 South Main Street, Waterbury, VT 05671-0603, (802) 241-3655.

Trail notes: This fairly easy round-trip hike of 2.3 miles leads to the open, craggy summit of Stowe Pinnacle, which is visible from the parking area. A great hike for young children—and quite popular with families—its summit offers excellent views, especially in a wide sweep from the northwest to southwest, including Camel's Hump to the southwest, Mount Mansfield to the west, and the ski town of Stowe in the valley separating the pinnacle from Mansfield.

The trail begins at the rear of the parking area. Following easy terrain at first, the blue-blazed path traverses areas which are often muddy. It ascends moderately through the woods to a junction with the Skyline Trail (marked by a sign) just over a mile from the parking lot. Turn right and hike uphill another tenth of a mile to the summit of Stowe Pinnacle. Return the way you came. See the special note in the description of Mount Hunger (hike number 10) for a way to link to two hikes on a nice ridge walk.

⑩ Mount Hunger

4.0 mi/3.0 hrs 

Location: In Putnam State Forest in Waterbury; Northern Vermont map page 174, grid c3.

User groups: Hikers and snowshoers. No wheelchair facilities. This trail is not suitable for bikes, horses, or skis. Dogs are prohibited. Hunting is allowed in season.

Access, fees: Parking and access are free. Trails are closed during the spring mud season, usually mid-April through mid-May.

Directions: Take Interstate 89 to exit 10 and turn north onto Route 100. Drive about three miles and turn right onto Howard Avenue. Continue four-tenths of a mile and turn left onto Maple Street. In a tenth of a mile, turn right onto Loomis Hill, then drive two miles and turn left onto the dirt Water Works Road. Follow it 1.5 miles to the parking area on the right.

Maps: The Vermont State Parks Map Atlas can be purchased for $5 plus tax at any park when open, or from the Vermont Department of Forests, Parks, and Recreation (see address below). The "Map and Guide to the Mount Mansfield Region," which does not show contours, is $2.95 from Huntington Graphics, P.O. Box 163, Huntington, VT 05462. For a topographic map of the area, request Stowe from the USGS.

Contact: Vermont Department of Forests, Parks, and Recreation, Barre District, 324 North Main Street, Barre, VT 05641, (802) 479-3241; main office, 103 South Main Street, Waterbury, VT 05671-0603, (802) 241-3655.

Trail notes: One of the nicest hikes in Vermont, yet requiring a fraction of the effort committed to many Green Mountain peaks,

Mount Hunger offers long views in virtually every direction from its 3,539-foot summit of bare rock. Dominating the western horizon is the long chain of the Green Mountains, with Camel's Hump the prominent peak to the southwest and Mount Mansfield, Vermont's highest, rising due west. Between Hunger and Mansfield lies a pastoral valley of open fields interspersed with sprawling forest. To the east, on a clear day, you will make out the White Mountains, particularly the towering wall of Franconia Ridge, and possibly even Mount Washington. Hike up here in late fall or winter, and you may see the Whites capped in white. I made the loop described in the special note below, over Hunger and Stowe Pinnacle, with two friends on a fall day when the foliage was near its peak, and we enjoyed a colorful show.

From the parking lot, the blue-blazed Waterbury Trail makes a moderately difficult ascent, passing some nice cascades, for nearly two miles before emerging above tree line about 100 yards below the summit. After reaching the summit, head back the way you came.

Special note: A ridge trail links the summit of Mount Hunger with Stowe Pinnacle (hike number 9); and by shuttling cars to the parking lots at each trailhead you can make this nice Worcester Range ridge walk of about seven miles (figure five hours). I recommend hiking up Mount Hunger and descending the Stowe Pinnacle end. From the summit of Hunger, look for the cairns and blazes of the Skyline Trail heading north. The trail dips back into the woods and remains in the trees, but it's an interesting, if somewhat rugged, walk through a lush subalpine forest on a trail which sees a fraction of the foot traffic seen on the primary trails up Hunger and Stowe Pinnacle. Some three miles or more from the top of Hunger, after the Skyline Trail passes over the wooded, 3,440-foot bump of Hogback Mountain, it descends, steeply in places, to a junction with the Pinnacle Trail. Bear left, reaching the top of Stowe Pinnacle in a tenth of a mile. Descend the Pinnacle Trail 1.1 miles to the trailhead parking lot.

11 Camel's Hump: Forest City/Burrows Trails Loop

6.4 mi/4.5 hrs 

Location: In Camel's Hump State Park in Huntington Center; Northern Vermont map page 174, grid c2.

User groups: Hikers and dogs. No wheelchair facilities. Dogs must be leashed above tree line. This trail may be difficult to snowshoe above tree line because of severe winter weather, and is not suitable for bikes, horses, or skis. Hunting is allowed in season.

Access, fees: Parking and access are free. The trails are closed to hiking during mud season, roughly mid-April through Memorial Day. Camping is prohibited except at the two Green Mountain Club cabins, Montclair Glen Lodge near the junction of the Burrows and Long Trails, and Gorham Lodge near the junction of the Long and Bamforth Ridge Trails; and at the Hump Brook tenting area, just off the Dean Trail. From Memorial Day weekend through Columbus Day, a Green Mountain Club caretaker is on duty and a $4-per-person nightly fee ($3 for GMC members) is collected to stay at the Montclair Glen Lodge and the Gorham Lodge.

Directions: In Huntington Center, 2.5 miles south of the post office in Huntington Village, turn onto Camel's Hump Road at signs for Camel's Hump State Park. Follow the dirt road, bearing right at forks (state park signs point the way). At 2.8 miles from Huntington Center, there is a small parking area on the right at the Forest City

Trailhead; you can start this loop from there (adding 1.5 miles to this hike's distance), or continue up the road another seven-tenths of a mile to a larger parking area at the Burrows Trailhead.

Maps: A basic trail map with state park information is available at the trailhead hiker register. The Green Mountain Club (see address below) sells sectional topographic maps of the Long Trail, either as a set of 21 for $7.95, or individually for $1 per map plus $1 postage; Camel's Hump is within Division IX, Birch Glen Camp to Bolton Mountain. For topographic maps of the area, request Huntington and Waterbury from the USGS.

Contact: Vermont Department of Forests, Parks, and Recreation, Essex Junction District, 111 West Street, Essex Junction, VT 05452, (802) 879-6565; main office, 103 South Main Street, Waterbury, VT 05671-0603, (802) 241-3655. Green Mountain Club, Route 100, RR 1, Box 650, Waterbury Center, VT 05677; (802) 244-7037.

Trail notes: With the only undeveloped alpine area in the Green Mountain State and a skyline that sets itself apart from everything else for miles, 4,083-foot Camel's Hump may be Vermont's finest peak. The views from its distinctive summit are among the best in New England. To the west are the Adirondacks and Lake Champlain; the Green Mountains stretch out in a long chain to the south; to the southeast rises the prominent mound of Mount Ascutney; to the northeast lie Mount Hunger and Stowe Pinnacle in the Worcester Range; far to the northeast, on a clear day, the White Mountains are visible; and to the north, when not smothered in clouds, are Bolton Mountain and Mount Mansfield.

Camel's Hump is one of the state's most popular peaks, too, attracting hundreds of hikers on nice weekend days in summer and fall. But twice I've had the summit all to myself, simply by hiking at times when other people don't hike. On one sunny but bitterly cold early spring afternoon (before mud season), I gazed through thin haze at the white caps of New Hampshire's Presidential Range and Franconia Ridge, seeming to float in the sky. The treeless summit of Camel's Hump hosts one of the state's few zones of alpine vegetation, plants threatened by heavy hiker use. Help protect them by walking only on the trail or bare rock.

You can hike this loop in either direction, but I recommend going from Forest City to the Long Trail and down the Burrows because the exposed ascent of the LT up Camel's Hump's southern ridge is a wonderful climb that builds excitement for the summit. (For a shorter hike, the Burrows round-trip to the summit is 5.4 miles.) The Forest City and Burrows Trails are well-worn paths and well marked with blue blazes; the Long Trail is blazed white. Trail junctions are marked with signs. From the Burrows Trailhead, turn right onto the connector trail leading a tenth of a mile to the Forest City Trail, then turn left onto it, hiking east. The trail ascends at a moderate grade, reaching the Long Trail about 1.6 miles from the Burrows Trailhead. Turn left (north) on the LT and follow it for nearly two miles to the 4,083-foot summit, climbing below and around spectacular cliffs. Beyond the summit, stay on the LT for another three-tenths of a mile to the Camel's Hump Hut Clearing, then turn left (west) on the Burrows Trail, which leads 2.4 miles back to the trailhead.

⑫ Camel's Hump: Long Trail/Bamforth Ridge

11.8 mi/8.0 hrs 

Location: In Camel's Hump State Park in North Duxbury; Northern Vermont map page 174, grid c2.

User groups: Hikers and dogs. No wheelchair facilities. Dogs must be leashed above tree line. This trail may be difficult to snowshoe above tree line because of severe winter weather, and is not suitable for bikes, horses, or skis. Hunting is allowed in season.

Access, fees: Parking and access are free. The trails are closed to hiking during mud season, roughly mid-April through Memorial Day. Camping is prohibited except at the two Green Mountain Club cabins, Montclair Glen Lodge near the junction of the Burrows and Long Trails, and Gorham Lodge near the junction of the Long and Bamforth Ridge Trails; and at the Hump Brook tenting area, just off the Dean Trail. From Memorial Day weekend through Columbus Day, a Green Mountain Club caretaker is on duty and a $4-per-person nightly fee ($3 for GMC members) is collected to stay at the Montclair Glen Lodge and the Gorham Lodge.

Directions: From the south, take Interstate 89 to exit 10. Turn south and drive about a half mile to the end of the road, and turn left onto U.S. 2 east. Continue 1.3 miles, then turn right onto Route 100 south. Proceed just two-tenths of a mile and turn right at a sign for the Duxbury Elementary School. Just two-tenths of a mile farther, bear right onto a dirt road at a sign for Camel's Hump. Five miles down that road, continue straight ahead at a sign directing you left for Camel's Hump Trails. The parking lot for the Long Trail/Bamforth Ridge Trail lies 2.7 miles farther down the road. From the north, take Interstate 89 to exit 11 for U.S. 2 east. Drive about five miles into Jonesville, and just beyond the post office (on the left), turn right, crossing the bridge over the Winooski River. At two-tenths of a mile from U.S. 2, turn left onto Duxbury Road and continue 3.3 miles to the Long Trail/Bamforth Ridge Trail parking area on the right.

Maps: A basic trail map with state park information is available at the trailhead hiker register. The Green Mountain Club (see address below) sells sectional topographic maps of the Long Trail, either as a set of 21 for $7.95, or individually for $1 per map plus $1 postage; Camel's Hump is within Division IX, Birch Glen Camp to Bolton Mountain. For topographic maps of the area, request Huntington and Waterbury from the USGS.

Contact: Vermont Department of Forests, Parks, and Recreation, Essex Junction District, 111 West Street, Essex Junction, VT 05452, (802) 879-6565; main office at 103 South Main Street, Waterbury, VT 05671-0603, (802) 241-3655. Green Mountain Club, Route 100, RR 1, Box 650, Waterbury Center, VT 05677; (802) 244-7037.

Trail notes: See the Camel's Hump: Forest City/Burrows Trails Loop (hike number 11) for more descriptive information about Camel's Hump. The Long Trail from the north constitutes the most arduous route to the 4,083-foot summit of Camel's Hump, and at 11.8 miles round-trip, the longest as well. The LT was relocated in 1996 onto this route, also known as the Bamforth Ridge Trail. (The former route of the LT, which passed the Honey Hollow tenting area, has been closed, as has the tenting area.) The LT ascends the rugged Bamforth Ridge, dipping and climbing repeatedly and often steeply, and traversing some boggy terrain. But open ledges at many points along the ridge offer the most sustained views of any route up Camel's Hump.

From the parking lot, follow the LT's white blazes south. The trail reaches the short spur path to Gorham Lodge at 5.2 miles, then climbs to Camel's Hump clearing at 5.6 miles. From the clearing, the trail grows fairly steep and rugged to the summit, 5.9 miles from the road. Return the way you came.

⑬ Camel's Hump: Forestry/Alpine Trails Loop

6.6 mi/4.5 hrs 

Location: In Camel's Hump State Park in North Duxbury; Northern Vermont map page 174, grid c2.

User groups: Hikers and dogs. No wheelchair facilities. Dogs must be leashed above tree line. This trail may be difficult to snowshoe above tree line because of severe winter weather, and is not suitable for bikes, horses, or skis. Hunting is allowed in season.

Access, fees: Parking and access are free. The trails are closed to hiking during mud season, roughly mid-April through Memorial Day. Winter parking is in the lot for Camel's Hump View, a half mile before the Couching Lion site. Camping is prohibited except at the two Green Mountain Club cabins, Montclair Glen Lodge near the junction of the Burrows and Long Trails, and Gorham Lodge near the junction of the Long and Bamforth Ridge Trails; and at the Hump Brook tenting area, just off the Dean Trail. From Memorial Day weekend through Columbus Day, a Green Mountain Club caretaker is on duty and a $4-per-person nightly fee ($3 for GMC members) is collected to stay at the Montclair Glen Lodge and the Gorham Lodge.

Directions: From the south, take Interstate 89 to exit 10. Turn south and drive about a half mile to the end of the road, and turn left onto U.S. 2 east. Continue 1.3 miles, then turn right onto Route 100 south. Proceed just two-tenths of a mile and turn right at a sign for the Duxbury Elementary School. Just two-tenths of a mile farther, bear right onto a dirt road at a sign for Camel's Hump. Five miles down that road, turn left at a sign for Camel's Hump Trails. Drive 1.2 miles and bear left over a bridge. Continue another 2.4 miles to the parking lot at the end of the road, at the so-called Couching Lion site. From the north, take Interstate 89 to exit 11 for U.S. 2 east. Drive about five miles into Jonesville, and just beyond the post office (on the left), turn right, crossing the bridge over the Winooski River. In two-tenths of a mile turn left onto Duxbury Road and continue six miles to the sign for Camel's Hump trails. Turn right, cross the bridge at 1.2 miles, and continue 2.4 miles to the Couching Lion site.

Maps: A basic trail map with state park information is available at the trailhead hiker register. The Green Mountain Club (see address below) sells sectional topographic maps of the Long Trail, either as a set of 21 for $7.95, or individually for $1 per map plus $1 postage; Camel's Hump is within Division IX, Birch Glen Camp to Bolton Mountain. For topographic maps of the area, request Huntington and Waterbury from the USGS.

Contact: Vermont Department of Forests, Parks, and Recreation, Essex Junction District, 111 West Street, Essex Junction, VT 05452, (802) 879-6565; main office, 103 South Main Street, Waterbury, VT 05671-0603, (802) 241-3655. Green Mountain Club, Route 100, RR 1, Box 650, Waterbury Center, VT 05677; (802) 244-7037.

Trail notes: The Forestry Trail may be the most popular route up a very popular mountain. (See the Camel's Hump: Forest City/Burrows Trails Loop, hike number 11, for more descriptive information about Camel's Hump.) This 6.6-mile loop includes an interesting variation from that route onto the Alpine Trail. From the parking lot, the blue-blazed Forestry Trail ascends at a moderate grade at first, but grows steeper as you climb higher. Sections of the trail are often wet, even into autumn. At 2.5 miles, turn left onto the yellow-blazed Alpine Trail, which is wooded and fairly rugged along this stretch. Within a half mile, you will pass near the wing of a WWII bomber that crashed into the mountain during a wartime training flight at night.

Just beyond the wreckage, the Alpine Trail meets the Long Trail; turn right (north) on the white-blazed LT, quickly emerging from the trees for your first sweeping views from below the towering cliffs on the south face of Camel's Hump. The Long Trail swings left below the cliffs and ascends the west face of the mountain to its open, 4,083-foot summit, two-tenths of a mile from the Alpine Trail. Continue on the Long Trail north over the summit, descending rocky terrain for three-tenths of a mile to Camel's Hump Hut Clearing. Turn right onto the Forestry Trail, which takes you down 3.1 miles to the parking area.

⑭ Camel's Hump View

0.2 mi/0.25 hr 

Location: In Camel's Hump State Park in North Duxbury; Northern Vermont map page 174, grid c2.

User groups: Hikers, dogs, skiers, snowshoers, and wheelchair users. Dogs must be on a leash. This trail is not suitable for bikes or horses. Hunting is allowed in season.

Access, fees: Parking and access are free. The trails in the park are closed to hiking during mud season, roughly mid-April through Memorial Day.

Directions: From the south, take Interstate 89 to exit 10. Turn south, drive about a half mile to the end of the road, and turn left onto U.S. 2 east. Continue 1.3 miles, then turn right onto Route 100 south. Proceed just two-tenths of a mile and turn right at a sign for the Duxbury Elementary School. Just two-tenths of a mile farther, bear right onto a dirt road at a sign for Camel's Hump. Five miles down that road, turn left at a sign for Camel's Hump Trails. Drive 1.2 miles and bear left over a bridge. Continue another 1.9 miles, turn left (a half mile before the Couching Lion site), and drive another two-tenths of a mile to the Lewis Place parking area. From the north, take Interstate 89 to exit 11 onto U.S. 2 east. Drive about five miles into Jonesville, and just beyond the post office (on the left), turn right, crossing the bridge over the Winooski River. At two-tenths of a mile from U.S. 2, turn left onto Duxbury Road and continue six miles to the sign for Camel's Hump Trails. Turn right, cross the bridge at 1.2 miles, and 1.9 miles past the bridge turn left for the Lewis Place parking area.

Maps: No map is necessary for this hike, although a basic trail map of Camel's Hump State Park is available at the trailhead hiker register at the Couching Lion site. For topographic maps of the area, request Huntington and Waterbury from the USGS.

Contact: Vermont Department of Forests, Parks, and Recreation, 103 South Main Street, Waterbury, VT 05671-0603; (802) 241-3655.

Trail notes: Here is an easy walk of just two-tenths of a mile round-trip to a striking view of Camel's Hump for folks not inclined to actually climb the mountain. It's also a nice trail for hikers or cross-country skiers looking for an unusual angle on arguably Vermont's most recognizable peak. From the parking lot, walk up the left fork of the Camel's Hump View Trail, crossing over Sinnott Brook on a wooden bridge and reaching a wooden bench on the right at a tenth of a mile. From the bench, look across a clearing for a view of Camel's Hump. You can turn back from here, or continue up the trail for a half-mile loop back to the parking lot. The Ridley Crossing ski trail diverges off this loop about halfway through it, leading to the Beaver Meadow Trail, where you would turn right to loop back to the main road just below the Couching Lion site.

⑮ The Long Trail: Route 17, Appalachian Gap, to the Winooski River

18.4 mi. one way/
2–3 days 

Location: Between Appalachian Gap and North Duxbury; Northern Vermont map page 174, grid c2.

User groups: Hikers and dogs. No wheelchair facilities. Dogs must be leashed above tree line. This trail may be difficult to snowshoe, and is not suitable for bikes, horses, or skis. Hunting is allowed in season.

Access, fees: Parking and access are free. The Long Trail is closed from Appalachian Gap to the Winooski River from mid-April through Memorial Day. Much of this section of the Long Trail is in Camel's Hump State Park; the remainder is on private land. Camping is prohibited except at the Green Mountain Club shelters and campsites: the Birch Glen Camp, 2.6 miles north of Route 17; the Cowles Cove shelter, 5.5 miles north of Route 17; the Montclair Glen Lodge near the junction of the Burrows and Long Trails, 10.6 miles north of Route 17; and the Gorham Lodge, near the junction of the Long and Bamforth Ridge Trails, 13.2 miles north of Route 17 and 5.2 miles from River Road. From Memorial Day weekend through Columbus Day, a Green Mountain Club caretaker is on duty and a $4-per-person nightly fee ($3 for GMC members) is collected to stay at the Montclair Glen Lodge and the Gorham Lodge.

Directions: You need to shuttle two vehicles for this one-way traverse. To hike south to north, as described here, leave one vehicle in the trailhead parking lot on River Road in North Duxbury (see Directions for Camel's Hump: Long Trail/Bamforth Ridge, hike number 12). Then drive to where the Long Trail crosses Route 17 in Appalachian Gap, three miles east of the Huntington Road and six miles west of Route 100 in Irasville.

Maps: A basic trail map is available at trailheads in Camel's Hump State Park (see hike number 11 to 14). The Green Mountain Club (see address below) sells sectional topographic maps of the Long Trail, either as a set of 21 for $7.95, or individually for $1 per map plus $1 postage; this hike begins in Division VIII, Cooley Glen shelter to Birch Glen Camp, and extends into Division IX, Birch Glen Camp to Bolton Mountain. For topographic maps of the area, request Mount Ellen, Huntington, and Waterbury from the USGS.

Contact: Vermont Department of Forests, Parks, and Recreation, Essex Junction District, 111 West Street, Essex Junction, VT 05452, (802) 879-6565; main office at 103 South Main Street, Waterbury, VT 05671-0603, (802) 241-3655. Green Mountain Club, Route 100, RR 1, Box 650, Waterbury Center, VT 05677; (802) 244-7037.

Trail notes: This 18.4-mile leg of the Long Trail is arguably its most spectacular stretch. The centerpiece of this hike is 4,083-foot Camel's Hump, but less well-known Burnt Rock Mountain offers one of the nicest views on the Long Trail; Molly Stark's Balcony is another choice spot, and the trail harbors some gems in the woods like Ladder Ravine. This is the northern section of the fabled Monroe Skyline (hike number 21). The one-way traverse covers rugged terrain and involves significant gain and loss in elevation; it can easily take three days.

This hike, especially the Camel's Hump area, is popular in summer and fall, and the shelters tend to fill up quickly on weekends. When above tree line, remember that the fragile alpine vegetation suffers under boots, so stay on the marked trail or on rocks. Also, be advised that water sources are few along the ridge, and generally found only at the shelters.

From Route 17, the Long Trail northbound climbs steeply out of Appalachian Gap for four-tenths of a mile, descends steeply, then climbs again to the top of Molly Stark Mountain at one mile from the road. At 1.3 miles, the trail passes over Molly Stark's Balcony, a rock outcropping atop a cliff rising above the trees, where you get a nice long view north toward Camel's Hump, and northeast to the Worcester Range, which includes Mount Hunger and Stowe Pinnacle. Descending more easily, the LT reaches the Beane Trail at 2.6 miles, which leads left (west) about 100 feet to the Birch Glen Camp, and nine-tenths of a mile to a road by which it is 1.5 miles to Hanksville. The LT follows easier ground from there, ascending gradually to Cowles Cove shelter at 5.5 miles. Climbing slightly still, the trail passes the Hedgehog Brook Trail at 6.4 miles, which descends right (east) 2.5 miles to a road two miles outside North Fayston. Then the Long Trail quickly grows more rugged, climbing to the open, rocky summit of Burnt Rock Mountain seven miles into this hike. At 3,168 feet, its summit should be wooded but was denuded by fires years ago, and today offers long views of the Green Mountains arcing southward, the hills of the Worcester Range to the east and the White Mountains beyond, the southern tip of Lake Champlain to the southwest, and New York's Adirondacks brooding darkly behind the lake.

Follow the blazes and cairns carefully as the trail makes numerous turns over Burnt Rock's bare crown. The LT re-enters the lush, wild forest, reaching Ladder Ravine at 7.4 miles, a perpetually wet place where a wooden ladder is employed to descend a short cliff. Continuing over rough terrain, the trail climbs over the wooded humps of Mounts Ira Allen (at 8.5 miles) and Ethan Allen's two peaks (at 9.5 and 9.6 miles), then descends past the Allis Trail at 10.4 miles; that trail leads straight ahead to Allis Lookout, where there is a view of the mountains to the north, and terminates at the Long Trail in three-tenths of a mile. The LT, meanwhile, swings left and descends to Montclair Glen Lodge at 10.6 miles. Just downhill from the cabin on the LT, the Forest City Trail departs left (west), dropping gradually for 2.2 miles to a road outside Huntington Center (see hike number 11).

The LT then begins the ascent of Camel's Hump, passing the Dean Trail in Wind Gap (at 10.8 miles) leading right (east) 2.3 miles to the Couching Lion site (see hike number 13). Traversing open ledges on the east side of Camel's Hump's southern ridge, the LT affords excellent views south along the Green Mountains, east in a wide sweep from Mount Ascutney southeast to the Worcester Range northeast. It then reenters the woods again briefly, climbing steeply to a junction at 12.3 miles with the Alpine Trail, which departs right (east) and provides an alternate route around the summit in bad weather, swinging north and reaching the Bamforth Ridge Trail/Long Trail in 1.7 miles. It is two-tenths of a mile more of steep, exposed hiking, with the trail swinging left around tall cliffs and ascending the west face up the rocky summit cone of Camel's Hump. (See hike number 11 for a more detailed description of the summit.) Dropping north off the summit, the LT reaches the Camel's Hump Hut Clearing at 12.8 miles, where the Forestry Trail leaves right (east), descending 3.1 miles to the Couching Lion site; and the Burrows Trail leaves left (west), descending 2.6 miles to a road outside Huntington Center. Reentering the woods, the LT—since being re-routed in 1996—now follows the old Bamforth Ridge Trail north, reaching the short side path left at 13.2 miles which leads to the Gorham Lodge. The descent from the lodge is rugged, dipping and climbing repeatedly and often steeply, and traversing some boggy terrain. But open ledges at many points along the ridge offer the best views of any trail on Camel's Hump. The LT reaches the parking lot on River Road at 18.4 miles.

16 Mount Philo

2.2 mi/1.5 hrs 

Location: In Mount Philo State Park, between North Ferrisburg and Charlotte; Northern Vermont map page 174, grid c1.

User groups: Hikers and snowshoers. No wheelchair facilities. This trail is not suitable for bikes, horses, or skis. Dogs are prohibited. Hunting is allowed in season.

Access, fees: An entrance fee of $2 is charged to persons 14 and older, and $1.50 for children age 4 to 13, from a week before Memorial Day through Columbus Day. Trails are closed during the spring mud season, usually mid-April through mid-May. The park road is not maintained in winter, making it a strenuous cross-country skiing route up the mountain.

Directions: From U.S. 7, about 1.2 miles north of North Ferrisburg and 2.5 miles south of the junction of U.S. 7 and Route F-5 in Charlotte, turn east onto State Park Road. Drive a half mile to a crossroads. Park off the road here, or continue straight ahead through the entrance to Mount Philo State Park and park at the roadside. State officials have plans for a parking lot inside that entrance.

Maps: While no map is necessary for this hike, a free, basic map is available to virtually all state parks. The Vermont State Parks Map Atlas can be purchased for $5 plus tax at any park when open, or from the Vermont Department of Forests, Parks, and Recreation (see address below). For a topographic map of the area, request Mount Philo from the USGS.

Contact: Mount Philo State Park, 5425 Mount Philo Road, Charlotte, VT 05445, (802) 425-2390. Vermont Department of Forests, Parks, and Recreation, 103 South Main Street, Waterbury, VT 05671-0603; (802) 241-3655.

Trail notes: The view from atop the cliffs of Mount Philo far exceeds the expectations I had while driving toward this tiny hill. The bucolic Champlain Valley sprawls before you, flanked by the long chain of the Green Mountains stretching southward and the brooding Adirondack Mountains rising across Lake Champlain. This 2.2-mile loop over the summit is somewhat steep in places, although not difficult. When the road is open, you can drive to the top of Philo and walk about a tenth of a mile to the cliff overlooks.

From the crossroads, walk up the park road about 100 yards and enter the woods on the left, following blue blazes. The trail—which tends to be muddy and slippery in spring—winds up Mount Philo, crossing the summit road once, to the overlooks. (This trail is not suitable for bikes or skis; bike riders and skiers should take the summit road up and down.) After taking in the views, continue past the summit overlooks on a dirt road for a tenth of a mile to a large parking lot, and descend the paved park road 1.2 miles back to the start of this hike.

17 Big Deer Mountain

4.2 mi/3.0 hrs 

Location: In Groton State Forest; Northern Vermont map page 174, grid c4.

User groups: Hikers and snowshoers. No wheelchair facilities. This trail is not suitable for bikes, horses, or skis. Dogs are prohibited. Hunting is allowed in season.

Access, fees: An entrance fee of $2 is charged to persons 14 and older, and $1.50 for children age 4 to 13, from a week before

Memorial Day through either Labor Day or Columbus Day, depending on the park. Trails are closed during the spring mud season, usually mid-April through mid-May. The road into the New Discovery Campground is closed and blocked by a gate when the park is closed, from Labor Day through Memorial Day weekend.

Directions: From Interstate 91, take exit 17 onto U.S. 302 west. Drive about 8.8 miles and turn right onto Route 232 north. Drive 9.4 miles and turn right into the New Discovery Campground. From Memorial Day weekend through Labor Day, continue a tenth of a mile past the open gate to a field, turn right, and drive to the picnic shelter on Osmore Pond to park. In winter, park at the gate without blocking it.

Maps: A free, basic map is available to virtually all state parks. The Vermont State Parks Map Atlas can be purchased for $5 plus tax at any park when open, or from the Vermont Department of Forests, Parks, and Recreation (see address below). For a topographic map of the area, request Marshfield from the USGS.

Contact: Vermont Department of Forests, Parks, and Recreation, Barre District, 324 North Main Street, Barre, VT 05641, (802) 479-3241; main office, 103 South Main Street, Waterbury, VT 05671-0603, (802) 241-3655.

Trail notes: I first discovered Groton State Forest, in Vermont's Northeast Kingdom, while on a bike tour several years ago; that time, I only spent a night in the campground. More recently, I returned with a friend to mountain bike its forest roads and hike up Big Deer Mountain, which has good views for a hill not even 2,000 feet high. This hike begins from different parking areas, depending upon whether the road into the New Discovery Campground is open.

In winter, parking at the gate, walk a tenth of a mile past the gate to a field; in summer, backtrack the road from the Osmore Pond picnic area to the field. Facing that field (as you would in winter, walking from the gate), turn left onto a dirt forest road and follow it three-tenths of a mile, then turn right onto the Big Deer Mountain Trail (marked by a sign). Follow the blue blazes through the woods on a trail that's mostly flat for 1.1 miles. Then, at a trail junction, continue straight ahead, climbing about 200 feet in elevation over six-tenths of a mile of rocky trail onto Big Deer Mountain. The trail ends at open ledges with a view to the south, overlooking Lake Groton. Just before the end of the trail, a side path leads left a short distance to another open ledge with a view east from high above Peacham Bog. On a clear day, you can see the White Mountains. Backtrack six-tenths of a mile to the junction and turn left onto the Big Deer Mountain Trail toward Osmore Pond. It descends gently, crosses a marshy area, passes over a slight rise, then descends more steeply to a trail junction near the south end of Osmore Pond, nine-tenths of a mile from the last junction. Turn right onto the Osmore Pond Hiking Loop, a rock-strewn but flat trail which parallels the pond's east shore and loops around its north end. In winter, about seven-tenths of a mile from the trail junction at the pond's south end, turn right again onto a connector trail leading back to the New Discovery campground. In summer, follow the loop trail around the pond to the picnic area.

⓲ Kingsland Bay State Park

1.0 mi/0.75 hr 

Location: In Ferrisburg; Northern Vermont map page 174, grid c1.

User groups: Hikers and snowshoers. No wheelchair facilities. This trail is not suitable for bikes, horses, or skis. Dogs are prohibited. Hunting is allowed in season.

Access, fees: An entrance fee of $2 is charged to persons 14 and older, and $1.50 for children age 4 to 13, from a week before Memorial Day through Labor Day. Trails are closed during the spring mud season, usually mid-April through mid-May. The park road is closed to traffic in the off-season, but you can walk the road, adding a mile round-trip to this hike's distance.

Directions: From the junction of U.S. 7 and Route 22A north of Vergennes, drive north on U.S. 7 for a half mile, then turn left (west) onto Tuppers Crossing Road. Proceed four-tenths of a mile and bear right onto Bottsford Road. Drive eight-tenths of a mile and continue straight through a crossroads onto Hawkins Road. Or, from North Ferrisburg, drive south on U.S. 7 for about four miles and turn right (west) onto Little Chicago Road. Continue a mile and turn right onto Hawkins. Follow Hawkins Road for 3.4 miles, then turn right at a sign into Kingsland Bay State Park. Follow the dirt park road about a half mile and park at the roadside near the tennis courts.

Maps: While no map is necessary for this hike, a free, basic map is available to virtually all state parks. The Vermont State Parks Map Atlas can be purchased for $5 plus tax at any park when open, or from the Vermont Department of Forests, Parks, and Recreation (see address below). For a topographic map of the area, request Westport from the USGS.

Contact: Kingsland Bay State Park, RR 1 Box 245, Ferrisburg, VT 05456; (802) 877-3445. Vermont Department of Forests, Parks, and Recreation, 103 South Main Street, Waterbury, VT 05671-0603; (802) 241-3655.

Trail notes: An unmarked but obvious trail begins behind the tennis courts and soon forks, creating a loop through the conifer woods on this point of land jutting into Lake Champlain which can be done in either direction. Much of the one-mile, easy trail remains in the woods, with limited views of the lake; but there is one clearing with a view northeast toward Camel's Hump and the Green Mountains.

⑲ Molly Stark's Balcony

2.6 mi/2.0 hrs 

Location: North of Appalachian Gap; Northern Vermont map page 174, grid d2.

User groups: Hikers, dogs, and snowshoers. No wheelchair facilities. Dogs must be on a leash. This trail is not suitable for bikes, horses, or skis. Hunting is allowed in season.

Access, fees: Parking and access are free. The Long Trail is closed from Appalachian Gap to the Winooski River from mid-April through Memorial Day. This stretch of the Long Trail passes through Camel's Hump State Park, and camping is prohibited except at the Green Mountain Club shelters. The Birch Glen Camp is on the LT, 1.3 miles north of Molly Stark's Balcony.

Directions: Drive to where the Long Trail crosses Route 17 in Appalachian Gap, three miles east of the Huntington Road and six miles west of Route 100 in Irasville.

Maps: The Green Mountain Club (see address below) sells sectional topographic maps of the Long Trail, either as a set of 21 for $7.95, or individually for $1 per map plus $1 postage; this hike is in Division VIII, Cooley Glen shelter to Birch Glen Camp. For a topographic map of the area, request Mount Ellen from the USGS.

Contact: Vermont Department of Forests, Parks, and Recreation, 103 South Main Street, Waterbury, VT 05671-0603; (802) 241-3655. Green Mountain Club, Route 100, RR 1, Box 650, Waterbury Center, VT 05677; (802) 244-7037.

Trail notes: From Molly Stark's Balcony, a rocky ledge atop a cliff jutting above the woods, you get a nice long view north toward Camel's Hump, and northeast to the Worcester Range, which includes Mount Hunger and Stowe Pinnacle. Though just a 2.6-mile round-trip, this hike is strenuous. The Long Trail northbound climbs steeply out of Appalachian Gap for four-tenths of a mile, drops steeply, then climbs again to the highest point on Molly Stark Mountain at one mile from the road. Continue north on the LT for three-tenths of a mile to the balcony, a small ledge on the right side of the trail immediately before another steep downhill. Return the way you came up.

20 Button Bay State Park

1.0 mi/0.75 hr 

Location: In Panton; Northern Vermont map page 174, grid d1.

User groups: Hikers, bikes, skiers, and snowshoers. Wheelchair users can drive the dirt road beyond the public parking lots to handicapped parking just 100 yards before the point on Lake Champlain. This trail is not suitable for horses. Dogs are prohibited. Hunting is allowed in season.

Access, fees: An entrance fee of $2 is charged to persons 14 and older, and $1.50 for children age 4 to 13, from a week before Memorial Day through Columbus Day. Trails are closed during the spring mud season, usually mid-April through mid-May. The park road is closed to traffic in the off-season, but you can walk the road, adding a mile round-trip to this hike's distance.

Directions: From the green in the center of Vergennes, drive south on Route 22A for a half mile and turn right onto Panton Road. Proceed 1.4 miles and turn right onto Basin Harbor Road. Continue 4.5 miles, then turn left onto Button Bay Road and follow it six-tenths of a mile to the entrance on the right to Button Bay State Park. Drive about a half mile down the park road to two gravel parking lots on the left, across from the pavilion.

Maps: While no map is necessary for this hike, a free, basic map is available to virtually all state parks. The Vermont State Parks Map Atlas can be purchased for $5 plus tax at any park when open, or from the Vermont Department of Forests, Parks, and Recreation (see address below). For a topographic map of the area, request Westport from the USGS.

Contact: Button Bay State Park, RD 3, Box 4075, Vergennes, VT 05491; (802) 475-2377. Vermont Department of Forests, Parks, and Recreation, 103 South Main Street, Waterbury, VT 05671-0603; (802) 241-3655.

Trail notes: This flat walk of a mile round-trip along a wide dirt road leads to Button Point, where the land thrusts a finger of rocks into Lake Champlain and the views encompass a wide sweep from Camel's Hump and the Green Mountains to the east, to the Adirondacks across the lake. From the parking lots, walk the gravel road a half mile to its end at Button Point. Return the same way.

21 The Monroe Skyline

47.4 mi. one way/ 5–6 days 

Location: Between Middlebury Gap and North Duxbury; Northern Vermont map page 174, grid d2.

User groups: Hikers and dogs. No wheelchair facilities. Dogs must be on a leash. This trail may be difficult to snowshoe because of severe winter weather, and is not suitable for bikes, horses, or skis. Hunting is allowed in season, but not near trails.

Access, fees: Parking and access are free. See specific access information for the three sections of the Long Trail covered separately (see below).

Directions: You need to shuttle two

vehicles for this one-way traverse. To hike south to north, as described here, leave one vehicle in the trailhead parking lot on River Road in North Duxbury (see Directions for Camel's Hump: Long Trail/Bamforth Ridge, hike number 12). Then, to reach the trailhead, drive to the large turnout on the south side of Route 125, immediately west of where the Long Trail crosses the road in Middlebury Gap, 5.6 miles east of Ripton and 6.4 miles west of Route 100 in Hancock.

Maps: The Green Mountain Club (see address below) sells sectional topographic maps of the Long Trail, either as a set of 21 for $7.95, or individually for $1 per map plus $1 postage; this hike covers Divisions VII, VIII, and IX. For topographic maps of the area, request Bread Loaf, Lincoln, Mount Ellen, Huntington, and Waterbury from the USGS.

Contact: Green Mountain Club, Route 100, RR 1, Box 650, Waterbury Center, VT 05677; (802) 244-7037.

Trail notes: When the nation's first long-distance hiking trail was in its formative years, this stretch of nearly 50 miles was not along the high mountain ridges it now traverses. It was mired down in the woods, where the state forestry officials who did much of the early work on the trail wanted it to be so they could access forest fires. Then along came Professor Will Monroe, a respected botanist and book author, who over several years beginning in 1916 became the catalyst behind the Green Mountain Club's effort to move the Long Trail up onto the rugged chain of peaks between Middlebury Gap and the Winooski River. Now dubbed the Monroe Skyline, this 47.4-mile section is widely considered the soul of the Long Trail, and is a much sought-after multi-day trek. For backpackers who want to sample the best of the Long Trail and have a week or less, this is the trip to take.

The Monroe Skyline links three sections of the Long Trail described elsewhere in this book. For details, see the descriptions for the following three hikes: The Long Trail: Route 125, Middlebury Gap, to the Lincoln-Warren Highway, Lincoln Gap (hike number 27); The Long Trail: Lincoln-Warren Highway, Lincoln Gap, to Route 17, Appalachian Gap (hike number 22); and The Long Trail: Route 17, Appalachian Gap, to the Winooski River (hike number 15).

22 The Long Trail: Lincoln-Warren Highway, Lincoln Gap, to Route 17, Appalachian Gap

11.6 mi. one way/8.5 hrs 5 10

Location: Between Lincoln Gap and Appalachian Gap; Northern Vermont map page 174, grid d2.

User groups: Hikers and dogs. No wheelchair facilities. Dogs must be on a leash. This trail may be difficult to snowshoe because of severe winter weather, and is not suitable for bikes, horses, or skis. Hunting is allowed in season, but not near trails.

Access, fees: Parking and access are free. The Long Trail is closed from Lincoln Gap to Appalachian Gap from mid-April through Memorial Day. No-trace camping is permitted within the Green Mountain National Forest, but north of the national forest boundary the Long Trail passes through private land, and camping is prohibited except at the Green Mountain Club's Glen Ellen Lodge cabin (located on the Barton Trail, two-tenths of a mile east of the Long Trail, 8.2 miles north of Lincoln Gap); and in summer, when a GMC caretaker is there, in the Stark's Nest, the upper chairlift station of the Mad River Glen Ski Area (9.1 miles north of Lincoln Gap), where a $4-per-person nightly fee ($3 for GMC members) is collected. From Memorial Day weekend through Columbus Day, a caretaker is on duty and the same nightly fee is collected at the Battell shelter, on the Long Trail 1.8 miles north of Lincoln Gap. The Theron Dean shelter is on the LT, 9.8 miles north of Lincoln Gap and 1.8 miles south of Appalachian Gap.

Directions: You need to shuttle two vehicles for this one-way traverse. To hike south to north, as described here, leave one vehicle where the Long Trail crosses Route 17 in Appalachian Gap, three miles east of the Huntington Road and six miles west of Route 100 in Irasville. Then drive to where the Long Trail crosses the Lincoln-Warren Highway in Lincoln Gap, 4.7 miles east of Lincoln and 4.7 miles west of Route 100 in Warren. There is parking two-tenths of a mile west of Lincoln Gap, as well as along the road in the vicinity of the trail crossing.

Maps: The Green Mountain Club (see address below) sells sectional topographic maps of the Long Trail, either as a set of 21 for $7.95, or individually for $1 per map plus $1 postage; this hike is in Division VIII, Cooley Glen shelter to Birch Glen Camp. For topographic maps of the area, request Lincoln and Mount Ellen from the USGS.

Contact: Green Mountain National Forest Supervisor, 231 North Main Street, Rutland, VT 05701; (802) 747-6700. Green Mountain Club, Route 100, RR 1, Box 650, Waterbury Center, VT 05677; (802) 244-7037.

Trail notes: This 11.6-mile stretch of the Long Trail traverses the high, narrow ridge of Lincoln Mountain, passing over its several summits, including spectacular Mount Abraham (4,006 feet, hike number 23) and two other summits with excellent views. One of the premier sections of the LT, it is also the middle portion of the fabled Monroe Skyline (hike number 21). While this can be done in a long and strenuous day, many people make a two-day backpacking trip of it, or hike it as a link in a longer outing on the LT.

This is a popular destination in summer and fall, and the shelters tend to fill up quickly on weekends. When above tree line, remember that the fragile alpine vegetation suffers under boots, so stay on the marked trail or on rocks. Also, be advised that water sources are few along the ridge, and generally found only at the shelters (although the spring at the Theron Dean shelter is not reliable in dry seasons).

From the Lincoln-Warren Highway, follow the white blazes of the Long Trail northbound, beginning the at-first gradual ascent of Mount Abraham. At 1.2 miles, the trail passes a pair of huge boulders named The Carpenters, after two trailworkers. At 1.7 miles, the Battell Trail veers left (west), leading two miles to a road; and a tenth of a mile farther, the LT reaches the Battell shelter. The trail then climbs more steeply, over rocky terrain and exposed slabs until emerging from the trees into the alpine zone atop Abraham, 2.6 miles from the road. The views stretch far down the Green Mountain chain to the south, east to the White Mountains, west to Lake Champlain and the Adirondacks, and north to the other peaks of Lincoln Mountain.

At 3.3 miles, a sign indicates the wooded summit of Little Abe; and a tenth of a mile farther the LT crosses Lincoln Peak, at 3,975 feet, where an observation deck to the right of the trail offers a 360-degree panorama. The LT passes through a cleared area above the Sugarbush Valley Ski Area just past the observation deck, bears left, and re-enters the forest. The hiking is fairly easy along the ridge, with little elevation shift. At four miles, the LT traverses the wooded summit of Nancy Hanks Peak, passes a Sugarbush chairlift at 4.7 miles, then climbs about 250 feet in elevation to the 4,022-foot summit of Cutts Peak, which has good views, at 5.9 miles. Just four-tenths of a mile farther, the trail passes over the wooded and viewless summit of Mount Ellen, at 4,083 feet tied with Camel's Hump for third-highest of Vermont's five "official" 4,000-footers. (Cutts does not qualify because there is not enough elevation gain and loss between it and Ellen.) The LT almost immediately passes a chairlift for the Sugarbush North Ski Area, bears left along a ski trail for 100 feet and re-enters the woods, descending very rocky ground, where footing is difficult.

At 6.7 miles, the LT leaves the national forest, and at 8.1 miles reaches a junction with the Jerusalem Trail, which departs left (west) and continues 2.5 miles to a road. Just a tenth of a mile farther, the LT reaches the Barton Trail, which leads to the right (east) two-tenths of a mile to the Glen Ellen Lodge. The LT then climbs steeply for a short distance to the height of General Stark Mountain (3,662 feet), at 8.5 miles, and reaches the Stark's Nest shelter at 9.1 miles. The LT follows a ski trail briefly, turns left into the woods, crosses a cross-country skiing trail, then descends steeply to the Theron Dean shelter at 9.8 miles. A path leads a short distance past the shelter to a good view of the mountains to the north. From the shelter, the LT drops steeply, passes another chairlift station at 10 miles, and reaches Route 17 at 11.6 miles.

23 Mount Abraham

5.2 mi/4.0 hrs 

Location: In the Green Mountain National Forest north of Lincoln Gap; Northern Vermont map page 174, grid d2.

User groups: Hikers and dogs. No wheelchair facilities. Dogs must be on a leash. This trail may be difficult to snowshoe because of severe winter weather, and is not suitable for bikes, horses, or skis. Hunting is allowed in season, but not near trails.

Access, fees: Parking and access are free. No-trace camping is permitted within the Green Mountain National Forest. From Memorial Day weekend through Columbus Day, a Green Mountain Club caretaker is on duty and a $4-per-person nightly fee ($3 for GMC members) is collected to stay at the Battell shelter, which is on the Long Trail 1.8 miles north of Lincoln Gap. The Long Trail is closed from Lincoln Gap to Appalachian Gap from mid-April through Memorial Day.

Directions: Drive to where the Long Trail crosses the Lincoln-Warren Highway in Lincoln Gap, 4.7 miles east of Lincoln and 4.7 miles west of Route 100 in Warren. There is parking two-tenths of a mile west of Lincoln Gap, as well as along the road in the vicinity of the trail crossing.

Maps: The Green Mountain Club (see address below) sells sectional topographic maps of the Long Trail, either as a set of 21 for $7.95, or individually for $1 per map plus $1 postage; this hike is in Division VIII, Cooley Glen shelter to Birch Glen Camp. For topographic maps of the area, request Lincoln and Mount Ellen from the USGS.

Contact: Green Mountain National Forest Supervisor, 231 North Main Street, Rutland, VT 05701; (802) 747-6700. Green Mountain Club, Route 100, RR 1, Box 650, Waterbury Center, VT 05677; (802) 244-7037.

Trail notes: At 4,006 feet in elevation, Mount Abraham is one of just five summits in Vermont which rises above 4,000 feet—and one of just four which thrusts a rocky crown above the trees. For the other three, see Killington Peak (hikes number 40 and 41), Camel's Hump (hikes number 11 to 14), and Mount Mansfield (hikes number 7 and 8). The 360-degree view from the top of Abraham stretches south along the Green Mountain chain to Killington, west to the Champlain Valley and the Adirondacks, east to the White Mountains on a clear day, and north along this high ridge whose south end Abraham anchors.

Remember that the fragile alpine vegetation above tree line suffers under boots, and to stay on the marked trail or on rocks. From Lincoln Gap, the hike to the summit is a steep, 5.2-mile round-trip. On the ascent, 1.2 miles from the road, the LT passes a pair of huge boulders known as The Carpenters, named for two trailworkers. It passes the Battell Trail at 1.7 miles, which veers left (west), leading two miles to a road; and the Battell shelter, 1.8 miles from the road. From Abraham's summit, you can continue north along this level, high ridge to 3,975-foot Lincoln Peak (making this hike's round-trip distance 6.8 miles), where an observation deck just to the right of the trail offers views in every direction.

Still feeling strong? Keep hiking north to Cutts Peak, which has good views, and then an easy four-tenths of a mile beyond Cutts to the wooded and viewless summit of another Vermont 4,000-footer, 4,083-foot Mount Ellen, making this marathon hike a 12.6-mile round-trip from Lincoln Gap. Turn around and descend the way you came up.

24 Eastwood's Rise and Mount Grant

7.8 mi/5.0 hrs 

Location: In the Green Mountain National Forest south of Lincoln Gap; Northern Vermont map page 174, grid d2.

User groups: Hikers and dogs. No wheelchair facilities. Dogs must be on a leash. This trail may be difficult to snowshoe because of severe winter weather, and is not suitable for bikes, horses, or skis. Hunting is allowed in season, but not near trails.

Access, fees: Parking and access are free. The road through Lincoln Gap is not maintained during winter. No-trace camping is permitted within the Green Mountain National Forest. The Cooley Glen shelter is eight-tenths of a mile south of Mount Grant on the Long Trail.

Directions: Drive to where the Long Trail crosses the Lincoln-Warren Highway in Lincoln Gap, 4.7 miles east of Lincoln and 4.7 miles west of Route 100 in Warren. There is parking two-tenths of a mile west of Lincoln Gap, and parking along the road in the vicinity of the trail crossing.

Maps: The Green Mountain Club (see address below) sells sectional topographic maps of the Long Trail, either as a set of 21 for $7.95, or individually for $1 per map plus $1 postage; this hike is in Division VIII, Cooley Glen shelter to Birch Glen Camp. For a topographic map of the area, request Lincoln from the USGS.

Contact: Green Mountain National Forest Supervisor, 231 North Main Street, Rutland, VT 05701; (802) 747-6700. Green Mountain Club, Route 100, RR 1, Box 650, Waterbury Center, VT 05677; (802) 244-7037.

Trail notes: This one hike really presents the possibility of two different hikes, one a fairly easy round-trip of just eight-tenths of a mile to Eastwood's Rise, a wide, flat ledge looking west all the way to New York's Adirondacks. Hikers seeking a longer outing can continue on to the summit of Mount Grant (3,623 feet), with its view south of the Green Mountains' Bread Loaf Wilderness, a 7.8-mile round-trip.

From Lincoln Gap, follow the white blazes of the Long Trail southbound. The trail passes Eastwood's Rise at four-tenths of a mile, another overlook called Sunset Ledge at 1.1 miles, then climbs steadily to Mount Grant at 3.9 miles. Hike back to the parking area along the same route.

25 Bread Loaf Mountain

8.4 mi/6.0 hrs 

Location: In the Green Mountain National Forest near South Lincoln; Northern Vermont map page 174, grid d2.

User groups: Hikers and dogs. No wheelchair facilities. Dogs must be on a leash. This trail may be difficult to snowshoe because of severe winter weather, and is not suitable for bikes, horses, or skis. Hunting is allowed in season, but not near trails.

Access, fees: Parking and access are free. No-trace camping is permitted within the Green Mountain National Forest. The Emily Proctor shelter is located at the junction of the Long Trail and Emily Proctor Trail, 3.5 miles into this hike. The Skyline Lodge cabin is a tenth of a mile east of the Long Trail via the Skylight Pond Trail, and nine-tenths of a mile south of the summit of Bread Loaf Mountain.

Directions: From the general store in the center of Lincoln, follow the road to South Lincoln for one mile and turn right at a sign for the Emily Proctor Trail. Drive 1.9 miles (it becomes a dirt road) and continue straight ahead onto South Lincoln Road for another two miles. Turn left onto USFS Road 201 and proceed three-tenths of a mile to parking on the left.

Maps: The Green Mountain Club (see address below) sells sectional topographic maps of the Long Trail, either as a set of 21 for $7.95, or individually for $1 per map plus $1 postage; this hike is in Division VII, Brandon Gap, Route 73, to Cooley Glen shelter. For topographic maps of the area, request Bread Loaf and Lincoln from the USGS.

Contact: Green Mountain National Forest Supervisor, 231 North Main Street, Rutland, VT 05701; (802) 747-6700. Green Mountain Club, Route 100, RR 1, Box 650, Waterbury Center, VT 05677; (802) 244-7037.

Trail notes: The overlook on Bread Loaf Mountain offers one of the best views on this section of the Long Trail, a wide sweep south and west of the Green Mountains, the Champlain Valley, and the Adirondack Mountains. The Emily Proctor Trail largely follows an old logging road, and crosses a tributary of the New Haven River three times, once on rocks. The crossings could be tricky in high water. The trail ascends moderately for much of its distance, turning steeper just before reaching the Long Trail at the Emily Proctor shelter, 3.5 miles from the parking area. Much of the approximately 2,000 feet of elevation gain on this hike is accomplished on the Emily Proctor Trail. Turn right and follow the LT southbound for seven-tenths of a mile to the wooded top of 3,835-foot Bread Loaf Mountain. Here, the LT swings left and a side path leads right for a tenth of a mile to the overlook.

Returning the way you came up, you might consider making the very worthwhile side trip to Mount Wilson (3,745 feet), which lies eight-tenths of a mile north of the Emily Proctor shelter on the Long Trail. The view from ledges just off the LT on Wilson—of the long chain of the Green Mountains stretching southward—is even nicer than from Bread Loaf. That detour makes this hike's round-trip distance 10 miles. For another hiking option, see the special note with Skylight Pond (hike number 28).

26 Cooley Glen Trail/Emily Proctor Trail Loop

12.5 mi/8.5 hrs 

Location: In the Green Mountain National Forest near South Lincoln; Northern Vermont map page 174, grid d2.

User groups: Hikers and dogs. No wheelchair facilities. Dogs must be on a leash. This trail may be difficult to snowshoe because of severe winter weather, and is not suitable for bikes, horses, or skis. Hunting is allowed in season, but not near trails.

Access, fees: Parking and access are free. The access road is not maintained for winter hiker access to the trailhead parking lot. No-trace camping is permitted within the Green Mountain National Forest. The

Cooley Glen shelter is at the junction of the Long Trail and the Cooley Glen Trail, 3.4 miles into this hike. The Emily Proctor shelter is located at the junction of the Long Trail and Emily Proctor Trail, 5.6 miles south of the Cooley Glen shelter.

Directions: From the general store in the center of Lincoln, follow the road to South Lincoln for one mile and turn right at a sign for the Emily Proctor Trail. Go 1.9 miles (it becomes a dirt road) and continue straight on South Lincoln Road for two miles. Turn left onto USFS Road 201 and drive three-tenths of a mile to parking on the left.

Maps: The Green Mountain Club (see address below) sells sectional topographic maps of the Long Trail, either as a set of 21 for $7.95, or individually for $1 per map plus $1 postage; this hike is in Division VII, Brandon Gap, Route 73, to Cooley Glen shelter. For topographic maps of the area, request Bread Loaf and Lincoln from the USGS.

Contact: Green Mountain National Forest Supervisor, 231 North Main Street, Rutland, VT 05701; (802) 747-6700. Green Mountain Club, Route 100, RR 1, Box 650, Waterbury Center, VT 05677; (802) 244-7037.

Trail notes: This 12.5-mile loop traverses three named 3,000-footers, Mounts Cleveland, Roosevelt, and Wilson, the last two of which have good views. From the parking area, take the Cooley Glen Trail, which climbs at a moderate grade east, then northeast, paralleling and once crossing a stream before reaching the Long Trail at 3.4 miles. The Cooley Glen shelter lies at this junction of trails. Turn right (south) on the white-blazed LT, climbing a half mile, steeply at times, to the wooded summit of 3,482-foot Mount Cleveland. The Long Trail follows a ridge through several short climbs and dips for 3.1 miles to the summit of Mount Roosevelt, at 3,528 feet, and a spot known as Killington View with a good view south and west of the mountains. Descending briefly off Roosevelt, the LT reaches the Clark Brook Trail in another four-tenths of a mile; that trail branches left (east), leading three miles to a road. The LT then ascends eight-tenths of a mile to Mount Wilson (3,745 feet) and the best view on this hike; follow the obvious side path about 100 feet to the left to an open ledge with a long view south down the backbone of the Green Mountains. Just eight-tenths of a mile farther south on the LT, turn right (north) onto the Emily Proctor Trail—near the shelter of the same name—and descend steadily for 3.5 miles to the parking area.

27 The Long Trail: Route 125, Middlebury Gap, to the Lincoln-Warren Highway, Lincoln Gap

17.4 mi. one way/ 2.0 days

Location: In the Green Mountain National Forest, between Middlebury Gap and Lincoln Gap; Northern Vermont map page 174, grid d2.

User groups: Hikers and dogs. No wheelchair facilities. Dogs must be on a leash. This trail may be difficult to snowshoe because of severe winter weather, and is not suitable for bikes, horses, or skis. Hunting is allowed in season, but not near trails.

Access, fees: Parking and access are free. The road through Lincoln Gap is not maintained during winter. No-trace camping is permitted within the Green Mountain National Forest. North from Route 125 on the Long Trail, it is 5.3 miles to the Skylight Pond Trail, which leads east a tenth of a mile to the Skyline Lodge cabin; 7.1 miles to the Emily Proctor shelter; and 12.7 miles to the Cooley Glen shelter (the last is 4.7 miles south of the Lincoln-Warren Highway).

Directions: You need to shuttle two

vehicles for this one-way traverse. To hike south to north, as described here, leave one vehicle where the Long Trail crosses the Lincoln-Warren Highway in Lincoln Gap, 4.7 miles east of Lincoln and 4.7 miles west of Route 100 in Warren. There is parking two-tenths of a mile west of Lincoln Gap, as well as along the road in the vicinity of the trail crossing. Then drive to the large turnout on the south side of Route 125, immediately west of where the Long Trail crosses the road in Middlebury Gap, 5.6 miles east of Ripton and 6.4 miles west of Route 100 in Hancock.

Maps: The Green Mountain Club (see address below) sells sectional topographic maps of the Long Trail, either as a set of 21 for $7.95, or individually for $1 per map plus $1 postage; this hike begins in Division VII, Brandon Gap, Route 73, to Cooley Glen shelter, and extends into Division VIII, Cooley Glen shelter to Birch Glen Camp. For topographic maps of the area, request Bread Loaf and Lincoln from the USGS.

Contact: Green Mountain National Forest Supervisor, 231 North Main Street, Rutland, VT 05701; (802) 747-6700. Green Mountain Club, Route 100, RR 1, Box 650, Waterbury Center, VT 05677; (802) 244-7037.

Trail notes: This fairly rugged stretch of the Long Trail passes over nine named 3,000-foot peaks in 17.4 miles. Although most of this ridge walk is wooded, there are several good, long views of the Green Mountains. This is also the southern section of the famous Monroe Skyline (hike number 21). Typical of New England's mountains, the Long Trail here takes you on a roller-coaster ride up and down these peaks in a series of short, often steep steps which can seem endless. But on my own extended trek on the Long Trail, this section whetted my appetite for the big peaks immediately north—especially the views from spots like Skylight Pond, Bread Loaf Mountain, and Mount Wilson.

From Route 125, the LT northbound climbs steeply for four-tenths of a mile to a junction with a blue-blazed trail branching right and leading four-tenths of a mile to Silent Cliff. This easy detour (which adds eight-tenths of a mile to this hike's distance) is one a hiker with his "trail legs" could make in 20 or 30 minutes round-trip, and leads to a ledge jutting out over thin air atop Silent Cliff, with a view of Middlebury Gap and the Middlebury Snow Bowl Ski Area, and west to the Champlain Valley and the Adirondacks on a clear day. Immediately before the cliff, a footpath veers right a few steps to Silent Cave, a cavelike passage beneath a massive boulder perched against the mountainside.

From the Silent Cliff Trail junction, the Long Trail swings left and ascends more moderately over 3,040-foot Burnt Hill at 2.1 miles from Route 125, passes the Burnt Hill Trail (which leads west 2.2 miles to a road), then traverses up and down several summits along the ridge: Kirby Peak (3,140 feet) at 2.7 miles, Mount Boyce (3,323 feet) at 3.6 miles, and Battell Mountain (3,482 feet) at five miles from Route 125. Between Kirby and Boyce, the trail passes Boyce shelter at 3.2 miles. There are a few limited views of surrounding mountains and valleys from along this part of the ridge. At 5.3 miles, the LT is crossed by the Skylight Pond Trail, which leads left (west) 2.3 miles to a road, and right (east) a tenth of a mile to Skyline Lodge and Skylight Pond, one of the most picturesque spots on this hike. I awoke one morning in Skyline Lodge early enough to catch the predawn sky lit up with vivid bands of red and yellow and fog filling the valleys between distant mountain ridges.

From the Skylight Pond Trail, the LT climbs about 400 feet in elevation to Bread Loaf Mountain, where at 6.4 miles a side path leads a tenth of a mile to a good overlook south of the long chain of the Green Mountains, and west to the Champlain Valley and Adirondack Mountains. At 7.1 miles, the LT passes the Emily Proctor shelter and the Emily Proctor Trail, which leads north 3.5 miles to a road outside South Lincoln. The LT then ascends about 300 feet to Mount Wilson at 7.9 miles; do not pass up the view from ledges about 100 feet off the trail (reached via a clear path) south down the long backbone of the Greens. The LT descends to a junction with the Clark Brook Trail at 8.7 miles, which leads east three miles to a road; then climbs less than 200 feet to reach the top of 3,528-foot Mount Roosevelt at 9.1 miles, and a spot called Killington View, with a good view south and west of the mountains.

After several more short climbs and descents, the trail passes over the wooded summit of Mount Cleveland (3,482 feet) at 12.2 miles and descends to the Cooley Glen shelter at 12.7 miles. From the shelter, the LT swings west and climbs 500 feet over eight-tenths of a mile to the summit of Mount Grant (3,623 feet) at 13.5 miles, where you get a view of the Bread Loaf Wilderness of the Green Mountains to the south. The LT continues north along the ridge, passing through an interesting birch forest to a broad view west all the way to the Adirondacks from an open ledge called Eastwood's Rise at 17 miles. The trail drops fairly easily to the Lincoln-Warren Highway in Lincoln Gap.

28 Skylight Pond

4.8 mi/3.2 hrs 

Location: In the Green Mountain National Forest, between Middlebury Gap and Lincoln Gap; Northern Vermont map page 174, grid d2.

User groups: Hikers and dogs. No wheelchair facilities. Dogs must be on a leash. This trail may be difficult to snowshoe because of severe winter weather, and is not suitable for bikes, horses, or skis. Hunting is allowed in season, but not near trails.

Access, fees: Parking and access are free. USFS Road 59 is not maintained in winter, but does dry out fairly quickly after the snow is gone in spring. No-trace camping is permitted within the Green Mountain National Forest. The Skyline Lodge cabin is a tenth of a mile off the Long Trail, 2.4 miles into this hike, at the end of the Skylight Pond Trail.

Directions: From Route 125, nine miles west of the junction of Routes 125 and 100 in Hancock, and 2.8 miles east of Ripton (or eight-tenths of a mile east of the Robert Frost Interpretive Trail parking lot), turn north onto USFS Road 59 and drive about 3.5 miles to parking for the Skylight Pond Trail.

Maps: The Green Mountain Club (see address below) sells sectional topographic maps of the Long Trail, either as a set of 21 for $7.95, or individually for $1 per map plus $1 postage; this hike is within Division VII, Brandon Gap, Route 73, to Cooley Glen shelter. For topographic maps of the area, request Bread Loaf and Lincoln from the USGS.

Contact: Green Mountain National Forest Supervisor, 231 North Main Street, Rutland, VT 05701; (802) 747-6700. Green Mountain Club, Route 100, RR 1, Box 650, Waterbury Center, VT 05677; (802) 244-7037.

Trail notes: I woke up alone in the Skyline Lodge one late-October morning, before dawn, and saw fire through a musty window. I stepped outside and stood in the chill for about 45 minutes, watching a spectacular sunrise come to life on the distant eastern horizon, with mountain ridges and fog-filled valleys in the middle distance and the whole scene reflected in Skylight Pond. This is a popular spot, no doubt because the lodge is one of the nicest cabins along the entire trail. This 4.8-mile hike can easily be done in a half day, but you just might be tempted to spend the night in the lodge and catch the sunrise. From the parking area, follow the Skylight Pond Trail, which ascends moderately for 2.3 miles to the Long Trail. It crosses the LT and continues a tenth of a mile to the lodge. Return the way you came.

Special note: Want to make a longer adventure of it? By shuttling two vehicles, you could combine this hike and Bread Loaf Mountain (hike number 25) by taking the Skylight Pond Trail to the pond, the Long Trail north over Bread Loaf Mountain to Mount Wilson, then backtracking on the LT and descending the Emily Proctor Trail, a 9.4-mile trek. From the Skylight Pond Trail parking area, continue driving north on USFS Road 59, bear right onto USFS Road 54, then turn right onto USFS Road 201 to reach the Emily Proctor Trail parking area.

29 Robert Frost Interpretive Trail

1.0 mi/0.75 hr 

Location: In the Green Mountain National Forest, between Ripton and Hancock; Southern Vermont map page 175, grid b2.

User groups: Hikers, dogs, skiers, and snowshoers. A portion of this trail is wheelchair accessible. Dogs must be on a leash. This trail is not suitable for bikes or horses. Hunting is allowed in season, but not near trails.

Access, fees: Parking and access are free.

Directions: Drive to the parking area on the south side of Route 125, 9.8 miles west of the junction of Routes 125 and 100 in Hancock, and two miles east of Ripton (also, a tenth of a mile west of the Robert Frost Wayside Area on Route 125).

Maps: No map is necessary for this hike. A brochure with information about this and other trails in the Middlebury and Rochester Districts of the national forest is available from the Green Mountain National Forest Supervisor (see address below). For a topographic map of the area, request Bread Loaf from the USGS.

Contact: Green Mountain National Forest Supervisor, 231 North Main Street, Rutland, VT 05701; (802) 747-6700.

Trail notes: This interpretive trail, beginning from the parking lot, makes a one-mile loop through various microenvironments, including forest, marsh, brooks, and an open meadow with a nice view of the Green Mountains. Along the trail are information boards identifying vegetation and containing pieces of verse from the famous New England poet for whom the trail is named. It's a tranquil place to visit under a blanket of snow, although the information boards may be covered by the white stuff, too.

30 Silent Cliff

1.6 mi/1.0 hr 

Location: In the Green Mountain National Forest at Middlebury Gap; Southern Vermont map page 175, grid b2.

User groups: Hikers and dogs. No wheelchair facilities. Dogs must be on a leash. This trail may be difficult to snowshoe because of severe winter weather, and is not suitable for bikes, horses, or skis. Hunting is allowed in season, but not near trails.

Access, fees: Parking and access are free. No-trace camping is permitted within the Green Mountain National Forest. The Boyce shelter is on the Long Trail, 3.2 miles north of Route 125 and 2.8 miles beyond the junction of the Long Trail and Silent Cliff Trail.

Directions: Drive to the large turnout on the south side of Route 125, immediately west of where the Long Trail crosses the road in Middlebury Gap, 5.6 miles east of Ripton and 6.4 miles west of Route 100 in Hancock.

Maps: The Green Mountain Club (see address below) sells sectional topographic maps of the Long Trail, either as a set of 21 for $7.95, or individually for $1 per map plus $1 postage; this hike is within Division VII, Brandon Gap, Route 73, to Cooley Glen shelter. For a topographic map of the area, request Bread Loaf from the USGS.

Contact: Green Mountain National Forest Supervisor, 231 North Main Street, Rutland, VT 05701; (802) 747-6700. Green Mountain Club, Route 100, RR 1, Box 650, Waterbury Center, VT 05677; (802) 244-7037.

Trail notes: The view from atop Silent Cliff, where a ledge juts out into thin air like a defiant chin, takes in a wide sweep of Middlebury Gap, the Middlebury Snow Bowl Ski Area across the gap, and west to the Champlain Valley and the Adirondacks on a clear day. While half the hike is steep, it's just 1.6 miles round-trip, and a good one for young children. From the parking area on Route 125, cross the road and follow the Long Trail northbound, climbing steeply for four-tenths of a mile. Turn right onto the blue-blazed Silent Cliff Trail, which leads four-tenths of a mile over much easier terrain to the cliff. Immediately before the cliff is Silent Cave, a steep and tight cavelike passage beneath a massive boulder perched against the mountainside—another attraction guaranteed to fascinate kids. Return the way you came up. You might combine this with the Middlebury Gap (hike number 33).

31 Texas Falls Nature Trail

1.0 mi/1.0 hr 

Location: In the Green Mountain National Forest, between Ripton and Hancock; Southern Vermont map page 175, grid b2.

User groups: Hikers, dogs, and snowshoers. No wheelchair facilities. Dogs must be on a leash. This trail is not suitable for bikes, horses, or skis. Hunting is allowed in season, but not near trails.

Access, fees: Parking and access are free. The Texas Falls Recreation Area is closed from 10 P.M. to 6 A.M. USFS Road 39 can be hazardous with snow and ice from late fall into spring.

Directions: From Route 125, 3.1 miles west of the junction of Routes 125 and 100 in Hancock, and 8.7 miles east of Ripton, turn north onto USFS Road 39 at a sign for Texas Falls. Drive a half mile to a turnout on the left.

Maps: No map is necessary for this hike. A brochure with information about this and other trails in the Middlebury and Rochester Districts of the national forest is available from the Green Mountain National Forest Supervisor (see address below). For a topographic map of the area, request Bread Loaf from the USGS.

Contact: Green Mountain National Forest Supervisor, 231 North Main Street, Rutland, VT 05701; (802) 747-6700.

Trail notes: Cross USFS Road 39 from the parking turnout, walk down a few steps, and you are at Texas Falls, where Texas Brook charges through a narrow, spectacular gorge. Cross the brook on a wooden bridge—with an excellent view of the gorge—to the start of the one-mile nature trail loop. Bearing left, the trail follows the brook upstream along a well-graded, easy path. Within a half mile, the trail swings right, ascends the hillside briefly, then swings right again, looping back to the start. It's a good hike to introduce young children to the national forest.

32 Falls of Lana and Rattlesnake Cliffs

4.8 mi/3.0 hrs 

Location: In the Green Mountain National Forest and Branbury State Park south of Middlebury; Southern Vermont map page 175, grid b2.

User groups: Hikers, dogs, and snowshoers. No wheelchair facilities. Dogs must be on a leash. This trail is not suitable for bikes, horses, or skis. Hunting is allowed in season, but not near trails.

Access, fees: Parking and access are free.

Directions: Drive to the parking area on the east side of Route 53, 5.3 miles north of the junction of Routes 53 and 73 in Forest Dale, and four-tenths of a mile south of the entrance to Branbury State Park.

Maps: A basic trail map with state park information is available from the Vermont Department of Forests, Parks, and Recreation (see address below). A similar, basic trail map with information about these and other trails in the Middlebury and Rochester Districts of the national forest is available from the Green Mountain National Forest Supervisor (see address below). For a topographic map of the area, request East Middlebury from the USGS.

Contact: Vermont Department of Forests, Parks, and Recreation, 103 South Main Street, Waterbury, VT 05671-0603; (802) 241-3655. Green Mountain National Forest Supervisor, 231 North Main Street, Rutland, VT 05701; (802) 747-6700.

Trail notes: On a crisp and clear mid-November day, with the leaves long dead on the ground, I made this 4.8-mile hike past the beautiful Falls of Lana and up to Rattlesnake Cliffs for a long, late-afternoon view stretching to New York's Adirondack Mountains. This moderate hike begins in Branbury State Park and enters the Green Mountain National Forest.

From the parking area, follow the wide woods road a half mile to the Falls of Lana. Be sure to look for faint side paths leading left to various viewpoints above the falls, which tumble well over 100 feet through several picturesque cascades and pools. Many hikers turn back from the Falls of Lana for a round-trip of just one mile, but this hike continues past the falls, crossing Sucker Brook in another tenth of a mile. (To the right of the bridge is the Falls picnic area.) Beyond the bridge, walk straight ahead onto the North Branch Trail, and then bear right within 100 feet at signs for Rattlesnake Cliffs and the North Branch Trail. Follow that trail for a tenth of a mile, then turn left at a sign onto the Aunt Jennie Trail. The trail ascends, steeply in some places, about one mile until you reach the junction with the Rattlesnake Cliffs Trail. Turn left and follow that trail a tenth of a mile to another junction. Bear left and hike two-tenths of a mile to the trail's end, atop cliffs with a sweeping view which encompasses tiny Silver Lake, the bigger Lake Dunmore, and the Adirondacks in the distance. Backtrack up the trail about 50 yards to a side path branching to the right; a big tree and wooden post may be blown down across the path. Continue on the path downhill for a tenth of a mile to another sweeping view, this one to the south. Backtrack again all the way to the Rattlesnake Cliffs Trail and descend to the parking area the same way you came up.

33 Middlebury Gap

6.4 mi/4.5 hrs 3 7

Location: In the Green Mountain National Forest at Middlebury Gap; Southern Vermont map page 175, grid b2.

User groups: Hikers and dogs. No wheelchair facilities. Dogs must be on a leash. This trail may be difficult to snowshoe because of severe winter weather, and is not suitable for bikes, horses, or skis. Hunting is allowed in season, but not near trails.

Access, fees: Parking and access are free. No-trace camping is permitted within the Green Mountain National Forest. The Sucker Brook shelter is on the Long Trail, 4.4 miles south of Route 125 and 1.2 miles beyond the turn-around point for this hike.

Directions: Drive to the large turnout on the south side of Route 125, immediately west of where the Long Trail crosses the road in Middlebury Gap, 5.6 miles east of Ripton and 6.4 miles west of Route 100 in Hancock.

Maps: The Green Mountain Club (see address below) sells sectional topographic maps of the Long Trail, either as a set of 21 for $7.95, or individually for $1 per map plus $1 postage; this hike is within Division VII, Brandon Gap, Route 73, to Cooley Glen shelter. For a topographic map of the area, request Bread Loaf from the USGS.

Contact: Green Mountain National Forest Supervisor, 231 North Main Street, Rutland, VT 05701; (802) 747-6700. Green Mountain Club, Route 100, RR 1, Box 650, Waterbury Center, VT 05677; (802) 244-7037.

Trail notes: Hiking the Long Trail south from Middlebury Gap will bring you past a series of views which, if neither sweeping nor grand, make for a pleasant jaunt on a relatively quiet section of the trail. From the road, the trail climbs slightly for four-tenths of a mile to a side path on the right which leads a tenth of a mile to Lake Pleiad and the site of a former shelter, where camping is now prohibited. Continuing south on the white-blazed Long Trail, you will cross a pair of ski area trails, then soon reach the first viewpoint, Robert Frost Lookout. The LT goes through some short ups and downs to Monastery Lookout, 2.6 miles from Middlebury Gap. The wooded summit of Worth Mountain lies just a tenth of a mile farther, then the trail descends for a half mile past other limited views to South Worth Lookout, 3.2 miles from the highway. Backtracking from here makes for a 6.4-mile round-trip. For a slightly longer outing, combine this hike with Silent Cliff (hike number 30).

34 The Long Trail: Route 73, Brandon Gap, to Route 125, Middlebury Gap

9.8 mi. one way/7.5 hrs 

Location: In the Green Mountain National Forest, between Brandon Gap and Middlebury Gap; Southern Vermont map page 175, grid b2.

User groups: Hikers and dogs. No wheelchair facilities. Dogs must be on a leash. This trail may be difficult to snowshoe because of severe winter weather, and is not suitable for bikes, horses, or skis. Hunting is allowed in season, but not near trails.

Access, fees: Parking and access are free. No-trace camping is permitted within the Green Mountain National Forest. The Sucker Brook shelter is on the Long Trail, 5.4 miles north of Route 73.

Directions: You need to shuttle two vehicles for this one-way traverse. To hike south to north, as described here, leave one vehicle in the large turnout on the south side of Route 125, immediately west of where the Long Trail crosses the road in Middlebury Gap, 5.6 miles east of Ripton and 6.4 miles west of Route 100 in Hancock. Then drive to the parking area immediately west of where the LT crosses Route 73 in Brandon Gap, 5.2 miles east of Forest Dale and 9.7 miles west of the Route 100 junction south of Rochester.

Maps: The Green Mountain Club (see address below) sells sectional topographic maps of the Long Trail, either as a set of 21 for $7.95, or individually for $1 per map plus $1 postage; this hike is within Division VII, Brandon Gap, Route 73, to Cooley Glen shelter. For topographic maps of the area, request Mount Carmel and Bread Loaf from the USGS.

Contact: Green Mountain National Forest

Supervisor, 231 North Main Street, Rutland, VT 05701; (802) 747-6700. Green Mountain Club, Route 100, RR 1, Box 650, Waterbury Center, VT 05677; (802) 244-7037.

Trail notes: The most spectacular natural feature along this 9.8-mile stretch of the Long Trail is the Great Cliff at Mount Horrid, but there are also nice views from points on the mostly wooded ridge north of Worth Mountain. The trail continues to grow more rugged, with repeated short but fairly steep climbs and descents and significant gains and losses in elevation, the biggest being the climb of about 1,200 feet from the road in Brandon Gap to the summit of 3,366-foot Gillespie Peak.

From Route 73, follow the white blazes of the Long Trail northbound. The trail makes quick left and right turns, enters the woods and begins a steep ascent of six-tenths of a mile to a junction with a blue-blazed side path leading right a tenth of a mile to the view of the gap from the Great Cliff at Mount Horrid. From that junction, the LT ascends more moderately, passing over the wooded summit of Mount Horrid (3,216 feet) at 1.2 miles. It then follows the forested ridge, with steep and rocky rises and dips, over Cape Lookoff Mountain at 1.7 miles, Gillespie Peak at 3.2 miles, and Romance Mountain's east summit (3,125 feet) at four miles, before descending to the Sucker Brook shelter at 5.4 miles. The trail then ascends, steeply at times, over Worth Mountain at 7.1 miles, and follows the ridge north of the mountain past some views to the east and west.

Gradually descending, the LT passes a chairlift station for the Middlebury Snow Bowl, crosses a pair of ski trails, then reaches a side path on the left at 9.4 miles which leads a tenth of a mile to Lake Pleiad and the former site of a shelter; camping is prohibited there. The trail then descends slightly to Route 125 at 9.8 miles.

35 Great Cliff of Mount Horrid

1.2 mi/1.0 hr 

Location: In the Green Mountain National Forest at Brandon Gap; Southern Vermont map page 175, grid b2.

User groups: Hikers, dogs, and snowshoers. No wheelchair facilities. Dogs must be on a leash. This trail is not suitable for bikes, horses, or skis. Hunting is allowed in season, but not near trails.

Access, fees: Parking and access are free. No-trace camping is permitted within the Green Mountain National Forest. The Sucker Brook shelter is on the Long Trail, 5.4 miles north of Route 73.

Directions: Drive to the parking area immediately west of where the Long Trail crosses Route 73 in Brandon Gap, 5.2 miles east of Forest Dale and 9.7 miles west of the Route 100 junction south of Rochester.

Maps: The Green Mountain Club (see address below) sells sectional topographic maps of the Long Trail, either as a set of 21 for $7.95, or individually for $1 per map plus $1 postage; this hike is within Division VII, Brandon Gap, Route 73, to Cooley Glen shelter. For a topographic map of the area, request Mount Carmel from the USGS.

Contact: Green Mountain National Forest Supervisor, 231 North Main Street, Rutland, VT 05701; (802) 747-6700. Green Mountain Club, Route 100, RR 1, Box 650, Waterbury Center, VT 05677; (802) 244-7037.

Trail notes: The Great Cliff of Mount Horrid scowls high above the highway in Brandon Gap, its scarred and crumbling face something of an anomaly in the rounded, generally heavily wooded Green Mountains. This hike, while just 1.2 miles round-trip, climbs quite steeply to the excellent view of the gap and mountains from the cliff. From Route 73, follow the white blazes of the Long Trail northbound. The trail turns left and right, enters the woods, and climbs for six-tenths of a mile to a junction with a blue-blazed side path on the right. Follow that side trail a tenth of a mile to the view from the cliff. Hike back the same way.

36 The Long Trail: U.S. 4, Sherburne Pass, to Route 73, Brandon Gap

20.7 mi. one way/
2.0 days

Location: Between Sherburne and Brandon Gap; Southern Vermont map page 175, grid b2.

User groups: Hikers and dogs. No wheelchair facilities. Dogs must be on a leash. This trail may be difficult to snowshoe because of severe winter weather, and is not suitable for bikes, horses, or skis. Hunting is allowed in season, but not near trails.

Access, fees: Parking and access are free. No-trace camping is permitted within the Green Mountain National Forest; elsewhere, camping is prohibited except at the Green Mountain Club cabins and shelters. The Long Trail is on private land from Sherburne Pass to the New Boston Trail, and within the Green Mountain National Forest north of the New Boston Trail. The Tucker Johnson shelter is 1.8 miles north of U.S. 4; the Rolston Rest shelter is 5.4 miles north of U.S. 4; the David Logan shelter is two-tenths of a mile west of the LT via the New Boston Trail, 13.1 miles into this hike; and the Sunrise shelter is at 19.8 miles (or nine-tenths of a mile south of Route 73).

Directions: You need to shuttle two vehicles for this one-way traverse. To hike south to north, as described here, leave one vehicle in the parking area immediately west of where the Long Trail crosses Route 73 in Brandon Gap, 5.2 miles east of Forest Dale and 9.7 miles west of the Route 100 junction south of Rochester. Then drive to the parking area across from the Inn at Long Trail, where the Long Trail/Appalachian Trail crosses U.S. 4 at the height-of-land in Sherburne Pass.

Maps: The Green Mountain Club (see address below) sells sectional topographic maps of the Long Trail, either as a set of 21 for $7.95, or individually for $1 per map plus $1 postage; this hike comprises Division VI, U.S. 4, Sherburne Pass, to Route 73, Brandon Gap. For topographic maps of the area, request Pico Peak, Chittenden, Mount Carmel, and Rochester from the USGS.

Contact: Green Mountain National Forest Supervisor, 231 North Main Street, Rutland, VT 05701; (802) 747-6700. Green Mountain Club, Route 100, RR 1, Box 650, Waterbury Center, VT 05677; (802) 244-7037.

Trail notes: This 20.7-mile stretch of the Long Trail is entirely within the woods and fairly flat, with only a few climbs and descents in which elevation gain or loss is no more than 500 feet. From the parking lot in Sherburne Pass, cross U.S. 4 and pick up the white-blazed Long Trail northbound, immediately east of the Inn at Long Trail. The LT coincides with the Appalachian Trail for a steep half mile uphill; then the AT branches right (east), and the LT continues north on more level terrain. A scenic option which is only slightly longer than staying on the LT is to turn left (west) at a half mile onto the Deer Leap Trail, which leads four-tenths of a mile out to the open ledges of Deer Leap Lookout (see hike number 38) and a good view from high above Sherburne Pass. The Deer Leap Trail loops north to rejoin the LT 1.3 miles from U.S. 4. The LT follows the wooded ridge to Tucker Johnson shelter, at 1.8 miles, then continues on fairly easy ground, following an old logging road for awhile. Watch closely for blazes; if you lose the trail, you could find yourself in a maze of woods roads.

The trail crosses the abandoned Chittenden-Pittsfield Road at 3.7 miles, which leads right (east) nine-tenths of a mile to Elbow Road (down which it's another 1.4 miles to Route 100). The LT reaches Rolston Rest shelter 5.4 miles from U.S. 4. The trail climbs over slight rises in the ridge; Chittenden Reservoir may be visible through the trees to the west. At 13.1 miles, the New Boston Trail departs left (west), reaching the David Logan shelter in two-tenths of a mile, and in 1.2 miles a public road which leads to Chittenden. The trail climbs and dips a bit more beyond this junction—over Mount Carmel without reaching its wooded, 3,361-foot summit, down through Wetmore Gap at 14 miles, over the east slope of Bloodroot Mountain, and descending through Bloodroot Gap at 16.5 miles. Passing over one more hill, the Long Trail descends at a very easy grade to Sunrise shelter at 19.8 miles. The trail continues descending another nine-tenths of a mile to Route 73; about two-tenths of a mile before the highway, you get a good view toward the Great Cliff of Mount Horrid.

37 Gile Mountain

1.4 mi/1.0 hr 

Location: In Norwich; Southern Vermont map page 175, grid b4.

User groups: Hikers, dogs, and snowshoers. No wheelchair facilities. The last half of this trail is not suitable for bikes or skis, and the entire trail is not suitable for horses. Hunting is allowed in season.

Access, fees: Parking and access are free.

Directions: From Interstate 91, take exit 13 and follow the signs into Norwich. From Dan and Whit's General Store in the town center, continue straight through town on Main Street for six-tenths of a mile and turn left onto Turnpike Road. Drive nine-tenths of a mile and bear left at a fork. In another 1.7 miles, drive straight onto the dirt Lower Turnpike Road. Drive 2.6 miles farther to a turnout on the left at a sign reading, "Parking for Tower Trail."

Maps: For a topographic map of the area, request Hanover from the USGS.

Contact: There is no contact organization or agency for this hike.

Trail notes: With a group of friends, I mountain biked in the Gile Mountain area and hiked to the fire tower on its summit one September afternoon. From atop the tower, we enjoyed a surprisingly sweeping panorama, from Mount Ascutney to the south; west to Killington and Abraham; northwest to Camel's Hump; northeast to Mount Moosilauke and Franconia Ridge in the White Mountains; and east to the ridge across the Connecticut River which connects, from north to south, Mount Cube, Smarts Mountain, Holt's Ledge, and Moose Mountain.

With this tower so easily accessible, this hike makes for a great place to catch the sunset, especially with the fall foliage at its peak. Follow the Tower Trail, climbing steadily for four-tenths of a mile, then crossing power lines. At seven-tenths of a mile, the trail reaches an abandoned fire ranger's cabin. Follow the trail a short distance beyond the cabin to the fire tower. Return the same way you came up.

38 Deer Leap Mountain

1.8 mi/1.5 hrs 

Location: In Sherburne; Southern Vermont map page 175, grid d2.

User groups: Hikers and dogs. No wheelchair facilities. This trail may be difficult to snowshoe and is not suitable for skis. Bikes, horses, and hunting are prohibited.

Access, fees: Parking and access are free.

Directions: Drive to the parking area across from the Inn at Long Trail, where the Long Trail/Appalachian Trail crosses U.S. 4 at the height-of-land in Sherburne Pass.

Maps: For a map of hiking trails, refer to map 5 in the "Map and Guide to the Appalachian Trail in New Hampshire/Vermont," an eight-map set for $10.95 from the Appalachian Trail Conference (see address below). The Green Mountain Club (see address below) sells sectional topographic maps of the Long Trail, either as a set of 21 for $7.95, or individually for $1 per map plus $1 postage; Deer Leap Mountain is within Division VI, Sherburne Pass to Brandon Gap. For a topographic map of the area, request Pico Peak from the USGS.

Contact: Green Mountain Club, Route 100, RR 1, Box 650, Waterbury Center, VT 05677; (802) 244-7037. Appalachian Trail Conference, P.O. Box 807, Harpers Ferry, WV 25425; (304) 535-6331.

Trail notes: Although steep for more than half its course, this 1.8-mile round-trip to the open ledges of Deer Leap Mountain meets the criteria for an excellent hike for very young hikers: it feels like a mountain to them, both in relative difficulty and the views which reward them. From the lookout, you peer way down on Sherburne Pass and across to the ski slopes of Pico Peak—and on a clear day, views extend west to New York's Adirondack Mountains.

From the parking area, cross busy U.S. 4 and pick up the white-blazed Long Trail northbound, which coincides here with the Appalachian Trail, entering the woods just east of the Inn at Long Trail. The trail immediately begins a steep, rocky climb of a half mile to a junction with the Deer Leap Trail. Turn left onto the latter and follow it an easier four-tenths of a mile to the ledges. Descend the same way.

---

39 Quechee Gorge

2.2 mi/1.2 hrs 

Location: In Quechee Gorge State Park; Southern Vermont map page 175, grid c4.

User groups: Hikers, dogs, skiers, and snowshoers. No wheelchair facilities. This trail is not suitable for bikes or horses. Hunting is prohibited.

Access, fees: Parking and access are free, except that skiers must pay $5 per person at Wilderness Trails to cover costs of grooming the trails. Most of this hike is within Quechee Gorge State Park, but the Beaver Dam Trail briefly exits the state park onto private property; take care not to wander off the trail.

Directions: From Interstate 89 southbound, take exit 1 onto U.S. 4 west and drive 2.5 miles to the east side of the U.S. 4 bridge over Quechee Gorge. From Interstate 89 northbound, take exit 1 and drive 3.2 miles to the gorge. Park at the gift shop or information booth on the east side of the bridge.

Maps: Get a map of ski trails at Wilderness Trails, behind the Marshland Farm; take Dewey's Mill Road between the gift shops on the east side of the bridge and follow it a mile. (Snowshoes and cross-country skis, for adults and children, can be rented there.) For a topographic map of the area, request Quechee from the USGS.

Contact: Vermont Department of Forests, Parks, and Recreation, 103 South Main Street, Waterbury, VT 05671-0603; (802) 241-3655. Friends of the Quechee Gorge, P.O. Box Q, Quechee, VT 05059.

Trail notes: This 150-foot-deep, narrow gorge along the Ottauquechee River has long attracted tourists to a bridge on U.S. 4 spanning the gorge. I first ventured into the gorge on cross-country skis several years ago, making this easy, 2.2-mile loop along the gorge and through the woods of tiny Quechee Gorge State Park. If you're skiing and interested in a longer outing, start from Wilderness Trails (see above), which maintains a system of ski trails adjacent to this loop. From the parking area, walk down the steps in front of the gift shop to the gorge trail and turn left (south), passing under the highway bridge. Follow the well-graded trail above the gorge downhill about a half mile to a bend in the river, where there is a bench. Turn left, continue about two-tenths of a mile along the river, then walk up a small hill with good views of the river and cross a small footbridge. Turn left onto the Beaver Dam Trail, marked by red wooden blocks on trees, which winds up through the state park, leaving the park boundaries briefly and crossing private property. That trail leads a mile to U.S. 4, at the entrance to the state park campground and a half mile east of the bridge. You can walk along the road back to the start of this hike, or, especially if on skis, cross the highway and walk behind the Wildflowers Restaurant to an "easiest" ski trail. Turn left and follow it a half mile back to the gorge trail. Turn left and continue a short distance back to the start of this hike.

40 Killington Peak: Bucklin Trail

7.4 mi/6.0 hrs 

Location: In Mendon and Sherburne; Southern Vermont map page 175, grid c2.

User groups: Hikers and dogs. No wheelchair facilities. This trail may be difficult to snowshoe due to severe winter weather, and is not suitable for skis. Bikes, horses, and hunting are prohibited.

Access, fees: Parking and access are free. Most of this hike takes place on private land. Camping is prohibited except at the Green Mountain Club cabins and shelters. The Cooper Lodge cabin is located at the junction of the Bucklin Trail and Long Trail.

Directions: From U.S. 4, 5.1 miles east of the northern junction of U.S. 4 and U.S. 7 in Rutland, and 4.1 miles west of the Long Trail/Appalachian Trail crossing of U.S. 4 in Sherburne Pass, turn south onto Wheelerville Road. Follow it for 4.1 miles to a turnout on the left.

Maps: For a map of hiking trails, refer to map 6 in the "Map and Guide to the Appalachian Trail in New Hampshire/Vermont," an eight-map set for $10.95 from the Appalachian Trail Conference (see address below). The Green Mountain Club (see address below) sells sectional topographic maps of the Long Trail, either as a set of 21 for $7.95, or individually for $1 per map plus $1 postage; Killington Peak is within Division V, Route 140 to Sherburne Pass. For a topographic map of the area, request Killington Peak from the USGS.

Contact: Green Mountain Club, Route 100, RR 1, Box 650, Waterbury Center, VT 05677; (802) 244-7037. Appalachian Trail Conference, P.O. Box 807, Harpers Ferry, WV 25425; (304) 535-6331.

Trail notes: This 7.4-mile hike provides a route of moderate distance and difficulty up Vermont's second-highest peak, 4,235-foot Killington, whose barren, rocky summit boasts one of the finest panoramas in the state. From the summit, where there are radio transmission facilities and a fire tower, the views extend to Mount Mansfield to the north, numerous other Green Mountains peaks to the north and south, Lake Champlain and the Adirondack Mountains to the west, Mount Ascutney to the southeast, and the White Mountains to the northeast.

From the parking area, take the blue-blazed Bucklin Trail. It follows an abandoned logging road, first on the north bank of Brewers Brook, then the south bank, for nearly two miles. It grows steeper beyond the logging road, reaching the Cooper Lodge and the Long Trail, which coincides here with the Appalachian Trail, at 3.5 miles. Continue uphill on the LT southbound, passing to the right of the lodge, a short distance to where the LT swings right and the spur trail to

Killington's summit continues straight ahead. Hike up the very steep and rocky spur trail for two-tenths of a mile to the summit. Hike back along the same route.

41 Killington Peak: the Long Trail

11.2 mi/8.0 hrs 

Location: In Sherburne; Southern Vermont map page 175, grid c2.

User groups: Hikers and dogs. No wheelchair facilities. This trail may be difficult to snowshoe and is not suitable for skis. Bikes, horses, and hunting are prohibited.

Access, fees: Parking and access are free. Parts of this hike are on private land. Camping is prohibited except at the Green Mountain Club cabins and shelters. The Pico Camp cabin is at the junction of the Long Trail and Pico Link, 2.5 miles south of Sherburne Pass. The Cooper Lodge cabin is located at the junction of the Bucklin Trail and LT, 5.4 miles from Sherburne Pass.

Directions: Drive to the parking area across from the Inn at Long Trail, where the Long Trail/Appalachian Trail crosses U.S. 4 at the height-of-land in Sherburne Pass.

Maps: For a map of hiking trails, refer to map 6 in the "Map and Guide to the Appalachian Trail in New Hampshire/Vermont," an eight-map set for $10.95 from the Appalachian Trail Conference (see address below). The Green Mountain Club (see address below) sells sectional topographic maps of the Long Trail, either as a set of 21 for $7.95, or individually for $1 per map plus $1 postage; Killington Peak is within Division V, Route 140 to Sherburne Pass. For topographic maps of the area, request Killington Peak and Pico Peak from the USGS.

Contact: Green Mountain Club, Route 100, RR 1, Box 650, Waterbury Center, VT 05677; (802) 244-7037. Appalachian Trail Conference, P.O. Box 807, Harpers Ferry, WV 25425; (304) 535-6331.

Trail notes: Although a fairly committing hike of more than 11 miles, the Long Trail from Sherburne Pass presents a good route to the crown of Vermont's second-highest peak, 4,235-foot Killington. With the trailhead at 2,150 feet, there's less elevation gain involved than taking the Bucklin Trail up Killington (hike number 40). And this hike also offers the option of bagging Pico Peak. On the craggy summit of Killington, where there are radio transmission facilities and a fire tower, the 360-degree views encompass Mount Mansfield to the north, numerous other Green Mountains peaks to the north and south, Lake Champlain and the Adirondack Mountains to the west, Mount Ascutney to the southeast, and the White Mountains to the northeast.

From the parking area at Sherburne Pass, follow the spur trail leading a tenth of a mile to the white-blazed Long Trail, which coincides here with the Appalachian Trail. (You could also walk east along U.S. 4 a short distance and turn right onto the LT southbound.) Turn right (south) onto the LT. It climbs gradually for six-tenths of a mile to a side path which leads a tenth of a mile right to a view from the top of a chairlift and alpine slide at the Pico Ski Area. Continuing its steady ascent, the LT reaches a ski trail at two miles and follows it for 300 yards before re-entering the woods. At 2.5 miles from the pass, the LT reaches Pico Camp. A side path, Pico Link, leads four-tenths of a mile up steep and rocky ground from behind Pico Camp to the 3,957-foot summit of Pico Mountain, where there are good views (adding eight-tenths of a mile to this hike's distance). Continue on the LT southbound, mostly contouring along the rugged ridge to Killington Peak. At 5.4 miles, the LT passes Cooper Lodge and reaches the junction with the spur trail to

Killington's summit. Turn left and climb the very steep and rocky spur for two-tenths of a mile to the open summit. Return the way you came up.

42 The Long Trail: Route 103, Clarendon Gorge, to U.S. 4, Sherburne Pass

16.7 mi. one way/
2.0 days 

Location: Between Shrewsbury and Sherburne; Southern Vermont map page 175, grid c2.

User groups: Hikers and dogs. No wheelchair facilities. This trail may be difficult to snowshoe and is not suitable for skis. Bikes, horses, and hunting are prohibited.

Access, fees: Parking and access are free. Except for a patch of state-owned land on Killington Peak, this hike is on private land; camping is prohibited except at the Green Mountain Club shelters. From Route 103, it is one mile north to the Clarendon shelter, reached via a short walk down a woods road from the Long Trail; 6.8 miles to the Governor Clement shelter; 11 miles to the Cooper Lodge cabin; and the Pico Camp cabin is 13.8 miles (the last is 2.5 miles south of U.S. 4).

Directions: You need to shuttle two vehicles for this one-way traverse. To hike south to north, as described here, leave one vehicle in the parking area across from the Inn at Long Trail, where the Long Trail/Appalachian Trail crosses U.S. 4 at the height-of-land in Sherburne Pass. Then drive to the parking area where the trail crosses Route 103, two miles east of U.S. 7 in Clarendon, and three miles west of Cuttingsville.

Maps: For a map of hiking trails, refer to map 6 in the "Map and Guide to the Appalachian Trail in New Hampshire/Vermont," an eight-map set for $10.95 from the Appalachian Trail Conference (see address below). The Green Mountain Club (see address below) sells sectional topographic maps of the Long Trail, either as a set of 21 for $7.95, or individually for $1 per map plus $1 postage; this hike is within Division V, Route 140, Wallingford Gulf, to U.S. 4, Sherburne Pass. For topographic maps of the area, request Rutland, Killington Peak, and Pico Peak from the USGS.

Contact: Green Mountain Club, Route 100, RR 1, Box 650, Waterbury Center, VT 05677; (802) 244-7037. Appalachian Trail Conference, P.O. Box 807, Harpers Ferry, WV 25425; (304) 535-6331.

Trail notes: For someone hiking the entire Long Trail from south to north, this stretch is where the trail begins to metamorphose from a casual walk in the woods with occasional views, to a more committing tromp through the mountains. The LT passes over its first 4,000-footer, Killington Peak—Vermont's second-tallest mountain, at 4,235 feet—grows more rugged, and involves much greater gain and loss of elevation. The views in every direction from the rocky, open summit of Killington, where there are radio transmission facilities and a fire tower, encompass Mount Mansfield to the north, numerous other Green Mountains peaks to the north and south, Lake Champlain and the Adirondack Mountains to the west, Mount Ascutney to the southeast, and the White Mountains to the northeast. Remember that weather at the higher elevations can turn wintry in any month.

From the parking area on Route 103, the white-blazed Long Trail, which coincides here with the Appalachian Trail, crosses the highway and employs wooden stepladders to get over barbed wire fencing enclosing a field. Crossing the field into the woods, the trail follows a woods road and climbs steeply through a narrow, boulder-strewn ravine. Above the ravine, the LT passes a view to the south and west (four-tenths of a mile from Route 103), then descends to another woods road, a mile from Route 103. To the right a short distance down the road is the Clarendon shelter. The LT crosses the road and a brook and ascends Beacon Hill at 1.5 miles, where there is a view south from an open area at the summit. The trail descends again, crosses Lottery Road at 1.9 miles, the dirt Keiffer Road at 3.6 miles, then, after following Northam Brook, turns right onto Cold River Road (also called Lower Road), at 3.9 miles. The LT soon re-enters the woods, following a ridge high above the Cold River, and descends steeply to cross the river's east branch on rocks, which could be tricky in times of high water. After paralleling the river's west branch, the trail crosses Upper Cold River Road at 5.4 miles.

At six miles, turn left onto a dirt road, walk over a bridge, then turn immediately right into the woods. The trail crosses one more road before reaching the Governor Clement shelter at 6.9 miles from Route 103. Passing the shelter, the trail follows a flat woods road for less than a half mile, then starts the long climb up Little Killington and Killington Peak, becoming increasingly rockier, with difficult footing, as the trail narrows through a dense spruce forest. You will gain nearly 2,400 feet in elevation. At nine miles, the LT crosses two small brooks that I've seen flowing well even during a dry autumn. The LT crosses a ski area trail on Killington, then reaches a junction at 9.8 miles with the Shrewsbury Peak Trail, which bears right and leads two miles to that peak (hike number 43), while the LT swings left.

After crossing another ski trail, the hiking grows easier, contouring around the south and west slopes of Killington Peak. At 10.9 miles, a side path bears right and climbs very steeply, over rocky terrain, two-tenths of a mile to the summit of Killington (included in this hike's mileage). Leave your pack behind for this side trip. The LT turns and descends briefly to the Cooper Lodge, then turns right in front of the cabin. The hiking becomes moderate to Pico Camp at 13.8 miles; here, a blue-blazed side trail, the Pico Link, leads steeply uphill for four-tenths of a mile to the summit of Pico, where there are views and a chairlift station. (This detour is not included in this hike's total distance.) The LT contours to a ski area trail at 14.2 miles, follows it downhill for 300 feet, then turns right into the woods. A steady descent brings you to U.S. 4 at Sherburne Pass.

43 Shrewsbury Peak

3.6 mi/2.5 hrs 

Location: In Coolidge State Forest outside North Shrewsbury; Southern Vermont map page 175, grid c2.

User groups: Hikers, dogs, and snowshoers. No wheelchair facilities. Dogs must be on a leash. This trail is not suitable for bikes, horses, or skis. Hunting is allowed in season.

Access, fees: Parking and access are free. The CCC Road can be difficult to drive, especially from the east, in muddy or icy conditions.

Directions: From Route 100, 3.1 miles south of its junction with U.S. 4 in West Bridgewater, and 2.2 miles north of its junction with Route 100A in Plymouth Union, turn west onto the dirt CCC Road at a sign for Meadowsweet Herb Farm. Drive 3.4 miles to a parking area on the right at a sign for the Coolidge State Forest. Or, from the center of North Shrewsbury, pick up the CCC Road (marked by a sign) heading east, which begins as pavement and turns to dirt. At 1.1 miles, bear right at a fork and continue 1.6 miles farther to the parking area on the left.

Maps: The Green Mountain Club (see

address below) sells sectional topographic maps of the Long Trail, either as a set of 21 for $7.95, or individually for $1 per map plus $1 postage; Shrewsbury and Killington peaks are within Division V, Route 140, Wallingford Gulf, to U.S. 4, Sherburne Pass. For a topographic map of the area, request Killington Peak from the USGS.

Contact: Vermont Department of Forests, Parks, and Recreation, 103 South Main Street, Waterbury, VT 05671-0603; (802) 241-3655. Green Mountain Club, Route 100, RR 1, Box 650, Waterbury Center, VT 05677; (802) 244-7037.

Trail notes: On a mid-November day, with an inch of snow turning everything white, I hiked to the summit of Shrewsbury Peak and enjoyed wonderfully long views in a wide sweep to the northeast, east, and south. In the clear air I saw all the way to Franconia Ridge in the White Mountains, Mount Ascutney to the east and Mount Monadnock to the southeast, and a long chain of the Green Mountains to the south. Through openings in the trees looking north, I even caught a glimpse of Killington, which can be reached via Shrewsbury Peak for a scenic if quite rugged round-trip hike of 10.2 miles.

The Shrewsbury Peak Trail is unmarked but obvious, and begins from the stone wall at the rear of the parking lot. Within two-tenths of a mile, it passes in front of a lean-to. Follow the blue blazes over moderate terrain, which grows steeper as the trail ascends into the subalpine hemlock and spruce forest. At 1.8 miles, you will emerge at an open area at the summit. To complete this hike, return the way you came. But you could continue on the Shrewsbury Peak Trail north. In two miles, turn right (north) on the white-blazed Long Trail and follow it 1.1 miles to the Killington Peak Spur Trail. Turn right and climb very steeply two-tenths of a mile to the summit of Killington.

44 Clarendon Gorge and Airport Lookout

1.8 mi/1.2 hrs 

Location: Between Shrewsbury and Clarendon; Southern Vermont map page 175, grid c2.

User groups: Hikers, dogs, and snowshoers. No wheelchair facilities. This trail is not suitable for skis. Bikes, horses, and hunting are prohibited.

Access, fees: Parking and access are free.

Directions: Drive to the parking area on Route 103, three miles west of Cuttingsville, and two miles east of U.S. 7 in Clarendon.

Maps: For a map of hiking trails, refer to map 6 in the "Map and Guide to the Appalachian Trail in New Hampshire/Vermont," an eight-map set for $10.95 from the Appalachian Trail Conference (see address below). The Green Mountain Club (see address below) sells sectional topographic maps of the Long Trail, either as a set of 21 for $7.95, or individually for $1 per map plus $1 postage; this hike is within Division V, Route 140, Wallingford Gulf, to U.S. 4, Sherburne Pass. For a topographic map of the area, request Rutland from the USGS.

Contact: Green Mountain Club, Route 100, RR 1, Box 650, Waterbury Center, VT 05677; (802) 244-7037. Appalachian Trail Conference, P.O. Box 807, Harpers Ferry, WV 25425; (304) 535-6331.

Trail notes: For the view down into Clarendon Gorge, one of the two attractions on this hike, you need only walk southbound on the white-blazed Long Trail/Appalachian Trail for a tenth of a mile to the suspension bridge spanning the dramatic chasm. But the added uphill climb of less than a mile to Airport Lookout is worth the small effort involved. Its open ledges atop low cliffs afford a view west of the Rutland Airport, the valley that U.S. 7 runs through, and the southern Adirondacks. Be careful scrambling around on these ledges; I nearly took a nasty fall there myself. From Airport Lookout, backtrack the way you came up.

45 The Long Trail: Route 140, Wallingford Gulf, to Route 103, Clarendon Gorge

6.3 mi. one way/3.5 hrs 

Location: Between Shrewsbury and Clarendon; Southern Vermont map page 175, grid c2.

User groups: Hikers, dogs, and snowshoers. No wheelchair facilities. This trail is not suitable for skis. Bikes, horses, and hunting are prohibited.

Access, fees: Parking and access are free. Except for a patch of state-owned land at Clarendon Gorge, this hike is on private land; camping is prohibited except at the Green Mountain Club Minerva Hinchey shelter, reached via a short side path off the Long Trail, 2.6 miles north of Route 140.

Directions: You need to shuttle two vehicles for this one-way traverse. To hike south to north, as described here, leave one vehicle in the parking area on Route 103, two miles east of U.S. 7 in Clarendon, and three miles west of Cuttingsville. Then drive to where the Long Trail/Appalachian Trail crosses Route 140, 3.5 miles east of U.S. 7 in Wallingford, and three miles west of the junction of Routes 140, 155, and 103 in East Wallingford.

Maps: For a map of hiking trails, refer to map 6 in the "Map and Guide to the Appalachian Trail in New Hampshire/Vermont," an eight-map set for $10.95 from the Appalachian Trail Conference (see address below). The Green Mountain Club (see address below) sells sectional topographic maps of the Long Trail, either as a set of 21 for $7.95, or individually for $1 per map plus $1 postage; this hike is within Division V, Route 140, Wallingford Gulf, to U.S. 4, Sherburne Pass. For topographic maps of the area, request Wallingford and Rutland from the USGS.

Contact: Green Mountain Club, Route 100, RR 1, Box 650, Waterbury Center, VT 05677; (802) 244-7037. Appalachian Trail Conference, P.O. Box 807, Harpers Ferry, WV 25425; (304) 535-6331.

Trail notes: This 6.3-mile, fairly easy stretch of the Long and Appalachian Trails offers no dramatic views—nothing more than a pleasant walk in the woods, or perhaps a safe and moderate route for a beginning winter hiker to try snowshoeing. Crossing Route 140 northbound, head diagonally to the left onto a dirt road and follow it uphill for a half mile before entering the forest. The trail ascends about 500 feet in elevation over Button Hill, the top of which is mostly wooded, then reaches the side path on the right at 2.6 miles which leads to the Minerva Hinchey shelter. Beyond the shelter, the LT climbs over a low, wooded hill, then descends and passes through Spring Lake Clearing, 3.2 miles from Route 140. It then follows a wooded ridge to Airport Lookout at 4.5 miles, where open ledges atop low cliffs offer a view west of the Rutland Airport, the valley that U.S. 7 runs through, and the southern Adirondacks. Descending, the trail reaches Clarendon Gorge, crossing the gorge on a suspension bridge which offers a dramatic view down into the chasm. Just a tenth of a mile farther, you reach Route 103.

46 White Rocks Cliff

2.6 mi/2.0 hrs 

Location: In the Green Mountain National Forest east of Wallingford; Southern Vermont map page 175, grid c2.

User groups: Hikers and dogs. No wheelchair facilities. Dogs must be on a leash. This trail may be difficult to snowshoe and is not suitable for skis. Bikes, horses, and hunting are prohibited.

Access, fees: Parking and access are free. Camping is prohibited except at the Green Mountain Club cabins and shelters. The Greenwall shelter is located a half mile north of the junction of the Keewaydin and Long Trails.

Directions: From Route 140, 4.1 miles west of the junction of Routes 140 and 155 in East Wallingford and 2.1 miles east of the junction of 140 and U.S. 7 in Wallingford, turn south onto the dirt Sugar Hill Road. Drive a tenth of a mile and turn right onto the dirt USFS Road 52 at a sign for the White Rocks Picnic Area. Continue a half mile to the White Rocks Recreation Area.

Maps: For a map of hiking trails, refer to map 6 in the "Map and Guide to the Appalachian Trail in New Hampshire/Vermont," an eight-map set for $10.95 from the Appalachian Trail Conference (see address below). The Green Mountain Club (see address below) sells sectional topographic maps of the Long Trail, either as a set of 21 for $7.95, or individually for $1 per map plus $1 postage; White Rocks Cliff is within Division IV, Mad Tom Notch to Route 140, Wallingford Gulf. For a topographic map of the area, request Wallingford from the USGS.

Contact: Green Mountain National Forest Supervisor, 231 North Main Street, Rutland, VT 05701; (802) 747-6700. Green Mountain Club, Route 100, RR 1, Box 650, Waterbury Center, VT 05677; (802) 244-7037. Appalachian Trail Conference, P.O. Box 807, Harpers Ferry, WV 25425; (304) 535-6331.

Trail notes: From the White Rocks Recreation Area, follow the Keewaydin Trail steeply uphill for eight-tenths of a mile to the Long Trail, which coincides here with the Appalachian Trail. Turn right (south) on the LT and hike three-tenths of a mile, then turn right (west) on the White Rocks Cliff Trail. That trail descends steeply for two-tenths of a mile and ends at the top of the cliffs, with good views of the valley south of Wallingford. There are numerous footpaths around the cliffs, but take care because the rock is loose and footing can be dangerous. Return the way you came up.

47 Mount Ascutney

6.8 mi/4.5 hrs 

Location: In Ascutney State Park in Windsor; Southern Vermont map page 175, grid c3.

User groups: Hikers and snowshoers. No wheelchair facilities. This trail is not suitable for bikes, horses, or skis. Dogs are prohibited. Hunting is allowed in season.

Access, fees: Parking and access are free. Trails are closed during the spring mud season, usually mid-April through mid-May.

Directions: If you have two vehicles, drive one to the Windsor Trail parking area at the end of this hike, reducing this hike's distance by the one mile of paved road separating the trailheads; otherwise, just note the location of the Windsor Trail on your way to the start of the Brownsville Trail. From the north, take Interstate 91 to exit 9, then U.S. 5 south into the center of Windsor; from the south, take Interstate 91 to exit 8, then U.S. 5 north into Windsor. At the junction of U.S. 5 and Route 44 in Windsor, turn west onto Route 44 and follow it for 3.3 miles to its junction with Route 44A. The Windsor Trail parking area is just 100 yards down Route 44A, on the right. Continue west on Route 44 for nine-tenths of a mile to parking on the left side of the road for the Brownsville Trail.

Maps: The Ascutney Trails Association (see address below) publishes a guidebook and map of Ascutney which costs $4. A free, basic map is available to virtually all state parks. The Vermont State Parks Map Atlas can be purchased for $5 plus tax from the Vermont Department of Forests, Parks, and Recreation (see address below). For a topographic map of the area, request Mount Ascutney from the USGS.

Contact: Ascutney State Park, Box 186, HCR 71, Windsor, VT 05089; (802) 674-2060. Vermont Department of Forests, Parks, and Recreation, 103 South Main Street, Waterbury, VT 05671-0603; (802) 241-3655. Ascutney Trails Association, P.O. Box 147, Windsor, VT 05089.

Trail notes: Mount Ascutney, at 3,150 feet, belongs to a class of small New England mountains which rise much higher than any piece of earth surrounding them—peaks like Monadnock (hikes number 80 to 82 in the New Hampshire chapter), Cardigan (hike number 71 in the New Hampshire chapter), and Wachusett (hikes number 36 to 39 in the Massachusetts chapter). The eroded core of a volcano that once rose to 20,000 feet, Ascutney soars above the Connecticut River Valley; its observation tower offers excellent views in a 360-degree panorama to the Green Mountains to the west, Monadnock to the southeast, Mounts Sunapee and Cardigan to the northeast, and the White Mountains beyond. The first trail up Ascutney was cut in 1825; today, several go up the mountain.

Follow the Brownsville Trail's white blazes, climbing steadily along a wide woods path. At 1.1 miles, the trail passes by the remains of the Norcross Quarry on the right, where granite was harvested until 1910. The trail continues upward, passing a short side path at 1.3 miles leading to an overlook. A second lookout is reached at two miles, offering a view eastward. At 2.3 miles, the trail crosses a grassy area atop wooded North Peak (2,660 feet). After reaching the Windsor Trail junction (on the left) at 2.9 miles, bear right for the summit. Just a tenth of a mile beyond that junction you will reach the remains of what was called the Stone Hut, a former shelter. An unmarked trail leads left seven-tenths of a mile to the Ascutney auto road; and to the right, a short path leads to Brownsville Rock, which offers good views north.

Continue up the Windsor Trail two-tenths of a mile to the summit observation tower. Descend the same route for three-tenths of a mile, then turn right to follow the white-blazed Windsor Trail down. The trail crosses the two branches of Mountain Brook, then parallels the brook on a wide, old woods road through a wild drainage. At 2.6 miles from the summit, you reach Route 44A and the parking area for the Windsor Trail. If you have no vehicle here, turn left and follow 44A onto Route 44 west for nine-tenths of a mile to the start of this hike.

48 The Long Trail: USFS Road 10 to Route 140

9.0 mi. one way/5.5 hrs 2 7

Location: In the Green Mountain National Forest, between Danby and Wallingford; Southern Vermont map page 175, grid d2.

User groups: Hikers, dogs, and snowshoers. No wheelchair facilities. Dogs must be on a leash. This trail is not suitable for skis. Bikes, horses, and hunting are prohibited.

Access, fees: Parking and access are free. USFS Road 10 is not maintained in winter. No-trace camping is permitted within the Green Mountain National Forest, except at Little Rock Pond, where camping within 200 feet of the shore is allowed at designated campsites only. From Memorial Day weekend through Columbus Day, a Green Mountain Club caretaker is on duty and a $4-per-person nightly fee ($3 for GMC members) is collected to stay at the Little Rock Pond and Lula Tye shelters and campsites. From USFS Road 10, the Lula Tye shelter is 1.8 miles north, the Little Rock Pond campsites two miles north, the Little Rock Pond shelter 2.5 miles, and the Greenwall shelter 7.2 miles.

Directions: You need to shuttle two vehicles for this one-way traverse. To hike south to north, as described here, leave one vehicle where the Long Trail/Appalachian Trail crosses Route 140, 3.5 miles east of U.S. 7 in Wallingford, and three miles west of the junction of Routes 140, 155, and 103 in East Wallingford. This hike begins at the parking lot on USFS Road 10 at Big Black Branch, 3.5 miles west of U.S. 7 in Danby and 13.6 miles north of Route 11 in Peru.

Maps: For a map of hiking trails, refer to map 6 in the "Map and Guide to the Appalachian Trail in New Hampshire/Vermont," an eight-map set for $10.95 from the Appalachian Trail Conference (see address below). The Green Mountain Club (see address below) sells sectional topographical maps of the Long Trail, either as a set of 21 for $7.95, or individually for $1 per map plus $1 postage; this hike is within Division IV, Mad Tom Notch to Route 140, Wallingford Gulf. For topographic maps of the area, request Danby and Wallingford from the USGS.

Contact: Green Mountain National Forest Supervisor, 231 North Main Street, Rut-land, VT 05701; (802) 747-6700. Green Mountain Club, Route 100, RR 1, Box 650, Waterbury Center, VT 05677; (802) 244-7037. Appalachian Trail Conference, P.O. Box 807, Harpers Ferry, WV 25425; (304) 535-6331.

Trail notes: The highlights of this fairly easy, nine-mile stretch of the Long Trail/Appalachian Trail, are Little Rock Pond and the view from White Rocks Cliff (see hike number 46 for a shorter hike to the cliffs). From the parking area on USFS Road 10, cross the road onto the white-blazed LT northbound. The trail follows Little Black Brook, passing the Lula Tye shelter at 1.8 miles, and reaching Little Rock Pond, a small mountain tarn, at two miles. A popular destination with hikers, the pond sits tucked beneath a low ridge; there's a nice view across the pond where the Long Trail first reaches it, at its southeast corner. Following the pond's east shore, the LT reaches the short side path to Little Rock Pond shelter a tenth of a mile beyond the pond, at 2.5 miles into this hike. The trail then climbs gently for 3.9 miles to a blue-blazed side path on the left, which leads steeply downhill for two-tenths of a mile to White Rocks Cliff, with good views of the valley south of Wallingford. Continuing north on the LT, you pass the Keewaydin Trail branching left in another three-tenths of a mile, then descend another half mile to the Greenwall shelter, at 7.2 miles into this hike. More easy walking for six-tenths of a mile brings you to a road; walk straight ahead on it for three-tenths of a mile, cross the dirt USFS Road 19 into the woods, and walk another easy mile to Route 140.

49 Big Branch Wilderness

14.0 mi/8.5 hrs or 1–2 days 

Location: In the Green Mountain National Forest east of Danby; Southern Vermont map page 175, grid d2.

User groups: Hikers and dogs. No wheelchair facilities. Dogs must be on a leash. The trailhead is not accessible by road in winter for skiing or snowshoeing. Bikes, horses, and hunting are prohibited.

Access, fees: Parking and access are free. USFS Road 10 is not maintained during the winter. No-trace camping is permitted within the Green Mountain National Forest, except at Griffith Lake, where camping within 200 feet of the shore is restricted to designated sites. The Griffith Lake campsite is on the Long Trail, seven miles south of USFS Road 10. The Peru Peak shelter lies seven-tenths of a mile farther south. From Memorial Day weekend through Labor Day, a Green Mountain Club caretaker is on duty and a $4-per-person nightly fee ($3 for GMC members) is collected to stay at both sites. The Big Branch shelter is on the LT, 1.3 miles south of USFS Road 10, and the Lost Pond shelter is three miles south of the road.

Directions: Drive to the parking lot on USFS Road 10 at Big Black Branch, 3.5 miles west of U.S. 7 in Danby and 13.6 miles north of Route 11 in Peru. To finish this hike on the Baker Peak and Lake Trails, as described in the special note (below), you must leave a vehicle at the start of the Lake Trail; from the crossroads in Danby, drive south on U.S. 7 for 2.1 miles and turn left onto Town Highway 5. Drive a half mile to parking on the left.

Maps: For a map of hiking trails, refer to map 7 in the "Map and Guide to the Appalachian Trail in New Hampshire/Vermont," an eight-map set for $10.95 from the Appalachian Trail Conference (see address below). The Green Mountain Club (see address below) sells sectional topographic maps of the Long Trail, either as a set of 21 for $7.95, or individually for $1 per map plus $1 postage; this hike is in Division IV, Mad Tom Notch to Route 140, Wallingford Gulf. For a topographic map of the area, request Danby from the USGS.

Contact: Green Mountain National Forest Supervisor, 231 North Main Street, Rutland, VT 05701; (802) 747-6700. Green Mountain Club, Route 100, RR 1, Box 650, Waterbury Center, VT 05677; (802) 244-7037. Appalachian Trail Conference, P.O. Box 807, Harpers Ferry, WV 25425; (304) 535-6331.

Trail notes: I pulled this hike out of the full segment of the Long Trail described in hike number 51 to highlight a section of the trail I particularly enjoy, from the roaring, rock-strewn bed of the Big Branch to the craggy heights of Baker Peak to placid Griffith Lake. This full trek is a fairly easy, 14-mile, out-and-back hike on the Long Trail from USFS Road 10 to Griffith Lake, which could be done in a day but is better spread over two days to enjoy the scenery. But I could also envision going no farther than any of the shelters along the way—even staying at the Big Branch shelter, a mere 1.3 miles into this hike, and hanging out by the river all day. Along the Big Branch are deep holes for fishing native brook and rainbow trout.

From the parking lot on USFS Road 10, walk east on the road for a tenth of a mile and turn right, entering the woods on the white-blazed Long Trail southbound, which coincides here with the Appalachian Trail. It's an easy hike to the Big Branch stream and shelter. The trail parallels the stream for a tenth of a mile, then turns right and crosses it on a suspension bridge, and swings immediately left to follow the stream for another tenth of a mile before turning right, away from the stream. Following an old woods road over flat terrain, the LT reaches the Lost Pond shelter, via a short side path, at three miles into this hike. The hiking remains relatively easy all the way to Baker Peak's open summit at five miles, where there is a wide view west of the valley around the town of Danby, and Dorset Peak across the valley. Descending west off Baker Peak along a ridge of rock for a tenth of a mile, the LT swings sharply left at a junction with the Baker Peak Trail. It then descends at a gentle angle to the east shore of Griffith Lake and the campsite there, at seven miles. Nearby, the Old Job Trail departs east and the Lake Trail departs west. This hike backtracks on the Long Trail to the road.

Special note: There are a couple of options to this hike. A one- or two-day, one-way traverse of eight miles begins at USFS Road 10 and descends from Baker Peak via the Baker Peak and Lake Trails (see directions above). For a 13.7-mile loop of one to two days, hike the LT south from USFS Road 10 to Griffith Lake, then loop back to the Big Branch suspension bridge on the Old Job Trail.

50 Griffith Lake and Baker Peak

8.5 mi/6.0 hrs 

Location: In the Green Mountain National Forest southeast of Danby; Southern Vermont map page 175, grid d2.

User groups: Hikers, dogs, and snowshoers. No wheelchair facilities. Dogs must be on a leash. This trail is not suitable for skis. Bikes, horses, and hunting are prohibited.

Access, fees: Parking and access are free. Camping is prohibited except at the Green Mountain Club cabins and shelters. The Griffith Lake camping area, with tentsites, is located a tenth of a mile south of the junction of the Lake and Long Trails. From Memorial Day weekend through Labor Day, a Green Mountain Club caretaker is on duty and a $4-per-person nightly fee ($3 for GMC members) is collected.

Directions: From the crossroads in Danby, drive south on U.S. 7 for 2.1 miles and turn left onto Town Highway 5. Drive a half mile to parking on the left for the Lake Trail.

Maps: For a map of hiking trails, refer to map 7 in the "Map and Guide to the Appalachian Trail in New Hampshire/Vermont," an eight-map set for $10.95 from the Appalachian Trail Conference (see address below). The Green Mountain Club (see address below) sells sectional topographic maps of the Long Trail, either as a set of 21 for $7.95, or individually for $1 per map plus $1 postage; Griffith Lake and Baker Peak are within Division IV, Mad Tom Notch to Route 140, Wallingford Gulf. For a topographic map of the area, request Danby from the USGS.

Contact: Green Mountain National Forest Supervisor, 231 North Main Street, Rutland, VT 05701; (802) 747-6700. Green Mountain Club, Route 100, RR 1, Box 650, Waterbury Center, VT 05677; (802) 244-7037. Appalachian Trail Conference, P.O. Box 807, Harpers Ferry, WV 25425; (304) 535-6331.

Trail notes: Baker Peak, though just 2,850 feet high, thrusts a rocky spine above the trees for great views of the valley around the little town of Danby. And Griffith Lake is one of several scenic ponds and lakes along the Long Trail. This 8.5-mile loop incorporates both places.

From the parking area, follow the Lake Trail. It ascends very gently at first, then steeply, and nearly levels off again before reaching the Long Trail—which coincides here with the Appalachian Trail—in 3.5 miles. Turning right (south), you can walk the LT for a tenth of a mile to the Griffith Lake camping area and access views of the lake. Spin around and hike north on the LT for 1.8 relatively easy miles to the Baker Peak Trail junction. Here, turn right with the LT and scramble up the long ridge of rock protruding from the earth for a tenth of a mile to the open summit of Baker Peak. Then backtrack, descending the Baker Peak Trail, past the Quarry View overlook, for a mile to the Lake Trail. Turn right (west) and descend another two miles to the parking area.

51 The Long Trail: Route 11/30 to USFS Road 10

17.3 mi. one way/ 2.0 days 

Location: In the Green Mountain National Forest east of Danby; Southern Vermont map page 175, grid d2.

User groups: Hikers and dogs. No wheelchair facilities. Dogs must be on a leash. This trail is not suitable for skis. The north end of this trail is not accessible by road in winter for snowshoeing. Bikes, horses, and hunting are prohibited.

Access, fees: Parking and access are free. USFS Road 10 is not maintained during the winter. No-trace camping is permitted within the Green Mountain National Forest, except at Griffith Lake, where camping within 200 feet of the shore is restricted to designated sites. Backpackers can stay overnight in the warming hut on Bromley Mountain's summit, beside the observation deck; there is no water source. The Bromley tenting area is eight-tenths of a mile north of Route 11/30, reached via a short spur trail off the Long Trail. The Mad Tom shelter is a tenth of a mile down a spur path off the Long Trail, 3.6 miles into this hike. The Peru Peak shelter sits beside the LT at 9.7 miles, the Griffith Lake campsite at 10.4 miles, the Lost Pond shelter at 14.3 miles, and the Big Branch shelter at 16 miles (the last 1.3 miles south of the parking lot on USFS Road 10). From Memorial Day weekend through Labor Day, a Green Mountain Club caretaker is on duty and a $4-per-person nightly fee ($3 for GMC members) is collected to stay at the Peru Peak shelter and the Griffith Lake campsite.

Directions: You need to shuttle two vehicles for this one-way traverse. To hike south to north, as described here, leave one vehicle in the parking lot on USFS Road 10 at Big Black Branch, 3.5 miles west of U.S. 7 in Danby and 13.6 miles north of Route 11 in Peru. Then drive to the parking lot on the north side of Route 11/30, six miles east of Manchester Center and 4.4 miles west of Peru.

Maps: For a map of hiking trails, refer to map 7 in the "Map and Guide to the Appalachian Trail in New Hampshire/Vermont," an eight-map set for $10.95 from the Appalachian Trail Conference (see address below). The Green Mountain Club (see address below) sells sectional topographic maps of the Long Trail, either as a set of 21 for $7.95, or individually for $1 per map plus $1 postage; this hike begins in Division III, Arlington-West Wardsboro Road to Mad Tom Notch, and extends into Division IV, Mad Tom Notch to Route 140, Wallingford Gulf. For topographic maps of the area, request Peru and Danby from the USGS.

Contact: Green Mountain National Forest Supervisor, 231 North Main Street, Rutland, VT 05701; (802) 747-6700. Green Mountain Club, Route 100, RR 1, Box 650, Waterbury Center, VT 05677; (802) 244-7037. Appalachian Trail Conference, P.O. Box 807, Harpers Ferry, WV 25425; (304) 535-6331.

Trail notes: I have a personal bias regarding the mountains—I prefer hikes with good views and which inspire a sense of solitude. Those two features are not always mutually compatible in New England. But when I hiked much of the Long Trail in October 1996, this fairly scenic stretch of the trail gave me just that sort of experience. Timing no doubt helped; I started my trip after the leaves had fallen off the trees. One of my favorite moments was standing alone on the summit of Styles Peak at sunset. Another was sitting on big rocks beside the roaring, clear waters of the Big Branch, with no one around. I'd recommend this 17.3-mile stretch for a moderate, two-day backpacking trip.

From the parking lot on Route 11/30, follow the white blazes of the Long Trail northbound, which here coincides with the Appalachian Trail. Watch closely for the blazes; many unmarked trails cross the LT on this side of Bromley. At eight-tenths of a mile into this hike, a spur trail leads 150 feet to the right to the Bromley tenting area. Two miles from the road, the LT grows steeper, and at 2.6 miles it emerges from the woods onto a wide ski trail. Hike up the ski trail two-tenths of a mile to the mountain's summit, where there are ski area buildings. To the right is an observation deck—which offers views in every direction—and the warming hut. The LT swings left from the ski trail, just before a chairlift, and descends a steep, rocky section. At 3.3 miles (a half mile beyond the summit), the LT climbs over the rugged, wooded north summit of Bromley, then descends to the side path leading left to the Mad Tom shelter at 3.6 miles. The trail then descends more easily to cross USFS Road 21 in Mad Tom Notch at 5.3 miles. There is a working water pump at the roadside. Continuing north, the LT makes a steady, though not difficult, ascent of nearly 1,000 feet in elevation to the 3,394-foot summit of Styles Peak, at 6.7 miles. While I mentioned enjoying the sunset from this summit, I couldn't actually see the sunset, but the wide view south and west showed me long shadows across the land, and Styles' own pyramidal shadow.

Following the ridge north, the LT dips slightly, then ascends slightly to the wooded summit of Peru Peak (3,429 feet) at 8.4 miles, where a side path leads 75 feet right to a largely obscured view eastward. Descending steeply, the trail reaches the Peru Peak shelter at 9.7 miles, with a good stream nearby. The LT crosses the stream on a wooden bridge and continues a flat seven-tenths of a mile to Griffith Lake at 10.4 miles, where there are tentsites. The Old Job Trail leaves right (east), swinging north to loop 5.3 miles back to the Long Trail at a point a tenth of a mile east of the Big Branch suspension bridge. The Lake Trail departs left (west) at 10.5 miles, descending 3.5 miles to Town Highway 5 in Danby (a half mile from U.S. 7).

The Long Trail continues north over easy terrain, then climbs to a junction, at 12.2 miles, with the Baker Peak Trail (which descends west for 2.9 miles to Town Highway 5 via the Lake Trail). Turn right with the LT and scramble up a spine of exposed rock for a tenth of a mile to the open summit of 2,850-foot Baker Peak, with great views of the valley around the little town of Danby. The trail then re-enters the forest, and traverses fairly easy terrain, reaching and following an old woods road to a junction, at 14.3 miles, with a short side path leading left to the Lost Pond shelter.

Continuing on the woods road, the LT reaches the Big Branch at 15.8 miles, swings left along it for a tenth of a mile, then crosses the river on a suspension bridge. The trail swings left again, following the boulder-choked river to the Big Branch shelter at 16 miles. Easy hiking for another 1.2 miles brings you to USFS Road 10. Turn left and walk the road for a tenth of a mile to the parking lot at the north end of this hike.

52 Styles Peak

2.8 mi/2.0 hrs 

Location: In the Peru Peak Wilderness in the Green Mountain National Forest west of Peru; Southern Vermont map page 175, grid d2.

User groups: Hikers, dogs, and snowshoers. No wheelchair facilities. Dogs must be on a leash. Bikes, horses, and hunting are prohibited.

Access, fees: Parking and access are free. USFS Road 21 is maintained in winter only to a point about 2.5 miles from the Long Trail. No-trace camping is permitted within the Green Mountain National Forest. The Peru Peak shelter is on the Long Trail, 4.4 miles north of USFS Road 21, and three miles north of the summit of Styles Peak. From Memorial Day weekend through Labor Day, a Green Mountain Club caretaker is on duty and collects a $4-per-person nightly fee.

Directions: Drive to the parking area on USFS Road 21, immediately west of the height-of-land in Mad Tom Notch and the Long Trail crossing, and 4.3 miles west of Route 11 in Peru.

Maps: For a trail map, see map 7 in the "Map and Guide to the Appalachian Trail in New Hampshire/Vermont," an eight-map set for $10.95 from the Appalachian Trail Conference (see address below). The Green Mountain Club (see address below) sells topographic maps of the Long Trail, either as a set of 21 for $7.95, or for $1 per map plus $1 postage; Styles Peak is in Division IV, Mad Tom Notch to Route 140, Wallingford Gulf. For a topographic map of the area, request Peru from the USGS.

Contact: Green Mountain National Forest Supervisor, 231 North Main Street, Rutland, VT 05701; (802) 747-6700. Green Mountain Club, Route 100, RR 1, Box 650, Waterbury Center, VT 05677; (802) 244-7037. Appalachian Trail Conference, P.O. Box 807, Harpers Ferry, WV 25425; (304) 535-6331.

Trail notes: Styles Peak, 3,394 feet high, has a small crag of a summit which affords views to the east and south of the southern Green Mountains and the rumpled landscape of southeastern Vermont and southwestern New Hampshire. This quiet spot is a great place to catch the sunrise, and with just 1.4 miles to hike uphill to reach the summit, getting here before dawn is a reasonable objective.

From the parking area, walk east a few steps on the road to the junction with the LT, and turn left (north). After passing a water pump, follow the white-blazed Long Trail, which coincides here with the Appalachian Trail, as it climbs steadily, and then steeply, to the open rocks atop Styles Peak. Return the way you came.

---

53 Bromley Mountain from Mad Tom Notch

5.0 mi/3.5 hrs 

Location: In the Green Mountain National Forest west of Peru; Southern Vermont map page 175, grid d2.

User groups: Hikers and dogs. No wheelchair facilities. Dogs must be on a leash. This trail may be difficult to snowshoe and is not suitable for skis. Bikes, horses, and hunting are prohibited.

Access, fees: Parking and access are free. USFS Road 21 is maintained in winter only to a point about 2.5 miles from the Long Trail. No-trace camping is permitted within the Green Mountain National Forest. The Mad Tom shelter is a tenth of a mile down a spur path off the Long Trail, 1.7 miles south of USFS Road 21. Backpackers can stay overnight in the warming hut on Bromley's summit, beside the observation deck; there is no water source.

Directions: Drive to the parking area on USFS Road 21, immediately west of the height-of-land in Mad Tom Notch and the Long Trail crossing, and 4.3 miles west of Route 11 in Peru.

Maps: For a map of hiking trails, refer to map 7 in the "Map and Guide to the Appalachian Trail in New Hampshire/Vermont," an eight-map set for $10.95 from the Appalachian Trail Conference (see address below). The Green Mountain Club (see address below) sells sectional topographic maps of the Long Trail, either as a set of 21 for $7.95, or individually for $1 per map plus $1 postage; Bromley Mountain is within Division III, Arlington-West Wardsboro Road to Mad Tom Notch. For a topographic map of the area, request Peru from the USGS.

Contact: Green Mountain National Forest Supervisor, 231 North Main Street, Rutland, VT 05701; (802) 747-6700. Green Mountain Club, Route 100, RR 1, Box 650, Waterbury Center, VT 05677; (802) 244-7037. Appalachian Trail Conference, P.O. Box 807, Harpers Ferry, WV 25425; (304) 535-6331.

Trail notes: This five-mile route from the north up 3,260-foot Bromley Mountain is a bit more wild and less trammeled than taking the Long Trail from the south (hikes number 51 and 54). A ski area in winter, Bromley offers some of the better views along the southern Long Trail from its summit observation deck.

From the parking lot, walk east on the road briefly, then turn right and follow the white blazes of the Long Trail southbound, which here coincides with the Appalachian Trail. (Across the road from this trailhead is a working water pump.) The trail ascends easily at first, passing the side path to Mad Tom Notch shelter at 1.7 miles. It then climbs more steeply, over rocky terrain, to Bromley's wooded north summit at two miles. After dipping slightly, it climbs to the open summit of Bromley Mountain, 2.5 miles from the road. Cross the clearing to the observation deck and warming hut. Descend the same way you came up.

54 Bromley Mountain from Route 11/30

5.6 mi/3.5 hrs 

Location: In the Green Mountain National Forest, between Peru and Manchester Center; Southern Vermont map page 175, grid d2.

User groups: Hikers, dogs, and snowshoers. No wheelchair facilities. Dogs must be on a leash. This trail is not suitable for skis. Bikes, horses, and hunting are prohibited.

Access, fees: Parking and access are free. No-trace camping is permitted within the Green Mountain National Forest. The Bromley tenting area is eight-tenths of a mile north of Route 11/30, reached via a short spur trail off the Long Trail. Backpackers can stay overnight in the warming hut on Bromley's summit, beside the observation deck; there is no water source.

Directions: Drive to the parking lot on the north side of Route 11/30, six miles east of Manchester Center and 4.4 miles west of Peru.

Maps: For a map of hiking trails, refer to map 7 in the "Map and Guide to the Appalachian Trail in New Hampshire/Vermont," an eight-map set for $10.95 from the Appalachian Trail Conference (see address below). The Green Mountain Club (see address below) sells sectional topographic maps of the Long Trail, either as a set of 21 for $7.95, or individually for $1 per map plus $1 postage; Bromley Mountain is within Division III, Arlington-West Wardsboro Road to Mad Tom Notch. For a topographic map of the area, request Peru from the USGS.

Contact: Green Mountain National Forest Supervisor, 231 North Main Street, Rutland, VT 05701; (802) 747-6700. Green Mountain Club, Route 100, RR 1, Box 650, Waterbury Center, VT 05677; (802) 244-7037. Appalachian Trail Conference, P.O. Box 807, Harpers Ferry, WV 25425; (304) 535-6331.

Trail notes: Bromley Mountain, a ski area in winter, offers some of the better views along the southern Long Trail from the observation deck on its 3,260-foot summit. This 5.6-mile route up Bromley is a popular hike and suffers from erosion and muddy ground in many places.

From the parking lot, follow the white blazes of the Long Trail northbound, which here coincides with the Appalachian Trail. Watch closely for the blazes; numerous unmarked trails cross the LT on this side of Bromley. At eight-tenths of a mile into this hike, a spur trail leads 150 feet to the right to the Bromley tenting area. About two miles from the road, the LT grows steeper, and at 2.6 miles it emerges from the woods onto a wide ski trail. Hike up the ski trail two-tenths of a mile to the mountain's summit, where there are ski area buildings. Turn right and walk 100 feet to the observation deck. The views extend in every direction. Stratton Mountain looms prominently to the south. Beside the tower is the warming hut. Descend the way you came up.

55 Spruce Peak

4.4 mi/2.5 hrs 

Location: In the Green Mountain National Forest south of Peru; Southern Vermont map page 175, grid d2.

User groups: Hikers, dogs, and snowshoers. No wheelchair facilities. Dogs must be on a leash. Bikes, horses, and hunting are prohibited.

Access, fees: Parking and access are free. No-trace camping is permitted within the Green Mountain National Forest. The Spruce Peak shelter is a tenth of a mile down a side path off the LT, 2.7 miles south of Route 11/30 and a half mile south of the side path to Spruce Peak.

Directions: Drive to the parking lot on the north side of Route 11/30, six miles east of Manchester Center and 4.4 miles west of Peru.

Maps: For a map of hiking trails, refer to map 7 in the "Map and Guide to the Appalachian Trail in New Hampshire/Vermont," an eight-map set for $10.95 from the Appalachian Trail Conference (see address below). The Green Mountain Club (see address below) sells sectional topographic maps of the Long Trail, either as a set of 21 for $7.95, or individually for $1 per map plus $1 postage; Spruce Peak is within Division III, Arlington-West Wardsboro Road to Mad Tom Notch. For a topographic map of the area, request Peru from the USGS.

Contact: Green Mountain National Forest Supervisor, 231 North Main Street, Rutland, VT 05701; (802) 747-6700. Green Mountain Club, Route 100, RR 1, Box 650, Waterbury Center, VT 05677; (802) 244-7037. Appalachian Trail Conference, P.O. Box 807, Harpers Ferry, WV 25425; (304) 535-6331.

Trail notes: This fairly easy hike of 4.4 miles takes you up to Spruce Peak, at 2,040 feet no more than a small bump along a wooded Green Mountain ridge, but a spot with a couple of good views west to the valley at Manchester Center and out to the Taconic Range. On my trip, I happened to time this hike perfectly, enjoying the view on a cloudless Indian summer day in October when the foliage in the valley below was at its peak.

From the parking area, cross Route 11/30 and follow the white blazes of the Long Trail southbound into the woods. The hiking is mostly easy, with the trail passing through an area of moss-covered boulders and rocks. At 2.2 miles from the road, turn right (west) onto a side path which leads about 300 feet to the summit of Spruce Peak. There is a limited view west at the actual summit; but just below the summit, a few steps off the path, is a better view. Return the way you hiked in.

56 The Long Trail: Arlington-West Wardsboro Road to Route 11/30

16.3 mi. one way/ 11.0 hrs or 1–2 days 

Location: In the Green Mountain National Forest, between Stratton and Peru; Southern Vermont map page 175, grid e2.

User groups: Hikers and dogs. No wheelchair facilities. Dogs must be on a leash. This trail is not suitable for skis. The south end of this trail is not accessible by road in winter for snowshoeing. Bikes, horses, and hunting are prohibited.

Access, fees: Parking and access are free. The Arlington-West Wardsboro Road is not maintained in winter. No-trace camping is permitted within the Green Mountain National Forest, except at Stratton Pond, where camping is restricted to Green Mountain Club cabins and shelters. Camping is prohibited on the upper slopes of Stratton Mountain, which is privately owned. The Vondell and Bigelow lean-to shelters on Stratton Pond lie two-tenths of a mile and a tenth of a mile, respectively, down the Lye Brook Trail from the Willis Ross Clearing on the Long Trail. From Memorial Day weekend through Columbus Day, a Green Mountain Club caretaker is on duty and a $4-per-person nightly fee ($3 for GMC members) is collected to stay at the Stratton Pond shelters and the North Shore Tenting Area, which lies a half mile down the North Shore Trail from its junction with the Long Trail, a tenth of a mile north of Willis Ross Clearing. The Williams B. Douglas shelter lies a half mile south of the LT on the Branch Pond Trail, 10.3 miles north of the Arlington-West Wardsboro Road; and the Spruce Peak shelter a tenth of a mile down a side path off the LT, at 13.6 miles into this hike.

Directions: You need to shuttle two vehicles for this one-way traverse. To hike south to north, as described here, leave one vehicle in the parking lot on the north side of Route 11/30, six miles east of Manchester Center and 4.4 miles west of Peru. Then drive to the large parking area on the Arlington-West Wardsboro Road, 13.3 miles east of U.S. 7 in Arlington and eight miles west of Route 100 in West Wardsboro.

Maps: For a map of hiking trails, refer to map 7 in the "Map and Guide to the Appalachian Trail in New Hampshire/Vermont," an eight-map set for $10.95 from the Appalachian Trail Conference (see address below). The Green Mountain Club (see address below) sells sectional topographic maps of the Long Trail, either as a set of 21 for $7.95, or individually for $1 per map plus $1 postage; this hike is within Division III, Arlington-West Wardsboro Road to Mad Tom Notch. For topographic maps of the area, request Stratton Mountain, Manchester, and Peru from the USGS.

Contact: Green Mountain National Forest Supervisor, 231 North Main Street, Rutland, VT 05701; (802) 747-6700. Green Mountain Club, Route 100, RR 1, Box 650, Waterbury Center, VT 05677; (802) 244-7037. Appalachian Trail Conference, P.O. Box 807, Harpers Ferry, WV 25425; (304) 535-6331.

Trail notes: The highlights of this 16.3-mile traverse of a southern stretch of the Long Trail are the 360-degree view from the observation tower on 3,936-foot Stratton Mountain, and beautiful Stratton Pond. But you also get a nice view from Spruce Peak, and the northern part of this trek will feel considerably more secluded than Stratton Pond or Mountain.

From the parking area, follow the white-blazed Long Trail north (which coincides here with the Appalachian Trail). It rises gently through muddy areas, growing progressively steeper—and passing one outlook south—over the 3.4-mile climb to Stratton's summit. A Green Mountain Club caretaker cabin is located on the edge of the summit clearing, and a caretaker is on duty during the late spring through fall hiking season to answer questions and assist hikers. After climbing the observation tower (see the trail notes for Stratton Mountain and Stratton Pond, hike number 57, for a description of what is visible from the tower), continue north on the LT, descending for 2.6 miles to Willis Ross Clearing on the east shore of Stratton Pond, the largest water body and one of the busiest spots on the Long Trail. The Lye Brook Trail leads left to the Bigelow and Vondell shelters, while the LT swings right, passing a junction with the North Shore Trail within a tenth of a mile. The LT contours, for easy hiking, to the Winhall River at 7.9 miles into this hike; the river is crossed on a bridge, and the trail enters the Lye Brook Wilderness.

At 10.3 miles, the Branch Pond Trail leads left (west) into the Lye Brook Wilderness and to the William B. Douglas shelter. Crossing a

 Northern Vermont Map—page 174

brook, the LT turns left and follows a wide logging road. At 11.4 miles, an unmarked side path leads about 200 feet to Prospect Rock, with a good view of Downer Glen. The LT turns right (northeast) off the road and climbs steadily before descending again to a side path, at 13.6 miles, leading a tenth of a mile to the Spruce Peak shelter, a cabin. After more easy hiking, at 14.1 miles, a side path leads about 300 feet left to the summit of Spruce Peak, where there is a limited view west. But just below the summit is a better view of the valley and the Taconic Mountains. Continuing north, the LT crosses easy ground for 2.2 miles, passing through an area of interesting, moss-covered boulders, to reach Routes 11/30 at 16.3 miles. Cross the highway to the parking lot.

57 Stratton Mountain and Stratton Pond

11.0 mi/7.0 hrs 

Location: In the Green Mountain National Forest, between Arlington and West Wardsboro; Southern Vermont map page 175, grid e2.

User groups: Hikers and dogs. No wheelchair facilities. Dogs must be on a leash. This trail is not suitable for skis. The trailhead is not accessible by road in winter for snowshoeing. Bikes, horses, and hunting are prohibited.

Access, fees: Parking and access are free. The Arlington-West Wardsboro Road is not maintained in winter. No-trace camping is permitted within the Green Mountain National Forest, except at Stratton Pond, where camping is restricted to Green Mountain Club cabins and shelters. Camping is prohibited on the upper slopes of Stratton Mountain, which is privately owned. The Vondell and Bigelow lean-to shelters on Stratton Pond lie two-tenths of a mile and a tenth of a mile, respectively, down the Lye Brook Trail from the Willis Ross Clearing on the Long Trail. From Memorial Day weekend through Columbus Day, a Green Mountain Club caretaker is on duty and a $4-per-person nightly fee ($3 for GMC members) is collected to stay at the Stratton Pond shelters and the North Shore Tenting Area, which lies a half mile down the North Shore Trail from its junction with the Long Trail, a tenth of a mile north of Willis Ross Clearing.

Directions: The hike begins from a large parking area on the Arlington-West Wardsboro Road, 13.3 miles east of U.S. 7 in Arlington and eight miles west of Route 100 in West Wardsboro.

Maps: For a map of hiking trails, refer to map 7 in the "Map and Guide to the Appalachian Trail in New Hampshire/Vermont," an eight-map set for $10.95 from the Appalachian Trail Conference (see address below). The Green Mountain Club (see address below) sells sectional topographic maps of the Long Trail, either as a set of 21 for $7.95, or individually for $1 per map plus $1 postage; Stratton Mountain and Pond are within Division III, Arlington-West Wardsboro Road to Mad Tom Notch. For a topographic map of the area, request Stratton Mountain from the USGS.

Contact: Green Mountain National Forest Supervisor, 231 North Main Street, Rutland, VT 05701; (802) 747-6700. Green Mountain Club, Route 100, RR 1, Box 650, Waterbury Center, VT 05677; (802) 244-7037. Appalachian Trail Conference, P.O. Box 807, Harpers Ferry, WV 25425; (304) 535-6331.

Trail notes: From the observation tower on top of Stratton Mountain, you get one of the most sweeping panoramas on the LT. And merely climbing the tower will be an adventure for children, as well as adults not accustomed to heights. For a shorter hike, you can make a 6.8-mile round-trip on the Long Trail to the 3,936-foot summit of Stratton and return the same way.

From the parking area, follow the white-blazed Long Trail north (which coincides here with the Appalachian Trail). It rises steadily, through muddy areas at the lower elevations, and passing one outlook south in the 3.4-mile climb—the last stretch of which grows steeper. On the 3,936-foot summit is the Green Mountain Club's caretaker cabin, and a caretaker is on duty during the late spring through fall hiking season to answer questions and assist hikers. Climb the fire tower, where the views take in Somerset Reservoir and Mount Greylock to the south, the Taconic Range to the west, Mount Ascutney to the northeast, and Mount Monadnock to the southeast.

Return the same way, or make an 11-mile loop by continuing north on the LT, descending for 2.6 miles to beautiful Stratton Pond, the largest water body and one of the busiest areas on the Long Trail. The Long Trail reaches the east shore of Stratton Pond at Willis Ross Clearing. From there, a loop of about 1.5 miles around the pond is possible, taking the Lye Brook Trail along the south shore, and the North Shore Trail back to the Long Trail, a tenth of a mile north of Willis Ross Clearing; that distance is not included in this hike's mileage. From the clearing, backtrack a tenth of a mile south on the LT and turn right onto the Stratton Pond Trail, and follow it for an easy 3.8 miles back to the Arlington-West Wardsboro Road. Turn left (east) and walk the road 1.1 miles back to the parking area.

58 The Long Trail: Route 9 to Arlington-West Wardsboro Road

22.3 mi. one way/
2–3 days

Location: In the Green Mountain National Forest, between Woodford and Stratton; Southern Vermont map page 175, grid e2.

User groups: Hikers, dogs, and snowshoers. No wheelchair facilities. Dogs must be on a leash. This trail is not suitable for skis. Bikes, horses, and hunting are prohibited.

Access, fees: Parking and access are free. The Arlington-West Wardsboro Road is not maintained in winter. No-trace camping is permitted within the Green Mountain National Forest. The Green Mountain Club Melville Nauheim shelter is located 1.5 miles north of Route 9 on the Long Trail, the Goddard shelter at 9.8 miles, the Caughnawaga and Kid Gore shelters at 14 miles, and the Story Spring shelter at 18.7 miles (or 3.6 miles south of the Arlington-West Wardsboro Road).

Directions: You need to shuttle two vehicles for this one-way traverse. To hike south to north, as described here, leave one vehicle in the roadside parking area where the Long Trail/Appalachian Trail crosses the Arlington-West Wardsboro Road, 13.3 miles east of U.S. 7 in Arlington and eight miles west of Route 100 in West Wardsboro. Then drive to the large parking lot at the Long Trail/Appalachian Trail crossing of Route 9, 5.2 miles east of Bennington and 2.8 miles west of Woodford.

Maps: For a map of hiking trails, refer to map 8 in the "Map and Guide to the Appalachian Trail in New Hampshire/Vermont," an eight-map set for $10.95 from the Appalachian Trail Conference (see address below). The Green Mountain Club (see address below) sells sectional topographic maps of the Long Trail, either as a set of 21 for $7.95, or individually for $1 per map plus $1 postage; this hike comprises Division II, Route 9 to Arlington-West Wardsboro Road. For topographic maps of the area, request Woodford, Sunderland, and Stratton Mountain from the USGS.

Contact: Green Mountain National Forest Supervisor, 231 North Main Street, Rutland, VT 05701; (802) 747-6700. Green Mountain

Club, Route 100, RR 1, Box 650, Waterbury Center, VT 05677; (802) 244-7037. Appalachian Trail Conference, P.O. Box 807, Harpers Ferry, WV 25425; (304) 535-6331.

Trail notes: While much of this 22.3-mile stretch of the Long Trail/Appalachian Trail remains in the woods, it makes for a nice walk along a wooded ridge, on a relatively easy backpacking trip which can be done in two days without extreme effort. And there are a few nice views, most particularly from the fire tower on the summit of 3,748-foot Glastenbury Mountain, which offers one of the finest panoramas I had on the Long Trail.

From the parking lot, follow the white blazes of the Long Trail northbound. The trail parallels City Stream briefly, then crosses it on a wooden bridge. Climbing steadily, the trail crosses an old woods road two-tenths of a mile from the highway, then passes between the twin halves of Split Rock, formerly one giant boulder, at six-tenths of a mile. At 1.5 miles, a side path leads right a short distance to the Nauheim shelter. Ascending north from the shelter, the trail crosses a power line atop Maple Hill at two miles which affords a view toward Bennington. The trail then traverses the more level terrain of a wooded ridge, crossing Hell Hollow Brook, a reliable water source, on a bridge at three miles.

Hiking easily, passing through a stand of beech trees, the LT reaches Little Pond Lookout at 5.7 miles, with a good view east, then Glastenbury Lookout, with its view of Glastenbury Mountain, at 7.4 miles. The trail then ascends about 600 feet at a moderate angle to Goddard shelter, at 9.8 miles. From the shelter, it's a not-too-rigorous, three-tenths-of-a-mile walk uphill on the LT to the summit of Glastenbury. From the fire tower, the 360-degree view encompasses the Berkshires, and most prominently Mount Greylock to the south, the Taconic Range to the west, Stratton Mountain to the north, and Somerset Reservoir to the east. Continuing north, the LT descends about 500 feet in elevation, then follows a wooded ridge, with slight rises and dips, for about four miles, finally descending at a moderate angle to a side path on the right at 14 miles which leads a tenth of a mile to the Kid Gore shelter. About a tenth of a mile farther north on the LT, the other end of that side loop reaches the LT near the Caughnawaga shelter. The LT then goes through more slight ups and downs before reaching the Story Spring shelter, 18.7 miles north of Route 9 and 3.6 miles south of the Arlington-West Wardsboro Road. The LT crosses USFS Road 71 at 20.3 miles, passes beaver ponds and traverses an area often wet and muddy, then crosses Black Brook, a reliable water source, on a wooden bridge at 21.3 miles. Paralleling the East Branch of the Deerfield River, the trail reaches the Arlington-West Wardsboro Road at 22.3 miles. Turn right (east) and walk 200 feet to the parking area.

59 Glastenbury Mountain

20.2 mi/2.0 days 

Location: In the Green Mountain National Forest, between Bennington and Woodford; Southern Vermont map page 175, grid e2.

User groups: Hikers, dogs, and snowshoers. No wheelchair facilities. Dogs must be on a leash. This trail is not suitable for skis. Bikes, horses, and hunting are prohibited.

Access, fees: Parking and access are free. No-trace camping is permitted within the Green Mountain National Forest. The Green Mountain Club Melville Nauheim shelter is located 1.5 miles north of Route 9 on the Long Trail, and the Goddard shelter 9.8 miles north of the highway.

Directions: Drive to the large parking lot

at the Long Trail/Appalachian Trail crossing of Route 9, 5.2 miles east of Bennington and 2.8 miles west of Woodford.

Maps: For a map of hiking trails, refer to map 8 in the "Map and Guide to the Appalachian Trail in New Hampshire/Vermont," an eight-map set for $10.95 from the Appalachian Trail Conference (see address below). The Green Mountain Club (see address below) sells sectional topographic maps of the Long Trail, either as a set of 21 for $7.95, or individually for $1 per map plus $1 postage; Glastenbury Mountain is within Division II, Route 9 to Arlington-West Wardsboro Road. For a topographic map of the area, request Woodford from the USGS.

Contact: Green Mountain National Forest Supervisor, 231 North Main Street, Rutland, VT 05701; (802) 747-6700. Green Mountain Club, Route 100, RR 1, Box 650, Waterbury Center, VT 05677; (802) 244-7037. Appalachian Trail Conference, P.O. Box 807, Harpers Ferry, WV 25425; (304) 535-6331.

Trail notes: While much of the southern third of the Long Trail, which coincides with the Appalachian Trail, remains in the woods, the fire tower on the summit of 3,748-foot Glastenbury Mountain offers a superb panorama of the gently rolling wilderness of the southern Green Mountains. The Berkshires, particularly Mount Greylock, are visible due south, the Taconic Range to the west, Stratton Mountain to the north, and Somerset Reservoir to the east. I stood up here one afternoon at the height of the fall foliage, and it turned out to be one of the finest views I had in my lengthy trek on the Long Trail.

This fairly easy, 20.2-mile round-trip is best spread over two days, with an overnight stay at the spacious Goddard shelter (or tenting in the area). Goddard, which has a nice view south to Greylock, can be a popular place on nice weekends in summer and fall. See the trail notes for The Long Trail: Route 9 to Arlington-West Wardsboro Road (hike number 58), for the description of this hike from Route 9 to the Goddard shelter. At the shelter, leave your packs behind for the three-tenths-of-a-mile walk uphill on the LT to the summit of Glastenbury and the fire tower. On the second day, you can return the same way you came in. Or, to avoid backtracking, hike the West Ridge Trail from Goddard shelter, a fairly easy route which leads 7.7 miles to the summit of Bald Mountain and a junction at 7.8 miles with the Bald Mountain Trail. Turn left on that trail and descend 1.9 miles to a public road. Turning right on the road, you will reach Route 9 in eight-tenths of a mile, 1.2 miles west of the parking lot where you began this hike.

60 The Long Trail: Massachusetts Line to Route 9

14.2 mi. one way/ 2.0 days

Location: In the Green Mountain National Forest, between Clarksburg, Massachusetts, and Woodford; Southern Vermont map page 175, grid e2.

User groups: Hikers, dogs, and snowshoers. No wheelchair facilities. Dogs must be on a leash. This trail is not suitable for skis. Bikes, horses, and hunting are prohibited.

Access, fees: Parking and access are free. No-trace camping is permitted within the Green Mountain National Forest. The Seth Warner shelter is two-tenths of a mile west of the Long Trail, reached via a side path off the LT, 2.8 miles north of the Massachusetts border. The Congdon Camp shelter is on the Long Trail, 10 miles north of the Massachusetts border and 4.2 miles south of Route 9.

Directions: You need to shuttle two vehicles for this one-way traverse. To hike south to north, as described here, leave one vehicle in the large parking lot at the Long Trail/Appalachian Trail crossing of Route 9, 5.2 miles east of Bennington and 2.8 miles west of Woodford. Then drive to one of two possible starts for this hike, both in Massachusetts. For the Pine Cobble start, from U.S. 7 in Williamstown, a mile south of the Vermont line and three-tenths of a mile north of the Hoosic River bridge, turn east on North Housac Road. Drive a half mile and turn right on Brooks Road. Drive seven-tenths of a mile and park in a dirt lot on the left marked by a sign reading, "Parking for Pine Cobble Trail." For the Appalachian Trail start, drive to the AT footbridge over the Hoosic River (where there is no convenient parking), on Route 2, 2.9 miles east of Williamstown center and 2.5 miles west of North Adams center.

Maps: For a map of hiking trails, refer to map 8 in the "Map and Guide to the Appalachian Trail in New Hampshire/Vermont," an eight-map set for $10.95 from the Appalachian Trail Conference (see address below). The Green Mountain Club (see address below) sells sectional topographic maps of the Long Trail, either as a set of 21 for $7.95, or individually for $1 per map plus $1 postage; this hike comprises Division I, Massachusetts-Vermont State Line to Bennington-Brattleboro Highway, Route 9. For topographic maps of the area, request Pownal, Stamford, Bennington, and Woodford from the USGS.

Contact: Green Mountain National Forest Supervisor, 231 North Main Street, Rutland, VT 05701; (802) 747-6700. Green Mountain Club, Route 100, RR 1, Box 650, Waterbury Center, VT 05677; (802) 244-7037. Appalachian Trail Conference, P.O. Box 807, Harpers Ferry, WV 25425; (304) 535-6331.

Trail notes: This southernmost stretch of the Long Trail—here coinciding with the Appalachian Trail—is for the most part an easy hike along a mostly flat, wooded ridge. The southern Green Mountains are not known for spectacular views; there are few on this hike. But this would be a good overnight backpacking trip for hikers who prefer a woods walk, or for a beginner backpacker. Because the southern terminus of the Long Trail lies in the forest on the Vermont-Massachusetts border, you have to access this hike via one of two trails, adding either 3.6 miles or four miles to this hike's distance.

The Pine Cobble Trail, the more interesting and slightly shorter of the two, reaches the LT in 3.6 miles; from the parking area (described above), walk east on Brooks Road for two-tenths of a mile and turn left on Pine Cobble Road. The trail begins a tenth of a mile up the road on the right and is marked by a sign. (See Pine Cobble, hike number 1 in the Massachusetts chapter, for details about this trail.)

The white-blazed Appalachian Trail takes four miles to reach the border of the two states, passing a view south to Mount Greylock from an old rockslide 2.4 miles from Route 2. From the state border, the Long Trail follows level, wooded terrain, crossing some old logging roads, for 2.6 miles to a junction with the Broad Brook Trail, which branches left (west), leading four miles to a road outside Williamstown. At 2.8 miles, the Seth Warner Trail leads left (west) two-tenths of a mile to the Seth Warner shelter. Continuing north, the LT crosses the dirt County Road at 3.1 miles, which connects Pownal and Stamford and may be passable by motor vehicle as far as the Long Trail. The LT ascends several hundred feet over a 3,000-foot hill, drops down the other side, then makes an easier climb over Consultation Peak (2,810 feet) before reaching Congdon Camp at 10 miles. At 10.5 miles, the LT crosses the Dunville Hollow Trail, which leads left (west) seven-tenths of a mile to a rough woods road (turning right onto that road, it is 1.8 miles to houses on Burgess Road and four miles Route 9, a mile east of Bennington). The LT follows more easy terrain before climbing slightly to the top of Harmon Hill (2,325 feet) at 12.5 miles, from which there are some views west toward Bennington and north toward Glastenbury Mountain. Continuing north, the trail descends at an easy grade for a mile, then drops steeply over the final half mile to Route 9.

Northern Vermont Map—page 174

Massachusetts

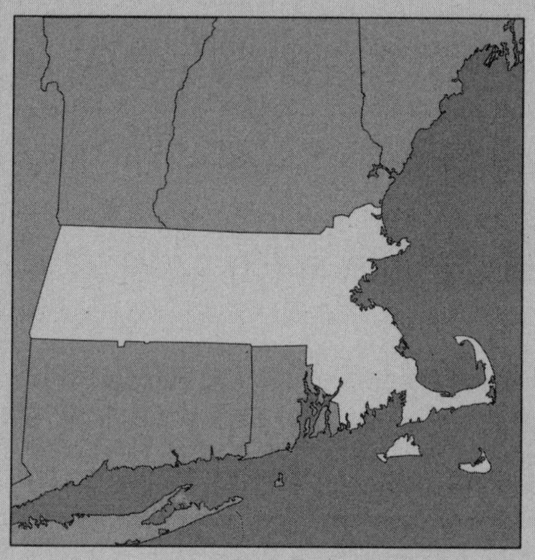

Overall Rating

1 2 3 4 5 6 7 8 9 10

Poor .... Fair .... Great

Difficulty

1 2 3 4 5

A stroll .... Moderate ...... A real butt-kicker!

Western Massachusetts

Adjoining Maps: North: Southern New Hampshire .... *page* 87
Southern Vermont .... *page* 175
East: Eastern Massachusetts .... *page* 239
South: Connecticut .... *pages* 320-321

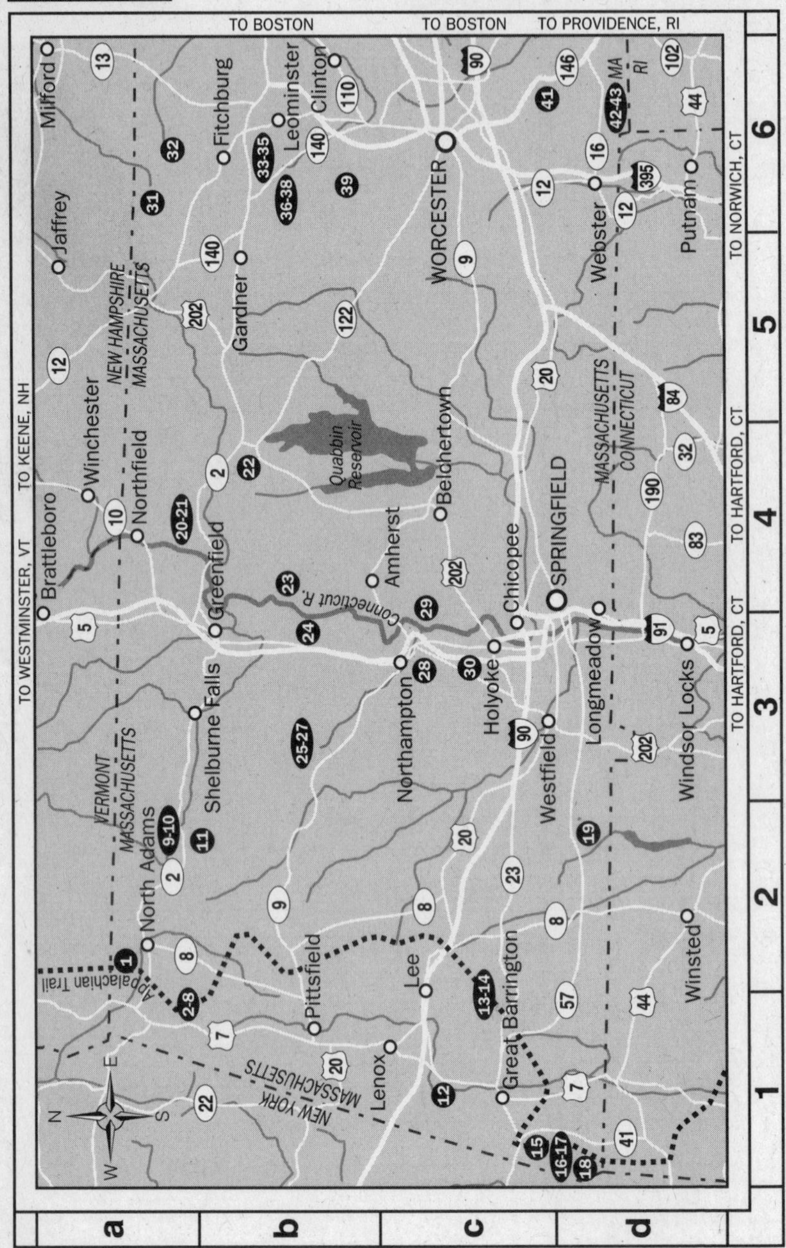

Eastern Massachusetts

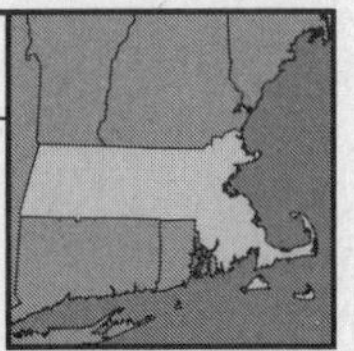

Adjoining Maps: North: Southern New Hampshire .... *page* 87
East: Cape Cod/Martha's Vineyard ..... *page* 240
West: Western Massachusetts .... *page* 238

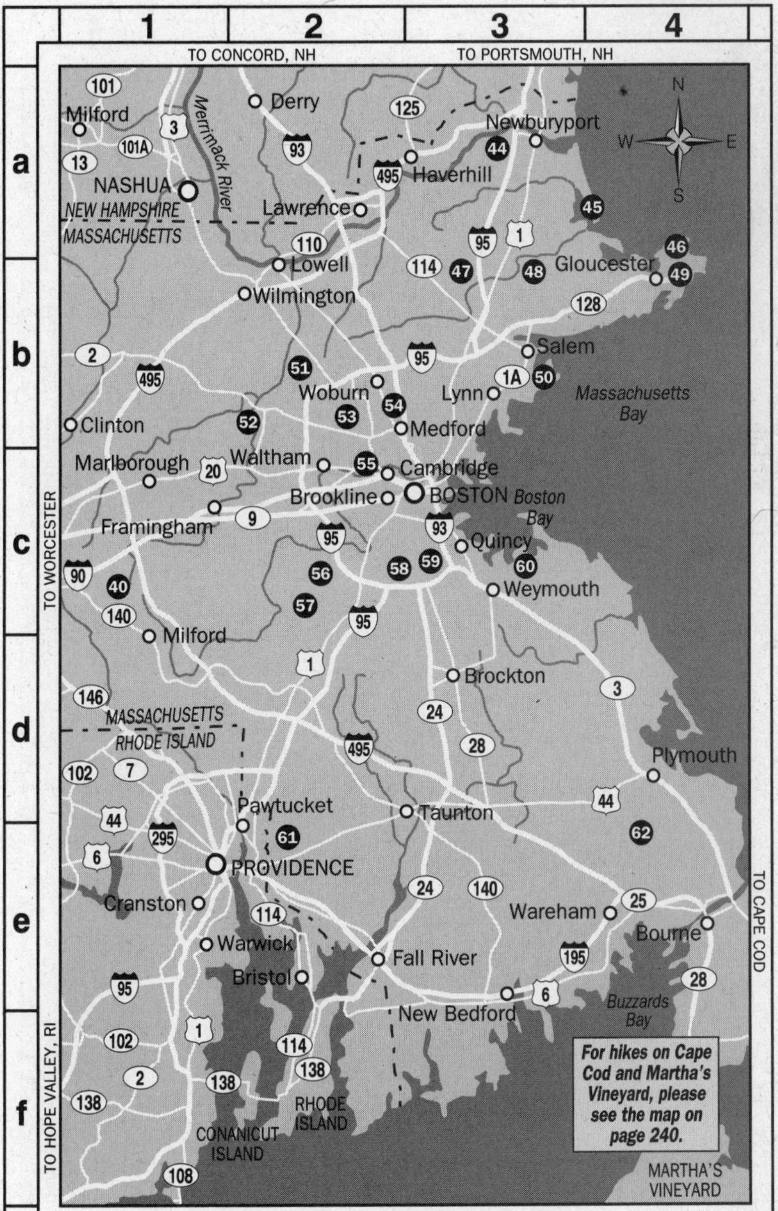

1 2 3 4

a b c d e f

TO CONCORD, NH
TO PORTSMOUTH, NH
TO WORCESTER
TO HOPE VALLEY, RI
TO CAPE COD

N S E W

101 Milford 3 101A 13 NASHUA Merrimack River Derry 93 125 Newburyport 44 495 Haverhill
NEW HAMPSHIRE
MASSACHUSETTS
Lawrence 45 95 1 110 Lowell 114 47 48 Gloucester 46 49 Wilmington 128
2 495 51 95 Salem 1A 50 Woburn Lynn 54 Massachusetts Bay Clinton 52 53 Medford
Marlborough 20 Waltham 55 Cambridge Brookline BOSTON Boston Bay Framingham 9 95 93 Quincy
90 40 56 58 59 60 Weymouth 57 140 95 Milford 1 Brockton 3
146 MASSACHUSETTS RHODE ISLAND 24 495 28 Plymouth 102 7
44 Pawtucket Taunton 44 295 61 62 6 PROVIDENCE 24 140
Cranston 114 Wareham 25 Bourne Warwick 195 Fall River Bristol 95 6 28 Buzzards Bay New Bedford
1 102 114 2 138 138 138 RHODE ISLAND CONANICUT ISLAND 108 MARTHA'S VINEYARD

For hikes on Cape Cod and Martha's Vineyard, please see the map on page 240.

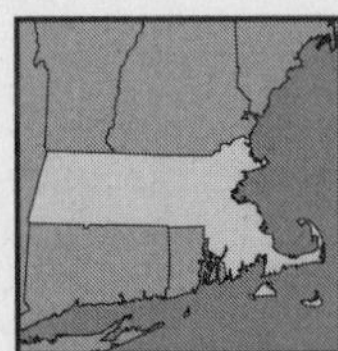

Cape Cod/Martha's Vineyard

Adjoining Maps: East: Eastern Massachusetts .... *page* 239

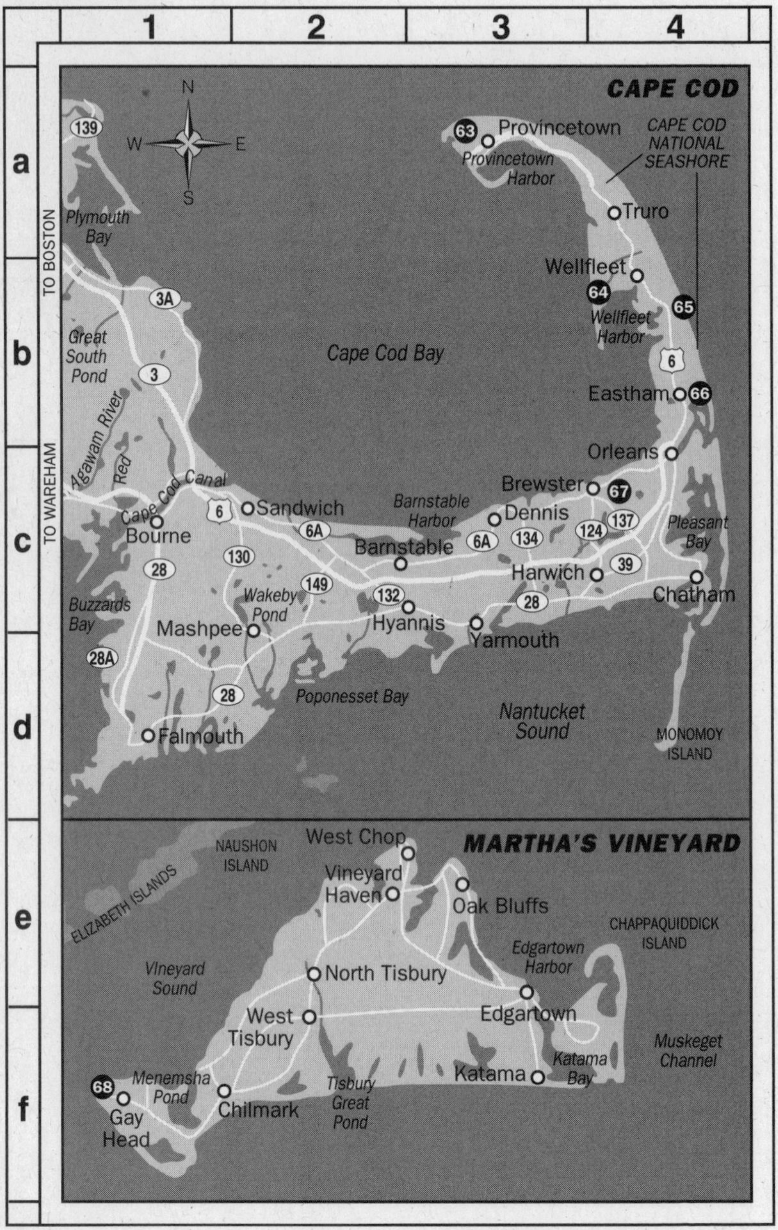

1 2 3 4

a b c d e f

TO BOSTON

TO WAREHAM

CAPE COD

N
W
E
S

139
Plymouth Bay
3A
Great South Pond
3
Agawam River
Red
Cape Cod Canal
Bourne
6
Sandwich
6A
130
28
149
Buzzards Bay
Wakeby Pond
Mashpee
28A
28
Falmouth
Poponesset Bay
Cape Cod Bay
Barnstable Harbor
Barnstable
132
Hyannis
Yarmouth
Dennis
6A
134
28
Nantucket Sound
63 Provincetown
Provincetown Harbor
CAPE COD NATIONAL SEASHORE
Truro
Wellfleet
64
Wellfleet Harbor
65
6
Eastham 66
Orleans
Brewster 67
124
137
Harwich
39
Pleasant Bay
Chatham
MONOMOY ISLAND

MARTHA'S VINEYARD

NAUSHON ISLAND
ELIZABETH ISLANDS
West Chop
Vineyard Haven
Oak Bluffs
Vineyard Sound
North Tisbury
West Tisbury
Edgartown Harbor
Edgartown
CHAPPAQUIDDICK ISLAND
Muskeget Channel
Katama
Katama Bay
Tisbury Great Pond
68
Menemsha Pond
Chilmark
Gay Head

Massachusetts features:

Eastern Massachusetts Map—page 239

MASSACHUSETTS

The Bay State may be second only to Maine among the New England states in the diversity of hiking opportunities. Although its highest peak, Mount Greylock, rises to just 3,487 feet, it and other summits in the Berkshires of western Massachusetts offer scenic, often rugged trails with occasional far-reaching views of these green, rounded hills. Low ranges like the Holyoke Range above the Connecticut River Valley, and isolated hills like Wachusett Mountain and Mount Watatic in central Massachusetts, boast surprisingly good views. The state also has one of the largest state park and forest systems in the country, with nearly 100 properties covering more than 270,000 acres, most of them crisscrossed by trails and old woods roads.

Three long-distance trails bisect the state north to south. In the west, the Appalachian Trail runs for 89 miles along the crest of the Berkshires. Bouncing along the Holyoke Range and through the hills of north-central Massachusetts on its 117-mile course from the Massachusetts-Connecticut line near Agawam and Southwick to the summit of Mount Monadnock in Jaffrey, New Hampshire, is the Metacomet-Monadnock Trail. The Midstate Trail extends 92 miles from the Rhode Island border in Douglas, Massachusetts, to the New Hampshire line in Ashburnham. While the AT is on federal land, the other two are largely on private land, and all three are maintained by volunteers.

Massachusetts also has nice seashore hikes—most notably in the Cape Cod National Seashore—and a few public bike paths which I've included because of their popularity and recreation potential.

Along the Appalachian Trail, dogs must be kept under control, and bikes, horses, hunting, and possession of firearms are prohibited. For information about the Appalachian Trail, contact the Appalachian Trail Conference (ATC), P.O. Box 807, Harpers Ferry, WV 25425; (304) 535-6331. Another

 Western Massachusetts Map—page 238

source is the Appalachian Mountain Club, Berkshire Chapter, P.O. Box 9369, North Amherst, MA 01059.

Dogs must be on a leash in state parks and forests. Horses are allowed in most state forests and parks, as is hunting in season. For maps or additional information about state parks, contact the Massachusetts Division of Forests and Parks, 100 Cambridge Street, 19th Floor, Boston, MA 02202; (617) 727-3180.

❶ Pine Cobble

3.4 mi/2.0 hrs 

Location: In Williamstown; Western Massachusetts map page 238, grid a2.

User groups: Hikers, dogs, and snowshoers. No wheelchair facilities. This trail is not suitable for bikes, horses, or skis. Hunting is prohibited.

Access, fees: Parking and access are free.

Directions: From U.S. 7 in Williamstown, a mile south of the Vermont state line and three-tenths of a mile north of the Hoosic River bridge, turn east on North Housac Road. Drive a half mile and turn right on Brooks Road. Continue seven-tenths of a mile and park in the dirt lot on the left side of the road marked by a sign reading "Parking for Pine Cobble Trail."

Maps: For a map of hiking trails, refer to map 1 in the "Map and Guide to the Appalachian Trail in Massachusetts and Connecticut," a five-map set for $16.95 from the Appalachian Trail Conference (see address below). For a topographic map of the area, request North Adams from the USGS.

Contact: Appalachian Trail Conference, P.O. Box 807, Harpers Ferry, WV 25425; (304) 535-6331.

Trail notes: I began backpacking Vermont's Long Trail from this access trail rather than using the Appalachian Trail (which crosses Route 2 in the Blackinton section of North Adams) because the view from Pine Cobble makes for a much more auspicious start to a 268-mile hike. The extensive quartzite ledges on the top of Pine Cobble offer excellent views of the Hoosic Valley, the low, green hills flanking the river, and towering Mount Greylock here in the northwest corner of Massachusetts. Ascending at an easy to moderate grade, this 3.4-mile trek (not including the half mile walked on pavement) is a good outing for young children.

From the parking area, walk east on Brooks Road for two-tenths of a mile and turn left on Pine Cobble Road. The trail begins a tenth of a mile up the road on the right and is marked by a sign. Follow the trail's blue blazes and well-worn path for 1.6 miles, to the point at which the blue blazes hook sharply left and a spur path leads to the right a tenth of a mile to Pine Cobble's summit. Take the spur path, soon reaching a ledge which offers a view west to the Taconic Range. Continue on a more faint footpath about 100 feet to reach the summit. The best views are from the open ledges about 30 feet beyond the summit. Looking south (right) you'll see Mount Greylock; east lie the woods and hills of the Clarksburg State Forest, and north (left) extends an array of hills traversed by Appalachian Trail hikers on their way into Vermont. Return the same way you came.

Special note: Hikers interested in a longer outing can continue north on the Pine Cobble Trail six-tenths of a mile to the Appalachian Trail, turn left (north), and hike another half mile to a nice view south of Mount Greylock from Eph's Lookout. The added distance makes the entire round-trip 5.6 miles.

❷ Money Brook Falls

5.0 mi/3.0 hrs 

Location: In Mount Greylock State Reservation in Williamstown, North Adams, Adams, and Lanesborough; Western Massachusetts map page 238, grid a1.

User groups: Hikers, dogs, and snowshoers. No wheelchair facilities. Dogs must be on a leash. This trail is not suitable for horses or skis. Bikes are prohibited. Hunting is allowed in season.

Access, fees: Parking and access are free. From the mid-December close of hunting season through about mid-May, roads within the state reservation are closed to vehicles (and groomed for snowmobiles), but Hopper Road is maintained to this trailhead. There is a lean-to and a dispersed backcountry camping zone along the Money Brook Trail.

Directions: From Route 43, 2.5 miles south of the junction of Routes 43 and 2 in Williamstown and 2.3 miles north of the junction of Route 43 and U.S. 7, turn east onto Hopper Road at a sign for Mount Hope Park. Drive 1.4 miles and bear left onto a dirt road. Continue seven-tenths of a mile to the parking area on the right.

Maps: A free trail map of Mount Greylock State Reservation is available at the visitors center or from the Massachusetts Division of Forests and Parks (see address below). The Holyoke Range/Mount Greylock/Pittsfield State Forest map is $2.95, and the more detailed "Mount Greylock State Reservation" shaded relief map is $5.95, both from the Appalachian Mountain Club, (800) 262-4455. The Mount Greylock Reservation Trail Map is $3.25 from New England Cartographics, (413) 549-4124. These trails are also covered on map 1 in the "Map and Guide to the Appalachian Trail in Massachusetts and Connecticut," a five-map set for $16.95 from the Appalachian Trail Conference (see address below). For topographic maps of the area, request North Adams and Cheshire from the USGS.

Contact: Mount Greylock State Reservation, P.O. Box 138, Lanesborough, MA 01237; (413) 499-4262 or (413) 499-4263. Massachusetts Division of Forests and Parks, 100 Cambridge Street, 19th Floor, Boston, MA 02202; (617) 727-3180. Appalachian Trail Conference, P.O. Box 807, Harpers Ferry, WV 25425; (304) 535-6331.

Trail notes: Money Brook Falls tumbles from an impressive height into a ravine choked with trees which haven't survived the steep, erosive terrain. Despite being one of the nicest natural features on the biggest hill in the Bay State, it may be its best-kept secret. The trail makes several stream crossings, some of which could be difficult in high water.

From the parking area, walk past the gate onto the Hopper Trail and follow a flat, grassy lane two-tenths of a mile. Where the Hopper Trail diverges right, continue straight ahead on the Money Brook Trail. It ascends gently at first, but after passing the Mount Prospect Trail junction at 1.5 miles, it goes through some short, steep stretches. At 2.4 miles, turn right onto a side path which leads a tenth of a mile to the falls. Hike back the way you came.

❸ Mount Greylock Circuit

12.0 mi/8.0 hrs  

Location: In Mount Greylock State Reservation in Williamstown, North Adams, Adams, and Lanesborough; Western Massachusetts map page 238, grid a1.

User groups: Hikers, dogs, and snowshoers. No wheelchair facilities. Dogs must be on a leash. This trail is not suitable for horses or skis. Bikes are prohibited. Hunting is allowed in season.

Access, fees: Parking and access are free. From the mid-December close of hunting season through about mid-May, roads within the state reservation are closed to vehicles (and groomed for snowmobiles), but Hopper Road is maintained to this trailhead. There is a lean-to and a dispersed backcountry camping zone along the Money Brook Trail.

Directions: From Route 43, 2.5 miles south of the junction of Routes 43 and 2 in Williamstown and 2.3 miles north of the junction of Route 43 and U.S. 7, turn east onto Hopper Road at a sign for Mount Hope Park. Drive 1.4 miles and bear left onto a dirt road. Continue seven-tenths of a mile to the parking area on the right.

Maps: A free, basic trail map of Mount Greylock State Reservation is available at the visitors center or from the Massachusetts Division of Forests and Parks (see address below). The Holyoke Range/Mount Greylock/Pittsfield State Forest map is $2.95, and the more detailed "Mount Greylock State Reservation" shaded relief map is $5.95, both from the Appalachian Mountain Club, (800) 262-4455. The Mount Greylock Reservation Trail Map is $3.25 from New England Cartographics, (413) 549-4124. These trails are also covered on map 1 in the "Map and Guide to the Appalachian Trail in Massachusetts and Connecticut," a five-map set for $16.95 from the Appalachian Trail Conference (see address below). For topographic maps of the area, request North Adams and Cheshire from the USGS.

Contact: Mount Greylock State Reservation, P.O. Box 138, Lanesborough, MA 01237; (413) 499-4262 or (413) 499-4263. Massachusetts Division of Forests and Parks, 100 Cambridge Street, 19th Floor, Boston, MA 02202; (617) 727-3180. Appalachian Trail Conference, P.O. Box 807, Harpers Ferry, WV 25425; (304) 535-6331.

Trail notes: In a desire to hike a loop around Massachusetts' highest peak, 3,491-foot Mount Greylock, taking in as many of its greatest features as possible on a day hike, I devised this 12-mile circuit. It climbs through and loops around the spectacular glacial cirque known as The Hopper, passes two waterfalls and over the summit, follows a stretch of the Appalachian Trail, and then descends through the rugged ravine of beautiful Money Brook. You could shave this distance by two miles by skipping the side trail to March Cataract Falls, and another mile by skipping Robinson Point.

From the parking area, walk past the gate onto the Hopper Trail and follow a flat, grassy lane two-tenths of a mile to where the Money Brook Trail leads straight ahead. Bear right with the Hopper Trail, ascending an old logging road, somewhat steeply at times, another two miles until you reach Sperry Road. Turn left and walk the road a tenth of a mile; just before the parking area on the right, turn left on a dirt campground road. Walk about 200 feet, past the Chimney Group Camping Area, and turn left at a sign for the March Cataract Falls Trail. It leads a mile, descending through switchbacks, to March Cataract Falls, a 30-foot falls which usually maintains a nice flow even during dry seasons.

Backtrack to Sperry Road, turn left and walk about 100 yards past the parking area, then turn left at a sign onto the Hopper Trail. The wide path climbs at a moderate grade past a short falls. Where the Deer Hill Trail diverges right, bear left. Within a mile of Sperry Road, where the Hopper Trail makes a sharp right, turn left onto the Overlook Trail. You will reach the first view of The Hopper within minutes, though trees partially obstruct it. A half mile down the Overlook Trail lies the second view, which is better; Stony Ledge is visible across The Hopper to the west. Continue on the Overlook Trail to the paved Notch Road, 1.2 miles from the

Hopper Trail. Turn left and walk the road downhill a tenth of a mile, past a day-use parking turnout, then turn left onto a trail marked by blue blazes. It descends steeply two-tenths of a mile to Robinson Point, and a view of The Hopper superior to anything on the Overlook Trail. Double back to the Overlook Trail, cross Notch Road, and follow the Overlook uphill for four-tenths of a mile to the white-blazed Appalachian Trail. Turn left on the AT, following it across the parking lot to the summit, where you'll find the War Memorial Tower and the Appalachian Mountain Club's Bascom Lodge. The best views are to the east from the meadow beyond the tower; there are also good views to the west. You can take the circular stairs up the tower for its panoramic vistas.

From the tower, follow the AT north. About a mile from the summit is a good view to the east. About 2.4 miles from the summit, a side trail leads left to Notch Road, but continue two-tenths of a mile straight ahead on the AT over Mount Williams, one of Greylock's summits. The AT swings left here, descending easily nine-tenths of a mile to Notch Road. Cross the road, and a tenth of a mile into the woods, turn left onto the Money Brook Trail; in two-tenths of a mile, pass a short side path leading to the Wilbur's Clearing shelter. The trail reaches a side path seven-tenths of a mile beyond the shelter which leads a short distance to spectacular Money Brook Falls. From that path, the Money Brook Trail follows Money Brook through a wild, narrow valley, with a few crossings that could be tricky in high water. Nearly a mile from the falls, the Mount Prospect Trail branches right; stay on the Money Brook Trail another 1.5 miles to the Hopper Trail—passing a dispersed camping zone just before reaching the Hopper Trail—then continue straight ahead two-tenths of a mile to return to the parking area.

4 Robinson Point

0.4 mi/0.5 hr 

Location: In Mount Greylock State Reservation in Williamstown, North Adams, Adams, and Lanesborough; Western Massachusetts map page 238, grid a1.

User groups: Hikers and dogs. No wheelchair facilities. Dogs must be on a leash. This trail is not suitable for horses or skis. The trailhead is not accessible by road in winter for snowshoeing. Bikes are prohibited. Hunting is allowed in season.

Access, fees: Parking and access are free. From the mid-December close of hunting season through about mid-May, roads within the state reservation are closed to vehicles (and groomed for snowmobiles). This trailhead is not accessible by car in the winter months.

Directions: From Route 2, 3.7 miles east of the junction of Routes 2 and 43 in Williamstown and 1.3 miles west of the junction of Routes 2 and 8A in North Adams, turn south onto Notch Road. Follow Notch Road up the mountain for 7.4 miles to a turnout for day-use parking on the right. From U.S. 7 in Lanesborough, 1.3 miles north of town center and 4.2 miles south of the Lanesborough/New Ashford line, turn east onto North Main Street. Drive seven-tenths of a mile and turn right onto Quarry Road. Continue six-tenths of a mile and bear left at a sign reading "Rockwell Road to Greylock." The Greylock Visitors Center is six-tenths of a mile farther up that road. From the visitors center, follow Rockwell Road up the mountain for 7.2 miles, then turn left onto Notch Road and continue nine-tenths of a mile to the day-use parking turnout on the left.

Maps: A free, basic trail map of Mount Greylock State Reservation is available at the visitors center or from the Massachusetts

Division of Forests and Parks (see address below). The Holyoke Range/Mount Greylock/Pittsfield State Forest map is $2.95, and the more detailed "Mount Greylock State Reservation" shaded relief map is $5.95, both from the Appalachian Mountain Club, (800) 262-4455. The Mount Greylock Reservation Trail Map is $3.25 from New England Cartographics, (413) 549-4124. These trails are also covered on map 1 in the "Map and Guide to the Appalachian Trail in Massachusetts and Connecticut," a five-map set for $16.95 from the Appalachian Trail Conference (see address below). For topographic maps of the area, request North Adams and Cheshire from the USGS.

Contact: Mount Greylock State Reservation, P.O. Box 138, Lanesborough, MA 01237; (413) 499-4262 or (413) 499-4263. Massachusetts Division of Forests and Parks, 100 Cambridge Street, 19th Floor, Boston, MA 02202; (617) 727-3180. Appalachian Trail Conference, P.O. Box 807, Harpers Ferry, WV 25425; (304) 535-6331.

Trail notes: The high ledge at Robinson Point offers one of the best views on Greylock of The Hopper, that huge glacial cirque carved out of the mountain's northwest flank. Visible are Stony Ledge, at the end of the ridge forming The Hopper's western wall, Williamstown in the valley beyond The Hopper's mouth, and the Taconic Range on the horizon. From the turnout, walk downhill just a few steps, then turn left onto a trail marked by blue blazes. It descends steeply two-tenths of a mile to Robinson Point. Return the same way.

5 Deer Hill Trail

2.2 mi/1.5 hrs 

Location: In Mount Greylock State Reservation in Williamstown, North Adams, Adams, and Lanesborough; Western Massachusetts map page 238, grid a1.

User groups: Hikers, dogs, and snowshoers. No wheelchair facilities. Dogs must be on a leash. This trail is not suitable for horses or skis. Bikes are prohibited. Hunting is allowed in season.

Access, fees: Parking and access are free. From the mid-December close of hunting season through about mid-May, roads within the state reservation are closed to vehicles (and groomed for snowmobiles). This trailhead is not accessible by car in winter. There is a lean-to for overnight camping along the Deer Hill Trail.

Directions: From Route 2, 3.7 miles east of the junction of Routes 2 and 43 in Williamstown and 1.3 miles west of the junction of Routes 2 and 8A in North Adams, turn south onto Notch Road. Follow Notch Road up the mountain for 8.3 miles and turn right onto Rockwell Road. Continue 1.7 miles, turn right onto Sperry Road, and drive six-tenths of a mile to the roadside parking. From U.S. 7 in Lanesborough, 1.3 miles north of town center and 4.2 miles south of the Lanesborough/New Ashford line, turn east onto North Main Street. Drive seven-tenths of a mile and turn right onto Quarry Road. Continue six-tenths of a mile and bear left at a sign reading "Rockwell Road to Greylock." The Greylock Visitors Center is six-tenths of a mile farther up that road. From the visitors center, follow Rockwell Road up the mountain for 5.5 miles, then turn left onto Sperry Road and continue six-tenths of a mile to the parking area.

Maps: A free, basic trail map of Mount Greylock State Reservation is available at the visitors center or from the Massachusetts Division of Forests and Parks (see address below). The Holyoke Range/Mount Greylock/Pittsfield State Forest map is $2.95, and the more detailed "Mount Greylock State Reservation" shaded relief map is $5.95, both from the Appalachian

Mountain Club, (800) 262-4455. The Mount Greylock Reservation Trail Map is $3.25 from New England Cartographics, (413) 549-4124. These trails are also covered on map 1 in the "Map and Guide to the Appalachian Trail in Massachusetts and Connecticut," a five-map set for $16.95 from the Appalachian Trail Conference (see address below). For topographic maps of the area, request North Adams and Cheshire from the USGS.

Contact: Mount Greylock State Reservation, P.O. Box 138, Lanesborough, MA 01237; (413) 499-4262 or (413) 499-4263. Massachusetts Division of Forests and Parks, 100 Cambridge Street, 19th Floor, Boston, MA 02202; (617) 727-3180. Appalachian Trail Conference, P.O. Box 807, Harpers Ferry, WV 25425; (304) 535-6331.

Trail notes: A friend and I actually backpacked this fairly easy two-mile loop past Deer Hill Falls and an interesting grove of tall hemlocks one weekend, and spent the night at the lean-to along the way, listening to coyotes in the darkness. If you have time, walk or drive the mile to the end of Sperry Road for the view from Stony Ledge of the huge glacial cirque on Greylock known as The Hopper, perhaps the finest view on the mountain.

From the parking area, walk back up Sperry Road (south) for four-tenths of a mile and turn right onto the Deer Hill Trail. The flat, wide path crosses a brook and within four-tenths of a mile makes a right turn, descending past a dark grove of tall hemlocks on the left and reaching the lean-to one mile from the road. Just beyond the lean-to, the trail descends steeply and crosses over a stream on a wooden bridge, then climbs steeply up to Deer Hill Falls. About two-tenths of a mile above the falls, make a right turn onto the Roaring Brook Trail, which leads back to the parking area in a tenth of a mile.

6 March Cataract Falls

2.0 mi/1.5 hrs 

Location: In Mount Greylock State Reservation in Williamstown, North Adams, Adams, and Lanesborough; Western Massachusetts map page 238, grid a1.

User groups: Hikers and dogs. No wheelchair facilities. Dogs must be on a leash. This trail is not suitable for horses or skis. The trailhead is not accessible by road in winter for snowshoeing. Bikes are prohibited. Hunting is allowed in season.

Access, fees: Parking and access are free. From the mid-December close of hunting season through about mid-May, roads in the state reservation are closed to vehicles (and groomed for snowmobiles). This trailhead is not accessible by car in winter.

Directions: From Route 2, 3.7 miles east of the junction of Routes 2 and 43 in Williamstown and 1.3 miles west of the junction of Routes 2 and 8A in North Adams, turn south onto Notch Road. Follow Notch Road up the mountain for 8.3 miles and turn right onto Rockwell Road. Continue 1.7 miles, turn right onto Sperry Road, and drive six-tenths of a mile to the roadside parking. From U.S. 7 in Lanesborough, 1.3 miles north of town center and 4.2 miles south of the Lanesborough/New Ashford line, turn east onto North Main Street. Drive seven-tenths of a mile and turn right onto Quarry Road. Continue six-tenths of a mile and bear left at a sign reading "Rockwell Road to Greylock." The Greylock Visitors Center is six-tenths of a mile farther up that road. From the visitors center, follow Rockwell Road up the mountain for 5.5 miles, then turn left onto Sperry Road and continue six-tenths of a mile to the parking area.

Maps: A free, basic trail map of Mount Greylock State Reservation is available at the visitors center or from the Massachusetts Division of Forests and Parks (see address below). The Holyoke Range/Mount Greylock/Pittsfield State Forest map is $2.95, and the more detailed "Mount Greylock State Reservation" shaded relief map is $5.95, both from the Appalachian Mountain Club, (800) 262-4455. The Mount Greylock Reservation Trail Map is $3.25 from New England Cartographics, (413) 549-4124. These trails are also covered on map 1 in the "Map and Guide to the Appalachian Trail in Massachusetts and Connecticut," a five-map set for $16.95 from the Appalachian Trail Conference (see address below). For topographic maps of the area, request North Adams and Cheshire from the USGS.

Contact: Mount Greylock State Reservation, P.O. Box 138, Lanesborough, MA 01237; (413) 499-4262 or (413) 499-4263. Massachusetts Division of Forests and Parks, 100 Cambridge Street, 19th Floor, Boston, MA 02202; (617) 727-3180. Appalachian Trail Conference, P.O. Box 807, Harpers Ferry, WV 25425; (304) 535-6331.

Trail notes: March Cataract Falls is a 30-foot-high curtain of water at the end of a fairly easy, one-mile trail beginning in the Sperry Road Campground. From the parking area, cross the road onto a dirt campground road. Walk that short half-circle road to the March Cataract Falls Trail, marked by a sign. It starts out on easy ground, then descends through switchbacks, reaching March Cataract Falls a mile from the campground. Head back along the same route.

7 Jones Nose

1.0 mi/0.75 hr 

Location: In Mount Greylock State Reservation in Williamstown, North Adams, Adams, and Lanesborough; Western Massachusetts map page 238, grid a1.

User groups: Hikers and dogs. No wheelchair facilities. Dogs must be on a leash. This trail is not suitable for horses or skis. The trailhead is not accessible by road in winter for snowshoeing. Bikes are prohibited. Hunting is allowed in season.

Access, fees: Parking and access are free. From the mid-December close of hunting season through about mid-May, roads in the state reservation are closed to vehicles (and groomed for snowmobiles). This trailhead is not accessible by car in winter.

Directions: From Route 2, 3.7 miles east of the junction of Routes 2 and 43 in Williamstown and 1.3 miles west of the junction of Routes 2 and 8A in North Adams, turn south onto Notch Road. Follow Notch Road up the mountain for 8.3 miles and turn right onto Rockwell Road. Continue 3.5 miles to the Jones Nose parking lot on the left. From U.S. 7 in Lanesborough, 1.3 miles north of the town center and 4.2 miles south of the Lanesborough/New Ashford line, turn east onto North Main Street. Drive seven-tenths of a mile and turn right onto Quarry Road. Continue six-tenths of a mile and bear left at a sign reading "Rockwell Road to Greylock." The Greylock Visitors Center is six-tenths of as mile farther up that road. From the visitors center, follow Rockwell Road up the mountain for 3.7 miles to the Jones Nose parking lot on the right.

Maps: A free, basic trail map of Mount Greylock State Reservation is available at the visitors center or from the Massachusetts Division of Forests and Parks (see address below). The Holyoke Range/Mount Greylock/Pittsfield State Forest map is $2.95, and the more detailed "Mount Greylock State Reservation" shaded relief map is $5.95, both from the Appalachian Mountain Club, (800) 262-4455. The Mount Greylock Reservation Trail Map is $3.25 from New England Cartographics, (413) 549-4124. These trails are also covered on map 1 in the "Map and Guide to the Appalachian Trail in Massachusetts and Connecticut," a five-map set for $16.95 from the Appalachian Trail Conference (see address below). For topographic maps of the area, request North Adams and Cheshire from the USGS.

Contact: Mount Greylock State Reservation, P.O. Box 138, Lanesborough, MA 01237; (413) 499-4262 or (413) 499-4263. Massachusetts Division of Forests and Parks, 100 Cambridge Street, 19th Floor, Boston, MA 02202; (617) 727-3180. Appalachian Trail Conference, P.O. Box 807, Harpers Ferry, WV 25425; (304) 535-6331.

Trail notes: Jones Nose is an open ledge on Greylock's southern ridge which offers a broad view of the mountains to the south and west—a nice spot to catch a sunset. From the parking area, walk north on the Jones Nose Trail. It passes through woods, crosses a meadow, then ascends steeply to a side path on the left, a half mile from the parking lot. Follow that path 40 feet to the viewpoint. Return the way you came.

8 Rounds Rock

1.0 mi/0.75 hr 

Location: In Mount Greylock State Reservation in Williamstown, North Adams, Adams, and Lanesborough; Western Massachusetts map page 238, grid a1.

User groups: Hikers and dogs. No wheelchair facilities. Dogs must be on a leash. This trail is not suitable for horses or skis. The trailhead is not accessible by road in winter for snowshoeing. Bikes are prohibited. Hunting is allowed in season.

Access, fees: Parking and access are free. From the mid-December close of hunting season through about mid-May, roads in the state reservation are closed to vehicles (and groomed for snowmobiles). This trailhead is not accessible by car in winter.

Directions: From Route 2, 3.7 miles east of the junction of Routes 2 and 43 in Williamstown and 1.3 miles west of the junction of Routes 2 and 8A in North Adams, turn south onto Notch Road. Follow Notch Road up the mountain for 8.3 miles and turn right onto Rockwell Road. Continue 4.2 miles to a turnout on the left, across from the Rounds Rock Trail. From U.S. 7 in Lanesborough, 1.3 miles north of the town center and 4.2 miles south of the Lanesborough/New Ashford line, turn east onto North Main Street. Drive seven-tenths of a mile and turn right onto Quarry Road. Continue six-tenths of a mile and bear left at a sign reading "Rockwell Road to Greylock." The Greylock Visitors Center is six-tenths of a mile farther up that road. From the visitors center, follow Rockwell Road up the mountain for three miles to a turnout on the right, across from the Rounds Rock Trail.

Maps: A free, basic trail map of Mount Greylock State Reservation is available at the visitors center or from the Massachusetts Division of Forests and Parks (see address below). The Holyoke Range/Mount Greylock/Pittsfield State Forest map is $2.95, and the more detailed "Mount Greylock State Reservation" shaded relief map is $5.95, both from the Appalachian Mountain Club, (800) 262-4455. The Mount Greylock Reservation Trail Map is $3.25 from New England Cartographics, (413) 549-4124. These trails are also covered on map 1 in the "Map and Guide to the Appalachian Trail in Massachusetts and Connecticut," a five-map set for $16.95 from the Appalachian Trail Conference (see address below). For topographic maps of the area, request North Adams and Cheshire from the USGS.

Contact: Mount Greylock State Reservation, P.O. Box 138, Lanesborough, MA 01237; (413) 499-4262 or (413) 499-4263. Massachusetts Division of Forests and Parks, 100 Cambridge Street, 19th Floor,

Boston, MA 02202; (617) 727-3180. Appalachian Trail Conference, P.O. Box 807, Harpers Ferry, WV 25425; (304) 535-6331.

Trail notes: This easy, one-mile loop to a pair of ledges offers some of the most dramatic views on Mount Greylock—for little effort. This is a terrific hike with young children, or to catch a sunset or the fall foliage. From the turnout, cross the road to the Rounds Rock Trail. Follow it through woods and across blueberry patches about a half mile to where a side path (at a sign which reads "scenic vista") leads left about 75 yards to a sweeping view south from atop a low cliff. Backtrack and turn left on the main trail, following it a tenth of a mile to another, shorter side path and a view south and west. Complete the loop on the Rounds Rock Trail by following it out to Rockwell Road. Turn right and walk the road about 150 yards back to the turnout.

9 Mohawk Trail

5.0 mi/3.5 hrs 

Location: In Mohawk Trail State Forest in Charlemont; Western Massachusetts map page 238, grid a2.

User groups: Hikers and dogs. No wheelchair facilities. Dogs must be on a leash. This trail would be difficult to snowshoe and is not suitable for bikes, horses, or skis. Hunting is allowed in season.

Access, fees: Parking and access are free.

Directions: The main entrance to the Mohawk Trail State Forest is on Route 2, 3.7 miles west of the junction of Routes 2 and 8A in Charlemont and one mile east of the Savoy/Charlemont line. Drive the state forest road for two-tenths of a mile, through a gate, and park just beyond the gate on the left, behind the headquarters building.

Maps: A free, basic trail and contour map of Mohawk Trail State Forest is available at the state forest headquarters, or from the Massachusetts Division of Forests and Parks (see address below). For a topographic map of the area, request Rowe from the USGS.

Contact: Mohawk Trail State Forest, P.O. Box 7, Route 2, Charlemont, MA 01339; (413) 339-5504. Massachusetts Division of Forests and Parks, 100 Cambridge Street, 19th Floor, Boston, MA 02202; (617) 727-3180.

Trail notes: This mostly wooded ridge walk follows a historical route: the original Mohawk Trail, used for hundreds of years by the area's native Americans. There is one good view along the ridge, from an open ledge on Todd Mountain overlooking the Cold River Valley. From the parking area, continue up the paved road, bearing left toward the camping area where the road forks, then bearing right at a sign for the Indian Trail at seven-tenths of a mile. The trail remains flat for only about 200 feet, then turns right and begins the steep and relentless ascent of a half mile to the ridge. This trail is not well marked, and can be easy to lose in a few places. Once atop the ridge, the walking grows much easier. Turn right onto the Todd Mountain Trail, following it a half mile to an open ledge with a good view. Double back to the Indian Trail and continue straight ahead (you will see disks on trees indicating that this is the old Mohawk Trail) on the easy, wide path that predates European settlement here by hundreds of years. About eight-tenths of a mile from the Todd Mountain Trail, the Indian/Mohawk Trail swings right and begins descending; double back from here and descend the Indian Trail back to the start.

10 Giant Trees of Clark Ridge

1.0 mi/2.0 hrs 

Location: In Mohawk Trail State Forest in Charlemont; Western Massachusetts map page 238, grid a2.

User groups: Hikers, dogs, and snowshoers. No wheelchair facilities. Dogs must be on a leash. This trail is not suitable for bikes, horses, or skis. Hunting is allowed in season.

Access, fees: Parking and access are free.

Directions: From Route 2, 1.6 miles west of the junction of Routes 2 and 8A in Charlemont and 2.1 miles east of the main entrance to the Mohawk Trail State Forest, turn north at a sign for Rowe/Monroe. Proceed 2.2 miles, bear left, and continue another eight-tenths of a mile to the Zoar picnic area on the left, where there is parking; or to parking a tenth of a mile farther on the right, immediately before the bridge over the Deerfield River.

Maps: A free, basic trail and contour map of Mohawk Trail State Forest is available at the state forest headquarters (reached via the state forest's main entrance; see directions), or from the Massachusetts Division of Forests and Parks (see address below). For a topographic map of the area, request Rowe from the USGS.

Contact: Mohawk Trail State Forest, P.O. Box 7, Route 2, Charlemont, MA 01339; (413) 339-5504. Massachusetts Division of Forests and Parks, 100 Cambridge Street, 19th Floor, Boston, MA 02202; (617) 727-3180.

Trail notes: If you're wondering how it could take two hours to walk a mile, then consider this: you may not even walk a mile, yet you may spend even longer in here. Unlike the other hikes in this book, this one doesn't follow an established trail. It begins on an abandoned, somewhat overgrown logging road and becomes a bushwhack. But the steep, rugged terrain you will encounter on the north flank of Clark Ridge is probably a big part of the reason loggers left so many giant trees untouched here over the past few centuries—a time period when most of New England was deforested. Within an area of about 75 acres are an uncounted number of sugar maple, red oak, white ash, beech, and other hardwoods reaching more than 120 feet into the sky, and 200 to 300 years old. One respected regional expert has identified a 160-foot white pine here as the tallest living thing in New England. It would be impossible for me to direct you to particular trees, and equally difficult for you to identify any individual tree by its height without the proper equipment. But, just as I did, I think you will find walking around in this cathedral of bark to be a rare and stirring experience.

From either parking area, walk across the bridge and immediately turn left, following a faint footpath down across a wash and a cleared area and onto a distinct trail—actually, an abandoned logging road. The road dissipates within about a half mile; but you need only walk a quarter of a mile or so, then turn right and bushwhack uphill. You will soon find yourself craning your neck constantly. Be sure to remember how to find your way back to the logging road.

⓫ The Lookout

2.2 mi/1.5 hrs

Location: In Mohawk Trail State Forest in Charlemont; Western Massachusetts map page 238, grid a2.

User groups: Hikers, dogs, and snowshoers. No wheelchair facilities. Dogs must be on a leash. The trail is not suitable for bikes, horses, or skis. Hunting is allowed in season.

Access, fees: Parking and access are free.

Directions: The trail begins opposite a turnout and picnic area on Route 2 in Charlemont, nine-tenths of a mile west of the main entrance to the Mohawk Trail State Forest and a tenth of a mile east of the Charlemont/Savoy line.

Maps: A free, basic trail and contour map of Mohawk Trail State Forest is available at the state forest headquarters, or from the Massachusetts Division of Forests and Parks (see address below). For a topographic map of the area, request Rowe from the USGS.

Contact: Mohawk Trail State Forest, P.O. Box 7, Route 2, Charlemont, MA 01339; (413) 339-5504. Massachusetts Division of Forests and Parks, 100 Cambridge Street, 19th Floor, Boston, MA 02202; (617) 727-3180.

Trail notes: Here's an easy 2.2-mile walk through the quiet woods of Mohawk Trail State Forest to a lookout with a good view east of the Deerfield River Valley and Charlemont. Friends and I encountered a rugged grouse on this trail one snowless March day. From the parking area, cross the highway to the Totem Trail, which begins behind a stone marker for the state forest. The trail is obvious and well marked, crossing a small brook and reaching the overlook in 1.1 miles. Hike back along the same route.

⓬ Monument Mountain

1.6 mi/1.2 hrs 

Location: In Great Barrington; Western Massachusetts map page 238, grid c1.

User groups: Hikers and snowshoers. No wheelchair facilities. Bikes, dogs, horses, hunting, and skis are prohibited.

Access, fees: Parking and access are free. The Monument Mountain Reservation is open to the public from sunrise to sunset.

Directions: The trails begin at a large turnout and picnic area along U.S. 7 in Great Barrington, 1.1 miles south of the Stockbridge town line and 1.7 miles north of the junction with Route 183.

Maps: A map of trails is posted on an information board at the picnic area. A map is also available from the Trustees of Reservations (see address below). For topographic maps of the area, request Great Barrington and Stockbridge from the USGS.

Contact: Trustees of Reservations, 572 Essex Street, Beverly, MA 01915-1530, (508) 921-1944; or the Trustees' Western Regional Office, Mission House, P.O. Box 792, Stockbridge, MA 01262; (413) 298-3239.

Trail notes: Perhaps the finest hike in an area that rivals the Mount Greylock region for the best hiking in southern New England, Monument Mountain thrusts a spectacular gray-white quartzite ridge into the sky. Its summit, Squaw Peak, rises to 1,640 feet and offers three-state views in all directions from atop cliffs. Arguably even more dramatic, though, are the cliffs south of Squaw Peak, and the detached rock pinnacle known as Devil's Pulpit. A good time to come here is mid-June, when the mountain laurel blooms. Monument's vertical rock is also popular with the area's rock climbers. In fact, this unique hill has been popular since at least the nineteenth century: in 1850, so legend goes, Nathaniel Hawthorne, Oliver Wendell Holmes, and Herman Melville picnicked together on Monument's summit. And William Cullen Bryant wrote a poem titled "Monument Mountain" relating the tale of an Indian maiden who, spurned in love, leapt to her death from the cliffs. Your hike may be less historic, and less traumatic, than either of those, but Monument Mountain is one not to miss.

This fairly easy, 1.6-mile hike ascends and descends the Hickey Trail, but you may enjoy making a loop hike, going up the Hickey and coming down the 1.3-mile Indian Monument Trail, which joins up with the Hickey below the summit. At the picnic area, a sign describes the trail heading south, the Indian Monument, as easier, and the Hickey, which heads north, as steeper. The Hickey actually grows steep for only a short section below the summit, and is otherwise a well-graded and well-maintained trail. Follow the white blazes. You'll parallel a brook with a small waterfall. Nearing the summit ridge, watch for a trail entering on the right; that's the Indian Monument Trail, and you'll want to be able to distinguish it from the Hickey on your way back down. From the summit, continue following the white blazes south about a quarter mile, passing a pile of rocks, till you reach the cliffs. Devil's Pulpit is the obvious pinnacle at the far end of the cliffs.

⓭ Wildcat Loop

9.5 mi/6.0 hrs 

Location: In Beartown State Forest in Monterey; Western Massachusetts map page 238, grid c1.

User groups: Hikers, bikes, and dogs. No wheelchair facilities. Dogs must be on a leash. Horses, skis, and snowshoes are prohibited. Hunting is allowed in season.

Access, fees: Parking and access are free. Beartown State Forest is closed from 8 P.M. to a half hour before sunrise between May 1 and October 31, and from a half hour after sunset to a half hour before sunrise between November 1 and April 30.

Directions: Beartown State Forest is on Blue Hill Road, which runs north off Route 23, 2.4 miles west of the Monterey General Store and 1.8 miles east of the junction with Route 57. Follow Blue Hill Road seven-tenths of a mile to the forest headquarters on the left. Continuing north on Blue Hill Road, you will pass the Appalachian Trail crossing at 1.3 miles from the headquarters; at 1.5 miles, turn right onto Benedict Pond Road (shown as Beartown Road on the park map). Follow signs past the hiking trailhead and swimming area to the campground parking area.

Maps: A contour map of trails (designating uses allowed on each trail) is available in boxes at the state forest headquarters, at the parking area for hiking, at a trail information kiosk at the swimming area and bathrooms, and at the campground. You can also contact the Massachusetts Division of Forests and Parks (see address below). For topographic maps of the area, request Great Barrington and Otis from the USGS.

Contact: Beartown State Forest, Blue Hill Road, P.O. Box 97, Monterey, MA 01245-0097; (413) 528-0904. Massachusetts Division of Forests and Parks, 100 Cambridge Street, 19th Floor, Boston, MA 02202; (617) 727-3180.

Trail notes: I included this trail primarily for mountain bikers (a 2.5-hour ride for them) looking for a challenging bounce up and down a heavily rutted and rock-strewn old woods road. I emerged from this ride covered with a thick paste of mud and sweat—and with a newfound respect for Beartown's hills. As a hike, it represents a rugged, six-hour outing through quiet woods, though it tends to get muddy in some spots.

From the campground, head up Beartown Road a short distance and turn left onto the Wildcat Trail, which is marked by a sign and is just beyond a right bend in the road. This old woods road rolls up and down a few hills, passing through areas that tend to be muddy, especially in spring. After about 3.5 miles, the trail ends at paved Beartown Road. Turn right, cross over West Brook, and turn left onto Beebe Trail, another woods road marked by a sign. The Beebe loops less than two miles back to Beartown Road. Turn left and follow the paved road back to the campground. For a longer route, you can link up with the Sky Peak and Turkey Trails.

⓮ Benedict Pond and The Ledges

2.5 mi/1.5 hrs 

Location: In Beartown State Forest in Monterey; Western Massachusetts map page 238, grid c1.

User groups: Hikers, dogs, and snowshoers. No wheelchair facilities. Dogs must be on a leash. Bikes, horses, and skis are prohibited. Hunting is allowed in season.

Access, fees: Parking and access are free. Beartown State Forest is closed from 8 P.M. to a half hour before sunrise between May 1 and October 31, and from a half hour after sunset to a half hour before sunrise between November 1 and April 30.

Directions: Beartown State Forest is on Blue Hill Road, which runs north off Route 23, 2.4 miles west of the Monterey General Store and 1.8 miles east of the junction with Route 57. Follow Blue Hill Road seven-tenths of a mile to the forest headquarters on the left. Continuing north on Blue Hill Road, you will pass the Appalachian Trail crossing 1.3 miles from the headquarters; at 1.5 miles, turn right onto Benedict Pond Road (shown as Beartown Road on the park map). Follow signs to the trailhead in a dirt parking area; a sign marks the Pond Loop Trail. A short distance farther up the road are public bathrooms and a state forest campground.

Maps: A contour map of trails (designating uses allowed on each trail) is available in boxes at the state forest headquarters, at the trailhead parking area, at a trail information kiosk at the swimming area and bathrooms, and at the campground. You can also contact the Massachusetts Division of Forests and Parks (see address below). This section of the Appalachian Trail is covered on map 3 in the "Map and Guide to the Appalachian Trail in Massachusetts and Connecticut," a five-map set for $16.95 from the Appalachian Trail Conference (see address below). For topographic maps of the area, request Great Barrington and Otis from the USGS.

Contact: Beartown State Forest, Blue Hill Road, P.O. Box 97, Monterey, MA 01245-0097; (413) 528-0904. Massachusetts Division of Forests and Parks, 100 Cambridge Street, 19th Floor, Boston, MA 02202; (617) 727-3180. Appalachian Trail Conference, P.O. Box 807, Harpers Ferry, WV 25425; (304) 535-6331.

Trail notes: This hike makes a loop around pristine Benedict Pond, a place with rich bird life—I heard three or four woodpeckers hard at work one morning and saw one fairly close up. When I stopped to eat by the pond's shore, a pair of Canada geese with two goslings in tow swam up and waddled ashore not eight feet from me as I sat quietly; and the gander stood sentry over me while his family grazed on grass.

From the trailhead, follow the Pond Loop Trail to the pond's eastern end, where it merges with the white-blazed Appalachian Trail. Turn left. The trails soon reach a woods road and split again. Turn right onto the AT, ascending a low hillside. Where the AT hooks right and crosses a brook, continue straight ahead on a short side path to an impressive beaver dam that has flooded a swamp. Backtrack, cross the brook on the AT, and within several minutes you will reach The Ledges, with a view west toward East Mountain, Mount Everett, and on a clear day the Catskills in New York. Backtrack on the AT to the woods road and turn right onto the Pond Loop Trail. Watch for where the trail bears left off the woods road (at a sign and blue blazes). The trail passes through the state forest campground on the way back to the parking area.

⓯ Jug End

2.2 mi/2.0 hrs 

Location: In Egremont; Western Massachusetts map page 238, grid c1.

User groups: Hikers, dogs, and snowshoers. No wheelchair facilities. This trail is not suitable for skis. Bikes, horses, and hunting are prohibited.

Access, fees: Parking and access are free.

Directions: From the junction of Routes 23 and 41 in Egremont, drive south on Route 41 for a tenth of a mile and turn right onto Mount Washington Road. Continue eight-tenths of a mile and turn left on Avenue Road. At a half mile, bear to the left onto Jug End Road, and continue three-tenths of a mile to a turnout on the right where the Appalachian Trail emerges from the woods. Park in the turnout.

Maps: Refer to map 3 in the "Map and Guide to the Appalachian Trail in Massachusetts and Connecticut," a five-map set for $16.95 from the Appalachian Trail Conference (see address below). For topographic maps of the area, request Ashley Falls and Great Barrington from the USGS.

Contact: Appalachian Trail Conference, P.O. Box 807, Harpers Ferry, WV 25425; (304) 535-6331.

Trail notes: I hiked up to Jug End on a morning when a leaden sky threatened rain and clouds hung low on many of the bigger hills in this part of the southern Berkshires. I considered not even making the hike of barely more than two miles—but ultimately went up and encountered some exciting conditions. At the "summit," I stood in an icy wind watching low clouds drift across the valley between rounded mountains. The view from the open ledges above cliffs at Jug End is well worth the short, if steep, hike.

From the turnout, follow the Appalachian Trail steeply uphill. Within three-tenths of a mile, the trail starts up the steep side of the ridge, reaching the first open views at about seven-tenths of a mile from the road. Jug End's summit, with good views northward of the valley and the surrounding green hills of the southern Berkshires, is 1.1 miles from the road. After you've taken in the views, head back to the parking area the same way you hiked up.

⓰ Mount Everett

5.4 mi/3.5 hrs 

Location: In Mount Washington; Western Massachusetts map page 238, grid c1.

User groups: Hikers, dogs, and snowshoers. No wheelchair facilities. This trail is not suitable for skis. Bikes, horses, and hunting are prohibited.

Access, fees: Parking and access are free.

Directions: From the junction where Routes 23 and 41 split in Egremont, follow Route 41 south for 5.2 miles to a turnout on the right. A kiosk and blue blazes mark the start of the Race Brook Trail.

Maps: The combined Southwest Massachusetts/Mount Tom and Holyoke Range/Wachusett/Dogtown trail map costs $2.95 from the Appalachian Mountain Club, (800) 262-4455. A free, rough trail and contour map of Mount Washington State Forest, which covers Mount Everett, is available at the state forest headquarters or from the Massachusetts Division of Forests and Parks (see address below). These trails are also covered on map 4 in the "Map and Guide to the Appalachian Trail in Massachusetts and Connecticut," a five-map set for $16.95 from the Appalachian Trail Conference (see address below). For a topographic map of the area, request Ashley Falls from the USGS.

Contact: Mount Washington State Forest, RD 3 East Street, Mount Washington, MA 01258; (413) 528-0330. Massachusetts Division of Forests and Parks, 100 Cambridge Street, 19th Floor, Boston, MA 02202; (617) 727-3180. Appalachian Trail Conference, P.O. Box 807, Harpers Ferry, WV 25425; (304) 535-6331.

Trail notes: Mount Everett, at 2,602 feet, is among the larger of those little hills in southwestern Massachusetts, with the green, rounded tops and steep flanks, that seem close enough for someone standing in the valley to reach out and touch. Long views east from atop Everett suggest it as a good place to catch the sunrise. As a bonus, on the way there you'll pass several waterfalls.

From the kiosk, follow the Race Brook Trail. Not far up the trail, a sign marks a side path leading right to a view of the lower falls along Race Brook. The main trail bears left and grows steeper just before crossing the brook below upper Race Brook Falls, some 80 feet high—an impressive sight at times of high runoff, most common in the spring. Above the falls, you reach a ledge with a view east. The trail then descends slightly to a third crossing of the brook.

At the Appalachian Trail, marked by signs, turn right (north) for the summit of Everett, seven-tenths of a mile distant. You will be walking on bare rock exposed by the footsteps of the many hikers who have come before you—hundreds of whom were backpacking the entire AT from Georgia to Maine. Notice how thin the soil is beside the trail, and you will understand how hiker traffic has eroded the soil on the trail. The views eastward begin before the summit, where only stunted trees and vegetation grow; in this rural southwest corner of Massachusetts, you survey the valley and an expanse of wooded hills with few signs of human presence. An abandoned fire tower marks the summit; walk toward it to a spot with views west toward the Catskills. Hike down along the same route.

17 Bash Bish Falls

0.5 mi/0.75 hr 

Location: In Bash Bish Falls State Park in Mount Washington; Western Massachusetts map page 238, grid c1.

User groups: Hikers, dogs, and snowshoers. No wheelchair facilities. Dogs must be on a leash. This trail is not suitable for bikes, horses, or skis. Hunting is allowed in season.

Access, fees: Parking and access are free.

Directions: From the junction of Routes 23 and 41 in Egremont, drive south on Route 41 for a tenth of a mile and turn right onto Mount Washington Road. Follow the signs several miles to Bash Bish Falls State Park and a turnout on the left. To reach the Mount Washington State Forest headquarters, follow the signs from Mount Washington Road.

Maps: Although no map is needed for this hike, a free trail map of the area is available at the Mount Washington State Forest headquarters, or from the Massachusetts Division of Forests and Parks (see address below). This area is covered in the combined Southwest Massachusetts/Mount Tom and Holyoke Range/Wachusett/Dogtown trail map, which is $2.95 from the Appalachian Mountain Club, (800) 262-4455. For a topographic map of the area, request Ashley Falls from the USGS.

Contact: Mount Washington State Forest, RD 3 East Street, Mount Washington, MA 01258; (413) 528-0330. Massachusetts Division of Forests and Parks, 100 Cambridge Street, 19th Floor, Boston, MA 02202; (617) 727-3180.

Trail notes: After driving one of the most winding roads in Massachusetts, you hike this short trail to what may be the state's most spectacular waterfall. The stream tumbles down through a vertical stack of giant boulders—splitting into twin columns of water around one huge, triangular block—then settles briefly in a clear, deep pool at the base of the falls before dropping in a foaming torrent through the water-carved rock walls of Bash Bish Gorge. The falls are, predictably, enhanced by spring rains and snowmelt. The Bash Bish Falls Trail is well marked with blue triangles, and a quarter-mile walk downhill from the roadside turnout leads to the falls.

⓲ Alander Mountain

6.0 mi/3.0 hrs 

Location: In Mount Washington State Forest in Mount Washington; Western Massachusetts map page 238, grid d1.

User groups: Hikers, bikes, dogs, horses, skiers, and snowshoers. No wheelchair facilities. Dogs must be on a leash. Hunting is allowed in season.

Access, fees: Parking and access are free. Backcountry camping is available in the Mount Washington State Forest, at 15 wilderness campsites just off this trail 1.5 miles from the trailhead, and in a cabin that sleeps six just below Alander's summit. The cabin (which has a wood-burning stove) and the campsites are filled on a first-come, first-served basis.

Directions: From the junction of Routes 23 and 41 in Egremont, drive south on Route 41 for a tenth of a mile and turn right onto Mount Washington Road. Follow the signs several miles to the Mount Washington State Forest headquarters on the right. The blue-blazed Alander Mountain Trail begins at a kiosk behind the headquarters.

Maps: The combined Southwest Massachusetts/Mount Tom and Holyoke Range/Wachusett/Dogtown trail map is $2.95 from the Appalachian Mountain Club, (800) 262-4455. A free, rough trail and contour map of Mount Washington State Forest is available at the state forest headquarters or from the Massachusetts Division of Forests and Parks (see address below). For a topographic map of the area, request Ashley Falls from the USGS.

Contact: Mount Washington State Forest, RD 3 East Street, Mount Washington, MA 01258; (413) 528-0330. Massachusetts Division of Forests and Parks, 100 Cambridge Street, 19th Floor, Boston, MA 02202; (617) 727-3180.

Trail notes: Less than a mile from the New York border and a few miles from Connecticut, Alander Mountain (2,240 feet) has two broad, flat summits, the westernmost having the best views of the southern Berkshires and of hills and farmland in New York all the way to the Catskill Mountains. An open ridge running south from the summit offers sweeping views. I rode my mountain bike as far as I could up the Alander Mountain Trail one spring afternoon, then hiked to the summit. Dark storm clouds drifted over the hills to the east, and shafts of sunlight daubed bright splotches over the green mountainsides while hawks floated on thermals overhead. While this is a wonderful hike, I think biking or skiing as far as possible up the trail adds another dimension to this little adventure.

From the kiosk behind the headquarters, the Alander Mountain Trail gradually ascends a woods road for much of its distance, then narrows to a trail and grows steeper. Just past the cabin, a sign points left to the east loop and right to the west loop; the west loop offers great views to the north, east, and south, and the east loop is worth checking out, too. Three old concrete blocks, probably the foundation of a former fire tower, sit at the summit. Continue over the summit on the white-blazed South Taconic Trail for views westward into New York. Then turn back and descend the way you came up.

Special note: During the winter months, be sure to watch out for snowmobiles.

⓳ Hubbard River Gorge

4.5 mi/2.5 hrs  

Location: In Granville State Forest in Granville; Western Massachusetts map page 238, grid d2.

User groups: Hikers, bikes, dogs, skiers, and snowshoers. No wheelchair facilities. Dogs must be on a leash. Sections of the trail would be difficult on a bike or skis (and could be icy in winter). Horses are prohibited. Hunting is allowed in season, except on Sundays or within 150 feet of a paved road or bike trail.

Access, fees: Parking and access are free.

Directions: From the junction of Routes 189 and 57, drive six miles west on Route 57 (eight-tenths of a mile west of the general store in West Granville) and turn left onto West Hartland Road. In another six-tenths of a mile, you pass a sign for the Granville State Forest; the rough dirt road heading left from that point is where this loop hike will emerge. Continue another three-tenths of a mile, cross the bridge over the Hubbard River, and park in the dirt lot on the left. The state forest headquarters is on West Hartland Road, six-tenths of a mile beyond the bridge.

Maps: A free map of hiking trails is available at the state forest headquarters or from the Massachusetts Division of Forests and Parks (see address below). For a topographic map of the area, request Southwick from the USGS.

Contact: Granville State Forest, 323 West Hartland Road, Granville, MA 01034; (413) 357-6611. Massachusetts Division of Forests and Parks, 100 Cambridge Street, 19th Floor, Boston, MA 02202; (617) 727-3180.

Trail notes: This loop features the highlight of this out-of-the-way state forest—the Hubbard River Gorge, which drops 450 feet over 2.5 miles through numerous falls. I've done this hike in winter, when ice made the going treacherous and beautiful in places, and in a spring rain and hailstorm when the river swelled with runoff.

From the dirt lot, backtrack over the bridge and turn right onto the paved road leading a half mile to Hubbard River Campground; the Hubbard River Trail begins at the end of the road. (When the metal gate at the road to the campground is open, usually mid-May to mid-October, you can drive to the road's cul-de-sac and park at the trailhead for a shorter loop of about 2.5 miles on the Hubbard River and Woods Trails.) Follow an old woods road, marked by blue triangles bearing a hiker symbol, southeast along the Hubbard River. After turning briefly away from the river, the road hugs the rim of the spectacular gorge, passing many spots that afford views of the river. The trail parallels the river for about a mile; then the Woods Trail branches left and circles back to the Hubbard River Trail, where you'll turn right to return to the campground road. This loop continues a bit farther on the Hubbard River Trail, then swings left at the blue arrows onto the Ore Hill Trail, which ascends a small hill through pleasant forest and follows the state forest boundary back to West Hartland Road. Turn left and walk the road back to the dirt lot. In spring the Ore Hill Trail can be flooded and muddy, so you may want to take the shorter loop.

Special note: If you want to cross-country ski elsewhere in the state forest, check out the short but scenic Beaver Pond Loop beyond the forest headquarters on West Hartland Road, or the loop from the headquarters on the CCC and Corduroy Trails. One last note: This quiet corner of Massachusetts is a wonderful area to drive through—or, better yet, bicycle. The villages of Granville and West Granville are both on the National Register of Historic Districts.

20 Northfield Mountain: Rose Ledge

5–6 mi/3.5 hrs  

Location: In Northfield; Western Massachusetts map page 238, grid a4.

User groups: Hikers, dogs, and snowshoers. No wheelchair facilities. Dogs must

be on a leash. Bikes, horses, hunting, and skis are prohibited from parts of this trail.

Access, fees: No fee is charged for parking or trail use, with the exception of a trail fee for cross-country skiing. Bikers must register once per season at the visitors center, and horseback riders must check in for parking and trail information; helmets are required for both biking and riding. Trails are often closed to bikes and horses during mud season, usually until late April.

Directions: The Northfield Mountain Visitors Center is off Route 63, 5.8 miles south of its junction with Route 10 and 2.5 miles north of Route 2. The visitors center is open from 9 A.M. to 5 P.M., Wednesday through Sunday, spring through fall. The cross-country center is open 9 A.M. to 5 P.M. every day during the ski season.

Maps: A trail map is available at the visitors center. For topographic maps of the area, request Northfield and Orange from the USGS.

Contact: Northfield Mountain Recreation and Environmental Center, 99 Millers Falls Road (Route 63), Northfield, MA 01360; (413) 659-3714.

Trail notes: Owned by Northeast Utilities, the Northfield Mountain Recreation and Environmental Center's 25 miles of hiking and multi-use trails comprises one of the best trail systems open year-round in Massachusetts. The Metacomet-Monadnock Trail is not far from this system, and can be reached via a marked trail off the 10th Mountain Trail near Bugaboo Pass. Other activities, including orienteering, canoeing on the nearby Connecticut River, and educational programs, are conducted through the center. This hike takes in some of the mountain's best features—including the Rose Ledge cliffs and a view of the reservoir at the 1,100-foot summit—but many other loop options are possible here.

From the parking lot, follow the wide carriage road of the 10th Mountain Trail to the right. At the sign, turn left onto a footpath, the Rose Ledge Trail (marked here by blue diamonds). Follow the trail across a carriage road, then turn right where the trail follows orange blazes. Cross two carriage roads, Hemlock Hill and Jug End. Then the Rose Ledge Trail forks: the left branch traverses above the cliffs, and the right branch below them. Either is a nice hike, and both branches link at the opposite end of the cliffs.

This hike begins above the cliffs, with some views of nearby wooded hills, then drops below them for close-up views of the cliffs themselves. Bear left at the fork, and just before reaching the wide carriage road called Rock Oak Ramble, turn right at an easily overlooked trail leading downhill (parallel to Rock Oak Ramble). Reaching the Lower Ledge Trail, turn left and cross Rock Oak Ramble. You're soon walking below the cliffs, and may see rock climbers on them; be careful of loose rock falling from above if you venture near the cliff base. After rejoining the Rose Ledge Trail, continue straight on the Mariah Foot Trail to the Hill 'n Dale carriage road; turn right, then left onto the 10th Mountain carriage road. At a junction marked number 32 (corresponding to the trail map), turn right for the summit, which has a reservoir viewing platform. Descend to junction 32 and turn left on 10th Mountain, right on Hill 'n Dale, right at junction 16 onto Rock Oak Ramble, left at junction 8 onto Hemlock Hill, then right onto the orange-blazed Rose Ledge Trail, backtracking to the parking lot.

21 Crag Mountain

3.4 mi/2.0 hrs 

Location: In Northfield; Western Massachusetts map page 238, grid a4.

User groups: Hikers, dogs, and snowshoers. No wheelchair facilities. The trail is not suitable for bikes, horses, or skis. This hike is on private land; assume that hunting is allowed unless otherwise posted.

Access, fees: Parking and access are free.

Directions: From Route 10/63 in Northfield, about two-tenths of a mile south of the town center and three-tenths of a mile north of the southern junction of Routes 10 and 63, turn west onto Maple Street, which becomes Gulf Road. Drive 3.1 miles to a turnout on the right, where the white blazes of the Metacomet-Monadnock Trail enter the woods.

Maps: The Guide to the Metacomet-Monadnock Trail, which includes maps, is $6.95 from New England Cartographics, P.O. Box 9369, North Amherst, MA 01059; (413) 549-4124. For a topographic map of the area, request Northfield from the USGS.

Contact: Appalachian Mountain Club Berkshire Chapter, P.O. Box 9369, North Amherst, MA 01059.

Trail notes: This easy hike leads to Crag Mountain, a rocky outcropping on the ridge with excellent views. Follow the white-blazed Metacomet-Monadnock Trail south. The trail crosses one wet area, rises gently through a mixed deciduous and conifer forest, and reaches Crag's open summit 1.7 miles from the road. The views take in the Berkshires and the southern Green Mountains of Vermont to the west and northwest, Mount Monadnock to the northeast, the hills of central Massachusetts to the east, and the Northfield Mountain Reservoir, Mount Toby, and Sugarloaf Mountain to the south. Hike back along the same route.

22 Bear's Den

0.2 mi/0.5 hr 

Location: In New Salem; Western Massachusetts map page 238, grid b4.

User groups: Hikers and snowshoers. No wheelchair facilities. This trail is not suitable for bikes, dogs, horses, or skis. Hunting is prohibited.

Access, fees: Parking and access are free. The reservation closes at sunset.

Directions: From the junction of U.S. 202 and Route 122 in New Salem, follow U.S. 202 south for four-tenths of a mile. Turn right onto Elm Street, drive seven-tenths of a mile, then turn left onto Neilson Road. Drive a half mile and park at the roadside. The entrance is on the right, where a short trail leads to the gorge.

Maps: No map is necessary for this short and easy walk.

Contact: Trustees of Reservations, 572 Essex Street, Beverly, MA 01915-1530; (508) 921-1944.

Trail notes: This compact but dramatic gorge along the Middle Branch of the Swift River is a beautiful spot just minutes from the road. Follow the trail up and left to reach the rim of the gorge, where you can stand at the brink of a precipitous drop to the river. Then double back and follow the trail downhill, to the banks of the river, where the foundations of an old grist mill still stand. A sign near the beginning of the trail relates some of this spot's history: how a settler killed a black bear here, thus explaining the name Bear's Den; and how the Wampanoag Indian chief King Phillip supposedly met with other chiefs here in 1675, during their wars with European settlers in the Connecticut Valley.

23 Mount Toby

5.0 mi/2.5 hrs 

Location: In Sunderland; Western Massachusetts map page 238, grid b4.

User groups: Hikers, dogs, and snowshoers. No wheelchair facilities. Dogs must be on a leash. Parts of the trail are not suitable for bikes, horses, or skis, but Summit Road is open to them (see the trail notes below). Hunting is allowed in season.

Access, fees: Parking and access are free.

Directions: The Mount Toby Summit Road is off Reservation Road, which comes off Route 47, nine-tenths of a mile south of its junction with Route 63 and just north of the Sunderland town line (there may not be a sign for Reservation Road). Follow it for a half mile and park in a dirt lot on the right, just past the sign for the Mount Toby Forest.

Maps: The Mount Toby trail map is $3.25 from New England Cartographics, P.O. Box 9369, North Amherst, MA 01059; (413) 549-4124. For topographic maps of the area, request Greenfield and Williamsburg from the USGS.

Contact: There is no contact agency for this hike.

Trail notes: The well-maintained Summit Road provides a route to the top of Mount Toby that can be hiked easily—or biked or skied by anyone seeking a fairly challenging climb and a fast descent. The hike described here descends the steeper Telephone Line Trail; skiers or bikers should descend the Summit Road instead. Toby's 1,269-foot summit is wooded, but a fire tower open to the public offers a 360-degree panorama with views stretching 50 miles across five states on a clear day.

The Summit Road begins behind the Mount Toby Forest sign (don't turn right onto the orange-blazed Robert Frost Trail, although that is an alternate descent route). Frequent white blazes begin a short distance down the road. After less than a mile, the Telephone Line Trail diverges right. Approaching the summit, the road coincides with the orange-blazed Robert Frost Trail. From the fire tower, follow the power lines down to the Summit Road. Another option is to pick up the Robert Frost Trail, which diverges left about halfway down the Telephone Line Trail and also leads back to the start of the Summit Road.

24 South Sugarloaf Mountain

1.5 mi/1.5 hrs 

Location: In Mount Sugarloaf State Reservation in South Deerfield; Western Massachusetts map page 238, grid b3.

User groups: Hikers and dogs. No wheelchair facilities. Dogs must be on a leash. This trail would be difficult to snowshoe, and is not suitable for bikes, horses, or skis. Hunting is prohibited.

Access, fees: Parking and access are free.

Directions: From the junction of Routes 47 and 116 in Sunderland, drive seven-tenths of a mile west on Route 116 and turn right onto Sugarloaf Road. The Mount Sugarloaf State Reservation Summit Road begins immediately on the right; park in the dirt lot along Sugarloaf Road just beyond the turn for the Summit Road.

Maps: For a free, basic map of hiking trails, contact the Mount Sugarloaf State Reservation or the Massachusetts Division of Forests and Parks (see addresses below). The Mount Toby trail map, which covers the Mount Sugarloaf State Reservation, is $3.25 from New England Cartographics, P.O. Box 9369, North Amherst, MA 01059; (413) 549-4124. For a topographic map of the area, request Williamsburg from the USGS.

Contact: Mount Sugarloaf State Reservation, Sugarloaf Street (Route 116), South Deerfield, MA 01373; (413) 665-2928. Massachusetts Division of Forests and Parks, 100 Cambridge Street, 19th Floor, Boston, MA 02202; (617) 727-3180.

Trail notes: At just 652 feet above sea level, South Sugarloaf is barely a hill—but one that rises abruptly from the flat valley, its cliffs looming over the wide Connecticut River. Reached via this short but strenuous hike, the summit of South Sugarloaf offers some of the best views of the Connecticut Valley in Massachusetts.

From the parking lot, the wide (though unmarked) West Side Trail leads into the woods. A side trail branches right immediately, soon leading across the Summit Road to the start of the Pocumtuck Ridge Trail, marked by a wooden post without a sign. (The Pocumtuck Ridge Trail can also be reached by walking up the Summit Road about 100 feet inside the gate.) Follow the blue blazes straight up the steep hillside under power lines; the trail finally makes several switchbacks just below the summit. It follows the edge of the fence, with sweeping views from atop the cliffs. An observation tower on the summit provides a 360-degree panorama.

Cross the summit to the lower parking lot, where the blue-blazed Pocumtuck Ridge Trail re-enters the woods and follows the clifftop, descending steeply and passing a fenced overlook. After crossing the Summit Road's hairpin turn, descend an old woods road to where the trail forks, and turn left onto the sporadically red-blazed West Side Trail. Just before reaching a dead-end paved road, the trail turns left, skirting the edges of fields and returning to the parking lot. If hiking a loop isn't important to you, go up the West Side Trail and the Pocumtuck Ridge Trail to the summit, then return the same way; though somewhat longer, it's a more pleasant hike than the lower stretch of the Pocumtuck Ridge Trail.

---

25 Fire Tower Hike

3.0 mi/2.0 hrs 

Location: In D.A.R. State Forest in Goshen; Western Massachusetts map page 238, grid b3.

User groups: Hikers, dogs, and snowshoers. No wheelchair facilities. Dogs must be on a leash. This trail is not suitable for bikes, horses, or skis. Hunting is prohibited.

Access, fees: There is a $2 charge for parking between Memorial Day and Labor Day.

Directions: From Interstate 91 northbound, take exit 19 onto Route 9 west. In Goshen, turn right onto Route 112 north. The park entrance will be on your right. From Interstate 91 southbound, take exit 25 for Route 116 west. In Ashfield, turn left onto Route 112 south. The park entrance will be on your left. In summer, park in the second lot along Moore Hill Road, located just past the left turn for the boat launch and nature center. In winter, park in the first lot, near the bathrooms and warming hut (Moore Hill Road is not maintained beyond that point).

Maps: A free, basic trail map, which is not perfectly accurate on trail locations but is useful, is available at the state forest or from the Massachusetts Division of Forests and Parks, 100 Cambridge Street, 19th Floor, Boston, MA 02202; (617) 727-3180.

Contact: D.A.R. State Forest, Route 112, Goshen, Massachusetts, (413) 268-7098; or mail to East Street, Williamsburg, MA 01096.

Trail notes: This 1,500-acre state forest has a network of fun forest roads for mountain biking or cross-country skiing, hiking trails through interesting woodlands, and a hilltop fire tower that affords 360-degree views of the countryside. (See hike numbers 26 and 27 for two other possibilities.) This hike follows the Long Trail (not to be confused with the trail running the length of Vermont), which begins between the boat launch and the night registration office and makes a circuitous route of about 1.5 miles through the state forest to the fire tower. Climbing the tower's steps, you get a 360-degree panorama of the surrounding countryside, with views stretching to Mount Monadnock to the northeast, the

Holyoke Range and Mount Tom to the southeast, and Mount Greylock to the northwest. Descend the same way you hiked up.

26 D.A.R. State Forest Ski Touring Loop

6.0 mi/3.5 hrs 

Location: In D.A.R. State Forest in Goshen; Western Massachusetts map page 238, grid b3.

User groups: Hikers, bikes, dogs, horses, skiers, and snowshoers. No wheelchair facilities. Dogs must be on a leash. Hunting is prohibited.

Access, fees: There is a $2 charge for parking between Memorial Day and Labor Day.

Directions: From Interstate 91 northbound, take exit 19 onto Route 9 west. In Goshen, turn right onto Route 112 north. The park entrance will be on your right. From Interstate 91 southbound, take exit 25 for Route 116 west. In Ashfield, turn left onto Route 112 south. The park entrance will be on your left. In summer, park in the second lot along Moore Hill Road, located just past the left turn for the boat launch and nature center. In winter, park in the first lot, near the bathrooms and warming hut (Moore Hill Road is not maintained beyond that point).

Maps: A free, basic trail map, which is not perfectly accurate on trail locations but is useful, is available at the state forest or from the Massachusetts Division of Forests and Parks, 100 Cambridge Street, 19th Floor, Boston, MA 02202; (617) 727-3180.

Contact: D.A.R. State Forest, Route 112, Goshen, Massachusetts, (413) 268-7098; or mail to East Street, Williamsburg, MA 01096.

Trail notes: I've included this loop for cross-country skiers looking for a moderate ski tour and a nice view from a fire tower. The approximately six-mile route largely follows state forest roads that are not maintained in winter; a friend and I skied this one winter when we could not find snow in much of Massachusetts and southern New Hampshire, and we found plenty of it in D.A.R. State Forest. From spring through fall, the road that this route follows is maintained for vehicular traffic; the better choice for a hike during that time would be hike number 25, the Fire Tower Hike.

Head out from the first parking lot on Moore Hill Road, ascending to the fire tower; a sign will direct you to it. If you climb the tower's steps, you will enjoy a 360-degree panorama of the surrounding countryside, with views stretching to Mount Monadnock to the northeast, the Holyoke Range and Mount Tom to the southeast, and Mount Greylock to the northwest. Backtrack down from the tower, but before reaching Moore Hill Road, turn right onto another woods road, Oak Hill Road, which descends steeply to a junction with Wing Hollow Road. Turn left and continue until you reach pavement; carry your skis about a quarter mile, then turn left onto Moore Hill Road and head up the long climb back up over the hill and down to the parking area. You could also combine this with hike number 27 out to Balancing Rock, though short sections of that trail might be difficult on skis (we skied out there and had a ball, though). Don't expect many signs marking roads or trails.

27 Balancing Rock

1.0 mi/0.75 hr 

Location: In D.A.R. State Forest in Goshen; Western Massachusetts map page 238, grid b3.

User groups: Hikers, dogs, skiers, and snowshoers. No wheelchair facilities. Dogs must be on a leash. This trail is not suitable for horses. Hunting is prohibited.

Access, fees: There is a $2 charge per

vehicle for parking between Memorial Day and Labor Day.

Directions: From Interstate 91 northbound, take exit 19 onto Route 9 west. In Goshen, turn right onto Route 112 north. The park entrance will be on your right. From Interstate 91 southbound, take exit 25 for Route 116 west. In Ashfield, turn left onto Route 112 south. The park entrance will be on your left. In summer, park in the second lot along Moore Hill Road, located just past the left turn for the boat launch and nature center. In winter, park in the first lot, near the bathrooms and warming hut (Moore Hill Road is not maintained beyond that point).

Maps: A free, basic trail map, which is not perfectly accurate on trail locations but is useful, is available at the state forest or from the Massachusetts Division of Forests and Parks, 100 Cambridge Street, 19th Floor, Boston, MA 02202; (617) 727-3180.

Contact: D.A.R. State Forest, Route 112, Goshen, Massachusetts, (413) 268-7098; or mail to East Street, Williamsburg, MA 01096.

Trail notes: Here is a hike of about one mile that is both worthwhile and easy—even for young children—which leads to an interesting glacial erratic out in the woods. A friend and I skied these trails to find the boulder wearing a cap of white one winter afternoon.

Head south along the woods road opposite the second parking lot, following the blue blazes. At the intersection of several trails, turn left onto the trail with orange blazes and follow it all the way to Balancing Rock, a truck-size boulder in the woods. Continue to follow the orange blazes past Balancing Rock, paralleling a stone wall at one point, back to a wide trail in the dark woods, where you'll turn right and return shortly to the start of the orange-blazed trail. At this point turn left and retrace your route back to the parking lot.

28 Norwottuck Trail

10.1 mi. one way/5.0 hrs 

Location: In Northampton; Western Massachusetts map page 238, grid c3.

User groups: Hikers, bikes, dogs, skiers, snowshoers, and wheelchair users. Dogs must be on a leash. Horses and hunting are prohibited.

Access, fees: Parking and access are free.

Directions: To reach the western end of the trail from the south, take Interstate 91 to exit 19. Down the off-ramp, drive straight through the intersection and turn right into the Connecticut River Greenway State Park/Elwell Recreation Area. From the north, take Interstate 91 to exit 20. Turn left at the traffic lights and drive 1.5 miles to the Elwell Recreation Area on the left. The trail can also be accessed from four other parking areas: behind the Bread and Circus store in the Mountain Farms Mall on Route 9 in Hadley, 3.7 miles from the Elwell Recreation Area parking lot; near the junction of Mill Lane and Southeast Street off Route 9 in Amherst; on Station Road in Amherst (reached via Southeast Street off Route 9), 1.6 miles from the trail's eastern terminus; and at its eastern terminus, on Warren Wright Road in Belchertown.

Maps: A brochure/map is available at both trailheads. For topographic maps of the area, request Easthampton and Holyoke from the USGS.

Contact: Elwell State Park, 136 Damon Road, Northampton, MA 01060; (413) 586-8706. Massachusetts Division of Forests and Parks, 100 Cambridge Street, 19th Floor, Boston, MA 02202; (617) 727-3180.

Trail notes: The 10.1-mile-long Norwottuck Trail is a paved bike path which follows a former railroad bed from Northampton, through Hadley and Amherst, into Belchertown. Its flat course provides a linear recreation area for walkers, runners, bicyclists, in-line skaters, cross-country skiers, snowshoers, and people in wheelchairs. As with any bike or pedestrian path, it is popular with families because it provides a refuge from traffic. The place many users access the trail from is the large parking lot at its western end; but that is often full, so it's wise to try one of the other access points among those listed above, in the directions. Park officials are hoping to complete an extension of the Norwottuck to Woodmont Road in Northampton—eventually reaching Look Park—by 1998.

29 Mount Holyoke

3.2 mi/2.0 hrs 

Location: In Skinner State Park in Hadley; Western Massachusetts map page 238, grid c3.

User groups: Hikers, dogs, and snowshoers. No wheelchair facilities. Dogs must be on a leash. This trail is not suitable for bikes, horses, or skis. Hunting is prohibited.

Access, fees: Parking and access are free.

Directions: From the junction of Routes 47 and 9 in Hadley, drive south on Route 47 for 4.9 miles (you will see the Summit House on the ridge of Mount Holyoke straight ahead). Across from the Hockanum Cemetery, turn left, continue a tenth of a mile, and park at the roadside where the white blazes of the Metacomet-Monadnock Trail enter the woods on the right. Or, from the junction of Routes 47 and 116 in South Hadley, drive north on Route 47 for 2.7 miles and turn right at Hockanum Cemetery, then continue a tenth of a mile to the trailhead.

Maps: A free trail map of Skinner State Park is available at the Halfway House on Mountain Road (off Route 47) when a staff person is there; at the Notch Visitors Center on Route 116, where the Metacomet-Monadnock Trail crosses the road and enters Holyoke Range State Park in Amherst; or from the Massachusetts Division of Forests and Parks (see address below). The combined Southwest Massachusetts/Mount Tom and the Holyoke Range/Wachusett/Dogtown trail map and the combined Mount Toby/Mount Tom and the Holyoke Range/Mount Greylock/Pittsfield State Forest maps each are $2.95 from the Appalachian Mountain Club, (800) 262-4455. The Holyoke Range/Skinner State Park (Western section) Trail Map is $3.25, and guide to the Metacomet-Monadnock Trail is $6.95, from New England Cartographics, P.O. Box 9369, North Amherst, MA 01059; (413) 549-4124. For a topographic map of the area, request Mount Holyoke from the USGS.

Contact: Skinner State Park, Route 47, Box 91, Hadley, MA 01035; (413) 586-0350 or (413) 253-2883. Massachusetts Division of Forests and Parks, 100 Cambridge Street, 19th Floor, Boston, MA 02202; (617) 727-3180. Appalachian Mountain Club, Berkshire Chapter, P.O. Box 9369, North Amherst, MA 01059.

Trail notes: Along the up-and-down ridge of Mount Holyoke, the Summit House stands out prominently, easily visible to motorists on Interstate 91 several miles to the west. While mostly wooded, this rugged ridgeline has several overlooks which afford splendid views west of the Connecticut Valley and to the Berkshires, and some views southward.

Follow the Metacomet-Monadnock Trail east from the road, immediately climbing a steep hillside; the trail soon swings north and ascends the ridge, reaching first views in just over a half mile. At 1.6 miles, the trail passes by the Summit House, which is open sporadically, when staffed; the views of the Connecticut Valley from here are excellent. You can return the way you came up, or continue over the summit, crossing the paved Mountain Road, and turning right (south) in Taylor's Notch onto the red-blazed Dry Brook Trail. Follow it down that small valley, trending to the southwest and finally to the west and back to your vehicle.

30 Mount Tom

5.4 mi/2.5 hrs 

Location: In Mount Tom State Reservation in Holyoke; Western Massachusetts map page 238, grid c3.

User groups: Hikers and snowshoers. No wheelchair facilities. Dogs must be on a leash. This trail is not suitable for skis. Bikes, horses, and hunting are prohibited.

Access, fees: Parking and access are free, except on weekends and holidays from Memorial Day weekend through Columbus Day, when $2 per vehicle is charged for parking.

Directions: Take Interstate 91 to exit 18, then U.S. 5 south for roughly 3.3 miles. Turn right onto Smiths Ferry Road, at the entrance to Mount Tom State Reservation. Follow the road for nearly a mile, passing under Interstate 91 (immediately after which the reservation headquarters are on the right), to a horseshoe-shaped parking area on the right. The parking is about two-tenths of a mile before the stone house interpretive center, where Smiths Ferry Road meets Christopher Clark Road, and just beyond a paved, dead-end road.

Maps: A free map of hiking trails is available at the reservation headquarters and the stone house, or from the Massachusetts Division of Forests and Parks, 100 Cambridge Street, 19th Floor, Boston, MA 02202; (617) 727-3180. The combined Southwest Massachusetts/Mount Tom and Holyoke Range/Wachusett/Dogtown trail map is $2.95 from the Appalachian Mountain Club, (800) 262-4455. The Mount Tom Reservation trail map is $3.25 from New England Cartographics, P.O. Box 9369, North Amherst, MA 01059; (413) 549-4124. For topographic maps of the area, request Mount Tom, Easthampton, Mount Holyoke, and Springfield North from the USGS.

Contact: Mount Tom State Reservation, P.O. Box 985, Northampton, MA 01061; (413) 527-4805 or (413) 534-1186.

Trail notes: One of the most popular stretches of the 98-mile Metacomet-Monadnock Trail is the traverse of the Mount Tom Ridge. A steep mountainside capped by tall basalt cliffs defines Mount Tom's west face, and the trail follows the brink of that precipice for nearly two miles, treating the hiker to commanding views west as far as the Berkshires on a clear day.

From the parking area, walk up the paved road toward the stone house for about 75 yards. Turn right and enter the woods at a trail marked by white rectangular blazes and a triangular marker for the Metacomet-Monadnock Trail. Within minutes, the trail veers right and climbs steeply toward Goat Peak. Pass a good view westward, then reach the open clearing of Goat Peak, where the lookout tower offers a 360-degree panorama. Double back to Smiths Ferry Road, turn right, walk about 75 yards, and then enter the woods on the left, following the white blazes of the Metacomet-Monadnock. It crosses the Quarry Trail, then ascends the ridge. Numerous side paths lead to the right to great views from the cliffs, each view better than the last until you reach the summit of Mount Tom, where there are radio and television transmission stations. Retrace your steps on the Metacomet-Monadnock Trail to your car.

31 Mount Watatic and Nutting Hill

2.8 mi/1.5 hrs 

Location: In Ashburnham; Western Massachusetts map page 238, grid a6.

User groups: Hikers, dogs, and snowshoers. No wheelchair facilities. This trail is not suitable for bikes, horses, or skis. Hunting is allowed in season.

Access, fees: Parking and access are free.

Directions: The trailhead parking area is on the north side of Route 119 in Ashburnham, 1.4 miles west of its junction with Route 101.

Maps: For a contour map of hiking trails, obtain the Wapack Trail map available for $3 from the Friends of the Wapack (see address below). For a topographic map of the area, request Ashburnham from the USGS.

Contact: Friends of the Wapack, P.O. Box 115, West Peterborough, NH 03468. Midstate Trail Committee, Stanton Whitman, 17 Stoneleigh Road, Worcester, MA 01606.

Trail notes: Mount Watatic's 1,832-foot elevation barely qualifies it as anything but a big hill. But the pair of barren, rocky summits offer excellent views of nearby peaks such as Wachusett and Monadnock, as well as the entire Wapack Range extending north—and, on a clear day, landmarks as distant as Mount Greylock, the White Mountains of New Hampshire, and the Boston skyline. Watatic can feel like a bigger mountain, especially when the wind kicks up on its exposed crown. This loop uses the Wapack and Midstate Trails to encompass Nutting Hill, whose flat, open summit offers some views. Both trails are well blazed with yellow triangles.

From the parking area, follow an old woods road north, ascending gradually. At three-tenths of a mile, the Wapack Trail—also known in this section as the Blueberry Ledge Trail—turns right (east), reaching the summit of Watatic in another mile. But this hike continues straight ahead on the Midstate Trail. Where the Midstate turns left onto a more narrow hiking trail a half mile farther, continue straight on the woods road, reaching the Wapack Trail within another two-tenths of a mile. It is nearly a mile from this point to Watatic's summit. Turn right (southeast), soon passing over the open top of Nutting Hill; watch for cairns leading directly over the hill and into the woods. Climbing Watatic's northwest slope, you'll pass somewhat overgrown trails of the former ski area. Just below the summit stands an abandoned fire tower, now closed and unsafe. From the summit, an unmarked path leads to the lower, southeast summit. Double back to the fire tower, turn left, and follow the Wapack, passing an open ledge with views and, farther down, an enormous split boulder. At the Midstate Trail junction, turn left for the parking area.

32 Willard Brook

2.0 mi/1.0 hr 

Location: In Willard Brook State Forest in Ashby; Western Massachusetts map page 238, grid a6.

User groups: Hikers, dogs, skiers, and snowshoers. No wheelchair facilities. Dogs must be on a leash. Bikes and horses are prohibited. Hunting is allowed in season.

Access, fees: Parking and access are free.

Directions: Park at the Damon Pond entrance off Route 119 in Ashby, 1.3 miles west of the Willard Brook State Forest headquarters and two-tenths of a mile east of the junction of Routes 119 and 31. The gate is closed in winter, so park in the roadside pullout.

Maps: A free, basic trail map of the state forest is available at the headquarters on Route 119 in West Townsend, just before the Ashby town line, or from the Massachusetts Division of Forests and Parks (see address below). For a topographic map of the area, request Ashburnham from the USGS.

Contact: Willard Brook State Forest, Route 119, West Townsend, MA 01474; (508) 597-

8802. Massachusetts Division of Forests and Parks, 100 Cambridge Street, 19th Floor, Boston, MA 02202; (617) 727-3180.

Trail notes: This easy walk hugs the rock-strewn Willard Brook through its tight valley. You'll walk through hemlock groves and among huge boulders. This is a good, gentle hike to introduce very young children to the woods. The trail begins from either side of the stone bridge over Willard Brook, just below Damon Pond. Toward the other (northeast) end of the trail, it ascends a hillside and reaches a forest road; turning left brings you shortly to the state forest headquarters. Most people just double back to the start. There are several miles of woods roads in the state forest open to other activities such as mountain biking or horseback riding.

0.7 mi/0.75 hr 

Location: In Leominster State Forest in Westminster; Western Massachusetts map page 238, grid b6.

User groups: Hikers, dogs, and snowshoers. No wheelchair facilities. Dogs must be on a leash. This trail is not suitable for bikes, horses, or skis. Hunting is allowed in season.

Access, fees: From May through October, a $2 parking fee is collected; a season pass costs $15. The parking lot may not always be plowed in winter; call the state forest headquarters for more information.

Directions: The hike begins from a large parking lot at the Crow Hills Pond Picnic Area along Route 31 on the Westminster–Princeton line, 2.2 miles south of the junction of Routes 31 and 2, and 1.5 miles north of the junction of Routes 31 and 140.

Maps: A free, basic trail map of Leominster State Forest is available at the state forest headquarters or from the Massachusetts Division of Forests and Parks (see address below). The Wachusett Mountain and Leominster State Forest Trail Map is $3.25 from New England Cartographics, P.O. Box 9369, North Amherst, MA 01059; (413) 549-4124. For a topographic map of the area, request Fitchburg from the USGS.

Contact: Leominster State Forest, Route 31, Princeton, MA 01541; (508) 874-2303. Massachusetts Division of Forests and Parks, 100 Cambridge Street, 19th Floor, Boston, MA 02202; (617) 727-3180.

Trail notes: The hike up Crow Hills, at the western edge of the more than 4,000-acre Leominster State Forest, is a short loop that can be done with young children, though it gets steep and rocky in brief sections (where snowshoeing could be tricky). Despite its brevity, it is one of the nicest in central Massachusetts, traversing the top of tall cliffs with commanding views of the wooded hills and ponds of the state forest and of Wachusett Mountain.

From the parking lot, cross Route 31 to a wide, well-marked trail entering the woods. Within 100 feet, the trail turns sharply left, then swings right and climbs fairly steeply to the base of cliffs 100 feet high in places. The trail then diverges right and left, both branches looping up to the top of the cliffs. You can hike the loop in either direction; this description leads to the right (counterclockwise). Walk below the cliff to where stones arranged in steps lead steeply uphill to a junction with the Midstate Trail, marked by yellow triangular blazes. Turn left, carefully following the trail atop the cliffs past several spots that offer sweeping views; the best views are at the far end of the cliffs. Wachusett Mountain, with its ski slopes, is visible to the southwest. Take care not to kick any loose stones; there often are rock climbers and hikers below. From the last open ledges, the Midstate Trail swings right, entering the woods again and continuing about 75 yards, then turning left and descending a steep, rocky gully. At its bottom, turn left again and, diverging from the Midstate, walk the trail around the base of the cliffs to the beginning of this loop. Turn right and descend to the parking lot.

34 Ball Hill Loop

3.5 mi/2.5 hrs 

Location: In Leominster State Forest in Westminster, Princeton, and Leominster; Western Massachusetts map page 238, grid b6.

User groups: Hikers, dogs, and snowshoers. No wheelchair facilities. Dogs must be on a leash. This trail is not suitable for bikes, horses, or skis. Hunting is allowed in season.

Access, fees: From May through October, a $2 parking fee is collected; a season pass costs $15. The parking lot may not always be plowed in winter; call the state forest headquarters for more information.

Directions: The hike begins from a large parking lot at the Crow Hills Pond Picnic Area along Route 31 on the Westminster–Princeton line, 2.2 miles south of the junction of Routes 31 and 2, and 1.5 miles north of the junction of Routes 31 and 140.

Maps: A free, basic trail map of Leominster State Forest is available at the state forest headquarters or from the Massachusetts Division of Forests and Parks (see address below). The Wachusett Mountain and Leominster State Forest Trail Map is $3.25 from New England Cartographics, P.O. Box 9369, North Amherst, MA 01059; (413) 549-4124. For a topographic map of the area, request Fitchburg from the USGS.

Contact: Leominster State Forest, Route 31, Princeton, MA 01541; (508) 874-2303. Massachusetts Division of Forests and Parks, 100 Cambridge Street, 19th Floor, Boston, MA 02202; (617) 727-3180.

Trail notes: Leominster State Forest has a network of marked trails and less-distinct footpaths weaving throughout it, most of them in its northern half, north of Rocky Pond Road/Parmenter Road. (South of that dirt road, which is not open to motor vehicles, the state forest is crossed mainly by old woods roads.) This hike ascends one of the low, wooded hills in the state forest, into an area I've wandered into countless times—having grown up in Leominster—but where I still run across trails I don't recognize, or end up someplace I did not expect to end up. There are myriad trails through here, and it's easy to get lost once you venture over Ball Hill.

From the parking area, walk across the earthen dike between the two halves of Crow Hills Pond, then turn right, following a blazed trail south along the shore of the pond. Within a half mile, turn left (east) onto the Rocky Pond Trail, which climbs, steeply for short stretches, up Ball Hill. Near the top of that hill, about one mile from the hike's start, is a spot where the trees thin enough to allow a partially obstructed view of the hills to the west. Anyone concerned about getting lost might want to turn back from here. Otherwise, continue over the hill, through quiet woods crossed by the occasional stone wall.

Descending the back side of the hill, ignore the trails branching off to the right. Turn left at the first opportunity; about 2.5 miles from the parking area, you will see a landfill through the trees at the edge of the state forest. The trail swings north, then west; continue bearing left at trail junctions. On your way back you will pass through a wet area, over a low hillock, and eventually reach the paved parking lot at the public beach at the north end of Crow Hills Pond. Cross the parking lot to the south (left), picking up the trail again for the short walk back to the dike across the pond.

35 Leominster Forest Roads Loop

5.5 mi/3.0 hrs 

Location: In Leominster State Forest in Westminster, Princeton, and Leominster; Western Massachusetts map page 238, grid b6.

User groups: Hikers, bikes, dogs, skiers, and snowshoers. No wheelchair facilities. Dogs must be on a leash. Horses are prohibited. Hunting is allowed in season.

Access, fees: From May through October, a $2 parking fee is collected; a season pass costs $15. The parking lot may not always be plowed in winter; call the state forest headquarters for more information.

Directions: The hike begins from a large parking lot at the Crow Hills Pond Picnic Area along Route 31 on the Westminster–Princeton line, 2.2 miles south of the junction of Routes 31 and 2, and 1.5 miles north of the junction of Routes 31 and 140.

Maps: A free, basic trail map of Leominster State Forest is available at the state forest headquarters or from the Massachusetts Division of Forests and Parks (see address below). The Wachusett Mountain and Leominster State Forest Trail Map is $3.25 from New England Cartographics, P.O. Box 9369, North Amherst, MA 01059; (413) 549-4124. For a topographic map of the area, request Fitchburg from the USGS.

Contact: Leominster State Forest, Route 31, Princeton, MA 01541; (508) 874-2303. Massachusetts Division of Forests and Parks, 100 Cambridge Street, 19th Floor, Boston, MA 02202; (617) 727-3180.

Trail notes: This loop of approximately 5.5 miles largely follows old woods roads through the southern half of Leominster State Forest, making it particularly fun on cross-country skis or a mountain bike. I've skied this loop and other roads in here many times; I especially enjoy coming to this state forest in winter. There are small hills along these roads—nothing which is difficult to hike, but which can make skiing or biking fairly strenuous.

From the parking lot, cross the picnic area and the earthen dike dividing the two halves of Crow Hills Pond. Across the dike, turn right (south), following the trail along the pond and past it, about seven-tenths of a mile to the rough, dirt Rocky Pond Road (which is not open to motor vehicles). Cross Rocky Pond Road onto Wolf Rock Road and continue about a half mile. Where the road forks, bear right, then watch for an unmarked footpath diverging left within two-tenths of a mile (if you reach the state forest boundary near private homes, you've gone too far). Follow that winding, narrow path through the woods—I've seen tracks of deer, rabbit, and other animals here in winter—less than a half mile to Wolf Rock Road and turn right. You will descend a steep hill on the road, then turn left onto Center Road and follow it about 1.2 miles to Parmenter Road. Turn left (west), climbing a hill and crossing from Leominster into Princeton, where the road becomes Rocky Pond Road. From the road's high point, continue west for less than a mile to the junction of Rocky Pond Road, Wolf Rock Road, and the trail from Crow Hills Pond; turn right on the trail to return to this hike's start.

Special note: Short sections of this loop follow hiking trails that would be difficult on a bike. Cyclists might instead begin this loop from the dirt parking area and gate where Rocky Pond Road crosses Route 31, six-tenths of a mile south of the main parking area described in the directions above. Pedal east on Rocky Pond Road for about four-tenths of a mile, then turn right onto the wide Wolf Rock Road. A half mile farther, where the road forks, bear left, staying on Wolf Rock, which leads to Center

Road and the continuation of this hike (described above).

36 Wachusett Mountain: Balanced Rock

0.6 mi/0.5 hr 

Location: In Wachusett Mountain State Reservation in Princeton; Western Massachusetts map page 238, grid b6.

User groups: Hikers dogs, and snowshoers. No wheelchair facilities. Dogs must be on a leash. This trail is not suitable for skis. Bikes and horses are prohibited. Hunting is allowed in season.

Access, fees: Parking and access are free.

Directions: From Route 140, 2.2 miles south of the junction of Routes 140 and 2 in Westminster, or 1.8 miles north of the junction of Routes 140 and 31, turn onto Mile Hill Road, following signs to the Wachusett Mountain Ski Area. Drive a mile and turn right into the ski area parking lot, then cross to the rear of the lot, behind the lodge. The Wachusett Mountain State Reservation Visitors Center is farther up Mile Hill Road.

Maps: A free contour map of hiking trails is available at the visitors center or from the Massachusetts Division of Forests and Parks (see address below). The combined Southwest Massachusetts/Mount Tom and Holyoke Range/Wachusett/Dogtown trail map is $2.95 from the Appalachian Mountain Club, (800) 262-4455 (the Wachusett and Dogtown maps don't show contours). The Wachusett Mountain/Leominster State Forest Trail Map is available for $3.25 from New England Cartographics, P.O. Box 9369, North Amherst, MA 01059. For topographic maps of the area, request Sterling and Fitchburg from the USGS.

Contact: Wachusett Mountain State Reservation, Mountain Road, P.O. Box 248, Princeton, MA 01541; (508) 464-2987. Massachusetts Division of Forests and Parks, 100 Cambridge Street, 19th Floor, Boston, MA 02202; (617) 727-3180.

Trail notes: Balanced Rock is a glacial erratic boulder which well lives up to its name. Pick up the yellow triangular blazes of the Midstate Trail at the rear of the parking lot. Here, the trail is also known as the Balanced Rock Trail. Follow it, climbing gently, for three-tenths of a mile to Balanced Rock. To finish this hike, return the way you came. Hikers looking for a bit more of an outing can continue on the Midstate Trail to the summit via the Semuhenna and Harrington Trails, then descend the Old Indian Trail back to the Midstate to return, a loop of several miles; consult the map and inquire at the visitors center for specific distances.

37 Wachusett Mountain: Pine Hill Trail

2.0 mi/1.5 hrs 

Location: In Wachusett Mountain State Reservation in Princeton; Western Massachusetts map page 238, grid b6.

User groups: Hikers, dogs, and snowshoers. No wheelchair facilities. Dogs must be on a leash. This trail is not suitable for skis. Bikes and horses are prohibited. Hunting is allowed in season.

Access, fees: Parking and access are free.

Directions: From Route 140, 2.2 miles south of the junction of Routes 140 and 2 in Westminster, or 1.8 miles north of the junction of Routes 140 and 31, turn onto Mile Hill Road, following signs to the Wachusett Mountain Ski Area. Drive a mile and turn right into the ski area parking lot; then cross to the rear of the lot, behind the lodge. The Wachusett Mountain State Reservation Visitors Center is farther up Mile Hill Road.

Maps: A free contour map of hiking trails is available at the visitors center or from the

Massachusetts Division of Forests and Parks (see address below). The combined Southwest Massachusetts/Mount Tom and Holyoke Range/Wachusett/Dogtown trail map is $2.95 from the Appalachian Mountain Club, (800) 262-4455 (the Wachusett and Dogtown maps do not show contours). The Wachusett Mountain/Leominster State Forest trail map is available for $3.25 from New England Cartographics, P.O. Box 9369, North Amherst, MA 01059. For topographic maps of the area, request Sterling and Fitchburg from the USGS.

Contact: Wachusett Mountain State Reservation, Mountain Road, P.O. Box 248, Princeton, MA 01541; (508) 464-2987. Massachusetts Division of Forests and Parks, 100 Cambridge Street, 19th Floor, Boston, MA 02202; (617) 727-3180.

Trail notes: At 2,006 feet and the biggest hill in central Massachusetts, Wachusett may be better known for its downhill ski area. But the state reservation has a fairly extensive network of fine hiking trails, including a section of the Midstate Trail that passes over the summit. The summit offers views in all directions—on a clear day, you can see Monadnock to the north and the Boston skyline 40 miles to the east. Trail junctions are marked with signs.

From the visitors center parking lot, follow the Bicentennial Trail to the first trail branching off to the right—the Pine Hill Trail, actually an old ski trail and the most direct route to the summit, about a half mile. The trail ascends at a moderate grade over fairly rocky terrain. After checking out the views from various spots on the broad summit, cross it and look for the sign for the Harrington Trail. Descending the Harrington, you soon cross the paved summit road; after re-entering the woods, take a short side path left off the Harrington to enjoy a long view west over the sparsely populated hills and valleys of central Massachusetts. Backtrack and descend the Harrington to the Link Trail and turn left. Cross the Mountain House Trail, then bear left onto the Loop Trail, which descends to the Bicentennial. Turn left for the visitors center.

38 Redemption Rock to Wachusett Mountain

1.8 mi/1.0 hr  

Location: In Princeton; Western Massachusetts map page 238, grid b6.

User groups: Hikers, dogs, and snowshoers. No wheelchair facilities. The trail is not suitable for bikes, horses, or skis. Hunting is allowed in season except where otherwise posted.

Access, fees: Parking and access are free.

Directions: The hike begins from the small parking lot at Redemption Rock along Route 140 in Princeton, 3.1 miles south of the junction of Routes 140 and 2 in Westminster, and nine-tenths of a mile north of the junction of Routes 140 and 31 in Princeton.

Maps: The Wachusett Mountain and Leominster State Forest Trail Map, which shows this section of the Midstate Trail, is $3.25 from New England Cartographics, P.O. Box 9369, North Amherst, MA 01059; (413) 549-4124. The "Midstate Trail Guide" is available in local stores or from the Midstate Trail Committee (see address below). For topographic maps of the area, request Fitchburg and Sterling from the USGS.

Contact: Trustees of Reservations, 572 Essex Street, Beverly, MA 01915; (508) 921-1944. Midstate Trail Committee, Stanton Whitman, 17 Stoneleigh Road, Worcester, MA 01606; (508) 853-3751.

Trail notes: When I was a young boy, an uncle and aunt took my brothers and sister and I to Redemption Rock, a massive, flat-topped boulder just off the roadside. We climbed around on it, thinking we were on some great adventure—which, of course, we were. Years later, I took my young nephew and niece to Redemption Rock, and let them have their own little adventure. Legend has it that a Concord settler named John Hoar sat atop that boulder with members of a band of King Phillip's Indians in 1676 to negotiate the release of Mary Rowlandson, wife of the minister in the nearby town of Lancaster, whom the Indians abducted and held captive for 11 weeks.

This is a fun spot for young children, and the walk through the woods to the base of Wachusett Mountain and back follows a fairly quiet stretch of the Midstate Trail where you might see a deer or grouse. After exploring Redemption Rock, which sits beside the parking area, follow the yellow triangular blazes of the Midstate Trail into the woods. Watch closely for the blazes; side trails branch off the Midstate. It proceeds generally westward through the woods, climbing slightly and traversing some rocky stretches of trail and some wet areas, reaching Mountain Road and the parking lot for the Wachusett Mountain Ski Area in nine-tenths of a mile. Turn around and return the way you came. Or combine this with Wachusett Mountain Balanced Rock (hike number 36), which begins across the ski area parking lot.

39 Wachusett Meadow to Wachusett Mountain

6.2 mi/3.5 hrs 

Location: In Princeton; Western Massachusetts map page 238, grid b6.

User groups: Hikers and snowshoers. No wheelchair facilities. This trail is not suitable for horses. Bikes, dogs, hunting, and skis are prohibited.

Access, fees: A fee of $3 per adult and $2 per child is charged at Wachusett Meadow to nonmembers of the Massachusetts Audubon Society. The Wachusett Meadow Visitors Center parking lot is open dawn to dusk, Tuesday through Sunday, and on many Monday holidays.

Directions: From the junction of Routes 62 and 31 in Princeton center, drive west on Route 62 for a half mile and turn right onto Goodnow Road at a sign for the Wachusett Meadow Sanctuary. Continue a mile to the end of the paved road and park at the sanctuary visitors center.

Maps: A map of Wachusett Meadow is available at an information board beside the parking lot. A free contour map of hiking trails in the Wachusett Mountain State Reservation is available at the state reservation or from the Massachusetts Division of Forests and Parks (see address below). The Wachusett Mountain/Leominster State Forest Trail Map is available for $3.25 from New England Cartographics, P.O. Box 9369, North Amherst, MA 01059. The combined Southwest Massachusetts/Mount Tom and Holyoke Range/Wachusett/Dogtown trail map is $2.95 from the Appalachian Mountain Club, (800) 262-4455 (the Wachusett and Dogtown maps don't show contours). The "Midstate Trail Guide" is available in local stores or from the Midstate Trail Committee (see address below). For a topographic map of the area, request Sterling from the USGS.

Contact: Massachusetts Audubon Society Wachusett Meadow Wildlife Sanctuary, 113 Goodnow Road, Princeton, MA 01541; (508) 464-2712. Massachusetts Audubon Society Headquarters, 208 South Great Road, Lincoln, MA 01773; (617) 259-9500. Wachusett Mountain State Reservation, Mountain Road, P.O. Box 248, Princeton, MA 01541; (508) 464-2987. The Massachusetts Division of Forests and Parks, 100 Cambridge Street, 19th Floor, Boston, MA 02202; (617) 727-3180. Midstate Trail Committee, Stanton Whitman, 17 Stoneleigh Road, Worcester, MA 01606; (508) 853-3751.

Trail notes: Much of this stretch of the Midstate Trail is relatively flat and easy; the hike only grows steep for the final three-tenths-of-a-mile climb to the summit of Wachusett Mountain, where there are long views in every direction. Visitors to Wachusett Meadow, a 977-acre nature preserve, might want to check out the loop of about 1.5 miles over Brown Hill, whose open crown affords 360-degree views. You also shouldn't miss the 300-year-old Crocker maple, one of the largest sugar maples in the country, with a circumference of more than 15 feet. It sits on the west edge of the meadow, a very short detour off this hike's route, and it is guaranteed to awe children.

From the parking area, walk north into the meadow on the Mountain Trail, then turn left in the middle of the meadow at post six, heading for the woods and reaching a junction with the Midstate Trail about two-tenths of a mile from the parking lot. Turn right (north), following the Midstate over easy terrain through the woods. The trail crosses a dirt road about a mile from the hike's start, passes over a small hill, then crosses paved Westminster Road at 1.8 miles. After crossing a field, the trail enters the woods again, ascending a low hill and passing just below its summit. (You can bushwhack a short distance off-trail to the hilltop and see a wind farm of windmills, then double back to the trail.) After crossing paved Administration Road, the Midstate Trail—here also called the Harrington Trail—reaches a junction with the Semuhenna Trail one mile from Westminster Road. The Semuhenna/Midstate turns left, but this hike continues straight up the Harrington another three-tenths mile to the summit of Wachusett Mountain. Hike back the way you came.

Special note: To avoid backtracking, and for a somewhat shorter hike, shuttle vehicles to Wachusett Meadow and the Wachusett Mountain State Reservation Visitors Center, and do this hike one way, then descend the Pine Hill Trail and Bicentennial Trail to the Wachusett Mountain Visitors Center, as described in the Redemption Rock to Wachusett Mountain hike (hike number 38).

40 Whistling Cave

3.0 mi/1.5 hrs 

Location: In Upton State Forest in Upton; Eastern Massachusetts map page 239, grid c1.

User groups: Hikers dogs, and snowshoers. No wheelchair facilities. Dogs must be on a leash. Bikes, horses, and skis are prohibited. Hunting is allowed in season.

Access, fees: Parking and access are free.

Directions: From Interstate 495, take exit 21B for West Main Street, Upton, and drive 3.7 miles south to the junction of High Street, Hopkinton Road, and Westboro Road; there will be a pond to the left. (That junction can be reached in the other direction from Route 140 in Upton center by taking North Main Street for a half mile.) Turn north onto Westboro Road, drive two miles, then turn right at the sign for Upton State Forest. Bear right onto a dirt road and stop at the map box. Then continue down that dirt road a short distance to a parking lot at a gate.

Maps: A free map is available at the state forest entrance, or from the Massachusetts Division of Forests and Parks (see address below). For a topographic map of the area, request Milford from the USGS.

Contact: Upton State Forest, 205 Westboro Road, Upton, MA 01568; (508) 529-6923. Massachusetts Division of Forests and Parks, 100 Cambridge Street, 19th Floor, Boston, MA 02202; (617) 727-3180.

Trail notes: Whistling Cave is not a cave but two large boulders, one leaning against the other, with a small passageway beneath them. It's located in an interesting little wooded stream valley littered with such boulders. Trails are well blazed and forest road intersections are marked by signs, and the state forest has many more miles of both trails and roads.

From the parking lot, head past the gate on a dirt forest road to the junction of Loop Road and Park Road. Bear right on Park Road, passing one blue-blazed trail on the left (which may not appear on the map). Continue up a gentle hill to a pullout on the left. The Whistling Cave Trail, marked by a sign and blazed with blue triangles, begins there. It soon drops over ledges and down a steep embankment, then levels out. You'll cross a couple of small brooks, then enter the area of boulders. Whistling Cave is right on the trail at the far end of this area, shortly after you start up a hillside. Just beyond it, the trail ends at the junction of Middle and Loop Roads. (To reach Whistling Cave on bikes, horses, or skis, take Loop Road to this intersection, then walk or attempt to ski to the boulders, and double back.) You can return on either Loop Road or Middle Road; the former remains a forest road, while the latter eventually narrows to an easy trail marked by blue triangles.

41 Purgatory Chasm

0.5 mi/0.5 hr 

Location: In Purgatory Chasm State Reservation in Sutton; Western Massachusetts map page 238, grid c6.

User groups: Hikers and dogs. No wheelchair facilities. Dogs must be on a leash. The trail may be difficult to snowshoe, depending on snow conditions, and is not suitable for bikes, horses, or skis. Hunting is allowed in season.

Access, fees: Parking and access are free. Purgatory Chasm State Reservation is open sunrise to sunset daily, year-round.

Directions: From Route 146 in Northbridge, take the exit for Purgatory Road. Turn west on Purgatory Road and drive six-tenths of a mile to parking on the left, beside a pavilion and information kiosk.

Maps: A free map of hiking trails is available at the information kiosk and from the Massachusetts Division of Forests and Parks (see address below). For topographic maps of the area, request Milford and Worcester South from the USGS.

Contact: Purgatory Chasm State Reservation, Purgatory Road, Sutton, MA 01590; (508) 234-3733. Massachusetts Division of Forests and Parks, 100 Cambridge Street, 19th Floor, Boston, MA 02202-0001; (617) 727-3180.

Trail notes: You scramble over rocks into the mouth of a chasm stretching a quarter mile before you, its floor littered with huge boulders. The air is often at least 10 degrees cooler than in the parking lot you've just left behind. Rock walls rise as high at 70 feet on either side of this narrow defile called Purgatory Chasm. Geologists theorize that the chasm was created by catastrophic force, when melting glacial ice suddenly released torrents of flood water that shattered this gap through the granite bedrock. As if clinging to its prehistoric roots, Purgatory Chasm today is known to harbor pockets of ice into May and June. Although the scrambling can be difficult for people who are uncomfortable moving over rocks, this half-mile loop is a good one for children.

From the information kiosk, walk toward the pavilion, but before reaching it turn right where blue blazes lead down through the chasm; you may see rock climbers on the walls. At the chasm's far end, poke your head inside the aptly named Coffin, a tight space among the boulders to the right of the trail. Then turn left and follow the blue blazes uphill onto the rim above the chasm, past deep cracks that have been given such names as Fat Man's Misery and the Corn Crib. The blue blazes will lead you back to the parking lot.

42 Midstate Trail Loop

6.5 mi/3.5 hrs 

Location: In Douglas State Forest in Douglas; Western Massachusetts map page 238, grid d6.

User groups: Hikers, bikes, dogs, horses, skiers, and snowshoers. No wheelchair facilities. Dogs must be on a leash. Hunting is allowed in season.

Access, fees: Access is free. Parking is free except from Memorial Day to Labor Day, when there is a $2-per-vehicle fee to park near the beach and boat ramp. The fee can be avoided by accessing the state forest at other roadside parking areas. Consult the map for other access points.

Directions: From Interstate 395, take exit 2 for Route 16 east. Drive 5.1 miles and turn right onto Cedar Road (there may be no street sign) at the sign for Douglas State Forest. Drive 1.8 miles to a crossroads at Southwest Main Street, and proceed straight through onto Wallum Street. At nine-tenths of a mile farther, turn right into the state forest and drive seven-tenths of a mile to an information panel where a box contains maps. Bear right and continue a short distance to a parking lot.

Maps: A free trail map and informational brochure are available at the park entrance, or through the Massachusetts Division of Forests and Parks (see address below). For a topographic map of the area, request Webster from the USGS.

Contact: Douglas State Forest, Wallum Lake Road, RR 01, Box 161D30, Douglas, MA 01516; (508) 476-7872. Massachusetts Division of Forests and Parks, 100 Cambridge Street, 19th Floor, Boston, MA 02202; (617) 727-3180. Midstate Trail Committee, Stanton Whitman, 17 Stoneleigh Road, Worcester, MA 01606.

Trail notes: This loop, mostly on forest roads, uses the Midstate Trail to explore the big piece of Douglas State Forest that lies south of Route 16. The state forest also extends north of the highway, and is worth exploring further. The sections of this loop that employ forest roads are easy or moderately difficult for mountain bikers, but the stretches of it that follow a rougher trail are more difficult. It's fairly flat, but crosses some streams and gets rocky in places. The Midstate is well blazed with yellow triangles, but most other forest roads are not marked; use the map.

The Midstate Trail is accessed via the Coffeehouse Loop's southern arm, a forest road beginning at the south end of the parking lot. When you reach the Midstate, turn right (north) onto it. The Midstate makes several turns. Some three miles out, the Midstate reaches a T intersection at a forest road; you'll probably hear traffic on Route 16 to the left. This loop turns right, following that forest road south. At a fork, bear right and shortly cross the dirt Southwest Main Street (where, if you turned left, you would shortly reach the intersection of Cedar Road and Wallum Street). The next intersection reconnects you with the Midstate Trail; backtrack on the Midstate southbound to return.

43 Coffeehouse Loop

2.2 mi/1.5 hrs  

Location: In Douglas State Forest in Douglas; Western Massachusetts map page 238, grid d6.

User groups: Hikers, dogs, skiers, and snowshoers. No wheelchair facilities. Dogs must be on a leash. Bikes and horses are prohibited on part of this loop. Hunting is allowed in season.

Access, fees: Access is free. Parking is free

except from Memorial Day to Labor Day, when there is a $2-per-vehicle fee to park near the beach and boat ramp. The fee can be avoided by accessing the state forest at other roadside parking areas. Consult the map for other access points.

Directions: From Interstate 395, take exit 2 for Route 16 east. Drive 5.1 miles and turn right onto Cedar Road (there may be no street sign) at the sign for Douglas State Forest. Drive 1.8 miles to a crossroads at Southwest Main Street, and proceed straight through onto Wallum Street. At nine-tenths of a mile farther, turn right into the state forest and drive seven-tenths of a mile to an information panel where a box contains maps. Bear right and continue a short distance to a parking lot.

Maps: A free trail map and informational brochure are available at the park entrance, or through the Massachusetts Division of Forests and Parks (see address below). For a topographic map of the area, request Webster from the USGS.

Contact: Douglas State Forest, Wallum Lake Road, RR 01, Box 161D30, Douglas, MA 01516; (508) 476-7872. Massachusetts Division of Forests and Parks, 100 Cambridge Street, 19th Floor, Boston, MA 02202; (617) 727-3180. Midstate Trail Committee, Stanton Whitman, 17 Stoneleigh Road, Worcester, MA 01606.

Trail notes: This relatively flat trail makes an easy loop through peaceful woods, with the terrain growing slightly rocky in some places. Easy to follow, with trail junctions clearly marked with signs, this hike also offers access to a longer outing on the Midstate Trail for those with extra time and energy. The loop begins at the north end of the parking lot, eventually reaches and coincides for a short distance with the Midstate Trail southbound, then diverges left from the Midstate Trail and returns to the parking lot via a forest road.

44 Maudslay State Park

2.5 mi/1.5 hrs 

Location: In Newburyport; Eastern Massachusetts map page 239, grid a3.

User groups: Hikers, bikes, dogs, horses, skiers, and snowshoers. No wheelchair facilities. Dogs must be on a leash. Hunting is prohibited.

Access, fees: A special-use permit is required for weddings, family reunions, and school groups. Parking and access are free. The park is open from 8 A.M. to sunset. Picnickers are welcome.

Directions: From Interstate 95, take exit 57 in Newburyport for Route 113 west. Drive a half mile, then turn right onto Hoyt's Lane/Gypsy Lane. At the end of the road, turn right (in front of the park headquarters) onto Pine Hill Road and right again into the parking lot.

Maps: A free, good trail map, including historical information and the seasons for viewing various park flora in bloom, is available at park headquarters (see address below). A more basic map is also available free from the Massachusetts Division of Forests and Parks, 100 Cambridge Street, 19th Floor, Boston, MA 02202; (617) 727-3180. For a topographic map of the area, request Newburyport from the USGS.

Contact: Maudslay State Park, Curzon's Mill Road, Newburyport, MA 01950; (508) 465-7223.

Trail notes: This 480-acre park on the Merrimack River was the nineteenth-century estate of the Moseleys, one of New England's wealthiest families. George Washington visited this area in 1789, and a regular ferry crossed the river here in the seventeenth century. Today, you can hike trails through its many gardens and one of the largest naturally occurring mountain laurel stands in eastern Massachusetts, and over grounds where more flowers and plants bloom than I could begin to list. Mid-June is the time to catch the brilliant white flowers of the mountain laurel. The park sponsors numerous educational and recreational events.

From the parking lot, walk past the headquarters and turn right at a green gate onto Hedge Drive, a dirt road lined with trees and hedges. Near a small building, turn left and follow that road a short distance to its intersection with another road. You are across from the vegetable garden. Turn left, walk past buildings, and enter the Italian Garden. Walk straight through it onto a path that passes an old well, cross the dirt Main Road, and walk through a courtyard to the Merrimack River Trail, which is marked by blue, white, and green blazes. Straight ahead is the Merrimack River. Turn right onto the Merrimack River Trail; follow it along the hilltop and down into woods. After crossing two brooks on wooden bridges, the trail bears left onto another road and crosses over a dam at the end of the Flowering Pond. Here you reach the Laurel Walk, where the Merrimack River Trail branches right and left. The area to the left is closed from November 1 to March 31; take the right branch during these months. Otherwise, turn left and follow the Merrimack River Trail along the riverbank. When it meets the Castle Hill Trail (and the Merrimack River Trail's other branch), turn left and stay with the Merrimack River Trail until you reach the end of a tree-lined road on your right; the Castle Hill Trail follows it up onto Castle Hill, where there are views of the state park and this corner of the Merrimack Valley. Over the hilltop, turn right onto one road and quickly left onto another, then right onto Line Road. It leads straight onto the Main Road (backtracking over the Merrimack River Trail 's right branch). Take the stone bridge over the Flowering Pond; turn left onto the Pasture Trail and follow it back to the parking lot.

45 Bar Head Drumlin/ Plum Island

3.0 mi/1.5 hrs 

Location: In Sandy Point State Reservation in Ipswich; Eastern Massachusetts map page 239, grid a4.

User groups: Hikers and snowshoers. No wheelchair facilities. This trail rarely receives enough snow for skis or snowshoes and is not suitable for bikes or horses. Dogs are prohibited. Hunting is allowed in season.

Access, fees: The fee for entering the Parker River National Wildlife Refuge is $5 per vehicle or $2 for anyone entering on foot or a bike.

Directions: Take U.S. 1 to the downtown Newburyport exit. Turn east on Water Street and follow it about 3.5 miles out to Plum Island. Take the first right after the bridge, to the Parker River National Wildlife Refuge. From the refuge entrance, drive 6.5 miles to lot 7 and park.

Maps: For topographic maps of the area, request Ipswich and Newburyport from the USGS.

Contact: Salisbury Beach State Reservation, (508) 462-4481.

Trail notes: This easy hike combines a walk along a sandy beach and a rocky shoreline with a hike onto a glacial drumlin, an oval mound of earth deposited by a receding glacier 10,000 years ago. Today, several plant and animal species rarely found near a sandy beach thrive on Bar Head Drumlin. Fifty feet high and covering 15 acres, the drumlin is shrinking under constant erosion by the ocean. Nearby, the sprawling Parker River National Wildlife Refuge is home to numerous bird species in summer, including cormorants, herons, kingfishers, and ducks. The refuge also offers hiking opportunities. Across from lot 7 is an observation tower with a view of the refuge's marshlands.

From lot 7, follow the boardwalk onto the beach and turn right for the drumlin. Below the eroded cliffs of Bar Head, you'll walk a rock-strewn beach. Beyond the drumlin, the beach again becomes sandy. Follow the waterline around to the right until you reach a fence at the wildlife refuge boundary. Turn right, and follow an overgrown road along the refuge boundary to a parking lot for the state reservation. Cross the lot to an unmarked, overgrown trail leading up onto Bar Head. Although the trees and brush atop the drumlin are too dense and high to afford views, a few side trails to the cliffs permit views of the beach and ocean. The trail leads over Bar Head and back to the beach near the boardwalk where you started.

46 Halibut Point State Park

0.5 mi/0.5 hr 

Location: In Halibut Point State Park in Rockport; Eastern Massachusetts map page 239, grid a4.

User groups: Hikers and dogs. No wheelchair facilities. Dogs must be on a leash. This trail rarely receives enough snow for skis or snowshoes and is not suitable for bikes or horses. Hunting is prohibited.

Access, fees: From Memorial Day weekend to Columbus Day weekend, hours are 8 A.M. to 8 P.M. and a small fee (which was $2 in 1996, but may increase soon) is charged for parking. For the rest of the year, the park is open at no charge during the daylight hours.

Directions: From the junction of Routes 128 and 127, follow Route 127 north (on Eastern Avenue) toward Rockport. After three miles, turn left onto Railroad Avenue, which is still Route 127. After another 2.4 miles, turn right onto Gott Avenue. The parking lot is on the right a short distance up the road.

Maps: A free trail map is available at the park. A basic trail map is also available from the Massachusetts Division of Forests and Parks, 100 Cambridge Street, 19th Floor, Boston, MA 02202; (617) 727-3180.

Contact: Halibut Point State Park, Gott Avenue, Rockport, MA 01966; (508) 546-2997. Trustees of Reservations, 572 Essex Street, Beverly, MA 01915; (508) 921-1944.

Trail notes: Halibut Point State Park is built around the site of the former Babson Farm granite quarry, which operated for nearly a century and is now filled with water, creating a small pond ringed by the sheer "cliffs" of the quarry walls. I visited late one spring day, when the low sun was highlighting thin clouds creating beautiful reflections in the pond. The park's name derives from "Haul About Point," the name given to the 50-foot granite cliff at the water's edge by sailors tacking around the point to approach Cape Ann.

From the parking lot, cross Gott Avenue, following signs to the park entrance. A short trail through trees leads to the quarry. The park headquarters is to the left. Take the trail that goes around the quarry to the right. You'll pass a mooring stone—an enormous granite slab sunk underwater to anchor an oak post used as a mooring for fishermen's boats. Then turn onto a trail branching to the right, toward the ocean. The shore here is very rocky, an extremely wild place when the surf is high—be sure not to get too close to the water because the riptide is very powerful. Walk to the left along the shore, then follow a trail back up toward the quarry. To return, walk around the quarry to the left, which will take you back to the entrance trail.

47 Bald Hill

3.0 mi/2.0 hrs 

Location: In Boxford State Forest; Eastern Massachusetts map page 239, grid b3.

User groups: Hikers, bikes, dogs, horses, skiers, and snowshoers. No wheelchair facilities. Dogs must be on a leash. Hunting is allowed in season.

Access, fees: Parking and access are free.

Directions: From Interstate 95 in Boxford, take exit 51 for Endicott Road. Drive west, and turn right onto Middleton Road. After passing Fuller Lane on the right, continue on Middleton Road another eight-tenths of a mile. Park at a roadside turnout on the left.

Maps: A free trail map is available through the Massachusetts Division of Forests and Parks, 100 Cambridge Street, 19th Floor, Boston, MA 02202; (617) 727-3180.

Contact: Harold Parker State Forest, 1951 Turnpike Road, North Andover, MA 01845-6326; (508) 686-3391.

Trail notes: Here is yet another sizable chunk of state land on the North Shore with a wealth of trails ideal for many activities. This loop takes you through the forest's southeast corner and over Bald Hill, but there's lots more to this place worth checking out. You may stumble across old gravestones or home foundations. This loop largely follows forest roads, but the terrain can be rocky and rugged, a challenge on a mountain bike. Many trail intersections have numbered markers that correspond to numbers on the trail map. The forest tends toward the soggy, meaning a plague of mosquitoes in spring and early summer. Avoid digging up the trails with mountain bikes in mud season—but this is a primo riding destination during summer and fall.

From the turnout, head past the gate onto the dirt Bald Hill Road. Past Crooked Pond, at intersection 14, bear left, and left again at intersection 13. Farther along, turn right, climbing fairly steeply up Bald Hill. On its open summit, cross the field to the left and pick up a forest road heading back down. Bear right. You'll pass a stone foundation at the former Russell-Hooper farmhouse site (marked by a small sign). Just beyond it, to the right of the trail, is the Russell-Hooper barn site. Follow the trail around to the right. At intersection 8A, turn right; eventually, you'll follow white blazes. At intersection 26, turn right again, and follow this trail back to intersection 13.

48 Bradley Palmer State Park

2.5 mi/1.5 hrs 

Location: In Topsfield; Eastern Massachusetts map page 239, grid b3.

User groups: Hikers, bikes, dogs, horses, skiers, and snowshoers. No wheelchair facilities. Dogs must be on a leash. Hunting is allowed in season.

Access, fees: Parking and access are free.

Directions: From U.S. 1 in Topsfield, turn east onto Ipswich Road (at a traffic light). Drive 1.2 miles, and turn right onto Asbury Street. The state park entrance is on the left a short distance down the road. Park in a dirt area just before the state park headquarters.

Maps: A free, fairly accurate trail map is available at the park headquarters (see address below), or through the Massachusetts Division of Forests and Parks, 100 Cambridge Street, 19th Floor, Boston, MA 02202; (617) 727-3180.

Contact: Bradley Palmer State Park, Asbury Street, Topsfield, MA 01983; (508) 887-5931.

Trail notes: Bradley Palmer is just a great multi-use recreational area. I lived on the North Shore a number of years ago, and this park was my favorite local place to cross-country ski. Its moderately sloping hills, wide forest roads, and rugged trails also offer very interesting and varied mountain biking and hiking. And the wildlife here might surprise you: two friends of mine were mountain biking here when an owl with a squirrel in its talons swept just over their heads. This hike merely introduces you to this park; you can explore it further on your own.

From the parking area, cross the paved road and head onto a broad forest road. Bear left and start climbing Blueberry Hill (a rigorous climb on a bike). Take the third right onto another forest road, then the second left to reach the open hilltop. If you imagine entering the hilltop meadow at six o'clock, then cross the hilltop and trend right, toward a road entering the woods at about three o'clock. Watch for a more narrow trail exiting left off that road, and follow it down a steep hill. Bear right onto another trail, which leads down to the Ipswich River and land in the Essex County Greenbelt. Turn left along a trail paralleling the river; you will begin seeing the blue blazes, with a paw print on them, of the Discover Hamilton Trail. Where a footbridge leads right over the river, turn left up a forest road. At a long, wide meadow, turn right and continue onto a forest road back to the park headquarters.

49 Dogtown

8.8 mi/5.0 hrs 

Location: In Gloucester and Rockport; Eastern Massachusetts map page 239, grid b4.

User groups: Hikers, bikes, and dogs. No wheelchair facilities. This trail rarely receives enough snow for skis or snowshoes and is not suitable for horses. Hunting is permitted in season.

Access, fees: Parking and access are free.

Directions: From the Grant Circle Rotary on Route 128 in Gloucester, take Route 127 (Washington Street) north for nine-tenths of a mile and turn right onto Reynard Street. Follow Reynard to a left onto Cherry Street. Then turn right onto the access road to Dogtown, 1.5 miles from Grant Circle Rotary. Drive less than a half mile to a parking area and a gate.

Maps: A free trail map of Dogtown is available from Gloucester Chamber of Commerce (see phone number below). The combined Southwest Massachusetts/Mount Tom and Holyoke Range/Wachusett/Dogtown trail map is $2.95 from the Appalachian Mountain Club, (800) 262-4455. For a topographic map of the area, request Rockport from the USGS.

Contact: Gloucester Chamber of Commerce, (508) 283-1601.

Trail notes: This patch of untamed woods in the heart of Cape Ann has become a favorite among local hikers and mountain bikers, for its rugged trails, glacial erratic boulders scattered through the forest—and the legacy of a wealthy financier named Roger Babson. Earlier in this century, Babson hired stonecutters to carve sayings into rocks here like "Get a Job" and "Never Try Never Win." The old woods roads along this hike carry names, but are not maintained thoroughfares for motor vehicles; many are very difficult to negotiate even for experienced mountain bikers. This nearly nine-mile route through Dogtown could take five hours hiking, three to four hours on bikes.

From the parking area, go around the gate and follow the rough dirt Dogtown Road, passing to the left of old cellar holes, for 1.2 miles to Dogtown Square, a junction of trails where a rock is inscribed "D.T. SQ." From Dogtown Square, turn right onto a rock-strewn dirt road and follow it for a tenth of a mile, then turn right again (where the red blazes of the Beaver Dam Trail branch left) onto the Tent Rock Trail, sometimes called the Boulder Trail. It continues for a mile to Babson Reservoir, along the way passing the large boulders inscribed with messages such as "Truth," "Industry," and "Help Mother." From the nice view of the reservoir, the trail turns left, crosses railroad tracks, and reaches the rough dirt Old Rockport Road behind Blackburn Industrial Park, 1.4 miles from Dogtown Square. Turn left and follow the road 1.2 miles to the Babson Museum on Eastern Avenue (Route 127). Behind the museum, turn left onto the red-blazed Beaver Dam Trail. Crossing the railroad tracks, then a brook four times, the trail passes over a small hill, takes a sharp right and reaches Dogtown Square 1.4 miles from the museum. Turn right onto Wharf Road and follow it four-tenths of a mile to Common Road. Turn right onto the Whale's Jaw Trail, pass a huge boulder called Peter's Pulpit at about three-tenths of a mile, and reach the Whale's Jaw at eight-tenths of a mile, another massive boulder. Backtrack the same way to Dogtown Square, and follow Dogtown Road back to the parking area.

50 Chandler Hovey Park

0.2 mi/0.25 hr 

Location: In Marblehead; Eastern Massachusetts map page 239, grid b3.

User groups: Hikers only. No wheelchair facilities. This trail rarely receives enough snow for skis or snowshoes and is not suitable for bikes or horses. Dogs and hunting are prohibited.

Access, fees: Parking and access are free.

Directions: From the junction of Routes 114 and 129 in Marblehead, turn east onto Route 129. Drive one block to where Route 129 turns right, and continue straight ahead onto Ocean Avenue. Follow it nearly a mile, passing Devereaux Beach, onto Marblehead Neck. Bear left onto Harbor Avenue and follow it nearly a mile; it merges onto Ocean Avenue again. Continue two-tenths of a mile, turn left onto Follett Street, and proceed a tenth of a mile to the parking lot at the end of the road. If the gate is closed, park on the street.

Maps: No map is necessary for this short walk, but for topographic maps of the area, request Lynn and Salem from the USGS.

Contact: Marblehead Parks and Recreation Department, (617) 631-3350.

Trail notes: This town park on Marblehead Neck is a postage stamp-sized parcel of public land amid some of the most stately houses on Massachusetts' North Shore. The sea crashes up against a classic, New England rocky shoreline, a beautiful place at any time of year, in any weather. I especially like coming out here on a stormy day, when no one else is around. There is no trail; from the parking lot, simply wander out onto the rocks.

51 Great Meadows National Wildlife Refuge

2.0 mi/1.5 hrs 

Location: In Concord; Eastern Massachusetts map page 239, grid b2.

User groups: Hikers, dogs, skiers, snowshoers, and wheelchair users. Dogs must be on a leash. Bikes, horses, and hunting are prohibited.

Access, fees: Parking and access are free.

Directions: From the junction with Route 2A in Concord center, follow Route 62 east for 1.3 miles, then turn left onto Monsen Road. Drive three-tenths of a mile, then turn left at the sign for the Great Meadows National Wildlife Refuge. Drive to the dirt lot at the end of the road.

Maps: A map of hiking trails and a number of brochures about Great Meadows, including a list of bird species sighted here, are available at the trailhead. For a topographic map of the area, request Maynard from the USGS.

Contact: Great Meadows National Wildlife Refuge, Refuge Manager, Weir Hill Road, Sudbury, MA 01776; (617) 443-4661.

Trail notes: Although most visitors here are bird-watchers, even the casual walker can't help but be impressed by the profusion of winged creatures on this 3,000-acre refuge stretching along 12 miles of the Concord River. From great blue herons and osprey to songbirds and wood ducks, 221 species of birds have been observed here. The Dike Trail around the broad wetlands is considered one of the best birding sites in the state. I watched a great blue not 50 feet away slowly stalking a meal across a shallow marsh. Bring binoculars if you have them. Besides birds, animals such as deer, muskrats, foxes, raccoons, cottontail rabbits, and weasels call the refuge home. With all the standing water here, you can bet there are lots of bugs too, especially in spring. Interestingly, relics of human habitation here date back to 5500 B.C.

Before you begin your hike, check out the view from the observation tower beside the parking lot. Then pick up the Dike Trail, to the right of the tower, which traverses the meadows between the Upper and Lower Pools. On the other side, the trail reaches the banks of the Concord River (where canoeists pull ashore to walk the trail). Turn left, following the trail along the Upper Pool about a quarter mile to the refuge boundary, marked by signs. Turn back, and follow the trail around the Lower Pool. You can either double back or, where the Lower Pool ends, take the Edge Trail through the woods back to the entrance road. Turn right on the road to return to the parking lot.

Special note: You can canoe the gentle Sudbury and Concord Rivers through the refuge and put ashore here to walk this trail. Depending on how long a day trip you want, put in along either Route 27, Route 117, or Route 62 and take out along Route 225 on the Carlisle–Bedford line.

52 Walden Pond

1.7 mi/1.0 hr 

Location: In Walden Pond State Park Reservation in Concord; Eastern Massachusetts map page 239, grid b2.

User groups: Hikers, skiers, and snowshoers. Wheelchairs can access the beginning of this trail above the beach on Walden Pond. Bikes, dogs, horses, and hunting are prohibited.

Access, fees: There is a $2 fee for parking levied daily from Memorial Day through Labor Day; a season pass costs $15. Park officials may close the entrance if the park reaches capacity. The park is open to the public from 5 A.M. to sunset; check for the closing time posted in the parking lot.

Directions: From the junction of Routes 2 and 126 in Concord, drive south on Route 126 for three-tenths of a mile to the Walden Pond State Reservation entrance and parking lot on the left.

Maps: A free map that shows trails and contour lines, and an informational brochure about Walden Pond, are available outside the Shop at Walden Pond, next to the park office at the south end of the parking lot. The map can also be obtained from the Massachusetts Division of Forests and Parks (see address below). For a topographic map of the area, request Maynard from the USGS.

Contact: Walden Pond State Park Reservation, 915 Walden Street (Route 126), Concord, MA 01742; (508) 369-3254. Massachusetts Division of Forests and Parks,

100 Cambridge Street, 19th Floor, Boston, MA 02202; (617) 727-3180. The Shop at Walden Pond, (508) 287-5477.

Trail notes: In 1845, a 27-year-old former schoolteacher named Henry David Thoreau came to Walden Pond to live on 14 acres owned by his friend, Ralph Waldo Emerson. Thoreau built a small one-room cabin and began his "experiment in simplicity," living a largely sustenance lifestyle on the pond. At the time, much of Concord was already deforested and the land converted to farms, but the woods around Walden Pond had remained untouched because the sandy soil was not very fertile. Two years, two months, and two days later, Thoreau closed up his house and returned to village life in Concord. Emerson sold the cabin to his gardener. (The cabin no longer stands, but a replica can be seen beside the parking lot.) In 1854, Thoreau published *Walden, or Life in the Woods*—still considered a classic of American literature. Ever since, Walden Pond has stood as a symbol of the American conservation movement.

Today, Walden Pond sits in the middle of a small patch of woods within earshot of busy highways and a railroad line, yet it remains popular with hikers and cross-country skiers, as well as fishermen and canoeists (a boat launch is on the right side of Route 126 just beyond the parking area). Songbirds, Canada geese, and ducks are commonly seen here; I once was captivated by the sight of a blue jay bathing itself at the water's edge.

From the parking lot, cross Route 126 and walk downhill to the pond. From either end of the beach, the Pond Path circles the pond, usually staying just above the shoreline but offering almost constant pond views. It's a wide, mostly flat trail, easy to ski. A short side trail, marked by a sign along the Pond Path, leads to Thoreau's house site. Stay on trails—erosion is a problem here.

53 Minuteman Bikeway

11.0 mi/5.5 hrs 

Location: In Somerville, Cambridge, Arlington, Lexington, and Bedford; Eastern Massachusetts map page 239, grid b2.

User groups: Hikers, bikes, dogs, and wheelchair users. This trail does not usually receive enough snow for skis or snowshoes and is not suitable for horses. Hunting is prohibited.

Access, fees: Parking and access are free.

Directions: The Minuteman Bikeway can be accessed from numerous points for walks or rides of virtually any distance. Its endpoints are behind the T station in Davis Square, between Holland Street and Meacham Road in Somerville; and at the junction of Railroad Avenue and Loomis Street in Bedford. Access points include Massachusetts Avenue in Cambridge at Cameron Avenue and Harvey Street, four-tenths of a mile south of Route 16; the Alewife T station at the junction of Routes 2 and 16; a parking lot on Lake Street in Arlington just west of the traffic lights at Brooks Avenue; Swan Place and Mystic Street in Arlington center, near the junction of Routes 2A and 60 (where the Bikeway crosses Massachusetts Avenue); Park Avenue in Arlington (via a stairway) just north of Massachusetts Avenue; Maple Street (Route 2A) in Lexington; Woburn Street in Lexington just west of Massachusetts Avenue; Hancock and Meriam Streets (at a large parking lot), off Bedford Street (Route 4 and Route 225) and the Lexington Battle Green; and Bedford Street (Route 4 and Route 225) between North Hancock and Revere Streets in Lexington.

Maps: A brochure and map of the Bikeway is available from the Arlington Planning Department (see address below). "Boston's Bikemap," a detailed bicycling map of the metropolitan area that covers the Minuteman Bikeway, is available for $5 from BikeMaps Massachusetts, P.O. Box 1035, Cambridge, MA 02140; (617) 868-8948. For topographic maps of the area, request Boston South, Boston North, and Maynard from the USGS.

Contact: The Friends of the Minuteman Bikeway, c/o Planning and Community Development Department, Town Hall, 730 Massachusetts Avenue, Arlington, MA 02174; (617) 641-4891. Rails to Trails Conservancy, 1400 16th Street Northwest, Suite 300, Washington, DC 20036; (202) 797-5400.

Trail notes: The paved Bikeway follows a former railroad bed and is popular with walkers, runners, bicyclists, families, in-line skaters, and—when there's snow—cross-country skiers. Many people, particularly students, use the Bikeway to commute to work and classes. The Bikeway passes mainly through forest in Bedford and Lexington, and through a nice wetland in Lexington as well. From Arlington into Cambridge and Somerville, the bikeway becomes increasingly an urban recreation path.

54 Middlesex Fells Skyline Trail

7.0 mi/4.0 hrs 

Location: In Middlesex Fells Reservation in Medford; Eastern Massachusetts map page 239, grid b2.

User groups: Hikers and dogs. No wheelchair facilities. Dogs must be on a leash. This trail rarely receives enough snow for snowshoes and is not suitable for horses or skis. Bikes and hunting are prohibited.

Access, fees: Parking and access are free.

Directions: Take Interstate 93 to exit 33 in Medford. From the traffic circle, turn onto South Border Road. Drive two-tenths of a mile and turn into a parking area on the right, at Bellevue Pond.

Maps: A good contour map of trails in the Middlesex Fells is available for $4 from the Metropolitan District Commission North Region headquarters, (617) 662-5230, or the Friends of the Middlesex Fells Reservation (see address below).

Contact: The Friends of the Middlesex Fells Reservation, P.O. Box 560057, West Medford, MA 02156; (617) 396-5118.

Trail notes: This may be the premier hiking circuit in the Fells, a 2,000-acre piece of woods in an urban wilderness. You can actually find quiet and solitude along parts of this trail—although traffic on the interstate can be heard at times, and the Fells as a whole sees heavy recreational use. The trail loops around the Winchester Reservoirs, passing through forest and traversing countless rocky ledges, some with good views of the Fells, an isolated pocket of woodlands amid the urban sprawl, and occasionally the Boston skyline. ("Fells" is a Saxon word for rocky hills.) Perhaps the best view is from atop Pine Hill, near the start of this loop, which overlooks Boston's skyline and the Blue Hills to the south; climb the stone Wright's Tower on the hill. The white blazes of the Skyline Trail are generally easy to follow, but it crosses many other paths and forest roads, which can cause confusion. The trail dries out fairly quickly after the snow melts—it's a nice hike on the first warm day of spring. Bikes are prohibited from this trail, and it's not suited to skiing, but there are many forest roads and trails forming a network through the Fells that offer good mountain biking and cross-country skiing.

From the parking lot, walk along the right side of Bellevue Pond and onto a wide forest road at the opposite end of the pond. Look for the white-blazed trail leading to the right, up Pine Hill. The loop eventually brings you back to this intersection.

55 Paul Dudley White Charles River Bike Path

14.0 mi/6.0 hrs 

Location: In Boston, Cambridge, and Watertown; Eastern Massachusetts map page 239, grid c2.

User groups: Hikers, bikes, dogs, and wheelchair users. Dogs must be on a leash. This path rarely receives enough snow for skis and is not suitable for snowshoeing. Horses and hunting are prohibited.

Access, fees: Parking and access are free.

Directions: The bike path runs for seven miles along both sides of the Charles River, from the Boston Museum of Science on the O'Brien Highway (Route 28) to Watertown Square in Watertown (the junction of Routes 16 and 20), forming a 14-mile loop. It is accessible from numerous points in Boston, Cambridge, and Watertown, including the footbridges over Storrow Drive in Boston, although not from the Longfellow and B.U. bridges on the Boston side.

Maps: "Boston's Bikemap," a detailed bicycling map of the metropolitan area which covers the Paul Dudley White Charles River Bike Path, is available for $5 from Rubel BikeMaps, Box 1035, Cambridge, MA 02140. For a topographic map of the area, request Boston South from the USGS.

Contact: Metropolitan District Commission, 20 Somerset Street, Boston, MA 02108.

Trail notes: The paved Paul Dudley White Bike Path along both banks of the Charles River teems with activity weekday evenings and weekends—walkers, runners, in-line skaters, bicyclists, skateboarders, people of all ages out getting exercise in the middle of the city. It is easily reached from colleges like M.I.T., Boston University, and Harvard, and it accesses riverside attractions like the Esplanade and Hatch Shell. The bike path provides a more convenient, more pleasant, and often faster means of getting around the city than driving or using public transportation. It also has great skyline views of Boston from the Cambridge side. For the 20th anniversary Earth Day concert several years ago, when literally hundreds of thousands of concertgoers jammed the Esplanade and Storrow Drive was closed to motor vehicles, a friend and I easily biked to the show, then left without getting stuck in the crowds afterward. Some sections of the path are quite wide, others no wider than a pair of bikes; likewise, some stretches see much heavier use than others. Bicycling fast can be difficult when the path is crowded, and numerous crossings of busy streets necessitate frequent stops. The entire path forms a 14-mile loop between the Museum of Science and Watertown Square, and can be traveled in either direction.

56 Noanet Peak

4.0 mi/2.0 hrs 

Location: In Dover; Eastern Massachusetts map page 239, grid c2.

User groups: Hikers, dogs, skiers, and snowshoers. No wheelchair facilities. Bikes and horses are allowed by permit only (see below). Hunting is prohibited.

Access, fees: Parking and access are free. The Noanet Woodlands Reservation closes at sunset. A biking permit can be obtained at the Noanet Woodlands ranger station at the Caryl Park entrance on weekends and holidays, or from the Southeast Region office of the Trustees of Reservations, 2468B Washington Street, Canton, MA 02021; (617) 821-2977. For a horse permit, contact the Superintendent, Rocky Woods Reservation, P.O. Box 352 (64 Hartford Street), Medfield, MA 02052; (508) 359-6333.

Directions: From Interstate 95 (Route 128), take exit 17 onto Route 135 west.

Drive about six-tenths of a mile and turn left at the traffic lights onto South Street. Drive seven-tenths of a mile and bear left at a fork. After another 1.4 miles, turn left onto Chestnut Street. Cross the Charles River and enter Dover; the road becomes Dedham Street. Two miles past the river, turn left into Caryl Park.

Maps: A trail map is posted on an information board at the trailhead. Major trail junctions in Noanet are marked with numbered signs that correspond to markings on the map. For topographic maps of the area, request Boston South, Framingham, Medfield, and Norwood from the USGS.

Contact: Trustees of Reservations, 572 Essex Street, Beverly, MA 01915-1530; (508) 921-1944.

Trail notes: The 591-acre Noanet Woodlands is a surprisingly quiet and secluded-feeling patch of forest plunked down in the middle of suburbia. I suspect it comes as a shock to many first-time hikers of 387-foot Noanet Peak to find that virtually the only sign of civilization visible from that barren knob of rock is the Boston skyline 20 miles away—floating on the horizon like the Emerald City. You have to scan the unbroken forest and rolling hills for a glimpse of another building. And you may hear no other sounds than the breeze and singing of birds.

The yellow-blazed Caryl Trail begins at one end of the parking lot. Follow it to junction 6 and turn left onto an unmarked trail. Pass a trail entering on the right; at the next junction, turn right, then left up a hill. You'll soon reach the open ledge atop Noanet Peak. Double back about 100 feet from the summit and walk straight onto a trail marked by a small sign prohibiting bikes. This path follows the crest of a wooded ridge, slowly descending to the Caryl Trail; turn left. At junction 18, walk straight onto the blue-blazed Peabody Trail. Pass ponds and the site of an old mill on the right. (From 1815 to 1876, Noanet Brook powered the Dover Union Iron Company, until a flood breached the huge dam at Noanet Falls. In 1954, then-owner Amelia Peabody rebuilt the dam.) Bear left through junction 4, and turn right onto the Caryl Trail again, which leads back to the parking lot.

57 Rocky Woods Reservation

2.3 mi/1.5 hrs 

Location: In Medfield; Eastern Massachusetts map page 239, grid c2.

User groups: Hikers, bikes, dogs, horses, skiers, and snowshoers. No wheelchair facilities. Dogs must be on a leash in the parking and picnic areas. Hunting is prohibited.

Access, fees: An entrance fee of $2.50 per person is levied only on weekends and holidays, with children under 12 free. The reservation is open daily from sunrise to sunset.

Directions: From Interstate 95 (Route 128) in Westwood, take exit 16B onto Route 109, driving west for 5.7 miles. Take a sharp right onto Hartford Street and continue six-tenths of a mile to the reservation entrance on the left. Or, from the junction of Routes 27 and 109 in Medfield, drive 1.7 miles east on Route 109 and bear left on Hartford Street. On weekdays, park in the first lot on the left; on weekends, park in the larger lot at the end of the entrance road.

Maps: A trail map is available for $2 from the ranger on duty weekends and holidays. Trail intersections numbered on the map correspond to numbered signs on the trails. For a topographic map of the area, request Medfield and Norwood from the USGS.

Contact: Trustees of Reservations, 572 Essex Street, Beverly, MA 01915-1530, (508) 921-1944; or the Southeast Region office, 2468B Washington Street, Canton, MA 02021; (617) 821-2977.

Trail notes: This 488-acre patch of woodlands, rich in birds and other wildlife, boasts more than 12 miles of cart paths and foot trails, and is popular with locals for activities from walking to cross-country skiing and fishing (catch and release only). There are many more loop possibilities besides the one described here.

From the far end of the second parking lot, follow the Quarry Trail a tenth of a mile along the shore of Chickering Pond. Bear left at trail junction 2, continue a tenth of a mile, then continue straight through junction 3. At trail junction 4, a half mile from junction 3, cross the Harwood Notch Trail diagonally, staying on the Quarry Trail. A quarter mile farther, at junction 7, turn right on the Ridge Trail and walk seven-tenths of a mile. Bear right at junction 6, turn left immediately after that at junction 5, and follow the cart path more than a half mile back to junction 2. The pond and parking area lie straight ahead.

58 Blue Hills: Skyline Trail Loop

4.5 mi/2.5 hrs 

Location: In the Blue Hills Reservation in Canton; Eastern Massachusetts map page 239, grid c2.

User groups: Hikers and dogs. No wheelchair facilities. Dogs must be on a leash. This trail is not suitable for skis or snowshoes. Bikes and hunting are prohibited.

Access, fees: Parking and access are free.

Directions: From Interstate 93, take exit 2B onto Route 138 north. Continue for nearly a half mile, passing the Howard Johnson's, to a commuter parking lot on the left. The reservation headquarters is at 695 Hillside Street in Milton, reached via the reservation entrance on Route 138, before the Howard Johnson's, or from Randolph Avenue (Interstate 93 exit 5).

Maps: A trail map of the Blue Hills is available for $1 at the reservation headquarters (see address below). Maps are also available through the Friends of the Blue Hills, the Audubon Society at the Metropolitan District Commission Trailside Museum, or the MDC (see addresses below). And the Appalachian Mountain Club (800-262-4455) sells a Blue Hills trail map (no contours) for $2.95. For a topographic map of the area, request Norwood from the USGS.

Contact: Blue Hills Reservation Headquarters, 695 Hillside Street, Milton, MA 02186. Friends of the Blue Hills, 1894 Canton Avenue (Route 138), Milton, MA 02186; (617) 326-2543. The Audubon Society at the Metropolitan District Commission Trailside Museum, 1904 Canton Avenue (Route 138), Milton, MA 02186; (617) 333-0690. Metropolitan District Commission, 2173 Washington Street, Canton, MA 02021; (617) 698-1802.

Trail notes: With 5,800 acres of forest spread over 20 hilltops, the Blue Hills Reservation in Quincy, Braintree, Randolph, Canton, and Milton comprises the largest tract of open space in Greater Boston. It hosts a broad diversity of flora and fauna, including the timber rattlesnake, which you are extremely unlikely to encounter, given the snakes' fear of people. The reservation harbors an extensive network of trails and carriage roads—but be aware that some are unmarked and confusing, and many are rocky and surprisingly rugged. At 635 feet, Great Blue Hill, near the reservation's western end, is the park's highest point and probably its most popular hike.

This 4.5-mile loop on the north and south branches of the Skyline Trail passes over Great Blue and four other hills, incorporating several good views—the best being the panorama from the stone tower on Great Blue, reached near this hike's end. In fact, while the tower, built of native granite, is less than 50 years old, it symbolizes this high point's long history. Patriots used it as a lookout during the Revolutionary War, lighting beacons up here to warn of any British attack; and for several hundred years, fires have been lit on Great Blue to celebrate historic occurrences, beginning with the repeal of the Stamp Act and including the signing of the Declaration of Independence.

From the parking lot, walk back toward the Howard Johnson's, watching for blue blazes that cross the road within 100 feet, and enter the woods at a granite post inscribed with the words "Skyline Trail." The trail ascends steeply for a half mile, reaching open ledges and the carriage road just below the summit. Turn right on the carriage road, where blue blazes are often marked on stones (which could be covered by snow in winter). Pass the path leading to the summit (there aren't any views, and the observatory is private property), and within one-tenth of a mile turn right with the blue blazes onto a footpath marked by a post inscribed "South Skyline Trail." It descends ledges with good views of the Boston skyline and Houghton Pond, enters the woods, and, within a mile of Great Blue, reaches wooded Houghton Hill. Descend a short distance to Hillside Street, cross it and turn left, and follow the blue blazes about 150 feet to where the blazes direct you back across the street toward the reservation headquarters (passing a post marked "North Skyline Trail"). Walk up the driveway and left of the headquarters onto a carriage path. In about 75 feet, turn right at a sign onto the North Skyline Trail. In minutes you'll reach an open ledge on Hancock Hill with a view of Great Blue Hill.

Continuing over Hemenway Hill and Wolcott Hill in the next mile, watch for side paths leading right to views of Boston. The Skyline Trail drops downhill, crosses a carriage path, then climbs the north side of Great Blue to the stone tower. Climb the stairs to the tower for a sweeping view of woods, city, and ocean. From the tower's observation deck, looking west (out over the stone building beside the tower), you may see Mount Wachusett. Standing on the side of the tower facing Boston, look left: on a clear day, Mount Monadnock rises between two tall radio towers in the distance. Descend the stone tower and turn right on the Skyline Trail, circling around Great Blue, past the posts marking the South and North Skyline Trail branches. Make a left turn at the third Skyline Trail post and descend a half mile to Route 138, where you began this hike.

59 Blue Hills: Rattlesnake and Wampatuck Hills

2.2 mi/1.5 hrs 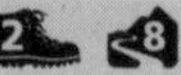

Location: In the Blue Hills Reservation in Braintree; Eastern Massachusetts map page 239, grid c3.

User groups: Hikers and dogs. No wheelchair facilities. Dogs must be on a leash. This trail is not suitable for skis or snowshoes. Bikes and hunting are prohibited.

Access, fees: Parking and access are free. This trail is closed from 8 P.M. to dawn.

Directions: From Interstate 93 in Braintree, take exit 6 and follow signs to Willard Street. About a mile from the highway, watch for the ice rink on the left. Drive two-tenths of a mile beyond the rink and turn left on Hayden Street, then immediately left again on Wampatuck Road. Drive another two-tenths of a mile and park at the roadside on the right, where a post marks the Skyline Trail. The reservation headquarters is at 695 Hillside Street in Milton, reached via the reservation entrance on Route 138, before the Howard Johnson's, or from Randolph Avenue (Interstate 93 exit 5).

Maps: A trail map of the Blue Hills is avail-

Western Massachusetts Map—page 238

able for $1 at the reservation headquarters (see address below). Maps are also available through the Friends of the Blue Hills, the Audubon Society at the Metropolitan District Commission Trailside Museum, or the MDC (see addresses below). The Appalachian Mountain Club (800-262-4455) sells a Blue Hills trail map (no contours) for $2.95. For a topographic map of the area, request Norwood from the USGS.

Contact: Blue Hills Reservation Headquarters, 695 Hillside Street, Milton, MA 02186. Friends of the Blue Hills, 1894 Canton Avenue (Route 138), Milton, MA 02186; (617) 326-2543. The Audubon Society at the Metropolitan District Commission Trailside Museum, 1904 Canton Avenue (Route 138), Milton, MA 02186; (617) 333-0690. Metropolitan District Commission, 2173 Washington Street, Canton, MA 02021; (617) 698-1802.

Trail notes: While many hikers flock to the west side of the reservation and to Great Blue Hill, the east side of the reservation remains a fairly well-kept secret—and the views from there are arguably better than those from Great Blue Hill. Standing in a warm summer breeze on Rattlesnake Hill one afternoon, gazing out over an expanse of woods to the Boston skyline in the distance, I listened, and listened . . . and realized I couldn't hear any traffic. I heard only the breeze and the singing of birds, despite having left the interstate behind just a half hour earlier and hiked merely a half mile.

From the roadside parking area, follow the Skyline Trail, which quickly ascends a short but steep hillside to a view of the thickly forested, rolling hills of the reservation and the Boston skyline beyond. The trail bends around an old quarry now filled with water, and about a half mile from the road reaches the rocky top of Rattlesnake Hill, with excellent views of the hills and skyline. Wampatuck Hill, with more good views, lies less than a half mile farther. Return the same way.

60 World's End Reservation

2.9 mi/1.5 hrs 

Location: In Hingham; Eastern Massachusetts map page 239, grid c3.

User groups: Hikers, bikes, dogs, skiers, and snowshoers. No wheelchair facilities. Dogs must be on a leash. Horses and hunting are prohibited.

Access, fees: There is an entrance fee of $3.50 per person (family passes are available). The reservation is open from sunrise to sunset.

Directions: From the junction of Routes 228 and 3A, drive north on 3A for six-tenths of a mile. Turn right on Summer Street, drive three-tenths of a mile, proceed straight through the traffic lights, then continue another eight-tenths of a mile to the World's End Reservation entrance.

Maps: A map of the carriage paths and trails is available for $1 at the entrance. For a topographic map of the area, request Hull from the USGS.

Contact: Trustees of Reservations, 572 Essex Street, Beverly, MA 01915-1530; (508) 921-1944.

Trail notes: This 250-acre peninsula in Hingham nearly became a community of 163 homes in the late 1800s, when then-landowner John Brewer hired none other than the famous landscape architect Frederick Law Olmsted to design a landscape of carriage paths lined by English oaks and native hardwoods. That much was accomplished, but the Brewer family continued to farm the land rather than develop it. Today, thanks to the Trustees of Reservations, this string of four low hills rising above Hingham Harbor provides local people with a wonderful recreation area for walking, running, or cross-country skiing. Bird-watchers flock here, particularly in spring and fall to observe migratory species. From various spots, you'll enjoy views of the Boston skyline, Hingham Harbor, and across the Weir River to Hull. Although the carriage paths are wide and safe, watch out for poison ivy in the fields. This hike loops around the property's perimeter, but four miles of carriage paths and three miles of foot trails, all interconnected, offer many other possible routes for exploration.

From the entrance, walk straight (northwest) along the flat carriage path for a quarter mile, then bear left around the west flank of Planter's Hill. A quarter mile past Planter's, cross the narrow land bar between the harbor and river, and turn left onto another carriage road. This follows a half-mile curve around a hillside; then turn left at the next junction of carriage paths. After another half mile, bear left again, reaching the land bar a quarter mile farther. Bear left, continue three-tenths of a mile, then turn right and walk nearly four-tenths of a mile back to the entrance.

61 Caratunk Wildlife Refuge

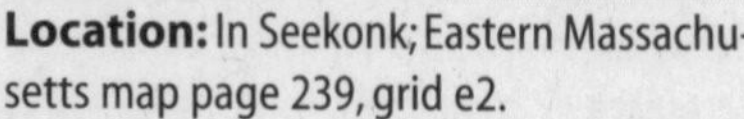

2.0 mi/1.0 hr 

Location: In Seekonk; Eastern Massachusetts map page 239, grid e2.

User groups: Hikers, skiers, and snowshoers. No wheelchair facilities. Bikes, dogs, horses, and hunting are prohibited.

Access, fees: A donation of $1 is requested for nonmembers of the Audubon Society. The refuge is open daily, sunrise to sunset. Visitors should stay on trails.

Directions: From Interstate 95 in Attleboro, take exit 2 onto Newport Avenue southbound (Route 1A). Drive 1.8 miles from the interstate, turn left onto Armistice Boulevard (Route 15), and follow it 1.2 miles to its end. Turn right onto Route 152 south, continue six-tenths of a mile, then turn left at a church onto Brown Avenue. Proceed eight-tenths of a mile farther to the refuge entrance on the right.

Maps: A map is available at the refuge. For a topographic map of the area, request Providence from the USGS.

Contact: Caratunk Wildlife Refuge, 301 Brown Avenue, Seekonk, MA 02771; (508) 761-8230. Audubon Society of Rhode Island, 12 Sanderson Road, Smithfield, RI 02917; (401) 949-5454.

Trail notes: Bird-watchers will want to visit here during April and May or from late August through October to catch the migratory birds, but this easy, two-mile walk mostly through woods is a nice outing any time of year. There are a few trail options in the refuge, all of them well blazed; this loop, mostly on the blue trail, is the longest, winding through much of the property, past open fields, wetlands, and two small ponds.

From the parking lot, walk to the right of the building, past the information kiosk and along the right edge of the field. Soon, a short side path loops into the woods to the right, bringing you along a bog, then back out to the field. Walk a short distance farther along the field, then turn right onto the red trail. After passing through a pine grove and skirting the far edge of the same field where you began, turn right onto the yellow trail, then bear left onto the blue trail. At the edge of Muskrat Pond, turn right, staying on blue past Ice Pond, crossing power lines, passing another pond and through the beech woods and a hemlock stand; you will pass several trail junctions and loop back to the bog, where you begin backtracking on the blue trail. After crossing the power lines and passing Ice Pond in the other direction, stay on blue past one junction with the yellow trail, then bear left onto the yellow trail at the next junction. Upon reaching the field, turn right on the red trail and follow it around the field back to the refuge office and parking lot.

62 Myles Standish State Forest Loop

11.0 mi/6.0 hrs 

Location: In Carver; Eastern Massachusetts map page 239, grid e4.

User groups: Hikers, bikes, dogs, skiers, and snowshoers. No wheelchair facilities. Dogs must be on a leash. Horses are prohibited. Hunting is allowed in season.

Access, fees: Parking and access are free.

Directions: From Interstate 495, take exit 2 on the Middleborough–Wareham line onto Route 58 north. Drive 2.5 miles to where Route 58 turns left, but continue straight ahead, following signs for the state forest. Proceed another eight-tenths of a mile and turn right onto Cranberry Road, then drive 2.8 miles to the state forest headquarters and a parking lot on the left.

Maps: A free, basic trail map of Myles Standish State Forest is available at the state forest headquarters or from the Massachusetts Division of Forests and Parks (see address below). For topographic maps of the area, request Plymouth and Wareham from the USGS.

Contact: Myles Standish State Forest, Cranberry Road, P.O. Box 66, South Carver, MA 02366; (508) 866-2526. Massachusetts Division of Forests and Parks, 100 Cambridge Street, 19th Floor, Boston, MA 02202; (617) 727-3180.

Trail notes: Myles Standish State Forest sprawls over more than 14,000 acres, making it one of the largest public lands in Massachusetts. A gridwork of old woods roads cuts through this pine barrens, along with a hiking trail and a paved bicycle path. This loop from the forest headquarters, which I did one November afternoon on my mountain bike, connects several dirt woods roads, and much of its course is reserved for skiers in winter (who have to watch out for snowmobiles on other roads in Myles Standish). The grid pattern of roads and signs at many intersections makes navigating through this vast, ubiquitous landscape easier than it might otherwise be; but bring a map. Although the terrain is mostly flat, there are slight rises and dips that can make the workout a little harder on a bike or skis. Also, sand traps crop up periodically, spanning the roads, and I found a few of them impossible to pedal across; fortunately, none were very big. Distances in this description are estimates based on the map provided by the state.

From the parking lot, head back out onto Cranberry Road, turn right, then immediately right again past the headquarters building onto paved Lower College Pond Road into the state forest. Within a half mile, bicyclists and skiers can turn left onto the paved bike path, which leads to the dirt Halfway Pond Road; others will continue a quarter mile on Lower College Pond Road to the Halfway Pond Road intersection. Turn left onto Halfway Pond Road, follow it a half mile to a crossroads, and turn right onto Jessup Road. Continue about seven-tenths of a mile and bear right at a sign reading "Ebeeme Road," which is shown as Jessup Road on the state map. A half mile farther, at a crossroads, turn right onto Federal Pond Road. Follow it a mile, crossing the bridle trail, a gas line right-of-way, Kamesit Way, and turn right onto Sabbatia Road. Continue a mile, then turn left onto Three Cornered Pond Road. Reaching the paved Lower College Pond Road within a quarter mile, turn right, then bear left immediately and proceed straight onto the bridle path (don't turn left onto another branch of the bridle path), marked by a horse symbol sign. In a quarter mile, at the next intersection, turn left onto Negas Road, continue a half mile, then turn left onto paved Upper College Pond Road. Proceed nearly a half mile and turn right onto Three Cornered Pond Road. Three-quarters of a mile farther, turn right again onto Cobb Road and follow it three-quarters of a mile to its end. Turn right onto Halfway Pond Road, go about two-tenths of a mile, then take the first left. In about three-tenths of a mile, turn left again onto Doctor's Pond Road, go a half mile, then turn right onto Webster Springs Road. Follow it nearly a mile, crossing paved Circuit Drive, a dirt road, the bike path, and the bridle path before reaching Upper College Pond Road. Turn left, following the paved road nearly a half mile to its end. Turn right on paved Fearing Pond Road and continue a half mile back to the forest headquarters.

63 Province Lands Trail

6.0 mi/3.0 hrs 

Location: In the Cape Cod National Seashore in Provincetown; Cape Cod/Martha's Vineyard map page 240, grid a3.

User groups: Hikers, bikes, dogs, and wheelchair users. Dogs must be on a leash. This trail rarely receives enough snow for skis or snowshoes. Horses and hunting are prohibited.

Access, fees: Parking and access are free. Trails are closed to the public between midnight and 6 A.M. The Province Lands Visitors Center on Race Point Road is open daily from 9 A.M. to 4:30 P.M.

Directions: Drive U.S. 6 east to Provincetown. At the traffic lights on U.S. 6, turn right onto Race Point Road. Continue to the Beech Forest parking area on the left; the Province Lands Visitors Center is a short distance farther on the right.

Maps: A guide to national seashore bike trails is available at the Province Lands and Salt Pond Visitor Centers (in Eastham). A detailed map of roads and bike paths on Cape Cod and the Islands and Cape Ann and the North Shore is available for $5 from BikeMaps Massachusetts, P.O. Box 1035, Cambridge, MA 02140; (617) 868-8948. For a topographic map of the area, request Provincetown from the USGS.

Contact: Superintendent, Cape Cod National Seashore, South Wellfleet, MA 02663; (508) 349-3785. Salt Pond Visitors Center, (508) 255-3421.

Trail notes: Though designed for bikers, this trail is used by hikers, runners, in-line skaters, and others, and it's good for wheelchairs, too. The paved bikeway makes a circuitous loop through forest, past ponds, and over sprawling sand dunes—it may be the most interesting bike path I've ever pedaled. Be sure to take the spur path a half mile out to Race Point (included in the above mileage figure), which is the tip of Massachusetts and a great place for whale-watching during the seasonal migrations, when the whales often swim close to shore. Heed the center dividing line on this path, especially through its many blind corners. Pick up the bike path from the Beech Forest parking lot; the loop returns here.

64 Great Island Trail

6.0 mi/3.5 hrs 

Location: In the Cape Cod National Seashore in Wellfleet; Cape Cod/Martha's Vineyard map page 240, grid b4.

User groups: Hikers only. No wheelchair facilities. This trail rarely receives enough snow for skis or snowshoes. Bikes, dogs, horses, and hunting are prohibited.

Access, fees: Parking and access are free.

Trails are closed to the public between midnight and 6 A.M. The Salt Pond Visitors Center is open daily from 9 A.M. to 4:30 P.M.

Directions: From the Salt Pond Visitors Center at the Doane Road exit in Eastham, drive U.S. 6 east for 8.2 miles. Turn left at the sign for Wellfleet center and harbor. Drive four-tenths of a mile and turn left at the sign for Blue Harbor. In another six-tenths of a mile you will reach the marina; turn right, following the road (with the water on your left) for 2.5 miles to the Great Island parking lot on the left.

Maps: An information board is at the trailhead, and information about the trail is available at the Salt Pond Visitors Center. A detailed map of roads and bike paths on Cape Cod and the Islands and Cape Ann and the North Shore is available for $5 from BikeMaps Massachusetts, P.O. Box 1035, Cambridge, MA 02140; (617) 868-8948. For a topographic map of the area, request Wellfleet from the USGS.

Contact: Superintendent, Cape Cod National Seashore, South Wellfleet, MA 02663; (508) 349-3785. Salt Pond Visitors Center, (508) 255-3421.

Trail notes: A friend and I took this hike in late afternoon on a warm spring day, as the sinking sun ignited the dunes a vivid yellow, a sharp contrast against the cobalt sky. We watched dozens of tiny crabs scatter from us in a wave of motion that for an instant made me think the sand was inexplicably sliding in one direction. We watched high, thin cirrus clouds create a rainbow halo around the sun. We saw no one else in three hours on this trail—except a lone sea kayaker paddling the glassy waters of the bay far offshore. The beach here is a great place to watch the sun set over Cape Cod Bay.

From the parking lot, the trail enters the woods, following a wide forest road. An optional side loop (adding two miles to the hike) leads to the Tavern Site, so named because fragments of a seventeenth-century tavern were excavated there; nothing remains today, however. The main trail leads over Great Beach Hill—which has no views—and out to the grasslands separating the beach from the forest. Follow that old road around to Jeremy Point overlook, where the dunes end abruptly and you reach the beach on Cape Cod Bay. At low tide, the long spit out to Jeremy Point may be walkable, but be aware that it disappears under the ocean when the tide rises. Return the way you came.

65 Atlantic White Cedar Swamp

1.0 mi/0.75 hr 

Location: In the Cape Cod National Seashore in South Wellfleet; Cape Cod/Martha's Vineyard map page 240, grid b4.

User groups: Hikers only. The Marconi station is wheelchair accessible. This trail rarely receives enough snow for skis or snowshoes. Bikes, dogs, horses, and hunting are prohibited.

Access, fees: Parking and access are free. Trails are closed to the public between midnight and 6 A.M. The Salt Pond Visitors Center is open daily from 9 A.M. to 4:30 P.M.

Directions: Drive U.S. 6 east to Eastham. Five miles beyond the Doane Road exit for the Salt Pond Visitors Center, turn right at signs for the Marconi station and continue to the parking lot. The Marconi station, which has historical displays, is between the lot and the beach. The trail begins at the parking lot.

Maps: A trail guide is available at the trailhead. Maps and information about the national seashore are available at the Salt Pond Visitors Center. A detailed map of roads and bike paths on Cape Cod and the Islands and Cape Ann and the North Shore is available for $5 from BikeMaps Massachusetts, P.O. Box 1035, Cambridge, MA 02140; (617) 868-8948. For a topographic map of the area, request Wellfleet from the USGS.

Contact: Superintendent, Cape Cod National Seashore, South Wellfleet, MA 02663; (508) 349-3785. Salt Pond Visitors Center, (508) 255-3421.

Trail notes: I consider this one of the highlights of the national seashore—and almost as much for the site's historic significance as for this short but uniquely beautiful swamp trail. It was from this spot, on January 18, 1903, that the Italian Guglielmo Marconi transmitted a 48-word message to England and received an immediate reply—the first two-way transoceanic communication and first wireless telegram between America and Europe. The four huge towers that once stood here are long gone; in fact, more than half the land where they stood has since eroded into the sea. With the way the ocean and wind continually batter this narrowest section of Cape Cod—the peninsula spans barely a mile across here—one has to wonder how many years will elapse before the elements cut the outer Cape off completely from the mainland.

The Atlantic White Cedar Swamp Trail begins among stunted oak and pine trees. But as you descend, albeit slightly and at a very gentle grade, the trees grow taller—they are more protected from the harsh ocean climate in this hollow of sorts. Pitch pine, black and white oak, golden beach-heather, and broom crowberry thrive, though many are still twisted in the manner characteristic of a place buffeted by almost constant winds. A boardwalk winds through the swamp, an eerie depression formed, like other "kettles" on the Cape, by a melting glacial ice block. The swamp's peat floor reaches down 24 feet. Cedars crowd in on the boardwalk, some leaning over it—the sense of intimacy with this odd little forest overwhelms. The trail emerges abruptly from the swamp onto an old sand road that leads back to the parking lot.

66 Nauset Marsh

1.2 mi/0.75 hr 

Location: In the Cape Cod National Seashore in Eastham; Cape Cod/Martha's Vineyard map page 240, grid b4.

User groups: Hikers only. No wheelchair facilities. This trail rarely receives enough snow for skis or snowshoes. Bikes, dogs, horses, and hunting are prohibited.

Access, fees: Parking and access are free. Trails are closed to the public between midnight and 6 A.M. The Salt Pond Visitors Center is open daily from 9 A.M. to 4:30 P.M.

Directions: Drive U.S. 6 east to Eastham. Take the exit for Doane Road, following signs for national seashore information to the Salt Pond Visitors Center.

Maps: A trail guide is available in a box at the trailhead, and maps and information about the national seashore are available in the visitors center. A detailed map of roads and bike paths on Cape Cod and the Islands and Cape Ann and the North Shore is available for $5 from BikeMaps Massachusetts, P.O. Box 1035, Cambridge, MA 02140; (617) 868-8948. For a topographic map of the area, request Orleans from the USGS.

Contact: Superintendent, Cape Cod National Seashore, South Wellfleet, MA 02663; (508) 349-3785. Salt Pond Visitors Center, (508) 255-3421.

Trail notes: This easy-to-follow trail has numerous interpretive signs with information about its abundant flora, and a good view of Nauset Marsh. From the visitors center parking lot, start out on the Buttonbush Trail for the Blind, which leads shortly to the Nauset Marsh Trail. It passes through pitch pine, black cherry, and eastern red cedar trees, then follows the edge of Salt Pond. (The pond was created when a glacier receded and left behind enormous salt blocks, which eventually melted, leaving kettle ponds such as this one in their wake. The ocean later broke through a land barrier to infiltrate Salt Pond.) The trail then turns away from the channel connecting pond to ocean and enters a forest of honeysuckle and cedar. It passes an open overlook above Nauset Marsh, which at one time was navigable. After entering a forest of red cedar and bayberry, it passes a side path leading nearly a mile to a good view of the marsh at a spot marked by the Doane Memorial, a plaque paying tribute to a family that once owned land here. The loop culminates near the visitors center parking lot.

67 Cape Cod Rail Trail

24.5 mi. one way/12.0 hrs

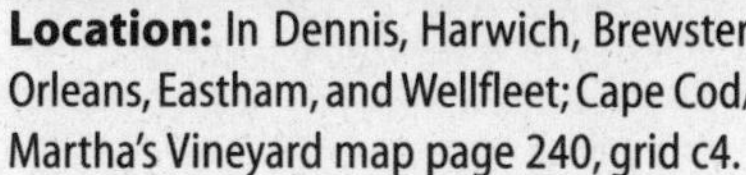

Location: In Dennis, Harwich, Brewster, Orleans, Eastham, and Wellfleet; Cape Cod/Martha's Vineyard map page 240, grid c4.

User groups: Hikers, bikes, dogs, horses, and wheelchairs users. Dogs must be on a leash. This trail rarely receives enough snow for skis or snowshoes. Hunting is prohibited.

Access, fees: Parking and access are free.

Directions: To reach the western end of the trail, from U.S. 6 in Dennis, take exit 9 onto Route 134 south. Proceed through two traffic signals to a large parking lot on the left for the Cape Cod Rail Trail. The eastern terminus is at Lecount Hollow Road in South Wellfleet, near the Cape Cod National Seashore's Marconi Visitors Center and off U.S. 6. The trail can be accessed at numerous points along its path.

Maps: The "Cape Cod & the Islands Bicycle Map," a detailed bicycling map which covers the Cape Cod Rail Trail, is available for $5 from Rubel BikeMaps, Box 1035, Cambridge, MA 02140. (On that map's flip side is the "Cape Ann & North Shore Bicycle Map.") For topographic maps of the area, request Dennis, Harwich, and Orleans from the USGS.

Contact: Nickerson State Park, P.O. Box 787, Brewster, MA 02631; (508) 896-3491. Massachusetts Division of Forests and Parks, 100 Cambridge Street, 19th Floor, Boston, MA 02202; (617) 727-3180.

Trail notes: Following a former railroad bed, the paved Cape Cod Rail Trail extends for 24.5 miles from Route 134 in South Dennis to Lecount Hollow Road in South Wellfleet, near the Cape Cod National Seashore's Marconi Visitors Center, making for about a two-hour bike ride. The mostly flat, paved trail crosses cranberry bogs, forests, and several roads, providing numerous access and egress points, including at the entrance to Nickerson State Park on Route 6A in Brewster, and at Locust Road in Eastham, which is off U.S. 6 near the Cape Cod National Seashore's Salt Pond Visitors Center on Doane Road. The trail passes through Nickerson, which has its own system of hiking trails and a bike path, and it connects with bike paths at the national seashore. The rail trail is very much a citizen's path—every time I've biked on it, it has been busy with cyclists, in-line skaters, walkers, adults, and children. As such, it can be difficult to bike at a fast pace, but a scenic and safe outing for a family.

68 Gay Head

3.0 mi/1.5 hrs

Location: In Gay Head on Martha's Vineyard; Cape Cod/Martha's Vineyard map page 240, grid f1.

User groups: Hikers only. No wheelchair facilities. This trail rarely receives enough snow for skis or snowshoes and is not suitable for bikes or horses. Dogs and hunting are prohibited.

Access, fees: A $15 fee for parking is charged from Memorial Day weekend through mid-October, although cyclists, walkers, or anyone not parking a vehicle can access the beach free. Three seasonal ferry services make regular trips, from May to October, to Vineyard Haven or Oak Bluffs from Falmouth, (508) 548-4800, and Hyannis, (508) 778-2600, on Cape Cod as well as from New Bedford, Massachusetts, (508) 997-1688. The Steamship Authority, (508) 477-8600, carries vehicles and passengers from Woods Hole on Cape Cod to Vineyard Haven year-round and Woods Hole to Oak Bluffs from May 15 through October 15.

Directions: The cliffs at Gay Head are on Moshup Beach at the western tip of Martha's Vineyard, in the town of Gay Head, and at the end of the State Road, which crosses the island from Vineyard Haven. Ferry services make regular trips to Vineyard Haven and Oak Bluffs from Falmouth and Hyannis on Cape Cod, as well as from New Bedford, Massachusetts (see additional ferry information above).

Maps: Although no map is needed for this hike, for a topographic map of the area, request Squibnocket from the USGS.

Contact: Gay Head Town Hall, 65 State Road, Gay Head, MA 02535; (508) 645-2300.

Trail notes: The vibrant pastels of the clay cliffs at Gay Head, the westernmost point of the island of Martha's Vineyard, are an eye-catching attraction at any time of day, but particularly striking at sunset, when the sun's low, long rays bring out the layered browns, yellows, reds, whites, and deep grays. This hike is an easy walk along Moshup Beach, and popular with tourists. From the parking lot, follow the sandy trail, sometimes crossing boardwalk, which parallels Moshup Road. Within minutes you are on the beach; turn right and follow the beach to the cliffs. At high tide, you may have difficulty walking to the far end of the cliffs. Head back the way you came.

Rhode Island

Overall Rating

1 2 3 4 5 6 7 8 9 10

Poor .... Fair .... Great

Difficulty

1 2 3 4 5

A stroll .... Moderate ...... A real butt-kicker!

Rhode Island

Adjoining Maps:

North: Massachusetts .... *pages* 238–239
East: Eastern Massachusetts .... *page* 239
West: Eastern Connecticut .... *page* 321

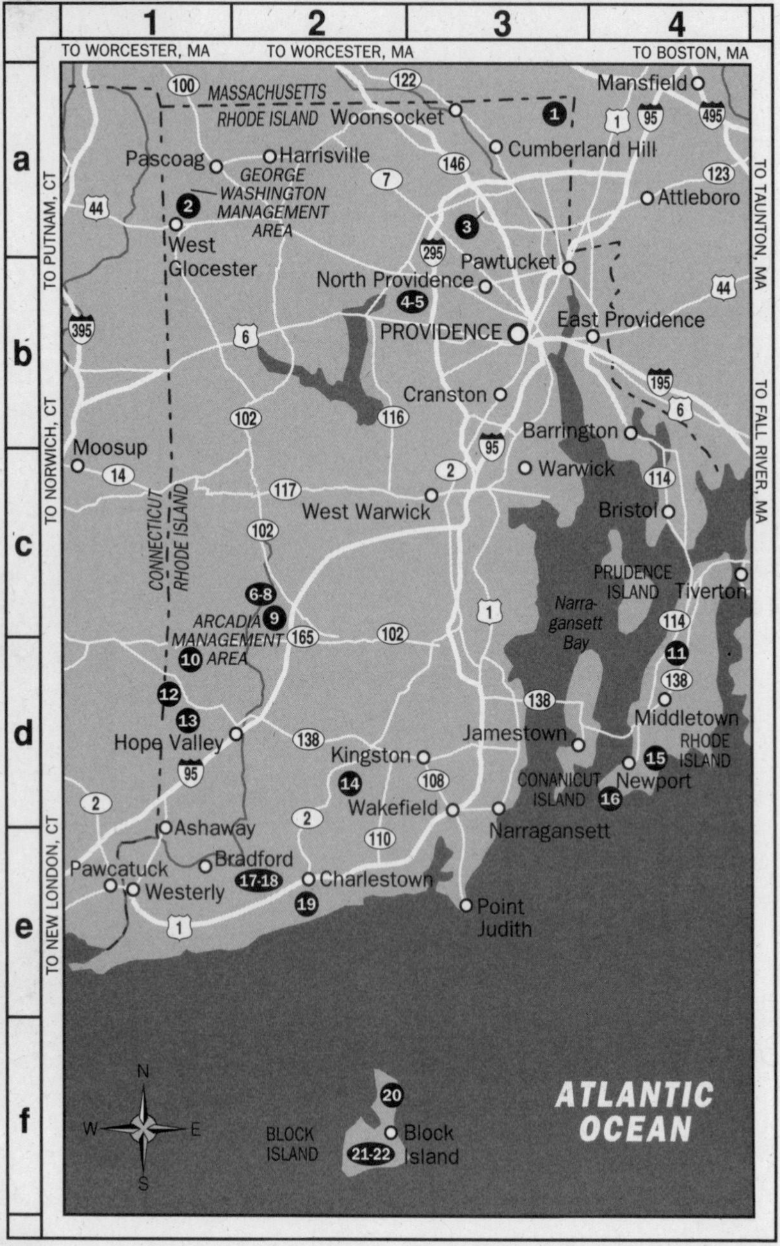

1 2 3 4

a b c d e f

TO WORCESTER, MA
TO WORCESTER, MA
TO BOSTON, MA
TO PUTNAM, CT
TO NORWICH, CT
TO NEW LONDON, CT
TO TAUNTON, MA
TO FALL RIVER, MA
MASSACHUSETTS
RHODE ISLAND
CONNECTICUT
RHODE ISLAND
Mansfield
Woonsocket
Cumberland Hill
Attleboro
Pascoag
Harrisville
GEORGE WASHINGTON MANAGEMENT AREA
West Glocester
Pawtucket
North Providence
PROVIDENCE
East Providence
Cranston
Barrington
Warwick
West Warwick
Bristol
Moosup
PRUDENCE ISLAND
Tiverton
Narragansett Bay
ARCADIA MANAGEMENT AREA
Middletown
RHODE ISLAND
Hope Valley
Jamestown
Kingston
Newport
CONANICUT ISLAND
Wakefield
Narragansett
Ashaway
Bradford
Pawcatuck
Westerly
Charlestown
Point Judith
ATLANTIC OCEAN
BLOCK ISLAND
Block Island
N
W
E
S
100 122 1 95 495 146 7 123 44 295 44 395 6 195 6 102 116 95 14 2 117 114 102 1 114 165 102 138 138 138 95 108 2 2 110 1
1 2 3 4-5 6-8 9 10 11 12 13 14 15 16 17-18 19 20 21-22

Rhode Island features:

RHODE ISLAND

The country's smallest state and one of its flattest, Rhode Island doesn't entice hikers and backpackers from great distances in order to sample its trails, as do states like Maine, New Hampshire, and Vermont. But locals enjoy its relatively shorter and easier hikes, which are scattered across the Ocean State in an abundance that surprised me when I first started visiting.

Most of the hikes here are in either state parklands or private preserves. Each state park's management issues regulations specific to its property, and many impose restrictions on bikes and require that dogs be kept on a leash. The two premier public lands are the George Washington Management Area, in the state's northwest corner, and the Arcadia Management Area, in the southwest corner.

Several of the hikes covered in this guide are in bird sanctuaries or other places known among bird-watchers; the state's woods and waters are a popular stop for migratory birds along the Atlantic Flyway. The private preserves are often open only to hikers; some require a small fee.

Rhode Island's winters rarely see enough snow for cross-country skiing or snowshoeing. But many public lands, like the Arcadia Management Area, harbor a wealth of dirt roads perfect for mountain biking. Respect postings that prohibit bikes from certain trails. Hunting is generally allowed in season on any land that is not posted specifically prohibiting it. Arcadia Management Area requires trail users to wear fluorescent orange during the hunting season.

Rhode Island Map—page 300

❶ Diamond Hill

0.5 mi/0.5 hr 

Location: In Diamond Hill State Park in Cumberland; Rhode Island map page 300, grid a3.

User groups: Hikers, bikes, dogs, horses, skiers, and snowshoers. No wheelchair facilities. Hunting is allowed in season.

Access, fees: Parking and access are free.

Directions: From Interstate 295, take exit 11 for Route 114 northbound and follow it 3.7 miles north to a dirt lot on the right at the base of the Diamond Hill cliff.

Maps: For a topographic map of the area, request Attleboro from the USGS.

Contact: Rhode Island Division of Parks and Recreation, 2321 Hartford Pike, Johnston, RI 02919; (401) 277-2632.

Trail notes: Here's a short walk atop a tall cliff to good views of the hills surrounding Route 114 and Diamond Hill State Park. Unfortunately, this place is marred by litter and graffiti. A cleanup by a local group would do wonders for the experience of this hike. From the dirt lot, follow the right fork of the trail as it works up the right side of the cliffs. Don't venture onto the cliff face, where there is much loose rock. You'll reach the top within minutes; then hike carefully along the cliff's edge, where the many footpaths can cause confusion. The trail traverses the top of the cliff and descends the other side of the hill, returning to the dirt parking lot.

❷ Walkabout Trail

2–8 mi/1–4 hrs 

Location: In the George Washington Management Area in Chepachet; Rhode Island map page 300, grid a1.

User groups: Hikers, dogs, horses, and snowshoers. No wheelchair facilities. Dogs must be on a leash. Bikes and skis are prohibited. Hunting is allowed in season.

Access, fees: Parking and access are free.

Directions: The entrance is off U.S. 44, eight-tenths of a mile east of its junction with Route 94, at a sign for the George Washington Camping Area. Proceed past the gatehouse; at three-tenths of a mile from U.S. 44, turn left (across from a trail marked by orange, red, and blue blazes—this hike's terminus). The Walkabout Trail begins a short distance farther, on the right, across from a parking area.

Maps: A trail map is available at the park headquarters on U.S. 44 in Glocester. You can also obtain the George Washington Management Area map from the Appalachian Mountain Club, (800) 262-4455. For a topographic map of the area, request Thompson, Connecticut, from the USGS.

Contact: George Washington Management Area, RR 2, Box 2185, Chepachet, RI 02814; (401) 568-2013. Rhode Island Division of Forest Environment, 260 Arcadia Road, Hope Valley, RI 02832; (401) 539-2356. The North-South Trail, when completed (possibly by 1999), will extend about 72 miles through western Rhode Island, linking many existing trail systems, including trails through the George Washington Management Area. For maps and a brochure, contact the Rhode Island Department of Environmental Management, 83 Park Street, Providence, RI 02903; (401) 277-2776.

Trail notes: The George Washington Management Area is one of the two nicest backcountry parklands in Rhode Island, and the Walkabout is its signature hiking trail. Mostly flat, it winds along the shores of largely undeveloped ponds and through quiet woodlands punctuated by glacial erratics, crossing myriad brooks and streams. In fact, the first nice view of Bowdish Reservoir occurs not far down the trail, at a large rock. This is a wet place that can be buggy in spring.

The trail offers three options—the eight-mile orange loop, the six-mile red loop, and the two-mile blue loop—all of them well blazed and all beginning from the same parking lot. The possibilities in this "remote" corner of tiny Rhode Island begin with the Walkabout, but the forest roads here open up much more terrain for easy skiing or mountain biking.

3 Lime Rock Preserve

2.0 mi/1.5 hrs 

Location: In Lincoln; Rhode Island map page 300, grid a3.

User groups: Hikers, bikes, dogs, horses, skiers, and snowshoers. No wheelchair facilities. Hunting is allowed in season.

Access, fees: Parking and access are free. The preserve is open to hikers year-round from dawn to dusk.

Directions: From Route 146 northbound, take the exit for Route 123 westbound, proceed to the traffic lights, and turn right. Drive 1.7 miles; at the Blackstone Valley Historical Society building, turn left onto Wilbur Road and drive another half mile. Watch closely for a small dirt driveway on the right; there's no sign, but information boards are set back from the road. From Route 146 southbound, take the Route 246 exit, turn right and drive three-tenths of a mile, then turn left on Wilbur Road.

Maps: For a topographic map of the area, request Attleboro from the USGS.

Contact: The Nature Conservancy, 45 South Angell Street, Providence, RI 02906; (401) 331-7110.

Trail notes: This nature preserve in Lincoln offers a nice walk in the woods along a long-abandoned electric railroad bed and around a pond. The forest is punctuated by rock ledges and wildflowers. From the dirt driveway, follow the railroad bed. Initially it sits low and may be flooded—you can easily hike the higher ground to either side—but it gradually rises high above the surrounding terrain. Within about a half mile, just before you reach a point where the railroad bed passes above a nice little stream valley, turn onto a trail diverging right (the first you will encounter on that side). It leads to the far end of the pond that soon becomes visible through the trees, and across an earthen dam where you will get a good view of the pond. Across the dam, ledges rise high up a hillside. Turn left with the trail, circling the pond and eventually reaching the rail bed again, where turning left returns you to the parking area.

4 Powder Mill Ledges

2.0 mi/1.0 hr 

Location: In Smithfield; Rhode Island map page 300, grid b3.

User groups: Hikers only. No wheelchair facilities. These trails rarely receive enough snow for snowshoes and are not suitable for skis. Bikes, dogs, horses, and hunting are prohibited.

Access, fees: Parking and access are free. Trails are open to the public from dawn to dusk every day.

Directions: From U.S. 44 in Smithfield, turn south on Route 5. Immediately on the left is the entrance to Powder Mill Ledges, at the headquarters of the Audubon Society of Rhode Island.

Maps: A map is available in the Audubon Society Visitors Center, which is open Tuesday through Friday from noon to 5 P.M., and Saturday from noon to 4 P.M. For a topographic map of the area, request North Scituate from the USGS.

Contact: Audubon Society of Rhode Island, 12 Sanderson Road, Smithfield, RI 02917; (401) 949-5454.

Trail notes: The three well-marked loop trails through this bird sanctuary lead you along open meadows, a small pond and boggy areas, and through pine forest. The orange loop offers a self-guided tour of its vegetation; pick up a pamphlet at the visitors center. Although at times the sound of traffic from nearby U.S. 44 is audible, the song of birds is constant. This is a nice local walk, not to mention a good place for birding. A lengthy list of the month's bird sightings is posted on an information board outside the visitors center. On the spring day of my visit, species checked off the list included the red-tailed hawk, downy woodpecker, black-capped chickadee, and white-breasted nuthatch. The center conducts regular educational and children's programs as well.

Pick up the trail behind the information board. This hike links all three loops around the refuge perimeter, the first blazed orange, the second blue, and the third yellow, but you can easily make a shorter loop. The yellow loop—the longest and outermost of the three—follows power lines for a time and can be very hot on a sunny summer day.

5 Snake Den

0.5 mi/0.5 hr 

Location: In Snake Den State Park in Johnston; Rhode Island map page 300, grid b3.

User groups: Hikers, dogs, skiers, and snowshoers. No wheelchair facilities. This trail is not suitable for bikes or horses. Hunting is prohibited.

Access, fees: Parking and access are free.

Directions: From U.S. 44, follow Route 5 southbound for six-tenths of a mile, turn right onto Brown Avenue, and drive four-tenths of a mile to a pullout on the right across from a wide, unmarked trail blocked by large rocks. From U.S. 6, 2.6 miles west of Interstate 295, turn north onto Brown Avenue and drive two miles to the pullout on the left.

Maps: For a topographic map of the area, request North Scituate from the USGS.

Contact: Rhode Island Division of Parks and Recreation, 2321 Hartford Pike, Johnston, RI 02919; (401) 277-2632.

Trail notes: The Snake Den is a narrow defile in the woods, barely more than 100 yards long, with broken rock ledges rising as much as 40 feet above the trail on one side. A short, easy walk, it's a good place to bring young children, though you'll want to watch out for loose rock on the ledges. From the pullout, follow the wide trail into the woods, bearing right where it forks. Within minutes, you drop down into the Snake Den; the trail leads straight through it and continues into the woods beyond. It is possible—exercising appropriate caution—to scramble up through natural breaks, or gullies, in the ledges and get atop these low cliffs, then take a trail that loops back to where you started hiking; or you can access the trail over the ledges from the opposite end of the cliffs.

6 Stepstone Falls

3.4 mi/2.5 hrs 

Location: In the Arcadia Management Area in Exeter; Rhode Island map page 300, grid c2.

User groups: Hikers, dogs, skiers, and snowshoers. No wheelchair facilities. Dogs must be on a leash from March 1 through August 15. Bikes and horses are prohibited. Hunting is allowed in season; all trail users are required to wear at least 200 square inches of fluorescent orange, as a cap and/or vest, during the hunting season (from the second Saturday of October through the last day of February).

Access, fees: Parking and access are free.

Austin Farm Road is closed to motor vehicles at Escoheag Hill Road during the winter. Other roads open to traffic in summer but closed in winter include Brook Trail, Barber Trail, and Blitzkrieg Trail.

Directions: From the junction of Routes 3 and 165 in Exeter, drive west on Route 165 for about 5.5 miles and turn right onto the paved Escoheag Hill Road. Continue another mile and turn right onto the dirt Austin Farm Road. Two roads diverge here; take the left one, drive past an Arcadia Management Area office (where maps may be available), and, about a mile from Escoheag Hill Road, pull into a parking area on the left, immediately before the bridge over Falls River. To reach the Arcadia Management Area headquarters from the junction of Routes 3 and 165, drive west on Route 165 for 1.5 miles and turn left onto Arcadia Road. Continue 2.5 miles to a T intersection, turn left, and drive six-tenths of a mile to the headquarters on the right.

Maps: A free trail map is available at the Arcadia headquarters and in various parking lots in the management area. The George Washington Management Area/Arcadia Management Area/Blue Hills (Massachusetts) map, which shows trails but not contour lines, is $2.95 from the Appalachian Mountain Club, (800) 262-4455. For topographic maps of the area, request Hope Valley and Voluntown from the USGS.

Contact: Rhode Island Division of Forest Environment, Arcadia Headquarters, 260 Arcadia Road, Hope Valley, RI 02832; (401) 539-2356. The headquarters is open from 8:30 A.M. to 4 P.M. weekdays.

Trail notes: The Ben Utter Trail, marked by a sign at the back of the parking area, parallels Falls River, actually a small, stone-littered brook. Relatively flat, the trail follows the brook for 1.7 miles to Stepstone Falls, where water tumbles through a series of short ledges, the highest about two feet tall. I walked this trail on a beautiful Saturday morning in August and, surprisingly, had it all to myself. Follow the yellow blazes and the obvious footpath all the way to the falls, then double back the way you came. The trail actually ends at the dirt Falls River Road, just beyond the falls, which is reached via Escoheag Hill Road; by shuttling cars, you could make this a 1.7-mile walk and not have to double back.

Special note: For a nice combination of hikes, link this one with Penny Hill (hike number 7), which begins from the same parking area.

7 Penny Hill

1.6 mi/1.0 hr 

Location: In the Arcadia Management Area in Exeter; Rhode Island map page 300, grid c2.

User groups: Hikers, dogs, and snowshoers. No wheelchair facilities. Dogs must be on a leash from March 1 through August 15. Bikes and horses are prohibited. Hunting is allowed in season; all trail users are required to wear at least 200 square inches of fluorescent orange, as a cap and/or vest, during the hunting season (from the second Saturday of October through the last day of February).

Access, fees: Parking and access are free. Austin Farm Road is closed to motor vehicles at Escoheag Hill Road during the winter. Other roads open to traffic in summer but closed in winter include Brook Trail, Barber Trail, and Blitzkrieg Trail.

Directions: From the junction of Routes 3 and 165 in Exeter, drive west on Route 165 for about 5.5 miles and turn right onto the paved Escoheag Hill Road. Continue another mile and turn right onto the dirt Austin Farm Road. Two roads diverge here; take the left one, drive past an Arcadia Management Area office (where maps may be available), and, about a mile from Escoheag Hill Road, pull into a parking area on the left, immediately before the bridge over Falls River. To reach the Arcadia Management Area headquarters from the junction of Routes 3 and 165, drive west on Route 165 for 1.5 miles and turn left onto Arcadia Road. Continue 2.5 miles to a T intersection, turn left, and drive six-tenths of a mile to the headquarters on the right.

Maps: A free trail map is available at the Arcadia headquarters and in various parking lots in the management area. The George Washington Management Area/Arcadia Management Area/Blue Hills (Massachusetts) map, which shows trails but not contour lines, is $2.95 from the Appalachian Mountain Club, (800) 262-4455. For topographic maps of the area, request Hope Valley and Voluntown from the USGS.

Contact: Rhode Island Division of Forest Environment, Arcadia Headquarters, 260 Arcadia Road, Hope Valley, RI 02832; (401) 539-2356. The headquarters is open from 8:30 A.M. to 4 P.M. weekdays.

Trail notes: Although trees largely block any view from the summit of 370-foot Penny Hill, this hike offers an appealing walk through the woods to hilltop ledges that young kids would enjoy scrambling around on. From the parking area, cross the bridge over Falls River and ignore the first yellow-blazed trail entering the woods on the right. About 75 feet past the bridge, turn right into the woods on the yellow-blazed Breakheart Trail. The trail crosses a brook in an area that is often muddy, emerges from the woods within a half mile of the start to cross Austin Farm Road again, then ascends moderately to the craggy height of Penny Hill. From there, the Breakheart Trail descends to the east, but this hike returns the way you came.

Special note: For a nice combination of hikes, link this one with Stepstone Falls (hike number 6), which begins from the same parking area.

---

8 Breakheart Pond Loop

2.0 mi/1.0 hr 

Location: In the Arcadia Management Area in Exeter; Rhode Island map page 300, grid c2.

User groups: Hikers, dogs, skiers, and snowshoers. No wheelchair facilities. Dogs must be on a leash from March 1 through August 15. Bikes and horses are prohibited. Hunting is allowed in season; all trail users are required to wear at least 200 square inches of fluorescent orange, as a cap and/or vest, during the hunting season (from the second Saturday of October through the last day of February).

Access, fees: Parking and access are free. Austin Farm Road is closed to motor vehicles at Escoheag Hill Road during the winter. Other roads open to traffic in summer but closed in winter include Brook Trail, Barber Trail, and Blitzkrieg Trail.

Directions: From the junction of Routes 3 and 165 in Exeter, drive west on Route 165 for 2.9 miles and turn right at the sign for Camp E-Hun-Tee onto the dirt Frosty Hollow Road. Follow that road for 1.6 miles and turn right onto the dirt Austin Farm Road. Continue another half mile to the road's end at Breakheart Pond. Park in the lot to the right. To reach the Arcadia Management Area headquarters from the junction of Routes 3 and 165, drive west on Route 165 for 1.5 miles and turn left onto Arcadia Road. Continue 2.5 miles to a T intersection, turn left, and drive six-tenths of a mile to the headquarters on the right.

Maps: A free map of trails and roads is available at the Arcadia Management Area headquarters and in various parking lots in the management area. The George Washington Management Area/Arcadia Management Area/Blue Hills (Massachusetts) map, which shows trails but not contour lines, is $2.95 from the Appalachian Mountain Club, (800) 262-4455. For topographic maps of the area, request Hope Valley and Voluntown from the USGS.

Contact: Rhode Island Division of Forest Environment, Arcadia Headquarters, 260 Arcadia Road, Hope Valley, RI 02832; (401) 539-2356. The headquarters is open from 8:30 A.M. to 4 P.M. weekdays.

Trail notes: This relatively flat, 1.5-mile loop around Breakheart Pond provides a good introduction to hiking in Arcadia. The views of the pond are better from the trail on its west bank, which you reach during the second half of this hike. From the parking area, pick up the Breakheart Trail—marked by a sign—and follow its yellow blazes counter-clockwise around the pond. Views of the water are few here, though you could bushwhack off the trail to the shore. Reaching the pond's north end in about seven-tenths of a mile, turn left with the blazed trail, cross a brook on a wooden footbridge beside a small beaver dam, and reach a junction of trails. Turn left and you'll soon come upon the pond's west shore, with decent views of Breakheart Pond. The loop finishes in the parking area.

9 Forest Roads Loop

8.0 mi/4.0 hrs  

Location: In the Arcadia Management Area in Exeter; Rhode Island map page 300, grid c2.

User groups: Hikers, bikes, dogs, horses, skiers, and snowshoers. No wheelchair facilities. Dogs must be on a leash from March 1 through August 15. Hunting is allowed in season; all trail users are required to wear at least 200 square inches of fluorescent orange, as a cap and/or vest, during the hunting season (from the second Saturday of October through the last day of February).

Access, fees: Parking and access are free. Austin Farm Road is closed to motor vehicles at Escoheag Hill Road during the winter. Other roads open to traffic in summer but closed in winter include Brook Trail, Barber Trail, and Blitzkrieg Trail.

Directions: From the junction of Routes 3 and 165 in Exeter, drive west on Route 165 for three miles and turn right onto the dirt road marked Brook Trail. Park in the large dirt lot immediately on the right. To reach the Arcadia Management Area headquarters from the junction of Routes 3 and 165, go west on Route 165 for 1.5 miles and turn left onto Arcadia Road. Drive 2.5 miles to a T intersection, turn left, and drive six-tenths of a mile to the headquarters on the right.

Maps: A free trail map is available at the Arcadia headquarters and in various parking lots in the management area. The George Washington Management Area/Arcadia Management Area/Blue Hills (Massachusetts) map, which shows trails but not contour lines, is $2.95 from the Appalachian Mountain Club, (800) 262-4455. For topographic maps of the area, request Hope Valley and Voluntown from the USGS.

Contact: Rhode Island Division of Forest Environment, Arcadia Headquarters, 260 Arcadia Road, Hope Valley, RI 02832; (401) 539-2356. The headquarters is open from 8:30 A.M. to 4 P.M. weekdays.

Trail notes: I've included this eight-mile loop on dirt roads through Arcadia less for hikers than as a fairly easy outing for novice mountain bikers, including children, and—on those rare occasions when snow falls—cross-country skiers. I biked this loop to reach foot trails I wanted to hike: Breakheart Pond (hike number 8), Penny Hill (hike number 7), and Stepstone Falls (hike number 6). In fact, the start of the trail to the Mount Tom Cliffs (hike number 10) lies just a half mile west, on Route 165, of the parking area where this loop begins and ends. Be aware that some of these dirt roads are open to motor vehicles.

From the parking area, follow the dirt Brook Trail a short distance north and turn right on the first dirt road you encounter, passing a gate. Within a quarter mile, pass another gate and turn left on the dirt Frosty Hollow Road. Continue about 1.5 miles to the dirt Austin Farm Road and turn right, reaching the foot of Breakheart Pond in a half mile, where you'll have a good view of the pond. Retrace that half mile and continue west on Austin Farm Road for another 2.2 miles, cross a bridge over the Falls River (where the Penny Hill and Stepstone Falls hikes begin), and go another half mile before turning left on the dirt Barber Road. Within two miles, the road leads to a T intersection; turn left, cross Falls River again, then turn right on the Brook Trail and follow it about a half mile back to the parking area.

10 Mount Tom Cliffs

2.8 mi/1.5 hrs 

Location: In the Arcadia Management Area in Exeter; Rhode Island Map page 300, grid d1.

User groups: Hikers, dogs, and snowshoers. No wheelchair facilities. Dogs must be on a leash from March 1 through August 15. Bikes and horses are prohibited. Hunting is allowed in season; all trail users are required to wear at least 200 square inches of fluorescent orange, as a cap and/or vest, during the hunting season (from the second Saturday of October through the last day of February).

Access, fees: Parking and access are free. Austin Farm Road is closed to motor vehicles at Escoheag Hill Road during the winter. Other roads open to traffic in summer but closed in winter include Brook Trail, Barber Trail, and Blitzkrieg Trail.

Directions: From the junction of Routes 3 and 165 in Exeter, drive west on Route 165 for 3.6 miles. Immediately after crossing the bridge over the Wood River, turn left at the sign for the hunter checking station into a large dirt parking lot beside a Quonset hut. To reach the Arcadia Management Area headquarters from the junction of Routes 3 and 165, drive west on Route 165 for 1.5 miles and turn left onto Arcadia Road. Continue 2.5 miles to a T intersection, turn left, and drive six-tenths of a mile to the headquarters on the right.

Maps: A free trail map is available at the Arcadia headquarters and in various parking lots in the management area. The George Washington Management Area/Arcadia Management Area/Blue Hills (Massachusetts) map, which shows trails but not contour lines, is $2.95 from the Appalachian Mountain Club, (800) 262-4455. For topographic maps of the area, request Hope Valley and Voluntown from the USGS.

Contact: Rhode Island Division of Forest Environment, Arcadia Headquarters, 260 Arcadia Road, Hope Valley, RI 02832; (401) 539-2356. The headquarters is open from 8:30 A.M. to 4 P.M. weekdays.

Trail notes: The cliffs that form the low ridge of Mount Tom offer what are probably Arcadia's most sweeping views. From the back of the parking lot, follow the white blazes of the Mount Tom Trail into the woods. The trail is flat and wide at first, passing several giant anthills, maybe a foot high and two feet across, best observed from a comfortable distance. In about a half mile, turn left onto the dirt road called Blitzkrieg Trail; watch closely for the white blazes, which re-enter the woods on the right within a tenth of a mile, where the road crosses Parris Brook. The trail ascends easily for less than a mile until it reaches the open crest of the Mount Tom cliffs and a 270-degree panorama of gently rolling forest. Walk the trail over the ledges for about a tenth of a mile, until the trail begins descending into the woods again, then backtrack the way you came.

⓫ Norman Bird Sanctuary

2.0 mi/1.5 hrs 

Location: In Middletown; Rhode Island map page 300, grid d4.

User groups: Hikers only. No wheelchair facilities. The trail is not suitable for bikes, horses, skis, or snowshoes. Dogs and hunting are prohibited.

Access, fees: There is an entrance fee of $4 for adults, $3 for seniors, and $1 for children. Members of the private sanctuary and children under three are admitted free. The sanctuary is open Tuesday through Sunday, year-round, from 9 A.M. to 5 P.M., and is also open Mondays in summer and on holidays.

Directions: From Route 114, at the Middletown–Portsmouth town line, turn east onto Mitchell's Lane at a small sign for the Norman Bird Sanctuary. At 1.4 miles, turn left at a stop sign. Drive a half mile, then bear right at a fork and proceed another three-tenths of a mile to a four-way stop at a crossroads. Drive straight through the intersection and go another eight-tenths of a mile to the sanctuary entrance on the right.

Maps: A map and trail guide is available at the visitors center. For a topographic map of the area, request Prudence Island from the USGS.

Contact: Norman Bird Sanctuary, 583 Third Beach Road, Middletown, RI 02842; (401) 846-2577. Ask about guided group tours and workshops for adults and children.

Trail notes: This private sanctuary, established in 1949, comprises 450 acres and is home to creatures ranging from pheasants to foxes. It has eight miles of trails through forests, old fields, pastures, and swamps. The most popular trail here is the Hanging Rock Trail, which traverses the narrow crest of a spine of rock that seems wholly out of place rising 40 to 50 feet above the surrounding woods and marsh. Stunted trees, characteristic of high mountains, grow atop it. Although parts of the ridge are somewhat exposed, it's a fairly easy walk and great for kids. The sanctuary, as the name implies, is also a good spot for birding.

From the parking lot, walk past the visitors center (housed in a 125-year-old barn) onto the main path, and follow it a short distance; then turn left onto the Quarry Trail, passing a field with bird feeders. Turn right on the Blue Dot Trail, going by a former slate quarry on the left, now filled with water. Cross a boardwalk, climb a short hill past ledges, and at a T junction turn left again. Beyond the views of Gardner Pond, the trail turns sharply uphill onto the Hanging Rock Trail. Go left, following the increasingly open ridge to its end, where it terminates abruptly at a short cliff with views of Narragansett Bay. Double back, staying with the Hanging Rock Trail to its beginning, then turning right and following signs back to the barn.

⓬ Green Falls Pond

2.0 mi/1.0 hr 

Location: In Rockville; Rhode Island map page 300, grid d1.

User groups: Hikers only. No wheelchair facilities. This trail rarely receives enough snow for snowshoes and is not suitable for bikes, horses, or skis. A portion of this hike lies on private land, and use restrictions can change. Dogs are not allowed unless otherwise posted. Hunting is permitted in season unless otherwise posted.

Access, fees: Parking and access are free.

Directions: From Route 138 in Rockville, turn onto Camp Yawgoog Road and drive

3.8 miles, past Camp Yawgoog, and park in a turnout on the right.

Maps: The George Washington Management Area/Arcadia Management Area/Blue Hills (Massachusetts) map, which covers the area of Green Fall Pond, is $2.95 from the Appalachian Mountain Club, (800) 262-4455. For a topographic map of the area, request Voluntown from the USGS.

Contact: The Blue Trails Network—which includes the Narragansett Trail—is maintained by the nonprofit Connecticut Forest and Park Association, 16 Meriden Road, Rockfall, CT 06481-2961; (203) 346-2372. Pachaug State Forest, RFD 1, Voluntown, CT 06384; (860) 376-4075.

Trail notes: Here's a relatively easy two-mile walk through the woods—which happens to include some interesting, if brief, scrambling over rock ledges—to a scenic little pond. The Narragansett Trail actually follows the Rhode Island–Connecticut state line for a short distance before turning west into Connecticut and reaching the shore of Green Falls Pond. Although the blue-blazed trail continues west around the pond, my companion and I found it difficult to follow and returned the way we'd hiked in—but not until we had enjoyed the pond views for a while.

13 Long and Ell Ponds

0.5 mi/0.5 hr 

Location: In Rockville; Rhode Island map page 300, grid d1.

User groups: Hikers only. No wheelchair facilities. This trail rarely receives enough snow for snowshoes and is not suitable for skis. Bikes, dogs, horses, and hunting are prohibited.

Access, fees: Parking and access are free. The refuge is open from a half hour before sunrise to a half hour after sunset.

Directions: From Route 138 in Rockville, turn onto Winchek Road, follow it for a tenth of a mile, then turn onto Canonchet Road. Continue a half mile, bear right, and drive another mile to a small parking area on the left. There is also space for cars at the roadside just beyond the parking area.

Maps: The George Washington Management Area/Arcadia Management Area/Blue Hills (Massachusetts) map, which covers the area of Long and Ell Ponds, is $2.95 from the Appalachian Mountain Club, (800) 262-4455. For a topographic map of the area, request Voluntown from the USGS.

Contact: The Long Pond Woods Refuge is jointly managed by two conservation organizations and a state agency: the Nature Conservancy, 45 South Angell Street, Providence, RI 02906, (401) 331-7110; the Audubon Society of Rhode Island, 12 Sanderson Road, Smithfield, RI 02917, (401) 949-5454; and the Rhode Island Department of Environmental Management, (401) 277-3070.

Trail notes: This hike packs a lot of scenery into a short distance. From the parking area, the trail enters the woods, passing through thick stands of rhododendrons and mountain laurel and over myriad rocks and boulders. Reaching the top of a small hill, the trail's yellow blazes turn right, but this hike turns left, following an unmarked but obvious path. A quarter mile from the road, skirt to the right around cliffs and emerge on ledges overlooking scenic Long Pond. Hike back along the same route.

14 Great Swamp Management Area

5.5 mi/2.5 hrs 

Location: In West Kingston; Rhode Island map page 300, grid d2.

User groups: Hikers, bikes, dogs, horses, skiers, and snowshoers. No wheelchair facilities. Dogs must be on a leash. Hunting is allowed in season.

Access, fees: Parking and access are free.

Directions: From Route 138 in West Kingston, just west of the junction with Route 110, turn west onto Liberty Lane. Drive a mile to the road's end, then turn left onto the dirt Great Neck Road. Within a mile, you will pass the headquarters on the right. The dirt road ends one mile from Liberty Lane, at a big parking area.

Maps: A trail map is available at the management area headquarters. For a topographic map of the area, request Kingston from the USGS.

Contact: Rhode Island Division of Fish and Wildlife, 4808 Tower Hill Road, Wakefield, RI 02879; (401) 277-3075.

Trail notes: Popular with bird-watchers, the 3,349-acre Great Swamp, in the towns of South Kingston and Richmond, encompasses habitat ranging from freshwater wetlands to forest. More than two miles of pristine shoreline along Worden Pond is protected. Cottontail rabbit, white-tailed deer, fox, raccoon, coyote, mink, muskrat, wild turkey, grouse, and wood duck all call this vast preserve home. The best time for birding is during the spring migration in May.

This loop follows relatively flat, wide woods roads that make for easy biking or skiing (although snow is rare here) as well as hiking. From the parking area, go around the gate and follow the woods road straight (avoiding the side roads leading right) for a bit more than a mile, until you reach an old hangar and the shore of scenic Worden Pond. Double back on the woods road and take the second left turn onto another dirt road, which loops around the perimeter of the Great Swamp Impoundment, a man-made marsh of more than 130 acres and a good place for birding. Where that woods road ends beyond the swamp, turn left, then left again at the next junction to return to the parking area.

⑮ Newport Cliff Walk

6.0 mi/3.0 hrs 

Location: In Newport; Rhode Island map page 300, grid d4.

User groups: Hikers only. No wheelchair facilities. This trail is not suitable for bikes, dogs, horses, skis, or snowshoes. Hunting is prohibited.

Access, fees: Parking and access are free. The Cliff Walk is closed to the public between 9 P.M. and 6 A.M.

Directions: Take Route 114 to Route 138 to Route 138A in Newport (Memorial Boulevard). Follow it to Easton Beach and park. On foot, continue up Memorial Boulevard in the direction of the town center, walking a short distance to a large sign on the median strip indicating the start of the Cliff Walk, behind Cliff Walk Manor.

Maps: No map is necessary for this walk, but for a topographic map of the area, request Newport from the USGS.

Contact: Newport County Convention and Visitors Bureau, 23 America's Cup Ave., Newport, RI 02840; (800) 326-6030 or (401) 849-8098. The visitors bureau is open seven days a week, year-round, from 9 A.M. to 5 P.M.

Trail notes: Come here during the height of the summer tourist season, and the experience of your walk will suffer from the crowds, which often form a conga line along the trail's length. But come here in the off-season—during the spring or fall—and you will gain much more enjoyment from this scenic walk atop cliffs that fall away dramatically to the ocean. What is probably Rhode Island's most famous walk passes mansions built by some of the nation's wealthiest families in the late nineteenth and early twentieth centuries—including Rosecliff, the house used in the filming of *The Great Gatsby*.

This hike brings you along the Cliff Walk,

then down Bellevue Avenue for views of the mansions that are often better than the views from the Cliff Walk. Follow the wide walkway along the cliff tops; do not stray onto private property. Though the walk begins on flat and level ground, parts of it become rocky. After about three miles you emerge at the end of a side street, Ledge Road. Turn right and follow Ledge Road straight onto Bellevue Avenue. Walk down Bellevue, past the mansions, and back to Memorial Boulevard, then turn right to return to Easton Beach.

16 Brenton Point State Park

2.0 mi/1.0 hr 

Location: In Newport; Rhode Island map page 300, grid d4.

User groups: Hikers and dogs. A wheelchair-accessible paved sidewalk parallels the shoreline. This trail is not suitable for bikes, horses, skis, or snowshoes. Hunting is prohibited.

Access, fees: Parking and access are free.

Directions: Take Route 114 or Route 138 into Newport. Turn left onto Thames Street, then bear right into the through-lanes. Turn right (remaining on Thames) at the Newport Bay Club and Hotel. Turn right onto Wellington Street; follow it to its end, then turn right onto Harrison Street, passing Fort Adams State Park. At the end of the road, turn right onto Ocean Drive. Brenton Point State Park lies a short distance ahead; there are several places to park.

Maps: No map is necessary for this short walk, but for a topographic map of the area, request Newport from the USGS.

Contact: Rhode Island Division of Parks and Recreation, 2321 Hartford Pike, Johnston, RI 02919; (401) 277-2632.

Trail notes: This easy walk follows the rocky, wind-battered shoreline at Brenton Point. The land once belonged to the Budlong family, but before World War II the federal government took it over and built military facilities here. Later, the feds turned the land over to the state for this park. I recommend driving to the farthest parking lot on the right—beside a field popular among kite-flyers—then crossing the road and walking along the shore back in the direction you came by car. Clamber up onto a crooked stone jetty jutting a short distance into the ocean. Continue along the shore; you can walk for about a mile. Then double back to your car.

17 Vin Gormley Trail

8.0 mi/4.0 hrs 

Location: In Burlingame State Park in Charlestown; Rhode Island map page 300, grid e2.

User groups: Hikers only. No wheelchair facilities. This trail rarely receives enough snow for skis or snowshoes. Bikes, dogs, horses, and hunting are prohibited.

Access, fees: Parking and access are free.

Directions: Take U.S. 1 to Charlestown and the exit for Burlingame State Park. Drive six-tenths of a mile to the park entrance on the left. Watch for the yellow blazes of the Vin Gormley Trail, which crosses the parking lot.

Maps: A map of the Vin Gormley Trail is available at the state park campground office off Klondike Road in Charlestown, which is open weekdays year-round; and at the picnic area off Prosser Trail, which is open from Memorial Day to Labor Day. For a topographic map of the area, request Carolina from the USGS.

Contact: Burlingame State Park, 1 Burlingame Park Road, Charlestown, RI 02813; (401) 322-8910. Rhode Island Division of Parks and Recreation, 2321 Hartford Pike, Johnston, RI 02919; (401) 277-2632. The

North-South Trail, when completed (possibly by 1999), will extend about 72 miles through western Rhode Island, linking many existing trail systems, including trails in Burlingame State Park. For maps and a brochure, contact the Rhode Island Department of Environmental Management, 83 Park Street, Providence, RI 02903; (401) 277-2776.

Trail notes: The Vin Gormley Trail makes a big loop around Watchaug Pond in the state park, though it passes close enough to the pond to give you views of it only for a short time, while you're within the Audubon Society's Kimball Wildlife Refuge (hike number 18). Although the flat terrain here doesn't offer any compelling views, this trail is a nice walk along narrow footpaths, woods roads, and, for a short distance, a stretch of paved road. You'll cross several brooks and boardwalks through boggy areas. The entire trail is well blazed and easy to follow.

18 Kimball Wildlife Refuge

1.5 mi/0.75 hr 

Location: In Charlestown; Rhode Island map page 300, grid e2.

User groups: Hikers only. No wheelchair facilities. The trails rarely receive enough snow for snowshoes and are not suitable for skis. Bikes, dogs, horses, and hunting are prohibited.

Access, fees: Parking and access are free.

Directions: Take U.S. 1 to Charlestown and the exit for Burlingame State Park. Take the first left at a small sign for the Kimball Wildlife Refuge. Drive to the end of the road, turn left again, and proceed to a dirt parking lot near an information kiosk.

Maps: A basic trail map is available at the information kiosk next to the parking area. For a topographic map of the area, request Carolina from the USGS.

Contact: Kimball Wildlife Refuge, 180 Sanctuary Road, Charlestown, RI 02813. Audubon Society of Rhode Island, 12 Sanderson Road, Smithfield, RI 02917; (401) 949-5454.

Trail notes: Owned by the Audubon Society of Rhode Island, this 29-acre parcel of woodlands on Watchaug Pond, abutting Burlingame State Park, has three well-marked loop trails through the woods. This hike makes a loop around the refuge, incorporating sections of all three trails. Begin behind the information kiosk, turning left onto the red trail, then left at each successive junction with the orange, green, and blue trails. Spring, when flowers bloom and the songbirds return, is the time to visit this refuge.

19 Ninigret National Wildlife Refuge

1.4 mi/1.0 hr 

Location: In Charlestown; Rhode Island map page 300, grid e2.

User groups: Hikers only. No wheelchair facilities. This trail rarely receives enough snow for snowshoes and is not suitable for bikes, horses, or skis. Dogs and hunting are prohibited.

Access, fees: Parking and access are free.

Directions: Take U.S. 1 to Charlestown and the exit for Ninigret Park. Follow signs to the park, turn left into it, then follow signs to the nature trails and a parking lot on an old runway.

Maps: A map is posted in an information kiosk at the trailhead, and a look at it is really all that's needed for this hike. For topographic maps of the area, request Carolina and Quonochontaug from the USGS.

Contact: The U.S. Fish and Wildlife Service

refuge headquarters is in Shoreline Plaza on Old Post Road (Route 119) in Charlestown, (401) 364-9124. The office is open from 8 A.M. to 4:30 P.M. weekdays.

Trail notes: Established in 1971, the refuge occupies 407 acres of shrublands, grasslands, freshwater ponds, salt marshes, and a barrier beach around a former naval training site. This is a stopover area for migrating birds and a wintering spot for some bird species. Call the refuge headquarters for a list of bird species found at the national wildlife refuges of Rhode Island, including Ninigret. The hike follows wide dirt roads through marsh and out to the shore of the saltwater Ninigret Pond, and is a good place to see herons, cormorants, geese, and migrating songbirds. Hiking here one spring day, we saw a sea kayaker in the distance paddling surreptitiously out toward what looked like swans.

From the parking lot, walk on the runway to the left until you reach the kiosk at the start of the Grassy Point Nature Trail, which consists of two loops totaling 1.4 miles. Take the shorter loop first, beginning to the left of the kiosk and following the arrows, eventually returning to the kiosk. The second loop begins to the right. A wide spur road, not marked by arrows, diverges left from this trail out to Grassy Point, where an observation deck offers good views of the pond and its birds. At the end of the loop, walk down a runway back to the kiosk.

20 Block Island: Clay Head Trail and the Maze

0.7 mi/0.75 hr 

Location: On Block Island; Rhode Island map page 300, grid f2.

User groups: Hikers and dogs. No wheelchair facilities. Dogs must be on a leash. This trail rarely receives enough snow for skis or snowshoes and is not suitable for horses. Bikes and hunting are prohibited.

Access, fees: Access to hiking trails on the island is free.

Directions: Ferries to Block Island run year-round from Point Judith, Rhode Island, and in summer also from Providence and Newport, Rhode Island, and New London, Connecticut. From the island's ferry landing in Old Harbor, turn right on Water Street along the waterfront strip, left on Dodge Street, then right at the post office onto Corn Neck Road. Continue about 3.5 miles to a dirt road on the right marked by a post indicating the Clay Head Trail. Follow the dirt road a short distance to the trailhead (there is a rack for bikes).

Maps: Get basic maps of the island and its hiking trails (the latter is $1.25) from the Chamber of Commerce, which operates an information booth at the ferry landing in Old Harbor and an office around the corner on Water Street. The Moped Man, (401) 466-5011, across from the ferry landing at 435 Water Street, also has a basic map of island roads. For a topographic map, request Block Island from the USGS.

Contact: For ferry information, call (401) 783-4613. For information about Block Island, contact the Chamber of Commerce, Drawer D, Block Island, RI 02807; (401) 466-2982. Also try the Block Island Tourism Council at (800) 383-2474. For information about trails on conservation land, contact the Nature Conservancy's local office at (401) 466-2129, or its main office at 45 South Angell Street, Providence, RI 02906; (401) 331-7110.

Trail notes: As with the other trails on Block Island, the best way to explore this one is to ride a bicycle from the ferry landing in Old Harbor to the trailhead. Reasonably fit people could easily link this hike with the two other Block Island hikes in this chapter (hikes number 21 and 22) in a day.

Bikes can be brought over on the ferry for a few dollars, or rented in Old Harbor when you get off the ferry for about $10 a day. The best times to go are spring and fall, when hundreds of thousands of birds representing some 150 species descend on the island during their seasonal migrations—the Nature Conservancy describes Clay Head as one of the best spots in North America to see migratory songbirds in autumn. Tourists jam the island in July and August, the months to avoid.

The Clay Head Trail follows the top of bluffs, passing Clay Head Swamp, the edge of the Littlefield Farm, and numerous views of the bluffs and seashore. At first, several trails leading left into the dense scrub brush and forest are posted as private property. Once beyond those, however, you will see many unmarked trails diverging off the Clay Head Trail and weaving through a cooked-spaghetti tangle of footpaths called the Maze. These trails are fun to explore, though they can get confusing.

21 Block Island: Rodman's Hollow

0.5 mi/0.75 hr 

Location: On Block Island; Rhode Island map page 300, grid f2.

User groups: Hikers and dogs. No wheelchair facilities. Dogs must be on a leash. This trail rarely receives enough snow for skis or snowshoes and is not suitable for horses. Bikes and hunting are prohibited.

Access, fees: Access to hiking trails on the island is free.

Directions: Ferries to Block Island run year-round from Point Judith, Rhode Island, and in summer also from Providence and Newport, Rhode Island, and New London, Connecticut. From the island's ferry landing in Old Harbor, turn left on Water Street and head straight through an intersection, passing the First Baptist Church on your left, onto Spring Street. It runs straight onto Southeast Light Road, passing two trails leading to the Mohegan Bluffs. The road becomes Mohegan Trail, then hooks right and becomes Lakeside Drive. About four miles from Old Harbor, turn left onto Cooneymus Road. The road doglegs left, then right, then passes a stone wall and a sign on the left overlooking Rodman's Hollow. Just beyond that point, turn left onto the dirt Black Rock Road. A quarter mile farther is the trailhead, marked by a bike rack and a wooden turnstile. The road continues to a trail leading down to the beach.

Maps: Get basic maps of the island and its hiking trails (the latter is $1.25) from the Chamber of Commerce, which operates an information booth at the ferry landing in Old Harbor and an office around the corner on Water Street. The Moped Man, (401) 466-5011, across from the ferry landing at 435 Water Street, also has a basic map of island roads. For a topographic map, request Block Island from the USGS.

Contact: For ferry information, call (401) 783-4613. For information about Block Island, contact the Chamber of Commerce, Drawer D, Block Island, RI 02807; (401) 466-2982. Also try the Block Island Tourism Council at (800) 383-2474. For information about trails on conservation land, contact the Nature Conservancy's local office at (401) 466-2129, or its main office at 45 South Angell Street, Providence, RI 02906; (401) 331-7110.

Trail notes: A depression left by a receding glacier, Rodman's Hollow is a wild little corner of the island overgrown with dense brush. A loop trail cuts through it, cresting one small hill with sweeping views of the homes and rolling hills at the southern end of the island. Rodman's Hollow was the inspiration for the conservation movement of the 1970s that helped protect one-fourth of Block Island from development. It's also part of the Greenway, a network of interconnecting trail systems that includes the Enchanted Forest, Turnip Farm, and Fresh Swamp Preserve.

I recommend bicycling from the ferry landing in Old Harbor to this and other trails in this chapter (hike numbers 20 and 22). Bikes can be brought over on the ferry for a few dollars, or rented in Old Harbor when you get off the ferry for about $10 a day. The best times to visit are spring and fall, when hundreds of thousands of birds representing some 150 species descend on the island during their seasonal migrations. Avoid coming in July and August, when tourists crowd the island.

From just beyond the turnstile, follow the loop trail to the right; a sign indicates a "short loop" and a "long loop," but it's all one trail. The trail crests a hill at a wooden bench. From there, the path forks; following the right fork brings you back to Black Rock Road (where you would turn right to return to the trailhead). Bear left instead, following the trail through the hollow and eventually back to the spot where the path first split.

22 Block Island: Mohegan Bluffs

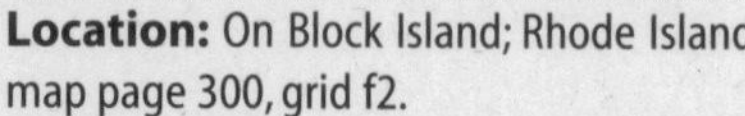
0.5 mi/0.75 hr

Location: On Block Island; Rhode Island map page 300, grid f2.

User groups: Hikers and dogs. No wheelchair facilities. Dogs must be on a leash. This trail rarely receives enough snow for skis or snowshoes and is not suitable for horses. Bikes and hunting are prohibited.

Access, fees: Access to hiking trails on the island is free.

Directions: Ferries to Block Island run year-round from Point Judith, Rhode Island, and in summer also from Providence and Newport, Rhode Island, and New London, Connecticut. From the island's ferry landing in Old Harbor, turn left on Water Street and head straight through an intersection, passing the First Baptist Church on your left, onto Spring Street. It in turn runs straight onto Southeast Light Road. About two miles from the ferry landing, a footpath on the left leads a short distance to Southeast Lighthouse, above the Mohegan Bluffs. A short distance up the road is a trailhead (with a rack for parking bicycles) leading to stairs that descend the bluffs to the beach.

Maps: Get basic maps of the island and its hiking trails (the latter is $1.25) from the Chamber of Commerce, which operates an information booth at the ferry landing in Old Harbor and an office around the corner on Water Street. The Moped Man, (401) 466-5011, across from the ferry landing at 435 Water Street, also has a basic map of island roads. For a topographic map, request Block Island from the USGS.

Contact: For ferry information, call (401) 783-4613. For information about Block Island, contact the Chamber of Commerce, Drawer D, Block Island, RI 02807; (401) 466-2982. Also try the Block Island Tourism Council at (800) 383-2474. For information about trails on conservation land, contact the Nature Conservancy's local office at (401) 466-2129, or its main office at 45 South Angell Street, Providence, RI 02906; (401) 331-7110.

Trail notes: Dubbed one of the "Last Great Places" in the Western Hemisphere by the Nature Conservancy, Block Island has evolved as a unique micro-environment since a glacier left 12 miles of ocean between it and mainland New England 10,000 years ago. More than 40 of its indigenous species are listed as rare or endangered. Just seven miles long and three miles wide, it has 32 miles of hiking trails.

The best way to explore Block Island's trails

is to ride a bicycle from the ferry landing in Old Harbor to the trailheads. That way, you see more trails and enjoy some scenic cycling on country roads through a landscape of rolling hills and open fields crisscrossed by an uncanny 2,042 miles of stone walls. Reasonably fit people could easily link this hike with the two other Block Island hikes in this chapter (hike numbers 20 and 21) in a day, by biking between them. Bikes can be brought over on the ferry for a few dollars, or rented in Old Harbor when you get off the ferry for about $10 a day. The best times to go are spring and fall, when hundreds of thousands of birds representing some 150 species descend on the island during their seasonal migrations. In May, the white blossoms of the shadblow are in bloom. Tourists jam the island in July and August, the months to avoid. Winters tend to be cold and windy.

This hike is actually two short walks near one another. The first leads to Southeast Lighthouse and great views of the spectacular Mohegan Bluffs. The lighthouse, built in 1873 on the eroding cliffs 150 feet above the sea, had to be moved back 200 feet in 1993 because the ocean had chewed away nearly all the land between it and the sea. Legend has it that in 1590 the island's first inhabitants, the Narragansett Indians—also known as the Manisses tribe, for the name they gave the island—drove a party of invading Mohegan Indians over the cliffs here.

From the second trailhead, a trail leads to a wooden staircase that drops steeply down to the rocky beach, a nice place to walk below the bluffs. Don't try scrambling around on the cliffs themselves, though—the soil and rocks are as loose as they appear, and dangerous rockslides occur frequently.

Connecticut

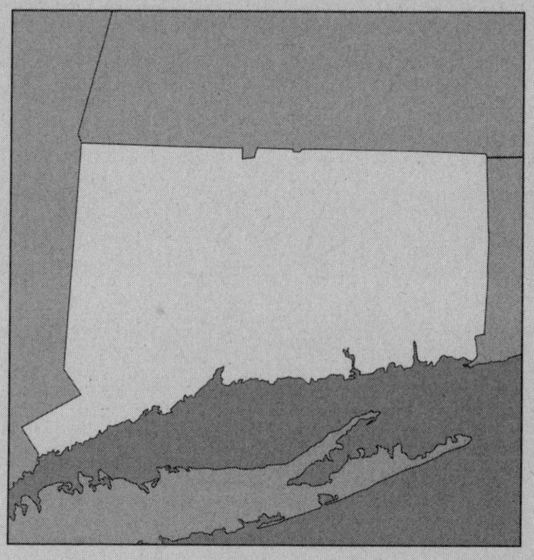

Overall Rating

1 2 3 4 5 6 7 8 9 10

Poor .... Fair .... Great

Difficulty

1 2 3 4 5

A stroll .... Moderate ...... A real butt-kicker!

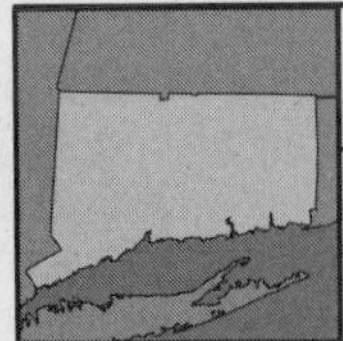

Western Connecticut

Adjoining Maps: North: Western Massachusetts .... *page* 238
East: Eastern Connecticut .... *page* 321

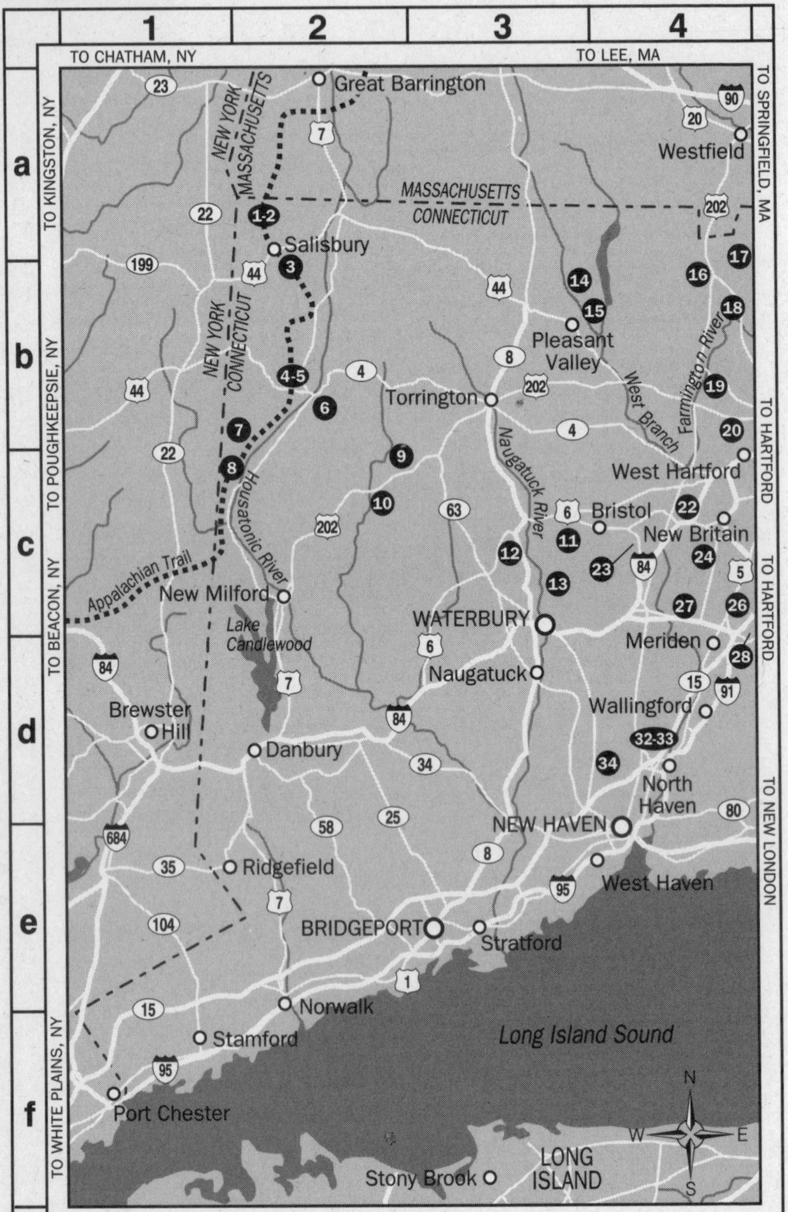

1 2 3 4
a b c d e f

TO CHATHAM, NY
TO LEE, MA
TO SPRINGFIELD, MA
TO HARTFORD
TO HARTFORD
TO NEW LONDON
TO KINGSTON, NY
TO POUGHKEEPSIE, NY
TO BEACON, NY
TO WHITE PLAINS, NY

Great Barrington
Westfield
NEW YORK
MASSACHUSETTS
MASSACHUSETTS
CONNECTICUT
NEW YORK
CONNECTICUT
Salisbury
Pleasant Valley
Torrington
West Branch
Farmington River
West Hartford
Housatonic River
Naugatuck River
Bristol
New Britain
Appalachian Trail
New Milford
Lake Candlewood
WATERBURY
Meriden
Naugatuck
Wallingford
Brewster Hill
Danbury
North Haven
NEW HAVEN
Ridgefield
West Haven
BRIDGEPORT
Stratford
Norwalk
Stamford
Long Island Sound
Port Chester
Stony Brook
LONG ISLAND
N
W
E
S

1-2 3 4-5 6 7 8 9 10 11 12 13 14 15 16 17 18 19 20 22 23 24 26 27 28 32-33 34

23 90 20 7 202 22 199 44 44 8 4 202 44 4 22 63 6 202 84 5 6 84 7 15 91 84 34 80 684 58 25 8 35 95 7 104 1 15 95

Eastern Connecticut

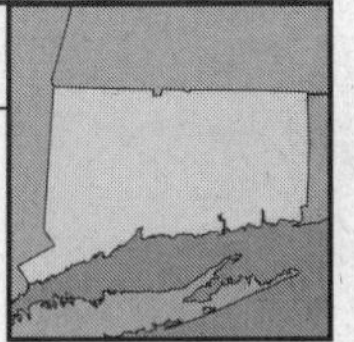

Adjoining Maps:

North: Western Massachusetts .... *page* 238
East: Rhode Island .... *page* 300
West: Western Connecticut .... *page* 320

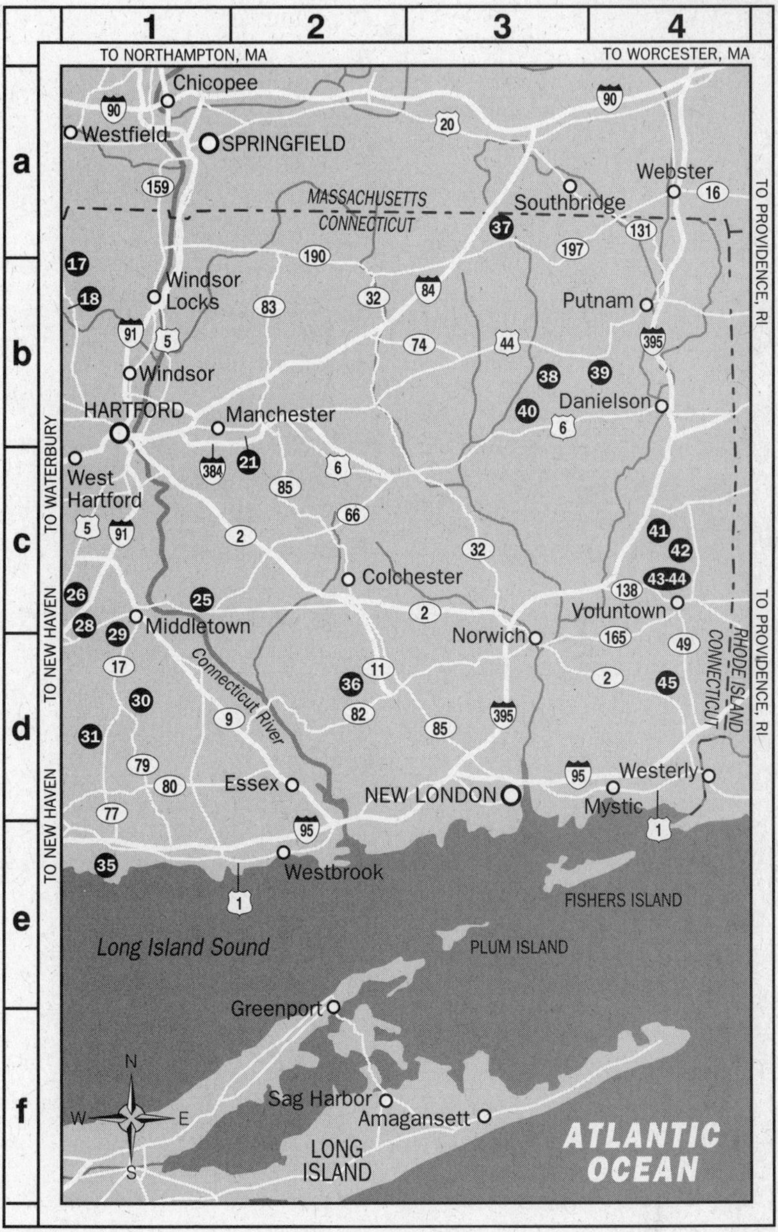

1 2 3 4

a b c d e f

TO NORTHAMPTON, MA
TO WORCESTER, MA
TO PROVIDENCE, RI
TO PROVIDENCE, RI
TO WATERBURY
TO NEW HAVEN
TO NEW HAVEN

Chicopee
Westfield
SPRINGFIELD
Webster
Southbridge
MASSACHUSETTS
CONNECTICUT
Windsor Locks
Putnam
Windsor
HARTFORD
Manchester
Danielson
West Hartford
Colchester
Voluntown
Middletown
Norwich
RHODE ISLAND
CONNECTICUT
Connecticut River
Essex
NEW LONDON
Westerly
Mystic
Westbrook
FISHERS ISLAND
PLUM ISLAND
Long Island Sound
Greenport
Sag Harbor
Amagansett
LONG ISLAND
ATLANTIC OCEAN
N
W
E
S

90 20 90 159 16 131 197 190 32 84 83 91 5 74 44 395 6 384 6 85 66 5 91 2 32 138 2 165 49 17 11 2 9 82 85 395 79 80 95 77 95 1 1

17 18 37 38 39 40 21 41 42 43-44 26 25 28 29 30 36 45 31 35

Connecticut features:

Western Connecticut Map—page 320

CONNECTICUT

When it comes to hiking in New England, the bigger peaks of the north country steal the show for spectacle and remoteness, and the lower-elevation, more densely populated southern regions dwell in their shadow. But that generality overlooks the extensive trail systems that have been developed in states like Connecticut.

The so-called Blue Trails Network comprises more than 700 miles of trail across Connecticut, many of them on private land and maintained by volunteer members of the nonprofit Connecticut Forest and Park Association. Numerous private preserves have trails open to the public. And from Macedonia Brook State Park and People's State Forest in the west, to Mashamoquet Brook State Park and Pachaug State Forest in the east, Connecticut is peppered with dozens of state lands ideal for activities from hiking and mountain biking to snowshoeing and cross-country skiing.

The character of trails varies across Connecticut. In the state's more rural western corners, the Appalachian Trail follows a chain of green hills above the beautiful valley of the Housatonic River. Above the Connecticut River Valley, hikes up onto the traprock ridges tend to entail short but steep climbs to open ledges with good views, where loose rock often makes footing difficult. East of the Connecticut Valley, the land flattens out more, with some gently rolling hills and extensive woodlands. Despite having some of New England's largest cities, much of Connecticut remains rural, with its trails more civilized than elsewhere in the region—shorter hikes with little elevation gain and loss, many of them offering bucolic views of a well-settled, pastoral landscape.

Most Blue Trails lie on private land, and the Connecticut Forest and Park Association has secured landowner permission only for hiker access. While uses can vary, assume that dogs, horses, and mountain bikes are not allowed unless a trail is specifically marked for them. Most Blue Trails are open to cross-country skiing. Assume that hunting is permitted in season unless the land is posted prohibiting it.

Along the Appalachian Trail, dogs must be kept under control, and horses, mountain bikes, hunting, and possession of firearms are prohibited—although that rule does not preclude hunters inadvertently wandering near the AT. Cross-country skiing and snowshoeing are permitted on the AT, and much of the trail in Connecticut presents easy to moderate terrain for snowshoeing.

In Connecticut state parks and forests, dogs must be on a leash and horses are allowed on trails and forest roads. Hunting is allowed in season in state forests, but not in state parks, and is prohibited on Sundays. Access fees are levied at some state lands, but most are free year-round.

Eastern Connecticut Map—page 321

❶ Bear Mountain

6.5 mi/4.0 hrs 

Location: In Salisbury; Western Connecticut map page 320, grid a2.

User groups: Hikers, dogs, and snowshoers. No wheelchair facilities. This trail is not suitable for skis. Bikes, horses, and hunting are prohibited.

Access, fees: Parking and access are free. Camping is prohibited except in designated shelters and campsites along the Appalachian Trail.

Directions: From the junction of Routes 44 and 41 in Salisbury, drive north on Route 41 for three miles to a parking area on the left for the Undermountain Trail.

Maps: For a trail map, refer to map 4 in the "Map and Guide to the Appalachian Trail in Massachusetts and Connecticut," a five-map set for $16.95 from the Appalachian Trail Conference (see address below). For topographic maps of the area, request Ashley Falls and Sharon from the USGS.

Contact: Appalachian Mountain Club's Mount Greylock Visitors Center, P.O. Box 1800, Lanesboro, MA 01237, (413) 443-0011; or the AMC's main office in Boston, (617) 523-0636. Appalachian Trail Conference, P.O. Box 807, Harpers Ferry, WV 25425; (304) 535-6331. The Blue Trails Network, Connecticut Forest and Park Association, (860) 346-2372.

Trail notes: This loop over the state's highest peak, 2,316-foot Bear Mountain, is one of the most popular hikes in Connecticut and a busy place on a nice weekend. Youth groups and backpackers make frequent use of the few legal campsites along the Appalachian Trail just south of Bear's summit. Still, even here you can avoid the crowds with an early start—or a well-planned late one. I started up this loop with a backpack at dusk one Saturday, as the last few day hikers were returning to their cars. A nearly full moon lit the trail for me, making for a beautiful—and solitary—2.4-mile walk to the Bond shelter camping area. Come morning, I hit the trail early and had the summit to myself. An interesting footnote, by the way, is that the summit of the state's highest mountain is not the highest point in Connecticut; that's actually on the southern slope of Mount Frissell, whose summit lies just over the line into Massachusetts, just northwest of Bear Mountain.

From the trailhead, follow the Undermountain Trail for 1.9 miles to its junction with the Appalachian Trail, marked by a sign. To the left (south), three camping areas are spread out along the AT, from a half mile to 1.7 miles distant. Turn right (north) on the AT for the summit of Bear. You'll break out of the trees for sweeping views; to the east, south, and west, survey the pastoral landscape of hills, dense forest, and tiny towns that makes up this rural northwest corner of Connecticut. The views are also excellent from the enormous stone pile on the summit. The AT steeply descends the north side of Bear Mountain, and the rocks may be slippery with water or even ice in late fall or early spring. A half mile beyond the summit, turn right onto Paradise Lane Trail, walk two miles to the Undermountain Trail, and turn left for the parking area.

❷ Lion's Head/Bald Peak

7.5 mi/4.5 hrs 

Location: In Salisbury; Western Connecticut map page 320, grid a2.

User groups: Hikers, dogs, and snowshoers. No wheelchair facilities. This trail is not suitable for skis. Bikes, horses, and hunting are prohibited.

Access, fees: Parking and access are free. Camping is prohibited except in designated shelters and campsites along the Appalachian Trail.

Directions: From the junction of Routes 44 and 41 in Salisbury, drive north on Route 41 for eight-tenths of a mile to a somewhat hidden parking area on the left for the Appalachian Trail.

Maps: For a map of hiking trails, refer to map 4 in the "Map and Guide to the Appalachian Trail in Massachusetts and Connecticut," a five-map set for $16.95 from the Appalachian Trail Conference (see address below). For topographic maps of the area, request Ashley Falls and Sharon from the USGS.

Contact: Appalachian Mountain Club's Mount Greylock Visitors Center, P.O. Box 1800, Lanesboro, MA 01237, (413) 443-0011; or the AMC's main office in Boston, (617) 523-0636. Appalachian Trail Conference, P.O. Box 807, Harpers Ferry, WV 25425; (304) 535-6331. The Blue Trails Network, Connecticut Forest and Park Association, (860) 346-2372.

Trail notes: The ridge shared by Bear Mountain and Lion's Head in Connecticut's northwestern corner may harbor the nicest stretch of the Appalachian Trail through Connecticut—and the view from Lion's Head nearly rivals that from the enormously popular Bear Mountain just a few miles to the north. After a pleasant walk through the woods for a few miles, you'll turn abruptly upward, scramble over exposed rock the last 50 feet to the summit of Lion's Head, and step up to wide views of hills, forest, and pastures. On our hike, we shared the summit with just a few Appalachian Trail through-hikers—people who had already walked more than 1,000 miles, yet stood awed by this view. Turning back from Lion's Head makes for a round-trip hike of 4.6 miles—but Bald Peak is worth the effort because you'll see nothing but unbroken forest and hills from its bare summit, and fewer hikers head all the way out there.

From the trailhead, follow the white blazes of the Appalachian Trail as it heads west, then swings northward. After you've gone about two miles, the blue-blazed Lion's Head Trail enters from the left, and the AT swings right and climbs steeply to the summit of Lion's Head. A ledge about 30 feet south of the actual summit offers the best view, encompassing the Twin Lakes, Prospect Mountain, and the Housatonic Valley. Continue north on the AT for a half mile and then turn left on the blue-blazed Bald Peak Trail, which leads you through woods for a mile to the summit of Bald Peak. Return the way you came.

❸ Prospect Mountain and Rand's View

5.2 mi/2.5 hrs 

Location: In Salisbury; Western Connecticut map page 320, grid b2.

User groups: Hikers, dogs, and snowshoers. No wheelchair facilities. Sections of this trail would be difficult to ski. Bikes, horses, and hunting are prohibited.

Access, fees: Parking and access are free. Camping is prohibited except in designated shelters and campsites along the Appalachian Trail.

Directions: From the junction of U.S. 7 and Route 126 in Falls Village, take Route 126 north for six-tenths of a mile and turn left on Point of Rocks Road. Drive a tenth of a mile and turn right on Water Street. Drive another three-tenths of a mile, cross the famous Iron Bridge (look for the white blazes of the Appalachian Trail, which crosses this bridge and enters the woods on the right), bear right after the bridge, then take an immediate right onto Housatonic River Road. Continue four-tenths of a mile to a parking area on the right marked by a sign reading "Car-top boat launch/Historic Trail." Park on the left, away from the boat launch area.

Maps: For a map of hiking trails, refer to map 4 in the "Map and Guide to the Appalachian Trail in Massachusetts and Connecticut," a five-map set for $16.95 from the Appalachian Trail Conference (see address below). For topographic maps of the area, request South Canaan and Sharon from the USGS.

Contact: Appalachian Mountain Club's Mount Greylock Visitors Center, P.O. Box 1800, Lanesboro, MA 01237, (413) 443-0011; or the AMC's main office in Boston, (617) 523-0636. Appalachian Trail Conference, P.O. Box 807, Harpers Ferry, WV 25425; (304) 535-6331. The Blue Trails Network, Connecticut Forest and Park Association, (860) 346-2372.

Trail notes: Rand's View has been praised as "the nicest view along the Appalachian Trail in Connecticut." That's a big claim, but a hiker standing at Rand's gazes north across a classic New England countryside of broad pastures and hills. In the left foreground rises the low ridge of Wetauwanchu Mountain. In the distance, from left to right, are Bear Mountain, Mount Everett in Massachusetts, and the abrupt end of the ridge at Jug End—a look into the future for an AT through-hiker reaching this spot, because the trail traverses that prominent ridge. On a clear day, you can see Mount Greylock, 50 miles away, on the center-right horizon.

From the parking area, cross Housatonic River Road to the left and pick up the white-blazed Appalachian Trail. The trail is gentle here, so you will quickly walk the two miles to the summit of Prospect Mountain, with its view of the nearby valley and hills to the north and east. Continue over Prospect another half mile to where the AT turns sharply right and a blue-blazed trail (marked by a sign) leads left a half mile to Limestone shelter. A second sign points to the right toward Rand's View, just 500 feet farther down the Appalachian Trail. Hike back along the same route.

4 Pine Knob Loop

2.5 mi/1.5 hrs 

Location: In Housatonic Meadows State Park in Sharon; Western Connecticut map page 320, grid b2.

User groups: Hikers, dogs, and snowshoers. No wheelchair facilities. Dogs must be on a leash. This trail is not suitable for skis. Bikes, horses, and hunting are prohibited.

Access, fees: Parking and access are free. Camping is prohibited except in designated shelters and campsites along the Appalachian Trail.

Directions: The trail begins at a parking area marked by a sign on U.S. 7 in Housatonic Meadows State Park, between the towns of Cornwall Bridge and West Cornwall, one mile north of the junction with Route 4 and four-tenths of a mile south of the entrance to the state park campground.

Maps: For a map of hiking trails, refer to map 4 in the "Map and Guide to the Appalachian Trail in Massachusetts and Connecticut," a five-map set for $16.95 from the Appalachian Trail Conference (see address below). For topographic maps of the area, request Ellsworth and Cornwall from the USGS.

Contact: Appalachian Mountain Club's Mount Greylock Visitors Center, P.O. Box 1800, Lanesboro, MA 01237, (413) 443-0011; or the AMC's main office in Boston, (617) 523-0636. Appalachian Trail Conference, P.O. Box 807, Harpers Ferry, WV 25425; (304) 535-6331. The Blue Trails Network, Connecticut Forest and Park Association, (860) 346-2372. Housatonic Meadows State Park, Cornwall Bridge, CT 06754; (860) 927-3238. Connecticut State Parks Division, 79

Elm Street, Hartford, CT 06106-5127; (860) 424-3200.

Trail notes: This loop hike leads to a pair of scenic views of the hills lining the Housatonic River Valley. From the parking area, follow the blue-blazed Pine Knob Loop Trail for two-tenths of a mile, and bear right where the trail forks. The trail ascends gradually over Pine Knob, arriving at the first view, among low pine trees, about one mile from the trailhead. Another two-tenths of a mile past that view, turn left (south) on the Appalachian Trail (marked by a sign), now following both white and blue blazes. The next view lies about a half mile beyond the trail junction, and it also looks southeast over the Housatonic Valley. Continuing south on the Appalachian Trail, you'll reach a junction (marked by a sign) in three-tenths of a mile where the AT leads straight ahead and this hike turns left, descending the blue-blazed Pine Knob Loop Trail. Bear right when the trail forks a half mile farther, and continue another two-tenths of a mile to the parking area.

5 Breadloaf Mountain

1.0 mi/0.75 hr 

Location: In Housatonic Meadows State Park in Sharon; Western Connecticut map page 320, grid b2.

User groups: Hikers, dogs, and snowshoers. No wheelchair facilities. Dogs must be on a leash. This trail is not suitable for skis. Bikes, horses, and hunting are prohibited.

Access, fees: Parking and access are free. Camping is prohibited except in designated shelters and campsites along the Appalachian Trail.

Directions: The trail begins at a parking area marked by a sign for the Mohawk Trail on U.S. 7 in Housatonic Meadows State Park, between the towns of Cornwall Bridge and West Cornwall, a tenth of a mile north of the junction with Route 4 and 1.4 miles south of the entrance to the state park campground.

Maps: For a map of hiking trails, refer to map 4 in the "Map and Guide to the Appalachian Trail in Massachusetts and Connecticut," a five-map set for $16.95 from the Appalachian Trail Conference (see address below). For topographic maps of the area, request Ellsworth and Cornwall from the USGS.

Contact: The Blue Trails Network, Connecticut Forest and Park Association, (860) 346-2372. Housatonic Meadows State Park, Cornwall Bridge, CT 06754; (860) 927-3238. Connecticut State Parks Division, 79 Elm Street, Hartford, CT 06106-5127; (860) 424-3200. Appalachian Trail Conference, P.O. Box 807, Harpers Ferry, WV 25425; (304) 535-6331.

Trail notes: I awoke one morning in the campground at Housatonic Meadows State Park to the sound of rain drumming on my tent, and thought, "No hiking today." But when I poked my head out of the tent and realized the rain amounted to little more than a steady but light shower, I headed for the Mohawk Trail leading up Breadloaf Mountain. This easy hike promised me a quick escape back to my car if the rain really intensified into a downpour—and, possibly, some interesting foul-weather views of the Housatonic River Valley. Sure enough, before long I stood on the summit of Breadloaf Mountain looking out over heavily wooded hillsides cloaked in gray, with wisps of clouds rising off them like a thousand question marks.

From the trailhead, follow the blue-blazed Breadloaf Mountain Trail all the way up to the 1,050-foot Breadloaf summit. The Appalachian Trail is located just a tenth of a mile beyond the summit, but this hike returns down the Breadloaf Mountain Trail to the parking area.

6 Echo Rock and Dudleytown

5.0 mi/2.5 hrs 

Location: In Cornwall; Western Connecticut map page 320, grid b2.

User groups: Hikers and snowshoers. No wheelchair facilities. Portions of this trail lie on private land, and use restrictions can change. Assume that bikes, dogs, and horses are not allowed unless a trail is specifically marked for them (although many landowners do not object to dogs). Most trails are open to cross-country skiing. Assume that hunting is allowed in season unless otherwise posted.

Access, fees: Parking and access are free.

Directions: At the junction of U.S. 7 and Route 4 in Cornwall Bridge, look for the sign marking the Mohawk Trail on the east side of the green, just north of Baird's General Store. Park in a turnout 75 yards farther east on Route 4.

Maps: For a topographic map of the area, request Cornwall from the USGS.

Contact: The Blue Trails Network, Connecticut Forest and Park Association, (860) 346-2372.

Trail notes: Expect pleasures more subtle than spectacular on this hike through a quiet wood and a "ghost town" to a view at Echo Rock of the Cornwall Valley and Mohawk Mountain. I had this trail all to myself one afternoon, enhancing the spookiness of Dudleytown, a long-abandoned community where today only a network of stone walls remains amid the dark pine forest. Veteran Appalachian Trail through-hikers may recall Dudleytown—the AT followed the 24-mile Mohawk Trail prior to being rerouted to the west side of the Housatonic River several years ago.

This trail is well marked with blue blazes, but goes through enough twists and turns that you can lose it easily if you're not watching closely for the blazes. From the parking area, walk back toward the green. At the Mohawk Trail sign, turn left up paved Dark Entry Road (there may not be a street sign), following blue blazes. The road becomes dirt and ends about a half mile from Route 4. Turn left onto an old woods road. The trail crosses Bonney Brook nearly a mile from Route 4, then parallels the gentle brook. About 1.5 miles out, cross the brook again, entering Dudleytown. A mile past Dudleytown, you'll reach Echo Rock, a slab on the right. Return the way you came.

7 Cobble Mountain and Pine Hill

2.5 mi/2.0 hrs 

Location: In Macedonia Brook State Park in Kent; Western Connecticut map page 320, grid b2.

User groups: Hikers, dogs, and snowshoers. No wheelchair facilities. Dogs must be on a leash. This trail is not suitable for skis. Bikes, horses, and hunting are prohibited.

Access, fees: Parking and access are free. Macedonia Brook State Park is open from 8 A.M. to sunset year-round.

Directions: From the junction of U.S. 7 and Route 341 in Kent, drive west on Route 341 for 1.8 miles. Turn right at the sign for Macedonia Brook State Park, then follow the signs to the park office, which is two miles from Route 341. Park in the pavilion lot on the right, a tenth of a mile beyond the office.

Maps: A basic map of hiking trails with park information is available at the park office. For topographic maps of the area, request Amenia, Ellsworth, Dover Plains, and Kent from the USGS.

Contact: Macedonia Brook State Park, 159 Macedonia Brook Road, Kent, CT 06757; (860) 927-3238. Connecticut State Parks Division, 79 Elm Street, Hartford, CT 06106; (860) 424-3200. The Blue Trails Network, Connecticut Forest and Park Association, (860) 346-2372.

Trail notes: This loop in Macedonia Brook State Park offers a range of hiking, from easy walking down a flat forest road to steep, rocky trail and summit views of hills unblemished by signs of development. It's a good hike for young children.

From the parking area, cross the road and pick up the Cobble Mountain Trail (marked by a sign). Follow its white blazes a quarter mile, and turn right onto the wide CCC Road (a grassy woods road). Watch for the blazes turning left into the woods again in another quarter mile. The trail then ascends Cobble Mountain, taking you over rock slabs as you near the top. About a half mile from the CCC Road, turn right (north) on the blue-blazed Macedonia Ridge Trail (formerly the route of the Appalachian Trail) and walk a tenth of a mile to the summit of Cobble Mountain, where open ledges offer views west all the way to the Catskills in New York. The trail follows these ledges for about 100 yards, then enters the woods again and descends steeply over rocky ground to a junction with the Pine Hill Trail (entering from the right) within a half mile. Bear left, staying on the Ridge Trail; you'll soon reach the top of Pine Hill, where ledges offer a nice view eastward. A quarter mile past Pine Hill, turn right onto the Old CCC Road and follow it straight for about a mile. Turn left on the white-blazed Cobble Mountain Trail to return to the pavilion parking area.

8 St. Johns Ledges and Caleb's Peak

2.4 mi/2.0 hrs 

Location: In Kent; Western Connecticut map page 320, grid c2.

User groups: Hikers, dogs, and snowshoers. No wheelchair facilities. This trail is not suitable for skis. Bikes, horses, and hunting are prohibited.

Access, fees: Parking and access are free. Camping is prohibited except in designated shelters and campsites along the Appalachian Trail. The dirt access road to the Appalachian Trail closes at sunset.

Directions: From Route 341 on the west side of the Housatonic River in Kent, turn north onto Skiff Mountain Road. Drive 1.1 miles and bear right onto a dirt road marked by a sign for the Appalachian National Scenic Trail. Continue another 1.6 miles to a turnout on the left where the white blazes of the Appalachian Trail enter the woods.

Maps: For a map of hiking trails, refer to map 5 in the "Map and Guide to the Appalachian Trail in Massachusetts and Connecticut," a five-map set for $16.95 from the Appalachian Trail Conference (see address below). For topographic maps of the area, request Ellsworth and Kent from the USGS.

Contact: Appalachian Mountain Club's Mount Greylock Visitors Center, P.O. Box 1800, Lanesboro, MA 01237, (413) 443-0011; or the AMC's main office in Boston, (617) 523-0636. Appalachian Trail Conference, P.O. Box 807, Harpers Ferry, WV 25425; (304) 535-6331. The Blue Trails Network, Connecticut Forest and Park Association, (860) 346-2372.

Trail notes: From atop the cliffs of the St. Johns Ledges, you enjoy a broad view of the bucolic Housatonic Valley to the east; I stood there one morning watching a hawk float on the warm breezes. Caleb's Peak offers a nice, if somewhat more limited, view to the south. This section of the AT includes a very steep tenth-of-a-mile stretch up large rocks laid out as steps by trail crews, and easy walking along the ridge from St. Johns Ledges to Caleb's Peak.

From the turnout, head west into the woods. Within about a tenth of a mile, an unmarked side path diverges left to low cliffs frequented by rock climbers. The white-blazed AT continues straight, turns left (southwest) and ascends below slab cliffs, then turns steeply upward, reaching St. Johns Ledges six-tenths of a mile from the road. Continue another six-tenths of a mile south on the AT to Caleb's Peak. Hike back along the same route.

9 Prospect Mountain

2.5 mi/1.5 hrs 

Location: In the Bantam section of Litchfield; Western Connecticut map page 320, grid c2.

User groups: Hikers and snowshoers. No wheelchair facilities. Portions of this trail lie on private land, and use restrictions can change. Assume that bikes, dogs, and horses are not allowed unless a trail is specifically marked for them (although many landowners do not object to dogs). Most trails are open to cross-country skiing. Assume that hunting is allowed in season unless otherwise posted.

Access, fees: Parking and access are free.

Directions: From the junction of U.S. 202 and Route 209 in Bantam (west of Litchfield), drive west on U.S. 202 for six-tenths of a mile and turn right onto Cathole Road. Drive 1.6 miles to a turnout on the left. There is no trail sign, but look for a rock with a blue blaze (difficult to see from the road) marking the trail.

Maps: For topographic maps of the area, request New Preston and Litchfield from the USGS.

Contact: The Blue Trails Network, Connecticut Forest and Park Association, 16 Meriden Road, Rockfall, CT 06481-2961; (860) 346-2372.

Trail notes: Although the start of this hike lacks much scenic appeal, ledges in two spots offer decent views of the forested hills of western Connecticut, including Mount Tom, with its distinctly visible observation tower. The trail also passes between interesting rock ledges just below the summit. Follow the blue blazes of the Mattatuck Trail through an area recovering from tornado damage, ascending steadily. The trail reaches a ridge crest, dips briefly through the ledges, then emerges from the woods onto a broad, open ledge with good views west to Mount Tom. Continue another tenth of a mile; where the trail turns sharply left, a footpath leads right up onto the summit ledges, with some views of the surrounding hills. Return the way you came.

10 Mount Tom State Park Tower

1.0 mi/0.75 hr 

Location: In Mount Tom State Park in Litchfield and Washington; Western Connecticut map page 320, grid c2.

User groups: Hikers and snowshoers. No wheelchair facilities. This trail is not suitable for skis. Bikes, dogs, horses, and hunting are prohibited.

Access, fees: On weekends from Memorial Day until Labor Day, a parking fee of $5 per day is charged to Connecticut residents and $8 to nonresidents; on weekdays during this period, residents pay $4 and nonresidents $5.

Directions: The entrance to Mount Tom State Park is along U.S. 202 between Woodville and Bantam and is marked by signs. Inside the park entrance, turn right into a parking lot marked by a sign for the picnic area and Tower Trail.

Maps: A trail map is available free from the Connecticut State Parks Division (see address below). For a topographic map of the area, request New Preston from the USGS.

Contact: The Connecticut State Parks Division, 79 Elm Street, Hartford, CT 06106-5127; (860) 424-3200.

Trail notes: This short, easy hike—a good one for young children—leads to a stone tower on Mount Tom's summit that you can climb to enjoy a 360-degree panorama of the western Connecticut countryside. From the parking lot, head up a dirt road to where it forks at a sign directing you up the right fork for the Tower Trail. At the next fork, bear right, following yellow blazes through a few more turns. The trail skirts a wet area, then turns right and climbs to the summit. Be careful not to turn onto a different trail on the descent.

11 Buttermilk Falls

0.2 mi/0.25 hr 

Location: In Plymouth; Western Connecticut map page 320, grid c3.

User groups: Hikers and snowshoers. No wheelchair facilities. This trail is not suitable for skis. Bikes, dogs, horses, and hunting are prohibited.

Access, fees: Parking and access are free.

Directions: Take U.S. 6 into Terryville (Plymouth). Turn south onto South Main Street, which makes a right turn in two-tenths of a mile and again in another 1.2 miles. After the second right, drive 1.3 miles and turn left onto Lane Hill Road. Drive two-tenths of a mile to a small turnout on the right marked by a sign for the Nature Conservancy, where the blue blazes of the Mattatuck Trail enter the woods. There are also turnouts along the road just before and beyond the trailhead.

Maps: No map is needed for this short walk, but for a topographic map of the area, request Thomaston from the USGS.

Contact: The Nature Conservancy, 55 High Street, Middletown, CT 06457-3788; (860) 344-0716. The Blue Trails Network, Connecticut Forest and Park Association, 16 Meriden Road, Rockfall, CT 06481-2961; (860) 346-2372.

Trail notes: As soon as you step out of your car, the sound of Buttermilk Falls reaches your ears. It's a short, relatively flat walk to the waterfall, which plummets about 100 feet through several drops. A popular place to bring young children, Buttermilk sees lots of visitors, especially on nice weekends in summer, so parking here can be difficult at times. The preserve also, unfortunately, attracts illegal after-hours activity; the Nature Conservancy makes periodic visits to clean up trash left by insensitive visitors. Consider lending a hand by picking up trailside litter on your visit here.

From the roadside parking area, the trail leads into the woods, traversing fairly level terrain a short distance to the falls, where you can easily walk uphill or down for various views on the waterfall.

12 Leatherman's Cave/ Crane Lookout

2.0 mi/1.0 hr 

Location: In Watertown; Western Connecticut map page 320, grid c3.

User groups: Hikers and snowshoers. No wheelchair facilities. Portions of this trail lie on private land, and use restrictions can change. Assume that bikes, dogs, and horses are not allowed unless a trail is specifically marked for them. Most trails are open to cross-country skiing. Assume that hunting is allowed in season unless otherwise posted.

Access, fees: Parking and access are free.

Directions: Take Route 8 to exit 39, then take U.S. 6 west. From the traffic lights at the junction of U.S. 6 and Route 109, drive nine-tenths of a mile farther west on U.S. 6 to a turnout on the right at a small sign for the Mattatuck Trail.

Maps: For a topographic map of the area, request Thomaston from the USGS.

Contact: The Blue Trails Network, Connecticut Forest and Park Association, 16 Meriden Road, Rockfall, CT 06481-2961; (860) 346-2372.

Trail notes: Leatherman's Cave is the sort of place that excites both children and adults: a jumble of giant boulders that have fallen from the cliff below Crane Lookout over the centuries. And the Mattatuck Trail sends hikers crawling through a dark, cool 50-foot passageway among the boulders.

From the turnout, cross the highway and follow the blue blazes of the Mattatuck Trail into the woods. You'll soon scramble up exposed rock and traverse a classic Connecticut rock ridge with views of rolling, wooded hills. Descending the other end, cross an unmarked trail; you'll soon reach a woods road and turn left, following it a short distance through an area that is sometimes wet. Bear right, then take the leftmost trail of the three before you, an eroded gully that ascends through a area that has been burned, probably by a small forest fire. At the next trail junction, turn left and walk out onto Crane Lookout, which offers views of the craggy hills to the north and of the industrial areas to the east. Leatherman's Cave is below you, out of sight. Double back and bear down and left with the blue blazes (the trail you followed onto Crane Lookout bears right). Take a left at the first of two successive trail junctions, descending quickly to Leatherman's Cave. Return to U.S. 6 the same way you came.

⓭ Hancock Brook: Lion Head Loop

2.5 mi/1.5 hrs 

Location: In the Waterville section of Waterbury; Western Connecticut map page 320, grid c3.

User groups: Hikers and snowshoers. No wheelchair facilities. Portions of this trail lie on private land, and use restrictions can change. Assume that bikes, dogs, and horses are not allowed unless a trail is specifically marked for them (although many landowners do not object to dogs). Most trails are open to cross-country skiing. Assume that hunting is allowed in season unless otherwise posted.

Access, fees: Parking and access are free.

Directions: Take exit 37 off Route 8 and head east a short distance to Thomaston Avenue (old Route 8). Turn right and drive 1.9 miles into Waterville, then turn left onto Sheffield Street. Follow it to the end and park at the roadside on the right just before the sand and gravel pit.

Maps: For a topographic map of the area, request Waterbury from the USGS.

Contact: The Blue Trails Network, Connecticut Forest and Park Association, 16 Meriden Road, Rockfall, CT 06481-2961; (860) 346-2372.

Trail notes: Okay, so after driving through industrial Waterville and parking next to a gravel pit, your expectations for this hike may be a bit modest. But after leaving the gravel pit behind, this actually becomes a decent little hike. The highlight is Hancock Brook, which I had the opportunity to see running full and rambunctious with spring runoff.

The trail begins at a post marked with a blue blaze. Walk the right edge of the gravel pit's property. At a rock where a blue arrow directs you into the woods, stop and look left; the gravel road leading uphill is where this loop finishes. Soon after entering the woods, the sound of heavy machinery is replaced by the sound of running water—or, rather, falling water—Hancock Brook drops steeply through a narrow ravine. Follow the wide and flat path of what resembles an old rail bed (watch on the right for a cascade tumbling into the brook on its opposite bank). Abundant hardwoods create a shady, cool corridor along the brook. Although it lies well down a steep embankment at the outset, the brook gradually rises nearly to the level of the trail. After the brook becomes more placid, the well-blazed trail turns left and ascends steeply up onto the open ledge of the Lion's Head, with decent views in all directions of the rolling hills of central Connecticut and the surrounding communities. Continue back, following the blazes to the gravel pit.

⓮ Jessie Gerard Trail

3.0 mi/2.0 hrs 

Location: In People's State Forest in Barkhamsted; Western Connecticut map page 320, grid b3.

User groups: Hikers and dogs. No wheelchair facilities. Dogs must be on a leash. This trail may be difficult to snowshoe because of steepness and ice, and is not suitable for bikes, horses, or skis. Hunting is prohibited.

Access, fees: Parking and access are free.

Directions: From the junction of Routes 318 and 181 in Pleasant Valley (Barkhamsted), drive east over the Farmington River bridge and take an immediate left onto East River Road. Proceed another 2.4 miles (passing a road on the right, marked by a sign, which leads to the state forest office), and park in the turnout on the left, across from a sign marking the Jessie Gerard Trail.

Maps: A free, noncontour map of hiking trails in the People's and American Legion State Forests is available at several locations, including boxes at the People's State Forest office and museum, the Austin F. Hawes Campground on West River Road (which runs north from the junction of Routes 318 and 181 in Barkhamsted), and the field office on West River Road. You can also try the Pleasant Valley Store or the Riverton Store (both stores are located in the center of those towns). For topographic maps of the area, request Winsted and New Hartford from the USGS.

Contact: People's State Forest, P.O. Box 1, Pleasant Valley, CT 06063; (860) 379-2469. Connecticut State Parks Division, 79 Elm Street, Hartford, CT 06106; (860) 424-3200.

Trail notes: This hike leads to open ledges at the Overlook and Chaugham Lookout, which offer spectacular views of the Farmington River Valley—and, a somewhat rare treat in Connecticut, a largely undeveloped landscape. You'll catch a fog over the river in the early morning when conditions are right, and the fall foliage show is five-star.

From the turnout, cross the road and follow the yellow-blazed trail on a steep and strenuous climb of the famous stone stairway known as the "299 Steps," paralleling the cascades of a brook. Shortly after a brook crossing, where the trail hooks right, look for trees with large woodpecker holes beside the trail on the right. Pass a waterfall, then follow the trail as it ascends more moderately. A bit more than a mile from the trailhead lies the Overlook, with the best views of this hike. Another three-tenths of a mile ahead is Chaugham Lookout; a few minutes beyond that, the trail passes between two enormous, twin glacial erratics called the Veeder Boulders. This hike doubles back from the boulders, though Greenswoods Road lies just three-tenths of a mile beyond them.

⓯ Braille Trail

0.3 mi/0.5 hr 

Location: In Barkhamsted; Western Connecticut map page 320, grid b4.

User groups: Hikers, dogs, and wheelchair users. This trail is closed in the winter. Bikes, horses, and hunting are prohibited.

Access, fees: Parking and access are free. The recreation area is open daily from 8 A.M. to 8 P.M., beginning April 1 until the first snowfall.

Directions: From the junction of Routes 318 and 181 in Pleasant Valley (Barkhamsted), drive east over the Farmington River bridge and follow Route 181 past the Pleasant Valley firehouse. Turn right onto Goosegreen Road, which is the first paved road on the right. Drive about a tenth of a mile and turn left into the Metropolitan District Commission's Goosegreen Recreation Area. Follow signs to the Braille Trail.

Maps: No map is needed for this short walk, but for a topographic map of the area, request New Hartford from the USGS.

Contact: Metropolitan District Commission, Supply Division, 39 Beachrock Road, Pleasant Valley, CT 06063, (860) 379-0938; or the MDC's main office in Hartford, (860) 278-7850.

Trail notes: Opened in 1994 on the shores of scenic Lake McDonough, this short, paved loop is designed for people with visual and other physical impairments and walkers who prefer a gentle grade. Managed by the Metropolitan District Commission, it has information signs in English and Braille, a guide rope for visitors to follow to each station, and signs that point out various features of geology, vegetation, and wildlife. And it's right on the water, with nice views of the lake and hills.

⑯ McLean Game Refuge Summit Hike Loop

2.6 mi/1.5 hrs 

Location: In Granby; Western Connecticut map page 320, grid b4.

User groups: Hikers, dogs, skiers, and snowshoers. No wheelchair facilities. Dogs must be on a leash. Bikes, horses, and hunting are prohibited.

Access, fees: Parking and access are free. The refuge trails are open daily from 8 A.M. to dusk.

Directions: From the junction in Granby where Routes 20, 10, and 189 and U.S. 202 merge, drive south on Route 10/U.S. 202 for one mile and turn right onto the entrance road (which is 1.6 miles north of the Simsbury town line). Park in the lot at the end of the road.

Maps: A map of hiking trails is posted with refuge regulations on an information board in the parking lot. For a topographic map of the area, request Tariffville from the USGS.

Contact: Trustees of the McLean Fund, 75 Great Pond Road, Simsbury, CT 06070; (860) 653-7869.

Trail notes: Former Senator George P. McLean created the 3,480-acre refuge that bears his name in an act of his will when he died in 1932. Woods roads and foot trails meander through the gentle, forested terrain. Several loops are possible.

This hike takes you to an overlook atop the Barndoor Hills with a nice view of a bucolic valley and wooded hills. From the parking lot, walk past the wooden gate and follow the woods road across a wooden bridge over Bissell Brook. Just beyond the bridge, turn right onto the Blue Loop. Follow the blue blazes through a mixed forest with slight ups and downs. At an intersection with a woods road, the Blue Loop turns left to return to the start, but you turn right, following the road through a dark hemlock grove. At a junction of woods roads, with a hillside of shattered rock on your left, a sign directs you to turn left for the summit of the Barndoor Hills. (Do not go straight onto Barndoor Hill Road.) Follow that road steadily uphill, then turn right onto the blue-blazed summit trail, leading soon to the open ledge with unobstructed views. Backtrack down the summit trail and turn left on the woods road, returning the way you came. But at the next junction of roads, bear right into the woods onto a trail marked by faded blue blazes. Within minutes, turn left onto another trail, which will deposit you onto the same woods road where the Blue Loop emerged earlier. Turn right to return to the parking lot, passing scenic Trout Pond on the way. On my hike by the pond, I happened upon a furry little yellow gosling that fled, squeaking in panic, at my approach. Moments later, three honking geese flew low overhead in perfect V formation.

17 Peak Mountain

2.0 mi/1.0 hr 

Location: In East Granby; Western Connecticut map page 320, grid b4.

User groups: Hikers and snowshoers. No wheelchair facilities. Portions of this trail lie on private land, and use restrictions can change. Assume that bikes, dogs, and horses are not allowed unless a trail is specifically marked for them (although many landowners do not object to dogs). Most trails are open to cross-country skiing. Assume that hunting is allowed in season unless otherwise posted.

Access, fees: Parking and access are free.

Directions: On Route 20 in East Granby, seven-tenths of a mile west of the junction with Route 187 and 2.6 miles east of the junction in Granby where Routes 20, 10, and 189 and U.S. 202 merge, turn north onto Newgate Road (there is a sign for the Old Newgate Prison, which is open to visitors). Pull into the turnout on the right; the blue-blazed Metacomet Trail enters the woods there.

Maps: For topographic maps of the area, request Tariffville and Windsor Locks from the USGS.

Contact: The Blue Trails Network, Connecticut Forest and Park Association, 16 Meriden Road, Rockfall, CT 06481-2961; (860) 346-2372.

Trail notes: Some might say that Peak Mountain, at 672 feet, is neither a peak nor a mountain. But the open ledges at its "summit" offer long views to the west and make a nice local spot to catch the sunset. From the turnout, follow the trail as it ascends a steep hillside, quickly reaching the ridge. Then turn left (north), following the blue blazes to the broad rock outcropping a mile from the trailhead. Either double back from here, or continue north along the ridge for nearly another mile to enjoy two more long views of the Granby area and the hills farther west, one from an open area and another from an outcropping. Then follow the Metacomet back to the trailhead.

18 Tariffville Gorge

0.4 mi/0.5 hr 

Location: Near East Granby, Bloomfield, and Simsbury; Western Connecticut map page 320, grid b4.

User groups: Hikers only. No wheelchair facilities. This trail would be difficult to snowshoe and is not suitable for bikes, dogs, horses, or skis. Hunting is prohibited.

Access, fees: Parking and access are free.

Directions: Take Route 189 north into Tariffville. Pass the town center, cross the Farmington River, and park on the other side of the bridge. The blue blazes of the Metacomet Trail enter the woods on the east side of the road.

Maps: For topographic maps of the area, request Tariffville and Windsor Locks from the USGS.

Contact: The Blue Trails Network, Connecticut Forest and Park Association, 16 Meriden Road, Rockfall, CT 06481; (860) 346-2372.

Trail notes: The short hike climbs a steep

hillside to one of the finest views along the Metacomet Trail; you look out over the village of Tariffville, the Farmington River, and surrounding hills from an open ledge hundreds of feet above the river. Because this hike is so short, you can do it at odd times of day—perhaps early morning, with a fog over the river, or toward evening, if a nice sunset is starting to take shape. Follow the blue blazes. Once you gain the ridgetop, it's a short walk to the open ledge overlooking the river.

19 Talcott Mountain

5.0 mi/3.0 hrs 

Location: In Talcott Mountain State Park in Bloomfield; Western Connecticut map page 320, grid b4.

User groups: Hikers, dogs, and snowshoers. No wheelchair facilities. Dogs must be on a leash. The trail is not suitable for bikes, horses, or skis. Hunting is prohibited.

Access, fees: Parking and access are free. The Heublein Tower and the small museum at the summit are open daily from June 1 to November 1, and on weekends in May.

Directions: This hike begins from the parking lot a tenth of a mile inside the entrance to Penwood State Park on Route 185, 1.2 miles west of the junction of Routes 178 and 185 in Bloomfield, and 1.7 miles east of the junction of Route 185 and Route 10/ U.S. 202 in Simsbury.

Maps: For a topographic map of the area, request Avon from the USGS.

Contact: Connecticut State Parks Division, 79 Elm Street, Hartford, CT 06106-5127; (860) 424-3200. The Blue Trails Network, Connecticut Forest and Park Association, 16 Meriden Road, Rockfall, CT 06481-2961; (860) 346-2372.

Trail notes: This five-mile round-trip hike takes in two of Connecticut's scenic attractions: the quarter mile of the Metacomet Trail along the exposed ridge in Talcott Mountain State Park ranks as one of the most scenic stretches of what may be the state's premier trail; and the Heublein Tower offers a 360-degree panorama of the surrounding countryside.

From the parking lot, follow the blue-blazed Metacomet south across Route 185 and into the woods. Within two-tenths of a mile, the trail crosses power lines; don't cross straight onto a woods road, but rather, bear right across the power lines, looking for a footpath and a blue blaze at the edge of the trees. The Metacomet then zigs and zags along various woods roads for nearly a mile, ascending gently to the ridge and more interesting hiking along a footpath through eastern hemlock trees. At 2.3 miles from the parking lot, the trail emerges onto an open ledge with a view stretching for miles out to the hills of western Connecticut. Just a tenth of a mile farther south, the trail passes by the impressive, 165-foot tower built in 1914 by Gilbert Heublein and used as his summer home until 1937. Continue a tenth of a mile past the tower on the Metacomet to a traprock ledge to the left of the picnic area for views of Farmington River Valley. Hike back the way you came.

20 West Hartford Reservoir

8.0 mi/4.0 hrs 

Location: In West Hartford; Western Connecticut map page 320, grid b4.

User groups: Hikers, bikes, dogs, horses, skiers, and snowshoers. No wheelchair facilities. Dogs must be on a leash. Hunting is prohibited.

Access, fees: Parking and access are free. The reservoir is open from 8 A.M. to 8 P.M. from mid-April through late October, and 8 A.M. to 6 P.M. during the rest of the year.

Directions: This loop begins from a dirt turnout on the south side of U.S. 44 in West Hartford, 2.1 miles east of the easternmost junction of U.S. 44 and Route 10 in Avon and a tenth of a mile west of a large paved parking lot and entrance to the reservoir area. You could also park in the paved lot and walk (or bike) up U.S. 44 to access this loop.

Maps: A good map of the West Hartford Reservoir Area (also called the Talcott Mountain Reservoir Area) can be ordered for $2 from the Metropolitan District Commission; call (860) 278-7850 and ask for West Hartford Filters. For a topographic map of the area, request Avon from the USGS.

Contact: Metropolitan District Commission, Supply Division, 39 Beachrock Road, Pleasant Valley, CT 06063; (860) 379-0938.

Trail notes: This roughly eight-mile loop is great for mountain bikers and cross-country skiers, although hikers and trail runners enjoy it as well. With an extensive network of trails and old woods roads weaving through the forest and around the water bodies here, the West Hartford Reservoir area is a popular local recreation spot. This loop encircles the southern half of the water district land, and there's a lot more exploration potential here. Trail maps are posted at several strategic junctions, but it's a good idea to carry one.

The first half of this hike is on the blue-blazed Metacomet Trail. From the turnout on U.S. 44, follow the blue blazes up onto the earthen dike and turn right (west), following the dike about 200 yards to a gate beside the highway (on your right). Turn left with the Metacomet, continuing along an old woods road until the trail hooks left, crossing a brook onto a footpath. The trail then passes through fairly open woods and over occasional rock ledges for more than two miles before emerging on the rough Dirt Rock Road. Turn right on the road, still following the Metacomet, descending a steep slope of broken rock. Within half a mile, bear left with the blue blazes, off the woods road and onto a path. About half a mile farther, turn left onto a paved section of Finger Rock Road, then right onto the paved Red Road. In about three-tenths of a mile, turn left onto a wide woods road, then take the next left (near a map board) onto the dirt Overlook Road.

Stay on Overlook for about 1.2 miles, and cross Reservoir Number 5 on a bridge, where you will enjoy some of the nicest views along this route of forest tightly embracing the waters of the reservoir on both sides of the bridge. Then take two lefts in rapid succession. You will be on the paved Reservoir Road Extension; follow it to the left around the end of the reservoir, through a quiet woods, then turn right onto the paved Northwest Road, which becomes dirt within about three-tenths of a mile. Continue about another three-tenths of a mile and take the first trail on the right. Stay left through the next two trail intersections, then bear right twice, the second time at the edge of an open meadow. Follow that obvious path, which leads onto the earthen dike, about 1.2 miles back to the turnout on U.S. 44.

21 Case Mountain

2.0 mi/1.0 hr 

Location: In the Highland Park section of Manchester; Eastern Connecticut map page 321, grid b1.

User groups: Hikers, bikes, dogs, skiers, and snowshoers. No wheelchair facilities. Dogs must be on a leash. Horses and hunting are prohibited.

Access, fees: Parking and access are free.

Directions: From Interstate 384 westbound, take exit 4 in Manchester. Turn right onto Highland Street, drive three-tenths of a mile, then turn right again onto Spring

Street. Continue another three-tenths of a mile to a parking turnout on the left just over a bridge. From Interstate 384 eastbound, take exit 4 in Manchester and turn right onto Spring Street. Continue two-tenths of a mile to the same parking turnout on the left.

Maps: A trail map is posted at several major trail junctions, and a free copy of the map is available through the Manchester Parks and Recreation Department (see address below). For topographic maps of the area, request Manchester and Rockville from the USGS.

Contact: Manchester Parks and Recreation Department, (860) 647-3084. The Blue Trails Network, Connecticut Forest and Park Association, 16 Meriden Road, Rockfall, CT 06481-2961; (860) 346-2372.

Trail notes: This fairly easy two-mile hike incorporates the Shenipsit and other trails through the Case Mountain Open Space to loop over the Lookout, a cleared area with limited views west toward Hartford. For the most part, this hike remains in the woods, but it's a nice refuge for a short hike in the midst of a fairly populous urban area. Trails are well blazed and generally easy to follow, and distances between junctions described here are rarely more than three-tenths of a mile.

From the parking area, walk past the gate, following the wide path of the white-blazed Carriage Road Trail about 150 yards, then turn right onto the red-blazed Highland Park Trail at a sign which reads "Trail to Lookout." Follow the red trail past a junction where the orange-blazed Boulder Trail diverges left, then turn right, following the white trail uphill a tenth of a mile to the Lookout, where there are limited views to the west. Turn left on the yellow-blazed Lookout Trail, which coincides briefly with the blue-blazed Shenipsit Trail; bear right on the yellow trail after the two split again. After crossing the white trail, turn left onto a newer trail blazed blue and yellow (watch closely for it). Turn left on the blue trail, walk 100 yards, then turn right on the white trail, which soon bears left off the woods road onto a footpath, leading straight onto the red trail. Upon rejoining the white trail, turn right and follow it back to the parking area.

22 Rattlesnake Mountain

5.4 mi/3.5 hrs 

Location: In Plainville; Western Connecticut map page 320, grid c4.

User groups: Hikers and snowshoers. No wheelchair facilities. Portions of this trail lie on private land, and use restrictions can change. Assume that bikes, dogs, and horses are not allowed unless a trail is specifically marked for them (although many landowners do not object to dogs). Most trails are open to cross-country skiing. Assume that hunting is allowed in season unless otherwise posted.

Access, fees: Parking and access are free.

Directions: This hike begins along Route 372 in Plainville, at a sign for the Metacomet Trail, 1.5 miles east of the junction with Route 10 and two miles west of exit 7 off Route 72. Parking here is difficult. Heed the no trespassing signs. You might ask permission to park at one of the gas stations just east of the trailhead on Route 372.

Maps: For a topographic map of the area, request New Britain from the USGS.

Contact: The Blue Trails Network, Connecticut Forest and Park Association, 16 Meriden Road, Rockfall, CT 06481-2961; (860) 346-2372.

Trail notes: Here's another relatively easy ridge walk that begins in a heavily industrialized area, yet leads to some fairly nice views from two clifftops. Follow the blue-blazed Metacomet Trail along a fence, then up a hillside into the woods. The trail makes numerous turns, finally reaching and following the western side of the low ridge past a couple of rock outcroppings with views west. At 1.7 miles, you reach the bare top of Pinnacle Rock, with views in all directions. You may see or hear rock climbers below; be careful not to dislodge any loose stones. Continue north, descending past an old stone foundation and crossing a dirt road; then the trail turns left and re-enters the woods. It eventually reaches Rattlesnake Mountain, ascending a slope of loose rocks and traversing below its vertical cliffs (another popular spot for climbers), passing through a tunnel-like passage in rocks.

The trail ascends around the end of the cliffs to the open ledges atop them, with good views to the north, east, and south (including Hartford's skyline to the northeast). A short distance farther along the Metacomet Trail lies Will Warren's Den, an area of huge boulders worth checking out before you retrace your steps on the return hike. (A local legend, which dates back to colonial times, has it that a man named Will Warren was flogged for not going to church and, in a fit of vengeance, he tried to burn down the entire village of Farmington. As a result, he was chased by the villagers into the nearby hills, where some Indian women hid him in this "cave.")

23 Compounce Ridge

2.5 mi. one way/2.0 hrs 

Location: In Southington; Western Connecticut map page 320, grid c4.

User groups: Hikers and snowshoers. No wheelchair facilities. Portions of this trail lie on private land, and use restrictions can change. Assume that bikes, dogs, and horses are not allowed unless a trail is specifically marked for them (although many landowners do not object to dogs). Most trails are open to cross-country skiing. Assume that hunting is allowed in season unless otherwise posted.

Access, fees: Parking and access are free.

Directions: Take two vehicles if possible. From the junction of Routes 72 and 229 in Bristol, drive south on Route 229 for three-tenths of a mile and turn right onto Lake Road. Drive 1.4 miles to the unmarked, dirt Cussgutter parking area on the right, just before the amusement park; leave a vehicle here, where this hike ends. Drive a second vehicle another 1.4 miles south on Route 229 and turn right onto Panthorn Trail, a paved residential street; at its end, the blue blazes of the Steep Climb Trail enter the woods. If you don't have two vehicles, you'll have to walk about 1.3 miles of road between the trailheads.

Maps: For a topographic map of the area, request Bristol from the USGS.

Contact: The Blue Trails Network, Connecticut Forest and Park Association, 16 Meriden Road, Rockfall, CT 06481-2961; (860) 346-2372.

Trail notes: This nice local ridge walk brings you to a pair of fine, open ledges with views east, Norton Outlook and Julian's Rock. From Panthorn Trail, the Steep Climb Trail does indeed ascend fairly steeply, crossing two brooks. At a half mile, turn right onto the Compounce Ridge Trail (CRT)—a part of the Tunxis Trail—and watch for a side path that leads right to an overlook. Continue uphill on the CRT to the bald cap of Norton Outlook, at 931 feet the actual high point of this ridge. On a clear day, you might see as far as Long Island to the south and Mount Tom in Massachusetts to the north. Norton is a mile from Panthorn Trail, and a logical turn-around point if you have just one vehicle parked there. The distance for hiking the trail in a loop is 3.7 miles.

This hike continues north on the CRT, descending to an unmarked trail junction and turning right. Soon you pass a low, overhanging cliff on your left and reach signs at the place where the Bobcat Trail crosses the CRT. Make a diagonal right on the CRT toward Julian's Rock, four-tenths of a mile from Norton Outlook, an open ridge of rock with expansive views east to the city of Southington and, in the background to the northeast, Hartford's skyline. At the next trail junction, turn left. The trail descends a slab into the woods. Where two streams meet in a nice little wooded drainage, turn right onto the Compounce Cascade Trail, which parallels scenic Cussgutter Brook for much of the descent to the Cussgutter parking area. Watch the blazes, and look particularly for a log bridge where the trail crosses the stream.

24 Ragged Mountain Preserve Trail

6.0 mi/4.0 hrs 

Location: In Berlin; Western Connecticut map page 320, grid c4.

User groups: Hikers, dogs, and snowshoers. No wheelchair facilities. Dogs must be on a leash. This trail is not suitable for bikes, horses, or skis. Hunting is prohibited.

Access, fees: Parking and access are free. Ragged Mountain Preserve closes at dusk.

Directions: From Route 71A in Berlin, 1.2 miles south of the junction of 71A and Route 372 and 1.2 miles north of the junction of 71A and Route 71, turn west onto West Lane. Proceed six-tenths of a mile to a turnout on the right at the gated entrance to the Ragged Mountain Preserve.

Maps: For topographic maps of the area, request New Britain and Meriden from the USGS.

Contact: The Blue Trails Network, Connecticut Forest and Park Association, 16 Meriden Road, Rockfall, CT 06481-2961; (860) 346-2372.

Trail notes: I did this six-mile loop on a blustery November afternoon when the leaves were down, giving me far more open views along the ridge than one has during summer or early fall. I also saw just three other hikers—and one deer. This is a great foliage hike, too, and much of the loop would be a nice ski tour, provided you don't mind lugging skis through the several short, difficult sections.

From the turnout, walk the woods road a tenth of a mile to the Ragged Mountain Preserve Trail loop. Follow its blue blazes with red dots to the left. Within half a mile you will reach the crest of tall cliffs high above Hart Ponds, with wide views to the southeast. The trail follows the clifftops along the southern edge of Ragged Mountain for the next mile or so, passing one cliff, at about 1.5 miles out, where a wall stands completely detached from the main cliff. Turn right onto the blue-blazed Metacomet Trail, which follows the west ridge of Ragged Mountain, high above Shuttle Meadow Reservoir, with excellent views to the south, west, and northwest. After dropping off the ridge, the Metacomet heads north; bear to the right (east) on the blue-red Ragged Mountain Preserve Trail, which eventually turns south through the woods, at one point climbing a slope of loose stones. The loop trail ends where you started; turn left and walk a tenth of a mile back to your vehicle.

25 Great Hill

1.0 mi/0.75 hr 

Location: In East Hampton; Eastern Connecticut map page 321, grid c1.

User groups: Hikers and snowshoers. No wheelchair facilities. Portions of this trail lie on private land, and use restrictions can change. Assume that bikes, dogs, and horses are not allowed unless a trail is specifically marked for them (although many landowners do not object to dogs). Most trails are open to cross-country skiing.

Assume that hunting is allowed in season unless otherwise posted.

Access, fees: Parking and access are free.

Directions: From the junction of Routes 66 and 151 in Cobalt (East Hampton), turn north onto Depot Hill Road, drive a tenth of a mile, then bear right, uphill, following the road another tenth of a mile. Turn right onto Gadpouch Road and proceed half a mile (the road becomes dirt) to a small dirt parking area on the right.

Maps: For a topographic map of the area, request Middle Haddam from the USGS.

Contact: The Blue Trails Network, Connecticut Forest and Park Association, 16 Meriden Road, Rockfall, CT 06481-2961; (860) 346-2372.

Trail notes: This fairly easy hike of just one mile round-trip leads to interesting quartz ledges with a good view over Great Hill Pond and the Connecticut River Valley. On the way to the ledges, the trail passes below low, rugged cliffs that young children would have a little adventure on.

From the parking area, cross the road and follow the blue-blazed Shenipsit Trail into the woods. The trail is easy at first, then begins slabbing up Great Hill, traversing ledges. Atop the hill, the Shenipsit makes a hairpin turn with two quick, sharp right turns; at the second of those, a white-blazed side trail leads to the left about a tenth of a mile to interesting quartz ledges with a good view over Great Hill Pond and the Connecticut River Valley. Return the way you came.

26 Chauncey Peak/Lamentation Mountain

4.2 mi/3.0 hrs 

Location: In Giuffrida Park and Lamentation Mountain State Park in Middletown; Eastern Connecticut map page 321, grid c1.

User groups: Hikers and snowshoers. No wheelchair facilities. Portions of this trail lie on private land, and use restrictions can change. Assume that bikes, dogs, and horses are not allowed unless a trail is specifically marked for them (although many landowners do not object to dogs). Most trails are open to cross-country skiing. Assume that hunting is allowed in season unless otherwise posted.

Access, fees: Parking and access are free.

Directions: Take Interstate 91 to exit 20 in Middletown. Head west on Country Club Road, which becomes Westfield Road; 2.5 miles from the highway—where the Mattabesett Trail enters the woods on the right—bear right and continue a tenth of a mile to the parking area on the right at Giuffrida Park.

Maps: A map of Giuffrida Park trails is available at the caretaker's house across the road from the parking lot. For a topographic map of the area, request Meriden from the USGS.

Contact: The Blue Trails Network, Connecticut Forest and Park Association, 16 Meriden Road, Rockfall, CT 06481-2961; (860) 346-2372.

Trail notes: Chauncey Peak and Lamentation Mountain comprise one of the finest hikes along the Mattabesett Trail, if not among all the traprock ridge walks of the Connecticut River Valley. Although it entails some steep hiking for brief periods, this 4.2-mile trip amply rewards you for the effort.

From the parking lot, cross the field below the dam and bear right onto a flat trail, following it a tenth of a mile to the blue-blazed Mattabesett. Turn left, soon climbing steeply to the summit of Chauncey at four-tenths of a mile, where you walk along the brink of a sheer cliff overlooking a pastoral countryside of fields and woods. Continue along the Mattabesett around the upper edge of a quarry to the open ridge and a view at eight-tenths of a mile from high above Crescent Lake—I stood up here one afternoon, watching the glasslike water perfectly mirror the sky. Walk the open ridge with long views, mostly to the west, for about two-tenths of a mile, then descend a steep hillside of loose rocks. At 1.2 miles, cross a small brook, then begin climbing Lamentation, reaching the first view at 1.7 miles. From here, walk the ridge for four-tenths of a mile—with nearly constant views south, west, and north—to the "summit," or high point on the ridge, at 2.1 miles. Visible are the Sleeping Giant to the south and Castle Crag to the west. Hike back along the same route.

27 Castle Crag/West Peak

6.0 mi/3.5 hrs 

Location: In Hubbard Park in Meriden; Western Connecticut map page 320, grid c4.

User groups: Hikers and snowshoers. No wheelchair facilities. Portions of this trail lie on private land, and use restrictions can change. Assume that bikes, dogs, and horses are not allowed unless a trail is specifically marked for them (although many landowners do not object to dogs). Most trails are open to cross-country skiing. Assume that hunting is allowed in season unless otherwise posted.

Access, fees: Parking and access are free.

Directions: Take Interstate 691 to exit 4. Turn east, continue eight-tenths of a mile, and take a left into Hubbard Park. Continue two-tenths of a mile and bear right, then go another tenth of a mile to a stop sign and turn left. Follow that road three-tenths of a mile to its end, passing under the highway. Turn left and drive another 1.1 miles, along the Merimere Reservoir, and park at a barricade at the end of the reservoir.

Maps: For a topographic map of the area, request Meriden from the USGS.

Contact: The Blue Trails Network, Connecticut Forest and Park Association, 16 Meriden Road, Rockfall, CT 06481-2961; (860) 346-2372.

Trail notes: This popular six-mile hike to a small, castlelike stone tower is one of the area's nicest, and a great adventure for children, because it follows the crest of high cliffs for much of its distance. You can cut the hike in half by just going to Castle Crag.

From the parking area, walk across the dam bridge. At its far end, pick up the blue-blazed Metacomet Trail, which turns left into a rock-strewn gully, then immediately left again, climbing a hillside out of the gully. An easy hike, with a few short, steep sections, brings you to the crest of the ridge high above Merimere Reservoir and sweeping views of the surrounding hills and the city of Meriden. Follow the trail along the ridge, passing several viewpoints. At 1.5 miles, you will reach Castle Crag, where the castle stands atop cliffs; you can climb its stairs for a 360-degree panorama. To make this a three-mile round-trip, return the way you came.

To continue on to West Peak for the full hike, cross the parking lot at Castle Crag to a blue arrow marking the Metacomet Trail, which follows the edge of woods along the tops of cliffs with almost constant views. The trail parallels the road to Castle Crag for about three-tenths of a mile, then turns left and descends fairly steeply for two-tenths of a mile. At the bottom of the hill, turn right onto an old woods road for about 50 feet, then right onto a footpath (watch for the blue blazes), slabbing uphill. Within a tenth of a mile, you will pass below cliffs, then ascend a short hillside to a woods road. Turn left and walk the road about 75 yards to where it terminates atop high cliffs with a commanding view. To the south lies the profile of the Sleeping Giant, a chain of low hills just north of New Haven that resembles a man lying on his back. To return to this hike's start, you can backtrack the way you came, or, for an easier descent, follow the paved West Peak Road. Backtrack on the woods road, past the trail to the end of the paved road (there are transmission towers to the left). Follow the road downhill, passing the right turn which leads to Castle Crag, all the way back to the reservoir dam, about an hour's walk (roughly three miles).

28 Mount Higby

2.4 mi/1.5 hrs 

Location: In Middlefield; Western Connecticut map page 320, grid c4.

User groups: Hikers and snowshoers. No wheelchair facilities. Portions of this trail lie on private land, and use restrictions can change. Assume that bikes, dogs, and horses are not allowed unless a trail is specifically marked for them (although many landowners do not object to dogs). Most trails are open to cross-country skiing. Assume that hunting is allowed in season unless otherwise posted.

Access, fees: Parking and access are free.

Directions: Drive to the eastern terminus of Interstate 691 in Middlefield, where it becomes Route 66. At the junction of Routes 66 and 147, park behind Guida's Restaurant.

Maps: For a topographic map of the area, request Middletown from the USGS.

Contact: The Blue Trails Network, Connecticut Forest and Park Association, 16 Meriden Road, Rockfall, CT 06481-2961; (860) 346-2372.

Trail notes: Unfortunately, you never escape the sounds of traffic on this fairly easy, 2.4-mile walk, but it leads through a nice forest to a good spot to catch the sunset over the Meriden cityscape.

From the parking lot, pick up the trail marked by blue blazes with purple dots, which begins beside the restaurant. (Don't take the trail from the rear of the lot marked only with a sign reading "no snowmobiles.") This connector trail follows flat ground for nearly four-tenths of a mile to the blue-blazed Mattabesett Trail (by turning left here, you could reach Route 66 in a tenth of a mile). Bear right onto the Mattabesett and continue three-tenths of a mile to where it turns sharply right and climbs fairly steeply onto the ridge, an ascent that is brief but can leave you short of breath. About 1.2 miles from the parking lot, you will reach the Pinnacle, a tall rock outcropping offering long views in nearly every direction, especially to the west. Return the way you came.

29 Wadsworth Falls State Park

3.2 mi/1.5 hrs 

Location: In the Rockfall section of Middlefield; Eastern Connecticut map page 321, grid d1.

User groups: Hikers, skiers, and snowshoers. No wheelchair facilities. Dogs must be on a leash. The side trail is not suitable for bikes, horses, and skis (see trail notes below). Hunting is prohibited.

Access, fees: From Memorial Day through Labor Day, an entrance fee of $5 per vehicle is charged to Connecticut residents and $8 to nonresidents on weekends and holidays, while residents pay $4 and nonresidents pay $5 on weekdays. Access is free the rest of the year. The state park is open from 8 A.M. to sunset.

Directions: From the junction of Routes 66 and 157 in Middletown, drive south on Route 157 for 1.5 miles and turn left into the state park entrance and parking lot.

Maps: Trail maps are available at the information board beside the parking lot. For a topographic map of the area, request Middletown from the USGS.

Contact: Connecticut State Parks Division, 79 Elm Street, Hartford, CT 06106-5127; (860) 424-3200.

Trail notes: The highlight of this flat, easy, 3.2-mile jaunt through the woods is the two waterfalls along the way—the first a tall cascade, the second a thundering column of water. The park is a great spot for an after-work or weekend walk, run, or cross-country ski, with several other trails to access besides this route.

Behind the bathrooms off the parking lot, pick up the orange-blazed Main Trail, a wide, mostly flat path. In a half mile, opposite a park map board, grows a giant mountain laurel. Continue on the Main Trail for two-tenths of a mile, then bear right at a sign for Little Falls, following a blue trail two-tenths of a mile to where the Coginchaug River tumbles 40 feet through a series of ledges. Rejoining the Main Trail above Little Falls, turn right. At 1.5 miles from the start, the Main Trail ends at a paved road. Turn right and follow the road a tenth of a mile to a parking area on the right; then follow the sound of crashing water about 100 yards to the Big Falls. Follow your steps back the same way to the parking lot.

30 Coginchaug Cave

1.4 mi/1.0 hr 

Location: In Durham; Eastern Connecticut map page 321, grid d1.

User groups: Hikers and snowshoers. No wheelchair facilities. Portions of this trail lie on private land, and use restrictions can change. Assume that bikes, dogs, and horses are not allowed unless a trail is specifically marked for them (although many landowners do not object to dogs). Most trails are open to cross-country skiing. Assume that hunting is allowed in season unless otherwise posted.

Access, fees: Parking and access are free.

Directions: From the junction of Routes 17 and 79 in Durham, drive south on Route 79 for eight-tenths of a mile and turn left onto Old Blue Hills Road. Bear right immediately, following blue blazes on the utility poles for seven-tenths of a mile to the end of the road, where there is limited parking.

Maps: For a topographic map of the area, request Durham from the USGS.

Contact: The Blue Trails Network, Connecticut Forest and Park Association, 16 Meriden Road, Rockfall, CT 06481-2961; (860) 346-2372.

Trail notes: This quiet stretch of the Mattabesett Trail leads to a huge overhanging rock wall known as Coginchaug Cave—an easy round-trip of 1.4 miles. Many years ago the cave supposedly sheltered Indians.

From the parking area, follow the rough jeep road 100 feet and turn right with the blue blazes onto a footpath into the woods. The trail crosses one small brook, makes a very short but steep climb of a hillock, and circles around exposed ledges in the forest to the "cave," seven-tenths of a mile from the hike's start. Return the way you came.

31 Bluff Head/ Totoket Mountain

2.5 mi/1.5 hrs 

Location: In North Guilford; Eastern Connecticut map page 321, grid d1.

User groups: Hikers and snowshoers. No wheelchair facilities. Portions of this trail lie on private land, and use restrictions can change. Assume that bikes, dogs, and horses are not allowed unless a trail is specifically marked for them (although many landowners do not object to dogs). Most trails are open to cross-country skiing. Assume that hunting is allowed in season unless otherwise posted.

Access, fees: Parking and access are free.

Directions: From the junction of Routes 77 and 80 in Guilford, drive north on Route 77 for 4.3 miles and turn left into an unmarked dirt parking area.

Maps: For a topographic map of the area, request Durham from the USGS.

Contact: The Blue Trails Network, Connecticut Forest and Park Association, 16 Meriden Road, Rockfall, CT 06481-2961; (860) 346-2372.

Trail notes: After a brief, steep climb, the trail follows the edge of high cliffs all the way to the rocky outcropping known as Bluff Head, with an almost continuous view east of the forest and low hills in this rural corner of southern Connecticut. From the parking area, follow the blue blazes of the Mattabesett Trail to the left (south) for about 50 feet, where the trail turns right and ascends steeply. After about two-tenths of a mile, it levels out and follows a low ridge to an overlook at four-tenths of a mile. From here, a trail leaves to the left (west); you will return to it, but this hike continues north on the Mattabesett another eight-tenths of a mile to Bluff Head, a high outcrop atop cliffs with wide and long views to the north, east, and south. Double back on the Mattabesett to the trail junction at the first overlook and turn right (west). Descend about three-tenths of a mile, then turn left and follow a woods road two-tenths of a mile back to your vehicle.

32 Sleeping Giant State Park Blue-White Loop

5.6 mi/4.5 hrs  

Location: In Hamden; Western Connecticut map page 320, grid d4.

User groups: Hikers, dogs, and snowshoers. No wheelchair facilities. Dogs must be on a leash. Bikes, horses, hunting, and skis are prohibited.

Access, fees: From Memorial Day through Labor Day, an entrance fee of $5 per vehicle is charged to Connecticut residents and $8 to nonresidents on weekends and holidays. The park closes at sunset.

Directions: From Route 10 in Hamden, about 1.4 miles north of the junction of Routes 10 and 40, turn east onto Mount Carmel Avenue. Continue two-tenths of a mile to the state park entrance and parking on the left, across from Quinnipiac College.

Maps: A basic trail map is available at the state park and from the Connecticut State Parks Division (see address below). For topographic maps of the area, request Mount Carmel and Wallingford from the USGS.

Contact: Sleeping Giant State Park Association, P.O. Box 14, Quinnipiac College, Hamden, CT 06518. Connecticut State Parks Division, 79 Elm Street, Hartford, CT 06106-5127; (860) 424-3200. Connecticut Forest and Park Association, 16 Meriden Road, Rockfall, CT 06481-2961; (860) 346-2372.

Trail notes: The Sleeping Giant is a chain of low hills which, from a distance, resemble a giant lying on his back. Sleeping Giant State Park now consists of 1,500 acres and has more than 30 miles of trails, although the Sleeping Giant Park Association's goal is to expand the park to 2,000 acres.

This fairly rugged, 5.6-mile loop on the blue and white trails passes over all of the major features of the giant—including the towering cliffs at his "chin"—and numerous ledges with excellent views. It is one of the most scenic hikes in the state. Besides the Tower Trail (hike number 33), the blue-blazed Quinnipiac Trail is the only trail in the park that leads to the stone tower, which can be climbed for panoramic views of the countryside and New Haven Harbor. While the loop could be done in either direction, I suggest hiking it counter-clockwise, starting on the white trail. The only drawback of going in this direction is that you will have to descend—rather than climb, which is easier—the steep, exposed slabs on the south slope of the Head (via the blue trail); this section can be hazardous when wet. (To avoid the slabs descent, backtrack north on the blue trail from the "chin's" clifftops to the wide Tower Trail, which provides an easy descent to the parking area.) On the other hand, hiking this loop counter-clockwise allows you to finish this hike with the cliff walks over the Head, which boasts the most striking and precipitous cliffs in the park. I won't bother describing every turn on this hike—they are myriad—but the trails are well blazed and the map is good.

From the parking lot, follow the paved road about a tenth of a mile to the picnic grounds and watch for the white-blazed trail branching to the right. Follow the white trail eastward across the park for nearly three miles, to where it crosses the blue-blazed trail near Hezekiah's Knob; turn left onto the blue trail and follow it back, passing by the stone tower and finishing over the Head. After descending steeply to the south off the Head, watch for a connector trail leading to the left (east) back to the picnic area. If you miss the first connector trail and start seeing Mount Carmel Avenue through the woods, take the violet-blazed trail, which will also lead you back to the picnic area.

33 Sleeping Giant State Park Tower Trail

3.2 mi/1.5 hrs 

Location: In Hamden; Western Connecticut map page 320, grid d4.

User groups: Hikers and snowshoers. No wheelchair facilities. Dogs must be on a leash. Bikes, horses, hunting, and skis are prohibited.

Access, fees: From Memorial Day through Labor Day, an entrance fee of $5 per vehicle is charged to Connecticut residents and $8 to nonresidents on weekends and holidays. The park closes at sunset.

Directions: From Route 10 in Hamden, about 1.4 miles north of the junction of Routes 10 and 40, turn east onto Mount Carmel Avenue. Continue two-tenths of a mile to the state park entrance and parking on the left, across from Quinnipiac College.

Maps: A basic trail map is available at the state park and from the Connecticut State Parks Division (see address below). For topographic maps of the area, request Mount Carmel and Wallingford from the USGS.

Contact: Sleeping Giant Park Association, P.O. Box 14, Quinnipiac College, Hamden, CT 06518. Connecticut State Parks Division, 79 Elm Street, Hartford, CT 06106-5127; (860) 424-3200. Connecticut Forest and Park Association, 16 Meriden Road, Rockfall, CT 06481-2961; (860) 346-2372.

Trail notes: This relatively easy, 3.2-mile round-trip leads to Sleeping Giant State Park's stone tower, which has stairs leading to its top and panoramic views of the countryside and south to New Haven Harbor.

From the parking area, walk the paved road about 100 feet and turn right at a large sign for the Tower Trail. It rises gently, following the carriage road 1.6 miles to the stone tower. Climb the steps in the tower to its top, where you may find yourself standing in a strong breeze, looking out over the New Haven skyline and the long ridge of the Sleeping Giant stretching off to the east and west. Retrace your steps to return to the parking area.

34 West Rock Ridge State Park

10.0 mi/6.5 hrs 

Location: In Hamden, Bethany, and Woodbridge; Western Connecticut map page 320, grid d4.

User groups: Hikers, dogs, and snowshoers. No wheelchair facilities. Dogs must be on a leash. The trail is not suitable for bikes, horses, or skis. Hunting is prohibited.

Access, fees: Parking and access are free.

Directions: From Route 10 in Hamden, about 1.5 miles north of the junction of Routes 10 and 40, turn west onto West Woods Road. Follow it nine-tenths of a mile to its end; turn left onto Shepard Avenue, then immediately right again onto the continuation of West Woods Road. Proceed half a mile and bear right onto Choate; follow it to its end, and turn left onto West Woods Road again. Follow it to the town line, where it becomes Brook Road. Just beyond the town line, drive straight through an intersection with a stop sign and continue another four-tenths of a mile. Park in a turnout on the left where the blue blazes with red dots marking the Sanford Feeder Trail enters the forest on an old woods road blocked by a chain. There may be no trail sign.

Maps: For topographic maps of the area, request New Haven and Mount Carmel from the USGS.

Contact: The Blue Trails Network, Connecticut Forest and Park Association, 16 Meriden Road, Rockfall, CT 06481-2961; (860) 346-2372. Connecticut State Parks Division, 79 Elm Street, Hartford, CT 06106-5127; (860) 424-3200.

Trail notes: This is an out-and-back hike along the West Rock Ridge, which offers views to the east and southeast of the New Haven area. As such, you can walk any distance desired and turn back, although the first views of houses and other buildings in Hamden and the New Haven skyline in the distance are reached after 1.8 miles.

From the turnout, follow the blue blazes with red dots marking the Sanford Feeder Trail along various woods roads for six-tenths of a mile, then turn right (uphill) onto the blue-blazed Regicides Trail. Within two-tenths of a mile, the trail reaches and parallels paved Baldwin Road, which runs through West Rock Ridge State Park and is only open during the warmer months. The trail crosses the road six-tenths of a mile after first reaching it; continue four-tenths of a mile along the Regicides Trail to the first view. The trail re-enters the woods, then crosses Baldwin Road again a tenth of a mile beyond that first viewpoint. Over the next roughly 3.5 miles, the Regicides Trail passes several more outlooks. Return along the same route.

35 Westwoods Preserve

2.0 mi/1.0 hr

Location: In Guilford; Eastern Connecticut map page 321, grid e1.

User groups: Hikers, dogs, skiers, and snowshoers. No wheelchair facilities. Dogs must be on a leash. Only a portion of this trail is suitable for bikes and horses. Hunting is allowed in season.

Access, fees: Parking and access are free.

Directions: Take Interstate 95 to exit 58 in Guilford. Drive south on Route 77 for half a mile and turn right onto U.S. 1 heading south. Continue two-tenths of a mile and turn left onto River Road, then go another six-tenths of a mile and turn right onto Water Street (Route 146). Follow it eight-tenths of a mile, turn right onto Sam Hill Road, and park in the turnout immediately on the left.

Maps: A map board is posted at the trailhead, and maps of Westwoods Preserve are sold in several local stores. For a topographic map of the area, request Guilford from the USGS.

Contact: Guilford Land Conservation Trust, P.O. Box 200, Guilford, CT 06437.

Trail notes: With 1,000 acres, Westwoods is a popular local place for hiking, cross-country skiing, and mountain biking because of its network of intersecting trails and the feeling of remoteness it inspires just a few miles from busy Interstate 95 and a short drive from New Haven. From the parking area, follow the obvious trail a tenth of a mile, then turn left onto the white-blazed trail. You will soon pass a side path leading left to large stone blocks; this detour rejoins the white trail within a tenth of a mile. The white trail continues past marshes on the left and Lost Pond, a protected little body of water ringed by woods and bordering on a wildlife refuge, so expect to see lots of birds like egrets, ducks, and osprey. The trail turns back into the woods, passing numerous glacial erratics, including one boulder split into two halves, between which grows a stout cedar tree. Where the white trail ends, turn right onto the orange trail, following it back to the parking area.

36 Devils Hopyard State Park Vista Trail Loop

2.5 mi/1.5 hrs 2 7

Location: In East Haddam; Eastern Connecticut map page 321, grid d2.

User groups: Hikers, dogs, and snowshoers. No wheelchair facilities. Dogs must be on a leash. This trail is not suitable for bikes or skis. Horses and hunting are prohibited.

Access, fees: Parking and access are free. The park closes at sunset.

Directions: From the center of Millington, north of the state park, drive east on Haywardville Road for seven-tenths of a mile and turn right onto Hopyard Road at a sign for Devils Hopyard State Park. Continue eight-tenths of a mile and turn left at a sign for Chapman Falls (a tenth of a mile beyond the park headquarters). Turn immediately left into the parking lot. Or from the junction of Routes 82 and 158 in East Haddam, south of the park, drive two-tenths of a mile east on Route 82 and turn left onto Hopyard Road. Continue 3.5 miles, then turn right at the sign for Chapman Falls, and left into the parking lot.

Maps: A map of the state park is posted at an information board across the street from the parking lot. For topographic maps of the area, request Colchester and Hamburg from the USGS.

Contact: Connecticut State Parks Division, 79 Elm Street, Hartford, CT 06106-5127; (860) 424-3200.

Trail notes: This 2.5-mile loop hike through Devils Hopyard State Park in a more rural section of central Connecticut is mostly wooded, but begins with spectacular Chapman Falls, which thunders loudly as it crashes down, frothing white, for 40 or 50 feet over several rock ledges. The trail then passes a beautiful view from an open ledge—be sure to take the time to enjoy the vistas, including a dark gorge along the Eight Mile River. I enjoyed a very peaceful, late-afternoon walk through here one cool November day.

From the parking lot, cross the road to the map board beside thundering Chapman Falls. Follow the footpath past the falls for a tenth of a mile to the picnic area and the covered bridge. Once over the bridge, turn left, following the orange blazes of the Vista Trail. Within the first half mile you will cross a brook on stones, which could be tricky in high water. The trail passes through a hemlock grove and some wet areas, and at 1.3 miles reaches an open ledge with a pastoral view to the south. The trail, which can be tricky to follow from here, descends to the right through mountain laurel, then mixed forest, reaching the Eight Mile River just downstream from a gorge. Before the gorge, the trail turns right, climbing a hillside and eventually reaching an old woods road that leads back to the covered bridge. Backtrack from there to the parking lot.

37 Breakneck Pond

6.5 mi/4.5 hrs 

Location: In Bigelow Hollow State Park and Nipmuck State Forest in Union; Eastern Connecticut map page 321, grid a3.

User groups: Hikers, dogs, and snowshoers. No wheelchair facilities. Dogs must be on a leash; horses can access the woods roads on this hike (see trail notes below). This trail is not suitable for bikes. Hunting is allowed in season in state forests, but not in state parks, and is prohibited on Sundays. This hike begins in Bigelow Hollow State Park, but most of it is within Nipmuck State Forest.

Access, fees: Parking and access are free. Bigelow Hollow State Park closes at sunset.

Directions: From the north, take Interstate 84 to exit 74. Follow Route 171 east for 2.4 miles, to the junction with Route 190. Turn left, staying on Route 171; proceed 1.4 miles, then turn left into Bigelow Hollow State Park. Continue seven-tenths of a mile to the picnic area parking lot and trailhead. From the south, take Interstate 84 to exit 73. Turn right onto Route 190 east, follow it for two miles, then turn right onto Route 171 and continue 1.4 miles to the state park entrance.

Maps: A basic trail map is available free at the trailhead and from the Connecticut State Parks Division (see address below). For topographic maps of the area, request Eastford, Westford, and Southbridge from the USGS.

Contact: Connecticut State Parks Division, 79 Elm Street, Hartford, CT 06106-5127; (860) 424-3200. The Blue Trails Network, Connecticut Forest and Park Association, 16 Meriden Road, Rockfall, CT 06481-2961; (860) 346-2372.

Trail notes: Located in one of the more rural parts of Connecticut, this 6.5-mile loop through Bigelow Hollow State Park and Nipmuck State Forest circles around picturesque Breakneck Pond, a long, narrow—and most notably in the Constitution State, undeveloped—finger of fresh water hidden away in quiet woods. For its relative sense of remoteness, scenic qualities, and even the bit of rugged trail along the pond's west shore, this is one of my favorite hikes in the state.

From the parking area, cross the road to the information board at the trailhead, where maps are available. The trail immediately splits; bear right onto the white-blazed East Ridge Trail. Within a tenth of a mile, it reaches and turns left onto an old logging road, following it 1.1 miles to a trail junction near the south end of Breakneck Pond. Turn left onto the Breakneck Pond View Trail, marked by blue blazes with white dots. The trail crosses a wet area and emerges at the pond's southern end, where you get a first view of nearly the full length of the approximately 1.5-mile-long pond. I first stood at this spot while accompanying a trail maintenance crew from the Connecticut Forest and Park Association. More than a year later, eager to hike around the pond, I returned with a friend and we made this loop in later afternoon without encountering another soul.

The trail then bears right off the logging road onto a footpath (still following the blue-white blazes). That footpath hugs the pond's western shore for the next two miles, traversing rocky ground in a thick forest with almost constant pond views—the most difficult stretch of this hike. Near the pond's north end, turn right at a trail junction, following the View Trail across an outlet stream (on rocks and a log); then turn right again (south) onto the blue-blazed Nipmuck Trail. The Nipmuck soon bears right off a logging road and becomes a footpath for two miles along the pond's eastern shore. Now you will have nearly constant views in the other direction, looking west across the pond, giving you a whole new perspective on it. At the next trail junction, turn right with the white blazes of the East Ridge Trail, walk about a tenth of a mile to the first trail junction you reached on this hike, then turn left and follow the East Ridge Trail along the logging road for the 1.1 miles back to the trailhead.

38 Natchaug State Forest Road Loop

4.0 mi/2.0 hrs 

Location: In Eastford; Eastern Connecticut map page 321, grid b3.

User groups: Hikers, bikes, dogs, horses, skiers, and snowshoers. No wheelchair facilities. Dogs must be on a leash. Hunting is allowed in season.

Access, fees: Parking and access are free.

Directions: From Interstate 395, take exit 93 for Dayville, onto Route 101 west. In Phoenixville, turn right (south) onto Route 198. Watch for a sign and the park entrance on the left. Follow the main park road to the headquarters building, and park at a roadside pullout across from the large maintenance building.

Maps: A free trail map is available at the park, outside the maintenance building across from the parking area; or from the Connecticut State Parks Division (see address below). For a topographic map of the area, request Hampton from the USGS.

Contact: Natchaug State Forest, Star Route Pilfershire Road, Eastford, CT 06242; (860) 974-1562. Connecticut State Parks Division, 79 Elm Street, Hartford, CT 06106-5127; (860) 424-3200.

Trail notes: This loop, ideal for mountain bikers, cross-country skiers, or hikers looking for an easy woods walk, introduces you to a 12,500-acre patch of state forest cut by several trails and forest roads, including the Natchaug Trail. Get a map and explore. Some major trail junctions are marked by numbered signs.

From the parking area, double back on the park road a short distance to where it hooks right; continue straight onto the gravel Kingsbury Road. Go past trail junction 5, where a gas line right-of-way leads left, to junction 6, where you'll turn left. Bear right around a horse camp, then bear left at the next fork. The trail descends, and just before crossing a brook you turn left; you're now on the gas line right-of-way, which leads back to junction 5 on Kingsbury Road. Bear in mind that snowmobilers use these trails in winter, as do hunters in late fall.

39 Mashamoquet Brook State Park

3.5 mi/2.0 hrs 

Location: In Mashamoquet; Eastern Connecticut map page 321, grid b4.

User groups: Hikers, bikes, dogs, skiers, and snowshoers. No wheelchair facilities. Bikes are not allowed during the spring mud season, from April through mid-May. Dogs must be on a leash. This trail is not suitable for horses. Hunting is prohibited.

Access, fees: Parking and access are free.

Directions: From Interstate 395, take exit 93 for Dayville, onto Route 101 west. In Pomfret, beyond the junction with Route 169 and U.S. 44, watch for a sign and the park entrance on the left.

Maps: A free trail map is available from the park office or the Connecticut State Parks Division (see addresses below). For a topographic map of the area, request Danielson from the USGS.

Contact: Mashamoquet Brook State Park, Pomfret Center, CT 06259; (860) 928-6121. Connecticut State Parks Division, 79 Elm Street, Hartford, CT 06106; (860) 424-3200.

Trail notes: Mashamoquet dispels any suggestion that Connecticut's northeast corner is flat and uninteresting. This hike almost immediately ascends a hillside, then winds through forested hills and a classic, glacier-scoured landscape of rocky ledges and boulders. (Short sections will be very difficult on skis; I had to remove and carry mine a few times.) This is a great hike for young children. All trails are well marked.

From the first picnic area, head a short distance up the road and cross Mashamoquet Brook on a wooden bridge. Follow the trail to the right and uphill. The blue-blazed trail branches to the right; stay on the red-blazed trail. Shortly after crossing Wolf Den Drive, you'll see Table Rock on the left, two flat boulders stacked like a table. Beyond it, the blue and red trails converge and enter an area of rocky ledges. A plaque mounted on a rock on the right marks the site of the Wolf Den, where in 1742 Israel Putnam crept into the cavelike channel in the boulders and shot what was reputedly the last wolf in Connecticut, an animal suspected of killing numerous sheep in the area. Continue following the blue blazes to the Indian Chair—another unique rock formation—through more ledges, across an open field, and finally to the first junction with the red-blazed trail.

40 Orchard Hill Lookout

2.0 mi/1.0 hr 

Location: In Chaplin; Eastern Connecticut map page 321, grid b3.

User groups: Hikers, dogs, skiers, and snowshoers. No wheelchair facilities. This trail is not suitable for horses. Hunting is allowed in season.

Access, fees: Parking and access are free.

Directions: From the junction of Routes 44 and 198 in Eastford, drive south on Route 198, past the entrance to Natchaug State Forest, into Chaplin. Turn left onto Morey Road, cross a bridge over a stream, and turn right onto Marcy Road. About two-tenths of a mile farther, the blue-blazed Natchaug Trail crosses Marcy Road. Park here along the roadside.

Maps: For topographic maps of the area, request Hampton and Spring Hill from the USGS.

Contact: The Blue Trails Network, Connecticut Forest and Park Association, (860) 346-2372.

Trail notes: This hike does not lead to any spectacular views, or orchards, for that matter; it's simply a pleasant little stroll through the woods to a lookout where, when the leaves are down, the view of the valley to the west is only partly obscured by trees. The trail is well blazed, so you're not likely to even need a map. It does cross one brook and a stone wall where skiers might have to walk, but otherwise the slope is gentle. I hiked this late one winter Monday afternoon, when there was no one else around. The forest was quiet, and the low-angle light from the sun was throwing long shadows behind bare trees and giving the snow subtle yellow highlights.

41 Devil's Den

1.0 mi/0.5 hr 

Location: In Plainfield; Eastern Connecticut map page 321, grid c4.

User groups: Hikers and snowshoers. No wheelchair facilities. Portions of this trail lie on private land, and use restrictions can change. Assume that bikes, dogs, and horses are not allowed unless a trail is specifically marked for them (although many landowners do not object to dogs). Most trails are open to cross-country skiing. Assume that hunting is allowed in season unless otherwise posted.

Access, fees: Parking and access are free.

Directions: From Interstate 395, take exit 88 in Plainfield and Route 14A east for 1.6 miles. Turn right on Spaulding Road and drive two miles to its end. Turn left on Flat Rock Road, and continue another seven-tenths of a mile; just beyond where the road becomes pavement, park in a turnout on the left.

Maps: Although a map is not necessary for this hike, for topographic maps of the area, request Plainfield and Oneco from the USGS.

Contact: The Blue Trails Network, Connecticut Forest and Park Association, 16 Meriden Road, Rockfall, CT 06481-2961; (860) 346-2372.

Trail notes: This relatively flat hike follows a rough woods road for a half mile to a faint side path on the right. That path—easily overlooked—leads 30 feet downhill to ledges in the woods that feature cavelike cavities and a narrow passageway known as Devil's Den. While unspectacular and lacking any views, this is a peaceful, enjoyable local walk.

From the parking area, walk out via the road (now impassable by car), which here is the blue-blazed Quinebaug Trail. Watch for a faint path on the right, just after walking a slight downhill over a slab in the road, and before the road levels out. If you reach the yellow-blazed Pachaug-Quinebaug Trail, you went about a tenth of a mile past Devil's Den. Return the way you came.

42 Pachaug State Forest Rhododendron Sanctuary

0.4 mi/0.25 hr 

Location: In Pachaug State Forest in Voluntown; Eastern Connecticut map page 321, grid c4.

User groups: Hikers, dogs, and snowshoers. No wheelchair facilities. Dogs must be on a leash. This trail is not suitable for bikes, horses, or skis. Hunting is allowed in season.

Access, fees: Parking and access are free.

Directions: The main entrance to Pachaug State Forest is Headquarters Road, which is off Route 49, 7.9 miles south of its junction with Route 14A and six-tenths of a mile north of Route 138 in Voluntown. Follow Headquarters Road eight-tenths of a mile, bear left at a fork, and drive another tenth of a mile to a field and parking; to the right is a sign at the entrance to the Rhododendron Sanctuary. To reach the state forest headquarters, follow Headquarters Road for three-tenths of a mile from Route 49, turn right, and continue another tenth of a mile to the office on the left.

Maps: A free map of Pachaug State Forest is available at the state forest headquarters, or from the Connecticut State Parks Division (see addresses below). For topographic maps of the area, request Voluntown, Jewett City, Oneco, and Plainfield from the USGS.

Contact: Pachaug State Forest, RFD 1, Voluntown, CT 06384; (860) 376-4075. Connecticut State Parks Division, 79 Elm Street, Hartford, CT 06106-5127; (860) 424-3200. The Blue Trails Network, Connecticut Forest and Park Association, (860) 346-2372.

Trail notes: This short, easy walk begins to the right of the field parking area, at the sign for the Rhododendron Sanctuary. Follow the blue-blazed Pachaug Trail into a stand of huge wild rhododendrons sprawling over the forest floor. The trail loops about four-tenths of a mile through the woods and emerges on the dirt Cutoff Road, two-tenths of a mile beyond the entrance to the Rhododendron Sanctuary and at the start of the hike up Mount Misery (hike number 43); the two make for a good combination. Otherwise, you can walk through the rhododendron stand, then double back to the parking area by walking out the same way you came in.

43 Mount Misery

1.0 mi/0.75 hr 

Location: In Pachaug State Forest in Voluntown; Eastern Connecticut map page 321, grid c4.

User groups: Hikers, dogs, and snowshoers. No wheelchair facilities. Dogs must be on a leash. The trail is not suitable for bikes, horses, or skis. Hunting is allowed in season.

Access, fees: Parking and access are free.

Directions: The main entrance to Pachaug State Forest is Headquarters Road, which is off Route 49, 7.9 miles south of its junction with Route 14A and six-tenths of a mile north of Route 138 in Voluntown. Follow Headquarters Road eight-tenths of a mile, bear left at a fork, and drive another tenth of a mile to a field. Bear right on the dirt Cutoff Road and drive another two-tenths of a mile to a turnout on the right about 125 feet beyond a left turn for the campground. To reach the state forest headquarters, follow Headquarters Road for three-tenths of a mile from Route 49, turn right, and continue another tenth of a mile to the office on the left.

Maps: A free map of Pachaug State Forest is available at the state forest headquarters, or from the Connecticut State Parks Division (see addresses below). For topographic maps of the area, request Voluntown, Jewett City, Oneco, and Plainfield from the USGS.

Contact: Pachaug State Forest, RFD 1, Voluntown, CT 06384; (860) 376-4075. Connecticut State Parks Division, 79 Elm Street, Hartford, CT 06106-5127; (860) 424-3200. The Blue Trails Network, Connecticut Forest and Park Association, (860) 346-2372.

Trail notes: Not expecting to find any real views from a 441-foot hill in eastern Connecticut, I scrambled over rocks to the "summit" of Mount Misery—and was surprised by a sweeping view of forested countryside from atop low cliffs. This one-mile round-trip hike is fairly flat for much of its length and a good one for young children. The Pachaug Trail enters the woods diagonally across Cutoff Road from the turnout, about 50 feet before the turnout and 75 feet beyond the road to the campground. Follow its blue blazes up Mount Misery, then explore the views from atop Misery's ridge of low cliffs. Return the way you came. You may want to combine this hike with the Rhododendron Sanctuary (hike number 42), also along the Pachaug Trail.

44 Pachaug State Forest Roads Loop

9.0 mi/4.5 hrs 

Location: In Pachaug State Forest in Voluntown; Eastern Connecticut map page 321, grid c4.

User groups: Hikers, bikes, dogs, horses, skiers, and snowshoers; check with state forest authorities in winter to find out which roads are open to skiers. No wheelchair facilities. Dogs must be on a leash. Hunting is allowed in season.

Access, fees: Parking and access are free.

Directions: The main entrance to Pachaug State Forest is Headquarters Road, which is off Route 49, 7.9 miles south of its junction with Route 14A and six-tenths of a mile north of Route 138 in Voluntown. Follow Headquarters Road eight-tenths of a mile, bear right at a fork onto Trail 1 Road, and drive another tenth of a mile to parking on the right at a picnic area. To reach the state forest headquarters, follow Headquarters Road for three-tenths of a mile from Route 49, turn right, and continue another tenth of a mile to the office on the left.

Maps: A free map of Pachaug State Forest is available at the state forest headquarters, or from the Connecticut State Parks Division (see addresses below). For topographic maps of the area, request Voluntown, Jewett City, Oneco, and Plainfield from the USGS.

Contact: Pachaug State Forest, RFD 1, Voluntown, CT 06384; (860) 376-4075. Connecticut State Parks Division, 79 Elm Street, Hartford, CT 06106-5127; (860) 424-3200. The Blue Trails Network, Connecticut Forest and Park Association, (860) 346-2372.

Trail notes: With miles of dirt roads laced throughout the sprawling Pachaug State Forest, the area is fertile ground for a long loop ride on a mountain bike. The loop described here covers about nine miles and much of the state forest—including, somewhat surprisingly, a few pretty good hills and a 20-minute side hike over 441-foot Mount Misery, which offers a sweeping view of forested countryside from atop low cliffs. This loop would make a good outing on skis as well, but there are better hiking options in Pachaug.

From the picnic area, head out Trail 1 Road, which becomes dirt within about 150 feet. Pass a dirt road entering from the right and cross Gardner Road within the first mile. Follow Trail 1 Road another mile or more to a paved road and turn left. In about a half mile, turn left at a four-way intersection onto the dirt Breakneck Hill Road. Within a mile, turn left onto the first major dirt road, Lawrence Road, and begin a long descent. Reaching a T intersection, turn right on Forest Road, climb a hill, then turn left on Cutoff Road, descending again. Turn onto the first dirt road on the right (watch for it), Firetower Road, and follow it a half mile to a gate. Before passing the gate, turn left down the side dirt road, which ends within a few hundred feet at a pair of trails leading up Mount Misery.

Hike the trail on the right, which traverses below low cliffs, circles around Mount Misery, then turns left (uphill) on the blue-blazed Pachaug Trail heading toward the summit. After checking out the view, continue over the top of Mount Misery, following the blue blazes back. Go back to the gate and turn left past it, following Firetower Road another half mile or more to another gate. Continue around the gate and turn left; this is Trail 1 Road. Follow it more than a mile back to the picnic area.

45 High and Bullet Ledges

4.4 mi/2.5 hrs 

Location: In North Stonington; Eastern Connecticut map page 321, grid d4.

User groups: Hikers and snowshoers. No wheelchair facilities. Portions of this trail lie on private land, and use restrictions can change. Assume that bikes, dogs, and horses are not allowed unless a trail is specifically marked for them (although many landowners do not object to dogs). Most trails are open to cross-country skiing. Assume that hunting is allowed in season unless otherwise posted.

Access, fees: Parking and access are free.

Directions: Drive Route 2 to North Stonington, and turn off the highway onto Main Street at the sign for the village. Drive four-tenths of a mile and turn onto Wyassup Road. Continue 3.1 miles, turn left onto Wyassup Lake Road, and follow it seven-tenths of a mile to parking at a boat launch area on the right.

Maps: Although a map is not necessary for this hike, for topographic maps of the area, request Old Mystic and Ashaway from the USGS.

Contact: The Blue Trails Network, Connecticut Forest and Park Association, 16 Meriden Road, Rockfall, CT 06481-2961; (860) 346-2372.

Trail notes: This relatively easy hike—with just a couple of steep, if short, climbs—on a 2.2-mile stretch of the blue-blazed Narragansett Trail brings you to two very different ledges hidden away in the woods. Neither offers any views; the appeal here lies in a quiet walk through the forest and a pair of interesting rock formations.

From the parking lot, continue a tenth of a mile farther down the road to where blue blazes turn left onto a woods road. Follow it a quarter mile, then continue straight ahead with the blue blazes, while the woods road bears left. The trail ascends a steep hillside, turns right, and reaches High Ledge just eight-tenths of a mile from the parking area. The trail circles the small ledge, then follows another woods road, descending somewhat, and passing below the base of a cliff some 40 feet high. At the cliff's far side, the trail turns right, ascends left of the cliff, and reaches its top–Bullet Ledge, 2.2 miles from the parking area. Head back to the parking lot the same way you came.

Eastern Connecticut Map—page 321

New England's Best Hikes

Best Hikes

Can't decide where to hike this weekend?
Here are my picks for the best hikes in New England in 23 categories:

Fall Foliage Viewing

Maiden Cliff, ME (page 53)

North Traveler Mountain, ME (page 8)

Sabattus Mountain, ME (page 80)

Tumbledown Mountain via any trail, ME (pages 67-68)

Mount Chocorua via any trail, NH (pages 153–154)

Mount Kearsarge, NH (page 160)

Mount Monadnock via any trail, NH (pages 166–167)

Mounts Lincoln and Lafayette, NH (page 137)

Squam Mountains, NH (page 157)

Webster Cliffs, NH (page 122)

Welch and Dickey, NH (page 150)

Camel's Hump via any trail, VT (pages 187–191)

Falls of Lana and Rattlesnake Cliffs, VT (page 207)

Mount Hunger, VT (page 186)

Mount Pisgah, VT (page 181)

Stowe Pinnacle, VT (page 185)

Stratton Mountain and Stratton Pond, VT (page 231)

Monument Mountain, MA (page 253)

Noanet Peak, MA (page 287)

Rounds Rock, MA (page 250)

Mount Tom Cliffs, RI (page 308)

Jessie Gerard Trail, CT (page 333)

Lion's Head/Bald Peak, CT (page 324)

Mount Tom State Park Tower, CT (page 330)

Prospect Mountain and Rand's View, CT (page 325)

Sunrises

Cadillac Mountain via any trail, ME (pages 46–47)

The Mahoosuc Range, ME (page 74)

Mount Katahdin: the Abol Trail, ME (page 16)

Twins-Bonds Traverse, NH (page 140)

Skylight Pond, VT (page 205)

Bar Head Drumlin/Plum Island, MA (page 279)

Halibut Point State Park, MA (page 280)

Mount Everett, MA (page 256)

Bear Mountain, CT (page 324)

Mount Tom State Park Tower, CT (page 330)

Sunsets

Doubletop Mountain, ME (page 22)

Isle au Haut: Eben's Head, ME (page 34)

The Carter Range, NH (pages 114–115)

Great Bay National Estuarine Reserve: Sandy Point Trail, NH (page 164)

Presidential Range Traverse, NH (page 104)

Falls of Lana and Rattlesnake Cliffs, VT (page 207)

Gile Mountain, VT (page 212)

Mount Philo, VT (page 194)

Gay Head, MA (page 297)

Great Island Trail, MA (page 294)

Mount Tom, MA (page 267)

Peak Mountain, CT (page 335)

Tree Viewing

Kilkenny Traverse, NH (page 94)

Rogers Ledge, NH (page 93)

Atlantic White Cedar Swamp, MA (page 295)

Giant Trees of Clark Ridge, MA (page 251)

Wachusett Meadow to Wachusett Mountain, MA (page 274)

Walkabout Trail, RI (page 302)

For Children up to Age 7

The Bubbles/Eagle Lake Loop, ME (page 43)

Sabattus Mountain, ME (page 80)

Screw Auger Falls, ME (page 71)

Elephant Head, NH (page 120)

Lonesome Lake, NH (page 133)

Mount Kearsarge, NH (page 160)

Mount Major, NH (page 160)

North Pack Monadnock, NH (page 166)

Sabbaday Falls, NH (page 149)

West Rattlesnake, NH (page 158)

Deer Leap Mountain, VT (page 212)

Stowe Pinnacle, VT (page 185)

Crow Hills, MA (page 269)

Monument Mountain, MA (page 253)

Purgatory Chasm, MA (page 276)

South Sugarloaf Mountain, MA (page 262)

Snake Den, RI (page 304)

Leatherman's Cave/Crane Lookout, CT (page 331)

Mount Tom State Park Tower, CT (page 330)

Sleeping Giant State Park Tower Trail, CT (page 346)

For Children Age 8 and Older

The Beehive, ME (page 50)

Doubletop Mountain, ME (page 22)

Piazza Rock and The Caves, ME (page 66)

Table Rock: Grafton Notch, ME (page 70)

Tumbledown Mountain Brook Trail, ME (page 68)

Arethusa Falls and Frankenstein Cliff, NH (page 123)

Mount Cardigan: East Side Loop, NH (page 159)

Mount Chocorua via any trail, NH (pages 153–154)

Mount Monadnock via any trail, NH (pages 166–167)

Welch and Dickey, NH (page 150)

Falls of Lana and Rattlesnake Cliffs, VT (page 207)

Money Brook Falls, MA (page 244)

Mount Watatic and Nutting Hill, MA (page 267)

Block Island: Clay Head Trail and the Maze, RI (page 314)

Bear Mountain, CT (page 324)

Scenic Gorges

Gulf Hagas, ME (page 32)

Pollywog Gorge, ME (page 29)

Emerald Pool, NH (page 118)

Clarendon Gorge and Airport Lookout, VT (page 218)

Quechee Gorge, VT (page 213)

Texas Falls Nature Trail, VT (page 207)

Bear's Den, MA (page 261)

Hubbard River Gorge, MA (page 258)

Tariffville Gorge, CT (page 335)

Coastline or Island Hikes

Moonlight Hikes

Ponds or Lakes

Waterfalls

Swimming Holes

Gulf Hagas, ME (page 32)

100-Mile Wilderness, ME (page 24)

Screw Auger Falls, ME (page 71)

Step Falls, ME (page 72)

Emerald Pool, NH (page 118)

Mount Tripyramid, NH (page 149)

Easy Backpacking

Half a 100-Mile Wilderness (northern half), ME (page 28)

Russell Pond/Davis Pond loop, ME (page 10)

Kilkenny Traverse, NH (page 94)

Glastenbury Mountain, VT (page 233)

The Long Trail: Route 11/30 to USFS Road 10, VT (page 224)

Difficult Backpacking

Bigelow Range, ME (page 55)

The Mahoosuc Range, ME (page 74)

100-Mile Wilderness, ME (page 24)

Saddleback Range, ME (page 63)

The Carter Range, NH (page 114–115)

Presidential Range Traverse, NH (page 104)

Twins-Bonds Traverse, NH (page 140)

The Long Trail: Route 17, Appalachian Gap, to the Winooski River, VT (page 192)

The Long Trail: Route 103, Clarendon Gorge, to U.S. 4, Sherburne Pass, VT (page 216)

The Monroe Skyline, VT (page 197)

Summits

Bigelow Mountain, ME (page 57)

The Mahoosuc Range (Goose Eye Mountain), ME (page 74)

Mount Abraham, ME (page 60)

Mount Katahdin via any trail, ME (pages 14–17)

North Traveler Mountain, ME (page 8)

The Owl, ME (page 20)

Saddleback Mountain and The Horn, ME (page 65)

Mount Adams via any trail, NH (pages 99–100)

Mount Chocorua via any trail, NH (pages 153–154)

Mount Hight/Carter Dome/Carter Notch, NH (page 114)

Mount Madison via any trail, NH (pages 99 and 101)

Table Rock: Dixville Notch, NH (page 91)

Camel's Hump via any trail, VT (pages 187–191)

Mount Abraham, VT (page 200)

Monument Mountain, MA (page 253)

Lion's Head/Bald Peak, CT (page 324)

Educational Nature Walks

Great Bay National Estuarine Reserve: Sandy Point Trail, NH (page 164)

Robert Frost Interpretive Trail, VT (page 206)

Atlantic White Cedar Swamp, MA (page 295)

Great Meadows National Wildlife Refuge, MA (page 283)

Norman Bird Sanctuary, RI (page 309)

Powder Mill Ledges, RI (page 303)

Solitude and Remoteness

North Traveler Mountain, ME (page 8)

Old Blue Mountain, ME (page 69)

100-Mile Wilderness, ME (page 24)

Peak of the Ridges, ME (page 9)

White Cap Mountain, ME (page 31)

Diamond Peaks, NH (page 91)

North Percy Peak, NH (page 93)

North Twin Mountain, NH (page 130)

Pemigewasset Wilderness Traverse, NH (page 141)

Sugarloaf Mountain, NH (page 92)

Breakneck Pond, CT (page 349)

Easy, Scenic Walks

Kidney Pond Loop, ME (page 23)

Ocean Path, ME (page 52)

Screw Auger Falls, ME (page 71)

Step Falls, ME (page 72)

Emerald Pool, NH (page 118)

Sabbaday Falls, NH (page 149)

Smuggler's Notch, VT (page 182)

Gay Head, MA (page 297)

Maudslay State Park, MA (page 278)

Nauset Marsh, MA (page 296)

Rounds Rock, MA (page 250)

World's End Reservation, MA (page 291)

Norman Bird Sanctuary, RI (page 309)

Mount Tom State Park Tower, CT (page 330)

Pachaug State Forest Rhododendron Sanctuary, CT (page 352)

Bird-Watching

Beaver Brook, NH (page 170)

Great Bay National Estuarine Reserve: Sandy Point Trail, NH (page 164)

Caratunk Wildlife Refuge, MA (page 292)

Great Meadows National Wildlife Refuge, MA (page 283)

Wachusett Meadow to Wachusett Mountain, MA (page 274)

Block Island, RI (pages 314–316)

Kimball Wildlife Refuge, RI (page 313)

Ninigret National Wildlife Refuge, RI (page 313)

Norman Bird Sanctuary, RI (page 309)

Powder Mill Ledges, RI (page 303)

Westwoods Preserve, CT (page 347)

Mountain Biking

Jordan Pond/Eagle Lake/Bubble Pond Carriage Road Loop, ME (page 44)

Jordan Pond/Sargent Mountain Carriage Road Loop, ME (page 42)

Bear Brook State Park Bike Race Loop, NH (page 163)

Pawtuckaway State Park, NH (page 164)

Dogtown, MA (page 282)

Leominster Forest Roads Loop, MA (page 271)

Myles Standish State Forest Loop, MA (page 293)

Province Lands Trail, MA (page 294)

Forest Roads Loop, RI (page 307)

Pachaug State Forest Roads Loop, CT (page 353)

West Hartford Reservoir, CT (page 336)

Mountain Ridges

Rugged Mountain Terrain

Cross-Country Skiing

Beaver Brook, NH (page 170)

Pawtuckaway State Park, NH (page 164)

Pemigewasset Wilderness Traverse, NH (page 141)

D.A.R. State Forest Ski Touring Loop, MA (page 264)

Leominster Forest Roads Loop, MA (page 271)

Myles Standish State Forest Loop, MA (page 293)

Walden Pond, MA (page 284)

Pachaug State Forest Roads Loop, CT (page 353)

Wadsworth Falls State Park, CT (page 343)

Westwoods Preserve, CT (page 347)

Index

BOLD PAGE NUMBERS INDICATE MAIN LISTINGS

A

B

D

E

F

H

O

Q

R

U

V

W

Y

Z

Acknowledgments

I had much help in putting together this book. I want to thank the many people who accompanied me on these trails, in particular my fiancée and hiking partner, Penny Beach. My parents, Henry and Joanne Lanza, deserve recognition—both of them for putting up with a son who has showed up at their door a few times since they first got rid of him, and my mom for also being a good hiking partner. Of the friends who have shared trails with me, Mike Casino warrants a special thanks for enduring innumerable miles in my company (and I still hope and pray he will again quit his job and have more free time).

Others I want to thank include: Keith Ratner, Gerry Prutsman, Mike Cunningham, Rod Venterea, Mike and Rick Baron, Diane Mailloux, Brion O'Connor, Julie Lanza, Nicholas Lanza, Brittany Lanza, Stephen Lanza, Rod and Ann Beach, Betsy Beach, Dan Corley, Ruth Corley, Brendan Corley, Jessica Corley, Mike Hannigan, Joe Albee, Matt Walsh, Jim and Annette Ermini, Doug Thompson, Steve and Denise Buck, Carol and Denis Lavoie, Bill Mistretta, Christine Raymond, Lance Riek, Eddie Maxwell, Topher Sharp, Mark Bogacz, Mark Fenton, Todd Balf, and Tim Symonds.

There were also many helpful people at various organizations and public agencies, including: Acadia National Park; the Appalachian Mountain Club; the Appalachian Trail Conference; the Ascutney Trails Association; Baxter State Park; the Bigelow Preserve; the Cape Cod National Seashore; the Chatham Trails Association; the Connecticut Forest and Park Association; the Connecticut State Parks Division; the DeLorme Mapping Company; the Friends of the Blue Hills; the Friends of the Middlesex Fells; the Friends of the Wapack; the Green Mountain Club; the Green Mountain National Forest; the Maine Appalachian Trail Club; the Maine Bureau of Parks and Lands; the Massachusetts Division of Forests and Parks; the Metropolitan District Commission (Hartford, CT); the Midstate Trail Committee; the Monadnock-Sunapee Greenway Trail Club; New England Cartographics; the New Hampshire Division of Parks and Recreation; the Randolph Mountain Club; the Rhode Island Division of Fish and Wildlife; the Rhode Island Division of Forest Environment; the Rhode Island Division of Parks and Recreation; cartographer Ed Rolfe; Trails Illustrated; the Trustees of Reservations; the Vermont Department of Forests, Parks, and Recreation; the White Mountain National Forest; the Williams Outing Club; and the Wonalancet Out Door Club.

About the Author

Freelance writer and photographer **Michael Lanza** syndicates a weekly column about outdoor activities in New England in more than a dozen daily newspapers throughout the region. He also contributes to outdoor publications such as *AMC Outdoors*, *Appalachia*, *Backpacker*, *Outside*, and *Walking*.

A native of Leominster, Massachusetts, Lanza graduated with a B.S. in photojournalism from Syracuse University in 1983 and spent 10 years as a reporter and editor at newspapers in Massachusetts and New Hampshire. An avid backpacker and climber, he has hiked extensively in the western United States as well as New England. He now lives in Lebanon, New Hampshire, with his fiancée, Penny Beach.

Credits

Editor in Chief	Donna Leverenz
Developmental Editor	Rebecca Poole Forée
Senior Editor	Jean Linsteadt
Associate Editor	Karin Mullen
Production Coordinator	Alexander Lyon
Production Assistant	Leigh Anna Mendenhall
Acquisitions Editor	Judith Pynn
Cover Photo	Mount Desert Island, Maine Walter Bibikow/ The Picture Cube, Inc.

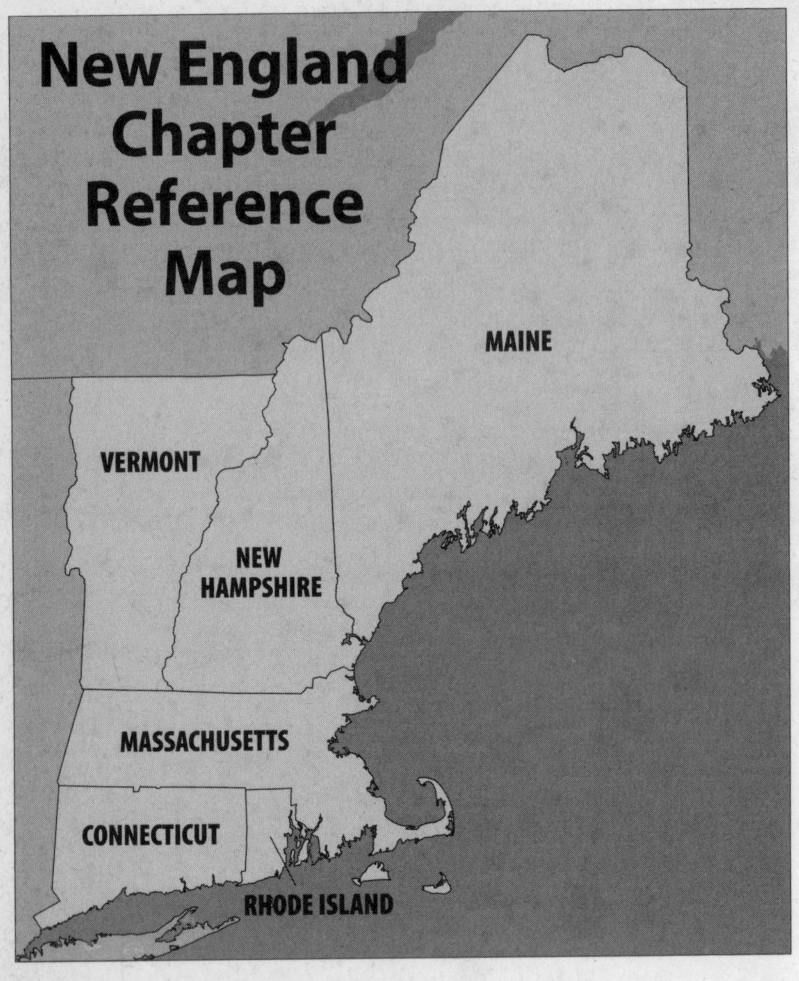
New England Chapter Reference Map
MAINE
VERMONT
NEW HAMPSHIRE
MASSACHUSETTS
CONNECTICUT
RHODE ISLAND